D0170515

# THE JANUARY 6 REPORT

FINDINGS FROM THE SELECT COMMITTEE TO
INVESTIGATE THE ATTACK ON THE U.S. CAPITOL
WITH REPORTING, ANALYSIS AND VISUALS
BY THE NEW YORK TIMES

The
New York
Times

12
TWELVE

NEWYORK BOSTON

Copyright © 2022 by The New York Times

Cover design by The New York Times. Cover photograph by Erin Schaff/ The New York Times.
Cover copyright © 2022 by Hachette Book Group, Inc.

Hachette Book Group supports the right to free expression and the value of copyright. The purpose of copyright is to encourage writers and artists to produce the creative works that enrich our culture.

The scanning, uploading, and distribution of this book without permission is a theft of the author's intellectual property. If you would like permission to use material from the book (other than for review purposes), please contact permissions@hbgusa.com. Thank you for your support of the author's rights.

Twelve
Hachette Book Group
1290 Avenue of the Americas, New York, NY 10104
twelvebooks.com
twitter.com/twelvebooks

First Edition: December 2022

Twelve is an imprint of Grand Central Publishing. The Twelve name and logo are trademarks of Hachette Book Group, Inc.

The publisher is not responsible for websites (or their content) that are not owned by the publisher.

The Hachette Speakers Bureau provides a wide range of authors for speaking events. To find out more, go to www.hachettespeakersbureau.com or call (866) 376-6591.

Library of Congress Control Number: 2022944213

ISBNs: 978-1-5387-4215-0 (paperback), 978-1-5387-4216-7 (ebook)

Printed in the United States of America

# Contents

# Introduction

BY LUKE BROADWATER

A loudspeaker in the Capitol crackled with a dire warning on the afternoon of Jan. 6, 2021, as I sat at my desk in the Senate press gallery.

"External security threat," I scribbled in my notepad, writing down what I was hearing. "Stay away from exterior windows and doors." And then: "Seek cover."

I jumped out of my chair to peer out the third-floor window and saw a horde of supporters of President Donald J. Trump swarming across the pristinely maintained Capitol grounds. They were kicking over bike racks and making their way to the doors of the building. I had covered large protests before, but this had taken a turn. There was something different, something darker in their eyes.

All of a sudden, Laura Lytle, the director of the press gallery, rounded me up with the other journalists in the office and began rushing us into the Senate gallery, overlooking the floor. Senators, including a number of octogenarians, were assembled there to certify the electoral vote count to confirm Joseph R. Biden Jr.'s victory, checking the final constitutional box to his election as president. Their presence made the Senate chamber, which was guarded by Capitol Police officers who were responsible for protecting them, the safest place to be.

"In or out!" Ms. Lytle yelled to stragglers as she herded us in. "In or out! We are locking the door!"

Observing the arcane rules of the Senate, I foolishly left my laptop and cellphone outside the chamber, effectively cutting myself off from the world. As I looked down from the balcony, I had no way of knowing that the chaos I had just seen outside was coming straight toward us.

Hundreds of rioters, believing Mr. Trump's lie of a stolen election, had started to storm the building. They were beating police officers, shattering doors and windows, and, I would later learn, chanting "Hang Mike Pence," the vice president. I couldn't see it at the time, but as they rampaged through the Capitol, they scrawled MURDER THE MEDIA on a door, smashed television cameras, and assaulted and robbed my colleague Erin Schaff, a *New York Times* photographer.

In the Senate chamber, I could feel a surge of panic. On the floor below, Senator Amy Klobuchar, Democrat of Minnesota, looked at her phone and called out,

A violent mob carrying Trump campaign flags swarmed the Capitol complex on Jan. 6, 2021, in an effort to disrupt Congress's certification of electoral votes to formally declare President-elect Joseph R. Biden Jr.'s victory. *Ashley Gilbertson/VII/Redux, for The New York Times Magazine*

"Shots fired!" Senator Todd Young, Republican of Indiana, spotted an open door and demanded that it be locked. Senator Mitt Romney of Utah threw up his arms in exasperation and yelled, "This is what you've gotten, guys," evidently addressing his fellow Republicans, some of whom were challenging Mr. Biden's victory.

Mr. Pence, who only minutes before had been presiding over the Senate, had been hustled out of the chamber. Security officials were increasingly worried about the deteriorating situation. One officer pulled Senator Chuck Schumer of New York, the chamber's top Democrat, by his collar: "We've got to move, Senator." Officers helped elderly lawmakers from their desks and through a side door.

From the balcony, reporters began calling down to the chamber: "What about us?"

It felt as if we were on our own.

Lytle told us to head toward the Capitol's basement tunnel system, and we dashed out, gathering up our belongings and starting down the hallway. The fear in people's voices was now discernible.

Outside the chamber, I was reunited with my phone and a flood of text messages.

"Where are you?"

"Luke, you need to respond."

One from my friend Erica L. Green, a fellow *Times* reporter, was at the top of the screen: "Luke, you have to fucking say something."

Only later would I learn that we had left the chamber just a minute before the mob arrived in the hallway outside.

One minute was all that stood between us and the rioters.

I grabbed my gear and jumped into an elevator to the basement with Andy Taylor from The Associated Press and Jazmine Ulloa from *The Boston Globe*. I later learned that had the elevator stopped on the first floor, we would have been face to face with the mob.

We rushed past a phalanx of police officers and through the Capitol's underground network of tunnels. Ahead of me was Senator Mitch McConnell of Kentucky, the Republican leader, a polio survivor who walks with a limp, being practically carried by his security detail, their hands beneath his arms to steady him as they rushed him along. Minutes earlier, he had been delivering a speech on the Senate floor warning that if Republicans followed Mr. Trump's lies of a stolen election, democracy would enter a "death spiral."

It seemed clear Mr. McConnell had waited too long to denounce the fiction that Mr. Trump had spun. Now he was fleeing from a mob that believed it.

We made it to a secure area, and I sat on the floor, my back pressed against a wall. In that moment, I was much more angry than I was afraid.

I thought about how everyone who had spread the lies that led us to this point— including some of the senators sheltering in a safe room one door down from me— knew better. Or at least they should have known better. I thought of how they had fooled millions of people into believing that the election was stolen. Now thousands of those believers were here in one of the most sacred places in American democracy, smashing things and injuring people for what they thought was a righteous cause.

I wasn't the only journalist feeling that way. Sitting in that secure area, my peers— including reporters from conservative outlets—were growing frustrated with the senators who had encouraged the myths. I recall one shouting to a Republican lawmaker as he passed by, "Are you proud of yourself, senator?"

I opened my laptop.

I knew what I could do as a journalist: I could tell the truth. I could report the facts as they happened. I could call out the lies.

My colleagues Nick Fandos and Jonathan Martin were in that small space too, already at work. My editor, Julie Davis, messaged me with an assignment for the next day's paper. Together with Emily Cochrane, a colleague who had been trapped in the House chamber on the other end of the Capitol when the rioters stormed in, we started to write.

Evacuated and safe, the other journalists and I carried on with our work, protected by the First Amendment. We weren't heroes. That title goes to the officers from the Capitol and Metropolitan Police forces, who beat back the attackers and ensured the transfer of power between presidential administrations. (I would come to know several of those officers over beers in the months that followed.) We did our jobs the best we could as the room filled with tactical law enforcement teams.

In a secure room adjacent to ours, senators began speaking in hushed tones about whether and how to proceed with the electoral count. According to our sources, some were suggesting delaying the certification until another day or moving it to a safer spot away from the Capitol.

Applause erupted from inside the room. We later learned that that was the moment when lawmakers agreed they would return to the Senate chamber that night to finish counting the votes.

"We will not be deterred from finishing the job," Ms. Klobuchar told me.

Shortly after 8 p.m., federal agents and police officers escorted us and the lawmakers back to the Senate chamber. As we moved through the Capitol, I realized I was walking alongside two Senate aides who were carrying the wooden chests that held the Electoral College certificates that Congress had met to count when the rioters stormed in. In the mayhem of a hasty evacuation, those aides had the instinct to carry the chests with them, protecting the official record of Mr. Biden's election as president.

It struck me that I was watching history in action. The very ballots the mob had sought to block were being returned to the chamber.

Still, even after the Senate reconvened, it took hours for lawmakers to approve Mr. Biden's victory. Some Republicans continued to object, perpetuating the lie that the result was illegitimate even after they had seen how much it had cost the country.

By the time Mr. Pence announced the certification of Mr. Biden's win, it was 3:41 a.m. on Jan. 7.

My colleagues and I paired up and carpooled to help everyone arrive home safely. I remember walking through my door around 5:30 a.m.

The next few weeks were pretty rough; I had trouble sleeping, and almost everybody I knew who was in the building that day went to therapy. There were feelings of anger, anxiety and claustrophobia.

The *Times*'s executive editor, Dean Baquet, scheduled a call with the reporters who had been at the Capitol on Jan. 6. "We'll never forget what you guys did for the paper that day," he told us.

When I returned to the building, a 7-foot-tall fence topped with razor wire surrounded it.

The violence of Jan. 6 was horrific, but it also gave me a sense of professional purpose. I had been at *The Times* for less than six months when rioters stormed the Capitol, and I was trying to find my footing at one of the biggest newspapers in the country. What stayed with me was what I had told myself in the hallway as the riot engulfed the building: I could tell the truth. I could report the facts as they happened. And I could call out the lies.

# How a Presidential Rally Turned Into a Capitol Rampage

# How the Mob Entered the Capitol in 80 Minutes

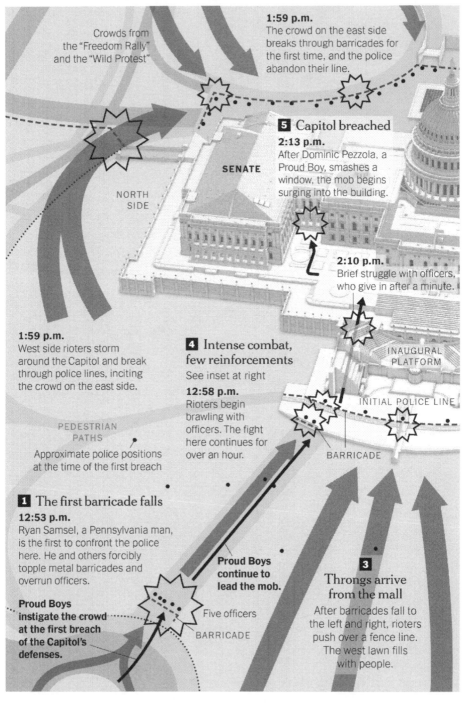

Crowds from the "Freedom Rally" and the "Wild Protest"

**1:59 p.m.**
The crowd on the east side breaks through barricades for the first time, and the police abandon their line.

SENATE

NORTH SIDE

**5 Capitol breached**
**2:13 p.m.**
After Dominic Pezzola, a Proud Boy, smashes a window, the mob begins surging into the building.

**2:10 p.m.**
Brief struggle with officers, who give in after a minute.

**1:59 p.m.**
West side rioters storm around the Capitol and break through police lines, inciting the crowd on the east side.

**4 Intense combat, few reinforcements**
See inset at right
**12:58 p.m.**
Rioters begin brawling with officers. The fight here continues for over an hour.

INAUGURAL PLATFORM

INITIAL POLICE LINE

PEDESTRIAN PATHS
Approximate police positions at the time of the first breach

BARRICADE

**1 The first barricade falls**
**12:53 p.m.**
Ryan Samsel, a Pennsylvania man, is the first to confront the police here. He and others forcibly topple metal barricades and overrun officers.

**Proud Boys instigate the crowd at the first breach of the Capitol's defenses.**

**Proud Boys continue to lead the mob.**

Five officers

BARRICADE

**3**
**Throngs arrive from the mall**
After barricades fall to the left and right, rioters push over a fence line. The west lawn fills with people.

✦ Breach of barricade, police line or building    • Approximate police positions

**12:45 p.m.**
Pipe bomb found at the Republican National Committee headquarters. Another pipe bomb is discovered at the Democratic National Committee soon afterward.

A few dozen officers line a barricade along the east perimeter.

**2:06 p.m.**
Crowd reaches the eastern doors of the Capitol.

EAST SIDE

BARRICADE

NEW JERSEY AVE.

HOUSE

SOUTH SIDE

TERRACE

FENCE LINE (APPROXIMATE)

WEST SIDE

TERRACE    **2:10 p.m.**
Rioters reach the terrace

**1:14 p.m.**
Reinforcements from the district's Metropolitan Police Department arrive to bolster the Capitol Police line.

SCAFFOLDING OVER STAIRS

OPENING

**1:53 p.m.**
Incited by the Proud Boys, the mob repeatedly pushes back officers guarding this stairway to the terrace.

WEST LAWN

**2** Another quick breach

FENCE

**12:55 p.m.**
Inspired by the breach near the Peace Monument, another part of the crowd pushes through police barricades.

About five officers

Paths of rioters and positions of fences, barricades and individual officers are approximate.

THE NEW YORK TIMES

# The Paths the Mob Takes Through the Capitol

☼ Breaches    ✸ Violent clashes    ➡ Route of mob    → Routes of others

**2:26 p.m.**
Vice President Mike Pence is evacuated from his office next to the Senate chamber.

**2:44 p.m.**
Rioters enter the Senate chamber.

**2:25 p.m.**
A second breach. The mob inside opens these doors and holds back a police officer as rioters stream into the Rotunda.

**2ND FLOOR**

SENATE CHAMBER

ROTUNDA

STAIRWELLS

**2:30 p.m.**
The police begin to evacuate the Senate chamber of all lawmakers and staff members who remain inside.

**2:15 p.m.**
Officer Goodman leads the mob up a staircase, away from the Senate chamber, and into a hall where police reinforcements are waiting.

**2:24 p.m.**
Rioters overrun officers guarding the Crypt, giving them access to the rest of the building.

**2:18 p.m.**
Rioters overpower officers trying to contain them.

**2:14 p.m.**
Officer Eugene Goodman of the Capitol Police first encounters some members of the mob here.

**1ST FLOOR**

CRYPT

Capitol breached
**2:13 p.m.**
Dominic Pezzola, a Proud Boy, smashes a window with a stolen police shield while other rioters break a nearby door, allowing the mob to stream in.

Note: For clarity, not all interior rooms and hallways are shown.

Dotted lines indicate travel between floors.

**2:44 p.m.**
After rioters smash through windows to the Speaker's Lobby, Ashli Babbitt is shot and killed by a Capitol Police officer as she tries to vault through the opening.

**2:23 p.m.**
Rioters freely move through Statuary Hall toward the House, which is still in session.

**2:35 p.m.**
Rioters overrun officers guarding the House.

**2:41 p.m.**
Rioters open a second set of doors from inside.

STATUARY HALL

HOUSE CHAMBER

**2:30–3:15 p.m.**
Rioters ransack Speaker Nancy Pelosi's office suite while her aides shelter inside a conference room.

**2:36 p.m.**
Rioters reach a door to the House chamber, and soon smash the glass panels.

**2:39 p.m.**
Representatives begin evacuating the House.

EAST SIDE OF CAPITOL

WEST SIDE OF CAPITOL

# Critical Moments in the Attack on the Capitol

# A Timeline of Events on Jan. 6

**9:00** A.M.  Start of the "Save America" rally at the Ellipse.

**10:00** A.M.  Start of the "Wild Protest," on the northeast lawn of the Capitol, and the "Freedom Rally."

**10:12** A.M.  A small group of protesters is already present at the police barriers on the Capitol's east side.

**10:45** A.M.  Scores of Proud Boys begin marching from the Ellipse to the Capitol.

**12:00** P.M.  President Donald J. Trump begins his speech at the Ellipse.

**12:17** P.M.  "We're going to walk down to the Capitol," Mr. Trump says.

**12:47** P.M.  The Proud Boys move to a police barricade at an entrance to the northwest Capitol lawn, near the Peace Monument.

**12:53** P.M.  The protest turns violent when Proud Boys and others overpower the police at the northwest barricade.

**12:55** P.M.  The mob breaches a second barricade at the west lawn, near the Garfield Monument.

**12:58** P.M.  The mob easily pushes back the Capitol Police to the inauguration platform and begins brawling with officers.

**1:00** P.M.  The joint session of Congress to certify the election result begins in the House chamber.

**1:05** P.M.  Vice President Mike Pence issues a statement saying he will not oppose the certification of Joseph R. Biden Jr.'s victory.

**1:12** P.M.  Mr. Trump's speech ends.

**1:14** P.M.  Metropolitan Police officers arrive to reinforce the Capitol Police. A Metropolitan

Police inspector calls for more backup.

**Around 1:15** P.M.  Mr. Trump argues with the Secret Service inside the presidential S.U.V. about his demand to go to the Capitol, which is refused.

**1:19** P.M.  Mr. Trump returns to the White House in his motorcade.

**1:23–1:26** P.M.  Rioters spread word of "reinforcements" coming from Ellipse. Those on the east side are encouraged by the breakthrough on the west.

**1:25** P.M.  After being told about the riot at the Capitol, Mr. Trump enters the private dining room off the Oval Office. He begins watching Fox News, which is showing live footage of the attack.

**1:49** P.M.  Mr. Trump tweets a link to a recording of his Ellipse speech, in which he told his supporters to go to the Capitol and "fight like hell."

**1:49–1:50** P.M.  The Capitol Police ask the sergeant-at-arms to request the National Guard. The Metropolitan Police declare the situation a riot.

**1:49–2:24** P.M.  A series of White House officials — including Mr. Trump's chief of staff, his White House counsel, his spokeswoman and his daughter Ivanka — try unsuccessfully to persuade him to make a public statement to call off the mob.

**1:53** P.M.  A mob including members of the Proud Boys forces its way up the northwest scaffolding staircase.

**1:59** P.M.  Incited by rioters

arriving from the west side, the crowd on the east side breaks through barricades for the first time, and the police abandon their line.

**2:06** P.M.  The eastern crowd ascends two staircases and reaches the locked doors of the Capitol.

**2:10** P.M.  The western crowd surges up the scaffolding staircase, breaks through the last police line and gains access to the Capitol terrace.

**2:10** P.M.  The Capitol Police Board gives approval to request the National Guard.

**2:12–2:13** P.M.  A Proud Boy, Dominic Pezzola, breaks a Capitol window, and a man named Michael Sparks vaults through. Rioters begin streaming into the building.

**2:13** P.M.  An objection by Senator James Lankford, Republican of Oklahoma, to the certification of Mr. Biden's victory is interrupted as the Senate goes into recess.

**2:14–2:24** P.M.  Mr. Pence's Secret Service detail calls for his office door, near the Senate chamber, to be secured more heavily and works to try to secure a safe evacuation route for him from the Capitol. They have begun to fear for their lives, talking over a secure radio channel about saying goodbye to their loved ones.

**2:15** P.M.  Officer Eugene Goodman of the Capitol Police leads a group of rioters away from unguarded doors of the Senate.

**2:15** P.M.  Speaker Nancy Pelosi is evacuated, followed quickly by Representative Steny H. Hoyer, Democrat of Maryland and the majority leader.

**2:18** P.M. The House recesses and locks down.

**2:23** P.M. In a clash with rioters near the inaugural platform, Officer Brian D. Sicknick of the Capitol Police is attacked with chemical spray. He dies a day later.

**2:24** P.M. Mr. Trump tweets: "Mike Pence didn't have the courage to do what should have been done."

**2:24–2:25** P.M. Rioters breach a police line in the Crypt, enter the Rotunda and open the eastern doors to the mob outside.

**2:26** P.M. Mr. Pence is evacuated.

**2:26** P.M. The House briefly resumes its certification session. It will recess four minutes later.

**2:28** P.M. Officers stop rioters outside the House. They break through eight minutes later and reach the House chamber doors.

**2:28** P.M. In a conference call, Lt. Gen. Walter E. Piatt of the Army tells Chief Steven Sund of the Capitol Police that he doesn't "like the visual" of sending National Guard troops to the Capitol but will ask for Defense Department permission.

**2:30** P.M. Lawmakers remaining in the Senate Chamber are evacuated.

**2:30–3:15** P.M. Rioters ransack Speaker Nancy Pelosi's office suite while her aides shelter across the hall.

**2:33** P.M. Rioters try but fail to break through locked doors into one of Ms. Pelosi's offices, where some of her staff members are hiding.

**2:35** P.M. A group of Oath Keepers in military garb ascends the main eastern staircase and soon enters the Capitol.

**2:38** P.M. Mr. Trump tweets "Please support our Capitol Police and Law Enforcement. They are truly on the side of our Country. Stay peaceful!" His spokeswoman tells a colleague shortly after that he resisted using the word "peace" at all.

**2:39** P.M. Lawmakers and staff in the House begin to evacuate through the Speaker's Lobby.

**2:40** P.M. The police on the west side retreat to the inauguration tunnel, and rioters soon arrive. It will be the site of some of the day's most brutal fighting.

**2:42** P.M. Rioters reach the doors to the Speaker's Lobby, which have been barricaded with furniture. One uses his fist and a helmet to break a large window in the door.

**2:44** P.M. Rioters breach the Senate chamber, which is now empty, shouting, "Treason! Treason!" On the House side, Ashli Babbitt tries to climb into the Speaker's Lobby through the broken window and is shot to death by a plainclothes Capitol Police officer.

**2:47** P.M. Metropolitan Police officers in riot gear begin to remove rioters from the northwest terrace.

**3:04** P.M. Christopher C. Miller, the acting defense secretary, approves full activation of the D.C. National Guard. He will not approve an operational plan for another hour and a half.

**3:19** P.M. Rioters drag Officer Michael Fanone of the Metropolitan Police and a colleague into the crowd. They beat Officer Fanone before returning him to the police line.

**4:03** P.M. Mr. Trump, having finally agreed to call on his supporters to go home, goes to the Rose Garden to record a message. He throws out the script, which condemned violence, and concludes by saying of the rioters, "We love you, you're very special."

**4:17** P.M. Mr. Trump tweets his "go home" message.

**4:19–4:27** P.M. Rosanne Boyland, a rioter, falls unconscious during a surge into the tunnel. She is pronounced dead later that day.

**5:02** P.M. National Guard troops depart the D.C. armory, two miles from the Capitol.

**5:04** P.M. Officers use tear gas and flashbangs to clear the inauguration tunnel and terrace.

**5:34** P.M. Rioters are finally pushed off the west lawn. The House sergeant-at-arms says the Capitol is secure.

**5:40** P.M. The first National Guard officers arrive on Capitol grounds.

**6:00** P.M. Curfew begins.

**6:01** P.M. Mr. Trump tweets his final message of the day, appearing to justify what happened at the Capitol: "These are the things and events that happen when a sacred landslide election victory is so viciously and unceremoniously stripped away from great patriots who have been badly & unfairly treated for so long."

**8:00** P.M. The Capitol Police declare the Capitol and surrounding areas secure.

**9:12** P.M. The House resumes debate.

# The Story So Far

BY LUKE BROADWATER, ALAN FEUER, MAGGIE HABERMAN,
KATIE BENNER AND MICHAEL S. SCHMIDT

Like 9/11, Jan. 6 needs no year attached to convey its dark place in American history. On that Wednesday afternoon, 64 days after Election Day 2020, a mob of President Donald J. Trump's supporters assaulted the Capitol, disrupting the official count of the electoral votes confirming that Joseph R. Biden Jr. would be the next president of the United States.

It was the most brutal attack on the building since the War of 1812, injuring more than 150 police officers and sending lawmakers and Vice President Mike Pence fleeing for their lives; at least seven people died in connection with the rampage. But "Jan. 6" has also become shorthand for something bigger: a monthslong campaign by Mr. Trump and his allies to subvert American democracy and cling to power by overturning an election.

In the immediate aftermath, the House impeached Mr. Trump on a charge of incitement of insurrection. Republicans orchestrated his acquittal in the Senate, where a majority favored his removal from office, but the vote fell short of the two-thirds necessary under the Constitution. Republicans blocked the creation of an independent commission to investigate the attack, but House Democrats set up a special committee to do that work.

Over more than a year, the Select Committee to Investigate the January 6th Attack on the United States Capitol conducted more than 1,000 interviews, obtained more than 1 million documents and issued more than 100 subpoenas. Its hearings in June and July 2022 produced blockbuster revelations, with an average of 13.8 million Americans tuning in. After the hearings began, the panel received more than 10,000 submissions to its tip line. As they drew to a close, the panel issued a subpoena to Mr. Trump himself, directing him to produce a wide range of material related to nearly every aspect of his plot to cling to the presidency; he never complied.

At the final presentation of its findings in late December of 2022, the committee formally accused Mr. Trump of committing four federal crimes and recommended that the Justice Department prosecute him for inciting insurrection, conspiracy to defraud the United States, obstruction of an act of Congress and conspiracy to make a

Tear gas and pepper spray were used as rioters clashed with law enforcement outside the building. One of the biggest questions in the aftermath of the attack was whether it was planned and carried out by organized groups. *Kenny Holston for The New York Times*

false statement. It was the first time in American history that Congress had referred a former president for criminal prosecution, and the coda to the committee's 18-month investigation into Mr. Trump's effort to overturn the 2020 election.

The evidence, the committee wrote, "has led to an overriding and straightforward conclusion: The central cause of Jan. 6 was one man, former President Donald Trump, who many others followed. None of the events of Jan. 6 would have happened without him."

The committee named five Trump allies—Mark Meadows, Rudolph W. Giuliani, John Eastman, Jeffrey Clark and Kenneth Chesebro—as potential co-conspirators with Mr. Trump in actions that it said warranted investigation. The charges would carry prison sentences, some of them lengthy, if federal prosecutors chose to pursue them.

The committee also released a 154-page executive summary of its 200,000-word final report, presenting evidence from its 10 previous public hearings and an astonishing narrative of Mr. Trump's efforts to effectively overthrow the government he led.

Mr. Trump responded by calling the committee a "kangaroo court."

The result is the investigative report that follows, the most authoritative account to date of how and why American democracy faltered on Jan. 6, 2021—and how close it came to collapsing.

It details the extent of Mr. Trump's bid to hold on to power after he lost the 2020 election, an effort that is as chilling as it was audacious. The president tried one tactic after another, leading a federal judge to conclude that he had engaged in a criminal

"All the News That's Fit to Print"

**The New York Times**

Late Edition
Today, plenty of sunshine, a bit less wind for most, high 45. Tonight, clear, a light breeze, low 31. Tomorrow, partly sunny, cooler, high 42. Weather map appears on Page 302.

VOL. CLXX ... No. 58,931     © 2021 The New York Times Company     NEW YORK, THURSDAY, JANUARY 7, 2021     $3.00

# TRUMP INCITES MOB

## *RAMPAGE IN CAPITOL FORCES EVACUATIONS; IT'S 'PART OF HIS LEGACY,' A REPUBLICAN SAYS*

### Lawmakers Back Biden's Victory in Arizona

By NICHOLAS FANDOS and EMILY COCHRANE

WASHINGTON — Congress moved late Wednesday toward confirming President-elect Joseph R. Biden Jr.'s victory after a mob of loyalists urged on by President Trump stormed and occupied the Capitol, disrupting the final electoral count in a shocking display of violence that shook the core of American democracy.

There was no parallel in modern American history, with insurgents acting in the president's name vandalizing Speaker Nancy Pelosi's office, smashing windows, looting, art and briefly taking control of the Senate chamber, where they took turns posing for photographs with fists up on the dais where Vice President Mike Pence had just been presiding. Outside the building, they erected a gallows, punctured the tires of a police SUV, and left a note on its windshield saying, "PELOSI IS SATAN."

By the time the Senate reconvened, hours after lawmakers had been evacuated from a Capitol overrun by rebels carrying pro-Trump paraphernalia, one of the nation's most polarizing moments had yielded an unexpected window of solidarity that briefly eclipsed partisan division. Republicans and Democrats locked arms to denounce the violence and express their determination to carry out what they called a constitutionally sacrosanct function.

"To those who wreaked havoc in our Capitol today, you did not win," Mr. Pence said in a sharp break from Mr. Trump, who had praised the mob. "Violence never wins. Freedom wins. And this is still the people's house."

Senator Mitch McConnell, Republican of Kentucky and the majority leader, said the "failed insurrection" had only clarified Congress's purpose.

"They tried to disrupt our democracy," he said. "They failed."

Under pressure from their colleagues, some Republicans who had planned several hours of objections to Mr. Biden's victory agreed to drop their challenges, though Senator Josh Hawley of Missouri was expected to press forward with a challenge to Pennsylvania's electors. Lawmakers met into the night to debate and vote on an objection to Arizona's results lodged just before the violence...

After scaling the walls outside the Capitol on Wednesday afternoon, some in the crowd made it into the House chamber as lawmakers and others scrambled for cover.

### President Lit Fuse for Chaos, Biden Declares

By MICHAEL D. SHEAR and JIM TANKERSLEY

WASHINGTON — President-elect Joseph R. Biden Jr...

### Americans at the Gates: The Trump Era's Inevitable Denouement

By PETER BAKER

WASHINGTON — So this is how it ends. The presidency of Donald John Trump, rooted from the beginning in anger, division and conspiracy-mongering, comes to a close with a violent...

...citadel of American democracy. Police officers brandishing guns in an armed standoff to defend the House chamber. Tear gas deployed in the Rotunda. Lawmakers in hiding. Extremists standing in the vice president's spot on the Senate dais and sitting at the desk of the speaker...

**4 Years of Provocation End With Invasion of Seat of Democracy**

...from the Oval Office that have left the country more polarized than in generations. Those who warned of worst-case scenarios only to be dismissed as alarmists found some of their darkest fears realized. By day's end, even some Republicans suggested...

---

The violence that unfolded on Jan. 6, 2021, was the most severe assault on the Capitol since British troops set the building ablaze during the War of 1812. "Those who warned of worst-case scenarios only to be dismissed as alarmists found some of their darkest fears realized," wrote Peter Baker, The Times's chief White House correspondent.

conspiracy. There was a failed legal strategy that clogged the courts with fantastical conspiracy theories about voter fraud, then a plot to twist the Justice Department into backing Mr. Trump's repeated lie that the election had been rigged. He and his allies pressured state officials into defying the will of voters; they considered directing the military or the Homeland Security Department to seize voting machines. And Mr. Trump tried an elaborate scheme to put forward false electors in states that Mr. Biden had won and to subvert the electoral count in Congress—the final constitutional box to check before his opponent could become president—trying to bully Mr. Pence into taking part.

When none of it worked, the investigation found, Mr. Trump knowingly urged an armed mob of his supporters to march to the Capitol while Congress was meeting to affirm his loss, unleashing a brutal effort to disrupt the peaceful transfer of power. When he was told that he could not join them, the president raged at the Secret Service and spent hours in the West Wing refusing to call off his supporters. He sympathized with the mob as they attacked police officers and ransacked the Capitol while chanting "Hang Mike Pence!"

The attack would fail; lawmakers ultimately returned to the Capitol to complete the electoral count that confirmed Mr. Biden's victory. But it would leave a scar on American history.

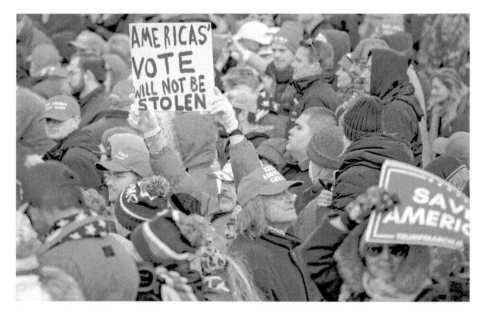

President Donald J. Trump's supporters at a rally before the riot. As Congress prepared to certify the victory of his successor, he continued a monthslong effort to delegitimize the election that helped set in motion hours of violence. *Pete Marovich for The New York Times*

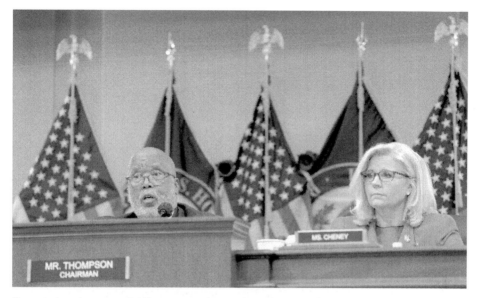

Democrats set up a special House committee to investigate the Jan. 6 assault. Led by Representatives Bennie Thompson, Democrat of Mississippi, and Liz Cheney, Republican of Wyoming, the panel held a series of public hearings over the summer of 2022 to examine President Donald J. Trump's actions and the events of that day. *Doug Mills/The New York Times*

## Planting Seeds of Doubt

For years, Mr. Trump railed against contests in which he had failed, disliked the outcome or feared he might be defeated. He objected nearly two decades ago to the results of the Emmys and falsely claimed that President Barack Obama had not won the popular vote. He asserted that Senator Ted Cruz of Texas "stole" a primary victory from him in Iowa in 2016 and predicted—before he defeated Hillary Clinton that year to win the presidency—that the general election would be "rigged." In the months leading up to the 2020 election, trailing in the polls, he again predicted that he would be cheated out of a victory and refused to commit to a peaceful transfer of power.

But what might have once been seen as political bluster or a character defect metastasized in Mr. Trump's case into what the Jan. 6 committee would come to refer to as the Big Lie, a sprawling undertaking that extended from the West Wing to the fringes of the far right. The narrative held that he had won the election, but it had been stolen from him by Democrats who had engaged in widespread voter fraud. Mr. Trump encouraged the lie in its various forms, indulging in increasingly outlandish fictions, spreading disinformation about the election results and encouraging his followers to challenge the vote at every step: in the courts, at statehouses and in the streets.

The lie found an eager audience in a broader movement fueled by far-right groups

From left, Sgt. Aquilino A. Gonell of the U.S. Capitol Police, Officers Michael Fanone and Daniel Hodges of the Metropolitan Police, and Officer Harry Dunn of the Capitol Police were sworn in before testifying to the House committee on July 27, 2021. "All of them were telling us, 'Trump sent us,'" Sergeant Gonell told the panel about the rioters as he tearfully recounted defending Congress on Jan. 6. *Oliver Contreras for The New York Times*

that believe that the United States, with its increasing racial and ethnic diversity, is being taken from them. For years, allies of Mr. Trump had promoted the false "Stop the Steal" narrative that elections were being stolen in districts across the country, particularly in cities with large numbers of Black and Latino voters who typically support Democrats. That narrative gained steam months before the 2020 election, when some of Mr. Trump's staunchest allies raised doubts about the security of mail-in ballots—an option that was expanded during the coronavirus pandemic—and began to spread claims that China or other nations would interfere in the election, to the president's detriment.

After he lost, the "Stop the Steal" narrative became a self-fulfilling prophecy and then a movement, promoted by a cast of lawyers, provocateurs, ideologues and others with an interest in keeping Mr. Trump in power—including some who had received, or would benefit from, a presidential pardon.

Perhaps the biggest promoter of the lie was Rudolph W. Giuliani, Mr. Trump's personal lawyer, who was already under federal investigation for his activities in Ukraine and traveled around the United States after the election to hold hearings and collect dubious affidavits about how the vote was purportedly stolen.

Others who played a critical role in advancing the false claims included the lawyers Sidney Powell and L. Lin Wood, against whom a federal judge has ordered sanctions;

the former national security adviser Michael T. Flynn, who was pardoned by Mr. Trump weeks after the election despite twice pleading guilty to lying to the F.B.I.; Patrick M. Byrne, the former chief executive of Overstock; Mike Lindell, the chief executive of MyPillow; Phil Waldron, a retired Army colonel; and Ron Watkins, the administrator of the online message board 8kun, who played a major role in spreading the baseless QAnon conspiracy theory that top Democrats worship Satan and run a child-trafficking ring.

At Mr. Wood's estate in South Carolina and at offices and hotels in the Washington area—including the Willard Intercontinental and the Trump International Hotels—assorted Trump allies met to plan strategies to overturn the election.

Their ideas relied on a range of conspiracy theories: that fraud had been perpetrated by dead voters in Philadelphia and election workers in Georgia; that defense contractors in Italy had used satellites to flip votes; that Hugo Chávez, the former president of Venezuela, who died in 2013, was somehow involved.

Some strategies were especially tangled and outlandish, but they would play an outsize role in the effort to persuade not only the courts but also the American public that the election was tainted.

In August 2020, before any presidential votes were cast, Mr. Waldron, an information warfare expert with a longstanding interest in China's purported involvement in election interference, developed a relationship with Allied Security Operations, a cybersecurity company in Texas.

Mr. Waldron has claimed that Allied Security discovered that the Chinese Communist Party had developed a way to flip votes on U.S. tabulation machines, particularly those built by Dominion Voting Systems. Those allegations about Dominion became the centerpiece of four federal lawsuits, laced with conspiracy theories, that Ms. Powell filed in late November and early December 2020 in a bid to reverse the election results.

But as Mr. Trump worked to overturn the election, he was told repeatedly—including by his own Justice Department—that his claims were false.

In the chaotic post-election period, a hotline that Mr. Trump's legal team had set up for fraud allegations was flooded with unverified claims. A truck driver for the United States Postal Service in Pennsylvania asserted without evidence that he drove thousands of phony ballots from New York to Pennsylvania. Republican voters in Arizona complained that some ballots had not been counted because they were marked with Sharpie pens that could not be read by voting machines.

Mr. Trump was aware of many of these reports and spoke about them often with aides and officials, raising various theories about voting fraud even as they debunked them one by one.

"When you gave him a very direct answer on one of them, he wouldn't fight us on it," Richard P. Donoghue, a former top Justice Department official, recalled in an interview with the House select committee. "But he would move to another allegation."

In testimony before the panel, Mr. Donoghue and Jeffrey A. Rosen, the acting attorney general, described how they had tried to fight Mr. Trump's conspiracy theories and false claims of fraud: It was a high-stakes game of Whac-a-Mole against an array of figures who were responding to the president's demand for evidence of wrongdoing by feeding him a steady stream of dubious material.

After receiving a video detailing the baseless "Italygate" conspiracy theory that Italian defense contractors had used satellite technology to convert votes for Mr. Trump to Mr. Biden, Mr. Donoghue wrote in an email that it was "pure insanity," testifying to the Jan. 6 committee that it was "patently absurd."

When Justice Department officials told Mr. Trump that they had not found widespread election fraud, he replied, according to Mr. Donoghue's testimony: "That is not what I'm asking you to do. I'm asking you to say it was corrupt and leave the rest to me and the Republican congressmen."

## Fighting in the Courts

Even before Election Day, Mr. Trump made clear that he planned to wage a legal battle, if necessary, to try to hold on to the White House. Two days before the vote, he stood in front of reporters in North Carolina and declared that as soon as the election was over, "We're going in with our lawyers."

For the next six weeks or so, the lawyers did go in—again and again—filing suits challenging the results. They fought in city courts, county courts and federal courts in key swing states from Georgia to Nevada. More than 60 lawsuits were ultimately filed by an army of lawyers, some employed by Mr. Trump's Republican allies, others working directly for his campaign.

This unfolded even as the president's own aides and advisers were telling him that he had been soundly—and legally—defeated.

According to testimony provided to the House committee by Jason Miller, a senior campaign adviser, a campaign data expert informed Mr. Trump shortly after the election "in pretty blunt terms that he was going to lose." A week or so later, the Cybersecurity and Infrastructure Security Agency, part of the Department of Homeland Security, announced that there was no evidence of fraud in the election.

That finding was backed by Attorney General William P. Barr, who alerted Mr. Trump privately in November and acknowledged publicly on Dec. 1 that the Justice Department had not found any evidence of fraud "on a scale that could have effected a different outcome in the election."

In the end, Mr. Trump's legal scorecard was abysmal. He won only one case, on a minor technical point affecting a small batch of votes in Pennsylvania.

Using the courts was Mr. Trump's first—and in a way, his most conventional—method of trying to stave off defeat.

He quickly turned to more unconventional methods.

Trump supporters outside the Senate chamber, after clashing with law enforcement officers and storming barricades to breach the Capitol. Calls for violence against lawmakers and taking over the building had circulated online for months. *Erin Schaff/The New York Times*

As early as August 2020, Mr. Trump reached out to a well-known Republican lawyer, Cleta Mitchell, to assemble an election litigation team, according to recent court papers.

After the election, a team of lawyers led by Mr. Giuliani and including Ms. Powell and Jenna Ellis oversaw the basic strategy used to manage cases handled by local lawyers in courts across the country. The cases fell into three broad categories.

The first was suits alleging what could be called traditional voting fraud. In Michigan, for instance, claims were made that poll workers had altered dates on absentee ballots. In Georgia, accusations arose that phony ballots had been sent to counting stations after hours. In Arizona, in what some of Mr. Trump's allies would call Sharpiegate, Republicans complained that dozens—maybe hundreds—of ballots had not been counted because voters had been told to fill them out with felt-tipped Sharpies instead of ballpoint pens.

A second batch of lawsuits focused on highly technical procedural issues related to changes made to the voting process during the coronavirus pandemic. Many of these suits raised questions about arcane matters like deadlines for submitting materials confirming the identities of mail-in voters or about the legitimacy of ballot drop boxes. They often hinged on complex arguments about the scope of state lawmakers' power to establish election rules.

The third category focused on a bizarre conspiracy theory that Chinese software companies, Swiss bankers, Venezuelan officials and the liberal financier George Soros had joined forces to hack Dominion voting machines in a plot to siphon votes from Mr. Trump. Filed in the Democratic strongholds of Atlanta, Detroit, Milwaukee and Phoenix, these suits became collectively known as the Krakens—a reference by Ms. Powell to a mythological, havoc-wreaking sea beast.

Even before the suits were filed, Trump campaign officials looked into some of the claims about Dominion and found that they had no merit. Eventually, the Kraken cases were laughed out of court.

Still, despite their outlandish content, Mr. Trump kept coming back to them. He mentioned the Dominion conspiracy theory several times on Jan. 2, 2021, in a phone call with Georgia's Republican secretary of state, Brad Raffensperger, whom he asked to "find 11,780" votes to help him win the state. (That call is now the subject of a criminal investigation in Georgia.)

After scores of cases were rejected—often with scathing words from judges—the State of Texas tried a Hail Mary, filing an unusual request directly to the Supreme Court that challenged election procedures in four key swing states: Georgia, Michigan, Pennsylvania and Wisconsin.

The Texas lawsuit asked the court to block those states from casting their electoral votes for Mr. Biden and to shift the selection of electors to the states' Republican legislatures. That would have effectively handed Mr. Trump the election and required the justices to throw out millions of votes.

The Supreme Court—in the hands of a conservative majority bolstered by three Trump appointees—rebuffed the effort in a brief, unsigned order, saying that Texas lacked the standing to pursue the case.

With the courts closing off as an avenue to keep Mr. Trump in power, he and his allies moved on to a series of largely ad hoc but stunningly antidemocratic efforts to reverse the election.


## A Showdown Over Executive Power

It was Dec. 17, 2020, three days after electors in state capitols across the country cast their Electoral College votes to formally confirm that Mr. Biden had been elected the 46th president of the United States. Under ordinary circumstances, that would have been accepted as the end of the election.

But Mr. Flynn, the onetime national security adviser, had other ideas.

Appearing on Newsmax, the conservative news channel, Mr. Flynn said that Mr. Trump "could immediately, on his order, seize every single" voting machine in the country.

"He could also order, within the swing states, if he wanted to, he could take military capabilities, and he could place them in those states and basically rerun an election in each of those states," said Mr. Flynn, whose pardon for lying to F.B.I. agents investigating his ties to Russia had been issued less than a month earlier.

"It's not unprecedented," he said, adding that while he was not advocating the use of martial law, it had been used dozens of times in American history.

A day later, Mr. Flynn was in the Oval Office, pressing his case directly to the president along with Ms. Powell and others. They came armed with draft executive orders that they wanted him to sign, partly based on the conspiracy theories about voting machine fraud that Mr. Waldron promoted.

On one side in the meeting were Ms. Powell and Mr. Flynn, who complained in front of West Wing officials—including Eric Herschmann, a lawyer in the White House Counsel's Office—that they were failing to fight hard enough for Mr. Trump. Ms. Powell and Mr. Flynn, asserting that foreign adversaries like China, Iran and Venezuela had used Dominion voting machines to flip votes for Mr. Biden, said that the president should use his authority to defend the United States, seize the machines and preserve them as evidence, and rerun the election.

On the other side were staff members like Mr. Herschmann, who initially took the lead in pushing back against Ms. Powell and Mr. Flynn and then called for West Wing aides to have the White House counsel, Pat A. Cipollone, join them.

As the meeting grew heated, Mr. Cipollone would tell the select committee, other plans were discussed—including to grant Ms. Powell a security clearance and name her special counsel, putting her in charge of Mr. Trump's legal effort to contest the election results.

The meeting was described in jolting detail during a public hearing by the House select committee as one of the most unhinged of the Trump presidency. It lasted hours, past midnight, moving from the Oval Office to other areas of the West Wing before ending in the presidential residence. It devolved into shouting that could be heard outside the room, with participants hurling insults and, at one point, nearly coming to blows. Some people left in tears.

Mr. Herschmann described a particularly intense moment in which Mr. Flynn "screamed at me that I was a quitter," to which he eventually yelled back: "Either come over or sit your f-ing ass back down."

The showdown came at a time when similar ideas were swirling among the president's allies. The House committee heard witness testimony that in the lead-up to and in the days after that moment, there were discussions in the White House about Mr. Trump asking about invoking martial law or the Insurrection Act, which would have allowed him to use active-duty troops for a specific purpose, according to a person familiar with the committee's work.

Mr. Giuliani was among those arguing against the idea of having the military commandeer voting machines. But around the same time, at Mr. Trump's direction, Mr. Giuliani called the Homeland Security Department to ask whether a civilian agency could do so. Kenneth T. Cuccinelli II, the acting deputy homeland security secretary, dismissed the idea, but Mr. Trump continued to ask about it in the days afterward.

In the end, the draft executive orders that Ms. Powell had brought to Mr. Trump went unsigned.

## A Hostile Takeover Attempt

At 3 p.m. on Sunday, Jan. 3, 2021, Jeffrey Clark, the acting head of the Justice Department's civil division and an expert in environmental law, strode into the conference room of his boss, Mr. Rosen, the acting attorney general who had taken over weeks earlier from Mr. Barr.

Mr. Clark had some remarkable but by that point not entirely surprising news: Mr. Trump had offered him the job of running the Justice Department, effective that day. Mr. Rosen was told he could stay on as the No. 2 if he wished. Mr. Rosen replied that he was not about to be fired by a subordinate and that he would take the matter directly to Mr. Trump.

The maneuvering for control of the Justice Department was a closely held secret at that point, but it underscored the lengths to which Mr. Trump was willing to go to forestall his defeat.

Over the span of several weeks, a battle raged among camps in the administration and among the president's allies over who would lead the Justice Department while it was under intense pressure from him to do more to investigate and validate his wide-ranging and unsupported claims that he had been robbed of re-election.

Over a few tense days, Mr. Trump brought to a head a plan that would have pushed aside Mr. Rosen, who had refused his entreaties, in favor of Mr. Clark, a loyalist who was eagerly promoting steps like having the Justice Department send Georgia officials a letter stating that voter fraud allegations could invalidate the state's Electoral College results—a message with no basis in fact.

Mr. Barr had previously dismissed allegations of widespread fraud, but Mr. Trump was not about to give up. He and his allies, including a band of Republican House members and several conservative lawyers, contacted Justice Department leaders nearly every day leading up to Jan. 6—sometimes multiple times a day—with demands for fraud investigations and other steps to overturn the election.

Representative Scott Perry, Republican of Pennsylvania, for instance, worked with Mr. Clark to try to persuade Georgia officials to withdraw the state's results. Others pushed the department to bring the fight to the Supreme Court.

The pressure campaign ramped up on Dec. 14, 2020, when Mr. Trump announced that the department's No. 2 official at the time, Mr. Rosen, would replace Mr. Barr. An aide to the president emailed Mr. Rosen talking points about voter fraud in Michigan and problems with Dominion Voting Systems machines, the first of many conspiracy theories that Mr. Rosen and his team would examine and debunk.

The next day in the Oval Office, Mr. Trump pressed Mr. Rosen to appoint a special counsel to investigate Dominion's machines and other issues. He wanted the department to support lawsuits that sought to overturn the election. Mr. Rosen rebuffed the requests, as he would for the next 19 days, reiterating Mr. Barr's statement that there was no widespread fraud.

Mr. Trump said the Justice Department was not fighting hard enough for him.

Mr. Rosen and other department officials hoped that the facts would eventually persuade the president to acknowledge his loss. They had no idea that Mr. Perry had secretly introduced Mr. Trump to Mr. Clark as the Justice Department ally he had longed for, one who would put the department to work disputing the election results.

Inklings of deeper trouble came on Dec. 27, when Mr. Rosen and his top deputy, Mr. Donoghue, told Mr. Trump that no evidence supported the lawsuits he had filed. Reports of corruption in swing states had not been borne out.

It was then that Mr. Trump instructed the pair to call the election "corrupt" and leave the rest to him and "the R. congressmen," according to Mr. Donoghue's notes on the meeting, which he would testify referred to Republican members of Congress.

Giving a hint of his intentions, Mr. Trump said that "people tell me Jeff Clark is great, I should put him in," Mr. Donoghue later testified. That day, Mr. Perry also called Mr. Donoghue to tell him that Mr. Clark could "do something" about the president's claims.

During tense conversations with Mr. Clark, Mr. Rosen and Mr. Donoghue learned that he was working on a plan with Mr. Trump's allies to overturn the results in Georgia. Mr. Clark asked Mr. Rosen to send a proposed letter falsely informing Georgia officials that a federal investigation could invalidate the state's results. Mr. Rosen refused.

At the White House, the president's chief of staff, Mark Meadows, briefed Mr. Rosen and Mr. Donoghue on Italygate, the groundless story about people in Italy remotely tampering with voting machines in the United States.

By New Year's Eve, Mr. Rosen and Mr. Donoghue had grown deeply concerned. They had rebuffed outlandish demands to lobby the Supreme Court, appoint special counsels and give credence to wild conspiracy theories. But they struggled to handle Mr. Clark, who wanted a department official to falsely say at a news conference that fraud inquiries had cast doubt on the election result.

Mr. Rosen and Mr. Donoghue forbade him from talking to Mr. Trump.

On Jan. 2, Mr. Clark revealed that he had secretly conducted a witness interview in connection with an election fraud allegation that had already been disproved. And he raised the prospect with Mr. Rosen that Mr. Trump could install him as the acting attorney general, but he offered a deal: He would decline any such offer if Mr. Rosen would send the sham letter to Georgia officials. Mr. Donoghue shut down the plan.

Mr. Clark then secretly spoke with Mr. Trump, in defiance of orders. On Jan. 3, Mr. Clark informed Mr. Rosen that the president intended to replace him.

Unwilling to be pushed out without a fight, Mr. Rosen worked with Mr. Cipollone,

# TRUMP LED ATTEMPTED COUP, PANEL SAYS

### He Is Accused of Spurring Jan. 6 Mob and Endorsing Pence's Hanging

**By LUKE BROADWATER**

WASHINGTON — The House Select Committee to Investigate the Jan. 6 Attack on the United States Capitol opened a landmark set of hearings on Thursday by showing video of aide after aide to former President Donald J. Trump testifying that his claims of a stolen election were false, as the panel laid out in meticulous detail the extent of the former president's efforts to overturn his defeat and keep himself in office.

Over about two hours, the panel offered new information about what it characterized as an attempted coup orchestrated by Mr. Trump that culminated in the deadliest assault on the Capitol in centuries. Its leaders revealed that investigators heard testimony that Mr. Trump endorsed the hanging of his own vice president as a mob of his supporters descended on Congress. They also said they had evidence that members of Mr. Trump's cabinet discussed invoking the 25th Amendment after the riot to remove him from office.

The session kicked off an ambitious effort by the nine-member committee, which was formed in July after Republicans blocked the creation of a nonpartisan commission to investigate the attack, to lay

The prime-time hearing, which unfolded in the historic Cannon House Office Building in a hall adorned with Corinthian columns and crystal chandeliers, featured dramatic video of how the Proud Boys, a right-wing extremist group, led the assault on the Capitol, and the emotional testimony of a U.S. Capitol Police officer who suffered a traumatic brain injury at the hands of the mob.

"What I saw was a war scene," Officer Caroline Edwards, one of the more than 150 officers injured in the campaign, testified after watching video of the moments when she was overrun by the mob. "I saw officers on the ground. They were bleeding. They were throwing up."

She added: "I was slipping on people's blood. It was carnage. It was chaos."

Officer Edwards's appearance reflected the potency of the committee's seamless two-hour presentation — including never-before-seen video — in bringing home the violence of that day all over again.It came as the committee began to publicly tell the story of how a sitting president undertook unprecedented efforts to overturn a democratic election and keep himself in power, resting the mantle of American de-

"Our democracy remains in danger," Representative Bennie Thompson, center, chair of the Jan. 6 House committee, said Thursday.

**Told of Injuries,** | **Portrait of a Power Grab by a Would-Be Autocrat**

The House committee investigating the Jan. 6 attack held its first prime-time televised hearing in a landmark series on June 9, 2022, kicking off its ambitious effort to lay out the full story of the assault on American democracy, orchestrated by a sitting president, that led to the deadly riot.

the White House counsel and an ally, to convene a meeting with Mr. Trump that evening, a Sunday. Before going to the White House, Mr. Donoghue hosted a conference call with several of the department's top leaders, laying out Mr. Clark's machinations and Mr. Rosen's upcoming fight for his job.

Should Mr. Rosen be fired, he asked, what would the group do?

Shocked, the officials agreed to resign en masse if Mr. Rosen was forced out. Their plan brought to mind the so-called Saturday Night Massacre, when Attorney General Elliot L. Richardson and his deputy resigned rather than carry out President Richard M. Nixon's order to fire the special prosecutor investigating him.

The showdown at the White House that evening was extraordinary even by the standards of the Trump administration. The president opened the Oval Office meeting around 6 p.m. with a blunt statement: "One thing we know is you, Rosen, aren't going to do anything to overturn the election," Mr. Rosen later testified.

Mr. Cipollone called Mr. Clark's plan to send the proposed letter to Georgia officials a "murder-suicide pact," participants in the meeting later testified. The Justice Department officials warned that firing Mr. Rosen would cause a mass resignation at the agency.

In a heated moment, Mr. Donoghue said that Mr. Clark "wouldn't even know how to find his way" to the F.B.I. director's office and was "not even competent to serve as the attorney general," he later told investigators.

When Mr. Clark protested, Mr. Donoghue told investigators, he snapped. "You're an environmental lawyer," he said he told Mr. Clark. "How about you go back to your office, and we'll call you when there's an oil spill."

Only in the final stages of the roughly three-hour meeting did Mr. Trump relent. The plan to install Mr. Clark to lead the Justice Department was shelved, and the letter to Georgia officials was never sent.

But the president was still not ready to let go of his election fraud claims. He said that he would fire the U.S. attorney in Atlanta, who quit upon hearing of the threat. Soon after the end of the Oval Office meeting, Mr. Donoghue recounted to Senate investigators, Mr. Trump alerted him to a report that a Department of Homeland Security agent had found a truck filled with shredded ballots near Atlanta.

The Justice Department, the F.B.I. and the Homeland Security Department later concluded that the only ballots that were destroyed were from previous elections. They had been cleared out to make room for storage of the 2020 ballots.

Thwarted in his attempt to execute a hostile takeover of the Justice Department, Mr. Trump and his team still had another strategy.

## Pressuring Pence

On Nov. 5, 2020, as his father waited for key states to finish counting their votes, Donald Trump Jr. texted a series of suggestions to Mr. Meadows, the White House chief of staff, for how the president could stay in power.

One message referred to Jan. 6, 2021, when the vice president would oversee the official congressional count of the Electoral College votes—typically a routine process. The message described the date as a last-ditch option, one that would be meaningful only if the Trump forces could engineer a situation in which neither Mr. Trump nor Mr. Biden was found to have amassed enough votes to prevail.

That plan had been pushed by Stephen K. Bannon, Mr. Trump's informal adviser and former White House counselor.

This tactic would involve two strands. The first was to create at least the appearance that there were alternate slates of pro-Trump electors from swing states that Mr. Biden had clearly won. That plan is now under scrutiny by federal prosecutors. The second was to persuade Mr. Pence, who would preside over Congress's count on Jan. 6 in his capacity as the president of the Senate, to disrupt the certification of Mr. Biden's victory.

Between Nov. 5, 2020, and Jan. 6, 2021, Mr. Pence was subjected to an intense pressure campaign from a range of Mr. Trump's associates outside government—including John Eastman, a lawyer working with the president—and from Mr. Trump himself. During that time, Mr. Pence had his counsel research what his powers were with regard to Jan. 6; over time, he made clear to the president that he did not believe he had the authority that Mr. Trump insisted he did.

The plan to replace legitimate electors for Mr. Biden with alternate electors for Mr. Trump ramped up days after the election. Ms. Mitchell, the pro-Trump lawyer, emailed Mr. Eastman, a former clerk for Justice Clarence Thomas, to assign him the task of producing a memo to create a legal framework to challenge the electoral certification in Congress.

"Why couldn't state legislatures reclaim that constitutional duty and designate the electors," Ms. Mitchell wrote to Mr. Eastman on Nov. 5, adding: "A movement is stirring. But needs constitutional support."

Mr. Eastman, Ms. Mitchell and others had been preparing to fight the results since well before Election Day. But the effort "kicked into high gear" four days afterward, on Nov. 7, when Mr. Eastman met with Mr. Trump's campaign team in Philadelphia to assist with the preparation of an election challenge, according to a filing by Mr. Eastman in a civil case.

Within days, members of Mr. Trump's legal team were exchanging written ideas about how to submit to Congress slates of pro-Trump electors in states won by Mr. Biden.

Lawyers working on the proposal made clear they knew that the pro-Trump electors they were putting forward might not hold up to legal scrutiny.

"We would just be sending in 'fake' electoral votes to Pence so that 'someone' in Congress can make an objection when they start counting votes, and start arguing that the 'fake' votes should be counted," Jack Wilenchik, a Phoenix-based lawyer who helped organize pro-Trump electors in Arizona, wrote on Dec. 8, 2020, to Boris Epshteyn, a strategic adviser for the Trump campaign, according to internal emails reviewed by *The New York Times*.

Some involved in the plan worried that it could "appear treasonous."

One lawyer, Kenneth Chesebro, wrote a series of memos in November and December 2020 describing how the plan could be carried out, though he said various state laws made it "somewhat dicey" and "very problematic" in some jurisdictions.

A federal judge has found that one of those memos—a missive sent to Mr. Eastman and Mr. Giuliani on Dec. 13 advising how the Senate could reject Mr. Biden's victory— "likely furthered the crimes of obstruction of an official proceeding and conspiracy to defraud the United States."

As lawyers were working to put into action the alternate elector plan, so were other members of Mr. Trump's team.

Michael A. Roman and Gary Michael Brown, the director and the deputy director of Election Day operations for Mr. Trump's campaign, began participating in the efforts to encourage state legislators to appoint "alternate" slates of electors, according to the House committee.

Angela McCallum, the Trump campaign's national executive assistant, made calls to

President Donald J. Trump rallied thousands of his supporters with an incendiary speech at the Ellipse, south of the White House, just before a large mob of them marched to the Capitol on Jan. 6. "We will never give up," the president told the crowd. "We will never concede." *Pete Marovich for The New York Times*

state legislators, telling them there was an effort in multiple states to keep Mr. Trump in office and asking for their support. "You do have the power to reclaim your authority and send a slate of electors that will support President Trump and Vice President Pence," she told one in Michigan, according to a voice message made public in December 2020.

Mr. Trump personally called Republican members of the Wayne County Board of Canvassers amid an effort to rescind the certification of the county's election results.

Eventually, the Republican National Committee was brought in. Ronna McDaniel, the chairwoman, testified before the House committee that during a call with Mr. Trump, he put Mr. Eastman on the phone with her "to talk about the importance of the R.N.C. helping the campaign gather these contingent electors."

Around the same time, the White House Counsel's Office told Mr. Meadows and Republican members of Congress that the plan to use so-called alternate electors was not "legally sound," but they pressed on.

On Jan. 2, Mr. Eastman and Mr. Giuliani joined Mr. Trump on a call with hundreds of state lawmakers. The president told the legislators they were the best chance to change the certified results of the presidential election in certain states. "You're the ones that are going to make the decision," he said.

Ultimately, groups of Republicans in seven states signed documents presenting themselves as either authorized or alternate electors.

But no state legislature or governor agreed to certify those slates as authentic. Out of options, Mr. Trump was left trying to pressure his vice president to unilaterally reject electoral votes for Mr. Biden when Congress met on Jan. 6.

On Jan. 4, 2021, Mr. Trump and Mr. Eastman met with Mr. Pence and his team in the Oval Office about the plan, which Mr. Eastman conceded in front of the president violated the Electoral Count Act, according to testimony to the House committee by Greg Jacob, the vice president's top lawyer. That session was followed by another on Jan. 5, during which Mr. Eastman again sought to persuade Mr. Jacob to go along with the scheme.

As Mr. Trump became more aggressive toward a number of officials, Mr. Pence told the president directly that he did not believe he had the power to delay the certification.

That day, Mr. Pence's chief of staff, Marc Short, called the lead Secret Service agent on the vice president's detail to his office in the West Wing to warn him that the tension between Mr. Trump and Mr. Pence was about to become public. The president was going to turn on the vice president, and they might have a security risk because of it, Mr. Short said, according to two people familiar with the conversation.

The next morning, Jan. 6, with his adult children and his aides milling around the Oval Office, Mr. Trump called the vice president's residence to push one last time. Just before Mr. Pence headed to the Capitol, people familiar with the discussion said shortly afterward, Mr. Trump told him: "You can either go down in history as a patriot, or you can go down in history as a pussy."

Outside at the Ellipse, a fervently pro-Trump crowd was waiting.

## From Protest to Riot

Like so many things during Mr. Trump's time in the White House, it started with a tweet.

On Dec. 19, 2020, six weeks after losing the election, Mr. Trump took to Twitter and issued a call to his supporters to join him in Washington for a last-ditch rally to protest the results of the vote. A date was set for Jan. 6, 2021—the day Congress would oversee the final certification of the count.

"Be there," Mr. Trump wrote, "will be wild!"

The response online was huge and instantaneous. Within hours, the president's words were amplified by a network of right-wing activists and hard-core conservatives in Congress. In the offline world, pro-Trump organizers set to work obtaining permits and portable toilets; people across the country started to mobilize, making travel plans and arranging for hotel rooms.

Ultimately, hundreds of thousands of Trump supporters descended on Washington that day, and many listened to the president deliver an incendiary speech at the Ellipse near the White House. They heard his claims that the election had been stolen and his encouragement to "fight like hell" to save the country. Thousands heeded his call to march from the Ellipse to the Capitol.

Ten minutes after Mr. Trump posted his tweet, Michael Coudrey, an associate of the "Stop the Steal" activist Ali Alexander, reposted it with more than 5,000 retweets. The right-wing outlet Gateway Pundit soon published an article about the tweet and a similar video that the president released that night. Mr. Trump's social media guru, Dan Scavino Jr., posted the article on Twitter and soon had more than 20,000 retweets.

The amplification continued all that day and for weeks afterward. Far-right extremist groups were among those that reacted the most forcefully, acquiring protective gear, setting up private channels of communication and, in one case, readying heavily armed "quick reaction forces" to be staged outside Washington. (In November 2022, Stewart Rhodes, the leader of the Oath Keepers militia, was convicted of seditious conspiracy for his role in the events of Jan. 6; top members of the Proud Boys were indicted on similar charges.)

By the first week in January, the Capitol Police's intelligence division, which draws on information from the F.B.I. and the Department of Homeland Security, issued a report warning of desperation about "the last opportunity to overturn the results of the presidential election" and the potential for significant danger to federal law enforcement and the public. On the morning of Jan. 6, top White House officials warned Mr. Meadows that law enforcement was reporting that multiple people were arriving at Mr. Trump's rally at the Ellipse carrying weapons such as knives, guns, bear spray, body armor, spears and flagpoles.

The president had been told they were armed, according to the testimony of Cassidy Hutchinson, Mr. Meadows's top aide. But Mr. Trump, preoccupied with the apparent size of the crowd, asked for metal detectors to be removed from the Ellipse so his supporters could get closer to the stage—a request that was rebuffed. He encouraged them to go to the Capitol anyway.

"You will never take back our country with weakness," Mr. Trump told the crowd.

As he spoke, a group of his supporters, including members of the Proud Boys, began breaching security barriers outside the Capitol and clashing with police officers defending the building. Once he finished speaking, Mr. Trump demanded that his presidential motorcade take him to the Capitol to join the throng and became "irate" when he was told he could not go because of security concerns, Ms. Hutchinson later testified.

On the Capitol grounds, the mob grew increasingly violent, erecting a gallows, brutalizing law enforcement officers and disrupting the electoral count underway in the Capitol, sending lawmakers and the vice president fleeing with the mahogany boxes containing the ballots. As rioters chanted "Hang Mike Pence," Mr. Eastman, the lawyer who had been pushing the plan to block or delay the certification, sent a hostile message to Mr. Jacob, Mr. Pence's counsel, blaming the vice president for the violence.

"The 'siege' is because YOU and your boss did not do what was necessary to allow this to be aired in a public way so that the American people can see for themselves what happened," Mr. Eastman wrote.

Once he was back at the White House, Mr. Trump sat in his dining room off the Oval Office, watching the violence unfold on Fox News. For hours, he did nothing to stop the riot, despite repeated entreaties from his aides and advisers, Republican members of Congress and others.

A call from a Pentagon official to coordinate a response to the assault on the Capitol went unanswered because, according to one White House official, "the president didn't want anything done."

As the riot continued, Mr. Meadows left the dining room and told colleagues that Mr. Trump was complaining that the vice president was being whisked to safety as the mob chanted for his execution.

"He doesn't want to do anything," Mr. Meadows told Mr. Cipollone, the White House counsel.

"You heard him, Pat, he thinks Mike deserves it," Ms. Hutchinson said Mr. Meadows had responded. "He doesn't think they are doing anything wrong."

As aides, including his daughter Ivanka Trump, implored him to make a statement to quell the violence, the president refused to call for peace, according to testimony by Sarah Matthews, a deputy White House press secretary who resigned that day. It took more than three hours for Mr. Trump to tell the mob to disperse—and he did so grudgingly, altering a script he had been given to remove a condemnation of the violence.

In a video posted on Twitter, Mr. Trump told his supporters that there had been "an election that was stolen from us," but that it was time for them to go home peacefully. "We love you," he said. "You're very special."

---

An earlier version of this essay was published in The New York Times.

It took the police more than three hours to regain control of the Capitol complex. The assault resulted in one of the worst days of injuries for law enforcement in the United States since the Sept. 11, 2001, terrorist attacks. *Kenny Holston for The New York Times*

Officer Eugene Goodman of the Capitol Police diverted pro-Trump rioters from entering the Senate chamber, where lawmakers and Vice President Mike Pence were gathered on Jan. 6. Officer Goodman, whose actions were captured on video, was widely credited with saving lives. He was later awarded the Congressional Gold Medal for his bravery. *Ashley Gilbertson/VII/Redux, for The New York Times Magazine*

"All the News That's Fit to Print"

# The New York Times

Late Edition

Today, mostly sunny, seasonally warm, low humidity, high 84. Tonight, clear to partly cloudy, low 68. Tomorrow, sunny, very warm, high 88. Weather map is on Page B10.

VOL. CLXXI ... No. 59,469    © 2022 The New York Times Company    NEW YORK, WEDNESDAY, JUNE 29, 2022    $3.00

# ENRAGED TRUMP ENCOURAGED VIOLENCE AND SOUGHT TO JOIN MOB, AIDE TESTIFIES

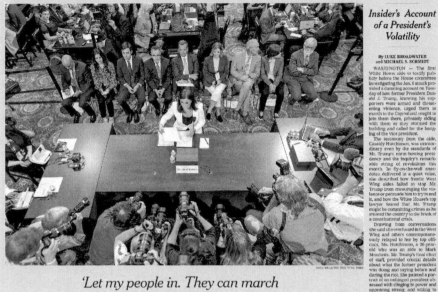

**Insider's Account of a President's Volatility**

By LUKE BROADWATER and MICHAEL S. SCHMIDT

WASHINGTON — The first White House aide to testify publicly before the House committee investigating the Jan. 6 attack provided a damning account on Tuesday of how former President Donald J. Trump, knowing his supporters were armed and threatening violence, urged them to march to the Capitol and sought to join them there, privately siding with them as they stormed the building and called for the hanging of the vice president.

The testimony from the aide, Cassidy Hutchinson, was extraordinary even by the standards of Mr. Trump's norm-busting presidency and the inquiry's remarkable string of revelations this month. In fly-on-the-wall anecdotes delivered in a quiet voice, she described how frantic West Wing aides failed to stop Mr. Trump from encouraging the violence or persuade him to try to end it, and how the White House's top lawyer feared that Mr. Trump might be committing crimes as he steered the country to the brink of a constitutional crisis.

Drawing from conversations she said she overheard in the West Wing and others contemporaneously relayed to her by top officials, Ms. Hutchinson, a 26-year-old who was an aide to Mark Meadows, Mr. Trump's final chief of staff, provided crucial details about what the former president was doing and saying before and during the riot. She painted a portrait of an unhinged president obsessed with clinging to power and appearing strong and willing to tolerate violence as a result — as long as it was not directed at him.

"They're not here to hurt me," she testified that Mr. Trump said as he demanded that security checkpoints be removed outside his rally on the Ellipse on Jan. 6, knowing that many of his supporters were armed and threatening violence. "Take the f-ing mags away. Let my people in. They can march to the Capitol from here."

'Let my people in. They can march to the Capitol from here. Let the people in.'

CASSIDY HUTCHINSON, former White House aide, summarizing Donald J. Trump's demand on Jan. 6, 2021, to remove metal detectors as a mob gathered at the Ellipse.

## Vivid Testimony Could Undercut A Possible Free-Speech Defense

By ALAN FEUER and GLENN THRUSH

It was one of the most dramatic moments in a presentation filled with them: Just before President Donald J. Trump went onstage near the White House last year, inquiry is focused on Mr. Trump remains unclear. But the revela-

**Witness Says President Knew of Weapons**

## Increasingly Unhinged as Power Slipped Away

By PETER BAKER

WASHINGTON — He flung his lunch across the room, smashing the plate in a fit of anger as ketchup dripped down the wall. He appeared to endorse supporters who wanted to hang his

NEWS ANALYSIS

**Trump's Erratic Actions Came as No Surprise at White House**

from her account was volatile.

or for that matter, many who had known him in the decades that preceded his life in politics. But hearing her recount it all under oath, on live television, brought home how much Mr. Trump and his White House spiraled in its perilous last chapter.

"This is f-ing crazy," Pat A. Cipollone, his White House counsel, said at one point.

It was an act of vanity by Mr. Trump, who wanted his crowd to appear as large as possible, that recalled his first day in office, which was consumed by his false claims about the size of the crowd at his inauguration. Ms. Hutchinson recounted it as she laid out a day of chaos in the White House

---

In the House committee's sixth hearing, Cassidy Hutchinson, a former White House aide, described in stunning testimony an unhinged President Donald J. Trump's actions. He was warned that his supporters were armed but expressed no concern because they were not a threat to him, she said.

*Edited by Julie Hirschfeld Davis and Richard W. Stevenson*

# The Committee and Staff

BY LUKE BROADWATER

## Representative Bennie Thompson

DOUG MILLS/THE NEW YORK TIMES

A nearly 30-year veteran of Congress when he was named to lead the House select committee to investigate the Jan. 6 attack, Representative Bennie Thompson, Democrat of Mississippi, was raised in the segregated Deep South, where his father could not vote and he received death threats because of his race early in his political career. After rising through the ranks of local politics in Bolton, Miss., he won a special election to Congress in 1993. There, he worked on higher education equity issues and steered large federal spending projects to his district, which includes the poverty-stricken Mississippi Delta and the majority-Black city of Jackson. At the start of the Jan. 6 committee's series of public hearings to lay out its findings in 2022, he said he took the attack on the Capitol personally. "I'm from a part of the country where people justify the actions of slavery, the Ku Klux Klan and lynching," Mr. Thompson said. "I'm reminded of that dark history as I hear voices today try and justify the actions of the insurrectionists on Jan. 6, 2021."

## Representative Liz Cheney

A deeply conservative Republican from ruby-red Wyoming who at the time of the Jan. 6 attack was her party's third-ranking leader in the House, Representative Liz Cheney, the daughter of former Vice President Dick Cheney, would initially have seemed like the last person to help lead a congressional investigation of how her party's president helped unleash an unprecedented assault on the Capitol. But following the riot, Ms. Cheney became an outspoken critic of President Donald J. Trump and his election lies. She broke with her party to support his impeachment on the charge of incitement of insurrection, and she was ousted from her leadership post for continuing to publicly condemn him and his actions. When Republicans blocked the creation of an independent, nonpartisan commission to investigate the Jan. 6 attack, House Democrats formed the select committee and ultimately asked her to join as its vice chairwoman. From that perch, she pushed to use Congress's investigative powers

aggressively to make a case that Mr. Trump should be prosecuted for his actions. Ms. Cheney's prominent role helped fuel a primary challenge from a Trump-backed candidate, Harriet Hageman, who defeated her in August 2022.

## Representative Zoe Lofgren

A close ally of Speaker Nancy Pelosi and one of four lawyers on the committee, Representative Zoe Lofgren, Democrat of California, is Congress's institutional memory on charging a president with high crimes and misdemeanors, having played a role in four impeachments of three presidents. As a young law student in 1974, she helped the House Judiciary Committee draft its Watergate charges against President Richard M. Nixon. Decades later, in 1998, she was a member of the committee when it voted to approve impeachment

charges against President Bill Clinton despite opposition from her and other Democrats, and in 2020, she was a House manager during Mr. Trump's first impeachment trial. Ms. Lofgren spoke on the House floor in 2021 in favor of impeaching Mr. Trump for incitement of insurrection following the Jan. 6 attack, and she also participated in efforts to rewrite the Electoral Count Act, a complex and little-known law that Mr. Trump and his allies tried to use to overturn the 2020 election in Congress.

## Representative Adam Kinzinger

Like Ms. Cheney, Representative Adam Kinzinger of Illinois was one of only 10 Republicans who voted to impeach Mr. Trump for what happened on Jan. 6. An Air Force veteran who served in both Iraq and Afghanistan and a six-term congressman, Mr. Kinzinger was outspoken even as the violence unfolded in condemning Mr. Trump's actions, calling the attack "a coup attempt." And unlike other Republicans who soon tempered their criticism, Mr. Kinzinger did not back down despite criticism

from his colleagues, his party and even members of his family, 11 members of which disowned him in a letter. Ms. Pelosi named him to the select committee after rejecting two lawmakers chosen by Republican leaders who had defended Mr. Trump after the riot, which prompted Republican leaders to boycott the panel entirely.

## Representative Adam B. Schiff

A former prosecutor who is also a favorite of Ms. Pelosi's, Representative Adam B. Schiff, Democrat of California and the chairman of the House Intelligence Committee, led the first impeachment of Mr. Trump on charges that he abused his office by attempting to withhold aid to Ukraine in exchange for an investigation into Joseph R. Biden Jr., a rival for the presidency. He brought the same understated style and sense of outrage on behalf of democracy to the investigation into Mr. Trump's role in the Jan. 6 attack. Mr. Schiff

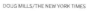

DOUG MILLS/THE NEW YORK TIMES

led the select committee's hearing that laid out how the former president and his allies pressured Republican officials in swing states to reverse his loss and pursued a plan to name fake slates of electors intended to tilt the Electoral College result in his favor.

## Representative Pete Aguilar

A former mayor of Redlands, Calif., Representative Pete Aguilar was the vice chairman of the House Democratic Caucus and the highest-ranking Latino in Congress. He led the questioning in the explosive public hearing in which the panel laid out how Mr. Trump continued to pressure Vice President Mike Pence to go along with his plan to unilaterally overturn his election defeat when Congress met to make an official count of the results, even though Mr. Trump was told it was unlawful.

DOUG MILLS/THE NEW YORK TIMES

## Representative Stephanie Murphy

The first Vietnamese American woman elected to the House, Representative Stephanie Murphy, Democrat of Florida, had a unique perspective on the threats to democracy laid bare on Jan. 6, given her family's escape from war-torn Vietnam and that country's history. Her background as a national security specialist for the Defense Department often involved working with what she described as struggling or nascent democracies abroad. Ms. Murphy helped to lead the hearing that focused on the role of domestic

HAIYUN JIANG/THE NEW YORK TIMES

violent extremist groups in orchestrating and carrying out the assault on the Capitol.

## Representative Jamie Raskin

The lead impeachment manager during Mr. Trump's Senate trial for incitement of insurrection, Representative Jamie Raskin, Democrat of Maryland, would go on to play an aggressive role in the Jan. 6 committee's investigation. The attack on the Capitol carried tragic personal significance for Mr. Raskin, who was a constitutional law professor and state legislator before winning election to Congress in 2016. The attack unfolded on his first day back on Capitol Hill after burying his son, Tommy Raskin, who died by suicide. Mr. Raskin was in the House chamber when the

KENNY HOLSTON FOR
THE NEW YORK TIMES

mob descended, and he began drafting an impeachment article against Mr. Trump later that day after he and other lawmakers had been taken to a secure location. He helped lead the hearing examining ties between Mr. Trump and the domestic violent extremist groups that participated in the riot.

## Representative Elaine Luria

The only politically endangered Democrat to sit on the Jan. 6 panel, Representative Elaine Luria of Virginia risked her job representing a swing district to be part of the investigation. "If I don't get re-elected because of this, that's OK," she told *The New York Times*. She served as a naval officer for 20 years and said constituents in her heavily military district took the Constitution and the nation's institutions seriously and would reward her efforts to expose the former president's attempts to subvert them. She

HAIYUN JIANG/THE NEW YORK TIMES

helped lead the questioning during the committee's prime-time hearing that focused on the 187-minute time period on Jan. 6 during which Mr. Trump did nothing while his supporters attacked the Capitol in his name. She was defeated in the midterm elections as the panel was in the throes of writing its report, one of only six Democratic incumbents to be beaten by a Republican in 2022.

## Timothy J. Heaphy

A former federal prosecutor, Timothy J. Heaphy served as the committee's chief investigative counsel, overseeing a staff of dozens of investigators. He previously served as the U.S. attorney for the Western District of Virginia during the Obama administration, where he led a number of high-profile prosecutions, and as the top lawyer for the University of Virginia, but he had never worked on Capitol Hill. As the lead investigator for the panel, he used prosecutorial tactics not generally employed by Congress, including link analysis, a data mapping technique often used by the F.B.I. to sort through reams of telephone records and metadata. Faced with more than a dozen Trump allies who refused to fully cooperate with the committee, his team of prosecutors took a page from mob cases, quietly turning at least six lower-level Trump staff members into witnesses who provided information about their bosses' activities. And Mr. Heaphy pushed for witness interviews to be recorded on video so they could be used in public hearings.

JASON ANDREW FOR
THE NEW YORK TIMES

## James Goldston

The former president of ABC News, James Goldston was hired by the committee to help distill a complex and multifaceted investigation into a made-for-television series of hearings that debuted in prime time in June 2022, drawing 20 million viewers. With a handful of production staff members, Mr. Goldston was in charge of sifting through and editing down hours of footage of the Capitol riot as it unfolded, including video from police body cameras, cellphones and hallway surveillance cameras as well as raw footage

DREW ANGERER/GETTY IMAGES

recorded by a documentarian. He also played a pivotal role in producing each hearing, packaging them as if they were episodes of a drama, complete with a tight script, surprises at key moments and cliffhangers to entice viewers to tune in for the next installment.

## John Wood

John Wood served as a senior investigative counsel for the committee, leading its "gold team" that investigated Mr. Trump's inner circle. Mr. Wood was a close associate of Ms. Cheney. He previously worked as a U.S. attorney during the George W. Bush administration and as a Supreme Court clerk for Justice Clarence Thomas. Mr. Wood left the committee in June 2022 to pursue a Senate bid in Missouri as an independent. He later abandoned that effort.

DOUG MILLS/THE NEW YORK TIMES

*Edited by Julie Hirschfeld Davis*

# Witnesses

BY LUKE BROADWATER, ALAN FEUER, MAGGIE HABERMAN,
KATIE BENNER AND MICHAEL S. SCHMIDT

## Officer Caroline Edwards

Caroline Edwards is believed to have been the first Capitol Police officer injured during the riot. She testified in chilling detail about what she experienced when the mob breached the police barricade where she was stationed protecting the Capitol. Officer Edwards was crushed beneath bike racks and knocked unconscious when the rioters overwhelmed her and a handful of other officers, and she sustained a traumatic brain injury. She told the committee that after regaining consciousness, she continued to fight off the crowd, slipping in blood and watching fellow officers writhing in pain and suffering from bear spray and tear gas as a combat-like scene unfolded around her. "It was carnage," she testified. "It was chaos. I can't even describe what I saw."

DOUG MILLS/THE NEW YORK TIMES

## Officer Michael Fanone

Michael Fanone, an officer with Washington's Metropolitan Police Department who was seriously injured during the Capitol riot, was one of the first witnesses to testify publicly before the committee. At a hearing in July 2021, Officer Fanone described how he had been beaten unconscious by the mob and subjected to repeated shocks with his own Taser, suffering a heart attack and a brain injury. He heard rioters calling for him to be killed with his own gun. The panel played video from Officer Fanone's body camera in which he could be heard pleading for mercy—"I've got

OLIVER CONTRERAS FOR
THE NEW YORK TIMES

kids," he muttered—before being carried off by fellow officers and losing consciousness. "I feel like I went to hell and back to protect them and the people in this room," Officer Fanone said in emotional testimony, referring to members of Congress. "But too many are now telling me that hell doesn't exist, or that hell actually wasn't that bad." Officer Fanone's experience prompted him to become something of an activist, and he ultimately left the force and became an on-air contributor for CNN on law enforcement issues.

## Officer Harry Dunn

Officer Harry Dunn of the Capitol Police, who was among the officers who fought off the rioters on Jan. 6, emerged as one of the leading voices condemning the violence and calling attention to the racism and brutality of the rioters. Officer Dunn told the committee that a rioter had used a racial slur against him, screaming that "This n— voted for Joe Biden!" The words that Officer Dunn spoke to another Black member of the Capitol Police in the Rotunda after the violence had ended were cited in the Senate's

JIM BOURG/REUTERS

impeachment trial of Mr. Trump. "I said, 'Is this America?' and I started crying," Officer Dunn recounted in an interview with *The Times*. "Tears are coming down my face. 'Is this America?'" Later, Officer Dunn urged the lawmakers leading the inquiry to uncover the full extent of Mr. Trump's role. "There was an attack carried out on Jan. 6, and a hitman sent them," he said. "I want you to get to the bottom of that."

## Officer Daniel Hodges

Officer Daniel Hodges, a member of the Metropolitan Police Department, was crushed in a door on Jan. 6 as he and other officers battled the mob in a tunnel-like entrance to the Capitol. He described to the panel how the rioters descended into "terrorism," booing and mocking the police as they hoisted American, Christian and Trump flags. As he was crushed in the door, a rioter attempted to gouge out his eye. "To my perpetual confusion, I saw the 'thin blue line' flag—a symbol of support for law enforcement—more than once being carried by the terrorists

OLIVER CONTRERAS FOR
THE NEW YORK TIMES

as they ignored our commands and continued to assault us," Officer Hodges said.

## Sgt. Aquilino A. Gonell

Sgt. Aquilino A. Gonell of the Capitol Police, a military veteran, told the committee of the clear message he heard from rioters as he fought to keep them out of the Capitol: "All of them were telling us, 'Trump sent us.'" Sergeant Gonell said what he went through on Capitol Hill that day had been more fearsome than any experience patrolling bomb-infested roads during an Army deployment in Iraq, denouncing what he called a "continued, shocking attempt to ignore or try to destroy the truth of what truly happened that day." Sergeant Gonell was forced to leave his career in policing because of injuries he sustained during the violence, a committee member said.

CHIP SOMODEVILLA/GETTY IMAGES

## William P. Barr

Shortly after the 2020 election, Attorney General William P. Barr gave prosecutors at the Justice Department the authority to investigate "specific allegations" of voter fraud. But privately, he soon came to believe that Mr. Trump's claims of election irregularities were unfounded and began pushing back aggressively on them. His public statement on Dec. 1, 2020, that there had been no widespread fraud in the election enraged Mr. Trump, who treated him to an Oval Office dressing-down. Mr. Barr soon resigned. In videotaped testimony played during the committee's hearings, he offered some of the most unvarnished assessments of Mr. Trump's fraud claims, calling them "bullshit," "complete nonsense" and "crazy stuff" and saying that his view at the time was that the president must have been "detached from reality" if he believed them. Mr. Barr told the panel that Mr. Trump was repeatedly told the election had not been stolen but that he never gave any "indication of interest in what the actual facts were."

OLIVER CONTRERAS FOR
THE NEW YORK TIMES

## Bill Stepien

Bill Stepien, Mr. Trump's campaign manager, participated in discussions with the president and his campaign staff about whether he had a path to victory after the 2020 balloting. Mr. Stepien told the House panel that he had told Mr. Trump on election night that he had no basis for declaring victory, but that Mr. Trump, who was being advised the opposite by Rudolph W. Giuliani, his personal

ANNA MONEYMAKER FOR
THE NEW YORK TIMES

lawyer, did so anyway. Mr. Stepien said there were essentially two teams advising Mr. Trump following the election and that his was "Team Normal." Mr. Stepien testified under subpoena and canceled an in-person appearance at a committee hearing because his wife was in labor. The panel instead used clips of his videotaped testimony.

## Byung J. "BJay" Pak

A former U.S. attorney in Atlanta, Byung J. "BJay" Pak testified to the Senate Judiciary Committee about his decision to resign in January 2021. At the time, Mr. Trump wanted to fire Mr. Pak over his refusal to back up the president's false claims of election fraud in Georgia. At a hearing of the Jan. 6 panel, Mr. Pak said his office had investigated wild claims promoted by Mr. Giuliani, about a suitcase full of ballots being brought in to change the election results. "The allegations made by Mr. Giuliani were false," Mr. Pak testified.

JASON ANDREW FOR
THE NEW YORK TIMES

## Al Schmidt

The sole Republican on the three-member Philadelphia County Board of Elections during the 2020 presidential balloting, Al Schmidt was targeted publicly by Mr. Trump after he defended the integrity of the city's vote-counting efforts. Days after the election, Mr. Schmidt appeared on television and said he had seen no evidence of widespread fraud in Philadelphia, adding that there had been "the most fantastical things on social media" alleging wrongdoing. The president lashed out at him on Twitter, questioning whether he was a Republican and saying that

JASON ANDREW FOR
THE NEW YORK TIMES

Mr. Schmidt "refuses to look at a mountain of corruption & dishonesty." Mr. Schmidt testified to the Jan. 6 committee that after Mr. Trump singled him out, the threats he had been receiving became more specific and graphic and included members of his family, their ages, his address and pictures of his home.

## Eric Herschmann

A top White House lawyer in the final year of the Trump administration, Eric Herschmann pushed back against people around Mr. Trump who were urging him to take extreme steps to overturn the election results. The committee used video clips from Mr. Herschmann's private testimony at key moments during the hearings, including several expletive-laced anecdotes in which he recounted rebuking individuals in the president's orbit who were advising him on ways to invalidate his defeat. Mr. Herschmann was present for an explosive, hourslong meeting in the Oval Office on Dec. 18, 2020, in which a group of outside allies of Mr. Trump, including the lawyer Sidney Powell and Michael T. Flynn, the former national security adviser, pressed outlandish claims of election fraud and urged Mr. Trump to sign an executive order to seize voting machines. Mr. Herschmann faced off with the group and then asked for aides to

get Pat A. Cipollone, the White House counsel, to join them. Mr. Herschmann also testified that the day after the riot, he told John Eastman, a lawyer who hatched a plan to have the vice president disrupt Congress's certification of the election, that he should get a good criminal defense lawyer. "You're going to need it," he recalled telling Mr. Eastman.

## Ivanka Trump

Ivanka Trump, Mr. Trump's elder daughter, served as one of his senior advisers in the White House. She testified behind closed doors for about eight hours before the House committee, and parts of her interview were featured in the panel's public hearings. She told the panel that she had accepted Mr. Barr's conclusion that there was no widespread fraud that tipped the election to Mr. Biden. "It affected my perspective," she said. "I respect Attorney General Barr, so I accepted what he was saying." That drew a

broadside from Mr. Trump. Ms. Trump's chief of staff at the White House, Julie Radford, testified that Ms. Trump had been shaken by her father's heated phone call with Mr. Pence on the morning of Jan. 6, in which the president used a misogynistic expletive to call out what he saw as Mr. Pence's cowardice for refusing to disrupt the certification of the election. Former administration officials also recounted how, during the riot, Ms. Trump was one of several advisers who tried repeatedly to persuade the president to call off the violence. A former White House press aide testified that when Mr. Trump resisted using the word "peace" in a tweet addressed to his rioting supporters, Ms. Trump suggested that he tell the crowd—which was already brutalizing police officers at the Capitol—to "stay peaceful," an obfuscation that the president accepted.

## Alex Cannon

The taped testimony of Alex Cannon, a lawyer who worked on the Trump campaign and for the Trump Organization, was featured at some of the committee's hearings, showing that top officials in Mr. Trump's campaign and his White House knew the election had not been stolen, even as the president claimed otherwise. Mr. Cannon told Mark Meadows, the White House chief of staff, that Trump allies had found no election issues that could reverse the results in key states. "So there's no there there," Mr. Meadows responded, according to Mr. Cannon.

HOUSE SELECT COMMITTEE.
VIA ASSOCIATED PRESS

## Jason Miller

Jason Miller, a senior adviser for the Trump campaign, told the committee in a deposition that Mr. Trump had been told soon after Election Day by a campaign data expert in "pretty blunt terms" that he was going to lose, suggesting that Mr. Trump was well aware that his months of assertions about a stolen election were false. Mr. Trump subsequently said he disagreed with the data expert's analysis, Mr. Miller said, because he thought he could win in court. Mr. Miller also told the panel that Mr. Giuliani, the former mayor of New York City, encouraged the president

VICTOR MORIYAMA FOR
THE NEW YORK TIMES

to say he had won the election on election night, even though votes were still being counted and his prospects of victory were not good. "The mayor was definitely intoxicated," Mr. Miller said in videotaped testimony played publicly by the committee.

## Greg Jacob

Few witnesses provided evidence as damning about the unlawful nature of the plot to overturn the 2020 election as Greg Jacob, the top White House lawyer to Mr. Pence. In a deposition, a series of emails turned over to the Jan. 6 committee and ultimately in-person testimony on Capitol Hill, Mr. Jacob described how Mr. Eastman, the architect of a plan embraced by Mr. Trump to use the vice president to nullify the election outcome, admitted to him that the strategy was illegal. Mr. Jacob played a pivotal role in the days before the Jan. 6 attack, advising Mr. Pence not to

KENNY HOLSTON FOR
THE NEW YORK TIMES

go along with the pressure campaign by Mr. Trump to throw out legitimate electoral votes for Mr. Biden. A memo written by Mr. Jacob warned the vice president that he would most likely lose in court if he delayed the vote certification. Existing laws "were already clear that the vice president did not possess the extraordinary powers others urged upon him," Mr. Jacob told the committee in a written statement.

## Marc Short

Marc Short, who served as chief of staff to Mr. Pence, testified privately before the House committee. Mr. Short was with Mr. Pence on Jan. 6 as a mob of Mr. Trump's supporters attacked the Capitol, and he provided the committee with firsthand knowledge of the effort by Mr. Trump and his allies to try to persuade the vice president to throw out legitimate electoral votes for Mr. Biden in favor of fake slates of pro-Trump electors. Mr. Short also told the panel that he grew so concerned about Mr. Trump's actions that

DOUG MILLS/THE NEW YORK TIMES

he presented a warning to a Secret Service agent: The president was going to publicly turn against the vice president, and there could be a security risk to Mr. Pence because of it.

## Rusty Bowers

Rusty Bowers, the speaker of the Arizona House of Representatives, testified publicly in painstaking and emotional detail about the pressure campaign he faced after the 2020 election, in which Mr. Trump lost his state. A Republican, Mr. Bowers told the House committee about the harassment he experienced outside his home from Trump supporters in the weeks before Jan. 6, recounting being called a pedophile and other epithets. Mr. Bowers, who spoke about the Constitution in reverential and spiritual

DOUG MILLS/THE NEW YORK TIMES

terms, had tears in his eyes as he described his gravely ill daughter enduring some of the harassment outside the house. (She died a few weeks after the riot.) He said the effort to persuade him to take steps to flip the outcome in Arizona to Mr. Trump's column began with pressure from Mr. Giuliani, who maintained that he had evidence of fraud. "Aren't we all Republicans here? I would think we would get a better reception," Mr. Bowers recalled Mr. Giuliani saying at one point. Eventually, he recalled, Mr. Giuliani said: "We've got lots of theories. We just don't have the evidence."

## Brad Raffensperger

Brad Raffensperger, Georgia's secretary of state, resisted efforts by Mr. Trump to overturn Mr. Biden's victory in his state. In a phone call on Jan. 2, 2021, that was recorded and leaked to the news media, Mr. Raffensperger, a Republican, was heard facing off against Mr. Trump and some of his lawyers and advisers, who presented a number of conspiracy theories that they argued could give Mr. Raffensperger reason to invalidate Mr. Biden's victory in Georgia. Mr. Raffensperger was heard repeatedly rejecting those arguments, as well as Mr. Trump's exhortation that he "find" 11,780 votes in the state—enough to declare Mr. Trump the winner of Georgia's 16 electoral votes. Mr. Raffensperger testified at a committee hearing that in the wake of the election, as he refuted Mr. Trump's claims of voter fraud in the state, his wife received "sexualized" threats by text and people broke into his daughter-in-law's house.

KENNY HOLSTON FOR
THE NEW YORK TIMES

## Gabriel Sterling

Gabriel Sterling, a top election official in Georgia who disputed Mr. Trump's false claims of fraud in the 2020 election, testified publicly before the Jan. 6 committee, along with Mr. Raffensperger, about how Mr. Trump had pressured them to produce more votes for him in the state, and the threats they endured for refusing to do so. Mr. Sterling and Mr. Raffensperger became vocal defenders of Georgia's election security in the weeks after the election, even as Mr. Trump and members of his campaign sought to discredit the

DOUG MILLS/THE NEW YORK TIMES

results and circulated conspiracy theories that the election had been rigged in favor of Mr. Biden. Unlike other state-level officials who did not publicly dispute Mr. Trump's false claims, Mr. Sterling repeatedly spoke out against the falsehoods in a prominent fashion. He told the committee in public testimony that a death threat he saw on Twitter featuring a noose prompted him to call a fiery news conference in which he angrily countered false claims of election fraud in Georgia and called on Mr. Trump to condemn threats against election officials, saying, "It has to stop."

## Wandrea Moss

An elections worker in Fulton County, Ga., Wandrea Moss, who goes by Shaye, became ensnared in Mr. Trump's election fraud lies when his allies baselessly claimed that she and her mother, Ruby Freeman, had taken 18,000 fraudulent ballots out of suitcases and put them through voting machines. Even though Fulton County and state election officials quickly debunked the accusations, the women were subjected to death threats and other harassment, and Mr. Trump himself invoked Ms. Freeman's

ROBERTO SCHMIDT/AFP—GETTY
IMAGES

name 18 times during his phone call with Mr. Raffensperger on Jan. 2, 2021. Ms. Moss testified in person before the Jan. 6 committee, and the panel also played clips of video-taped testimony from Ms. Freeman.

## Jeffrey A. Rosen

As acting attorney general, Jeffrey A. Rosen led the Justice Department during the final month of the Trump administration, when Mr. Trump and his allies most aggressively pressed federal and state officials to undo his loss in the 2020 election. He was thrust into the job by the departure of Mr. Barr, who left office as Mr. Trump attacked him for refusing to support his election fraud claims. Like Mr. Barr, Mr. Rosen repeatedly told the president that there was no credible evidence of widespread fraud and resisted

DOUG MILLS/THE NEW YORK TIMES

his entreaties to say publicly that there was. Mr. Rosen testified about a dramatic meeting in the Oval Office on Jan. 3, 2021, in which Mr. Trump threatened to replace him with Jeffrey Clark, a loyalist who had embraced the false claims of fraud, and top Justice Department officials said such an action would prompt mass resignations at the agency.

## Richard P. Donoghue

The acting deputy attorney general at the end of the Trump administration, Richard P. Donoghue was among the officials at the Justice Department who pushed back strongly on Mr. Trump's baseless claims of election fraud and resisted his pressure to say publicly that there were grounds to challenge the results. Mr. Donoghue's notes of one such conversation on Dec. 27, 2020, became crucial evidence in the investigation, showing how Mr. Trump had instructed him and Mr. Rosen to "say that the election

DOUG MILLS/THE NEW YORK TIMES

was corrupt" and "leave the rest to me." Mr. Donoghue testified about holding a phone call with senior Justice Department leaders in which they agreed to resign en masse if Mr. Rosen was ousted to make way for Mr. Clark. He also recounted telling Mr. Clark that he was not qualified to lead the department, saying: "You're an environmental lawyer. How about you go back to your office, and we'll call you when there's an oil spill?"

## Cassidy Hutchinson

As a special assistant to the president for legislative affairs in Mr. Trump's White House, Cassidy Hutchinson, 26, was an omnipresent aide to Mr. Meadows, the chief of staff, and witnessed many crucial conversations in the days leading up to the Jan. 6 attack and during the riot itself. Her decision once the hearings were already underway to testify publicly about what she saw and heard produced one of the most compelling moments of the investigation. She testified that the president knew that some of his supporters were

DOUG MILLS/THE NEW YORK TIMES

armed on Jan. 6 but that he wanted security checkpoints removed so that the crowd could mass near the White House for his speech at the Ellipse and then march to the Capitol. "They're not here to hurt me," she recalled him saying. She shared a story she said had been recounted to her about Mr. Trump lunging for the steering wheel of his vehicle after the Secret Service refused to drive him to the Capitol. And she said she had overheard Mr. Meadows tell a colleague as violence raged at the Capitol amid shouts of "Hang Mike Pence!" that Mr. Trump did not want to do anything to call off the mob because he thought that his supporters were not doing anything wrong and that Mr. Pence "deserves it."

## Pat A. Cipollone

The final White House counsel of Mr. Trump's presidency, Pat A. Cipollone defended the former president during his first impeachment trial. But Mr. Cipollone became a crucial witness in the Jan. 6 investigation, having repeatedly pushed back against Mr. Trump's efforts to overturn his 2020 election loss and then interacted with the president on the day of the riot. He participated in meetings with allies of Mr. Trump who pressed for the military to seize voting machines. He was also present when Mr. Barr offered his resignation after making clear that the

ANNA MONEYMAKER FOR
THE NEW YORK TIMES

Justice Department had found no widespread fraud in the 2020 election. Mr. Cipollone balked at acting on a plan proposed by Mr. Clark, a Trump loyalist at the Justice Department, to distribute official letters to state legislators falsely alerting them that the election might have been stolen and urging them to reconsider certified results. He called the letter "a murder-suicide pact." Mr. Cipollone was said to have heard Mr. Trump sympathize with the rioters during the attack on the Capitol, and he was also said to have told a White House aide earlier that day that if the president joined his supporters in marching there, "We're going to get charged with every crime imaginable."

## Anthony M. Ornato

A longtime Secret Service agent who had served presidents of both political parties before leading Mr. Trump's security detail, Anthony M. Ornato was installed in late 2019 as the deputy White House chief of staff for operations. The job placed Mr. Ornato at the epicenter of the Trump White House, steps from the Oval Office. From that perch, he was deeply involved in conversations about Mr. Trump's desire to march with his supporters to the Capitol on Jan. 6, something that Secret Service officials said would

SARAH SILBIGER/THE NEW YORK TIMES

be impossible to arrange and far too dangerous to pursue. According to Ms. Hutchinson's testimony to the committee, Mr. Ornato recounted to her how, when Mr. Trump was told he could not make the trip to Capitol Hill, the president lunged for the steering wheel of the vehicle he was riding in. Secret Service officials privately cast doubt on the story, but Mr. Ornato never publicly denied having told it. He retired from the Secret Service in August 2022.


## Jeffrey Clark

Jeffrey Clark, a former Justice Department official involved in Mr. Trump's frenzied efforts to overturn the 2020 election, repeatedly invoked his Fifth Amendment right against self-incrimination when he appeared before the Jan. 6 committee. A little-known official who led the agency's environment and natural resources division and was serving as the acting head of the civil division, Mr. Clark was the key man in Mr. Trump's plan to wield the Justice Department's power to try to stay in office. He not only

SUSAN WALSH/ASSOCIATED PRESS

embraced Mr. Trump's false election fraud claims but also pushed Mr. Rosen, the acting attorney general, to send a letter to election officials in Georgia falsely claiming that the Justice Department had "identified significant concerns" that may have affected the state's election results. Mr. Trump threatened to remove Mr. Rosen, who refused to go along with his plans, and install Mr. Clark, a loyalist, to do his bidding. During a heated showdown in the Oval Office, Justice Department officials warned of mass resignations should Mr. Trump follow through, and he backed down. In June 2022, federal agents searched Mr. Clark's home and seized his electronic devices.

# John Eastman

John Eastman, a lawyer who advised Mr. Trump on key elements of the effort to overturn the results of the 2020 election, also repeatedly invoked the Fifth Amendment in front of the Jan. 6 committee. A law professor in California, Mr. Eastman helped develop and promote a brazen plan to justify having Mr. Pence single-handedly block or delay certification of the Electoral College results confirming Mr. Biden's victory. In a series of meetings and phone calls, Mr. Trump and Mr. Eastman tried unsuccessfully to pressure Mr. Pence to put the plan into action

ANDY CROSS/MEDIANEWS GROUP/
THE DENVER POST, VIA GETTY IMAGES

when the vice president presided over a joint session of Congress on Jan. 6. A federal judge in California considering a civil suit concerning the release of Mr. Eastman's emails to the House committee concluded in March 2022 that Mr. Eastman and Mr. Trump most likely committed two felonies: obstruction of a proceeding before Congress and conspiracy to defraud the United States. Mr. Eastman was also instrumental in advising Mr. Trump to create alternate slates of electors backing Mr. Trump in key swing states won by Mr. Biden. These false pro-Trump electors were intended to give Mr. Pence a quasi-legal rationale for delaying or blocking the Electoral College certification on Jan. 6 or trying to throw the election to the House of Representatives. Federal agents armed with a search warrant seized Mr. Eastman's phone in June 2022.

# Matthew Pottinger

Matthew Pottinger, the former deputy national security adviser in the Trump White House, testified publicly before the House committee about why he tendered his resignation after watching Mr. Trump's response to the riot. Mr. Pottinger recalled his dismay at Mr. Trump's decision to tweet an attack on Mr. Pence as the assault on the Capitol was unfolding and the vice president was fleeing for his life, instead of trying to de-escalate the situation. "That was the moment that I decided that I was going to

DOUG MILLS/THE NEW YORK TIMES

resign, that that would be my last day at the White House," Mr. Pottinger said, referring to Mr. Trump's Twitter condemnation of Mr. Pence. "I simply didn't want to be associated with the events that were unfolding on the Capitol." He was the highest-ranking White House official to quit on Jan. 6.

## Sarah Matthews

Sarah Matthews, a deputy White House press secretary working in the West Wing, testified before the committee about the more than three hours on Jan. 6 during which Mr. Trump did nothing to quell the violence. Ms. Matthews quit that day. But before she departed, she saw efforts by the White House press secretary, Kayleigh McEnany, to have Mr. Trump issue some kind of statement deterring his supporters, hundreds of whom had swarmed the Capitol as Mr. Biden's Electoral College victory was being

certified. Ms. Matthews testified that Ms. McEnany had told her that Mr. Trump did not want to call on his supporters for "peace." Ms. Matthews told the committee that a tweet Mr. Trump sent during the riot in which he attacked Mr. Pence was like "pouring gasoline on the fire."

## Virginia "Ginni" Thomas

Virginia Thomas, a conservative activist and the wife of Justice Clarence Thomas, appeared before the Jan. 6 committee in late September 2022 to answer questions about her efforts to overturn the 2020 election. Ms. Thomas, who goes by Ginni, was in contact with Mr. Eastman, the conservative lawyer advising Mr. Trump who wrote a memo that Democrats and anti-Trump Republicans have likened to a blueprint for a coup. Ms. Thomas also exchanged text messages with Mr. Meadows, the White

House chief of staff; she urged him to challenge Mr. Biden's victory in the 2020 election, which she called a "heist," and indicated that she had reached out to Jared Kushner, the president's son-in-law, about Mr. Trump's efforts to use the courts to stay in power. She even suggested a lawyer to be put in charge of that effort. In closed-door testimony, Ms. Thomas told the committee that she had not discussed her election subversion attempts in detail with her husband and continued to falsely insist that the vote had been stolen.

*Edited by Julie Hirschfeld Davis*

# Other Characters

BY LUKE BROADWATER, ALAN FEUER, MAGGIE HABERMAN,
KATIE BENNER AND MICHAEL S. SCHMIDT

## Rudolph W. Giuliani

Mr. Giuliani, Mr. Trump's personal lawyer, who helped lead his legal efforts to overturn the results of the 2020 election, sat for a lengthy closed-door interview with the House committee. Mr. Giuliani was a key figure in Mr. Trump's attempts to stave off electoral defeat and was involved in plans to disrupt the normal workings of the Electoral College by persuading lawmakers in contested swing states to draw up alternate slates of electors claiming Mr. Trump as the victor in states actually won by

ERIN SCHAFF/THE NEW YORK TIMES

Mr. Biden. Mr. Giuliani was also instrumental in vetting a plan to use the Department of Homeland Security to seize voting machines and examine the data housed inside them for supposed evidence of fraud. At Mr. Trump's direction, Mr. Giuliani asked a top homeland security official if the department could legally take control of the machines—a notion the official shot down. The committee subpoenaed Mr. Giuliani and other members of a legal team that billed itself as an "elite strike force" and pursued a set of lawsuits on behalf of Mr. Trump promulgating conspiracy theories and making unsubstantiated claims of fraud in the election. On Jan. 6, speaking to the crowd of Trump supporters at the Ellipse before the mob began attacking the Capitol, Mr. Giuliani called for "trial by combat." Later, even as the building was under siege, both he and Mr. Trump called lawmakers in an attempt to delay the certification of Mr. Biden's victory. Prosecutors in Georgia have informed Mr. Giuliani that he is a target in a wide-ranging criminal investigation into election interference in that state.

## Cleta Mitchell

Cleta Mitchell, one of the key figures in a failed scheme to overturn Mr. Trump's defeat, was among a cadre of Republican lawyers who frantically compiled unsubstantiated accusations, debunked claims and an array of confusing and inconclusive eyewitness reports to build the case that the election was marred by fraud. Courts rejected the cases and election officials were unconvinced. She was also at the genesis of a plan to enlist the help of state lawmakers to create fake slates of electors; just two days after the

MATT ROURKE/ASSOCIATED PRESS

election, she sent an email suggesting the idea to Mr. Eastman, another lawyer close to Mr. Trump. "A movement is stirring," Ms. Mitchell wrote in the email, which was introduced as evidence at one of the Jan. 6 panel's hearings. "But needs constitutional support." Ms. Mitchell also participated in a call in which Mr. Trump tried to pressure Georgia's secretary of state to "find" enough votes to reverse his loss there.

## Sidney Powell

Ms. Powell, a lawyer who worked on many of the lawsuits with Mr. Giuliani, ran an organization that raised millions of dollars based on false claims that election machines were rigged. She was among the leading promoters of some of the most far-fetched and fantastical claims of widespread voter fraud, including a bizarre conspiracy theory alleging a vast plot by China, Venezuela and the financier George Soros to hack into Dominion Voting Systems machines to flip votes from Mr. Trump to Mr. Biden. In

DREW ANGERER/GETTY IMAGES

December 2020, she urged Mr. Trump to seize voting machines during a contentious White House meeting. Mr. Trump considered naming Ms. Powell to be a special counsel overseeing an investigation of voter fraud, even after his campaign had sought to distance itself from her as she aired wild and baseless claims about Dominion voting machines. Her organization, Defending the Republic, raised $14.9 million between December 2020 and July 2021.

## Michael T. Flynn

Mr. Trump's former national security adviser, Mr. Flynn emerged as one of the most extreme voices in the president's push to overturn the election. Mr. Flynn, who spent 33 years as an Army intelligence officer, attended a meeting in the Oval Office on Dec.

18, 2020, in which participants discussed seizing voting machines, declaring a national emergency, invoking certain national security emergency powers and continuing to spread the false message that the 2020 election had been tainted by widespread fraud. That meeting came after Mr. Flynn gave an interview to the right-wing media outlet Newsmax in which he talked about the supposed precedent for deploying military troops and declaring martial law to "rerun" the election.

TOM BRENNER FOR
THE NEW YORK TIMES

## Stephen K. Bannon

Stephen K. Bannon, a former top adviser to Mr. Trump, was convicted of two counts of contempt of Congress after he refused to comply with a subpoena from the committee. A day before the violence of Jan. 6, he made a prediction on his radio show that "all hell is going to break loose tomorrow," which the committee cited as evidence that "he had some foreknowledge about extreme events that would occur the next day." Investigators have also said that Mr. Bannon urged Mr. Trump in a conversation on Dec. 30 to focus his efforts on Jan. 6. Mr. Bannon was present at a meeting at the Willard InterContinental Hotel in Washington the day before the riot, when plans were discussed to try to overturn the election results the next day.

KENNY HOLSTON FOR
THE NEW YORK TIMES

## Mark Meadows

Mr. Meadows, the final White House chief of staff for Mr. Trump, was deeply involved in the effort to overturn the 2020 election. Although he refused to testify before the committee, he turned over around 9,000 pages of documents that helped jumpstart the panel's investigation. A former congressman from North Carolina who led the ultraconservative House Freedom Caucus, Mr. Meadows encouraged members of Congress to object to Mr. Biden's victory, and he pursued baseless allegations of voter fraud in several states. In addition, Mr. Meadows personally coordinated with rally planners who brought throngs of Mr. Trump's supporters to Washington on Jan. 6 to protest the president's election loss, and Mr. Meadows said he would line up the National Guard to protect them. As the assault on the Capitol was unfolding, Mr. Meadows received text messages from the president's son Donald Trump Jr. and the Fox News hosts

AL DRAGO FOR THE NEW YORK TIMES

Sean Hannity, Laura Ingraham and Brian Kilmeade urging that Mr. Trump speak out amid the violence. "I'm pushing it hard," Mr. Meadows responded to the younger Mr. Trump, though there is little evidence that he did so.

## Representative Scott Perry

AL DRAGO FOR THE NEW YORK TIMES

Representative Scott Perry, Republican of Pennsylvania, pressed Mr. Trump to appoint Mr. Clark, an official at the Justice Department, as his acting attorney general over the objections of top leaders at the department. Mr. Perry also introduced Mr. Clark to Mr. Trump. In the weeks after the election, Mr. Perry was among roughly a dozen Republican members of Congress involved in discussions with White House officials about overturning the election. Mr. Perry also endorsed the idea of encouraging Mr. Trump's supporters to march to the Capitol, the committee said. The panel issued a subpoena to Mr. Perry in May 2022, but he declined to comply. The F.B.I. seized his cellphone in August 2022.

## Representative Kevin McCarthy

JASON ANDREW FOR
THE NEW YORK TIMES

Representative Kevin McCarthy, Republican of California and the minority leader, refused to cooperate with a subpoena from the committee. Mr. McCarthy, who was nominated to be speaker after his party won control of the House in the midterm elections, had a heated phone call with Mr. Trump during the riot in which he implored the president to call off the mob. When Mr. Trump declined, according to Representative Jaime Herrera Beutler, a Washington Republican who said Mr. McCarthy recounted the exchange to her, Mr. Trump sided with the rioters, saying, "Well, Kevin, I guess these people are more upset about the election than you are." In the days after the attack, Mr. McCarthy took to the House floor and said: "The president bears responsibility for Wednesday's attack on Congress by mob rioters. He should have immediately denounced the mob when he saw what was unfolding." He also told fellow Republicans privately he planned to tell Mr. Trump to resign. He fought the creation of a Jan. 6 investigation and boycotted the committee after Democrats refused to seat Republicans who had defended Mr. Trump after the riot.

## Representative Jim Jordan

Representative Jim Jordan, Republican of Ohio and one of Mr. Trump's most outspoken defenders, was a key player in the effort to invalidate the election results, and he refused to cooperate with a subpoena from the committee. The panel informed Mr. Jordan in December 2021 that its investigators wanted to question him about his communications in the run-up to the Capitol riot, as well as his contact with Mr. Trump on the day of the violence. On Jan. 5, Mr. Jordan forwarded to Mr. Meadows a text message he had received from a lawyer and former Pentagon

MICHAEL A. MCCOY FOR
THE NEW YORK TIMES

inspector general outlining a legal strategy to overturn the election. "On Jan. 6, 2021, Vice President Mike Pence, as president of the Senate, should call out all electoral votes that he believes are unconstitutional as no electoral votes at all—in accordance with guidance from founding father Alexander Hamilton and judicial precedence," the text read. Mr. Jordan has acknowledged speaking with Mr. Trump on Jan. 6, though he has said he cannot remember how many times they spoke that day or when the calls occurred.

## Representative Mo Brooks

Representative Mo Brooks, Republican of Alabama, was a ringleader of the Republican effort to lodge formal challenges to the counting of electoral votes from battleground states on Jan. 6. He wore body armor as he addressed the throng of Trump supporters who gathered at the Ellipse near the White House that day, telling them to "start taking down names and kicking ass" and to "fight for America." He has said Mr. Trump pressured him repeatedly in the months afterward to help reinstate him to the office by illegally "rescinding" the results, removing Mr. Biden and forcing a

CHARITY RACHELLE FOR
THE NEW YORK TIMES

special election so that Mr. Trump could return to the presidency. "As a lawyer, I've repeatedly advised President Trump that Jan. 6 was the final election contest verdict and neither the U.S. Constitution nor the U.S. Code permit what President Trump asks," Mr. Brooks said in a statement. He implied that his refusal to go along with Mr. Trump's wishes prompted the former president to yank his endorsement of Mr. Brooks in the Republican primary for an Alabama Senate seat. Mr. Brooks ultimately lost in a runoff to Mr. Trump's preferred candidate.

## Representative Andy Biggs

Representative Andy Biggs, Republican of Arizona and the leader of the ultraconservative House Freedom Caucus at the time of the Capitol attack, tried to persuade state legislators to join Mr. Trump's push to overturn the 2020 election, and he refused to cooperate with the committee's subpoena. In a letter to Mr. Biggs, the panel's leaders wrote that they wanted to question him about evidence they had obtained about efforts by certain House Republicans to seek a presidential pardon after Jan. 6 in con-

nection with Mr. Trump's efforts to overturn the election. The committee also said it wanted to interview Mr. Biggs about a Dec. 21, 2020, meeting he attended at the White House with several other members of the Freedom Caucus about the plan to have Mr. Pence unilaterally refuse to count certain states' certified electoral votes on Jan. 6. The panel also wanted to question Mr. Biggs about Ali Alexander, a prominent organizer of so-called Stop the Steal rallies who said that he had "schemed" with Mr. Biggs, Mr. Brooks and Representative Paul Gosar, Republican of Arizona, to set in motion the events of Jan. 6.

*Edited by Julie Hirschfeld Davis*

Union Calendar No. XXX

117th Congress
2d Session

**HOUSE OF REPRESENTATIVES**

Report
117-000

# FINAL REPORT

OF THE

# SELECT COMMITTEE TO INVESTIGATE THE JANUARY 6TH ATTACK ON THE UNITED STATES CAPITOL

December 22, 2022
Committed to the Committee of the Whole House on the
State of the Union and ordered to be printed

U.S. GOVERNMENT PUBLISHING OFFICE
WASHINGTON : 2022

49-937

For sale by the Superintendent of Documents, U.S. Government Publishing Office
Internet: bookstore.gpo.gov  Phone: toll free (866) 512-1800; DC area (202) 512-1800
Fax: (202) 512-2104  Mail: Stop IDCC, Washington, DC 20402-0001

DAVID B. BUCKLEY *Staff Director*
KRISTIN L. AMERLING *Deputy Staff Director and Chief Counsel*
HOPE GOINS *Senior Counsel to the Chairman*
JOSEPH B. MAHER *Senior Counsel to the Vice Chair*
TIMOTHY J. HEAPHY *Chief Investigative Counsel*
JAMIE FLEET *Senior Advisor*
TIMOTHY R. MULVEY *Communications Director*
CANDYCE PHOENIX *Senior Counsel and Senior Advisor*
JOHN F. WOOD *Senior Investigative Counsel and Of Counsel to the Vice Chair*

KATHERINE B. ABRAMS, *Staff Associate*
TEMIDAYO AGANGA-WILLIAMS, *Senior Investigative Counsel*
ALEJANDRA APECECHEA, *Investigative Counsel*
LISA A. BIANCO, *Director of Member Services and Security Manager*
JEROME P. BJELOPERA, *Investigator*
BRYAN BONNER, *Investigative Counsel*
RICHARD R. BRUNO, *Senior Administrative Assistant*
MARCUS CHILDRESS, *Investigative Counsel*
JOHN MARCUS CLARK, *Security Director*
JACQUELINE N. COLVETT, *Digital Director*
HEATHER I. CONNELLY, *Professional Staff Member*
MEGHAN E. CONROY, *Investigator*
HEATHER L. CROWELL, *Printer Proofreader*
WILLIAM C. DANVERS, *Senior Researcher*
SOUMYALATHA O. DAYANANDA, *Senior Investigative Counsel*
STEPHEN W. DEVINE, *Senior Counsel*
LAWRENCE J. EAGLEBURGER, *Professional Staff Member*
KEVIN S. ELLIKER, *Investigative Counsel*
MARGARET E. EMAMZADEH, *Staff Associate*
SADALLAH A. FARAH, *Professional Staff Member*
DANIEL GEORGE, *Senior Investigative Counsel*
JACOB H. GLICK, *Investigative Counsel*
AARON S. GREENE, *Clerk*
MARC S. HARRIS, *Senior Investigative Counsel*
ALICE K. HAYES, *Clerk*
QUINCY T. HENDERSON, *Staff Assistant*
JENNA HOPKINS, *Professional Staff Member*
CAMISHA L. JOHNSON, *Professional Staff Member*

THOMAS E. JOSCELYN, *Senior Professional Staff Member*
REBECCA L. KNOOIHUIZEN, *Financial Investigator*
CASEY E. LUCIER, *Investigative Counsel*
DAMON M. MARX, *Professional Staff Member*
EVAN B. MAULDIN, *Chief Clerk*
YONATAN L. MOSKOWITZ, *Senior Counsel*
HANNAH G. MULDAVIN, *Deputy Communications Director*
JONATHAN D. MURRAY, *Professional Staff Member*
JACOB A. NELSON, *Professional Staff Member*
ELIZABETH OBRAND, *Staff Associate*
RAYMOND O'MARA, *Director of External Affairs*
ELYES OUECHTATI, *Technology Partner*
ROBIN M. PEGUERO, *Investigative Counsel*
SANDEEP A. PRASANNA, *Investigative Counsel*
BARRY PUMP, *Parliamentarian*
SEAN M. QUINN, *Investigative Counsel*
BRITTANY M. J. RECORD, *Senior Counsel*
DENVER RIGGLEMAN, *Senior Technical Advisor*
JOSHUA D. ROSELMAN, *Investigative Counsel*
JAMES N. SASSO, *Senior Investigative Counsel*
GRANT H. SAUNDERS, *Professional Staff Member*
SAMANTHA O. STILES, *Chief Administrative Officer*
SEAN P. TONOLLI, *Senior Investigative Counsel*
DAVID A. WEINBERG, *Senior Professional Staff Member*
AMANDA S. WICK, *Senior Investigative Counsel*
DARRIN L. WILLIAMS, JR., *Staff Assistant*
ZACHARY S. WOOD, *Clerk*

Rawaa Alobaidi
Melinda Arons
Steve Baker
Elizabeth Bisbee
David Canady
John Coughlin
Aaron Dietzen
Gina Ferrise
Angel Goldsborough
James Goldston
Polly Grube
L. Christine Healey
Danny Holladay
Percy Howard
Dean Jackson
Stephanie J. Jones
Hyatt Mamoun
Mary Marsh
Todd Mason
Ryan Mayers
Jeff McBride
Fred Muram
Alex Newhouse
John Norton
Orlando Pinder
Owen Pratt
Dan Pryzgoda
Brian Sasser
William Scherer
Driss Sekkat
Chris Stuart
Preston Sullivan
Brian Young

Innovative Driven

HOUSE OF REPRESENTATIVES,
SELECT COMMITTEE TO
INVESTIGATE THE
JANUARY 6TH ATTACK ON THE
UNITED STATES CAPITOL,
*Washington, DC,*
*December 22, 2022.*

Hon. CHERYL L. JOHNSON,
*Clerk, U.S. House of Representatives,*
*Washington, DC.*

DEAR MS. JOHNSON: By direction of the Select Committee to Investigate the January 6th Attack on the United States Capitol, I hereby transmit its final report pursuant to section 4(a) of House Resolution 503, 117th Congress.

Sincerely,

BENNIE G. THOMPSON,
*Chairman.*

# "THE LAST BEST HOPE OF EARTH"

**"I do solemnly swear that I will support and defend the Constitution of the United States against all enemies, foreign and domestic; that I will bear true faith and allegiance to the same; that I take this obligation freely, without any mental reservation or purpose of evasion; and that I will well and faithfully discharge the duties of the office on which I am about to enter: So help me God."**

All Members of the United States Congress take this sacred oath. On January 6, 2021, Democrats and Republicans agreed that we would fulfill this oath—and that we had an obligation to signal to the world that American Democracy would prevail.

In furtherance of fulfilling this duty, the Select Committee to Investigate the January 6th Attack on the United States Capitol was charged with investigating the facts, circumstances and causes that led to this domestic terror attack on the Capitol, the Congress and the Constitution.

We owe a debt of gratitude to Chairman Bennie Thompson, Vice Chair Liz Cheney, the patriotic Members of Congress and dedicated staff—who devoted themselves to this investigation, to uncovering the truth and to writing a report that is a "Roadmap for Justice."

The Select Committee to Investigate the January 6th Attack has succeeded in bringing clarity and demonstrating with painstaking detail the fragility of our Democracy. Above all, the work of the Select Committee underscores that our democratic institutions are only as strong as the commitment of those who are entrusted with their care.

As the Select Committee concludes its work, their words must be a clarion call to all Americans: to vigilantly guard our Democracy and to give our vote only to those dutiful in their defense of our Constitution.

Let us always honor our oath to, as Abraham Lincoln said, "nobly save, or meanly lose, the last best hope of earth." So help us God.

NANCY PELOSI
Speaker of the House

We were told to remove our lapel pins. At the start of every new Congress, House Members are presented with lapel pins. They are about the size of a quarter and carry a seal of a bald eagle.

On a routine day in the Capitol, there are thousands of tourists, advocates, and workers. Typically, the pins are an easy way to spot House Members.

However, on January 6, 2021, the pin that once was a badge of honor and distinction turned into a bullseye.

On that day, tear gas fogged the air as gunfire rang out, and a violent mob crashed against the sealed doors. Concerned for our safety, Capitol Police officers told us that our lapel pins would make us a target for rioters.

As the Capitol Police rushed Members of Congress and staff to safety, that simple and, in context, sensible warning stuck with me. On January 6, 2021, my colleagues and I came to work with the intent of fulfilling our oaths of office and constitutional duty to carry out the peaceful transfer of power. We were the people's representatives in the people's House doing the people's business. Sadly, on that day, the danger was too great for our work to continue and for us to remain in the Capitol. It was too dangerous to be identified as a representative of the American people.

I've been a Member of the House for nearly 30 years. In that time, there's not a day that goes by that I don't feel a profound sense of duty and responsibility to the men and women who sent me to Congress to be their voice. After all, I'm from a part of the country where, in my lifetime, Black people were excluded entirely from political processes. Jim Crow laws prevented my father from registering to vote, and tragically during his life, he never cast a vote.

For generations, the people in communities I represent have struggled to have their voices heard by their government. Therefore, I take my duties and responsibilities seriously, advocating for greater economic opportunity, robust infrastructure, better schools, and safer housing for my constituents.

However, that long struggle to overcome oppression and secure basic civil and human rights continues to be my highest priority. I am always mindful of the journey that brought me to Washington as a member of Congress to be the voice of the women and men of Mississippi. As a violent mob stormed the Capitol trying to take away people's votes, rioters carried the battle flag from a failed rebellion of confederate states. This moment resonated deeply with me because of my personal history. Additionally, I continually think about the ongoing struggle to ensure justice and equality for all Americans.

The Capitol building itself is a fixture in our country's history, of both good and bad. After all, this structure is among the most recognizable symbols of American democracy. The Capitol's shining dome, topped with the statue of goddess Freedom, was built partially by the labor of enslaved people in the 18th and 19th centuries. Dark chapters of America's history are written into the building's marble, sandstone, and mortar. And yet in the halls and chambers of this building, leaders of courage passed amendments to our Constitution and enacted the laws that banned slavery, guaranteed equal rights under the law, expanded the vote, promoted equality, and moved our country, and her people, forward. The Capitol Building itself is a symbol of our journey toward a more perfect union. It is a temple to our democracy.

Those great moments in our history have come when men and women put loyalty to our country and Constitution ahead of politics and party. They did the right thing. The work of the Select Committee certainly originates from the same tradition. Our bipartisan membership has moved politics to the side and focused on the facts, circumstances, and causes of January 6th.

When I think back to January 6th, after nearly a year and a half of investigation, I am frightened about the peril our democracy faced. Specifically, I think about what that mob was there to do: to block the peaceful transfer of power from one president to another based on a lie that the election was rigged and tainted with widespread fraud.

I also think about why the rioters were there, besieging the legislative branch of our government. The rioters were inside the halls of Congress because the head of the executive branch of our government, the then-President of the United States, told them to attack. Donald Trump summoned that mob to Washington, DC. Afterward, he sent them to the Capitol to try to prevent my colleagues and me from doing our Constitutional duty to certify the election. They put our very democracy to the test.

Trump's mob came dangerously close to succeeding. Courageous law enforcement officers put their lives on the line for hours while Trump sat in the White House, refusing to tell the rioters to go home, while watching the assault on our republic unfold live on television.

When it was clear the insurrection would fail, Trump finally called off the mob, telling them, "We love you." Afterward, Congress was able to return to this Capitol Building and finish the job of counting the Electoral College votes and certifying the election.

This is the key conclusion of the Select Committee, all nine of us, Republicans and Democrats alike.

But who knows what would have happened if Trump's mob had succeeded in stopping us from doing our job? Who knows what sort of constitutional grey zone our country would have slid into? Who would have been left to correct that wrong?

As required by House Resolution 503, which established the Select Committee, we've explored in great detail the facts, circumstances, and causes of the attack. This report will provide new details that supplement those findings the committee already presented during our hearings.

But there are some questions for which there are still no clear answers, even if all the facts, circumstances, and causes are brought to bear. The "What If?" questions. For the good of American democracy, those questions must never again be put to the test. So, while it's important that this report lays out what happened, it's just as important to focus on how to make sure that January 6th was a one-time event—to identify the ongoing threats that could lead us down that dangerous path again—with hopes and humble prayers that the committee's work is carried on through corrective action.

This report will provide greater detail about the multistep effort devised and driven by Donald Trump to overturn the 2020 election and block the transfer of power. Building on the information presented in our hearings earlier this year, we will present new findings about Trump's pressure campaign on officials from the local level all the way up to his Vice President, orchestrated and designed solely to throw out the will of the voters and keep him in office past the end of his elected term.

As we've shown previously, this plan faltered at several points because of the courage of officials (nearly all of them Republicans) who refused to go along with it. Donald Trump appeared to believe that anyone who shared his partisan affiliation would also share the same callous disregard for his or her oath to uphold the rule of law. Fortunately, he was wrong.

The failure of Trump's plan was not assured. To the contrary, Trump's plan was successful at several turns. When his scheme to stay in power through political pressure hit roadblocks, he relentlessly pushed ahead with a parallel plan: summoning a mob to gather in Washington, DC on January 6th, promising things "will be wild!"

That mob showed up. They were armed. They were angry. They believed the "Big Lie" that the election had been stolen. And when Donald Trump pointed them toward the Capitol and told them to "fight like hell," that's exactly what they did.

Donald Trump lit that fire. But in the weeks beforehand, the kindling he ultimately ignited was amassed in plain sight.

That's why as part of the Select Committee's investigation, we took a hard look at whether enough was done to mitigate that risk. Our investigative teams focused on the way intelligence was gathered, shared, and assessed. We probed preparations by law enforcement agencies and security responses on the day of the attack. We followed the money, to determine who paid for a number of events in the run-up to the attack and to gain a clearer understanding of the way the former President's campaign apparatus cashed in on the big lie. And we pulled back the curtain at certain major social media companies to determine if their policies and protocols were up to the challenge when the President spread a message of violence and his supporters began to plan and coordinate their descent on Washington.

The Select Committee's conclusion on these matters—particularly dealing with intelligence and law enforcement—is consistent with our broader findings about the causes of January 6th. Were agencies perfect in their preparations for January 6th and their responses as the violence unfolded? Of course not. Relevant oversight committees and watchdogs should continue to find efficiencies and improvements, some of which are laid out in Committee's recommendations.

But the shortfall of communications, intelligence and law enforcement around January 6th was much less about what they did or did not know. It was more about what they could not know. The President of the United States inciting a mob to march on the Capitol and impede the work of Congress is not a scenario our intelligence and law enforcement communities envisioned for this country. Prior to January 6th, it was unimaginable. Whatever weaknesses existed in the policies, procedures, or institutions, they were not to blame for what happened on that day.

And so, when I think about the ongoing threats—when I think about how to avoid having to confront those "What-Ifs?" in the future—my concerns are less with the mechanics of intelligence gathering and security posture, as important as those questions are. My concerns remain first and foremost with those who continue to seek power at the expense of American democracy.

What if those election officials had given in to Donald Trump's pressure? What if the Justice Department had gone along with Trump's scheme to declare the 2020 election fraudulent? What if the Vice President had tried to throw out electoral votes? What if the rioters bent on stopping the peaceful transfer of power hadn't been repelled?

To cast a vote in the United States of America is an act of both hope and faith. When you drop that ballot in the ballot box, you do so with the confidence that every person named on that ballot will hold up their end of the bargain. The person who wins must swear an oath and live up to it. The people who come up short must accept the ultimate results and abide by the will of the voters and the rule of law. This faith in our institutions and laws is what upholds our democracy.

If that faith is broken—if those who seek power accept only the results of elections that they win—then American democracy, only a few centuries old, comes tumbling down.

That's the danger.

What's the solution?

The Committee believes a good starting point is the set of recommendations we set forth in our report, pursuant to House Resolution 503. Driven by our investigative findings, these recommendations will help strengthen the guardrails of our democracy.

Beyond what we recommend, in my view and as I said during our hearings, the best way to prevent another January 6th is to ensure accountability for January 6th. Accountability at all levels.

I have confidence in our Department of Justice and institutions at the state and local level to ensure accountability under the law. As this report is released, we see those processes moving forward.

But preventing another January 6th will require a broader sort of accountability. Ultimately, the American people chart the course for our country's future. The American people decide whom to give the reins of power. If this Select Committee has accomplished one thing, I hope it has shed light on how dangerous it would be to empower anyone whose desire for authority comes before their commitment to American democracy and the Constitution.

I believe most Americans will turn their backs on those enemies of democracy.

But some will rally to the side of the election deniers, and when I think about who some of those people are, it troubles me deep inside. White supremacists. Violent extremists. Groups that subscribe to racism, anti-Semitism, and violent conspiracy theories; those who would march through the halls of the Capitol waving the Confederate battle flag.

These are people who want to take America backward, not toward some imagined prior greatness, but toward repression. These are people who want to roll back what we've accomplished. I believe that those who aligned with the scheme to overturn the election heeded Donald Trump's call to march on the Capitol because they thought taking up Donald Trump's cause was a way to advance their vile ambitions.

That is why I did not remove my lapel pin on January 6th.

Our country has come too far to allow a defeated President to turn himself into a successful tyrant by upending our democratic institutions, fomenting violence, and, as I saw it, opening the door to those in our country whose hatred and bigotry threaten equality and justice for all Americans.

We can never surrender to democracy's enemies. We can never allow America to be defined by forces of division and hatred. We can never go backward in the progress we have made through the sacrifice and dedication of true patriots. We can never and will never relent in our pursuit of a more perfect union, with liberty and justice for all Americans.

I pray that God continues to bless the United States of America.

BENNIE G. THOMPSON
Chairman

In April 1861, when Abraham Lincoln issued the first call for volunteers for the Union Army, my great-great grandfather, Samuel Fletcher Cheney, joined the 21st Ohio Volunteer Infantry. He fought through all four years of the Civil War, from Chickamauga to Stones River to Atlanta. He marched with his unit in the Grand Review of Troops up Pennsylvania Avenue in May 1865, past a reviewing stand where President Johnson and General Grant were seated.

Silas Canfield, the regimental historian of the 21st OVI, described the men in the unit this way:

> *Industry had taught them perseverance, and they had learned to turn aside for no obstacle. Their intelligence gave them a just appreciation of the value and advantage of free government, and the necessity of defending and maintaining it, and they enlisted prepared to accept all the necessary labors, fatigues, exposures, dangers, and even death for the unity of our Nation, and the perpetuity of our institutions.*[1]

I have found myself thinking often, especially since January 6th, of my great-great grandfather, and all those in every generation who have sacrificed so much for "the unity of our Nation and the perpetuity of our institutions."

At the heart of our Republic is the guarantee of the peaceful transfer of power. Members of Congress are reminded of this every day as we pass through the Capitol Rotunda. There, eight magnificent paintings detail the earliest days of our Republic. Four were painted by John Trumbull, including one depicting the moment in 1793 when George Washington resigned his commission, handing control of the Continental Army back to Congress. Trumbull called this, "one of the highest moral lessons ever given the world." With this noble act, George Washington established the indispensable example of the peaceful transfer of power in our nation.

Standing on the West Front of the Capitol in 1981, President Ronald Reagan described it this way:

> *To a few of us here today, this is a solemn and most momentous occasion, and yet in the history of our nation it is a commonplace occurrence. The orderly transfer of authority as called for in the Constitution routinely takes place, as it has for almost two centuries, and few of us stop to think how unique we really are. In the eyes of many in the world, this every-4-year ceremony we accept as normal is nothing less than a miracle.*

Every President in our history has defended this orderly transfer of authority, except one. January 6, 2021 was the first time one American President refused his Constitutional duty to transfer power peacefully to the next.

In our work over the last 18 months, the Select Committee has recognized our obligation to do everything we can to ensure this never happens again. At the outset of our investigation, we recognized that tens of millions of Americans had been persuaded by President Trump that the 2020 Presidential election was stolen by overwhelming fraud. We also knew this was flatly false, and that dozens of state and federal judges had addressed and resolved all manner of allegations about the election. Our legal system functioned as it should, but our President would not accept the outcome.

What most of the public did not know before our investigation is this: Donald Trump's own campaign officials told him early on that his claims of fraud were false. Donald Trump's senior Justice Department officials—each appointed by Donald Trump himself—investigated the allegations and told him repeatedly that his fraud claims were false. Donald Trump's White House lawyers also told him his fraud claims were false. From the beginning, Donald Trump's fraud allegations were concocted nonsense, designed to prey upon the patriotism of millions of men and women who love our country.

Most Americans also did not know exactly how Donald Trump, along with a handful of others, planned to defeat the transfer of Presidential power on January 6th. This was not a simple plan, but it was a corrupt one. This report lays that plan out in detail—a plan that ultimately had seven parts, anticipating that Vice President Pence, serving in his role as President of the Senate, would refuse to count official Biden electoral slates from multiple states. We understood from the beginning that explaining all the planning and machinations would be complex and would require many hours of public presentations and testimony. We also understood that our presentations needed to be organized into a series of hearings that presented the key evidence for the American public to watch live or streamed over a reasonable time period, rather than rely on second-hand accounts as reported by media organizations with their own editorial biases. We organized our hearings in segments to meet that goal. Tens of millions of Americans watched.

Among the most shameful findings from our hearings was this: President Trump sat in the dining room off the Oval Office watching the violent riot at the Capitol on television. For hours, he would not issue a public statement instructing his supporters to disperse and leave the Capitol, despite urgent pleas from his White House staff and dozens of others to do so. Members of his family, his White House lawyers, virtually all those around him knew that this simple act was critical. For hours, he would not do it. During this time, law enforcement agents were attacked and seriously injured, the Capitol was invaded, the electoral count was halted and the lives of those in the Capitol were put at risk. In addition to being unlawful, as described in this report, this was an utter moral failure—and a clear dereliction of duty. Evidence of this can be seen in the testimony of his White House Counsel and several other White House witnesses. No man who would behave that way at that moment in time can ever serve in any position of authority in our nation again. He is unfit for any office.

*      *      *      *      *

In presenting all of the information in our hearings, we decided that the vast majority of our witnesses needed to be Republicans. They were. We presented evidence from two former Trump Administration Attorneys General, a former White House Counsel, many former Trump-appointed White House, Justice Department, and Trump Campaign staff, a respected former conservative judge, the former Secretary of Labor, and many others.

Like our hearings, this report is designed to deliver our findings in detail in a format that is accessible for all Americans. We do so in an executive summary, while also providing immense detail for historians and others. We are also releasing transcripts and evidence for the public to review, consistent with a small number of security and privacy concerns. A section of this report also explains the legal conclusions we draw from the evidence, and our concerns about efforts to obstruct our investigation.

The Committee recognizes that this investigation is just a beginning; it is only an initial step in addressing President Trump's effort to remain in office illegally. Prosecutors are considering the implications of the conduct we describe in this report. As are voters. John Adams wrote in 1761, "The very ground of our liberties is the freedom of elections." Faith in our elections and the rule of law are paramount to our Republic. Election-deniers—those who refuse to accept lawful election results—purposely attack the rule of law and the foundation of our country.

As you read this report, please consider this: Vice President Pence, along with many of the appointed officials who surrounded Donald Trump, worked to defeat many of the worst parts of Trump's plan to overturn the election. This was not a certainty. It is comforting to assume that the institutions of our Republic will always withstand those who try to defeat our Constitution from within. But our institutions are only strong when those who hold office are faithful to our Constitution. We do not know what would have happened if the leadership of the Department of Justice declared, as Donald Trump requested, that the election was "corrupt," if Jeff Clark's letters to State Legislatures had been sent, if Pat Cipollone, Jeff Rosen, Richard Donoghue, Steve Engel and others were not serving as guardrails on Donald Trump's abuses.

Part of the tragedy of January 6th is the conduct of those who knew that what happened was profoundly wrong, but nevertheless tried to downplay it, minimize it or defend those responsible. That effort continues every day. Today, I am perhaps most disappointed in many of my fellow conservatives who know better, those who stood against the threats of communism and Islamic terrorism but concluded that it was easier to appease Donald Trump, or keep their heads down. I had hoped for more from them.

The late Charles Krauthammer wrote, "The lesson of our history is that the task of merely maintaining strong and sturdy the structures of a constitutional order is unending, the continuing and ceaseless work of every generation." This task is unending because democracy can be fragile and our institutions do not defend themselves.

The history of our time will show that the bravery of a handful of Americans, doing their duty, saved us from an even more grave Constitutional crisis. Elected officials, election workers, and public servants stood against Donald Trump's corrupt pressure. Many of our witnesses showed selfless patriotism and their words and courage will be remembered.

The brave men and women of the Capitol Police, Metropolitan Police and all the other law enforcement officers who fought to defend us that day undoubtedly saved lives and our democracy.

Finally, I wish to thank all who honorably contributed to the work of the Committee and to this Report. We accomplished much over a relatively short period of time, and many of you sacrificed for the good of your nation. You have helped make history and, I hope, helped right the ship.

LIZ CHENEY
Vice Chair

Contents . . . . . . . . . . . . . . . . . . . . . . . . . . . . . . . . . . . . . . . . . . . . . . . . Page

Contents . . . . . . . . . . . . . . . . . . . . . . . . . . . . . . . . . . . . . . . . . . . . . . . . . . . . . . . . . . . . . . . Page

Contents . . . . . . . . . . . . . . . . . . . . . . . . . . . . . . . . . . . . . . . . . . . . . . . . . . . . . Page

**NARRATIVE (CONTINUED)**

Contents . . . . . . . . . . . . . . . . . . . . . . . . . . . . . . . . . . . . . . . . . . . . . . . . Page

**NARRATIVE (CONTINUED)**

**RECOMMENDATIONS**

Contents............................................................. Page

**APPENDICES**

On October 31, 2022, in a Federal courthouse in Washington, DC, Graydon Young testified against Stewart Rhodes and other members of the Oath Keepers militia group. The defendants had been charged with seditious conspiracy against the United States and other crimes related to the January 6, 2021, attack on Congress.[1]

In his testimony that day, Young explained to the jury how he and other Oath Keepers were provoked to travel to Washington by President Donald Trump's tweets and by Trump's false claims that the 2020 Presidential election was "stolen" from him.[2] And, in emotional testimony, Young acknowledged what he and others believed they were doing on January 6th: attacking Congress in the manner the French had attacked the Bastille at the outset of the French Revolution.[3] Reflecting on that day more than a year and half later, Young testified:

> Prosecutor: And so how do you feel about the fact that you were pushing towards a line of police officers?
>
> Young: Today I feel extremely ashamed and embarrassed. . . .
>
> Prosecutor: How did you feel at the time?
>
> Young: I felt like, again, we were continuing in some kind of historical event to achieve a goal.
>
>                              * * *
>
> Prosecutor: Looking back now almost two years later, what would that make you as someone who was coming to D.C. to fight against the government?
>
> Young: I guess I was [acting] like a traitor, somebody against my own government.[4]

Young's testimony was dramatic, but not unique. Many participants in the attack on the Capitol acknowledged that they had betrayed their own country:

- Reimler: "And I'm sorry to the people of this country for threatening the democracy that makes this country so great . . . My participation in the events that day were part of an attack on the rule of law."[5]
- Pert: "I know that the peaceful transition of power is to ensure the common good for our nation and that it is critical in protecting our country's security needs. I am truly sorry for my part and accept full responsibility for my actions."[6]
- Markofski: "My actions put me on the other side of the line from my

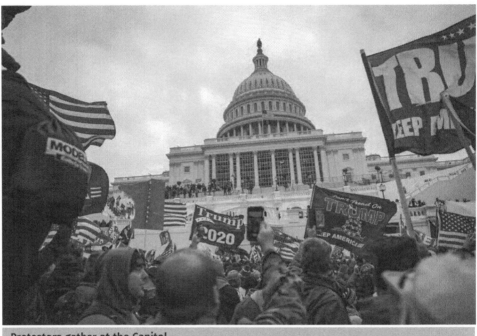

Protestors gather at the Capitol.

(Photo by Samuel Corum/Getty Images)

brothers in the Army. The wrong side. Had I lived in the area, I would have been called up to defend the Capitol and restore order . . . My actions brought dishonor to my beloved U.S. Army National Guard." [7]

- Witcher: "Every member—every male member of my family has served in the military, in the Marine Corps, and most have saw combat. And I cast a shadow and cast embarrassment upon my family name and that legacy." [8]
- Edwards: "I am ashamed to be for the first time in my 68 years, standing before a judge, having pleaded guilty to committing a crime, ashamed to be associated with an attack on the United States Capitol, a symbol of American democracy and greatness that means a great deal to me." [9]

Hundreds of other participants in the January 6th attack have pleaded guilty, been convicted, or await trial for crimes related to their actions that day. And, like Young, hundreds of others have acknowledged exactly what provoked them to travel to Washington, and to engage in violence. For example:

- Ronald Sandlin, who threatened police officers in the Capitol saying, "[y]ou're going to die," posted on December 23, 2020: "I'm going to be there to show support for our president and to do my part to stop the steal and stand behind Trump when he decides to cross the rubicon. If you are a patriot I believe it's your duty to be there. I see it as my civic responsibility." [10]

- Garret Miller, who brought a gun to the Capitol on January 6th, explained: "I was in Washington, D.C. on January 6, 2021, because I believed I was following the instructions of former President Trump and he was my president and the commander-in-chief. His statements also had me believing the election was stolen from him." [11]
- John Douglas Wright explained that he brought busloads of people to Washington, DC, on January 6th "because [Trump] called me there, and he laid out what is happening in our government." [12]
- Lewis Cantwell testified: If "the President of the United States . . . [is] out on TV telling the world that it was stolen, what else would I believe, as a patriotic American who voted for him and wants to continue to see the country thrive as I thought it was?" [13]
- Likewise, Stephen Ayres testified that "with everything the President was putting out" ahead of January 6th that "the election was rigged . . . the votes were wrong and stuff . . . it just got into my head." "The President [was] calling on us to come" to Washington, DC. [14] Ayres "was hanging on every word he [President Trump] was saying" [15] Ayres posted that "Civil War will ensue" if President Trump did not stay in power after January 6th. [16]

The Committee has compiled hundreds of similar statements from participants in the January 6th attack. [17]

House Resolution 503 instructed the Select Committee to "investigate and report upon the facts, circumstances, and causes relating to the January 6, 2021, domestic terrorist attack upon the United States Capitol Complex" and to "issue a final report" containing "findings, conclusions, and recommendations for corrective measures." The Select Committee has conducted nine public hearings, presenting testimony from more than 70 witnesses. In structuring our investigation and hearings, we began with President Trump's contentions that the election was stolen and took testimony from nearly all of the President's principal advisors on this topic. We focused on the rulings of more than 60 Federal and State courts rejecting President Trump's and his supporters' efforts to reverse the electoral outcome.

Despite the rulings of these courts, we understood that millions of Americans still lack the information necessary to understand and evaluate what President Trump has told them about the election. For that reason, our hearings featured a number of members of President Trump's inner circle refuting his fraud claims and testifying that the election was not in fact stolen. In all, the Committee displayed the testimony of more than four dozen Republicans—by far the majority of witnesses in our hearings—including two of President Trump's former Attorneys General, his former White House Counsel, numerous members of his White House staff, and the highest-ranking members of his 2020 election campaign, including his campaign manager and his campaign general counsel. Even key individuals who worked closely with President Trump to try to overturn the 2020 election on January 6th ultimately *admitted* that they lacked actual evidence sufficient to change the election result, and they *admitted* that what they were attempting was unlawful.[18]

This Report supplies an immense volume of information and testimony assembled through the Select Committee's investigation, including information obtained following litigation in Federal district and appellate courts, as well as in the U.S. Supreme Court. Based upon this assembled evidence, the Committee has reached a series of specific findings,[19] including the following:

1. Beginning election night and continuing through January 6th and thereafter, Donald Trump purposely disseminated false allegations of fraud related to the 2020 Presidential election in order to aid his effort to overturn the election and for purposes of soliciting contributions. These false claims provoked his supporters to violence on January 6th.

2. Knowing that he and his supporters had lost dozens of election lawsuits, and despite his own senior advisors refuting his election fraud claims and urging him to concede his election loss, Donald Trump refused to accept the lawful result of the 2020 election. Rather than honor his constitutional obligation to "take Care that the Laws be faithfully executed," President Trump instead plotted to overturn the election outcome.

3. Despite knowing that such an action would be illegal, and that no State had or would submit an altered electoral slate, Donald Trump corruptly pressured Vice President Mike Pence to refuse to count electoral votes during Congress's joint session on January 6th.

4. Donald Trump sought to corrupt the U.S. Department of Justice by attempting to enlist Department officials to make purposely false statements and thereby aid his effort to overturn the Presidential election. After that effort failed, Donald Trump offered the position of Acting Attorney General to Jeff Clark knowing that Clark intended to disseminate false information aimed at overturning the election.

5. Without any evidentiary basis and contrary to State and Federal law, Donald Trump unlawfully pressured State officials and legislators to change the results of the election in their States.

6. Donald Trump oversaw an effort to obtain and transmit false electoral certificates to Congress and the National Archives.

7. Donald Trump pressured Members of Congress to object to valid slates of electors from several States.

8. Donald Trump purposely verified false information filed in Federal court.

9. Based on false allegations that the election was stolen, Donald Trump summoned tens of thousands of supporters to Washington for January 6th. Although these supporters were angry and some were armed, Donald Trump instructed them to march to the Capitol on January 6th to "take back" their country.

10. Knowing that a violent attack on the Capitol was underway and knowing that his words would incite further violence, Donald Trump purposely sent a social media message publicly condemning Vice President Pence at 2:24 p.m. on January 6th.

11. Knowing that violence was underway at the Capitol, and despite his duty to ensure that the laws are faithfully executed, Donald Trump refused repeated requests over a multiple hour period that he instruct his violent supporters to disperse and leave the Capitol, and instead watched the violent attack unfold on television. This failure to act perpetuated the violence at the Capitol and obstructed Congress's proceeding to count electoral votes.

12. Each of these actions by Donald Trump was taken in support of a multi-part conspiracy to overturn the lawful results of the 2020 Presidential election.

13. The intelligence community and law enforcement agencies did successfully detect the planning for potential violence on January 6th, including planning specifically by the Proud Boys and Oath Keeper militia groups who ultimately led the attack on the Capitol. As January 6th approached, the intelligence specifically identified the potential for violence at the U.S. Capitol. This intelligence was shared within the executive branch, including with the Secret Service and the President's National Security Council.

14. Intelligence gathered in advance of January 6th did not support a conclusion that Antifa or other left-wing groups would likely engage in a violent counter-demonstration, or attack Trump supporters on January 6th. Indeed, intelligence from January 5th indicated that some left-wing groups were instructing their members to "stay at home" and not attend on January 6th.[20] Ultimately, none of these groups was involved to any material extent with the attack on the Capitol on January 6th.

15. Neither the intelligence community nor law enforcement obtained intelligence in advance of January 6th on the full extent of the ongoing planning by President Trump, John Eastman, Rudolph Giuliani and their associates to overturn the certified election results. Such agencies apparently did not (and potentially could not) anticipate the provocation President Trump would offer the crowd in his Ellipse speech, that President Trump would "spontaneously" instruct the crowd to march to the Capitol, that President Trump would exacerbate the violent riot by sending his 2:24 p.m. tweet condemning Vice President Pence, or the full scale of the violence and lawlessness that would ensue. Nor did law enforcement anticipate that President Trump would refuse to direct his supporters to leave the Capitol once violence began. No intelligence community advance analysis predicted exactly how President Trump would behave; no such analysis recognized the full scale and extent of the threat to the Capitol on January 6th.

16. Hundreds of Capitol and DC Metropolitan police officers performed their duties bravely on January 6th, and America owes those individuals immense gratitude for their courage in the defense of Congress and our Constitution. Without their bravery, January 6th would have been far worse. Although certain members of the Capitol Police leadership regarded their approach to January 6th as "all hands on deck," the Capitol Police leadership did not have sufficient assets in place to address the violent and lawless crowd.[21] Capitol Police leadership did not anticipate the scale of the violence that would ensue after President Trump instructed tens of thousands of his supporters in the Ellipse crowd to march to the Capitol, and then tweeted at 2:24 p.m. Although Chief Steven Sund raised the idea of National Guard support, the Capitol Police Board did not request Guard assistance prior to January 6th. The Metropolitan Police took an even more proactive approach to January 6th, and deployed roughly 800 officers, including responding to the emergency calls for help at the Capitol. Rioters still managed to break their line in certain locations, when the crowd surged forward in the immediate aftermath of Donald Trump's 2:24 p.m. tweet. The Department of Justice readied a group of Federal agents at Quantico and in the District of Columbia, anticipating that January 6th could become violent, and then deployed those agents once it became clear that police at the Capitol were overwhelmed. Agents from the Department of Homeland Security were also deployed to assist.

17. President Trump had authority and responsibility to direct deployment of the National Guard in the District of Columbia, but never gave

any order to deploy the National Guard on January 6th or on any other day. Nor did he instruct any Federal law enforcement agency to assist. Because the authority to deploy the National Guard had been delegated to the Department of Defense, the Secretary of Defense could, and ultimately did deploy the Guard. Although evidence identifies a likely miscommunication between members of the civilian leadership in the Department of Defense impacting the timing of deployment, the Committee has found no evidence that the Department of Defense intentionally delayed deployment of the National Guard. The Select Committee recognizes that some at the Department had genuine concerns, counseling caution, that President Trump might give an illegal order to use the military in support of his efforts to overturn the election.

* * *

This Report begins with a factual overview framing each of these conclusions and summarizing what our investigation found. That overview is in turn supported by eight chapters identifying the very specific evidence of each of the principal elements of President Trump's multi-part plan to overturn the election, along with evidence regarding intelligence gathered before January 6th and security shortfalls that day.

Although the Committee's hearings were viewed live by tens of millions of Americans and widely publicized in nearly every major news source,[22] the Committee also recognizes that other news outlets and commentators have actively discouraged viewers from watching, and that millions of other Americans have not yet seen the actual evidence addressed by this Report. Accordingly, the Committee is also releasing video summaries of relevant evidence on each major topic investigated.

This Report also examines the legal implications of Donald Trump and his co-conspirators' conduct and includes criminal referrals to the Department of Justice regarding President Trump and certain other individuals. The criminal referrals build upon three relevant rulings issued by a Federal district court and explain in detail how the facts found support further evaluation by the Department of Justice of specific criminal charges. To assist the public in understanding the nature and importance of this material, this Report also contains sections identifying how the Committee has evaluated the credibility of its witnesses and suggests that the Department of Justice further examine possible efforts to obstruct our investigation. We also note that more than 30 witnesses invoked their Fifth Amendment privilege against self-incrimination, others invoked Executive Privilege or categorically refused to appear (including Steve Bannon, who has since been convicted of contempt of Congress).

Finally, this report identifies a series of legislative recommendations, including the Presidential Election Reform Act, which has already passed the House of Representatives.

## EXECUTIVE SUMMARY: OVERVIEW OF THE EVIDENCE DEVELOPED

In the Committee's hearings, we presented evidence of what ultimately became a multi-part plan to overturn the 2020 Presidential election. That evidence has led to an overriding and straight forward conclusion: the central cause of January 6th was one man, former President Donald Trump, whom many others followed. None of the events of January 6th would have happened without him.

### THE BIG LIE

In the weeks before election day 2020, Donald Trump's campaign experts, including his campaign manager Bill Stepien, advised him that the election results would not be fully known on election night.[23] This was because certain States would not begin to count absentee and other mail-in votes until election day or after election-day polls had closed.[24] Because Republican voters tend to vote in greater numbers on election day and Democratic voters tend to vote in greater numbers in advance of election day, it was widely anticipated that Donald Trump could initially appear to have a lead, but that the continued counting of mail-in, absentee and other votes beginning election night would erode and could overcome that perceived lead.[25] Thus, as President Trump's campaign manager cautioned, understanding the results of the 2020 election would be a lengthy "process," and an initial appearance of a Trump lead could be a "red mirage."[26] This was not unique to the 2020 election; similar scenarios had played out in prior elections as well.[27]

Prior to the 2020 election, Donald Trump's campaign manager Bill Stepien, along with House Republican Leader Kevin McCarthy, urged President Trump to embrace mail-in voting as potentially beneficial to the Trump Campaign.[28] Presidential advisor and son-in-law Jared Kushner recounted others giving Donald Trump the same advice: "[M]ail in ballots could be a good thing for us if we looked at it correctly."[29] Multiple States, including Florida, had successfully utilized mail-in voting in prior elections, and in 2020.[30] Trump White House Counselor Hope Hicks testified: "I think he [President Trump] understood that a lot of people vote via absentee ballot in places like Florida and have for a long time and that it's worked fine."[31] Donald Trump won in numerous States that allowed no-excuse absentee voting in 2020, including Alaska, Florida, Idaho, Iowa, Kansas, Montana, North Carolina, North Dakota, Ohio, Oklahoma, South Dakota, and Wyoming.[32]

On election night 2020, the election returns were reported in almost exactly the way that Stepien and other Trump Campaign experts predicted, with the counting of mail-in and absentee ballots gradually diminishing President Trump's perceived lead. As the evening progressed, President Trump called in his campaign team to discuss the results. Stepien and other campaign experts advised him that the results of the election would not be known for some time, and that he could not truthfully declare victory.[33] "It was far too early to be making any calls like that. Ballots—ballots were still being counted. Ballots were still going to be counted for days."[34]

Campaign Senior Advisor Jason Miller told the Select Committee that he argued against declaring victory at that time as well, because "it was too early to say one way [or] the other" who had won.[35] Stepien advised Trump to say that "votes were still being counted. It's too early to tell, too early to call the race but, you know, we are proud of the race we run—we ran and we, you know, think we're—think we're in a good position" and would say more in the coming days.[36]

President Trump refused, and instead said this in his public remarks that evening: "This is a fraud on the American public. This is an embarrassment to our country. We were getting ready to win this election. Frankly, we did win this election. We did win this election . . . . We want all voting to stop."[37] And on the morning of November 5th, he tweeted "STOP THE COUNT!"[38] Halting the counting of votes at that point would have violated both State and Federal laws.[39]

According to testimony received by the Select Committee, the only advisor present who supported President Trump's inclination to declare victory was Rudolph Giuliani, who appeared to be inebriated.[40] President Trump's Attorney General, William Barr, who had earlier left the election night gathering, perceived the President's statement this way:

> [R]ight out of the box on election night, the President claimed that there was major fraud underway. I mean, this happened, as far as I could tell, before there was actually any potential of looking at evidence. He claimed there was major fraud. And it seemed to be based on the dynamic that, at the end of the evening, a lot of Democratic votes came in which changed the vote counts in certain States, and that seemed to be the basis for this broad claim that there was major fraud. And I didn't think much of that, because people had been talking for weeks and everyone understood for weeks that that was going to be what happened on election night . . . .[41]

President Trump's decision to declare victory falsely on election night and, unlawfully, to call for the vote counting to stop, was not a spontaneous decision. It was premeditated. The Committee has assembled a range of

President Trump declares victory in a speech at an election night party.
(Photo by Chip Somodevilla/Getty Images)

evidence of President Trump's preplanning for a false declaration of victory. This includes multiple written communications on October 31 and November 3, 2020, to the White House by Judicial Watch President Tom Fitton.[42] This evidence demonstrates that Fitton was in direct contact with President Trump and understood that President Trump would falsely declare victory on election night and call for vote counting to stop. The evidence also includes an audio recording of President Trump's advisor Steve Bannon, who said this on October 31, 2020, to a group of his associates from China:

> And what Trump's gonna do is just declare victory, right? He's gonna declare victory. But that doesn't mean he's a winner. He's just gonna say he's a winner . . . The Democrats—more of our people vote early that count. Theirs vote in mail. And so they're gonna have a natural disadvantage, and Trump's going to take advantage of it—that's our strategy. He's gonna declare himself a winner. So when you wake up Wednesday morning, it's going to be a firestorm . . . . Also, if Trump, if Trump is losing, by 10 or 11 o'clock at night, it's going to be even crazier. No, because he's gonna sit right there and say "They stole it. I'm directing the Attorney General to shut down all ballot places in all 50 states." It's

going to be, no, he's not going out easy. If Trump—if Biden's winning, Trump is going to do some crazy shit.[43]

Also in advance of the election, Roger Stone, another outside advisor to President Trump, made this statement:

I really do suspect it will still be up in the air. When that happens, the key thing to do is to claim victory. Possession is nine-tenths of the law. No, we won. Fuck you, Sorry. Over. We won. You're wrong. Fuck you.[44]

On election day, Vice President Pence's staff, including his Chief of Staff and Counsel, became concerned that President Trump might falsely claim victory that evening. The Vice President's Counsel, Greg Jacob, testified about their concern that the Vice President might be asked improperly to echo such a false statement.[45] Jacob drafted a memorandum with this specific recommendation: "[I]t is essential that the Vice President not be perceived by the public as having decided questions concerning disputed electoral votes prior to the full development of all relevant facts."[46]

Millions of Americans believed that President Trump was telling the truth on election night—that President Trump actually had proof the election was stolen and that the ongoing counting of votes was an act of fraud.

As votes were being counted in the days after the election, President Trump's senior campaign advisors informed him that his chances of success were almost zero.

Former Trump Campaign Manager Bill Stepien testified that he had come to this conclusion by November 7th, and told President Trump:

Committee Staff: What was your view on the state of the election at that point?

Stepien: You know, very, very, very bleak. You know, I—we told him—the group that went over there outlined, you know, my belief and chances for success at this point. And then we pegged that at, you know, 5, maybe 10 percent based on recounts that were—that, you know, either were automatically initiated or could be—could be initiated based on, you know, realistic legal challenges, not all the legal challenges that eventually were pursued. But, you know, it was—you know, my belief is that it was a very, very—5 to 10 percent is not a very good optimistic outlook.[47]

Trump Campaign Senior Advisor Jason Miller testified to the Committee about this exchange:

Miller: I was in the Oval Office. And at some point in the conversation Matt Oczkowski, who was the lead data person, was brought on, and I remember he delivered to the President in pretty blunt terms that he was going to lose.

Committee Staff: And that was based, Mr. Miller, on Matt and the data team's assessment of this sort of county-by-county, State-by-State results as reported?

Miller: Correct.[48]

In one of the Select Committee's hearings, former Fox News political editor Chris Stirewalt was asked what the chance President Trump had of winning the election after November 7th, when the votes were tallied and every news organization had called the race for now-President Biden. His response: "None."[49]

As the Committee's hearings demonstrated, President Trump made a series of statements to White House staff and others during this time period indicating his understanding that he had lost.[50] President Trump also took consequential actions reflecting his understanding that he would be leaving office on January 20th. For example, President Trump personally signed a Memorandum and Order instructing his Department of Defense to withdraw all military forces from Somalia by December 31, 2020, and from Afghanistan by January 15, 2021.[51] General Keith Kellogg (ret.), who had been appointed by President Trump as Chief of Staff for the National Security Council and was Vice President Pence's National Security Advisor on January 6th, told the Select Committee that "[a]n immediate departure that that memo said would have been catastrophic. It's the same thing what President Biden went through. It would have been a debacle."[52]

In the weeks that followed the election, President Trump's campaign experts and his senior Justice Department officials were informing him and others in the White House that there was no genuine evidence of fraud sufficient to change the results of the election. For example, former Attorney General Barr testified:

And I repeatedly told the President in no uncertain terms that I did not see evidence of fraud, you know, that would have affected the outcome of the election. And, frankly, a year and a half later, I haven't seen anything to change my mind on that.[53]

Former Trump Campaign lawyer Alex Cannon, who was asked to oversee incoming information about voter fraud and set up a voter fraud tip line, told the Select Committee about a pertinent call with White House Chief of Staff Mark Meadows in November 2020:

> Cannon: So I remember a call with Mr. Meadows where Mr. Meadows was asking me what I was finding and if I was finding anything. And I remember sharing with him that we weren't finding anything that would be sufficient to change the results in any of the key States.

> Committee Staff: When was that conversation?

> Cannon: Probably in November. Mid- to late November . . . .

> Committee Staff: And what was Mr. Meadows's reaction to that information?

> Cannon: I believe the words he used were: "So there is no there there?" [54]

President Trump's Campaign Manager Bill Stepien recalled that President Trump was being told "wild allegations" and that it was the Campaign's job to "track [the allegations] down":

> Committee Staff: You said that you were very confident that you were telling the President the truth in your dealings with [him]. And had your team been able to verify any of these allegations of fraud, would you have reported those to the President?

> Stepien: Sure.

> Committee Staff: Did you ever have to report that—

> Stepien: One of my frustrations would be that, you know, people would throw out, you know, these reports, these allegations, these things that they heard or saw in a State, and they'd tell President Trump. And, you know, it would be the campaign's job to track down the information, the facts. And, you know, President Trump, you know—if someone's saying, hey, you know, all these votes aren't counted or were miscounted, you know, if you're down in a State like Arizona, you liked hearing that. It would be our job to track it down and come up dry because the allegation didn't prove to be true. And we'd have to, you know, relay the news that, yeah, that tip that someone told you about those votes or that fraud or, you know, nothing came of it.

> That would be our job as, you know, the truth telling squad and, you know, not—not a fun job to be, you know, much—it's an easier job to

be telling the President about, you know, wild allegations. It's a harder job to be telling him on the back end that, yeah, that wasn't true.

Committee Staff: How did he react to those types of conversations where you [told] him that an allegation or another wasn't true?

Stepien: He was—he had—usually he had pretty clear eyes. Like, he understood, you know—you know, we told him where we thought the race was, and I think he was pretty realistic with our viewpoint, in agreement with our viewpoint of kind of the forecast and the uphill climb we thought he had.[55]

Trump Campaign Senior Advisor Jason Miller told the Committee that he informed President Trump "several" times that "specific to election day fraud and irregularities, there were not enough to overturn the election."[56]

Vice President Pence has also said publicly that he told President Trump there was no basis to allege that the election was stolen. When a reporter recently asked "Did you ever point blank say to the President [that] we lost this election?," Pence responded that "I did . . . Many times."[57] Pence has also explained:

There was never evidence of widespread fraud. I don't believe fraud changed the outcome of the election. But the President and the Campaign had every right to have those examined in court. But I told the President that, once those legal challenges played out, he should simply accept the outcome of the election and move on.[58]

The General Counsel of President Trump's campaign, Matthew Morgan, informed members of the White House staff, and likely many others, of the Campaign's conclusion that none of the allegations of fraud and irregularities could be sufficient to change the outcome of the election:

What was generally discussed on that topic was whether the fraud, maladministration, abuse, or irregularities, if aggregated and read most favorably to the campaign, would that be outcome determinative. And I think everyone's assessment in the room, at least amongst the staff, Marc Short, myself, and Greg Jacob, was that it was not sufficient to be outcome determinative.[59]

In a meeting on November 23rd, Barr told President Trump that the Justice Department was doing its duty by investigating every fraud allegation "if it's specific, credible, and could've affected the outcome," but that "they're just not meritorious. They're not panning out."[60]

Barr then told the Associated Press on December 1st that the Department had "not seen fraud on a scale that could have effected a different outcome in the election." [61] Next, he reiterated this point in private meetings with the President both that afternoon and on December 14th, as well as in his final press conference as Attorney General later that month.[62] The Department of Homeland Security had reached a similar determination two weeks earlier: "**There is no evidence that any voting system deleted or lost votes, changed votes, or was in any way compromised.**" [63]

In addition, multiple other high ranking Justice Department personnel appointed by President Trump also informed him repeatedly that the allegations were false. As January 6th drew closer, Acting Attorney General Rosen and Acting Deputy Attorney General Donoghue had calls with President Trump on almost a daily basis explaining in detail what the Department's investigations showed.[64] Acting Deputy Attorney General Richard Donoghue told the Select Committee that he and Acting Attorney General Rosen tried "to put it in very clear terms to the President. And I said something to the effect of 'Sir, we've done dozens of investigations, hundreds of interviews. The major allegations are not supported by the evidence developed. We've looked in Georgia, Pennsylvania, Michigan, Nevada. We're doing our job.'" [65] On December 31st, Donoghue recalls telling the President that "people keep telling you these things and they turn out not to be true." [66] And then on January 3rd, Donoghue reiterated this point with the President:

[A]s in previous conservations, we would say to him, you know, "We checked that out, and there's nothing to it." [67]

Acting Attorney General Rosen testified before the Select Committee that "the common element" of all of his communications with President Trump was President Trump urging the Department to find widespread fraud that did not actually exist. None of the Department's investigations identified any genuine fraud sufficient to impact the election outcome:

During my tenure as the Acting Attorney General, which began on December 24 of [2020], the Department of Justice maintained the position, publicly announced by former Attorney General William Barr, that the Department had been presented with no evidence of widespread voter fraud in a scale sufficient to change the outcome of the 2020 election.[68]

As President Trump was hearing from his campaign and his Justice Department that the allegations of widespread fraud were not supported by the evidence, his White House legal staff also reached the same conclusions, and agreed specifically with what Barr told President Trump. Both White House Counsel Pat Cipollone and White House Senior Advisor Eric Herschmann reinforced to President Trump that the Justice Department was doing its duty to investigate allegations of supposed voter fraud.[69]

Cipollone told the Select Committee that he "had seen no evidence of massive fraud in the election" and that he "forcefully" made this point "over and over again." For example, during a late-night group meeting with President Trump on December 18th, at which he and Herschmann urged Trump not to heed the advice of several election conspiracists at the meeting:

> Cipollone: They didn't think that we were, you know—they didn't think we believed this, you know, that there had been massive fraud in the election, and the reason they didn't think we believed it is because we didn't.

> Committee Staff: And you articulated that forcefully to them during the meeting?

> Cipollone: I did, yeah. I had seen no evidence of massive fraud in the election. . . . At some point, you have to deliver with the evidence. And I—again, I just to go back to what [Barr] said, he had not seen and I was not aware of any evidence of fraud to the extent that it would change the results of the election. That was made clear to them, okay, over and over again.[70]

Similarly, White House Attorney Eric Herschmann was also very clear about his views:

> [T]hey never proved the allegations that they were making, and they were trying to develop.[71]

In short, President Trump was informed over and over again, by his senior appointees, campaign experts and those who had served him for years, that his election fraud allegations were nonsense.

How did President Trump continue to make false allegations despite all of this unequivocal information? President Trump sought out those who were not scrupulous with the facts, and were willing to be dishonest. He found a new legal team to assert claims that his existing advisors and the Justice Department had specifically informed him were false. President Trump's new legal team, headed by Rudolph Giuliani, and their allies ultimately lost dozens of election lawsuits in Federal and State courts.

The testimony of Trump Campaign Manager Bill Stepien helps to put this series of events in perspective. Stepien described his interaction with Giuliani as an intentional "self-demotion," with Stepien stepping aside once it became clear that President Trump intended to spread falsehoods.

Stepien knew the President's new team was relying on unsupportable accusations, and he refused to be associated with their approach:

There were two groups of family. We called them kind of my team and Rudy's team. I didn't mind being characterized as being part of "team normal," as reporters, you know, kind of started to do around that point in time. [72]

Having worked for Republican campaigns for over two decades, Stepien said, "I think along the way I've built up a pretty good -- I hope a good reputation for being honest and professional, and I didn't think what was happening was necessarily honest or professional at that point in time." [73]

As Giuliani visited Campaign headquarters to discuss election litigation, the Trump Campaign's professional staff began to view him as unhinged.[74] In addition, multiple law firms previously engaged to work for the Trump Campaign decided that they could not participate in the strategy being instituted by Giuliani. They quit. Campaign General Counsel Matthew Morgan explained that he had conversations with "probably all of our counsel who [we]re signed up to assist on election day as they disengaged with the campaign." [75] The "general consensus was that the law firms were not comfortable making the arguments that Rudy Giuliani was making publicly." [76] When asked how many outside firms expressed this concern, Morgan recalled having "a similar conversation with most all of them." [77]

Stepien grew so wary of the new team that he locked Giuliani out of his office:

Committee Staff: Yeah. I'm getting the sense from listening to you here for a few hours that you sort of chose to pull back, that you were uncomfortable with what Mr. Giuliani and others were saying and doing and, therefore, you were purposefully stepping back from a day-to-day role as the leader of the campaign. Is that—I don't want to put words in your mouth. Is that accurate?

Stepien: That's accurate. That's accurate. You know, I had my assistant -- it was a big glass kind of wall office in our headquarters, and I had my assistant lock my door. I told her, don't let anyone in. You know, I'll be around when I need to be around. You know, tell me what I need to know. Tell me what's going on here, but, you know, you're going to see less of me.

And, you know, sure enough, you know, Mayor Giuliani tried to, you know, get in my office and ordered her to unlock the door, and she didn't do that, you know. She's, you know, smart about that. But your words are ones I agree with.[78]

Over the weeks that followed, dozens of judges across the country specifically rejected the allegations of fraud and irregularities being advanced by the Trump team and their allies. For example, courts described the arguments as "an amalgamation of theories, conjecture, and speculation," "allegations ... sorely wanting of relevant or reliable evidence," "strained legal arguments without merit," assertions that "did not prove by any standard of proof that any illegal votes were cast and counted," and even a "fundamental and obvious misreading of the Constitution." [79]

Reflecting back on this period, Trump Campaign Communications Director Tim Murtaugh texted colleagues in January 2021 about a news report that the New York State Bar was considering expelling Rudolph Giuliani over the Ellipse rally: "Why wouldn't they expel him based solely on the outrageous lies he told for 2 1/2 months?" [80]

This is exactly what ultimately came to pass. When suspending his license, a New York court said that Giuliani "communicated demonstrably false and misleading statements to courts, lawmakers and the public at large in his capacity as lawyer for former President Donald J. Trump and the Trump campaign in connection with Trump's failed effort at reelection in 2020." [81] The court added that "[t]he seriousness of [Giuliani's] uncontroverted misconduct cannot be overstated." [82]

Other Trump lawyers were sanctioned for making outlandish claims of election fraud without the evidence to back them up, including Sidney Powell, Lin Wood and seven other pro-Trump lawyers in a case that a Federal judge described as "a historic and profound abuse of the judicial process":

> It is one thing to take on the charge of vindicating rights associated with an allegedly fraudulent election. It is another to take on the charge of deceiving a federal court and the American people into believing that rights were infringed, without regard to whether any laws or rights were in fact violated. This is what happened here. [83]

A group of prominent Republicans have more recently issued a report—titled *Lost, Not Stolen*—examining "every count of every case brought in these six battleground states" by President Trump and his allies. The report concludes "that Donald Trump and his supporters had their day in court and failed to produce substantive evidence to make their case." [84] President Trump and his legal allies "failed because of a lack of evidence and not because of erroneous rulings or unfair judges . . . . In many cases, after making extravagant claims of wrongdoing, Trump's legal representatives showed up in court or state proceedings empty-handed, and then returned to their rallies and media campaigns to repeat the same unsupported claims." [85]

There is no reasonable basis for the allegation that these dozens of rulings by State and Federal courts were somehow politically motivated. [86] The outcome of these suits was uniform regardless of who appointed the judges.

One of the authors of *Lost, Not Stolen*, longtime Republican election lawyer Benjamin Ginsberg, testified before the Select Committee that "in no instance did a court find that the charges of fraud were real," without variation based on the judges involved.[87] Indeed, eleven of the judges who ruled against Donald Trump and his supporters were appointed by Donald Trump himself.

One of those Trump nominees, Judge Stephanos Bibas of the U.S. Court of Appeals for the Third Circuit, rejected an appeal by the Trump Campaign claiming that Pennsylvania officials "did not undertake any meaningful effort" to fight illegal absentee ballots and uneven treatment of voters across counties.[88] Judge Bibas wrote in his decision that "calling an election unfair does not make it so. Charges require specific allegations and then proof. We have neither here."[89] Another Trump nominee, Judge Brett Ludwig of the Eastern District of Wisconsin, ruled against President Trump's lawsuit alleging that the result was skewed by illegal procedures that governed drop boxes, ballot address information, and individuals who claimed "indefinitely confined" status to vote from home.[90] Judge Ludwig wrote in his decision, that "[t]his Court has allowed plaintiff the chance to make his case and he has lost on the merits" because the procedures used "do not remotely rise to the level" of breaking Wisconsin's election rules.[91]

Nor is it true that these rulings focused solely on standing, or procedural issues. As Ginsberg confirmed in his testimony to the Select Committee, President Trump's team "did have their day in court."[92] Indeed, he and his co-authors determined in their report that 30 of these post-election cases were dismissed by a judge after an evidentiary hearing had been held, and many of these judges explicitly indicated in their decisions that the evidence presented by the plaintiffs was wholly insufficient on the merits.[93]

Ultimately, even Rudolph Giuliani and his legal team acknowledged that they had no definitive evidence of election fraud sufficient to change the election outcome. For example, although Giuliani repeatedly had claimed in public that Dominion voting machines stole the election, he admitted during his Select Committee deposition that "I do not think the machines stole the election."[94] An attorney representing his lead investigator, Bernard Kerik, declared in a letter to the Select Committee that "it was impossible for Kerik and his team to determine conclusively whether there was widespread fraud or whether that widespread fraud would have altered the outcome of the election."[95] Kerik also emailed President Trump's chief of staff on December 28, 2020, writing: "We can do all the investigations we want later, but if the president plans on winning, it's the legislators that have to be moved and this will do just that."[96] Other Trump lawyers and supporters, Jenna Ellis, John Eastman, Phil Waldron, and Michael Flynn, all invoked their Fifth Amendment privilege against self-incrimination when

Rudolph Giuliani, Bernard Kerik, and other hold a press conference at Four Seasons Total Landscaping on November 7, 2020 falsely claiming Donald Trump had won the state of Pennsylvania.

(Photo by Chris McGrath/Getty Images)

asked by the Select Committee what supposed proof they uncovered that the election was stolen.[97] Not a single witness--nor any combination of witnesses--provided the Select Committee with evidence demonstrating that fraud occurred on a scale even remotely close to changing the outcome in any State.[98]

By mid-December 2020, Donald Trump had come to what most of his staff believed was the end of the line. The Supreme Court rejected a lawsuit he supported filed by the State of Texas in the Supreme Court, and Donald Trump had this exchange, according to Special Assistant to the President Cassidy Hutchinson:

> The President was fired up about the Supreme Court decision. And so I was standing next to [Chief of Staff Mark] Meadows, but I had stepped back . . . The President [was] just raging about the decision and how it's wrong, and why didn't we make more calls, and just this typical anger outburst at this decision . . . And the President said I think—so he had said something to the effect of, "I don't want people to know we lost, Mark. This is embarrassing. Figure it out. We need to figure it out. I don't want people to know that we lost."[99]

On December 14, 2020, the Electoral College met to cast and certify each State's electoral votes. By this time, many of President Trump's senior staff, and certain members of his family, were urging him to concede that he had lost.

Labor Secretary Gene Scalia told the Committee that he called President Trump around this time and gave him such feedback quite directly:

> [S]o, I had put a call in to the President—I might have called on the 13th; we spoke, I believe, on the 14th—in which I conveyed to him that I thought that it was time for him to acknowledge that President Biden had prevailed in the election . . . . But I communicated to the President that when that legal process is exhausted and when the electors have voted, that that's the point at which that outcome needs to be expected . . . . And I told him that I did believe, yes, that once those legal processes were run, if fraud had not been established that had affected the outcome of the election, that, unfortunately, I believed that what had to be done was concede the outcome.[100]

Deputy White House Press Secretary Judd Deere also told President Trump that he should concede. He recalled other staffers advising President Trump at some point to concede and that he "encouraged him to do it at least once after the electoral college met in mid-December." [101] White House Counsel Pat Cipollone also believed that President Trump should concede: "[I]f your question is did I believe he should concede the election at a point in time, yes, I did." [102]

Attorney General Barr told the Select Committee this: "And in my view, that [the December 14 electoral college vote] was the end of the matter. I didn't see—you know, I thought that this would lead inexorably to a new administration. I was not aware at that time of any theory, you know, why this could be reversed. And so I felt that the die was cast . . . ." [103]

Barr also told the Committee that he suggested several weeks earlier that the President's efforts in this regard needed to come to an end soon, in conversation with several White House officials after his meeting with Trump on November 23rd:

> [A]s I walked out of the Oval Office, Jared was there with Dan Scavino, who ran the President's social media and who I thought was a reasonable guy and believe is a reasonable guy. And I said, how long is he going to carry on with this 'stolen election' stuff? Where is this going to go?

> And by that time, Meadows had caught up with me and—leaving the office, and caught up to me and said that—he said, look, I think that he's becoming more realistic and knows that there's a limit to how far he can take this. And then Jared said, you know, yeah, we're working on this, we're working on it.[104]

Despite all that Donald Trump was being told, he continued to purposely and maliciously make false claims. To understand the very stark differences between what he was being told and what he said publicly and in fundraising solicitations, the Committee has assembled the following examples.

| Then-Deputy Attorney General Jeffrey Rosen (12/15/20): "And so he said, 'Well, what about this? I saw it on the videotape, somebody delivering a suitcase of ballots.' And we said, 'It wasn't a suitcase. It was a bin. That's what they use when they're counting ballots. It's benign.'" [105] | President Trump one week later (12/22/20): "There is even security camera footage from Georgia that shows officials telling poll watchers to leave the room before pulling suitcases of ballots out from under the tables and continuing to count for hours." [106] |
| --- | --- |
| Acting Deputy Attorney General Richard Donoghue (12/27 & 12/31/20): "I told the President myself that several times, in several conversations, that these allegations about ballots being smuggled in in a suitcase and run through the machine several times, it was not true, that we looked at it, we looked at the video, we interviewed the witnesses, that it was not true . . . . I believe it was in the phone call on December 27th. It was also in a meeting in the Oval Office on December 31st." [107] | President Trump later that week (1/2/21): "[S]he stuffed the machine. She stuffed the ballot. Each ballot went three times, they were showing: Here's ballot number one. Here it is a second time, third time, next ballot." [108] |
| GA Sec. State Brad Raffensperger (1/2/21): "You're talking about the State Farm video. And I think it's extremely unfortunate that Rudy Giuliani or his people, they sliced and diced that video and took it out of context." . . . "[W]e did an audit of that and we proved conclusively that they were not scanned three times. . . . Yes, Mr. President, we'll send you the link from WSB." [Trump]: "I don't care about a link. I don't need it." [109] | President Trump one day later (1/3/21): "I spoke to Secretary of State Brad Raffensperger yesterday about Fulton County and voter fraud in Georgia. He was unwilling, or unable, to answer questions such as the 'ballots under table' scam, ballot destruction, out of state 'voters', dead voters, and more. He has no clue!" [110] |

| | |
|---|---|
| *Attorney General Barr (12/1/20):* "Then he raised the 'big vote dump,' as he called it, in Detroit. And, you know, he said, people saw boxes coming into the counting station at all hours of the morning and so forth.... I said, 'Mr. President, there are 630 precincts in Detroit, and unlike elsewhere in the State, they centralize the counting process, so they're not counted in each precinct, they're moved to counting stations, and so the normal process would involve boxes coming in at all different hours.' And I said, 'Did anyone point out to you—did all the people complaining about it point out to you, you actually did better in Detroit than you did last time? I mean, there's no indication of fraud in Detroit.'" [111] | *President Trump one day later (12/2/20):* "I'll tell you what's wrong, voter fraud. Here's an example. This is Michigan. At 6:31 in the morning, a vote dump of 149,772 votes came in unexpectedly. We were winning by a lot. That batch was received in horror. . . . In Detroit everybody saw the tremendous conflict . . . there were more votes than there were voters." [112] |
| *Acting Deputy Attorney General Richard Donoghue (12/27/20):* "The President then continued, there are 'more votes than voters...'. But I was aware of that allegation, and I said, you know, that was just a matter of them 'comparing the 2020 votes cast to 2016 registration numbers.' That is 'not a valid complaint.'" [113] | *President Trump ten days later (1/6/21):* "More votes than they had voters. And many other States also." [114] |
| *Acting Deputy Attorney General Richard Donoghue (1/3/21):* "[W]e would say to him, you know, 'We checked that out, and there's nothing to it. . . . And we would cite to certain allegations. And so—like such as Pennsylvania, right. 'No, there were not 250,000 more votes reported than were actually cast. That's not true.' So we would say things like that." [115] | *President Trump three days later (1/6/21):* "In Pennsylvania, you had 205,000 more votes than you had voters. And the number is actually much greater than that now. That was as of a week ago. And this is a mathematical impossibility unless you want to say it's a total fraud." [116] |

| *GA Sec. State Brad Raffensperger (1/2/21):* | *President Trump two days later (1/4/21):* |
|---|---|
| [Trump]: "[I]t's 4,502 who voted, but they weren't on the voter registration roll, which they had to be. You had 18,325 vacant address voters. The address was vacant, and they're not allowed to be counted. That's 18,325."...<br><br>[Raffensperger]: "Well, Mr. President, the challenge that you have is the data you have is wrong." [117] | "4,502 illegal ballots were cast by individuals who do not appear on the state's voter rolls. Well, that's sort of strange. 18,325 illegal ballots were cast by individuals who registered to vote using an address listed as vacant according to the postal service." [118] |
| *GA Sec. of State Brad Raffensperger (1/2/21):* | *President Trump four days later (1/6/21):* |
| [Trump]: "So dead people voted, and I think the number is close to 5,000 people. And they went to obituaries. They went to all sorts of methods to come up with an accurate number, and a minimum is close to about 5,000 voters."...<br><br>[Raffensperger]: "The actual number were two. Two. Two people that were dead that voted. So that's wrong." [119] | "[T]he number of fraudulent ballots that we've identified across the state is staggering. Over 10,300 ballots in Georgia were cast by individuals whose names and dates of birth match Georgia residents who died in 2020 and prior to the election." [120] |
| *GA Sec. State General Counsel Ryan Germany (1/2/21):* | *President Trump four days later (1/6/21):* |
| [Trump]: "You had out-of-state voters. They voted in Georgia, but they were from out of state, of 4,925."... [Germany]: "Every one we've been through are people that lived in Georgia, moved to a different state, but then moved back to Georgia legitimately."... "They moved back in years ago. This was not like something just before the election. So there's something about that data that, it's just not accurate." [121] | "And at least 15,000 ballots were cast by individuals who moved out of the state prior to November 3rd election. They say they moved right back." [122] |

| | |
|---|---|
| *White House Press Secretary Kayleigh McEnany (n.d.):*<br>"[T]he one specific I remember referencing was I don't agree with the Dominion track." . . . "I specifically referenced waving him off of the Dominion theory earlier in my testimony." . . .<br>[Q] "Are you saying you think he still continued to tweet that after you waved him off of it?"<br>[A] "Yeah . . ."[123] | *President Trump:*<br>Between mid-November and January 5, 2021, President Trump tweeted or retweeted conspiracy theories about Dominion nearly three dozen times.[124] |
| *Trump Campaign Senior Advisor Jason Miller:*<br>"...the international allegations for Dominion were not valid."<br>[Q] "Okay. Did anybody communicate that to the President?"<br>[A]: "I know that that was—I know that was communicated. I know I communicated it"[125] | *President Trump:*<br>"You have Dominion, which is very, very suspect to start off with. Nobody knows the ownership. People say the votes are counted in foreign countries and much worse..."[126] |
| *Attorney General Barr (11/23/20):*<br>"I specifically raised the Dominion voting machines, which I found to be one of the most disturbing allegations— 'disturbing' in the sense that I saw absolutely zero basis for the allegations . . . I told him that it was crazy stuff and they were wasting their time on that and it was doing great, great disservice to the country."[127] | *President Trump three days later (11/26/20):*<br>"[T]hose machines are fixed, they're rigged. You can press Trump and the vote goes to Biden. . . . All you have to do is play with a chip, and they played with a chip, especially in Wayne County and Detroit."[128] |
| *Attorney General Barr (12/1/20):*<br>"I explained, I said, look, if you have a machine and it counts 500 votes for Biden and 500 votes for Trump, and then you go back later and you have a—you will have the 1,000 pieces of paper put through that machine, and you can see if there's any discrepancy . . . there has been no discrepancy."[129] | *President Trump one day later (12/2/20):*<br>"In one Michigan County, as an example, that used Dominion systems, they found that nearly 6,000 votes had been wrongly switched from Trump to Biden, and this is just the tip of the iceberg. This is what we caught. How many didn't we catch?"[130] |

| | |
|---|---|
| *Attorney General Barr (12/14/20):* "'I will, Mr. President. But there are a couple of things,' I responded. 'My understanding is that our experts have looked at the Antrim situation and are sure it was a human error that did not occur anywhere else. And, in any event, Antrim is doing a hand recount of the paper ballots, so we should know in a couple of days whether there is any real problem with the machines.'" [131] | *President Trump one day later (12/15/20):* "This is BIG NEWS. Dominion Voting Machines are a disaster all over the Country. Changed the results of a landslide election. Can't let this happen. . . ." [132] |
| *Then–Deputy Attorney General Jeffrey Rosen (12/15/20):* "[O]ther people were telling him there was fraud, you know, corruption in the election. The voting machines were no good. And we were telling him that is inconsistent, by 'we,' I mean Richard Donoghue and myself, that that was not what we were seeing." . . . "There was this open issue as to the Michigan report. And—I think it was Mr. Cuccinelli, not certain, but had indicated that there was a hand recount. And I think he said, 'That's the gold standard.'" [133] | *President Trump one day later (12/16/20):* "'Study: Dominion Machines shifted 2–3% of Trump Votes to Biden. Far more votes than needed to sway election.' Florida, Ohio, Texas and many other states were won by even greater margins than pro-jected. Did just as well with Swing States, but bad things happened. @OANN" [134] |
| *National Security Adviser Robert O'Brien (12/18/20):* "I got a call from, I think, Molly Michael in outer oval, the President's assistant, and she said, 'I'm connect-ing you to the Oval' . . . somebody asked me, was there—did I have any evidence of election fraud in the vot-ing machines or foreign interference in our voting machines. And I said, no, we've looked into that and there's no evidence of it." [135] | *President Trump one day later (12/19/20):* ". . . There could also have been a hit on our ridiculous voting machines during the election, which is now obvious that I won big, making it an even more corrupted embar-rassment for the USA. @DNI-_Ratcliffe @SecPompeo" [136] |

| *Acting Deputy AG Richard Donoghue (12/31/20):* | *President Trump two days later (1/2/21):* |
|---|---|
| "We definitely talked about Antrim County again. That was sort of done at that point, because the hand recount had been done and all of that. But we cited back to that to say, you know, this is an example of what people are telling you and what's being filed in some of these court filings that are just not supported by the evidence." [137] | "Well, Brad. Not that there's not an issue, because we have a big issue with Dominion in other states and perhaps in yours. . . . in other states, we think we found tremendous corruption with Dominion machines, but we'll have to see." . . . "I won't give Dominion a pass because we found too many bad things." [138] |
| *GA Sec. State Brad Raffensperger (1/2/21):* | *President Trump four days later (1/6/21):* |
| "I don't believe that you're really questioning the Dominion machines. Because we did a hand re-tally, a 100 percent re-tally of all the ballots, and compared them to what the machines said and came up with virtually the same result. Then we did the recount, and we got virtually the same result." [139] | "In addition, there is the highly troubling matter of Dominion Voting Systems. In one Michigan county alone, 6,000 votes were switched from Trump to Biden and the same systems are used in the majority of states in our country." . . . "There is clear evidence that tens of thousands of votes were switched from President Trump to former Vice President Biden in several counties in Georgia." [140] |

Evidence gathered by the Committee indicates that President Trump raised roughly one quarter of a billion dollars in fundraising efforts between the election and January 6th.[141] Those solicitations persistently claimed and referred to election fraud that did not exist. For example, the Trump Campaign, along with the Republican National Committee, sent millions of emails to their supporters, with messaging claiming that the election was "rigged," that their donations could stop Democrats from

Taped footage of William Barr speaking to the January 6th Select Committee is shown at one of its hearings.

(Photo by Mandel Ngan-Pool/Getty Images)

"trying to steal the election," and that Vice President Biden would be an "illegitimate president" if he took office.

Ultimately, Attorney General Barr suggested that the Department of Justice's investigations disproving President Trump's fraud claims may have prevented an even more serious series of events:

> [F]rankly, I think the fact that I put myself in the position that I could say that we had looked at this and didn't think there was fraud was really important to moving things forward. And I sort of shudder to think what the situation would have been if the position of the Department was, "We're not even looking at this until after Biden's in office." I'm not sure we would've had a transition at all.[142]

### RATHER THAN CONCEDE, DONALD TRUMP CHOOSES TO OBSTRUCT THE JANUARY 6TH PROCEEDING

President Trump disregarded the rulings of the courts and rejected the findings and conclusions and advice from his Justice Department, his campaign experts, and his White House and Cabinet advisors. He chose instead to try to overturn the election on January 6th and took a series of very specific steps to attempt to achieve that result.

A central element of Donald Trump's plan to overturn the election relied upon Vice President Mike Pence. As Vice President, Pence served as the President of the Senate, the presiding officer for the joint session of Congress on January 6th. Beginning in December, and with greater frequency as January 6th approached, Trump repeatedly and unlawfully pressured Pence in private and public to prevent Congress from counting lawful electoral votes from several States.

To understand the plan President Trump devised with attorney and law professor John Eastman, it is necessary to understand the constitutional structure for selecting our President.

At the Constitutional Convention 233 years ago, the framers considered but rejected multiple proposals that Congress itself vote to select the President of the United States.[143] Indeed the Framers voiced very specific concerns with Congress selecting the President. They viewed it as important that the electors, chosen for the specific purpose of selecting the President, should make the determination rather than Congress:

> It was desireable, that the sense of the people should operate in the choice of the person to whom so important a trust was to be confided. This end will be answered by committing the right of making it, not to any pre-established body, but to men, chosen by the people for the special purpose, and at the particular conjuncture.[144]

The Framers understood that a thoughtful structure for the appointment of the President was necessary to avoid certain evils: "Nothing was more to be desired, than that every practicable obstacle should be opposed to cabal, intrigue and corruption." [145] They were careful to ensure that "those who from situation might be suspected of too great devotion to the president in office" "were not among those that chose the president." [146] For that reason, "[n]o senator, representative, or other person holding a place of trust or profit under the United States, can be of the number of the electors." [147]

Article II of our Constitution, as modified by the Twelfth Amendment, governs election of the President. Article II created the electoral college, providing that the States would select electors in the manner provided by State legislatures, and those electors would in turn vote for the President. Today, every State selects Presidential electors by popular vote, and each State's laws provide for procedures to resolve election disputes, including through lawsuits if necessary. After any election issues are resolved in State or Federal court, each State's government transmits a certificate of the ascertainment of the appointed electors to Congress and the National Archives.

The electoral college meets in mid-December to cast their votes, and all of these electoral votes are then ultimately counted by Congress on January 6th. The Vice President, as President of the Senate, presides over the joint session of Congress to count votes. The Twelfth Amendment provides this straight forward instruction: "The president of the Senate shall, in the presence of the Senate and House of Representatives, open all the certificates and the votes shall then be counted; The person having the greatest number of votes for President shall be the President..." The Vice President has only a ministerial role, opening the envelopes and ensuring that the votes are counted. Likewise, the Electoral Count Act of 1887 provides no substantive role for the Vice President in counting votes, reinforcing that he or she can only act in a ministerial fashion—the Vice President may not choose, for example, to decline to count particular votes. In most cases (*e.g.*, when one candidate has a majority of votes submitted by the States) Congress has only a ministerial role, as well. It simply counts electoral college votes provided by each State's governor. Congress is not a court and cannot overrule State and Federal court rulings in election challenges.

As January 6th approached, John Eastman and others devised a plan whereby Vice President Pence would, as the presiding officer, declare that certain electoral votes from certain States *could not* be counted at the joint session.[148] John Eastman knew before proposing this plan that it was not legal. Indeed, in a pre-election document discussing Congress's counting of electoral votes, Dr. Eastman specifically disagreed with a colleague's proposed argument that the Vice President had the power to choose which envelopes to "open" and which votes to "count." Dr. Eastman wrote:

> I don't agree with this. The 12th Amendment only says that the President of the Senate opens the ballots in the joint session then, in the passive voice, that the votes shall then be counted. 3 USC § 12 [of the Electoral Count Act] says merely that he is the presiding officer, and then it spells out specific procedures, presumptions, and default rules for which slates will be counted. Nowhere does it suggest that the president of the Senate gets to make the determination on his own. § 15 [of the Electoral Count Act] doesn't either.[149]

Despite recognizing prior to the 2020 election that the Vice President had no power to refuse to count certain electoral votes, Eastman nevertheless drafted memoranda two months later proposing that Pence could do exactly that on January 6th—refuse to count certified electoral votes from Arizona, Georgia, Michigan, Nevada, New Mexico, Pennsylvania and Wisconsin.[150]

Eastman's theory was related to other efforts overseen by President Trump (described in detail below, *see infra*) to create and transmit fake electoral slates to Congress and the National Archives, and to pressure States to change the election outcome and issue new electoral slates. Eastman supported these ideas despite writing two months earlier that:

> Article II [of the Constitution] says the electors are appointed "in such manner as the Legislature thereof may direct," but I don't think that entitles the Legislature to change the rules after the election and appoint a different slate of electors in a manner different than what was in place on election day. And 3 U.S.C. §15 [of the Electoral Count Act] gives dispositive weight to the slate of electors that was certified by the Governor in accord with 3 U.S.C. §5.[151]

Even after Eastman proposed the theories in his December and January memoranda, he acknowledged in conversations with Vice President Pence's counsel Greg Jacob that Pence could not lawfully do what his own memoranda proposed.[152] Eastman admitted that the U.S. Supreme Court would unanimously reject his legal theory. "He [Eastman] had acknowledged that he would lose 9-0 at the Supreme Court."[153] Moreover, Eastman acknowledged to Jacob that he didn't think Vice President Al Gore had that power in 2001, nor did he think Vice President Kamala Harris should have that power in 2025.[154]

In testimony before the Select Committee, Jacob described in detail why the Trump plan for Pence was illegal:

> [T]he Vice President's first instinct, when he heard this theory, was that there was no way that our Framers, who abhorred concentrated power, who had broken away from the tyranny of George III, would ever have put one person—particularly not a person who had a direct interest in the outcome because they were on the ticket for the election—in a role to have decisive impact on the outcome of the election. And our review of text, history, and, frankly, just common sense, all confirmed the Vice President's first instinct on that point. There is no justifiable basis to conclude that the Vice President has that kind of authority.[155]

This is how the Vice President later described his views in a public speech:

> I had no right to overturn the election. The Presidency belongs to the American people, and the American people alone. And frankly,

there is no idea more un-American than the notion that any one person could choose the American President. Under the Constitution, I had no right to change the outcome of our election.[156]

But as January 6th approached, President Trump nevertheless embraced the new Eastman theories, and attempted to implement them. In a series of meetings and calls, President Trump attempted to pressure Pence to intervene on January 6th to prevent Congress from counting multiple States' electoral votes for Joe Biden. At several points in the days before January 6th, President Trump was told directly that Vice President Pence could not legally do what Trump was asking. For example, at a January 4th meeting in the Oval Office, Eastman acknowledged that any variation of his proposal— whether rejecting electoral votes outright or delaying certification to send them back to the States—would violate several provisions of the Electoral Count Act. According to Greg Jacob:

> In the conversation in the Oval Office on the 4th, I had raised the fact that . . . [Eastman's] preferred course had issues with the Electoral Count Act, which he had acknowledged was the case, that there would be an inconsistency with the Electoral Count Act[ ][157]

Jacob recorded Eastman's admission in an internal memo he drafted for Vice President Pence on the evening of January 4th: "Professor Eastman acknowledges that his proposal violates several provisions of statutory law."[158] And, during a phone call with President Trump and Eastman on the evening of January 5, 2021, Eastman *again* acknowledged that his proposal also would violate several provisions of the Electoral Count Act.

> [W]e did have an in-depth discussion about [the Electoral Count Act] in the subsequent phone calls as I walked him through provision after provision on the recess and on the fact that . . . Congressmen and Senators are supposed to get to object and debate. And he acknowledged, one after another, that those provisions would—in order for us to send it back to the States, we couldn't do those things as well. We can't do a 10-day, send it back to the States, and honor an Electoral Count Act provision that says you can't recess for more than one day and, once you get to the 5th, you have to stay continuously in session.[159]

As Pence's Chief of Staff, Marc Short, testified that the Vice President also repeatedly informed President Trump that the Vice President's role on January 6th was only ministerial.

Committee Staff: But just to pick up on that, Mr. Short, was it your impression that the Vice President had directly conveyed his position on these issues to the President, not just to the world through a Dear Colleague Letter, but directly to President Trump?

Marc Short: Many times.

Committee Staff: And had been consistent in conveying his position to the President?

Short: Very consistent. [160]

As the situation grew increasingly acrimonious, Vice President Pence's private counsel Richard Cullen contacted former Fourth Circuit Judge Michael Luttig, a renowned conservative judge for whom Eastman had previously clerked, and asked Luttig to make a public statement. On January 5th, Luttig wrote the following on Twitter: "The only responsibility and power of the Vice President under the Constitution is to faithfully count the electoral college votes as they have been cast." [161] As Judge Luttig testified in the Committee's hearings, "there was no basis in the Constitution or laws of the United States at all for the theory espoused by Eastman—at all. None." [162] Judge Luttig completely rejected Eastman's "blueprint to overturn the 2020 election" as "constitutional mischief" and 'the most reckless, insidious, and calamitous failure[ ] in both legal and political judgment in American history." [163]

Contemporaneous written correspondence also confirms both that: (1) Eastman himself recognized Pence could not lawfully refuse to count electoral votes, and (2) President Trump also knew this. While sheltering in a loading dock with the Vice President during the violent January 6th attack, Greg Jacob asked Eastman in an email, "Did you advise the President that in your professional judgment the Vice President DOES NOT have the power to decide things unilaterally?" Eastman's response stated that the President had "been so advised," but then indicated that President Trump continued to pressure the Vice President to act illegally: "But you know him—once he gets something in his head, it is hard to get him to change course." [164]

To be absolutely clear, no White House lawyer believed Pence could lawfully refuse to count electoral votes. White House Counsel Pat Cipollone told the Select Committee this:

I thought that the Vice President did not have the authority to do what was being suggested under a proper reading of the law. I conveyed that, ok? I think I actually told somebody, you know, in the Vice President's—"Just blame me." You know this is—I'm not a politician, you know . . . but, you know, I just said, "I'm a lawyer. This is my legal opinion." [165]

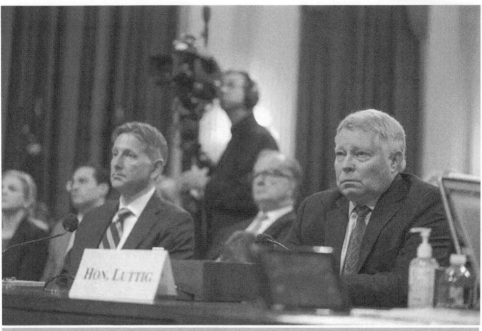

Greg Jacob and Judge Michael Luttig testify at January 6th Select Committee hearing.
(Photo by House Creative Services)

Cipollone also testified that he was "sure [he] conveyed" his views.[166] Indeed, other testimony from Cipollone indicates that Trump knew of Cipollone's view and suggests that Trump purposely excluded Cipollone from the meeting with Pence and Pence's General Counsel on January 4th.[167] Indeed, at one point, Cipollone confronted Eastman in the hallway outside the Oval Office and expressed his disapproval of and anger with Eastman's position. According to Jason Miller, "Pat Cipollone thought the idea was nutty and had at one point confronted Eastman basically with the same sentiment" outside the Oval Office.[168] Pat Cipollone did not deny having an angry confrontation with Eastman outside of the Oval Office—though he said he didn't have a specific recollection, he had no reason to contradict what Jason Miller said and, moreover, said that Eastman was aware of his views.[169]

Likewise, Eric Herschmann, another White House lawyer, expressed the same understanding that Eastman's plan "obviously made no sense" and "had no practical ability to work." [170] Herschmann also recounted telling Eastman directly that his plan was "completely crazy":

> And I said to [Eastman], hold on a second, I want to understand what you're saying. You're saying you believe the Vice President, acting as President of the Senate, can be the sole decisionmaker as to, under your theory, who becomes the next President of the

United States? And he said, yes. And I said, are you out of your F'ing mind, right. And that was pretty blunt. I said, you're completely crazy.[171]

Deputy White House Counsel Pat Philbin also had the same understanding.[172] Indeed, as Herschmann testified, even Rudolph Giuliani doubted that Vice President Mike Pence had any legal ability to do what Eastman had proposed.[173]

Despite all this opposition from all White House lawyers, Trump nevertheless continued to exert immense pressure on Pence to refuse to count electoral votes.

The pressure began before the January 4th Oval Office meeting with Pence, Eastman, Jacob, Short and Trump, but became even more intense thereafter. On the evening of January 5, 2021, the New York Times published an article reporting that "Vice President Mike Pence told President Trump on Tuesday that he did not believe he had the power to block congressional certification of Joseph R. Biden, Jr.'s victory in the Presidential election despite President Trump's baseless insistence that he did."[174] This reporting was correct—both as to the Vice President's power and as to Vice President Pence having informed President Trump that he did not have the authority to change the outcome of the election. But in response to that story, late in the evening before the January 6th joint session, President Trump dictated to Jason Miller a statement falsely asserting, "The Vice President and I are in *total agreement* that the Vice President has the power to act."[175] This statement was released at President Trump's direction and was false.[176]

Thereafter, Trump continued to apply public pressure in a series of tweets. At 1:00 a.m. on January 6th, "[i]f Vice President @Mike_Pence comes through for us, we will win the Presidency. Many States want to decertify the mistake they made in certifying incorrect & even fraudulent numbers in a process NOT approved by their State Legislatures (which it must be). Mike can send it back!"[177] At 8:17 a.m. on January 6th, he tweeted again: "States want to correct their votes, which they now know were based on irregularities and fraud, plus corrupt process never received legislative approval. All Mike Pence has to do is send them back to the States, AND WE WIN. Do it Mike, this is a time for extreme courage!"[178]

President Trump tried to reach the Vice President early in the morning of January 6th, but the Vice President did not take the call. The President finally reached the Vice President later that morning, shouting from the Oval Office to his assistants to "get the Vice President on the phone."[179] After again telling the Vice President that he had "the legal authority to send [electoral votes] back to the respective states," President Trump grew very heated.[180] Witnesses in the Oval Office during this call told the Select

President Trump speaks with Vice President Pence over the phone in the Oval Office on the morning of January 6th.
(Photo provided to the Select Committee by the National Archives and Records Administration)

Committee that the President called Vice President Pence a "wimp," [181] told him it would be "a political career killer" to certify the lawful electoral votes electing President Biden,[182] and accused him of "not [being] tough enough to make the call." [183] As Ivanka Trump would recount to her chief of staff moments later, her father called the Vice President "the p-word" for refusing to overturn the election.[184]

In response, Vice President Pence again refused to take any action other than counting the lawfully certified electoral votes of the States. But President Trump was angry and undeterred. After the conclusion of this call, he edited his speech for the Ellipse to insert language to which his lawyers objected—targeting Vice President Pence directly.[185]

Earlier that morning, Eric Herschmann had tried to remove the reference to Vice President Pence from the speech. As he told speechwriter Stephen Miller, he "didn't concur with the legal analysis" that John Eastman had advanced and believed it "wouldn't advance the ball" to discuss it publicly.[186] But after the call with Vice President Pence, speechwriters were instructed to reinsert the line. Although the final written draft of his speech referred to Pence just once—a line President Trump didn't end up reading[187]—the President went off-script five different times to pressure the Vice President:

"I hope Mike is going to do the right thing. I hope so. Because if Mike Pence does the right thing, we win the election," Trump first told the crowd.[188]

"Mike Pence is going to have to come through for us," Trump later said, "and if he doesn't, that will be a, a sad day for our country because you're sworn to uphold our Constitution."[189]

Addressing Pence directly, Trump told the assembled crowd: "Mike Pence, I hope you're going to stand up for the good of our Constitution and for the good of our country." Trump said at another point, "And if you're not, I'm going to be very disappointed in you. I will tell you right now. I'm not hearing good stories."[190]

"So I hope Mike has the courage to do what he has to do. And I hope he doesn't listen to the RINOs and the stupid people that he's listening to," Trump said.[191]

These statements to the assembled crowd at the Ellipse had Trump's intended effect—they produced substantial anger against Pence. When Pence released a statement confirming that he would not act to prevent Congress from counting electoral votes, the crowd's reaction was harshly negative.

> "I'm telling you what, I'm hearing that Pence—hearing the Pence just caved. No. Is that true? I didn't hear it. I'm hear — I'm hearing reports that Pence caved. No way. I'm telling you, if Pence caved, we're going to drag motherfuckers through the streets. You fucking politicians are going to get fucking drug through the streets."[192]

> Pence voted against Trump. [Interviewer: "Ok. And that's when all this started?"] Yup. That's when we marched on the Capitol.[193]

> "We just heard that Mike Pence is not going to reject any fraudulent electoral votes. [Other speaker: "Boo. You're a traitor!"] That's right. You've heard it here first. Mike Pence has betrayed the United States of America. [Other speaker: "Fuck you, Mike Pence!"] Mike Pence has betrayed this President and he has betrayed the people of the United States and we will never, ever forget." [Cheers][194]

> "This woman cames [sic] up to the side of us and she says Pence folded. So it was kind of, like, Ok, well — in my mind I was think-ing, well that's it. You know. Well, my son-in-law looks at me and he says I want to go in."[195]

> "[Q] "What percentage of the crowd is going to the Capitol?" [A] [Oath Keeper Jessica Watkins]: "One hundred percent. It has, it has spread like wildfire that Pence has betrayed us, and everybody's marching on the Capitol. All million of us. it's insane."[196]

"Bring him out. Bring out Pence. Bring him out. Bring out Pence. Bring him out. Bring out Pence. Bring him out. Bring out Pence."[197]

"Hang Mike Pence. Hang Mike Pence. Hang Mike Pence. Hang Mike Pence. Hang Mike Pence."[198]

Once Trump returned to the White House, he was informed almost immediately that violence and lawlessness had broken out at the Capitol among his supporters.[199] At 2:24 p.m., President Trump applied yet further pressure to Pence (*see infra*), posting a tweet accusing Vice President Mike Pence of cowardice for not using his role as President of the Senate to change the outcome of the election: "Mike Pence didn't have the courage to do what should have been done to protect our Country and our Constitution, giving States a chance to certify a corrected set of facts, not the fraudulent or inaccurate ones which they were asked to previously certify. USA demands the truth!"[200] Almost immediately thereafter, the crowd around the Capitol surged, and more individuals joined the effort to confront police and break further into the building.

The sentiment expressed in President Trump's 2:24 p.m. tweet, already present in the crowd, only grew more powerful as the President's words spread. Timothy Hale-Cusanelli—a white supremacist who expressed Nazi sympathies—heard about the tweet while in the Crypt around 2:25 p.m., and he, according to the Department of Justice, "knew what that meant." Vice President Pence had decided not to keep President Trump in power.[201] Other rioters described what happened next as follows:

Once we found out Pence turned on us and that they had stolen the election, like officially, the crowd went crazy. I mean, it became a mob. We crossed the gate.[202]

Then we heard the news on [P]ence . . . And lost it . . . So we stormed.[203]

They're making an announcement right now saying if Pence betrays us you better get your mind right because we're storming that building.[204]

Minutes after the tweet—at 2:35 p.m.—rioters continued their surge and broke a security line of the DC Metropolitan Police Department, resulting in the first fighting withdrawal in the history of that force.[205]

President Trump issued this tweet after he had falsely claimed to the angry crowd that Vice President Mike Pence could "do the right thing" and ensure a second Trump term, after that angry crowd had turned into a violent mob assaulting the Capitol while chanting, "Hang Mike Pence!"[206] and after the U.S. Secret Service had evacuated the Vice President from the Senate floor.[207] One minute after the President's tweet, at 2:25 p.m., the Secret Service determined they could no longer protect the Vice President in his ceremonial office near the Senate Chamber, and evacuated the Vice President and his family to a secure location, missing the violent mob by a mere 40 feet.[208]

Further evidence presented at our hearing shows the violent reaction following President Trump's 2:24 p.m. tweet and the efforts to protect Vice President Pence in the time that followed.[209]

The day after the attack on the Capitol, Eastman called Eric Herschmann to talk about continuing litigation on behalf of the Trump Presidential Campaign in Georgia. Herschmann described his reaction to Eastman this way:

> And I said to him, are you out of your F'ing mind? Right? I said, because I only want to hear two words coming out of your mouth from now on: Orderly transition. I said, I don't want to hear any other F'ing words coming out of your mouth, no matter what, other than orderly transition. Repeat those words to me." [210]

Herschmann concluded the call by telling Eastman: "Now I'm going to give you the best free legal advice you're ever getting in your life. Get a great F'ing criminal defense lawyer, you're going to need it," and hanging up the phone.[211]

In the course of investigating this series of facts, the Select Committee subpoenaed Eastman's emails from his employer, Chapman University.[212] Eastman sued to prevent Chapman from producing the emails, arguing that the emails were attorney-client privileged. Federal District Court Judge David Carter reviewed Eastman's emails *in camera* to determine, among other things, whether the emails had to be produced because they likely furthered a crime committed by one of Eastman's clients or by Eastman himself. In addition to reviewing the emails themselves, Judge Carter reviewed substantial additional evidence presented by the Select Committee and by Eastman.

After reciting a series of factual findings regarding President Trump's multi-part plan to overturn the election, Judge Carter concluded that President Trump likely violated two criminal statutes: 18 U.S.C. § 1512(c) (corruptly obstructing, impeding or influencing Congress's official proceeding to count electoral votes); and 18 U.S.C. § 371 (conspiring to defraud the United States). The Court also concluded that John Eastman likely violated at least one of these criminal laws. As to §1512(c), Judge Carter explained:

> Taken together, this evidence demonstrates that President Trump likely knew the electoral count plan had no factual justification.
>
> The plan not only lacked factual basis but also legal justification. . . .

The illegality of the plan was obvious. Our nation was founded on the peaceful transition of power, epitomized by George Washington laying down his sword to make way for democratic elections. Ignoring this history, President Trump vigorously campaigned for the Vice President to single-handedly determine the results of the 2020 election. . . . Every American—and certainly the President of the United States—knows that in a democracy, leaders are elected, not installed. With a plan this "BOLD," President Trump knowingly tried to subvert this fundamental principle. Based on the evidence, the Court finds it more likely than not that President Trump corruptly attempted to obstruct the Joint Session of Congress on January 6, 2021.[213]

As to 18 U.S.C. § 371, Judge Carter identified evidence demonstrating that both President Trump and John Eastman knew their electoral count plan was illegal, and knew it could not "survive judicial scrutiny" in any of its iterations:

Dr. Eastman himself repeatedly recognized that his plan had no legal support. . . . Dr. Eastman likely acted deceitfully and dishonestly each time he pushed an outcome-driven plan that he knew was unsupported by the law.[214]

Finally, Judge Carter concluded:

Dr. Eastman and President Trump launched a campaign to overturn a democratic election, an action unprecedented in American history. Their campaign was not confined to the ivory tower—it was a coup in search of a legal theory. The plan spurred violent attacks on the seat of our nation's government, led to the deaths of several law enforcement officers, and deepened public distrust in our political process.[215]

Judge Luttig reached similar conclusions during his live hearing testimony: "I have written, as you said, Chairman Thompson, that, today, almost two years after that fateful day in January 2021, that, still, Donald Trump and his allies and supporters are a clear and present danger to American democracy." [216]

During the hearing, Judge Luttig took issue with certain of Greg Jacob's characterizations of the 12th Amendment's text, explaining that the applicable text was not ambiguous in any way. The Committee agrees with Judge Luttig: the application of the Twelfth Amendment's text is plain in this context; it does not authorize Congress to second-guess State and Federal courts and refuse to count State electoral votes based on concerns about fraud. *See infra.* Although Jacob did not discuss his position in great detail during the hearing, his private testimony gives more insight on his actual views:

> In my view, a lot has been said about the fact that the role of the Vice President in the electoral count on January 6th is purely ministerial, and that is a correct conclusion. But if you look at the constitutional text, the role of Congress is purely ministerial as well. You open the certificates and you count them. Those are the only things provided for in the Constitution.[217]

## EFFORTS TO PRESSURE STATES TO CHANGE THE ELECTION OUTCOME, AND TO CREATE AND TRANSMIT FAKE ELECTION CERTIFICATES

Anticipating that the Eastman strategy for January 6th would be implemented, President Trump worked with a handful of others to prepare a series of false Trump electoral slates for seven States Biden actually won. President Trump personally conducted a teleconference with Eastman and Republican National Committee Chair Ronna McDaniel "a few days before December 14" and solicited the RNC's assistance with the scheme.[218] McDaniel agreed to provide that assistance.[219]

A series of contemporaneous documents demonstrate what President Trump and his allies, including attorney Kenneth Chesebro, were attempting to accomplish: they anticipated that the President of the Senate (which, under the Constitution, is the Vice President) could rely upon these false slates of electors on January 6th to justify refusing to count genuine electoral votes.[220]

The false slates were created by fake Republican electors on December 14th, at the same time the actual, certified electors in those States were meeting to cast their States' Electoral College votes for President Biden. By that point in time, election-related litigation was over in all or nearly all of the subject States, and Trump Campaign election lawyers realized that the fake slates could not be lawful or justifiable on any grounds. Justin Clark, the Trump Campaign Deputy Campaign Manager and Senior Counsel told the Select Committee that he "had real problems with the process." [221] Clark warned his colleagues, "unless we have litigation pending like in these States, like, I don't think this is appropriate or, you know, this isn't the right thing to do. I don't remember how I phrased it, but I got into a little bit of a back and forth and I think it was with Ken Chesebro, where I said, 'Alright, you know, you just get after it, like, I'm out.' " [222]

Matthew Morgan, the Trump Campaign General Counsel, told the Select Committee that without an official State certificate of ascertainment,[223] "the [fake] electors were, for lack of a better way of saying it, no good or not—not valid." [224]

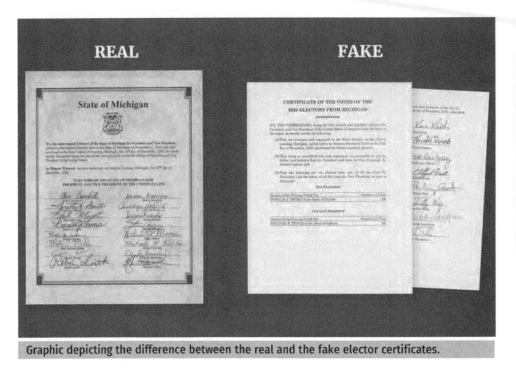

| REAL | FAKE |
|---|---|

Graphic depicting the difference between the real and the fake elector certificates.

The Office of White House Counsel also appears to have expressed concerns with this fake elector plan. In his interview by the Select Committee, White House Counsel Pat Cipollone acknowledged his view that by mid-December, the process was "done" and that his deputy, Pat Philbin, may have advised against the fake elector strategy.[225] In an informal Committee interview, Philbin described the fake elector scheme as one of the "bad theories" that were like "Whac-A-Mole" in the White House during this period.[226] Cipollone agreed with this characterization.[227]

In her testimony, Cassidy Hutchinson testified that she heard at least one member of the White House Counsel's Office say that the plan was not legal:

> Committee Staff: [T]o be clear, did you hear the White House Counsel's Office say that this plan to have alternate electors meet and cast votes for Donald Trump in States that he had lost was not legally sound?
>
> Hutchinson: Yes, sir.[228]

Multiple Republicans who were persuaded to sign the fake certificates also testified that they felt misled or betrayed, and would not have done so had they known that the fake votes would be used on January 6th without an intervening court ruling. One elector told the Select Committee that he thought his vote would be strictly contingent: "[I]t was a very consistent message that we were told throughout all of that, is this is the only reason why we're doing this, is to preserve the integrity of being able to have a challenge."[229]

The "Chairperson" of the Wisconsin fake electors, who was also at the time Chairman of the Wisconsin Republican Party, insisted in testimony to the Select Committee that he "was told that these would only count if a court ruled in our favor" and that he wouldn't have supported anyone using the Trump electors' votes without a court ruling.[230]

Despite the fact that all major election lawsuits thus far had failed, President Trump and his co-conspirators in this effort, including John Eastman and Kenneth Chesebro, pressed forward with the fake elector scheme. Ultimately, these false electoral slates, five of which purported to represent the "duly elected" electoral college votes of their States, were transmitted to Executive Branch officials at the National Archives, and to the Legislative Branch, including to the Office of the President of the Senate, Vice President Mike Pence.[231]

The fake electors followed Chesebro's step-by-step instructions for completing and mailing the fake certificates to multiple officials in the U.S. Government,[232] complete with registered mail stickers and return address labels identifying senders like the "Arizona Republican Party" and the "Georgia Republican Party."[233] The Wisconsin Republican Party's fake certificates apparently weren't properly delivered, however, so the Trump Campaign arranged to fly them to Washington just before the joint session on January 6th, and try to deliver them to the Vice President via Senator Ron Johnson and Representative Mike Kelly's offices.[234] Both Johnson and Kelly's offices attempted to do so, but Vice President Pence's aide refused the delivery.[235]

Despite pressure from President Trump, Vice President Pence and the Senate parliamentarian refused to recognize or count the unofficial fake electoral votes. Greg Jacob testified that he advised Vice President Pence on January 2nd that "none of the slates that had been sent in would qualify as an alternate slate" under the law and that the Senate Parliamentarian "was in agreement" with this conclusion.[236]

\* \* \*

In addition to this plan to create and transmit fake electoral slates, Donald Trump was also personally and substantially involved in multiple efforts to pressure State election officials and State legislatures to alter official lawful election results. As U.S. District Judge Carter stated in his June 7, 2022, opinion:

Dr. Eastman's actions in these few weeks [in December 2020] indicate that his and President Trump's pressure campaign to stop the electoral count did not end with Vice President Pence—it targeted every tier of federal and state elected officials. Convincing state legislatures to certify competing electors was essential to stop the count and ensure President Trump's reelection.[237]

Judge Carter also explained that "Dr. Eastman and President Trump's plan to disrupt the Joint Session was fully formed and actionable as early as December 7, 2020." [238]

Chapter 2 of this report provides substantial detail on many of President Trump's specific efforts to apply pressure to State officials and legislators. We provide a few examples here:

During a January 2, 2021, call, President Trump pressured Georgia's Republican Secretary of State Brad Raffensperger to "find 11,780 votes." During that call, President Trump asserted conspiracy theories about the election that Department of Justice officials had already debunked. President Trump also made a thinly veiled threat to Raffensperger and his attorney about his failure to respond to President Trump's demands: "That's a criminal, that's a criminal offense . . . That's a big risk to you and to Ryan, your lawyer . . . I'm notifying you that you're letting it happen." [239]

Judge Carter drew these conclusions:

Mr. Raffensperger debunked the President's allegations "point by point" and explained that "the data you have is wrong;" however, President Trump still told him, "I just want to find 11,780 votes." [240]

\* \* \*

President Trump's repeated pleas for Georgia Secretary of State Raffensperger clearly demonstrate that his justification was not to investigate fraud, but to win the election. . . . Taken together, this evidence demonstrates that President Trump likely knew the electoral count plan had no factual justification. The plan not only lacked factual basis but also legal justification.[241]

That call to Raffensperger came on the heels of President Trump's repeated attacks on Raffensperger, election workers, and other public servants about President Trump's loss in the election. A month earlier, the Georgia Secretary of State's Chief Operating Officer, Gabriel Sterling, had given this explicit public warning to President Trump and his team, a warning that the Select Committee has determined President Trump apparently saw and disregarded:[242]

[I]t has all gone too far. All of it. . . .

A 20-something tech in Gwinnett County today has death threats and a noose put out, saying he should be hung for treason because he was transferring a report on batches from an EMS to a county computer so he could read it.

It has to stop.

Mr. President, you have not condemned these actions or this language. Senators, you have not condemned this language or these actions. This has to stop. We need you to step up. And if you're going to take a position of leadership, show some.

My boss, Secretary Raffensperger—his address is out there. They have people doing caravans in front of their house, they've had people come onto their property. Tricia, his wife of 40 years, is getting sexualized threats through her cellphone.

It has to stop.

This is elections, this is the backbone of democracy, and all of you who have not said a damn word are complicit in this. It's too much....

What you don't have the ability to do—and you need to step up and say this—is stop inspiring people to commit potential acts of violence. Someone's going to get hurt. Someone's going to get shot. Someone's going to get killed.[243]

The stark warning was entirely appropriate, and prescient. In addition to the examples Sterling identified, President Trump and his team were also fixated on Georgia election workers Ruby Freeman and Wandrea "Shaye" Moss. He and Giuliani mentioned Freeman repeatedly in meetings with State legislators, at public rallies, and in the January 2nd call with Raffensperger. Referring to a video clip, Giuliani even accused Freeman and Moss of trading USB drives to affect votes "as if they [were] vials of heroin or cocaine."[244] This was completely bogus: it was not a USB drive; it was a ginger mint.[245]

After their contact information was published, Trump supporters sent hundreds of threats to the women and even showed up at Freeman's home.[246] As Freeman testified to the Select Committee, Trump and his followers' conduct had a profound impact on her life. She left her home based on advice from the FBI, and wouldn't move back for months.[247] And she explained, "I've lost my sense of security—all because a group of people, starting with Number 45 [Donald Trump] and his ally Rudy Giuliani, decided to scapegoat me and my daughter Shaye to push their own lies

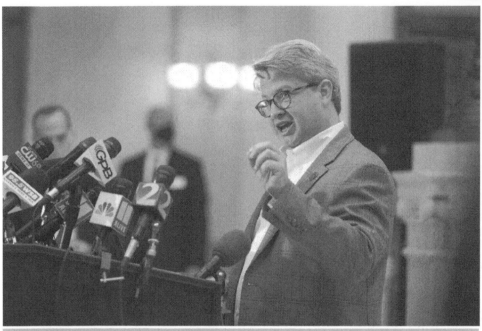

Gabriel Sterling at a press conference on November 6, 2020 in Atlanta, Georgia.
(Photo by Jessica McGowan/Getty Images)

about how the Presidential election was stolen." [248] The treatment of Freeman and Moss was callous, inhumane, and inexcusable. Rudolph Giuliani and others with responsibility should be held accountable.

In Arizona, a primary target of President Trump's pressure, and ire, was House Speaker Russell "Rusty" Bowers, a longtime Republican who had served 17 years in the State legislature. Throughout November and December, Bowers spoke to President Trump, Giuliani, and members of Giuliani's legal team, in person or on the phone. During these calls, President Trump and others alleged that the results in Arizona were affected by fraud and asked that Bowers consider replacing Presidential electors for Biden with electors for President Trump. [249] Bowers demanded proof for the claims of fraud, but never got it. At one point, after Bowers pressed Giuliani on the claims of fraud, Giuliani responded, "we've got lots of theories, we just don't have the evidence." [250] Bowers explained to Giuliani: "You are asking me do something against my oath, and I will not break my oath." [251]

President Trump and his supporters' intimidation tactics affected Bowers, too. Bowers's personal cell phone and home address were doxed, [252] leading demonstrators to show up at his home and shout insults until police arrived. One protestor who showed up at his home was armed and believed to be a member of an extremist militia. [253] Another hired a truck with a defamatory and profane allegation that Bowers, a deeply religious man, was a pedophile, and drove it through Bowers's neighborhood.[254] This, again, is the conduct of thugs and criminals, each of whom should be held accountable.

In Michigan, President Trump focused on Republican Senate Majority Leader Mike Shirkey and Republican House Speaker Lee Chatfield. He invited them to the White House for a November 20, 2020, meeting during which President Trump and Giuliani, who joined by phone, went through a "litany" of false allegations about supposed fraud in Michigan's election.[255] Chatfield recalled President Trump's more generic directive for the group to "have some backbone and do the right thing," which he understood to mean overturning the election by naming Michigan's Electoral College electors for President Trump.[256] Shirkey told President Trump that he wouldn't do anything that would violate Michigan law,[257] and after the meeting ended, issued a joint statement with Chatfield: "We have not yet been made aware of any information that would change the outcome of the election in Michigan and as legislative leaders, we will follow the law and follow the normal process regarding Michigan's electors, just as we have said throughout this election."[258]

When President Trump couldn't convince Shirkey and Chatfield to change the outcome of the election in Michigan during that meeting or in calls after, he or his team maliciously tweeted out Shirkey's personal cell phone number and a number for Chatfield that turned out to be wrong.[259] Shirkey received nearly 4,000 text messages after that, and another private citizen reported being inundated with calls and texts intended for Chatfield.[260]

None of Donald Trump's efforts ultimately succeeded in changing the official results in any State. That these efforts had failed was apparent to Donald Trump and his co-conspirators well before January 6th. By January 6th, there was no evidence at all that a majority of any State legislature would even attempt to change its electoral votes.[261]

This past October, U.S. District Court Judge David Carter issued a further ruling relating to one of President Trump's lawsuits in Georgia. Judge Carter applied the crime-fraud exception to attorney-client privilege again, and identified potential criminal activity related to a knowingly false representation by Donald Trump to a Federal court. He wrote:

> The emails show that President Trump knew that the specific numbers of voter fraud were wrong but continued to tout those numbers, both in court and in public.[262]

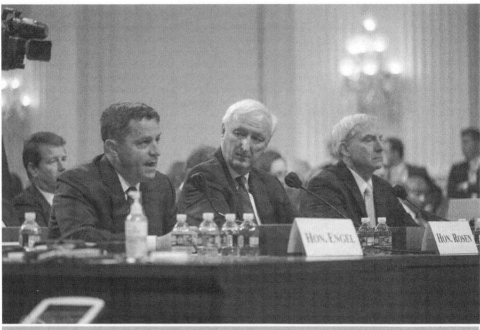

Steven Engel, Jeffrey Rosen and Richard Donoghue at a Select Committee hearing on June 23, 2022.

(Photo by House Creative Services)

As John Eastman wrote in an email on December 31, 2020, President Trump was "made aware that some of the allegations (and evidence proffered by the experts)" in a verified State court complaint was "inaccurate."[263] Dr. Eastman noted that "with that knowledge" President Trump could not accurately verify a Federal court complaint that incorporated by reference the "inaccurate" State court complaint: "I have no doubt that an aggressive DA or US Atty someplace will go after both the President and his lawyers once all the dust settles on this."[264] Despite this specific warning, "President Trump and his attorneys ultimately filed the complaint with the same inaccurate numbers without rectifying, clarifying, or otherwise changing them."[265] And President Trump personally "signed a verification swearing under oath that the incorporated, inaccurate numbers 'are true and correct' or 'believed to be true and correct' to the best of his knowledge and belief."[266] The numbers were not correct, and President Trump and his legal team knew it.

### EFFORTS TO CORRUPT THE DEPARTMENT OF JUSTICE

In the weeks after the 2020 election, Attorney General Barr advised President Trump that the Department of Justice had not seen any evidence to support Trump's theory that the election was stolen by fraud. Acting Attorney General Jeffrey Rosen and his Deputy repeatedly reinforced to President Trump that his claims of election fraud were false when they took over in mid-December. Also in mid-December 2020, Attorney General Barr announced his plans to resign. Between that time and January 6th, Trump spoke with Acting Attorney General Jeff Rosen and Acting Deputy Richard Donoghue repeatedly, attempting to persuade them and the Department of Justice to find factual support for his stolen election claims and thereby to assist his efforts to reverse election results.

As Rosen publicly testified, ". . . between December 23rd and January 3rd, the President either called me or met with me virtually every day, with one or two exceptions, like Christmas Day." [267] As discussed earlier, Justice Department investigations had demonstrated that the stolen election claims were false; both Rosen and Donoghue told President Trump this comprehensively and repeatedly.

One of those conversations occurred on December 27th, when President Trump called Rosen to go through a "stream of allegations" about the election.[268] Donoghue described that call as an "escalation of the earlier conversations" they had.[269] Initially, President Trump called Rosen directly. When Donoghue joined the call, he sought to "make it clear to the President [that] these allegations were simply not true." [270]

> So [the President] went through [the allegations]—in what for me was a 90-minute conversation or so, and what for the former Acting AG was a 2-hour conversation—as the President went through them I went piece by piece to say "no, that's false, that is not true," and to correct him really in a serial fashion as he moved from one theory to another.[271]

The President raised, among others, debunked claims about voting machines in Michigan, a truck driver who allegedly moved ballots from New York to Pennsylvania, and a purported election fraud at the State Farm Arena in Georgia.[272] None of the allegations were credible, and Rosen and Donoghue said so to the President.[273]

At one point during the December 27th call in which Donoghue refuted President Trump's fraud allegations, Donoghue recorded in handwritten notes a request President Trump made specifically to him and Acting Attorney General Rosen: "Just say the election was corrupt and leave the rest to me and the Republican Congressmen." [274] Donoghue explained: "[T]he Department had zero involvement in anyone's political strategy," and "he wanted us to say that it was corrupt." [275] "We told him we were not going to do that." [276] At the time, neither Rosen nor Donoghue knew the full extent to which Republican Congressmen, including Representative Scott Perry, were attempting to assist President Trump to overturn the election results.

The Committee's investigation has shown that Congressman Perry was working with one Department of Justice official, Jeffrey Clark, regarding the stolen election claims. Perry was working with Clark and with President Trump and Chief of Staff Mark Meadows with this goal: to enlist Clark to reverse the Department of Justice's findings regarding the election and help overturn the election outcome.[277]

After introducing Clark to the President, Perry sent multiple text messages to Meadows between December 26th and December 28th, pressing that Clark be elevated within the Department. Perry reminded Meadows that there are only "11 days to 1/6 . . . We gotta get going!," and, as the days went on, one asking, "Did you call Jeff Clark?"[278]

Acting Attorney General Rosen first learned about Clark's contact with President Trump in a call on Christmas Eve. On that call, President Trump mentioned Clark to Rosen, who was surprised to learn that Trump knew Clark and had met with him. Rosen later confronted Clark about the contact: "Jeff, anything going on that you think I should know about?"[279] Clark didn't "immediately volunteer" the fact that he had met with the President, but ultimately "acknowledged that he had been at a meeting with the President in the Oval Office, not alone, with other people."[280] Clark was "kind of defensive" and "somewhat apologetic," "casting it as that he had had a meeting with Congressman Perry from Pennsylvania and that, to his surprise, or, you know, he hadn't anticipated it, that they somehow wound up at a meeting in the Oval Office."[281] Clark's contact with President Trump violated both Justice Department and White House policies designed to prevent political pressure on the Department.[282]

While Clark initially appeared apologetic and assured Rosen that "[i]t won't happen again,"[283] he nevertheless continued to work and meet secretly with President Trump and Congressman Perry. Less than five days after assuring Rosen that he would comply with the Department's White House contacts policy, Clark told Rosen and Donoghue that he had again violated that policy. Donoghue confronted him: "I reminded him that I was his boss and that I had directed him to do otherwise."[284]

Around the same time, Representative Perry called Acting Deputy Attorney General Donoghue, criticized the FBI, and suggested that the Department hadn't been doing its job. Perry told Donoghue that Clark "would do something about this."[285]

On December 28th, Clark worked with a Department employee named Kenneth Klukowski—a political appointee who had earlier worked with John Eastman—to produce a draft letter from the Justice Department to the

State legislature of Georgia.[286] That letter mirrored a number of the positions President Trump and Eastman were taking at the time.[287] (Although both Clark and Eastman refused to answer questions by asserting their Fifth Amendment right against self-incrimination, evidence shows that Clark and Eastman were in communication in this period leading up to January 6th.[288] The draft letter to Georgia was intended to be one of several Department letters to State legislatures in swing States that had voted for Biden.[289]

The letter read: "The Department of Justice is investigating various irregularities in the 2020 election for President of the United States."[290] Clark continued: "The Department will update you as we are able on investigatory progress, but at this time we have identified significant concerns that may have impacted the outcome of the election in multiple States, including the State of Georgia."[291] This was *affirmatively untrue.* The Department had conducted many investigations of election fraud allegations by that point, but it absolutely did not have "significant concerns" that fraud "may have impacted the outcome of the election" in any State. Jeff Clark knew this; Donoghue confirmed it again in an email responding to Clark's letter: "[W]e simply do not currently have a basis to make such a statement. Despite dramatic claims to the contrary, we have not seen the type of fraud that calls into question the reported (and certified) results of the election."[292]

The letter also explicitly recommended that Georgia's State legislature should call a special session to evaluate potential election fraud. "In light of these developments, the Department recommends that the Georgia General Assembly should convene in special session so that its legislators are in a special position to take additional testimony, receive new evidence, and deliberate on the matter consistent with its duties under the U.S. Constitution."[293]

Clark's draft letter also referenced the fake electors that President Trump and his campaign organized—arguing falsely that there were currently two competing slates of legitimate Presidential electors in Georgia:[294]

> The Department believes that in Georgia and several other States, both a slate of electors supporting Joseph R. Biden, Jr., and a separate slate of electors supporting Donald J. Trump, gathered on [December 14, 2020] at the proper location to cast their ballots, and that both sets of those ballots have been transmitted to Washington, D.C., to be opened by Vice President Pence.[295]

This, of course, was part of Donald Trump and John Eastman's plan for January 6th. This letter reflects an effort to use the Department of Justice to help overturn the election outcome in Georgia and elsewhere. Rosen and Donoghue reacted immediately to this draft letter:

"[T]here's no chance that I would sign this letter or anything remotely like this," Donoghue wrote.[296] The plan set forth by Clark was "not even within the realm of possibility,"[297] and Donoghue warned that if they sent Clark's letter, it "would be a grave step for the Department to take and it could have tremendous Constitutional, political and social ramifications for the country."[298]

As Richard Donoghue testified when describing his response to Clark's proposed letter:

> Well, I had to read both the email and the attached letter twice to make sure I really understood what he was proposing because it was so extreme to me I had a hard time getting my head around it initially.
>
> But I read it, and I did understand it for what he intended, and I had to sit down and sort of compose what I thought was an appropriate response . . . .
>
> In my response I explained a number of reasons this is not the Department's role to suggest or dictate to State legislatures how they should select their electors. But more importantly, this was not based on fact. This was actually contrary to the facts as developed by Department investigations over the last several weeks and months.
>
> So, I respond to that. And for the department to insert itself into the political process this way I think would have had grave consequences for the country. It may very well have spiraled us into a constitutional crisis.[299]

Rosen and Donoghue also met with Clark about the letter. Their conversation "was a very difficult and contentious" one, according to Donoghue.[300] "What you're proposing is nothing less than the United States Justice Department meddling in the outcome of a Presidential election," Donoghue admonished Clark, to which Clark indignantly responded, "I think a lot of people have meddled in this election."[301]

Both Rosen and Donoghue refused to sign the letter, and confronted Clark with the actual results of the Department's investigations.[302] They also permitted Clark access to a classified briefing from the Office of the Director of National Intelligence ("ODNI") showing Clark that allegations he made to Rosen and Donoghue about foreign interference with voting machines were not true. According to Rosen, the decision to give Clark the briefing at that point "was a difficult question because, if he's going to brief the President, I reluctantly think it's probably better that he's heard from Director Ratcliffe than that he not, even if—I don't think he should brief the President. But, at this point, he's telling me that this is happening whether I agree with it or not. So, so I let him have that briefing."[303]

After Clark received the ODNI briefing, "he acknowledged [to Donoghue] that there was nothing in that briefing that would have supported his earlier suspicion about foreign involvement."[304] While Clark then dropped his claims about foreign interference, he continued to press to send the letter to Georgia and other States, despite being told that the Department of Justice investigations had found no fraud sufficient to overturn the election outcome in Georgia or any other States. This was an intentional choice by Jeff Clark to contradict specific Department findings on election fraud, and purposely insert the Department into the Presidential election on President Trump's behalf and risk creating or exacerbating a constitutional crisis.

By this point, President Trump recognized that neither Rosen nor Donoghue would sign the letter or support his false election claims. President Trump and his team then communicated further with Clark and offered him the job of Acting Attorney General. On January 2nd, Clark told Rosen that he "would turn down the President's offer if [Rosen] reversed [his] position and signed the letter" that he and Klukowski had drafted.[305] The next day, Clark decided to accept and informed Rosen, who then called White House Counsel to seek a meeting directly with President Trump. As Rosen put it, "I wasn't going to accept being fired by my subordinate, so I wanted to talk to the President directly."[306]

On January 3rd, that meeting was convened. Although contemporaneous White House documents suggest that Clark had *already* been appointed as the Acting Attorney General,[307] all the participants in the meeting other than Clark and President Trump aggressively opposed Clark's appointment.

At that point, Rosen decided to "broaden the circle" and ask that his subordinates inform all the other Assistant Attorneys General (AAGs) what was afoot.[308] Rosen wanted to know how the AAGs would respond if Jeff Clark was installed as the Acting Attorney General. Pat Hovakimian, who worked for Rosen, then set up a conference call. The AAGs almost immediately agreed that they would resign if Rosen was removed from office.[309]

Rosen, Donoghue, and Steve Engel, the Assistant Attorney General for the Office of Legal Counsel, attended the meeting. White House lawyers Pat Cipollone, Eric Herschmann and Pat Philbin joined as well.

When the meeting started, Clark attempted to defend his appointment. Clark declared that this was the "last opportunity to sort of set things straight with this defective election," and he had the "intelligence," the "will," and "desire" to "pursue these matters in the way that the President thought most appropriate."[310] Everyone else present disagreed that Clark could conceivably accomplish these things.

White House Counsel Pat Cipollone threatened to resign as well, describing Clark's letter as a "murder-suicide pact."[311] Cipollone warned that the letter would "damage everyone who touches it" and no one should have anything to do with it.[312]

President Trump asked Donoghue and Engel what they would do if Clark took office. Both confirmed they would resign.[313] Steve Engel recalled that the President next asked if he would resign:

> At some point, [] I believe Rich Donoghue said that senior Department officials would all resign if Mr. Clark were put in, and the President turned to me and said, "Steve, you wouldn't resign, would you?" I said, "Well, Mr. President, I've been with you through four Attorneys General, including two Acting Attorneys General, and I just couldn't be part of this if Mr. Clark were here." And I said, "And I believe that the other senior Department officials would resign as well. And Mr. Clark would be here by himself with a hostile building, those folks who remained, and nothing would get done."[314]

Donoghue added that they would not be the only ones to resign. "You should understand that your entire Department leadership will resign," Donoghue recalled saying. This included every Assistant Attorney General. "Mr. President, these aren't bureaucratic leftovers from another administration," Donoghue reminded Trump, "You picked them. This is your leadership team." Donoghue added, "And what happens if, within 48 hours, we have hundreds of resignations from your Justice Department because of your actions? What does that say about your leadership?"[315] Steve Engel then reinforced Donoghue's point, saying that Clark would be leading a "graveyard."

Faced with mass resignations and recognizing that the "breakage" could be too severe, Donald Trump decided to rescind his offer to Clark and drop his plans to use the Justice Department to aid in his efforts to overturn the election outcome.[316] The President looked at Clark and said, "I appreciate your willingness to do it. I appreciate you being willing to suffer the abuse. But the reality is, you're not going to get anything done. These guys are going to quit. Everyone else is going to resign. It's going to be a disaster. The bureaucracy will eat you alive. And no matter how much you want to get things done in the next few weeks, you won't be able to get it done, and it's not going to be worth the breakage."[317]

* * *

Evidence gathered by the Committee also suggests that President Trump offered Sidney Powell the position of Special Counsel for election

related matters during a highly charged White House meeting on December
18, 2020.[318] White House lawyers vehemently opposed Powell's appointment, and it also was not ultimately made formal.

## SUMMONING A MOB TO WASHINGTON, AND KNOWING THEY WERE ANGRY AND ARMED, INSTRUCTING THEM TO MARCH TO THE CAPITOL

In the early morning hours of December 19th, shortly after the contentious
December 18th White House meeting with Sidney Powell and others, Donald
Trump sent a tweet urging his supporters to travel to Washington for Janu-
ary 6th. In that tweet, President Trump attached false allegations that the
election was stolen and promised a "wild" time on January 6th.[319] This
Twitter invitation was followed by over a dozen other instances in which he
used Twitter to encourage supporters to rally for him in Washington, DC on
January 6th.[320]

The Committee has assembled detailed material demonstrating the
effects of these communications on members of far-right extremist groups,
like the Proud Boys, Oath Keepers, Three Percenters, and others, and on
individuals looking to respond to their president's call to action. President
Trump's supporters believed the election was stolen because they listened
to his words,[321] and they knew what he had called them to do; stop the certification of the electoral count.[322]

For example, one supporter, Charles Bradford Smith, noted on December 22, 2020, that "Trump is asking everyone to go" to Washington, DC on

January 6th "to fill the streets" on the "day Pence counts up the votes." [323] Derek Sulenta posted to Facebook on December 23, 2020, that "I'll be there Jan 6th to support the president no matter what happens" because "That's the day he called for patriots to show up." [324] By December 31, 2020, Robert Morss believed January 6th stood for the moment when "1776 Will Commence Again" because President Trump asked them to "Be there, Will be Wild." [325] Kenneth Grayson predicted what would eventually happen on January 6th, when on December 23, 2020, he wrote on Facebook that President Trump called people to Washington, DC through his December 19th tweet and then added "IF TRUMP TELLS US TO STORM THE FUKIN CAPITAL IMA DO THAT THEN!" [326] Some demonstrated their inspiration for January 6th by circulating flyers, which proclaimed "#OccupyCongress" over images of the United States Capitol. [327] Robert Gieswein, a Coloradan affiliated with Three Percenters who was among the first to breach the Capitol, said that he came to Washington, DC "to keep President Trump in." [328]

Chapter 8 of this report documents how the Proud Boys led the attack, penetrated the Capitol, and led hundreds of others inside. Multiple Proud Boys reacted immediately to President Trump's December 19th tweet and began their planning. Immediately, Proud Boys leaders reorganized their hierarchy, with Enrique Tarrio, Joseph Biggs, and Ethan Nordean messaging groups of Proud Boys about what to expect on January 6th. [329] Tarrio created a group chat known as the Ministry of Self-Defense for hand-selected Proud Boys whom he wanted to "organize and direct" plans for January 6th. [330] On social media, Tarrio referenced "revolt" and "[r]evolution," and conspicuously asked "What if we invade it?" on Telegram. [331] As of December 29, 2020, Tarrio told the group the events on January 6th would be "centered around the Capitol." [332]

At the time of publication of this report, prosecutions of certain Proud Boys are ongoing. To date, one Proud Boy has pled guilty to seditious conspiracy and other Proud Boys have pled guilty to other crimes, including conspiracy to obstruct Congress. [333] Jeremy Bertino, a Proud Boy who pled guilty to seditious conspiracy, admitted that he:

> understood from internal discussions among the Proud Boys that in the leadup to January 6, the willingness to resort to unlawful conduct increasingly included a willingness to use and promote violence to achieve political objectives. [334]

Moreover,

> Bertino believed that the 2020 election had been "stolen" and, as January 6, 2021, approached, believed that drastic measures,

including violence, were necessary to prevent Congress from certifying the Electoral College Vote on January 6, 2021. Bertino made his views in this regard known publicly, as well as in private discussions with MOSD leadership. Bertino understood from his discussions with MOSD leadership that they agreed that the election had been stolen, that the purpose of traveling to Washington, D.C., on January 6, 2021, was to stop the certification of the Electoral College Vote, and that the MOSD leaders were willing to do whatever it would take, including using force against police and others, to achieve that objective.[335]

As set out in Bertino's plea agreement, members of MOSD:

> openly discussed plans for potential violence at the Capitol [. . . and] members of MOSD leadership were discussing the possibility of storming the Capitol. Bertino believed that storming the Capitol would achieve the group's goal of stopping Congress from certifying the Electoral College Vote. Bertino understood that storming the Capitol or its grounds would be illegal and would require using force against police or other government officials.[336]

Another Proud Boy who has pled guilty to conspiracy and assault charges, Charles Donohoe, understood that the Proud Boys planned to storm the Capitol. Donohoe, a Proud Boys local chapter leader from North Carolina:

> was aware [as early as January 4, 2021] that members of MOSD leadership were discussing the possibility of storming the Capitol. Donohoe believed that storming the Capitol would achieve the group's goal of stopping the government from carrying out the transfer of presidential power.[337]

The Department of Justice has charged a number of Oath Keepers with seditious conspiracy. Specifically, the government alleges that "[a]fter the Presidential Election, Elmer Stewart Rhodes III conspired with his co-defendants, introduced below, and other co-conspirators, known and unknown to the Grand Jury, to oppose by force the lawful transfer of presidential power."[338] A jury agreed, convicting Stewart Rhodes and Kelly Meggs—the leader of the Florida Oath Keepers chapter—of seditious conspiracy. The jury also convicted Rhodes and Meggs, as well as fellow Oath Keepers Jessica Watkins, Kenneth Harrelson, and Thomas Caldwell,[339] of other serious felonies for their actions on January 6th.[340]

Meggs celebrated the December 19th tweet, sending an encrypted Signal message to Florida Oath Keepers that President Trump "wants us to make it WILD that's what he's saying. He called us all to the Capitol and wants us to make it wild!!! . . . Gentlemen we are heading to DC pack your shit!!" [341] Similarly, Oath Keeper Joshua James—who pleaded guilty to seditious conspiracy—told Oath Keepers that there was now a "NATIONAL CALL TO ACTION FOR DC JAN 6TH" following President Trump's words. [342]

Stewart Rhodes, the Oath Keepers' founder, felt that "the time for peaceful protest is over" after December 19th and, according to the government, "urged President Trump to use military force to stop the lawful transfer of presidential power, describing January 6, 2021, as "a hard constitutional deadline" to do so. [343] Rhodes created a "an invitation-only Signal group chat titled, 'DC OP: Jan 6 21'" on December 30, 2020, which he and other Oath Keepers, like Meggs and James, used to plan for January 6th, including by creating a "quick reaction force" of firearms to be stashed in Virginia. [344]

Multiple members of the Oath Keepers have pleaded guilty to seditious conspiracy. Brian Ulrich started planning for January 6th right after President Trump sent out his December 19th tweet. The Department of Justice summarized Ulrich's communications, as follows:

> Ulrich messaged the "Oath Keepers of Georgia" Signal group chat, "Trump acts now maybe a few hundred radicals die trying to burn down cities . . . Trump sits on his hands Biden wins . . . millions die resisting the death of the 1st and 2nd amendment." On December 20, 2020, an individual in the "Oath Keepers of Georgia" Signal group chat, who later traveled with Ulrich to Washington, D.C., and breached the Capitol grounds with Ulrich on January 6, 2021, messaged, "January 6th. The great reset. America or not." [345]

The Justice Department's Statement of Offense for Oath Keeper Joshua James provided these details:

> In advance of and on January 6, 2021, James and others agreed to take part in the plan developed by Rhodes to use any means necessary, up to and including the use of force, to stop the lawful transfer of presidential power. In the weeks leading up to January 6, 2021, Rhodes instructed James and other coconspirators to be prepared, if called upon, to report to the White House grounds to secure the perimeter and use lethal force if necessary against anyone who tried to remove President Trump from the White House, including the National Guard or other government actors who might be sent to remove President Trump as a result of the Presidential Election. [346]

The former President's call also galvanized Three Percenters to act. A group known as The Three Percenters Original sent a message to its members on December 16, 2020, noting they "stand ready and are standing by to answer the call from our President should the need arise" to combat the "pure evil that is conspiring to steal our country away from the american people" through the "2020 presidential election." [347] After President Trump's tweet, the group put out another letter instructing "any member who can attend . . . to participate" on January 6th because "[t]he President of the United States has put out a general call for the patriots of this Nation to gather" in Washington, DC.[348]

Other Three Percenter groups also responded. Alan Hostetter and Russell Taylor led a group of Three Percenters calling themselves the California Patriots—DC Brigade, who have been charged with conspiracy to obstruct Congress because they organized to fight to keep President Trump in power on January 6th after President Trump's December 19th tweet inspired them to come to Washington, DC.[349] On December 19th, Hostetter posted on Instagram:

> President Trump tweeted that all patriots should descend on Washington DC on Wednesday 1/6/2021. This is the date of the Joint Session of Congress in which they will either accept or reject the fake/phony/stolen electoral college votes.[350]

Between December 19th and January 6th, Hostetter, Taylor, and other members of the California Patriots—DC Brigade exchanged messages and posted to social media about bringing gear, including "weaponry," like "hatchet[s]," "bat[s]," or "[l]arge metal flashlights," and possibly "firearms," and, about being "ready and willing to fight" like it was "1776." Taylor even spoke in front of the Supreme Court on January 5, 2021, explaining that "[p]atriots" would "not return to our peaceful way of life until this election is made right . . . ." [351] On December 29, 2020, Taylor exclaimed "I personally want to be on the front steps and be one of the first ones to breach the doors!" [352]

Similarly, members of the Florida Guardians of Freedom, Three Percent sent around a flyer on December 24, 2020, saying they were "responding to the call from President Donald J. Trump to assist in the security, protection, and support of the people as we all protest the fraudulent election and re-establish liberty for our nation." [353] Their leader, Jeremy Liggett, posted a meme to Facebook stating that "3% Will Show In Record Numbers In DC" [354] and put out a "safety video" instructing people that they could bring "an expandable metal baton, a walking cane and a folding knife" [355] to Washington, DC on January 6th. Several have been arrested for participating in the violence around the tunnel on January 6th.[356]

When interviewed by the FBI on March 31, 2021, Danny Rodriguez—a Three Percenter from California who tased Officer Michael Fanone in the neck as rioters tried to break through a door on the west side of the Capitol—reflected on his decision to go to Washington, DC[357]:

Trump called us to D.C. . . . and he's calling for help—I thought he was calling for help. I thought he was—I thought we were doing the right thing. . . . [W]e thought we were going to hit it like a civil war. There was going to be a big battle. . . . I thought that the main fight, the main battle, was going to be in D.C. because Trump called everyone there.[358]

These groups were not operating in silos. Meggs bragged on Facebook that following President Trump's December 19th tweet he had formed an alliance between the Oath Keepers, the Florida Three Percenters, and the Proud Boys "to work together to shut this shit down."[359] On December 19th, Meggs called Enrique Tarrio and they spoke for more than three minutes.[360] Three days later, Meggs messaged Liggett, echoing his excitement about the December 19th tweet and specifically referencing the seat of Congress: "He called us all to the Capitol and wants to make it wild!!!"[361] Liggett said "I will have a ton of men with me" and Meggs replied that "we have made Contact [sic] with PB [Proud Boys] and they always have a big group. Force multiplier. . . . I figure we could splinter off the main group of PB and come up behind them. Fucking crush them for good."[362] Aside from Meggs, Stewart Rhodes brought in at least one local militia leader[363] and Three Percenters into the Oath Keepers January 6th planning chats that came about following President Trump's tweet.[364]

Even on January 6th, rioters referenced the tweet. An unknown rioter was caught on video as they ascended the Capitol steps saying "He said it was gonna be wild. He didn't lie."[365] MPD body-worn cameras captured Cale Clayton around 3:15 p.m. as he taunted officers from under the scaffolding: "Your fucking president told us to be here. You should be on this side, right here, going with us. You are an American citizen. Your fucking President told you to do that. You too. You too. You. All of you guys. That Tweet was for you guys. For us. For you."[366]

As January 6th neared, intelligence emerged indicating that January 6th was likely to be violent, and specifically that the Capitol was a target. On January 3rd, an intelligence summary informed Department of Justice officials of plans to "occupy the Capitol" and "invade" the Capitol on January 6th. This summarized a "SITE Intelligence Group" report about the "online rhetoric focused on the 6 Jan event." Some of the reporting includes: "Calls to occupy federal buildings." "intimidating Congress and invading the capitol building." The email also quoted WUSA9 local reporting: "one of the websites used for organizing the event was encouraging attendees to bring guns."

Acting Deputy Attorney General Richard Donoghue testified:

And we knew that if you have tens of thousands of very upset people showing up in Washington, DC, that there was potential for violence.[368]

At the same time, a Defense Department official predicted on a White House National Security Council call that violence could be targeted at the Capitol on January 6th. According to Chairman of the Joint Chiefs of Staff Gen. Mark Milley:

> So during these calls, I—I only remember in hindsight because he was almost like clairvoyant. [Deputy Secretary of Defense David] Norquist says during one of these calls, the greatest threat is a direct assault on the Capitol. I'll never forget it.[369]

Likewise, documentation received by the Committee from the Secret Service demonstrates a growing number of warnings both that January 6th was likely to be violent, and specifically that the Capitol would likely be the target, including intelligence directly regarding the Proud Boys and Oath Keepers militia groups.

Even two weeks ahead of January 6th, the intelligence started to show what could happen. On December 22, 2020, the FBI received a screenshot of an online chat among Oath Keepers, seemingly referring to the State capitols besieged by protesters across the country earlier that year: "if they were going to go in, then they should have went all the way."[370] "There is only one way. It is not signs. It's not rallies. It's fucking bullets," one user replied.[371]

A public source emailed the Secret Service a document titled "Armed and Ready, Mr. President," on December 24th, which summarized online comments responding to President Trump's December 19th tweet.[372] Protestors should "start marching into the chambers," one user wrote.[373] Trump "can't exactly openly tell you to revolt," another replied. "This is the closest he'll ever get."[374] "I read [the President's tweet] as armed," someone said.[375] "[T]here is not enough cops in DC to stop what is coming," replied yet another.[376] "[B]e already in place when Congress tries to get to their meeting," the comments continued, and "make sure they know who to fear.'"[377] "[W]aiting for Trump to say the word," a person said, and "this is what Trump expects," exclaimed another.[378] Capitol Police's head of intelligence, Jack Donohue, got the same compilation from a former colleague at the New York Police Department on December 28, 2020.[379]

On December 26, 2020, the Secret Service received a tip about the Proud Boys detailing plans to have "a large enough group to march into DC armed [that] will outnumber the police so they can't be stopped."[380] "Their plan is to literally kill people," the informant stated. "Please please take this tip seriously . . . "[381] On December 29, 2020, Secret Service forwarded related warnings to Capitol Police that pro-Trump demonstrators were being urged to "occupy federal building[s]," including "march[ing] into the capital building and mak[ing] them quake in their shoes by our mere presence." [382]

Civilians also tipped off Capitol Police about people bringing weapons to besiege the Capitol. One tipster, who had "track[ed] online far right extremism for years," emailed Capitol Police warning "I've seen countless tweets from Trump supporters saying they will be armed," and "I[']ve also seen tweets from people organizing to 'storm the Capitol' on January 6th." [383]

On December 29, 2020, Secret Service forwarded related warnings to Capitol Police that pro-Trump demonstrators were being urged to "occupy federal building," including "march[ing] into the capital building and mak-[ing] them quake in their shoes by our mere presence." [384] Indeed, a Secret Service intelligence briefing on December 30th entitled "March for Trump," highlighted the President's "Will be wild!" tweet alongside hashtags #WeAreTheStorm, #1776Rebel, and #OccupyCapitols, writing "President Trump supporters have proposed a movement to occupy Capitol Hill." [385]

On January 1, 2021, a lieutenant in the intelligence branch at DC Police forwarded a civilian tip about "a website planning terroristic behavior on Jan 6th, during the rally" to Capitol Police intelligence. [386] "There are detailed plans to storm federal buildings," including "the capitol in DC on Jan 6th," the tipster reported, linking to thedonald.win. [387]

On January 2, 2021, the FBI discovered a social media posting that read, "This is not a rally and it's no longer a protest. This is a final stand . . . many are ready to die to take back #USA . . . . And don't be surprised if we take the #capital building." [388]

On January 3, 2021, a Parler user's post—under the name 1776(2.0) Minuteman— noting "after weds we are going to need a new congress" and "Jan 6 may actually be their [Members of Congress] last day in office" reached the FBI and Capitol Police. [389]

The FBI field office in Norfolk, Virginia issued an alert to law enforcement agencies on January 5th tiled "Potential for Violence in Washington, D.C. Area in Connection with Planned 'StopTheSteal' Protest on 6 January 2021," which noted:

An online thread discussed specific calls for violence to include stating, "Be ready to fight. Congress needs to hear glass breaking, doors being kicked in, and blood . . . being spilled. Get violent . . . stop calling this a march, or rally, or a protest. Go there ready for war. We get our President or we die. NOTHING else will achieve this goal." [390]

In addition, the alert copied "perimeter maps [of the Capitol] and caravan pictures [that] were posted" on thedonald.win, particularly worrying that the "caravans . . . had the same colors as the sections of the perimeter" of the Capitol.[391] Secret Service also knew about caravans planning to come to DC to "Occupy the Capitol." [392]

That same day, representatives from DHS, FBI, DC's Homeland Security and Emergency Management Agency, Secret Service, DC Police, and Capitol Police shared a website, Red State Secession, which had a post titled "Why the Second American Revolution Starts Jan 6." A user asked visitors to post where they could find the home addresses of Democratic congressmen and "political enemies" and asked if "any of our enemies [will] be working in offices in DC that afternoon." [393] "What are their routes to and from the event?" the post continued.[394] "[T]he crowd will be looking for enemies." [395]

A Secret Service open-source unit flagged an account on thedonald.win that threatened to bring a sniper rifle to a rally on January 6th. The user also posted a picture of a handgun and rifle with the caption, "Sunday Gun Day Providing Overwatch January 6th Will be Wild." [396]

The Secret Service learned from the FBI on January 5th about right-wing groups establishing armed quick reaction forces in Virginia, where they could amass firearms illegal in DC[397] Trump supporters staged there waiting across the river "to respond to 'calls for help.'" [398] The Oath Keepers were such a group.[399]

President Trump's closest aides knew about the political power of sites like thedonald.win, which is where much of this violent rhetoric and planning happened. On December 30, 2020, Jason Miller—a Senior Adviser to and former spokesman for the former President—texted Chief of Staff Mark Meadows a link to the thedonald.win, adding "I got the base FIRED UP." [400] The link connected to a page with comments like "Gallows don't require electricity," "if the filthy commie maggots try to push their fraud through, there will be hell to pay," and Congress can certify Trump the winner or leave "in a bodybag." [401] Symbolic gallows were constructed on January 6th at the foot of the Capitol.[402]

After President Trump's signal, his supporters did not hide their plans for violence at the Capitol, and those threats made their way to national and local law enforcement agencies. As described in this report, the intelligence agencies did detect this planning, and they shared it with the White House and with the U.S. Secret Service.

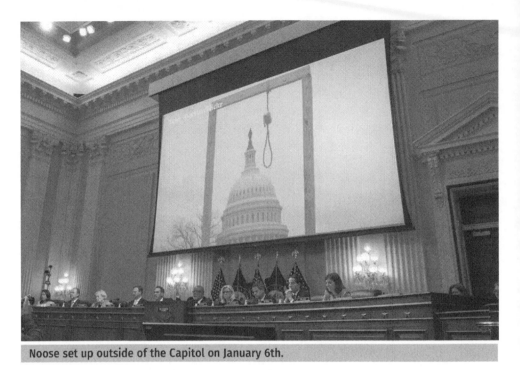
Noose set up outside of the Capitol on January 6th.

Testimony from White House staff also suggests real concerns about the risk of violence as January 6th approached. Cassidy Hutchinson, for example, testified about a conversation she had with her boss, Mark Meadows, on January 2nd:

I went into Mark's office, and he was still on his phone . . . . I said to Mark, "Rudy [Giuliani] said these things to me. What's going on here? Anything I should know about?"

This was—he was, like, looking at his phone. He was like, "Oh, it's all about the rally on Wednesday. Isn't that what he was talking to you about?"

I said, "Yeah. Yeah, sounds like we're going to the Capitol."

He said, "Yeah. Are you talking with Tony?"

"I'm having a conversation, sir."

He said—still looking at his phone. I remember he was scrolling. He was like, "Yeah. You know, things might get real, real bad on the 6th."

And I remember saying to him, "What do you mean?"

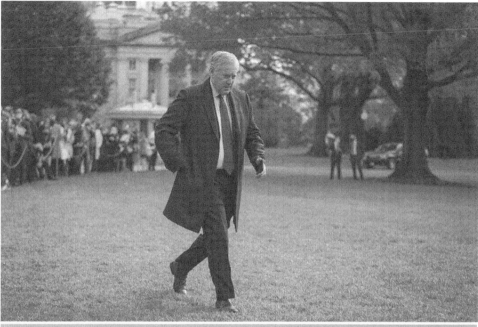

Mark Meadows walks along the South Lawn on October 30, 2020.
(Photo by Sarah Silbiger/Getty Images)

He was like, "I don't know. There's just going to be a lot of people here, and there's a lot of different ideas right now. I'm not really sure of everything that's going on. Let's just make sure we keep tabs on it." [403]

Hutchinson also testified about a conversation she had with Director of National Intelligence, Ratcliffe:

He had expressed to me that he was concerned that it could spiral out of control and potentially be dangerous, either for our democracy or the way that things were going for the 6th. [404]

Hope Hicks texted Trump Campaign spokesperson Hogan Gidley in the midst of the January 6th violence, explaining that she had "suggested . . . several times" on the preceding days (January 4th and January 5th) that President Trump publicly state that January 6th must remain peaceful and that he had refused her advice to do so. [405] Her recollection was that Herschmann earlier advised President Trump to make a preemptive public statement in advance of January 6th calling for no violence that day. [406] No such statement was made.

The District of Columbia Homeland Security office explicitly warned that groups were planning to "occupy the [Capitol] to halt the vote." [407]

[W]e got derogatory information from OSINT suggesting that some very, very violent individuals were organizing to come to DC, and not only were they organized to come to DC, but they were—these groups, these nonaligned groups were aligning. And so all the red flags went up at that point, you know, when you have armed militia, you know, collaborating with White supremacy groups, collaborating with conspiracy theory groups online all toward a common goal, you start seeing what we call in, you know, terrorism, a blended ideology, and that's a very, very bad sign. . . . [T]hen when they were clearly across—not just across one platform but across multiple platforms of these groups coordinating, not just like chatting, "Hey, how's it going, what's the weather like where you're at," but like, "what are you bringing, what are you wearing, you know, where do we meet up, do you have plans for the Capitol." That's operational—that's like preoperational intelligence, right, and that is something that's clearly alarming.[408]

Again, this type of intelligence was shared, including obvious warnings about potential violence prior to January 6th.[409] What was not shared, and was not fully understood by intelligence and law enforcement entities, is what role President Trump would play on January 6th in exacerbating the violence, and later refusing for multiple hours to instruct his supporters to stand down and leave the Capitol. No intelligence collection was apparently performed on President Trump's plans for January 6th, nor was there any analysis performed on what he might do to exacerbate potential violence. Certain Republican members of Congress who were working with Trump and the Giuliani team may have had insight on this particular risk, but none appear to have alerted the Capitol Police or any other law enforcement authority.

On January 2, 2021, Katrina Pierson wrote in an email to fellow rally organizers, "POTUS expectations are to have something intimate at the [E]llipse, and call on everyone to march to the Capitol."[410] And, on January 4, 2021, another rally organizer texted Mike Lindell, the MyPillow CEO, that President Trump would "unexpectedly" call on his supporters to march to the Capitol:

This stays only between us . . . . It can also not get out about the march because I will be in trouble with the national park service and all the agencies but POTUS is going to just call for it "unexpectedly."[411]

Testimony obtained by the Committee also indicates that President Trump was specifically aware that the crowd he had called to Washington was fired up and angry on the evening of January 5th. Judd Deere, a deputy

White House press secretary recalled a conversation with President Trump in the Oval Office on the evening of January 5th:

Judd Deere: I said he should focus on policy accomplishments. I didn't mention the 2020 election.

Committee Staff: Okay. What was his response?

Deere: He acknowledged that and said, "We've had a lot," something along those lines, but didn't—he fairly quickly moved to how fired up the crowd is, or was going to be.

Committee Staff: Okay. What did he say about it?

Deere: Just that they were—they were fired up. They were angry. They feel like the election's been stolen, that the election was rigged, that—he went on and on about that for a little bit. [412]

Testimony indicated that President Trump was briefed on the risk of violence on the morning of the 6th before he left the White House. Cassidy Hutchinson provided this testimony:

Vice Chair Cheney: So, Ms. Hutchinson, is it your understanding that Mr. Ornato told the President about weapons at the rally on the morning of January 6th?

Hutchinson: That is what Mr. Ornato relayed to me. [413]

The head of President Trump's security detail, Bobby Engel, told the Select Committee that when he shared critical information with White House Deputy Chief of Staff Anthony Ornato, it was a means of conveying that information with the Oval Office: "So, when it came to passing information to Mr. Ornato, I—my assumption was that it would get to the chief [of staff, Mark Meadows], or that he was sharing the information with the chief. I don't—and the filtering process, or if the chief thinks it needs to get to the President, then he would share it with the President." [414] Also, Engel confirmed that if "information would come to my attention, whether it was a protective intelligence issue or a concern or—primarily, I would—I would make sure that the information got filtered up through the appropriate chain usually through Mr. Ornato. So if I received a report on something that was happening in the DC area, I'd either forward that information to Mr. Ornato, or call him about that information or communicate in some way." [415]

The Select Committee also queried Deputy Chief of Staff Ornato this November about what he generally would have done in this sort of situation, asking him the following: "Generally you receive information about things like the groups that are coming, the stuff that we talked earlier. You would bring that to Mr. Meadows and likely did here, although you don't have a specific recollection?"[416] Ornato responded: "That is correct, sir."[417] Ornato also explained to the Committee that "… in my normal daily functions, in my general functions as my job, I would've had a conversation with him about all the groups coming in and what was expected from the secret service."[418] As for the morning of January 6th itself, he had the following answer:

> Committee Staff: Do you remember talking to Chief of Staff Mark Meadows about any of your concerns about the threat landscape going into January 6th?

> Ornato: I don't recall; however, in my position I would've made sure he was tracking the demos, which he received a daily brief, Presidential briefing. So he most likely was getting all this in his daily brief as well. I wouldn't know what was in his intelligence brief that day, but I would've made sure that he was tracking these things and just mentioned, "Hey, are you tracking the demos?" If he gave me a "yeah", I don't recall it today, but I'm sure that was something that took place.[419]

Ornato had access to intelligence that suggested violence at the Capitol on January 6th, and it was his job to inform Meadows and President Trump of that. Although Ornato told us that he did not recall doing so, the Select Committee found multiple parts of Ornato's testimony questionable. The Select Committee finds it difficult to believe that neither Meadows nor Ornato told President Trump, as was their job, about the intelligence that was emerging as the January 6th rally approached.

Hours before the Ellipse rally on January 6th, the fact that the assembled crowd was prepared for potential violence was widely known. In addition to intelligence reports indicating potential violence at the Capitol, weapons and other prohibited items were being seized by police on the streets and by Secret Service at the magnetometers for the Ellipse speech. Secret Service confiscated a haul of weapons from the 28,000 spectators who did pass through the magnetometers: 242 cannisters of pepper spray, 269 knives or blades, 18 brass knuckles, 18 tasers, 6 pieces of body armor, 3 gas masks, 30 batons or blunt instruments, and 17 miscellaneous items like scissors, needles, or screwdrivers.[420] And thousands of others purposely remained outside the magnetometers, or left their packs outside.[421]

Others brought firearms. Three men in fatigues from Broward County, Florida brandished AR-15s in front of Metropolitan police officers on 14th Street and Independence Avenue on the morning of January 6th.[422] MPD advised over the radio that one individual was possibly armed with a "Glock" at 14th and Constitution Avenue, and another was possibly armed

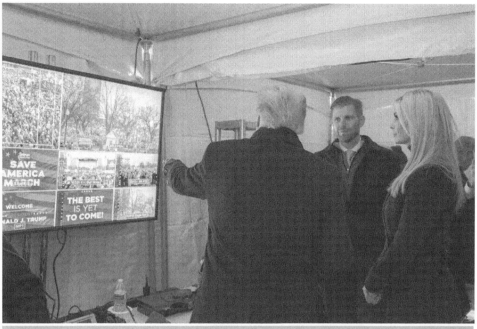

**President Trump looks backstage at the crowd gathered at the Ellipse.**
(Photo provided to the Select Committee by the National Archives and Records Administration)

with a "rifle" at 15th and Constitution Avenue around 11:23 a.m.[423] The National Park Service detained an individual with a rifle between 12 and 1 p.m.[424] Almost all of this was known before Donald Trump took the stage at the Ellipse.

By the time President Trump was preparing to give his speech, he and his advisors knew enough to cancel the rally. And he certainly knew enough to cancel any plans for a march to the Capitol. According to testimony obtained by the Select Committee, President Trump knew that elements of the crowd were armed, and had prohibited items, and that many thousands would not pass through the magnetometers for that reason. Testimony indicates that the President had received an earlier security briefing, and testimony indicates that the Secret Service mentioned the prohibited items again as they drove President Trump to the Ellipse.

Cassidy Hutchinson was with the President backstage. Her contemporaneous text messages indicate that President Trump was "effing furious" about the fact that a large number of his supporters would not go through the magnetometers:

Cassidy Hutchinson: But the crowd looks good from this vanish [sic] point. As long as we get the shot. He was fucking furious

Tony Ornato: He doesn't get it that the people on the monument side don't want to come in. They can see from there and don't want to come in. They can see from there and don't have to go through mags. With 30k magged inside.

Cassidy Hutchinson: That's what was relayed several times and in different iterations

Cassidy Hutchinson: Poor max got chewed out

Cassidy Hutchinson: He also kept mentioning [an off the record trip] to Capitol before he took the stage

Tony Ornato: Bobby will tell him no. It's not safe to do. No assets available to safely do it.[425]

And Hutchinson described what President Trump said as he prepared to take the stage:

When we were in the off-stage announce area tent behind the stage, he was very concerned about the shot. Meaning the photograph that we would get because the rally space wasn't full. One of the reasons, which I've previously stated, was because he wanted it to be full and for people to not feel excluded because they had come far to watch him at the rally. And he felt the mags were at fault for not letting everybody in, but another leading reason and likely the primary reasons is because he wanted it full and he was angry that we weren't letting people through the mags with weapons—what the Secret Service deemed as weapons, and are, are weapons. But when we were in the off-stage announce tent, I was a part of a conversation, I was in the vicinity of a conversation where I overheard the President say something to the effect of, "I don't F'ing care that they have weapons. They're not here to hurt me. Take the F'ing mags away. Let my people in. They can march to the Capitol from here. Let the people in. Take the F'ing mags away." [426]

The Secret Service special agent who drove the President after his speech told the Select Committee that Trump made a similar remark in the vehicle when his demand to go to the Capitol was refused—essentially that Trump did not believe his supporters posed a security risk to him personally.[427]

Minutes after the exchange that Hutchinson described—when President Trump took the stage—he pointedly expressed his concern about the thousands of attendees who would not enter the rally area and instructed Secret Service to allow that part of the crowd to enter anyway:

... I'd love to have if those tens of thousands of people would be allowed. The military, the secret service. And we want to thank you and the police law enforcement. Great. You're doing a great job. But I'd love it if they could be allowed to come up here with us. Is that possible? Can you just let [them] come up, please?[428]

Although President Trump and his advisors knew of the risk of violence, and knew specifically that elements of the crowd were angry and some were armed, from intelligence and law enforcement reports that morning, President Trump nevertheless went forward with the rally, and then specifically instructed the crowd to march to the Capitol: "Because you'll never take back our country with weakness. You have to show strength and you have to be strong. We have come to demand that Congress do the right thing and only count the electors who have been lawfully slated, lawfully slated."[429] Much of President Trump's speech was improvised. Even before his improvisation, during the review of President Trump's prepared remarks, White House lawyer Eric Herschmann specifically requested that "if there were any factual allegations, someone needed to independently validate or verify the statements."[430] And in the days just before January 6th, Herschmann "chewed out" John Eastman and told him he was "out of [his] F'ing mind" to argue that the Vice President could be the sole decision-maker as to who becomes the next President.[431] Herschmann told us, "I so berated him that I believed that theory would not go forward."[432] But President Trump made that very argument during his speech at the Ellipse and made many false statements. Herschmann attended that speech, but walked out during the middle of it.[433]

President Trump's speech to the crowd that day lasted more than an hour. The speech walked through dozens of known falsehoods about purported election fraud. And Trump again made false and malicious claims about Dominion voting systems.[434] As discussed earlier, he again pressured Mike Pence to refuse to count lawful electoral votes, going off script repeatedly, leading the crowd to believe falsely that Pence could and would alter the election outcome:

And I actually, I just spoke to Mike. I said: "Mike, that doesn't take courage. What takes courage is to do nothing. That takes courage." And then we're stuck with a president who lost the election by a lot and we have to live with that for four more years. We're just not going to let that happen . . . .

When you catch somebody in a fraud, you're allowed to go by very different rules.

So I hope Mike has the courage to do what he has to do. And I hope he doesn't listen to the RINOs and the stupid people that he's listening to."[435]

This characterization of Vice President Pence's decision had a direct impact on those who marched to and approached the Capitol, as illustrated by this testimony from a person convicted of crimes committed on January 6th:

So this woman came up to the side of us, and she, says, Pence folded. So it was kind of, like, okay. Well, in my mind I was thinking, "Well, that's it, you know." Well, my son-in-law looks at me, and he says, "I want to go in."[436]

Trump used the word "peacefully," written by speech writers, one time. But he delivered many other scripted and unscripted comments that conveyed a very different message:

Because you'll never take back our country with weakness. You have to show strength and you have to be strong. We have come to demand that Congress do the right thing and only count the electors who have been lawfully slated, lawfully slated. . . .

And we fight. We fight like hell. And if you don't fight like hell, you're not going to have a country anymore . . . .[437]

Trump also was not the only rally speaker to do these things. Giuliani, for instance, also said, "Let's have trial by combat."[438] Likewise, Eastman used his two minutes on the Ellipse stage to make a claim already known to be false—that corrupted voted machines stole the election.[439]

The best indication of the impact of President Trump's words, both during the Ellipse speech and beforehand, are the comments from those supporters who attended the Ellipse rally and their conduct immediately thereafter. Videoclips show several of the attendees on their way to the Capitol or shortly after they arrived:

I'm telling you what, I'm hearing that Pence—hearing the Pence just caved. No. Is that true? I didn't hear it. I'm hear—I'm hearing reports that Pence caved. No way. I'm telling you, if Pence caved, we're going to drag motherfuckers through the streets. You fucking politicians are going to get fucking drug through the streets.[440]

Yes. I guess the hope is that there's such a show of force here that Pence will decide do the right thing, according to Trump.[441]

Pence voted against Trump. [Interviewer: Ok. And that's when all this started?] Yup. That's when we marched on the Capitol.[442]

We just heard that Mike Pence is not going to reject any fraudulent electoral votes. [Other speaker: Boo. You're a traitor! Boo!] That's right. You've heard it here first. Mike Pence has betrayed the United States of America. [Other speaker: Boo! Fuck you, Mike Pence!] Mike Pence has betrayed this President and he has betrayed the people of the United States and we will never, ever forget. [Cheers][443]

[Q] What percentage of the crowd is going to the Capitol? [A] [Oath Keeper Jessica Watkins]: One hundred percent. It has, it has spread like wildfire that Pence has betrayed us, and everybody's marching on the Capitol. All million of us. It's insane. [444]

Another criminal defendant—charged with assaulting an officer with a flagpole and other crimes—explained in an interview why he went to the Capitol and fought:

Dale Huttle: We were not there illegally, we were invited there by the President himself. . . . Trump's backers had been told that the election had been stolen. . . .

Reporter Megan Hickey: But do you think he encouraged violence?

Dale Huttle: Well, I sat there, or stood there, with half a million people listening to his speech. And in that speech, both Giuliani and [Trump] said we were going to have to fight like hell to save our country. Now, whether it was a figure of speech or not—it wasn't taken that way.

Reporter Megan Hickey: You didn't take it as a figure of speech?

Dale Huttle: No.[445]

President Trump concluded his speech at 1:10 p.m.

Among other statements from the Ellipse podium, President Trump informed the crowd that he would be marching to the Capitol with them:

Now, it is up to Congress to confront this egregious assault on our democracy. And after this, we're going to walk down, **and I'll be there with you**, we're going to walk down, we're going to walk down. Anyone you want, but I think right here, **we're going to walk down to the Capitol**, and we're going to cheer on our brave senators and congressmen and women, and we're probably not going to be cheering so much for some of them.[446]

Hutchinson testified that she first became aware of President Trump's plans to attend Congress's session to count votes on or about January 2nd. She learned this from a conversation with Giuliani: "It's going to be great.

The President's going to be there. He's going to look powerful. He's—he's going to be with the members. He's going to be with the Senators." [447] Evidence also indicates that multiple members of the White House staff, including White House lawyers, were concerned about the President's apparent intentions to go to the Capitol. [448]

After he exited the stage, President Trump entered the Presidential SUV and forcefully expressed his intention that Bobby Engel, the head of his Secret Service detail, direct the motorcade to the Capitol. The Committee has now obtained evidence from several sources about a "furious interaction" in the SUV. The vast majority of witnesses who have testified before the Select Committee about this topic, including multiple members of the Secret Service, a member of the Metropolitan police, and national security and military officials in the White House, described President Trump's behavior as "irate," "furious," "insistent," "profane" and "heated." Hutchinson heard about the exchange second-hand and related what she heard in our June 28, 2022, hearing from Ornato (as did another witness, a White House employee with national security responsibilities, who shared that Ornato also recounted to him President Trump's "irate" behavior in the Presidential vehicle). Other members of the White House staff and Secret Service also heard about the exchange after the fact. The White House employee with national security responsibilities gave this testimony:

> Committee Staff: But it sounds like you recall some rumor or some discussion around the West Wing about the President's anger about being told that he couldn't go to the Capitol. Is that right?
>
> Employee: So Mr. Ornato said that he was angry that he couldn't go right away. In the days following that, I do remember, you know, again, hearing again how angry the President was when, you know, they were in the limo. But beyond specifics of that, that's pretty much the extent of the cooler talk. [449]

The Committee has regarded both Hutchinson and the corroborating testimony by the White House employee with national security responsibilities as earnest and has no reason to conclude that either had a reason to invent their accounts. A Secret Service agent who worked on one of the details in the White House and was present in the Ellipse motorcade had this comment:

> Committee Staff: Ms. Hutchinson has suggested to the committee that you sympathized with her after her testimony, and believed her account. Is that accurate?
>
> Special Agent: I have no—yeah, that's accurate. I have no reason—I mean, we—we became friends. We worked—I worked every day

with her for 6 months. Yeah, she became a friend of mine. We had a good working relationship. I have no reason—she's never done me wrong. She's never lied that I know of.[450]

The Committee's principal concern was that the President actually intended to participate personally in the January 6th efforts at the Capitol, leading the attempt to overturn the election either from inside the House Chamber, from a stage outside the Capitol, or otherwise. The Committee regarded those facts as important because they are relevant to President Trump's intent on January 6th. There is no question from all the evidence assembled that President Trump *did have that intent.*[451]

As it became clear that Donald Trump desired to travel to the Capitol on January 6th, a White House Security Official in the White House complex became very concerned about his intentions:

> To be completely honest, we were all in a state of shock. . . . it just—one, I think the actual physical feasibility of doing it, and then also we all knew what that implicated and what that meant, that this was no longer a rally, that this was going to move to something else if he physically walked to the Capitol. I—I don't know if you want to use the word "insurrection," "coup," whatever. We all knew that this would move from a normal, democratic, you know, public event into something else.[452]

President Trump continued to push to travel to the Capitol even after his return to the White House, despite knowing that a riot was underway. Kayleigh McEnany, the White House press secretary, spoke with President Trump about his desire to go to the Capitol after he returned to the White House from the Ellipse. "So to the best of my recollection, I recall him being—wanting to—saying that he wanted to physically walk and be a part of the march and then saying that he would ride the Beast if he needed to, ride in the Presidential limo."[453]

Later in the afternoon, Mark Meadows relayed to Cassidy Hutchinson that President Trump was still upset that he would not be able to go to the Capitol that day. As he told Hutchinson, "the President wasn't happy that Bobby [Engel] didn't pull it off for him and that Mark didn't work hard enough to get the movement on the books."[454]

### 187 MINUTES: TRUMP'S DERELICTION OF DUTY

Just after 1:00 p.m., Vice President Pence, serving as President of the Senate under Article I of the Constitution, gaveled the Congress into its Joint Session. President Trump was giving a speech at the Ellipse, which he concluded at 1:10 pm. For the next few hours, an attack on our Capitol occurred, perpetrated by Trump supporters many of whom were present at the Ellipse for President Trump's speech. More than 140 Capitol and Metropolitan police were injured, some very seriously.[455] A perimeter security line of Metropolitan Police intended to secure the Capitol against intrusion broke in the face of thousands of armed rioters—more than 2,000 of whom gained access to the interior of the Capitol building.[456] A woman who attempted to forcibly enter the Chamber of the House of Representatives through a broken window while the House was in session was shot and killed by police guarding the chamber. Vice President Pence and his family were at risk, as were those Secret Service professionals protecting him. Congressional proceedings were halted, and legislators were rushed to secure locations.

From the outset of the violence and for several hours that followed, people at the Capitol, people inside President Trump's Administration, elected officials of both parties, members of President Trump's family, and Fox News commentators sympathetic to President Trump all tried to contact him to urge him to do one singular thing—one thing that all of these people immediately understood was required: Instruct his supporters to stand down and disperse—to leave the Capitol.

As the evidence overwhelmingly demonstrates, President Trump specifically and repeatedly refused to do so—for multiple hours—while the mayhem ensued. Chapter 8 of this report explains in meticulous detail the horrific nature of the violence taking place, that was directed at law enforcement officers at the Capitol and that put the lives of American lawmakers at risk. Yet in spite of this, President Trump watched the violence on television from a dining room adjacent to the Oval Office, calling Senators to urge them to help him delay the electoral count, but refusing to supply the specific help that everyone knew was unequivocally required. As this report shows, when Trump finally did make such a statement at 4:17 p.m.—after hours of violence—the statement immediately had the expected effect; the rioters began to disperse immediately and leave the Capitol.[457]

To fully understand the President's behavior during those hours—now commonly known as the "187 minutes"—it is important to understand the context in which it occurred. As outlined in this report, by the afternoon of January 6th, virtually all of President Trump's efforts to overturn the outcome of the 2020 election had failed. Virtually all the lawsuits had already been lost. Vice President Mike Pence had refused Trump's pressure to stop the count of certain electoral votes. State officials and legislators had refused to reverse the election outcomes in every State where Trump and his team applied pressure. The Justice Department's investigations of alleged election fraud had all contradicted Trump's allegations.

The only factor working in Trump's favor that might succeed in materially delaying the counting of electoral votes for President-elect Biden was the violent crowd at the Capitol. And for much of the afternoon of January 6th, it appeared that the crowd had accomplished that purpose. Congressional leaders were advised by Capitol Police at one or more points during the attack that it would likely take several days before the Capitol could safely be reopened.[458]

By the time the President's speech concluded, the lawlessness at the United States Capitol had already begun, but the situation was about to get much worse.

By 1:25 p.m., President Trump was informed that the Capitol was under attack.

Minutes after arriving back at the White House, the President ran into a member of the White House staff and asked if they had watched his speech on television. "Sir, they cut it off because they're rioting down at the Capitol," the employee said. The President asked what they meant by that. "[T]hey're rioting down there at the Capitol," the employee repeated. "Oh really?" the President asked. "All right, let's go see."[459] A photograph taken by the White House photographer—the last one permitted until later in the day—captures the moment the President was made aware of the violent uprising at the Capitol.[460]

Not long thereafter, as thousands of Trump supporters from the Ellipse speech continued to arrive at the Capitol, the DC Metropolitan Police Department declared a riot at the Capitol at 1:49 p.m., the same time Capitol Police Chief Steven Sund informed the DC National Guard "that there was a dire emergency on Capitol Hill and requested the immediate assistance" of as many national guard troops as possible.[461]

No photographs exist of the President for the remainder of the afternoon until after 4 p.m. President Trump appears to have instructed that the White House photographer was not to take any photographs.[462] The Select Committee also was unable to locate any official records of President Trump's telephone calls that afternoon.[463] And the President's official Daily Diary contains no information for this afternoon between the hours of 1:19 p.m. and 4:03 p.m., at the height of the worst attack on the seat of the United States Congress in over two centuries.[464]

The Select Committee did, however, obtain records from non-official sources that contained data of some phone calls President Trump made that afternoon. Even though "he was placing lots of calls" that afternoon, according to his personal assistant,[465] the Select Committee was given no records of any calls from the President to security or law enforcement officials that afternoon, and that absence of data is consistent with testimony of witnesses who would have knowledge of any such calls, who said that he did not do so.[466] Based on testimony from President Trump's close aides, we know that President Trump remained in the Dining Room adjacent to the Oval Office for the rest of the afternoon until after 4:03 p.m.[467]

In fact, from cellular telephone records, it appears that at 1:39 p.m. and 2:03 p.m., after being informed of the riot at the Capitol, President Trump called his lawyer, Rudolph Giuliani. These calls lasted approximately four minutes and eight minutes, respectively.[468] And Press Secretary Kayleigh McEnany testified that President Trump also called a number of Senators.[469] The number or names of all such Members of Congress is unknown, although Senator Mike Lee (R–UT) received one such outgoing call from the President within the hour that followed.[470]

At 1:49 p.m., just as the DC Metropolitan Police officially declared a riot and the Capitol Police were calling for help from the National Guard to address the crisis, President Trump sent a tweet with a link to a recording of his speech at the Ellipse.[471]

At about that point, White House Counsel Pat Cipollone became aware of the Capitol riot. The Committee collected sworn testimony from several White House officials, each with similar accounts. The President's White House Counsel Pat Cipollone testified that he raced downstairs, and went to the Oval Office Dining Room as soon as he learned about the violence at the Capitol—likely just around or just after 2 p.m. Cipollone knew immediately that the President had to deliver a message to the rioters—asking them to leave the Capitol.

Here is how he described this series of events:

> . . . the first time I remember going downstairs was when people had breached the Capitol... But I went down with [Deputy White House Counsel] Pat [Philbin], and I remember we were both very upset about what was happening. And we both wanted, you know, action to be taken related to that . . . But we went down to the Oval Office, we went through the Oval office, and we went to the back where the President was. . . . I think he was already in the dining room . . . I can't talk about conversations [with the President]. I think I was pretty clear there needed to be an immediate and forceful response, statement, public statement, that people need to leave the Capitol now.[472]

Cipollone also left little doubt that virtually everyone among senior White House staff had the same view:

> There were a lot of people in the White House that day . . . Senior people who, you know, felt the same way that I did and who were working very hard to achieve that result. There were—I think

Ivanka was one of them. And Eric Herschmann was there, Pat Philbin was there, and a number of other people .... many people suggested it. .... Many people felt the same way. I'm sure I had conversations with Mark [Meadows] about this during the course of the day and expressed my opinion very forcefully that this needs to be done.[473]

Likewise, senior staff cooperated to produce a message for the President on a notecard, which read:

ANYONE WHO ENTERED THE CAPITOL ~~ILLEGALLY~~ WITHOUT PROPER AUTHORITY SHOULD LEAVE IMMEDIATELY.[474]

The President declined to make the statement. Cipollone also made it clear that the advice they were giving to the President never changed throughout this three-hour period. Trump refused to do what was necessary.

Committee Staff: [I]t sounds like you from the very onset of violence at the Capitol right around 2 o'clock were pushing for a strong statement that people should leave the Capitol. Is that right?

Cipollone: I was, and others were as well.[475]

Cassidy Hutchinson, who worked closely with Mark Meadows and sat directly outside his office, confirmed this account and described several additional details:

I see Pat Cipollone barreling down the hallway towards our office. And he rushed right in, looked at me, said, "Is Mark in his office?" And I said, "Yes." And on a normal day he would've said, "Can I pop in," or, "Is he talking to anyone," or, "Is it an appropriate time for me to go chat with him," and myself or Eliza would go let him in or tell him no. But after I had said yes, he just looked at me and started shaking his head and went over, opened Mark's office door, stood there with the door propped open, and said something to the—Mark was still sitting on his phone. I remember, like, glancing in. He was still sitting on his phone.

And I remember Pat saying to him something to the effect of, "The rioters have gotten to the Capitol, Mark. We need to go down and see the President now." And Mark looked up at him and said, "He doesn't want to do anything, Pat." And Pat said something to the effect of—and very clearly said this to Mark—something to the effect of, "Mark, something needs to be done, or people are going to die and the blood's gonna be on your F'ing hands. This is getting out of control. I'm going down there.[476]

The Select Committee believes that the entire White House senior staff was in favor of a Presidential statement specifically instructing the violent rioters to leave. But President Trump refused. White House Counsel Pat Cipollone answered certain questions from the Select Committee on this subject as follows:

Vice Chair Cheney: And when you talk about others on the staff thinking more should be done, or thinking that the President needed to tell people to go home, who would you put in that category?

Cipollone: Well, I would put . . . Pat Philbin, Eric Herschmann. Overall, Mark Meadows, Ivanka. Once Jared got there, Jared. General Kellogg. I'm probably missing some, but those are—Kayleigh I think was there. But I don't—Dan Scavino.

Vice Chair Cheney: And who on the staff did not want people to leave the Capitol?"

Cipollone: On the staff?

Vice Chair Cheney: In the White House?

Cipollone: I can't think of anybody on that day who didn't want people to get out of the Capitol once the—particularly once the violence started. No. I mean—

Mr. Schiff: What about the President?

Vice Chair Cheney: Yeah.

. . .

[Consultation between Mr. Cipollone and his counsel.]

Cipollone: Yeah. I can't reveal communications. But obviously I think, you know—yeah.[477]

The testimony of a White House employee with national security responsibilities also corroborated these facts. This employee testified about a conversation between Pat Cipollone and Eric Herschmann in which Herschmann indicated that the President did not want to do anything to halt the violence. That employee told the Select Committee that he overheard Herschmann saying something to the effect of "the President didn't want anything done."[478]

Deputy Press Secretary Judd Deere also testified to the Select Committee that as soon as it was clear that the Capitol's outer perimeter had been breached, he urged that the President make a statement telling the rioters to go home:

Committee Staff: And so what did you do at that point?

Judd Deere: If I recall, I went back up to [Press Secretary] Kayleigh [McEnany]'s office and indicated that we now likely needed to say something.

Committee Staff: Okay. And why did you think it was necessary to say something?

Deere: Well, I mean, it appears that individuals are storming the U.S. Capitol building. They also appear to be supporters of Donald Trump, who may have been in attendance at the rally. We're going to need to say something.

Committee Staff: And did you have a view as to what should be said by the White House?

Deere: If I recall, I told Kayleigh that I thought that we needed to encourage individuals to stop, to respect law enforcement, and to go home. . . . And it was—it was incumbent upon us to encourage those individuals, should they be supporters of ours, to stop.[479]

Testimony from both Deputy Press Secretary Matthews and White House Counsel Cipollone indicated that it would have been easy, and nearly instantaneous, for Trump to make a public statement insisting that the crowd disperse. As Matthews explained, he could have done so in under a minute:

> . . . it would take probably less than 60 seconds from the Oval Office dining room over to the Press Briefing Room. And, for folks that might not know, the Briefing Room is the room that you see the White House Press Secretary do briefings from with the podium and the blue backdrop. And there is a camera that is on in there at all times. And so, if the President had wanted to make a statement and address the American people, he could have been on camera almost instantly.[480]

Cipollone also shared that assessment:

> Committee Staff: Would it have been possible at any moment for the President to walk down to the podium in the briefing room and talk to the nation at any time between when you first gave him that advice at 2 o'clock and 4:17 when the video statement went out? Would that have been possible?

> Cipollone: Would it have been possible?"

> Committee Staff: Yes.

Cipollone: Yes, it would have been possible.[481]

At 2:13 p.m., rioters broke into the Capitol and flooded the building.[482]

As the violence began to escalate, many Trump supporters and others outside the White House began urgently seeking his intervention. Mark Meadows's phone was flooded with text messages. These are just some of them:

2:32 p.m. from Fox News anchor Laura Ingraham: "Hey Mark, The president needs to tell people in the Capitol to go home." [483]

2:35 p.m. from Mick Mulvaney: "Mark: he needs to stop this, now. Can I do anything to help?" [484]

2:46 p.m. from Rep. William Timmons (R–SC): "The president needs to stop this ASAP" [485]

2:53 p.m. from Donald Trump, Jr.: "He's got to condem [sic] this shit. Asap. The captiol [sic] police tweet is not enough." [486]

3:04 p.m. from Rep. Jeff Duncan (R–SC): "POTUS needs to calm this shit down" [487]

3:09 p.m. from former White House Chief of Staff Reince Priebus: "TELL THEM TO GO HOME !!!" [488]

3:13 p.m. from Alyssa Farah Griffin: "Potus has to come out firmly and tell protestors to dissipate. Someone is going to get killed." [489]

3:15 p.m. from Rep. Chip Roy (R–TX): "Fix this now." [490]

3:31 p.m. from Fox News anchor Sean Hannity: "Can he make a statement. I saw the tweet. Ask people to peacefully leave the capital [sic]" [491]

3:58 p.m. from Fox News anchor Brian Kilmeade: "Please get him on tv. Destroying every thing you guys have accomplished" [492]

Others on Capitol Hill appeared in the media, or otherwise appeared via internet. Representative Mike Gallagher (R–WI) issued a video appealing directly to the President:

Mr. President, you have got to stop this. You are the only person who can call this off. Call it off. The election is over. Call it off![493]

Some Members of Congress sent texts to President Trump's immediate staff or took to Twitter, where they knew the President spent time:

Sen. Bill Cassidy (R–LA) issued a tweet: @realDonaldTrump please appear on TV, condemn the violence and tell people to disband.[494]

Rep. Jaime Herrera Beutler (R—WA) sent a text to Mark Meadows: We need to hear from the president. On TV. I hate that Biden jumped him on it.[495]

Republican Leader Kevin McCarthy tried repeatedly to reach President Trump, and did at least once. He also reached out for help to multiple members of President Trump's family, including Ivanka Trump and Jared Kushner.[496] Kushner characterized Leader McCarthy's demeanor on the call as "scared":

Kushner: I could hear in his voice that he really was nervous, and so, obviously, I took that seriously. And, you know, I didn't know if I'd be able to have any impact, but I said, you know, it's better to at least try. And so I—like I said, I turned the shower off, threw on a suit, and, you know, and rushed into the White House as quickly as I could.

Committee Staff: Yeah. What did he ask you to do? When you say have an impact, what is it specifically that he needed your help with?

Kushner: I don't recall a specific ask, just anything you could do. Again, I got the sense that, you know, they were—they were—you know, they were scared.

Committee Staff: "They" meaning Leader McCarthy and people on the Hill because of the violence?

Kushner: That he was scared, yes.[497]

Kevin McCarthy told Fox News at 3:09 p.m. about his call with the President[498] and elaborated about its contents in a conversation with CBS News's Norah O'Donnell at around 3:30 p.m.:

O'Donnell: Have you spoken with the President and asked him to perhaps come to the Capitol and tell his supporters it's time to leave?

Leader McCarthy: I have spoken to the President. I asked him to talk to the nation and tell them to stop this. . . .

* * *

O'Donnell: The President invited tens of thousands of people to quote unquote stop the steal. I don't know if you heard his more-than-hour-long remarks or the remarks of his son, who was the wind-up. It was some heated stuff, Leader McCarthy. I just wonder whether someone is going to accurately call a spade a spade, and I am giving you the opportunity right now that your precious and beloved United States Capitol and our democracy is witnessing this. Call a spade a spade.

Leader McCarthy: I was very clear with the President when I called him. This has to stop. And he has to, he's gotta go to the American public and tell them to stop this.

\* \* \*

O'Donnell: Leader McCarthy, the President of the United States has a briefing room steps from the Oval Office. It is, the cameras are hot 24/7, as you know. Why hasn't he walked down and said that, now?

Leader McCarthy: I conveyed to the President what I think is best to do, and I'm hopeful the President will do it.[499]

The Committee has evidence from multiple sources regarding the content of Kevin McCarthy's direct conversation with Donald Trump during the violence.

Rep. Jaime Herrera Beutler (R–WA), to whom McCarthy spoke soon after, relayed more of the conversation between McCarthy and President Trump:

And he said [to President Trump], "You have got to get on TV. You've got to get on Twitter. You've got to call these people off." You know what the President said to him? This is as it's happening. He said, "Well Kevin, these aren't my people. You know, these are Antifa. And Kevin responded and said, "No, they're your people. They literally just came through my office windows and my staff are running for cover. I mean they're running for their lives. You need to call them off." And the President's response to Kevin to me was chilling. He said, "Well Kevin, I guess they're just more upset about the election, you know, theft than you are".[500]

Rep. Herrera Beutler's account of the incident was also corroborated by former Acting White House Chief of Staff Mick Mulvaney, who testified that Leader McCarthy told him several days later that President Trump had said during their call: "Kevin, maybe these people are just more angry about this than you are. Maybe they're more upset." [501]

Mulvaney was also trying to reach administration officials to urge President Trump to instruct his supporters to leave the Capitol.[502] As were many elected officials in both parties, including Nancy Pelosi and Chuck Schumer, and several Republican Members of Congress.[503]

As already noted, Cipollone and others in the White House repeatedly urged President Trump to tell his supporters to leave the Capitol. Cipollone described his conversations with Meadows after they failed to convince President Trump to deliver the necessary message:

> Committee Staff: Do you remember any discussion with Mark Meadows with respect to his view that the President didn't want to do anything or was somehow resistant to wanting to say something along the lines that you suggested.
>
> Pat Cipollone: Not just—just to be clear, many people suggested it.
>
> Committee Staff: Yeah.
>
> Cipollone: Not just me. Many people felt the same way. I'm sure I had conversations with Mark about this during the course of the day and expressed my opinion very forcefully that this needs to be done.[504]

* * *

> Committee Staff: So your advice was tell people to leave the Capitol, and that took over 2 hours when there were subsequent statements made, tweets put forth, that in your view were insufficient. Did you continue, Mr. Cipollone, throughout the period of time up until 4:17, continue, you and others, to push for a stronger statement?
>
> Cipollone: Yes.[505]

* * *

> Committee Staff: . . . at the onset of the violence when you first notice on television or wherever that rioters have actually breached the Capitol, did you have a conversation with Mark Meadows in which Meadows indicated he doesn't want to do anything, "he" meaning the President?
>
> Cipollone: I don't—I had a conversation I'm sure with Mark Meadows, I'm sure with other people, of what I thought should be done. Did Mark say that to me? I don't have a recollection of him saying that to me, but he may have said something along the lines.[506]

At 2:16 p.m., security records indicate that the Vice President was "being pulled" to a safer location.[507]

In an interview with the Select Committee, a White House Security Official on duty at the White House explained his observations as he listened to Secret Service communications and made contemporaneous entries into a security log. In particular, he explained an entry he made at 2:24 p.m.:

> Committee Staff: Ok. That last entry on this page is: "Service at the Capitol does not sound good right now."

Official: Correct.

Committee Staff: What does that mean?

Official: The members of the VP detail at this time were starting to fear for their own lives. There were a lot of—there was a lot of yelling, a lot of—I don't know—a lot [of] very personal calls over the radio. So—it was disturbing. I don't like talking about it, but there were calls to say good-bye to family members, so on and so forth. It was getting—for whatever the reason was on the ground, the VP detail thought that this was about to get very ugly.

Committee Staff: And did you hear that over the radio?

Official: Correct.

. . .

Committee Staff: ... obviously, you've conveyed that's disturbing, but what prompted you to put it into an entry as it states there, "Service at the Capitol—"

Official: That they're running out of options, and they're getting nervous. It sounds like that we came very close to either Service having to use lethal options or worse. At that point, I don't know. Is the VP compromised? Is the detail—like, I don't know. Like, we didn't have visibility, but it doesn't—if they're screaming and saying things, like, say good-bye to the family, like, the floor needs to know this is going to a whole another level soon.[508]

Also at 2:24 p.m., knowing the riot was underway and that Vice President Pence was at the Capitol, President Trump sent this tweet:

Mike Pence didn't have the courage to do what should have been done to protect our Country and our Constitution, giving States a chance to certify a corrected set of facts, not the fraudulent or inaccurate ones which they were asked to previously certify. USA demands the truth![509]

Evidence shows that the 2:24 p.m. tweet immediately precipitated further violence at the Capitol. Immediately after this tweet, the crowds both inside and outside of the Capitol building violently surged forward.[510] Outside the building, within ten minutes thousands of rioters overran the line on the west side of the Capitol that was being held by the Metropolitan Police Force's Civil Disturbance Unit, the first time in history of the DC Metro Police that such a security line had ever been broken.[511]

Virtually everyone on the White House staff the Select Committee interviewed condemned the 2:24 p.m. tweet in the strongest terms.

Police officers attempt to clear rioters inside the Capitol building.
(Photo by Brent Stirton/Getty Images)

Deputy National Security Adviser Matthew Pottinger told the Select Committee that the 2:24 p.m. tweet was so destructive that it convinced him to resign as soon as possible:

One of my aides handed me a sheet of paper that contained the tweet that you just read. I read it and was quite disturbed by it. I was disturbed and worried to see that the President was attacking Vice President Pence for doing his constitutional duty.

So the tweet looked to me like the opposite of what we really needed at that moment, which was a de-escalation. And that is why I had said earlier that it looked like fuel being poured on the fire.

So that was the moment that I decided that I was going to resign, that that would be my last day at the White House. I simply didn't want to be associated with the events with the events that were unfolding at the Capitol.[512]

Deputy Press Secretary Sarah Matthews had a similar reaction:

So it was obvious that the situation at the Capitol was violent and escalating quickly. And so I thought that the tweet about the Vice President was the last thing that was needed in that moment.

And I remember thinking that this was going to be bad for him to tweet this, because it was essentially him giving the green light to these people, telling them that what they were doing at the steps of the Capitol and entering the Capitol was okay, that they were justified in their anger.

And he shouldn't have been doing that. He should have been telling these people to go home and to leave and to condemn the violence that we were seeing.

And I am someone who has worked with him, you know, I worked on the campaign, traveled all around the country, going to countless rallies with him, and I have seen the impact that his words have on his supporters. They truly latch onto every word and every tweet that he says.

And so, I think that in that moment for him to tweet out the message about Mike Pence, it was him pouring gasoline on the fire and making it much worse.[513]

Deputy Press Secretary Judd Deere stated the following:

Committee Staff: What was your reaction when you saw that tweet?

Deere: Extremely unhelpful.

Committee Staff: Why?

Deere: It wasn't the message that we needed at that time. It wasn't going to—the scenes at the U.S. Capitol were only getting worse at that point. This was not going to help that.[514]

White House Counsel Pat Cipollone told the Select Committee, "I don't remember when exactly I heard about that tweet, but my reaction to it is that's a terrible tweet, and I disagreed with the sentiment. And I thought it was wrong." [515]

Likewise, Counselor to the President Hope Hicks texted a colleague that evening: "Attacking the VP? Wtf is wrong with him."[516]

At 2:26 p.m., Vice President Pence was again moved to a different location.[517]

President Trump had the TV on in the dining room.[518] At 2:38 p.m., Fox News was showing video of the chaos and attack, with tear gas filling the air in the Capitol Rotunda. And a newscaster reported, "[T]his is a very dangerous situation." [519] This is the context in which Trump sent the tweet.

Testimony obtained by the Committee indicates that President Trump knew about the rioters' anger at Vice President Pence and indicated something to the effect that the Vice President "deserves it." [520] As Cassidy Hutchinson explained:

I remember Pat saying something to the effect of, "Mark, we need to do something more. They're literally calling for the Vice President to be f'ing hung." And Mark had responded something to the effect of, "You heard him, Pat. He thinks Mike deserves it. He doesn't think they're doing anything wrong." To which Pat said something, "[t]his is f'ing crazy, we need to be doing something more," briefly stepped into Mark's office, and when Mark had said something—when Mark had said something to the effect of, "He doesn't think they're doing anything wrong," knowing what I had heard briefly in the dining room coupled with Pat discussing the hanging Mike Pence chants in the lobby of our office and then Mark's response, I understood "they're" to be the rioters in the Capitol that were chanting for the Vice President to be hung. [521]

Although White House Counsel Pat Cipollone was limited in what he would discuss because of privilege concerns, he stated the following:

Committee Staff: Do you remember any discussion at any point during the day about rioters at the Capitol chanting 'hang Mike Pence?'

Cipollone: Yes. I remember—I remember hearing that—about that. Yes.

Committee Staff: Yeah. And—

Cipollone: I don't know if I observed that myself on TV. I don't remember.

Committee Staff: I'm just curious, I understand the privilege line you've drawn, but do you remember what you can share with us about the discussion about those chants, the 'hang Mike Pence' chants?

Cipollone: I could tell you my view of that.

Committee Staff: Yeah. Please.

Cipollone: My view of that is that is outrageous.

Committee Staff: Uh-huh.

Cipollone: And for anyone to suggest such a thing as the Vice President of the United States, for people in that crowd to be chanting that I thought was terrible. I thought it was outrageous and wrong. And I expressed that very clearly to people.[522]

Almost immediately after the 2:24 p.m. tweet, Eric Herschmann went upstairs in the West Wing to try to enlist Ivanka Trump's assistance to persuade her father to do the right thing.[523] Ivanka rushed down to the Oval Office dining room. Although no one could convince President Trump to call for the violent rioters to leave the Capitol, Ivanka persuaded President Trump that a tweet could be issued to discourage violence against the police.

At 2:38 p.m., President Trump sent this tweet:

"Please support our Capitol Police and Law Enforcement. They are truly on the side of our Country. Stay peaceful!"[524]

While some in the meeting invoked executive privilege, or failed to recall the specifics, others told us what happened at that point. Sarah Matthews, the White House Deputy Press Secretary, had urged her boss, Kayleigh McEnany, to have the President make a stronger statement. But she informed us that President Trump resisted using the word "peaceful" in his message:

Committee Staff: Ms. Matthews, Ms. McEnany told us she came right back to the press office after meeting with the President about this particular tweet. What did she tell you about what happened in that dining room?

Sarah Matthews: When she got back, she told me that a tweet had been sent out. And I told her that I thought the tweet did not go far enough, that I thought there needed to be a call to action and he needed to condemn the violence. And we were in a room full of people, but people weren't paying attention. And so, she looked directly at me and in a hushed tone shared with me that the President did not want to include any sort of mention of peace in that tweet and that it took some convincing on their part, those who were in the room. And she said that there was a back and forth going over different phrases to find something that he was comfortable with. And it wasn't until Ivanka Trump suggested the phrase 'stay peaceful' that he finally agreed to include it.[525]

At 3:13 p.m., President Trump sent another tweet, but again declined to tell people to go home:

"I am asking for everyone at the U.S. Capitol to remain peaceful. No violence! Remember, WE are the Party of Law & Order—respect the Law and our great men and women in Blue. Thank you!"[526]

Almost everyone, including staff in the White House also found the President's 2:38 p.m. and 3:13 p.m. tweets to be insufficient because they did not instruct the rioters to leave the Capitol. As mentioned, President Trump's son, Donald Trump Jr., texted Meadows:

He's got to condem [sic] this shit. Asap. The captiol [sic] police tweet is not enough. [527]

Sean Hannity also texted Mark Meadows:

Can he make a statement. I saw the tweet. Ask people to peacefully leave the capital [sic].[528]

None of these efforts resulted in President Trump immediately issuing the message that was needed. White House staff had these comments:

Pottinger: Yeah. It was insufficient. I think what—you could count me among those who was hoping to see an unequivocal strong statement clearing out the Capitol, telling people to stand down, leave, go home. I think that's what we were hoping for.[529]

. . .

Matthews: Yeah. So a conversation started in the press office after the President sent out those two tweets that I deemed were insufficient. . . . I thought that we should condemn the violence and condemn it unequivocally. And I thought that he needed to include a call to action and to tell these people to go home.[530]

And they were right. Evidence showed that neither of these tweets had any appreciable impact on the violent rioters. Unlike the video-message tweet that did not come until 4:17 finally instructing rioters to leave, neither the 2:38 nor the 3:13 tweets made any difference.

At some point after 3:05 p.m. that afternoon, President Trump's Chief of Staff—and President Trump himself—were informed that someone had been shot.[531] That person was Ashli Babbitt, who was fatally shot at 2:44 p.m. as she and other rioters tried to gain access to the House chamber.[532] There is no indication that this affected the President's state of mind that day, and we found no evidence that the President expressed any remorse that day.

Meanwhile, leaders in Congress—including Speaker Pelosi, Senator Schumer, Senator McConnell—and the Vice President, were taking action. They called the Secretary of Defense, the Attorney General, governors and officials in Virginia, Maryland, and the District of Columbia, begging for assistance.[533]

President-elect Biden also broadcast a video calling on President Trump to take action:

I call on President Trump to go on national television now to fulfill his oath and defend the Constitution and demand an end to this siege.[534]

President Trump could have done this, of course, anytime after he learned of the violence at the Capitol. At 4:17 p.m., 187 minutes after finishing his speech (and even longer after the attack began), President Trump finally broadcast a video message in which he asked those attacking the Capitol to leave:

I know your pain. I know you're hurt. We had an election that was stolen from us. It was a landslide election, and everyone knows it, especially the other side, but you have to go home now. We have to have peace. [535]

President Trump's Deputy Press Secretary, Sarah Matthews testified about her reaction to this video message:

[H]e told the people who we had just watched storm our nation's Capitol with the intent on overthrowing our democracy, violently attack police officers, and chant heinous things like, "Hang Mike Pence," "We love you. You're very special." As a spokesperson for him, I knew that I would be asked to defend that. And to me, his refusal to act and call off the mob that day and his refusal to condemn the violence was indefensible. And so, I knew that I would be resigning that evening. [536]

By this time, the National Guard and other additional law enforcement had begun to arrive in force and started to turn the tide of the violence. Many of those attackers in the Capitol saw or received word of President Trump's 4:17 p.m. message, and they understood this message as an instruction to leave:[537]

- Stephen Ayres testified in front of the Select Committee that: "Well, we were there. As soon as that come out, everybody started talking about it, and it seemed like it started to disperse, you know, some of the crowd. Obviously, you know, once we got back to the hotel room, we seen that it was still going on, but it definitely dispersed a lot of the crowd." [538]
- Jacob Chansley, also known as the QAnon-Shaman answered President Trump's directive: "I'm here delivering the President's message. Donald Trump has asked everybody to go home." Another responded to Chansley: "That's our order." [539]
- Other unknown individuals also listened to President Trump's message while outside the Capitol, and responded: "He says, go home. He says, go home." And "Yeah. Here. He said to go home." [540]

At 6:01 p.m., President Trump sent his last tweet of the day, not condemning the violence, but instead attempting to justify it:

These are the things and events that happen when a sacred election landslide victory is so unceremoniously & viciously stripped away from great patriots who have been badly & unfairly treated for so long. Go home with love & in peace. Remember this day forever![541]

Staff in President Trump's own White House and campaign had a strong reaction to this message:

Sarah Matthews: At that point I had already made the decision to resign and this tweet just further cemented my decision. I thought that January 6, 2021, was one of the darkest days in our Nation's history and President Trump was treating it as a celebratory occasion with that tweet. And so, it just further cemented my decision to resign.[542]

Tim Murtaugh: I don't think it's a patriotic act to attack the Capitol. But I have no idea how to characterize the people other than they trespassed, destroyed property, and assaulted the U.S. Capitol. I think calling them patriots is a, let's say, a stretch, to say the least. . . . I don't think it's a patriotic act to attack the U.S. Capitol.[543]

Pat Cipollone: [W]hat happened at the Capitol cannot be justified in any form or fashion. It was wrong, and it was tragic. And a lot—and it was a terrible day. It was a terrible day for this country.[544]

Greg Jacob: I thought it was inappropriate. . . . To my mind, it was a day that should live in infamy.[545]

At 6:27 p.m., President Trump retired to his residence for the night. As he did, he had one final comment to an employee who accompanied him to the residence. The one takeaway that the President expressed in that moment, following a horrific afternoon of violence and the worst attack against the U.S. Capitol building in over two centuries, was this: "Mike Pence let me down."[546]

President Trump's inner circle was still trying to delay the counting of electoral votes into the evening, even after the violence had been quelled. Rudolph Giuliani tried calling numerous Members of Congress in the hour before the joint session resumed, including Rep. Jim Jordan (R–OH) and Senators Marsha Blackburn (R–TN), Tommy Tuberville (R–AL), Bill Hagerty (R–TN), Lindsey Graham (R–SC), Josh Hawley (R–MO), and Ted Cruz (R–TX).[547] His voicemail intended for Senator Tuberville at 7:02 p.m. that evening eventually was made public:

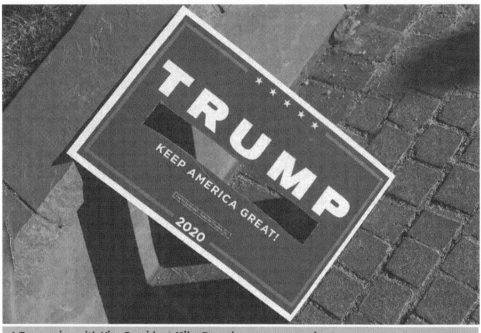

A Trump sign with Vice President Mike Pence's name removed.
(Photo by Michael Ciaglo/Getty Images)

Guiliani: Sen. Tuberville? Or I should say Coach Tuberville. This is Rudy Guiliani, the President's lawyer. I'm calling you because I want to discuss with you how they're trying to rush this hearing and how we need you, our Republican friends, to try to just slow it down so we can get these legislatures to get more information to you.[548]

Reflecting on President Trump's conduct that day, Vice President Pence noted that President Trump "had made no effort to contact me in the midst of the rioting or any point afterward."[549] He wrote that President Trump's "reckless words had endangered my family and all those serving at the Capitol."[550]

President Trump did not contact a single top national security official during the day. Not at the Pentagon, nor at the Department of Homeland Security, the Department of Justice, the F.B.I., the Capitol Police Department, or the D.C. Mayor's office.[551] As Vice President Pence has confirmed, President Trump didn't even try to reach his own Vice President to make sure that Pence was safe.[552] President Trump did not order any of his staff to facilitate a law enforcement response of any sort.[553] His Chairman of the Joint Chiefs of Staff—who is by statute the primary military advisor to the President—had this reaction:

General Milley: You know, you're the Commander in Chief. You've got an assault going on on the Capitol of the United States of America. And there's nothing? No call? Nothing? Zero?[554]

General Milley did, however, receive a call from President Trump's Chief of Staff Mark Meadows that day. Here is how he described that call:

He said, "We have to kill the narrative that the Vice President is making all the decisions. We need to establish the narrative, you know, that the President is still in charge and that things are steady or stable," or words to that effect. I immediately interpreted that as politics, politics, politics. Red flag for me, personally. No action. But I remember it distinctly. And I don't do political narratives.[555]

Some have suggested that President Trump gave an order to have 10,000 troops ready for January 6th.[556] The Select Committee found no evidence of this. In fact, President Trump's Acting Secretary of Defense Christopher Miller directly refuted this when he testified under oath:

Committee Staff: To be crystal clear, there was no direct order from President Trump to put 10,000 troops to be on the ready for January 6th, correct?

Miller: No. Yeah. That's correct. There was no direct—there was no order from the President.[557]

Later, on the evening of January 6th, President Trump's former campaign manager, Brad Parscale, texted Katrina Pierson, one of President Trump's rally organizers, that the events of the day were the result of a "sitting president asking for civil war" and that "This week I feel guilty for helping him win" now that ". . . a woman is dead." Pierson answered: "You do realize this was going to happen." Parscale replied: "Yeah. If I was Trump and knew my rhetoric killed someone." "It wasn't the rhetoric," Pierson suggested. But Parscale insisted: "Yes it was."[558]

### THE IMMEDIATE AFTERMATH OF JANUARY 6TH

In days following January 6th, President Trump's family and staff attempted repeatedly to persuade him not to repeat his election fraud allegations, to concede defeat, and to allow the transition to President Biden to proceed. Trump did make two video recordings, which initially appeared contrite. But evidence suggests that these statements were designed at least in part to ward off other potential consequences of January 6th, such as invocation of the 25th Amendment or impeachment.

In fact, Minority Leader Kevin McCarthy indicated after the attack, in a discussion with House Republican leaders, that he would ask President Trump to resign:

Rep. Cheney: I guess there's a question when we were talking about the 25th Amendment resolution, and you asked what would happen after he's gone? Is there any chance? Are you hearing that he might resign? Is there any reason to think that might happen?

Leader McCarthy: I've had a few discussions. My gut tells me no. I'm seriously thinking of having that discussion with him tonight. I haven't talked to him in a couple of days. From what I know of him, I mean, you guys all know him too, do you think he'd ever back away? But what I think I'm going to do is I'm going to call him. This is what I think. We know [the 25th Amendment resolution] will pass the House. I think there's a chance it will pass the Senate, even when he's gone. And I think there's a lot of different ramifications for that. . . . Again, the only discussion I would have with him is that I think this will pass, and it would be my recommendation you should resign.[559]

Before January 6th, Fox News personality Sean Hannity warned that January 6th could be disastrous:

Dec. 31, 2020 text from Sean Hannity to Mark Meadows: "We can't lose the entire WH counsels office. I do NOT see January 6 happening the way he is being told. After the 6 th [sic]. He should announce will lead the nationwide effort to reform voting integrity. Go to Fl and watch Joe mess up daily. Stay engaged. When he speaks people will listen." [560]

January 5, 2021 texts from Sean Hannity to Mark Meadows:

"Im very worried about the next 48 hours"

"Pence pressure. WH counsel will leave."

"Sorry, I can't talk right now."

"On with boss"[561]

A member of the Republican Freedom caucus also warned, on December 31, 2020, and on January 1, 2021:

The President should call everyone off. It's the only path. If we substitute the will of states through electors with a vote by Congress every 4 years . . . we have destroyed the electoral college . . . Respectfully.[562] If POTUS allows this to occur . . . we're driving a stake in the heart of the federal republic . . . [563]

After January 6th, Hannity worked to persuade President Trump to stop talking about election fraud, proposed that Trump pardon Hunter Biden, and discussed attending the Inauguration:

1. No more stolen election talk.
2. Yes, impeachment and 25th amendment are real, and many people will quit.
3. He was intrigued by the Pardon idea!! (Hunter)
4. Resistant but listened to Pence thoughts, to make it right.
5. Seemed to like attending Inauguration talk.[564]

Ultimately, President Trump took little of the advice from Hannity and his White House staff. A few days later, Hannity wrote again to Meadows and Jim Jordan:

Guys, we have a clear path to land the plane in 9 days. He can't mention the election again. Ever. I did not have a good call with him today. And worse, I'm not sure what is left to do or say, and I don t like not knowing if it's truly understood. Ideas?[565]

Likewise, despite her many contrary public statements, Republican Congresswoman Marjorie Taylor Greene privately texted her concerns on January 6th about a continuing and real threat of violence.

Mark I was just told there is an active shooter on the first floor of the Capitol Please tell the President to calm people This isn't the way to solve anything[566]

Donald Trump was impeached on January 13th. In a speech that day, Republican Leader Kevin McCarthy made this statement from the House floor, but voted against impeachment:

The President bears responsibility for Wednesday's attack on Congress by mob rioters. He should have immediately denounced the mob when he saw what was unfolding. These facts require immediate action by President Trump, accept his share of responsibility, quell the brewing unrest and ensure President-elect Biden is able to successfully begin his term. The President's immediate action also deserves congressional action, which is why I think a fact-finding commission and a censure resolution would be prudent.[567]

Later, McCarthy told members of the House Republican conference that Trump had acknowledged that he was at least partially responsible for the January 6th attack.

Kevin McCarthy speaks at a press conference at the Capitol building on August 27, 2021.
(Photo by Anna Moneymaker/Getty Images)

I asked him personally today, does he hold responsibility for what happened? Does he feel bad about what happened? He told me he does have some responsibility for what happened. And he need to acknowledge that.[568]

Since January 6th, President Trump has continued to claim falsely that the 2020 Presidential election was stolen. Not only that, he has urged other politicians to push this argument as well. Representative Mo Brooks has issued a public statement appearing to represent Trump's private views and intentions:

President Trump asked me to rescind the 2020 elections, immediately remove Joe Biden from the White House, immediately put President Trump back in the White House, and hold a new special election for the presidency.[569]

## REFERRALS TO THE U.S. DEPARTMENT OF JUSTICE SPECIAL COUNSEL AND HOUSE ETHICS COMMITTEE

The Committee's work has produced a substantial body of new information. We know far more about the President's plans and actions to overturn the election than almost all Members of Congress did when President Trump was impeached on January 13, 2021, or when he was tried by the Senate in February of that year. Fifty-seven of 100 Senators voted to convict President Trump at that time, and more than 20 others condemned the President's conduct and said they were voting against conviction because the President's term had already expired.[570] At the time, the Republican Leader of the U.S. Senate said this about Donald Trump: "A mob was assaulting the Capitol in his name. These criminals were carrying his banners, hanging his flags, and screaming their loyalty to him. It was obvious that only President Trump could end this. He was the only one who could."[571] House Republican Leader Kevin McCarthy, who spoke directly with President Trump during the violence of January 6th, expressed similar views both in private and in public. Privately, Leader McCarthy stated: "But let me be very clear to you and I have been very clear to the President. He bears responsibility for his words and actions. No if, ands or buts."[572] In public, Leader McCarthy concluded: "The President bears responsibility for Wednesday's attack on Congress by mob rioters."[573]

Today we know that the planning to overturn the election on January 6th was substantially more extensive, and involved many other players, and many other efforts over a longer time period. Indeed, the violent attack and invasion of the Capitol, and what provoked it, are only a part of the story.

From the outset of its hearings, the Committee has explained that President Trump and a number of other individuals made a series of very specific plans, ultimately with multiple separate elements, but all with one overriding objective: to corruptly obstruct, impede, or influence the counting of electoral votes on January 6th, and thereby overturn the lawful results of the election. The underlying and fundamental feature of that planning was the effort to get one man, Vice President Mike Pence, to assert and then exercise unprecedented and lawless powers to unilaterally alter the actual election outcome on January 6th. Evidence obtained by the Committee demonstrates that John Eastman, who worked with President Trump to put that and other elements of the plan in place, knew even before the 2020 Presidential election that Vice President Pence could not lawfully refuse to count official, certified electoral slates submitted by the Governors of the States.[574] Testimony and contemporaneous documentary evidence also indicate that President Trump knew that the plan was unlawful before January 6th.[575] When the Vice President's counsel wrote to Eastman on January 6th to ask whether the latter had informed the President that the Vice President did not have authority to decide the election unilaterally, Eastman responded: "He's been so advised," and added, "[b]ut you know him—once he gets something in his head, it is hard to get him to change course."[576]

Many of the other elements of President Trump's plans were specifically designed to create a set of circumstances on January 6th to assist President Trump in overturning the lawful election outcome during Congress's joint session that day. For example, President Trump pressured State legislatures to adopt new electoral slates that Vice President Pence could, unlawfully, count. Trump solicited State officials to "find" a sufficient number of votes to alter the final count, and instructed the Department of Justice to "just say that the election was was [sic] corrupt + leave the rest to me and the R[epublican] Congressmen." [577] President Trump offered the job of Acting Attorney General to Jeffrey Clark. As our evidence has unequivocally demonstrated, Clark intended to use that position to send a series of letters from the Department of Justice to multiple States falsely asserting that the Department had found fraud and urging those States to convene their legislatures to alter their official electoral slates.[578] And President Trump, with the help of the Republican National Committee and others, oversaw an effort to create and transmit to Government officials a series of intentionally false electoral slates for Vice President Pence to utilize on January 6th to alter or delay the count of lawful votes.[579]

Of course, other elements of the plan complemented these efforts too. As this Report documents, President Trump was advised by his own experts and the Justice Department that his election fraud allegations were false, and he knew he had lost virtually all the legal challenges to the election, but he nevertheless engaged in a successful but fraudulent effort to persuade tens of millions of Americans that the election was stolen from him. This effort was designed to convince Americans that President Trump's actions to overturn the election were justified. President Trump then urged his supporters to travel to Washington on January 6th to apply pressure to Congress to halt the count and change the election outcome, explaining to those who were coming to Washington that they needed to "take back" their country and "stop the steal." [580]

It is helpful in understanding these facts to focus on specific moments in time when President Trump made corrupt, dishonest, and unlawful choices to pursue his plans. For example, by December 14th when the electoral college met and certified Joe Biden's victory, President Trump knew that he had failed in all the relevant litigation; he had been advised by his own experts and the Justice Department that his election fraud claims were false; and he had been told by numerous advisors that he had lost and should concede. But despite his duty as President to take care that the laws are faithfully executed, he chose instead to ignore all of the judicial rulings and the facts before him and push forward to overturn the election. Likewise, in the days and hours before the violence of January 6th, President Trump knew that no State had issued any changed electoral slate. Indeed, neither President Trump nor his co-conspirators had any evidence that any majority of any State legislature was willing to do so. President Trump also knew that Vice President Pence could not lawfully refuse to count legitimate votes. Despite all of these facts, President Trump nevertheless proceeded to instruct Vice President Pence to execute a plan he already knew was illegal. And then knowing that a violent riot was underway, President Trump breached his oath of office; our Commander in Chief refused for hours to take the one simple step that his advisors were begging him to take—to instruct his supporters to disperse, stand down, and leave the Capitol. Instead, fully understanding what had unfolded at the Capitol, President Trump exacerbated the violence with a tweet attacking Vice President Pence.[581] Any rational person who had watched the events that day knew that President Trump's 2:24 p.m. tweet would lead to further violence. It did. And, at almost exactly the same time, President Trump continued to lobby Congress to delay the electoral count.

As the evidence demonstrates, the rioters at the Capitol had invaded the building and halted the electoral count. They did not begin to relent until President Trump finally issued a video statement instructing his supporters to leave the Capitol at 4:17 p.m., which had an immediate and helpful effect: rioters began to disperse[582]—but not before the Capitol was invaded, the election count was halted, feces were smeared in the Capitol, the Vice President and his family and many others were put in danger, and more than 140 law enforcement officers were attacked and seriously injured by mob rioters. Even if it were true that President Trump genuinely believed the election was stolen, *this is no defense*. No President can ignore the courts and purposely violate the law no matter what supposed "justification" he or she presents.

These conclusions are not the Committee's alone. In the course of its investigation, the Committee had occasion to present evidence to Federal District Court Judge David Carter, who weighed that evidence against submissions from President Trump's lawyer, John Eastman. Judge Carter considered this evidence in the context of a discovery dispute—specifically whether the Committee could obtain certain of Eastman's documents pursuant to the "crime-fraud" exception to the attorney-client privilege. That exception provides that otherwise privileged documents may lose their privilege if they were part of an effort to commit a crime or a fraud, in this case by President Trump. Judge Carter set out his factual findings, discussing multiple elements of President Trump's multi-part plan to overturn the election,[583] and then addressed whether the evidence, including Eastman's email communications, demonstrated that Trump and Eastman committed crimes. "Based on the evidence," Judge Carter explained, "the Court finds it more likely than not that President Trump corruptly attempted to obstruct the Joint Session of Congress on January 6, 2021," and "more likely than not that President Trump and Dr. Eastman dishonestly conspired to obstruct the Joint Session of Congress on January 6th." [584] Judge Carter also concluded that President Trump's and Eastman's "pressure campaign to stop the electoral count did not end with Vice President Pence—it targeted every tier of federal and state elected officials" [585] and was "a coup in search of a legal theory." [586] "The plan spurred violent attacks on the seat of our nation's government," Judge Carter wrote, and it threatened to "permanently end[] the peaceful transition of power. . . ." [587]

The U.S. Department of Justice has been investigating and prosecuting persons who invaded the Capitol, engaged in violence, and planned violence on that day. The Department has charged more than 900 individuals, and nearly 500 have already been convicted or pleaded guilty as we write. [588] As the Committee's investigation progressed through its hearings, public reporting emerged suggesting that the Department of Justice had also begun to investigate several others specifically involved in the events being examined by the Committee. Such reports indicated that search warrants had been issued, based on findings of probable cause, for the cell phones of John Eastman, Jeffrey Clark, and Representative Scott Perry. [589] Other reports suggested that the Department had empaneled one or more grand juries and was pursuing a ruling compelling several of this Committee's witnesses, including Pat Cipollone and Greg Jacob, to give testimony on topics for which President Trump had apparently asserted executive privilege. Recent reporting suggests that a Federal district court judge has now rejected President Trump's executive privilege claims in that context. [590]

Criminal referrals from a congressional committee are often made in circumstances where prosecutors are not yet known to be pursuing some of the same facts and evidence. That is not the case here. During the course of our investigation, both the U.S. Department of Justice and at least one local prosecutor's office (Fulton County, Georgia) have been actively conducting criminal investigations concurrently with this congressional investigation. [591] In fact, the U.S. Department of Justice has recently taken the extraordinary step of appointing a Special Counsel to investigate the former President's conduct. [592]

The Committee recognizes that the Department of Justice and other prosecutorial authorities may be in a position to utilize investigative tools, including search warrants and grand juries, superior to the means the Committee has for obtaining relevant information and testimony. Indeed, both the Department of Justice and the Fulton County District Attorney may now have access to witness testimony and records that have been unavailable to the Committee, including testimony from President Trump's Chief of Staff Mark Meadows, and others who either asserted privileges or invoked their Fifth Amendment rights.[593] The Department may also be able to access, via grand jury subpoena or otherwise, the testimony of Republican Leader Kevin McCarthy, Representative Scott Perry, Representative Jim Jordan and others, each of whom appears to have had materially relevant communications with Donald Trump or others in the White House but who failed to comply with the Select Committee's subpoenas.

Taking all of these facts into account, and based on the breadth of the evidence it has accumulated, the Committee makes the following criminal referrals to the Department of Justice's Special Counsel.

### I. Obstruction of an Official Proceeding (18 U.S.C. § 1512(c))

Section 1512(c)(2) of Title 18 of the United States Code makes it a crime to "corruptly" "obstruct[], influence[], or impede[] any official proceeding, or attempt[] to do so."[594] Sufficient evidence exists of one or more potential violations of this statute for a criminal referral of President Trump and others.[595]

*First*, there should be no question that Congress's joint session to count electoral votes on January 6th was an "official proceeding" under section 1512(c). Many Federal judges have already reached that specific conclusion.[596]

*Second*, there should be no doubt that President Trump knew that his actions were likely to "obstruct, influence or impede" that proceeding. Based on the evidence developed, President Trump was attempting to prevent or delay the counting of lawful certified electoral college votes from multiple States.[597] President Trump was directly and personally involved in this effort, personally pressuring Vice President Pence relentlessly as the joint session on January 6th approached.[598]

*Third*, President Trump acted with a "corrupt" purpose. Vice President Pence, Greg Jacob, and others repeatedly told the President that the Vice President had no unilateral authority to prevent certification of the election.[599] Indeed, in an email exchange during the violence of January 6th, Eastman admitted that President Trump had been "advised" that Vice President Pence could not lawfully refuse to count votes under the Electoral Count Act, but "once he gets something in his head, it's hard to get him to change course."[600] In addition, President Trump knew that he had lost dozens of State and Federal lawsuits, and that the Justice Department, his campaign and his other advisors concluded that there was insufficient fraud to alter the outcome. President Trump also knew that no majority of any State legislature had taken or manifested any intention to take any official action that could change a State's electoral college votes.[601] But President Trump pushed forward anyway. As Judge Carter explained, "[b]ecause

President Trump likely knew that the plan to disrupt the electoral count was wrongful, his mindset exceeds the threshold for acting 'corruptly' under § 1512(c)."[602]

Sufficient evidence exists of one or more potential violations of 18 U.S.C. § 1512(c) for a criminal referral of President Trump based solely on his plan to get Vice President Pence to prevent certification of the election at the joint session of Congress. Those facts standing alone are sufficient. But such a charge under that statute can also be based on the plan to create and transmit to the executive and legislative branches fraudulent electoral slates, which were ultimately intended to facilitate an unlawful action by Vice President Pence, to refuse to count legitimate, certified electoral votes during Congress's official January 6th proceeding.[603] Additionally, evidence developed about the many other elements of President Trump's plans to overturn the election, including soliciting State legislatures, State officials, and others to alter official electoral outcomes, provides further evidence that President Trump was attempting through multiple means to corruptly obstruct, impede, or influence the counting of electoral votes on January 6th. This is also true of President Trump's personal directive to the Department of Justice to "just say that the election was was [sic] corrupt + leave the rest to me and the R[epublican] Congressmen."[604]

We also stress in particular the draft letter to the Georgia legislature authored by Jeffrey Clark and another Trump political appointee at the Department of Justice. The draft letter embraces many of the same theories that John Eastman and others were asserting in President Trump's effort to lobby State legislatures. White House Counsel Pat Cipollone described that letter as "a murder-suicide pact," and other White House and Justice Department officials offered similar descriptions.[605] As described herein, that draft letter was intended to help persuade a State legislature to change its certified slate of electoral college electors based on false allegations of fraud, so Vice President Pence could unilaterally and unlawfully decide to count a different slate on January 6th.[606] The letter was transparently false, improper, and illegal. President Trump had multiple communications with Clark in the days before January 6th, and there is no basis to doubt that President Trump offered Clark the position of Acting Attorney General knowing that Clark would send the letter and others like it.[607]

Of course, President Trump is also responsible for recruiting tens of thousands of his supporters to Washington for January 6th, and knowing they were angry and some were armed, instructing them to march to the Capitol and "fight like hell."[608] And then, while knowing a violent riot was underway, he refused for multiple hours to take the single step his advisors and supporters were begging him to take to halt the violence: to make a public statement instructing his supporters to disperse and leave the Capitol.[609] Through action and inaction, President Trump corruptly obstructed, delayed, and impeded the vote count.

In addition, the Committee believes sufficient evidence exists for a criminal referral of John Eastman and certain other Trump associates under 18 U.S.C. §1512(c). The evidence shows that Eastman knew in advance of the 2020 election that Vice President Pence could not refuse to count electoral votes on January 6th.[610] In the days before January 6th, Eastman was warned repeatedly that his plan was illegal and "completely crazy," and would "cause riots in the streets."[611] Nonetheless, Eastman continued to assist President Trump's pressure campaign in public and in private, including in meetings with the Vice President and in his own speech at the Ellipse on January 6th. And even as the violence was playing out at the Capitol, Eastman admitted in writing that his plan violated the law but pressed for Pence to do it anyway.[612] In the immediate aftermath of January 6th, White House lawyer Eric Herschmann told Eastman that he should "[g]et a great F'ing criminal defense lawyer, you're going to need it."[613] Others working with Eastman likely share in Eastman's culpability. For example, Kenneth Chesebro was a central player in the scheme to submit fake electors to the Congress and the National Archives.

The Committee notes that multiple Republican Members of Congress, including Representative Scott Perry, likely have material facts regarding President Trump's plans to overturn the election. For example, many Members of Congress attended a White House meeting on December 21, 2020, in which the plan to have the Vice President affect the outcome of the election was disclosed and discussed. Evidence indicates that certain of those Members unsuccessfully sought Presidential pardons from President Trump after January 6th,[614] as did Eastman,[615] revealing their own clear consciousness of guilt.

### II. Conspiracy to Defraud the United States (18 U.S.C. § 371)

Section 371 of Title 18 of the U.S. Code provides that "[i]f two or more persons conspire either to commit any offense against the United States, or to defraud the United States, or any agency thereof in any manner or for any purpose, and one or more of such persons do any act to effect the object of the conspiracy, each shall be fined under this title or imprisoned not more than five years, or both." The Committee believes sufficient evidence exists for a criminal referral of President Trump and others under this statute.[616]

*First*, President Trump entered into an agreement with individuals to obstruct a lawful function of the government (the certification of the election). The evidence of this element overlaps greatly with the evidence of the section 1512(c)(2) violations, so we will not repeat it at length here. President Trump engaged in a multi-part plan described in this Report to obstruct a lawful certification of the election. Judge Carter focused his opinions largely on John Eastman's role, as Eastman's documents were at issue in that case, concluding that "the evidence shows that an agreement to enact the electoral count plan likely existed between President Trump and Eastman."[617] But President Trump entered into agreements—whether formal or informal[618]—with several other individuals who assisted with the multi-part plan. With regard to the Department of Justice, Jeffrey Clark stands out as a participant in the conspiracy, as the evidence suggests that Clark entered into an agreement with President Trump that if appointed Acting Attorney General, he would send a letter to State officials falsely stating that the Department of Justice believed that State legislatures had a sufficient factual basis to convene to select new electors. This was false—the Department of Justice had reached the conclusion that there was no factual basis to contend that the election was stolen. Again, as with section 1512(c), the conspiracy under section 371 appears to have also included other individuals such as Chesebro, Rudolph Giuliani, and Mark Meadows, but this Committee does not attempt to determine all of the participants of the conspiracy, many of whom refused to answer this Committee's questions.

*Second,* there are several bases for finding that the conspirators used "deceitful or dishonest means." For example, President Trump repeatedly lied about the election, after he had been told by his advisors that there was no evidence of fraud sufficient to change the results of the election.[619] In addition, the plot to get the Vice President to unilaterally prevent certification of the election was manifestly (and admittedly) illegal, as discussed above. Eastman and others told President Trump that it would violate the Electoral Count Act if the Vice President unilaterally rejected electors. Thus Judge Carter once again had little trouble finding that the intent requirement ("deceitful or dishonest means") was met, stating that "President Trump continuing to push that plan despite being aware of its illegality constituted obstruction by 'dishonest' means under § 371."[620] Judge Carter rejected the notion that Eastman's plan—which the President adopted and actualized—was a "good faith interpretation" of the law, finding instead that it was "a partisan distortion of the democratic process."[621] Similarly, both President Trump and Clark had been told repeatedly that the Department of Justice had found no evidence of significant fraud in any of its investigations, but they nonetheless pushed the Department of Justice to send a letter to State officials stating that the Department had found such fraud. And Georgia Secretary of State Brad Raffensperger and others made clear to President Trump that they had no authority to "find" him 11,780 votes, but the President relentlessly insisted that they do exactly that, even to the point of suggesting there could be criminal consequences if they refused.[622]

*Third*, there were numerous overt acts in furtherance of the agreement, including each of the parts of the President's effort to overturn the election. As Judge Carter concluded, President Trump and Eastman participated in "numerous overt acts in furtherance of their shared plan."[623] These included, but certainly were not limited to, direct pleas to the Vice President to reject electors or delay certification, including in Oval Office meetings and the President's vulgar comments to the Vice President on the morning of January 6th. Judge Carter also addressed evidence that President Trump knowingly made false representations to a court. Judge Carter concluded that Eastman's emails showed "that President Trump knew that the specific numbers of voter fraud" cited in a complaint on behalf of President Trump "were wrong but continued to tout those numbers, both in court and to the public." Judge Carter found that the emails in question were related to and in furtherance of a conspiracy to defraud the United States.[624]

In finding that President Trump, Eastman, and others engaged in conspiracy to defraud the United States under section 371, Judge Carter relied on the documents at issue (largely consisting of Eastman's own emails) and evidence presented to the court by this Committee. This Committee's investigation has progressed significantly since Judge Carter issued his first crime-fraud ruling in March 2022. The evidence found by this Committee and discussed in detail in this Report further documents that the conspiracy to defraud the United States under section 371 extended far beyond the effort to pressure the Vice President to prevent certification of the election. The Committee believes there is sufficient evidence for a criminal referral of the multi-part plan described in this Report under section 371, as the very purpose of the plan was to prevent the lawful certification of Joe Biden's election as President.

### III. Conspiracy to Make a False Statement (18 U.S.C. §§ 371, 1001)

President Trump, through others acting at his behest, submitted slates of fake electors to Congress and the National Archives. Section 1001 of Title 18 of the United States Code applies, in relevant part, to "whoever, in any matter within the jurisdiction of the executive, legislative, or judicial branch of the Government of the United States, knowingly and willfully—

(1) falsifies, conceals, or covers up by any trick, scheme, or device a material fact;

(2) makes any materially false, fictitious, or fraudulent statement or representation; or

(3) makes or uses any false writing or document knowing the same to contain any materially false, fictitious, or fraudulent statement or entry."

According to the Department of Justice, whether a false statement is criminal under section 1001 "depends on whether there is an affirmative response to each of the following questions:

1. Was the act or statement material?
2. Was the act within the jurisdiction of a department or agency of the United States?
3. Was the act done knowingly and willfully?" [625]

In addition, and as explained above, 18 U.S.C. § 371 makes it a crime to conspire to "commit any offense against the United States." [626]

The evidence suggests President Trump conspired with others to submit slates of fake electors to Congress and the National Archives. Sufficient evidence exists of a violation of 18 U.S.C. §§ 371 and 1001 for a criminal referral of President Trump and others.

As explained earlier and in Chapter 3 of this Report, the certifications signed by Trump electors in multiple States were patently false. Vice President Biden won each of those States, and the relevant State authorities had so certified. It can hardly be disputed that the false slates of electors were material, as nothing can be more material to the joint session of Congress to certify the election than the question of which candidate won which States. Indeed, evidence obtained by the Committee suggests that those attempting to submit certain of the electoral votes regarded the need to provide that material to Vice President Pence as urgent. [627]

There should be no question that section 1001 applies here. The false electoral slates were provided both to the executive branch (the National Archives) and the legislative branch. [628] The statute applies to "any matter within the jurisdiction of the executive, legislative, or judicial branch of the Government of the United States." [629] It is well established that false statements to Congress can constitute violations of section 1001. [630]

Finally, the false statement was made knowingly and willfully. There is some evidence suggesting that some signatories of the fake certificates believed that the certificates were contingent, to be used only in the event that President Trump prevailed in litigation challenging the election results in their States. That may be relevant to the question whether those electors knowingly and willfully signed a false statement at the time they signed the certificates. But it is of no moment to President Trump's conduct, as President Trump (including acting through co-conspirators such as John Eastman and Kenneth Chesebro) relied on the existence of those fake electors as a basis for asserting that the Vice President could reject or delay certification of the Biden electors. In fact, as explained earlier and in Chapter 5 of this Report, Eastman's memorandum setting out a six-step plan for over-turning the election on January 6th begins by stating that "7 states have transmitted dual slates of electors to the President of the Senate."

The remaining question is who engaged in this conspiracy to make the false statement to Congress under section 1001. The evidence is clear that President Trump personally participated in a scheme to have the Trump electors meet, cast votes, and send their votes to the joint session of Congress in several States that Vice President Biden won, and then his supporters relied on the existence of these fake electors as part of their effort to obstruct the joint session. Republican National Committee (RNC) Chairwoman Ronna McDaniel testified before this Committee that President Trump and Eastman directly requested that the RNC organize the effort to have these fake (i.e., Trump) electors meet and cast their votes.[631] Thus, the Committee believes that sufficient evidence exists for a criminal referral of President Trump for illegally engaging in a conspiracy to violate section 1001; the evidence indicates that he entered into an agreement with Eastman and others to make the false statement (the fake electoral certificates), by deceitful or dishonest means, and at least one member of the conspiracy engaged in at least one overt act in furtherance of the conspiracy (e.g., President Trump and Eastman's call to Ronna McDaniel).

### IV. "Incite," "Assist" or "Aid and Comfort" an Insurrection (18 U.S.C. § 2383)

Section 2383 of Title 18 of the United States Code applies to anyone who "incites, sets on foot, assists, or engages in any rebellion or insurrection against the authority of the United States or the laws thereof, or gives aid or comfort thereto."[632] The Committee recognizes that section 2383 does not require evidence of an "agreement" between President Trump and the violent rioters to establish a violation of that provision; instead, the President need only have incited, assisted, or aided and comforted those engaged in violence or other lawless activity in an effort to prevent the peaceful transition of the Presidency under our Constitution. A Federal court has already concluded that President Trump's statements during his Ellipse speech were "plausibly words of incitement not protected by the First Amendment."[633] Moreover, President Trump was impeached for "Incitement of Insurrection," and a majority of the Senate voted to convict, with many more suggesting they might have voted to convict had President Trump still been in office at the time.[634]

As explained throughout this Report and in this Committee's hearings, President Trump was directly responsible for summoning what became a violent mob to Washington, DC, urging them to march to the Capitol, and then further provoking the already violent and lawless crowd with his 2:24 p.m. tweet about the Vice President. Even though President Trump had repeatedly been told that Vice President Pence had no legal authority to stop the certification of the election, he asserted in his speech on January 6th that if the Vice President "comes through for us" that he could deliver victory to Trump: "[I]f Mike Pence does the right thing, we win the election." This created a desperate and false expectation in President Trump's mob that ended up putting the Vice President and his entourage and many others at the Capitol in physical danger. When President Trump tweeted at 2:24 p.m., he knew violence was underway. His tweet exacerbated that violence.[635]

During the ensuing riot, the President refused to condemn the violence or encourage the crowd to disperse despite repeated pleas from his staff and family that he do so. The Committee has evidence from multiple sources establishing these facts, including testimony from former White House Counsel Pat Cipollone. Although Cipollone's testimony did not disclose a number of direct communications with President Trump in light of concerns about executive privilege, the Department now appears to have obtained a ruling that Cipollone can testify before a grand jury about these communications. Based on the information it has obtained, the Committee believes that Cipollone and others can provide direct testimony establishing that President Trump refused repeatedly, for multiple hours, to make a public statement directing his violent and lawless supporters to leave the Capitol. President Trump did not want his supporters (who had effectively halted the vote counting) to disperse. Evidence obtained by the Committee also indicates that President Trump did not want to provide security assistance to the Capitol during that violent period.[636] This appalling behavior by our Commander in Chief occurred despite his affirmative constitutional duty to act to ensure that the laws are faithfully executed.[637]

The Committee believes that sufficient evidence exists for a criminal referral of President Trump for "assist[ing]" or "ai[ding] and comfort-[ing]" those at the Capitol who engaged in a violent attack on the United States. The Committee has developed significant evidence that President Trump intended to disrupt the peaceful transition of power and believes that the Department of Justice can likely elicit testimony relevant to an investigation under section 2383.

For example, Chief of Staff Mark Meadows told White House Counsel Pat Cipollone that the President "doesn't want to do anything" to stop the violence.[638] Worse, at 2:24 p.m., the President inflamed and exacerbated the mob violence by sending a tweet stating that the Vice President "didn't have the courage to do what should have been done." [639] The President threw gasoline on the fire despite knowing that there was a violent riot underway at the Capitol. Indeed, video and audio footage from the attack shows that many of the rioters specifically mentioned Vice President

Pence.[640] And immediately after President Trump sent his tweet, the violence escalated. Between 2:25 p.m. and 2:28 p.m., rioters breached the East Rotunda doors, other rioters breached the police line in the Capitol Crypt, Vice President Pence had to be evacuated from his Senate office, and Leader McCarthy was evacuated from his Capitol office.[641]

Evidence developed in the Committee's investigation showed that the President, when told that the crowd was chanting "Hang Mike Pence," responded that perhaps the Vice President deserved to be hanged.[642] And President Trump rebuffed pleas from Leader McCarthy to ask that his supporters leave the Capitol stating, "Well, Kevin, I guess these people are more upset about the election than you are." After hours of deadly riot, President Trump eventually released a videotaped statement encouraging the crowd to disperse, though openly professing his "love" for the members of the mob and empathizing with their frustration at the "stolen" election. President Trump has since expressed a desire to pardon those involved in the attack.[643]

Both the purpose and the effect of the President's actions were to mobilize a large crowd to descend on the Capitol. Several defendants in pending criminal cases identified the President's allegations about the "stolen election" as the key motivation for their activities at the Capitol. Many of them specifically cited the President's tweets asking his supporters to come to Washington, DC, on January 6th. For example, one defendant who later pleaded guilty to threatening House Speaker Nancy Pelosi texted a family member on January 6th to say: "[Trump] wants heads and I'm going to deliver." [644] Another defendant released a statement through his attorney stating: "I was in Washington, DC on January 6, 2021, because I believed I was following the instructions of former President Trump and he was my President and the commander-in-chief. His statements also had me believing the election was stolen from him." [645]

As the violence began to subside and law enforcement continued to secure the Capitol, President Trump tweeted again, at 6:01 pm to justify the actions of the rioters: "These are the things and events that happen," he wrote, when his so-called victory was "so unceremoniously & viciously stripped away. . . ." [646] When he wrote those words, he knew exactly what he was doing. Before President Trump issued the tweet, a White House staffer cautioned him that the statement would imply that he "had something to do with the events that happened at the Capitol"—but he tweeted it anyway.[647] The final words of that tweet leave little doubt about President Trump's sentiments toward those who invaded the Capitol: "Remember this day forever!" [648]

## V. Other Conspiracy Statutes (18 U.S.C. §§ 372 and 2384)

Depending on evidence developed by the Department of Justice, the President's actions with the knowledge of the risk of violence could also constitute a violation of 18 U.S.C. § 372 and § 2384, both of which require proof of a conspiracy. Section 372 prohibits a conspiracy between two or more persons "to prevent, by force, intimidation, or threat, any person from accepting or holding any office, trust, or place of confidence under the United States, or from discharging any duties thereof, or to induce by like means any officer of the United States to leave the place, where his duties as an officer are required to be performed, or to injure him in the discharge of his official duties."[649] Oath Keepers Kelly Meggs, Kenneth Harrelson, and Jessica Watkins were convicted of violating 18 U.S.C. § 372 in connection with the January 6th attack on the Capitol.[650] The Committee believes that former Chief of Staff Mark Meadows (who refused to testify and was held in contempt of Congress) could have specific evidence relevant to such charges, as may witnesses who invoked their Fifth Amendment rights against self-incrimination before this Committee.

Section 2384, the seditious conspiracy statute, prohibits "conspir[acy] to overthrow, put down, or to destroy by force the Government of the United States . . . or to oppose by force the authority thereof, or by force to prevent, hinder or delay the execution of any law of the United States . . . ."[651] A jury has already determined beyond a reasonable doubt that a conspiracy existed under section 2384, as the leader of the Oath Keepers and at least one other individual were convicted of seditious conspiracy under section 2384 for their actions related to the attack on the Capitol.[652] A trial regarding a series of other "Proud Boy" defendants may also address similar issues.[653]

The Department of Justice, through its investigative tools that exceed those of this Committee, may have evidence sufficient to prosecute President Trump under sections 372 and 2384. Accordingly, we believe sufficient evidence exists for a criminal referral of President Trump under these two statutes.

## VI. The Committee's Concerns Regarding Possible Obstruction of its Investigation

The Committee has substantial concerns regarding potential efforts to obstruct its investigation, including by certain counsel (some paid by groups connected to the former President) who may have advised clients to provide false or misleading testimony to the Committee.[654] Such actions could violate 18 U.S.C. §§ 1505, 1512. The Committee is aware that both the U.S. Department of Justice and the Fulton County District Attorney's Office have already obtained information relevant to these matters, including from the Committee directly. We urge the Department of Justice to examine the facts to discern whether prosecution is warranted. The Committee's broad concerns regarding obstruction and witness credibility are addressed in the Executive Summary to this Report.

## VII. ACCOUNTABILITY FOR THOSE WHO PLOTTED UNLAWFULLY TO OVERTURN THE ELECTION IS CRITICAL.

To date, the Justice Department has pursued prosecution of hundreds of individuals who planned and participated in the January 6th invasion of and attack on our Capitol. But the Department has not yet charged individuals who engaged in the broader plan to overturn the election through the means discussed in this Report. The Committee has concluded that it is critical to hold those individuals accountable as well, including those who worked with President Trump to create and effectuate these plans.

In his speech from the Ellipse on January 6th, President Trump recited a host of election fraud allegations he knew to be false, and then told tens of thousands of his angry supporters this:

> And fraud breaks up everything, doesn't it? When you catch some-body in a fraud, you're allowed to go by very different rules. So I hope Mike has the courage to do what he has to do. And I hope he doesn't listen to the RINOs and the stupid people that he's listening to. [655]

The meaning of President Trump's comments was sufficiently clear then, but he recently gave America an even more detailed understanding of his state of mind. Trump wrote that allegations of "massive fraud" related to the 2020 election "allow[] for the termination of all rules, regulations and articles, even those found in the Constitution." [656] And President Trump considered pardoning those involved in the attack and has since expressed a desire to pardon them—and even give them an apology—if he returns to the Oval Office.[657]

In the Committee's judgment, based on all the evidence developed, President Trump believed then, and continues to believe now, that he is above the law, not bound by our Constitution and its explicit checks on Presidential authority. This recent Trump statement only heightens our concern about accountability. If President Trump and the associates who assisted him in an effort to overturn the lawful outcome of the 2020 elec-tion are not ultimately held accountable under the law, their behavior may become a precedent, and invitation to danger, for future elections. A failure to hold them accountable now may ultimately lead to future unlawful efforts to overturn our elections, thereby threatening the security and viability of our Republic.

## VIII. REFERRAL OF MEMBERS TO THE HOUSE ETHICS COMMITTEE FOR FAILURE TO COMPLY WITH SUBPOENAS

During the course of the Select Committee's investigation of President Trump's efforts to subvert the election, the Committee learned that various Members of Congress had information relevant to the investigation. Accordingly, the Committee wrote letters to a number of Members involved in that activity inviting them to participate voluntarily in the Select Committee's investigation. None of the members was willing to provide information, which forced the Select Committee to consider alternative means of securing evidence about the conduct of these Members and the information they might have. On May 12, 2022, the Select Committee subpoenaed several members of Congress—including House Minority Leader Kevin McCarthy, Representative Jim Jordan, Representative Scott Perry, and Representative Andy Biggs—to obtain information related to the Committee's investigation.

This was a significant step, but it was one that was warranted by the certain volume of information these Members possessed that was relevant to the Select Committee's investigation, as well as the centrality of their efforts to President Trump's multi-part plan to remain in power.

Representative McCarthy, among other things, had multiple communications with President Trump, Vice President Pence, and others on and related to January 6th. For example, during the attack on the Capitol, Representative McCarthy urgently requested that the former President issue a statement calling off the rioters, to which President Trump responded by "push[ing] back" and said: "Well, Kevin, I guess these people are more upset about the election than you are." [658] And, after the attack, Representative McCarthy spoke on the House floor and said that, "[t]here is absolutely no evidence" that Antifa caused the attack on the Capitol and instead called on President Trump to "accept his share of responsibility" for the violence.[659] As noted above, Representative McCarthy privately confided in colleagues that President Trump accepted some responsibility for the attack on the Capitol.[660]

Representative Jordan was a significant player in President Trump's efforts. He participated in numerous post-election meetings in which senior White House officials, Rudolph Giuliani, and others, discussed strategies for challenging the election, chief among them claims that the election had been tainted by fraud. On January 2, 2021, Representative Jordan led a conference call in which he, President Trump, and other Members of Congress discussed strategies for delaying the January 6th joint session. During that call, the group also discussed issuing social media posts encouraging President Trump's supporters to "march to the Capitol" on the 6th.[661] An hour and a half later, President Trump and Representative

Jordan spoke by phone for 18 minutes.[662] The day before January 6th, Representative Jordan texted Mark Meadows, passing along advice that Vice President Pence should "call out all the electoral votes that he believes are unconstitutional as no electoral votes at all." [663] He spoke with President Trump by phone at least twice on January 6th, though he has provided inconsistent public statements about how many times they spoke and what they discussed.[664] He also received five calls from Rudolph Giuliani that evening, and the two connected at least twice, at 7:33 p.m. and 7:49 p.m.[665] During that time, Giuliani has testified, he was attempting to reach Members of Congress after the joint session resumed to encourage them to continue objecting to Joe Biden's electoral votes.[666] And, in the days following January 6th, Representative Jordan spoke with White House staff about the prospect of Presidential pardons for Members of Congress.[667]

Like Representative Jordan, Representative Perry was also involved in early post-election messaging strategy. Both Representative Jordan and Representative Perry were involved in discussions with White House officials about Vice President Pence's role on January 6th as early as November 2020.[668] Representative Perry was present for conversations in which the White House Counsel's Office informed him and others that President Trump's efforts to submit fake electoral votes were not legally sound.[669] But perhaps most pivotally, he was involved in President Trump's efforts to install Jeffrey Clark as the Acting Attorney General in December 2020 and January 2021. Beginning in early December 2020, Representative Perry suggested Clark as a candidate to Mark Meadows,[670] then introduced Clark to President Trump.[671] In the days before January 6th, Representative Perry advocated for President Trump to speak at the Capitol during the joint session, speaking to Mark Meadows on at least one occasion about it.[672] He was also a participant in the January 2, 2021, call in which Representative Jordan, President Trump, and others discussed issuing social media posts to encourage Trump supporters to march to the Capitol on January 6th.[673] After January 6th, Representative Perry reached out to White House staff asking to receive a Presidential pardon.[674]

Representative Biggs was involved in numerous elements of President Trump's efforts to contest the election results. As early as November 6, 2020, Representative Biggs texted Mark Meadows, urging him to "encourage the state legislatures to appoint [electors]." [675] In the following days, Representative Biggs told Meadows not to let President Trump concede his loss.[676] Between then and January 6th, Representative Biggs coordinated with Arizona State Representative Mark Finchem to gather signatures from Arizona lawmakers endorsing fake Trump electors.[677] He also contacted fake Trump electors in at least one State seeking evidence related to voter fraud.[678]

To date, none of the subpoenaed Members has complied with either voluntary or compulsory requests for participation.

Representative McCarthy initially responded to the Select Committee's subpoena in two letters on May 27 and May 30, 2022, in which he objected to the Select Committee's composition and validity of the subpoena and offered to submit written interrogatories in lieu of deposition testimony. Although the Select Committee did not release Representative McCarthy from his subpoena obligations, Representative McCarthy failed to appear for his scheduled deposition on May 31, 2022. The Select Committee responded to Representative McCarthy's letters this same day, rejecting his proposal to participate via written interrogatories and compelling his appearance for deposition testimony no later than June 11, 2022. Although Representative McCarthy again responded via letter on June 9, 2022, he did not appear for deposition testimony on or before the specified June 11, 2022, deadline.

Representative Jordan also responded to the Select Committee's subpoena just before his scheduled deposition in a letter on May 25, 2022, containing a variety of objections. Representative Jordan also requested material from the Select Committee, including all materials referencing him in the Select Committee's possession and all internal legal analysis related to the constitutionality of Member subpoenas. Although the Select Committee did not release Representative Jordan from his subpoena obligations, Representative Jordan failed to appear for his scheduled deposition on May 27, 2022. On May 31, 2022, the Select Committee responded to the substance of Representative Jordan's May 25th letter and indicated that Representative Jordan should appear for deposition testimony no later than June 11, 2022. On June 9, 2022, Representative Jordan again wrote to reiterate the points from his May 25th letter. That same day, Representative Jordan sent out a fundraising email with the subject line: "I'VE BEEN SUBPOENED." [679] Representative Jordan did not appear before the Select Committee on or before the June 11, 2022, deadline.

Representative Perry likewise responded to the Select Committee's subpoena on May 24, 2022, in a letter, "declin[ing] to appear for deposition" and requesting that the subpoena be "immediately withdrawn." [680] Although the Select Committee did not release Representative Perry from his subpoena obligations, Representative Perry failed to appear on May 26, 2022, for his scheduled deposition. Representative Perry sent a second letter to the Select Committee on May 31, 2022, with additional objections. That same day, the Select Committee responded to Representative Perry's letters and stated that he should appear before the Select Committee no later than June 11, 2022, for deposition testimony. Representative Perry responded via letter on June 10, 2022, maintaining his objections. He did not appear before the June 11, 2022, deadline.

Representative Biggs issued a press release on the day the Select Committee issued its subpoena, calling the subpoena "illegitimate" and "pure political theater." The day before his scheduled deposition, Representative Biggs sent a letter to the Select Committee with a series of objections and an invocation of Speech or Debate immunity. Although the Select Committee did not release Representative Biggs from his subpoena obligations, Representative Biggs did not appear for his scheduled deposition on May 26, 2022. On May 31, 2022, the Select Committee responded to the substance of Representative Biggs' May 25th letter and indicated that Representative Biggs should appear for deposition testimony no later than June 11, 2022. Although Representative Biggs responded with another letter on June 9th, he did not appear before the June 11, 2022, deadline.

Despite the Select Committee's repeated attempts to obtain information from these Members and the issuance of subpoenas, each has refused to cooperate and failed to comply with a lawfully issued subpoena. Accordingly, the Select Committee is referring their failure to comply with the subpoenas issued to them to the Ethics Committee for further action. To be clear, this referral is only for failure to comply with lawfully issued subpoenas.

The Rules of the House of Representatives make clear that their willful noncompliance violates multiple standards of conduct and subjects them to discipline. Willful non-compliance with compulsory congressional committee subpoenas by House Members violates the spirit and letter of House rule XXIII, clause 1, which requires House Members to conduct themselves "at all times in a manner that shall reflect creditably on the House." As a previous version of the House Ethics Manual explained, this catchall provision encompasses "'flagrant' violations of the law that reflect on 'Congress as a whole,' and that might otherwise go unpunished." [681] The subpoenaed House Members' refusal to comply with their subpoena obligations satisfies these criteria. A House Member's willful failure to comply with a congressional subpoena also reflects discredit on Congress. If left unpunished, such behavior undermines Congress's longstanding power to investigate in support of its lawmaking authority and suggests that Members of Congress may disregard legal obligations that apply to ordinary citizens.

For these reasons, the Select Committee refers Leader McCarthy and Representatives Jordan, Perry, and Biggs for sanction by the House Ethics Committee for failure to comply with subpoenas. The Committee also believes that each of these individuals, along with other Members who attended the December 21st planning meeting with President Trump at the

White House,[682] should be questioned in a public forum about their advance knowledge of and role in President Trump's plan to prevent the peaceful transition of power.

## EFFORTS TO AVOID TESTIFYING, EVIDENCE OF OBSTRUCTION, AND ASSESSMENTS OF WITNESS CREDIBILITY

More than 30 witnesses before the Select Committee exercised their Fifth Amendment privilege against self-incrimination and refused on that basis to provide testimony. They included individuals central to the investigation, such as John Eastman, Jeffrey Clark, Roger Stone, Michael Flynn, Kenneth Chesebro, and others.[683] The law allows a civil litigant to rely upon an "adverse inference" when a witness invokes the Fifth Amendment. "[T]he Fifth Amendment does not forbid adverse inferences against parties to civil actions . . .."[684] The Committee has not chosen to rely on any such inference in this Report or in its hearings.

We do note that certain witness assertions of the Fifth Amendment were particularly troubling, including this:

Vice Chair Cheney: General Flynn, do you believe the violence on January 6th was justified?

Counsel for the Witness: Can I get clarification, is that a moral question or are you asking a legal question?

Vice Chair Cheney: I'm asking both.

General Flynn: The Fifth.

Vice Chair Cheney: Do you believe the violence on January 6th was justified morally?

General Flynn: Take the Fifth.

Vice Chair Cheney: Do you believe the violence on January 6th was justified legally?

General Flynn: Fifth.

Vice Chair Cheney: General Flynn, do you believe in the peaceful transition of power in the United States of America?

General Flynn: The Fifth.[685]

President Trump refused to comply with the Committee's subpoena, and also filed suit to block the National Archives from supplying the Committee with White House records. The Committee litigated the National Archives case in Federal District Court, in the Federal Appellate Court for the District of Columbia, and before the Supreme Court. The Select Committee was successful in this litigation. The opinion of the D.C. Circuit explained:

> On January 6, 2021, a mob professing support for then-President Trump violently attacked the United States Capitol in an effort to prevent a Joint Session of Congress from certifying the electoral college votes designating Joseph R. Biden the 46th President of the United States. The rampage left multiple people dead, injured more than 140 people, and inflicted millions of dollars in damage to the Capitol. Then-Vice President Pence, Senators, and Representatives were all forced to halt their constitutional duties and flee the House and Senate chambers for safety.[686]

> Benjamin Franklin said, at the founding, that we have "[a] Republic"—"if [we] can keep it." The events of January 6th exposed the fragility of those democratic institutions and traditions that we had perhaps come to take for granted. In response, the President of the United States and Congress have each made the judgment that access to this subset of presidential communication records is necessary to address a matter of great constitutional moment for the Republic. Former President Trump has given this court no legal reason to cast aside President Biden's assessment of the Executive Branch interests at stake, or to create a separation of powers conflict that the Political Branches have avoided.[687]

Several other witnesses have also avoided testifying in whole or in part by asserting Executive Privilege or Absolute Immunity from any obligation to appear before Congress. For example, the President's Chief of Staff Mark Meadows invoked both, and categorically refused to testify, even about text messages he provided to the Committee. The House of Representatives voted to hold him in criminal contempt.[688] Although the Justice Department has taken the position in litigation that a former high level White House staffer for a former President is not entitled to absolute immunity,[689] and that any interests in the confidentiality of his communications with President Trump and others are overcome in this case, the Justice Department declined to prosecute Meadows for criminal contempt. The reasons for Justice's refusal to do so are not apparent to the Committee.[690] Commentators have speculated that Meadows may be cooperating in the Justice Department's January 6th investigation.[691] The same may be true for Daniel Scavino, President Trump's White House Deputy Chief of Staff for Communications and Director of Social Media, whom the House also voted to hold in contempt.[692]

Steve Bannon also chose not to cooperate with the Committee, and the Justice Department prosecuted him for contempt of Congress.[693] Bannon has been sentenced and is currently appealing his conviction. Peter Navarro, another White House Staffer who refused to testify, is currently awaiting his criminal trial.[694]

Although the Committee issued letters and subpoenas to seven Republican members of Congress who have unique knowledge of certain developments on or in relation to January 6th, none agreed to participate in the investigation; none considered themselves obligated to comply with the subpoenas. A number of these same individuals were aware well in advance of January 6th of the plotting by Donald Trump, John Eastman, and others to overturn the election, and certain of them had an active role in that activity.[695] None seem to have alerted law enforcement of this activity, or of the known risk of violence. On January 5th, after promoting unfounded objections to election results, Rep. Debbie Lesko appears to have recognized the danger in a call with her colleagues:

> I also ask leadership to come up with a safety plan for Members [of Congress]. . . . We also have, quite honestly, Trump supporters who actually believe that we are going to overturn the election, and when that doesn't happen—most likely will not happen—they are going to go nuts.[696]

During our hearings, the Committee presented the testimony of numerous White House witnesses who testified about efforts by certain Republican Members of Congress to obtain Presidential pardons for their conduct in connection with January 6th.[697] Cassidy Hutchinson provided extensive detail in this regard:

> Vice Chair Cheney: And are you aware of any members of Congress seeking pardons?

> Hutchinson: I guess Mr. Gaetz and Mr. Brooks, I know, have both advocated for there'd be a blanket pardon for members involved in that meeting, and a — a handful of other members that weren't at the December 21st meeting as the presumptive pardons. Mr. Gaetz was personally pushing for a pardon, and he was doing so since early December.

> I'm not sure why Mr. Gaetz would reach out to me to ask if he could have a meeting with Mr. Meadows about receiving a presidential pardon.

> Vice Chair Cheney: Did they all contact you?

> Hutchinson: Not all of them, but several of them did.

Vice Chair Cheney: So, you mentioned Mr. Gaetz, Mr. Brooks.

Hutchinson: Mr. Biggs did. Mr. Jordan talked about Congressional pardons, but he never asked me for one. It was more for an update on whether the White House was going to pardon members of Congress. Mr. Gohmert asked for one as well. Mr. Perry asked for a pardon, too. I'm sorry.

Vice Chair Cheney: Mr. Perry? Did he talk to you directly?

Hutchinson: Yes, he did.

Vice Chair Cheney: Did Marjorie Taylor Greene contact you?

Hutchinson: No, she didn't contact me about it. I heard that she had asked White House Counsel's Office for a pardon from Mr. Philbin, but I didn't frequently communicate with Ms. Greene.[698]

Many of these details were also corroborated by other sources. President Personnel Director Johnny McEntee confirmed that he was personally asked for a pardon by Representative Matt Gaetz (R–FL).[699] Eric Herschmann recalled that Representative Gaetz "... asked for a very, very broad pardon. . . . And I said Nixon's pardon was never nearly that broad." [700] When asked about reporting that Representatives Mo Brooks and Andy Biggs also requested pardons, Herschmann did not reject either possibility out of hand, instead answering: "It's possible that Representative Brooks or Biggs, but I don't remember." [701] The National Archives produced to the Select Committee an email from Representative Mo Brooks to the President's executive assistant stating that "President Trump asked me to send you this letter" and "... pursuant to a request from Matt Gaetz" that recommended blanket Presidential pardons to every Member of Congress who objected to the electoral college votes on January 6th.[702]

These requests for pardons suggest that the Members identified above were conscious of the potential legal jeopardy arising from their conduct. As noted *infra* 136, the Committee has referred a number of these individuals to the House Ethics Committee for their failure to comply with subpoenas, and believes that they each owe the American people their direct and unvarnished testimony.

The Select Committee has also received a range of evidence suggesting specific efforts to obstruct the Committee's investigation. Much of this evidence is already known by the Department of Justice and by other prosecutorial authorities. For example:

1. The Committee received testimony from a witness about her decision to terminate a lawyer who was receiving payments for the representation from a group allied with President Trump. Among other concerns expressed by the witness:

- The lawyer had advised the witness that the witness could, in certain circumstances, tell the Committee that she did not recall facts when she actually did recall them.
- During a break in the Select Committee's interview, the witness expressed concerns to her lawyer that an aspect of her testimony was not truthful. The lawyer did not advise her to clarify the specific testimony that the witness believed was not complete and accurate, and instead conveyed that, "They don't know what you know, [witness]. They don't know that you can recall some of these things. So you saying 'I don't recall' is an entirely acceptable response to this."
- The lawyer instructed the client about a particular issue that would cast a bad light on President Trump: "No, no, no, no, no. We don't want to go there. We don't want to talk about that."
- The lawyer refused directions from the client not to share her testimony before the Committee with other lawyers representing other witnesses. The lawyer shared such information over the client's objection.
- The lawyer refused directions from the client not to share information regarding her testimony with at least one and possibly more than one member of the press. The lawyer shared the information with the press over her objection.
- The lawyer did not disclose who was paying for the lawyers' representation of the client, despite questions from the client seeking that information, and told her, "we're not telling people where funding is coming from right now."
- The client was offered potential employment that would make her "financially very comfortable" as the date of her testimony approached by entities apparently linked to Donald Trump and his associates. Such offers were withdrawn or did not materialize as reports of the content of her testimony circulated. The client believed this was an effort to impact her testimony.

Further details regarding these instances will be available to the public when transcripts are released.

2. Similarly, the witness testified that multiple persons affiliated with President Trump contacted her in advance of the witness's testimony and made the following statements:

What they said to me is, as long as I continue to be a team player, they know that I am on the right team. I am doing the right thing. I am protecting who I need to protect. You know, I will continue to stay in good graces in Trump World. And they have reminded me a couple of times that Trump does read transcripts and just keep that in mind as I proceed through my interviews with the committee.

Here is another sample in a different context. This is a call received by one of our witnesses:

> [A person] let me know you have your deposition tomorrow. He wants me to let you know he's thinking about you. He knows you're a team player, you're loyal, and you're going do the right thing when you go in for your deposition.[703]

3. The Select Committee is aware of multiple efforts by President Trump to contact Select Committee witnesses. The Department of Justice is aware of at least one of those circumstances.
4. Rather than relying on representation by Secret Service lawyers at no cost, a small number of Secret Service agents engaged private counsel for their interviews before the Committee. [704] During one such witness's transcribed interview, a retained private counsel was observed writing notes to the witness regarding the content of the witness's testimony while the questioning was underway. The witness's counsel admitted on the record that he had done so.[705]

Recently, published accounts of the Justice Department's Mar-a-Lago investigation suggest that the Department is investigating the conduct of counsel for certain witnesses whose fees are being paid by President Trump's Save America Political Action Committee.[706] The public report implies the Department is concerned that such individuals are seeking to influence the testimony of the witnesses they represent.[707] This Committee also has these concerns, including that lawyers who are receiving such payments have specific incentives to defend President Trump rather than zealously represent their own clients. The Department of Justice and the Fulton County District Attorney have been provided with certain information related to this topic.

The Select Committee recognizes of course that most of the testimony we have gathered was given more than a year after January 6th. Recollections are not perfect, and the Committee expects that different accounts of the same events will naturally vary. Indeed, the lack of any inconsistencies in witness accounts would itself be suspicious. And many witnesses may simply recall different things than others.

Many of the witnesses before this Committee had nothing at all to gain from their testimony, gave straightforward responses to the questions posted, and made no effort to downplay, deflect, or rationalize. Trump Administration Justice Department officials such as Attorney General Barr,

Acting Attorney General Rosen, and Acting Deputy Attorney General Dono-ghue are good examples. Multiple members of President Trump's White House staff were also suitably forthcoming, including Sarah Matthews, Matthew Pottinger, Greg Jacob, and Pat Philbin, as were multiple career White House, military and agency personnel whose names the Committee agreed not to disclose publicly; as were former Secretary of Labor Eugene Scalia, Bill Stepien, and certain other members of the Trump Campaign. The Committee very much appreciates the earnestness and bravery of Cassidy Hutchinson, Rusty Bowers, Shaye Moss, Ruby Freeman, Brad Raffensperger, Gabriel Sterling, Al Schmidt, and many others who provided important live testimony during the Committees hearings.[708]

The Committee, along with our nation, offers particular thanks to Offi-cers Caroline Edwards, Michael Fanone, Harry Dunn, Aquilino Gonell, and Daniel Hodges, along with hundreds of other members of law enforcement who defended the Capitol on that fateful day, all of whom should be com-mended for their bravery and sacrifice. We especially thank the families of Officer Brian Sicknick, Howard Liebengood and Jeffrey Smith, whose loss can never be repaid.

The Committee very much appreciates the invaluable testimony of Gen-eral Milley and other members of our military, Judge J. Michael Luttig, and the important contributions of Benjamin Ginsberg and Chris Stirewalt. This, of course is only a partial list, and the Committee is indebted to many others, as well.

The Committee believes that White House Counsel Pat Cipollone gave a particularly important account of the events of January 6th, as did White House lawyer, Eric Herschmann. For multiple months, Cipollone resisted giving any testimony at all, asserting concerns about executive privilege and other issues, until after the Committee's hearing with Hutchinson. When he did testify, Cipollone corroborated key elements of testimony given by several White House staff, including Hutchinson—most impor-tantly, regarding what happened in the White House during the violence of January 6th—but also frankly recognized the limits on what he could say due to privilege: "Again, I'm not going to get into either my legal advice on matters, and the other thing I don't want to do is, again, other witnesses have their own recollections of things." Cipollone also told the Committee that, to the extent that other witnesses recall communications attributable to White House counsel that he does not, the communications might have been with his deputy Pat Philbin, or with Eric Herschmann, who had strong feelings and was particularly animated about certain issues.[709]

Of course, that is not to say that all witnesses were entirely frank or forthcoming. Other witnesses, including certain witnesses from the Trump White House, displayed a lack of full recollection of certain issues, or were not otherwise as frank or direct as Cipollone. We cite two examples here, both relating to testimony played during the hearings.

Kayleigh McEnany was President Trump's Press Secretary on January 6th. Her deposition was taken early in the investigation. McEnany seemed to acknowledge that President Trump: (1) should have instructed his violent supporters to leave the Capitol earlier than he ultimately did on January 6th;[710] (2) should have respected the rulings of the courts;[711] and (3) was wrong to publicly allege that Dominion voting machines stole the election.[712] But a segment of McEnany's testimony seemed evasive, as if she was testifying from pre-prepared talking points. In multiple instances, McEnany's testimony did not seem nearly as forthright as that of her press office staff, who testified about what McEnany said.

For example, McEnany disputed suggestions that President Trump was resistant to condemning the violence and urging the crowd at the Capitol to act peacefully when they crafted his tweet at 2:38 p.m. on January 6th.[713] Yet one of her deputies, Sarah Matthews, told the Select Committee that McEnany informed her otherwise: that McEnany and other advisors in the dining room with President Trump persuaded him to send the tweet, but that ". . . she said that he did not want to put that in and that they went through different phrasing of that, of the mention of peace, in order to get him to agree to include it, and that it was Ivanka Trump who came up with 'stay peaceful' and that he agreed to that phrasing to include in the tweet, but he was initially resistant to mentioning peace of any sort." [714] When the Select Committee asked "Did Ms. McEnany describe in any way how resistant the President was to including something about being peaceful," Matthews answered: "Just that he didn't want to include it, but they got him to agree on the phrasing 'stay peaceful.'" [715]

The Committee invites the public to compare McEnany's testimony with the testimony of Pat Cipollone, Sarah Matthews, Judd Deere, and others.

Ivanka Trump is another example. Among other things, Ivanka Trump acknowledged to the Committee that: (1) she agreed with Attorney General Barr's statements that there was no evidence of sufficient fraud to overturn the election; (2) the President and others are bound by the rulings of the courts and the rule of law; (3) President Trump pressured Vice President Pence on the morning of January 6th regarding his authorities at the joint session of Congress that day to count electoral votes; and (4) President Trump watched the violence on television as it was occurring.[716] But again, Ivanka Trump was not as forthcoming as Cipollone and others about President Trump's conduct.

Indeed, Ivanka Trump's Chief of Staff Julie Radford had a more specific recollection of Ivanka Trump's actions and statements. For example, Ivanka

Trump had the following exchange with the Committee about her attendance at her father's speech on January 6th that was at odds with what the Committee learned from Radford:

> Committee Staff: It's been reported that you ultimately decided to attend the rally because you hoped that you would calm the President and keep the event on an even keel. Is that accurate?
>
> Ivanka Trump: No. I don't know who said that or where that came from.[717]

However, this is what Radford said about her boss's decision:

> Committee Staff: What did she share with you about why it was concerning that her father was upset or agitated after that call with Vice President Pence in relation to the Ellipse rally? Why did that matter? Why did he have to be calmed down, I should say.
>
> Radford: Well, she shared that he had called the Vice President a not—an expletive word. I think that bothered her. And I think she could tell based on the conversations and what was going on in the office that he was angry and upset and people were providing misinformation. And she felt like she might be able to help calm the situation down, at least before he went on stage.
>
> Committee Staff: And the word that she relayed to you that the President called the Vice President—apologize for being impolite—but do you remember what she said her father called him?
>
> Radford: The "P" word.[718]

When the Committee asked Ivanka Trump whether there were "[a]ny particular words that you recall your father using during the conversation" that morning with Vice President Pence, she answered simply: "No."[719]

In several circumstances, the Committee has found that less senior White House aides had significantly better recollection of events than senior staff purported to have.

The Select Committee also has concerns regarding certain other witnesses, including those who still rely for their income or employment on organizations linked to President Trump, such as the America First Policy Institute. Certain witnesses and lawyers were unnecessarily combative, answered hundreds of questions with variants of "I do not recall" in circumstances where that answer seemed unbelievable, appeared to testify from lawyer-written talking points rather than their own recollections, provided highly questionable rationalizations or otherwise resisted telling the truth. The public can ultimately make its own assessment of these issues when it reviews the Committee transcripts and can compare the accounts of different witnesses and the conduct of counsel.

One particular concern arose from what the Committee realized early on were a number of intentional falsehoods in former White House Chief of Staff Mark Meadows's December 7, 2021 book, *The Chief's Chief.*[720] Here is one of several examples: Meadows wrote, "When he got offstage, President Trump let me know that he had been speaking metaphorically about going to the Capitol."[721] Meadows goes on in his book to claim that it "was clear the whole time" President Trump didn't intend to go to the Capitol.[722] This appeared to be an intentional effort to conceal the facts. Multiple witnesses directly contradicted Meadows's account about President Trump's desire to travel to the Capitol, including Kayleigh McEnany, Cassidy Hutchinson, multiple Secret Service agents, a White House employee with national security responsibilities and other staff in the White House, a member of the Metropolitan Police and others. This and several other statements in the Meadows book were false, and the Select Committee was concerned that multiple witnesses might attempt to repeat elements of these false accounts, as if they were the party line. Most witnesses did not, but a few did.

President Trump's desire to travel to the Capitol was particularly important for the Committee to evaluate because it bears on President Trump's intent on January 6th. One witness account suggests that President Trump even wished to participate in the electoral vote count from the House floor, standing with Republican Congressmen, perhaps in an effort to apply further pressure to Vice President Mike Pence and others.[723]

Mark Meadows's former Deputy Chief of Staff for Operations Anthony Ornato gave testimony consistent with the false account in Meadows book. In particular, Ornato told the Committee that he was not aware of a genuine push by the President to go to the Capitol, suggesting instead that "it was one of those hypotheticals from the good idea fairy . . . [b]ecause it's ridiculous to think that a President of the United States can travel especially with, you know, people around just on the street up to the Capitol and peacefully protest outside the Capitol...."[724] He told the Select Committee that the only conversation he had about the possibility of the President traveling to the Capitol was in a single meeting officials from the President's advance team,[725] and his understanding is that this idea "wasn't from the President."[726] Two witnesses before the Committee, including a White House employee with national security responsibilities and Hutchinson, testified that Ornato related an account of President Trump's "irate" behavior when he was told in the Presidential SUV on January 6th that he would not be driven to the Capitol.[727] Both accounts recall Ornato doing so from his office in the White House, with another member of the Secret Service present.[728] Multiple other witness accounts indicate that the President genuinely was "irate," "heated," "angry," and "insistent" in the Presidential vehicle.[729] But Ornato professed that he did not recall either communication, and that he had no knowledge at all about the President's anger.[730]

Likewise, despite a significant and increasing volume of intelligence information in the days before January 6th showing that violence at the Capitol was indeed possible or likely, and despite other intelligence and law enforcement agencies similar conclusions,[731] Ornato claimed never to have reviewed or had any knowledge of that specific information[732] He testified that he was only aware of warnings that opposing groups might "clash on the Washington Monument" and that is what he "would have briefed to [Chief of Staff] Meadows."[733] The Committee has significant concerns about the credibility of this testimony, including because it was Ornato's responsibility to be aware of this information and convey it to decision-makers.[734] The Committee will release Ornato's November Transcript so the public can review his testimony on these topics.

## SUMMARY: CREATION OF THE SELECT COMMITTEE; PURPOSES.

In the week after January 6th, House Republican Leader Kevin McCarthy initially supported legislation to create a bipartisan commission to investigate the January 6th attack on the United States Capitol, stating that "the President bears responsibility for Wednesday's attack on Congress by mob rioters" and calling for creation of a "fact-finding commission."[735] Leader McCarthy repeated his support for a bipartisan commission during a press conference on January 21st: "The only way you will be able to answer these questions is through a bipartisan commission."[736]

On February 15th, House Speaker Nancy Pelosi announced in a letter to the House Democratic Caucus her intent to establish the type of independent commission McCarthy had supported, to "investigate and report on the facts and causes relating to the January 6, 2021 domestic terrorist attack upon the United States Capitol Complex."[737] A few days thereafter, Leader McCarthy provided the Speaker a wish list that mirrored "suggestions from the Co-Chairs of the 9/11 Commission" that he and House Republicans hoped would be included in the House's legislation to establish the Commission.[738]

In particular, Leader McCarthy requested an equal ratio of Democratic and Republican nominations, equal subpoena power for the Democratic Chair and Republican Vice Chair of the Commission, and the exclusion of predetermined findings or outcomes that the Commission itself would produce. Closing his letter, Leader McCarthy quoted the 9/11 Commission

Co-Chairs, writing that a "bipartisan independent investigation will earn credibility with the American public." [739] He again repeated his confidence in achieving that goal. [740] In April 2021, Speaker Pelosi agreed to make the number of Republican and Democratic Members of the Commission equal, and to provide both parties with an equal say in subpoenas, as McCarthy had requested. [741]

In May 2021, House Homeland Security Committee Chairman Bennie G. Thompson began to negotiate more of the details for the Commission with his Republican counterpart, Ranking Member John Katko. [742] On May 14th, Chairman Thompson announced that he and Ranking Member Katko had reached an agreement on legislation to "form a bipartisan, independent Commission to investigate the January 6th domestic terrorism attack on the United States Capitol and recommend changes to further protect the Capitol, the citadel of our democracy." [743]

On May 18th, the day before the House's consideration of the Thompson-Katko agreement, Leader McCarthy released a statement in opposition to the legislation. [744] Speaker Pelosi responded to that statement, saying: "Leader McCarthy won't take yes for an answer." [745] The Speaker referred to Leader McCarthy's February 22nd letter where "he made three requests to be addressed in Democrats' discussion draft." [746] She noted that "every single one was granted by Democrats, yet he still says no." [747]

In the days that followed, Republican Ranking Member Katko defended the bipartisan nature of the bill to create the Commission:

*As I have called for since the days just after the attack, an independent, 9/11-style review is critical for removing the politics around January 6 and focusing solely on the facts and circumstances of the security breach at the Capitol, as well as other instances of violence relevant to such a review. Make no mistake about it, Mr. Thompson and I know this is about facts. It's not partisan politics. We would have never gotten to this point if it was about partisan politics.* [748]

That evening, the House passed the legislation to establish a National Commission to Investigate the January 6th Attack on the United States Capitol Complex in a bipartisan fashion, with 35 Republicans joining 217 Democrats voting in favor and 175 Republicans voting against. [749] In the days thereafter, however, only six Senate Republicans joined Senate Democrats in supporting the legislation, killing the bill in the Senate. [750]

On June 24th, Speaker Pelosi announced her intent to create a House select committee to investigate the attack. [751] On June 25th, Leader McCarthy met with DC Metropolitan Police Officer Michael Fanone, who was seriously injured on January 6th.[752] Officer Fanone pressed Leader McCarthy "for a commitment not to put obstructionists and the wrong people in that position." [753]

On June 30th, the House voted on H. Res. 503 to establish a 13-Member Select Committee to Investigate the January 6th Attack on the United States Capitol by a vote of 222 Yeas and 190 Nays with just two Republicans supporting the measure: Representative Liz Cheney and Representative Adam Kinzinger.[754] On July 1st, Speaker Pelosi named eight initial Members to the Select Committee, including one Republican: Representative Cheney.[755]

On July 17th, Leader McCarthy proposed his selection of five members:

*Representative Jim Jordan, Ranking Member of the House Judiciary Committee;*

*Representative Kelly Armstrong of North Dakota; House Energy and Commerce Committee;*

*Representative Troy Nehls, House Transportation & Infrastructure and Veterans' Affairs Committees.*

*Representative Jim Banks, Armed Services, Veterans' Affairs and Education and Labor Committees;*

*Representative Rodney Davis, Ranking Member of the Committee on House Administration.*[756]

Jordan was personally involved in the acts and circumstances of January 6th, and would be one of the targets of the investigation. By that point, Banks had made public statements indicating that he had already reached his own conclusions and had no intention of cooperating in any objective investigation of January 6th, proclaiming, for example, that the Select Committee was created ". . . solely to malign conservatives and to justify the Left's authoritarian agenda." [757]

On July 21st, Speaker Nancy Pelosi exercised her power under H. Res. 503 not to approve the appointments of Representatives Jordan or Banks, expressing "concern about statements made and actions taken by these Members" and "the impact their appointments may have on the integrity of the investigation." [758] However, she also stated that she had informed Leader McCarthy ". . . that I was prepared to appoint Representatives Rodney Davis, Kelly Armstrong and Troy Nehls, and requested that he recommend two other Members." [759]

In response, Leader McCarthy elected to remove all five of his Republican appointments, refusing to allow Representatives Armstrong, Davis and Nehls to participate on the Select Committee.[760] On July 26, 2021, Speaker Pelosi then appointed Republican Representative Adam Kinzinger.[761] In resisting the Committee's subpoenas, certain litigants attempted to argue that the Commission's Select Committee's composition violated House Rules or H. Res. 503, but those arguments failed in court.[762]

## SELECT COMMITTEE WITNESSES WERE ALMOST ENTIRELY REPUBLICAN

In its ten hearings or business meetings, the Select Committee called live testimony or played video for several dozen witnesses, the vast majority of whom were Republicans. A full list is set forth below.

### Republicans:

- **John McEntee** (served as Director of the White House Presidential Personnel Office in Trump Administration)
- **Judd Deere** (served as Deputy Assistant to the President and White House Deputy Press Secretary in the Trump Administration)
- **Jared Kushner** (served as a Senior Advisor to President Donald Trump)
- **Pat Cipollone** (served as White House Counsel for President Donald Trump)
- **Eric Herschmann** (served as a Senior Advisor to President Donald Trump)
- **Kayleigh McEnany** (served as White House Press Secretary in Trump Administration)
- **Derek Lyons** (served as White House Staff Secretary and Counselor to the President in the Trump Administration)
- **Cassidy Hutchinson** (served as Assistant to Chief of Staff Mark Meadows in the Trump Administration)
- **Matt Pottinger** (served as Deputy National Security Advisor in the Trump Administration)
- **Ben Williamson** (served as Senior Advisor to Chief of Staff Mark Meadows)
- **Sarah Matthews** (served as Deputy Press Secretary in the Trump Administration)
- **William Barr** (served as Attorney General in the Trump Administration)
- **Mike Pompeo** (served as Director of the Central Intelligence Agency and Secretary of State in the Trump Administration)
- **Ivanka Trump** (served as a Senior Advisor and Director of the Office of Economic Initiatives and Entrepreneurship in the Trump Administration)
- **Donald Trump Jr.** (eldest child of Donald Trump)
- **Molly Michael** (served as Deputy Assistant to the President and Executive Assistant to the President)
- **Tim Murtaugh** (served as Director of Communications for the Trump 2020 Presidential campaign)

- **Richard Donoghue** (served as Acting Deputy Attorney General in the Trump Administration)
- **Jeffrey Rosen** (served as Acting Attorney General in the Trump Administration)
- **Steven Engel** (served as Assistant Attorney General for the Office of Legal Counsel in the Trump Administration)
- **Marc Short** (served as Chief of Staff to Vice President Mike Pence)
- **Greg Jacob** (served as Counsel to Vice President Mike Pence)
- **Keith Kellogg** (served as National Security Advisor to Vice President Mike Pence)
- **Chris Hodgson** (served as Director of Legislative Affairs for Vice President Mike Pence)
- **Douglas Macgregor** (served as advisor to the Secretary of Defense in the Trump Administration)
- **Jason Miller** (served as spokesman for the Donald Trump 2016 Presidential Campaign and was a Senior Adviser to the Trump 2020 Presidential Campaign)
- **Alex Cannon** (Counsel for the Trump 2020 Presidential Campaign)
- **Bill Stepien** (served as the Campaign Manager for the Trump 2020 Presidential Campaign and was the White House Director of Political Affairs in the Trump Administration from 2017 to 2018)
- **Rudolph Giuliani** (an attorney for Donald Trump)
- **John Eastman** (an attorney for Donald Trump)
- **Michael Flynn** (served as National Security Advisor in the Trump Administration)
- **Eugene Scalia** (served as the Secretary of Labor in the Trump Administration)
- **Matthew Morgan** (General Counsel for the Trump 2020 Presidential Campaign)
- **Sidney Powell** (an attorney and advisor to Donald Trump)
- **Jeffrey Clark** (served as Acting Assistant Attorney General for the Civil Division in the Trump Administration)
- **Cleta Mitchell** (an attorney working with the Trump 2020 Presidential Campaign)
- **Ronna Romney McDaniel** (Chair of the Republican National Committee)
- **Justin Clark** (served as Deputy Campaign Manager for the Trump 2020 Presidential Campaign)
- **Robert Sinners** (Georgia State Director of Election Day Operations for the Trump 2020 Presidential Campaign)
- **Andrew Hitt** (Wisconsin Republican Party Chair)
- **Laura Cox** (Michigan Republican Party Chair)

- **Mike Shirkey** (Majority Leader, Michigan State Senate)
- **Bryan Cutler** (Speaker, Pennsylvania House of Representatives)
- **Rusty Bowers** (Speaker, Arizona House of Representatives)
- **Brad Raffensperger** (Georgia Secretary of State)
- **Gabriel Sterling** (Georgia Secretary of State, Chief Operating Officer)
- **BJay Pak** (served as United States Attorney for the Northern District of Georgia in the Trump Administration)
- **Al Schmidt** (City Commissioner of Philadelphia)
- **Chris Stirewalt** (Fox News Political Editor)
- **Benjamin Ginsberg** (Election Attorney)
- **J. Michael Luttig** (Retired judge for the U.S. Court of Appeals for the Fourth Circuit and informal advisor to Vice President Mike Pence)
- **Katrina Pierson** (served as a liaison for the White House and organizers at Donald Trump's "Save America" rally on January 6)
- **Nicholas Luna** (served as Personal Aide to President Trump)
- **Stephen Miller** (served as Senior Advisor to President Trump)
- **Vincent Haley** (served as Deputy Assistant to the President and Advisor for Policy, Strategy and Speechwriting in the Trump Administration)
- **Julie Radford** (Chief of Staff to Ivanka Trump in the Trump Administration)
- **Mick Mulvaney** (former Acting Chief of Staff and Special Envoy for Northern Ireland in the Trump Administration)
- **Elaine Chao** (Secretary of Transportation in the Trump Administration)
- **Roger Stone** (Trump associate)

Democrats:

- **Jocelyn Benson** (Michigan Secretary of State)

Other:

- **U.S. Capitol Police Officer Harry Dunn**
- **DC Metropolitan Police Officer Michael Fanone**
- **U.S. Capitol Police Sgt. Aquilino Gonell**
- **DC Metropolitan Police Officer Daniel Hodges**
- **General Mark Milley** (Chairman of the Joint Chiefs of Staff)
- **U.S. Capitol Police Officer Caroline Edwards**
- **Nick Quested** (award-winning British filmmaker)
- **Robert Schornack** (sentenced to 36 months' probation)
- **Eric Barber** (charged with theft and unlawful demonstration in the Capitol)
- **John Wright** (awaiting trial for felony civil disorder and other charges)
- **George Meza** (Proud Boy)

- **Daniel Herendeen** (sentenced to 36 months' probation for role in Capitol attack)
- **Matthew Walter** (Proud Boy)
- **Wandrea ArShaye "Shaye" Moss** (Georgia election worker)
- **Ruby Freeman** (Georgia election worker)
- **Anika Collier Navaroli** (former Twitter employee)
- **White House Security Official**
- **Jim Watkins** (Founder and owner, 8kun)
- **Jody Williams** (former owner of TheDonald.win)
- **Dr. Donell Harvin** (Chief of Homeland Security and Intelligence for the government of the District of Columbia)
- **Kellye SoRelle** (attorney for Oath Keepers)
- **Shealah Craighead** (White House Photographer)
- **Jason Van Tatenhove** (former Oath Keepers spokesperson)
- **Stephen Ayres** (plead guilty to disorderly and disruptive conduct related to Capitol attack)
- **Sgt. Mark Robinson** (Ret.) (Metropolitan Police Department)
- **Janet Buhler** (plead guilty to charges related to the Capitol attack)

# 1

# THE BIG LIE

Late on election night 2020, President Donald J. Trump addressed the nation from the East Room of the White House. When Trump spoke, at 2:21 a.m. on November 4th, the President's re-election was very much in doubt. Fox News, a conservative media outlet, had correctly called Arizona for former Vice President Joseph R. Biden. Every Republican presidential candidate since 1996 had won Arizona. If the President lost the State, and in the days ahead it became clear that he had, then his campaign was in trouble. But as the votes continued to be counted, President Trump's apparent early lead in other key States—States he needed to win—steadily shrank. Soon, he would not be in the lead at all—he'd be losing.

So, the President of the United States did something he had planned to do long before election day: he lied.

"This is a fraud on the American public. This is an embarrassment to our country," President Trump said. "We were getting ready to win this election," the President continued. "Frankly, we did win this election. We did win this election." Trump claimed, without offering any evidence, that a "major fraud" was occurring "in our nation." [1]

Neither of President Trump's claims were true. He had no basis for claiming victory or that fraud was taking place. Millions of votes still had not been counted. The States were simply tabulating the ballots cast by the American people. Trump's own campaign advisors told him to wait—that it was far too early to declare victory.

As the evening progressed, President Trump called in his campaign team to discuss the results. Trump Campaign Manager William Stepien and other campaign experts advised him that the results of the election would not be known for some time, and that he could not truthfully declare victory. Stepien was of the view that, because ballots were going to be counted for days, "it was far too early to be making any proclamation [about having won the election]." Stepien told President Trump that his recommendation was to say, "votes are still being counted. It's ... too early to call the race." [2]

Jason Miller, another senior Trump Campaign advisor, told the Select Committee that he argued in conversations with Stepien and others that night against declaring victory at the time as well, because "it was too early to say one way [or] the other" who had won. Miller recalled recommending that "we should not go and declare victory until we had a better sense of the numbers." [3]

According to testimony received by the Committee, the only advisor present who supported President Trump's inclination to declare victory was Rudy Giuliani, who, according to Miller, was "definitely intoxicated" that evening. [4]

President Trump's decision to declare victory falsely on election night and, unlawfully, to call for the vote counting to stop, was not a spontaneous decision. It was premeditated. The Committee has assembled a range of evidence of President Trump's preplanning for a false declaration of victory. This includes multiple written communications on October 31st and November 3, 2020, to the White House by Judicial Watch President Tom Fitton.[5] This evidence demonstrates that Fitton was in direct contact with President Trump and understood that he would falsely declare victory on election night and call for vote counting to stop. The evidence also includes an audio recording of President Trump's advisor Steve Bannon, who said this on October 31, 2020, to a group of his associates from China:

> And what Trump's going to do is just declare victory, right? He's gonna declare victory. But that doesn't mean he's the winner. He's just gonna say he's a winner. . . . The Democrats, more of our people vote early that count. Their vote in mail. And so they're gonna have a natural disadvantage, and Trump's going to take advantage of it. That's our strategy. He's gonna declare himself a winner. So when you wake up Wednesday morning, it's going to be a firestorm. . . . Also, if Trump, if Trump is losing, by ten or eleven o'clock at night, it's going to be even crazier. No, because he's gonna sit right there and say 'They stole it. I'm directing the Attorney General to shut down all ballot places in all 50 states. It's going to be, no, he's not going out easy. If Trump—if Biden's winning, Trump is going to do some crazy shit.[6]

Also in advance of the election, Roger Stone, another outside advisor to President Trump, made this statement:

I really do suspect it will still be up in the air. When that happens, the key thing to do is to claim victory. Possession is 9/10s of the law. No, we won. Fuck you, Sorry. Over. We won. You're wrong. Fuck you.[7]

In the days after the election, the President's own campaign team told him he had lost and there was no evidence of significant fraud. When his campaign staff wouldn't tell him what he wanted to hear, President Trump replaced them with what Attorney General William Barr described as a "clown car" of individuals willing to promote various conspiracy theories.[8]

But Donald Trump was no passive consumer of these lies. He actively propagated them. Time and again President Trump was informed that his election fraud claims were not true. He chose to spread them anyway. He did so even after they were legally tested and rejected in dozens of lawsuits. Not even the electoral college's certification of former Vice President Biden's victory on December 14, 2020, stopped the President from lying. Throughout, the Big Lie remained central to President Trump's efforts to block the peaceful transfer of power on January 6, 2021.

### 1.1 THE BIG LIE REFLECTED DELIBERATE EXPLOITATION OF THE "RED MIRAGE"

President Trump's "Big Lie" on election night was based on simple differences in how Americans vote. In 2020, it was well-known that Democrats were much more likely to vote via mail-in ballots than in person in 2020. On the other hand, Republicans generally preferred to vote in person on election day.[9] In key swing States with tight margins between the candidates, the election day votes would favor President Trump and disproportionately be counted first. Mail-in ballots, which would favor former Vice President Biden, would disproportionately be counted later. In some States it would take days to process the remaining mail-in ballots.

The timing of how votes are counted created the potential for what is known as a "Red Mirage"—or an illusion of a Republican (Red) victory in the early stages of vote counting. President Trump would appear to be in the lead on election night, but this was not the whole picture. Many mail-in votes for former Vice President Biden would not be counted on election day. Therefore, the actual winner would likely not be known on election night.

The "Red Mirage" phenomenon was widely known prior to the 2020 presidential election. Chris Stirewalt was the head of the Fox News elections desk that correctly called Arizona for Biden. Stirewalt and his team tried to warn viewers of the Red Mirage. He testified that over the past 40 or 50 years, "Americans have increasingly chosen to vote by mail or early or absentee," and that "Democrats prefer that method of voting more than

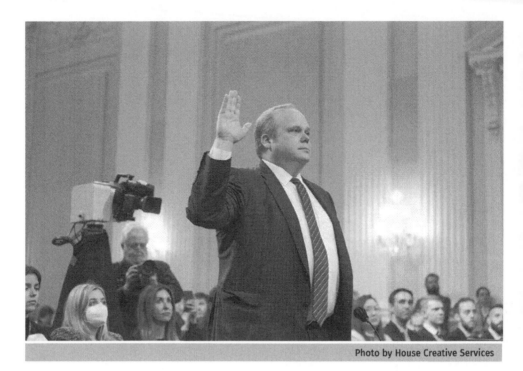

Photo by House Creative Services

Republicans do." [10] In nearly "every election," Stirewalt elaborated, "Republicans win Election Day and Democrats win the early vote, and then you wait and start counting." It "[h]appens every time." [11]

President Trump's campaign team made sure the President was briefed on the timing of vote tallying. Stepien, his campaign manager, told the Select Committee that President Trump was reminded on election day that large numbers of mail-in ballots would still remain to be counted over the coming days. [12] Stepien added that he personally reminded the President that while early returns may be favorable, the counting would continue: "I recounted back to 2016 when I had a very similar conversation with him on election day... I recounted back to that conversation with him in which I said, just like I said in 2016 was going to be a long night, I told him in 2020 that, you know, it was going to be a process again, as, you know, the early returns are going to be positive. Then we're going to, you know, be watching the returns of ballots as, you know, they rolled in thereafter." [13]

Ordinarily, the "Red Mirage" anomaly does not create problems in the election process because candidates wait for the votes to be tallied before declaring victory or conceding. As Stirewalt emphasized, prior to President Trump, "no candidate had ever tried to avail themselves of this quirk in the election counting system." [14]

CHAPTER 1

President Trump, however, made a different choice. In an extraordinary breach of the American democratic process, he decided to exploit the potential for confusion about the staggered timing of vote counting to deceive the American public about the election results. He and his allies foreshadowed this decision in their statements in the months leading up to the November 2020 election.

## 1.2  TRUMP'S PRE-ELECTION PLANS TO DECLARE VICTORY

On Halloween, advisor Steve Bannon, who had served four years earlier as Donald Trump's 2016 campaign manager, laid out the election night plan. "What Trump's gonna do is just declare victory. Right? He's gonna declare victory. But that doesn't mean he's a winner," Bannon told a private audience. "He's just gonna *say* he's a winner." [15]

Bannon explained that the Democrats "[would] have a natural disadvantage" on election night, because more Democrats would vote by mail than Republicans and it would take time to count the mail-in ballots. This would give President Trump the illusion of a lead. "And Trump's going to take advantage of it," Bannon said. "That's our strategy. He's gonna declare himself a winner." [16]

In an interview on Fox News the morning of the election, Bannon insisted that President Trump needed to address the nation that night, to "provide the narrative engine for how we go forward." [17] During an episode of his podcast later that same day, Bannon clarified what he meant: President Trump is "going to claim victory. Right? He's going to claim victory." [18]

Tom Fitton drafted a victory statement for the President to read on election night.[19] On October 31st, he emailed the statement to President Trump's assistant, Molly Michael, and social media guru, Dan Scavino. Fitton wrote that election day, November 3rd, was the "deadline by which voters in states across the country *must* choose a president." Fitton argued that counting ballots that arrived after election day would be part of an effort by "partisans" to "overturn" the election results.[20]

Of course, that claim wasn't true—mail-in ballots are regularly processed after election day. Regardless, Fitton encouraged the President to pre-emptively declare victory. "We had an election today—and I won," Fitton wrote for President Trump.[21] Early in the evening on election day, Fitton emailed Michael again to say he had "[j]ust talked to him [President Trump] about the draft [statement]." [22] Later that evening, before President Trump made his election night remarks, Michael replied that she was "...redelivering to him [President Trump] now." [23]

October 31, 2020

He's just gonna say he's a winner.

Photo by Alex Wong/Getty Images

Roger Stone, President Trump's longtime political confidante, told several associates just prior to the election that Trump needed to declare victory—especially if the race wasn't called on election day. "Let's just hope we are celebrating" on election night, Stone said. "I really do suspect it will still be up in the air. When that happens, the key thing to do is claim victory." Stone elaborated with colorful language. "Possession is nine-tenths of the law. No, we won. Fuck you. Sorry. Over. We won. You're wrong. Fuck you." [24]

Indeed, published reports echoed these warnings about President Trump's election strategy. Two days before the election, Jonathan Swan of *Axios* reported that President Trump "has told confidants he'll declare victory on Tuesday night if it looks like he's 'ahead.'" [25] Swan added that "Trump's team is preparing to falsely claim that mail-in ballots counted after Nov. 3—a legitimate count expected to favor Democrats—are evidence of election fraud." [26] If the vote tally swung against Trump after election night in States such as Pennsylvania, then the Trump team would claim the Democrats had "stolen" the election. [27] Fox News election analysis Chris Stirewalt testified that he and his team "had gone to pains" to inform viewers that early votes would favor Republicans but the lead would be illusory "because the Trump campaign and the President had made it clear that they were going to try to exploit this anomaly."[28] Others warned that President Trump could exploit the Red Mirage as well.[29]

## 1.3  TRUMP'S PRE-ELECTION EFFORTS TO DELEGITIMIZE THE ELECTION PROCESS

President Trump also paved the way for his false election-night declaration of victory by blanketing voters with a blizzard of lies and statements delegitimizing mail-in voting in the middle of a deadly pandemic and consistently questioning the security of ballots. President Trump used the president's bully pulpit, including his heavily-trafficked Twitter feed, to tell one lie after another.

The Select Committee found dozens of instances in which President Trump claimed that mail-in voting would produce a "rigged" election. Trump repeatedly denounced mail-in voting on Twitter, during interviews, and even during the presidential debate. Here is a small sample of President Trump's attempts to delegitimize mail-in balloting.

On April 7, 2020, President Trump claimed:

*Mail ballots are a very dangerous thing for this country, because they're cheaters. They go and collect them. They're fraudulent in many cases.... These mailed ballots come in. The mailed ballots are corrupt, in my opinion. And they collect them, and they get people to go in and sign them. And then they—they're forgeries in many cases. It's a horrible thing.[30]*

The following day, April 8, President Trump tweeted:

*Republicans should fight very hard when it comes to statewide mail-in voting. Democrats are clamoring for it. Tremendous potential for voter fraud, and for whatever reason, doesn't work out well for Republicans. @foxandfriends[31]*

On May 24, President Trump tweeted:

*The United States cannot have all Mail In Ballots. It will be the greatest Rigged Election in history. People grab them from mailboxes, print thousands of forgeries and "force" people to sign. Also, forge names. Some absentee OK, when necessary. Trying to use Covid for this Scam![32]*

On September 17, President Trump falsely alleged that mail-in ballots were ripe for foreign interference:

*@TrueTheVote There is a group of people (largely Radical Left Democrats) that want ELECTION MAYHEM. States must end this CRAZY mass*

*sending of Ballots. Also, a GIFT to foreign interference into our election!!! Stop it now, before it is too late.*[33]

Before the election, as President Trump campaigned against mail-in voting, Bill Stepien sought an intercession. Along with House Minority Leader Kevin McCarthy, Stepien attempted to convince the President that mail-in voting was "not…a bad thing for his campaign."[34] They argued that President Trump's decision to discourage mail-in voting, while "urging [his] voters to vote only on election day leaves a lot to chance" and would fail to take advantage of a superior grassroots operation that could encourage Trump voters to return their ballots.[35] President Trump did not heed their warning. He continued to demonize mail-in voting. The Red Mirage was a key part of his "Big Lie."

Ominously, President Trump consistently refused to commit to accepting the outcome of the election. During an interview on Fox News in July, Chris Wallace asked: "Can you give a direct answer [if] you will accept the election?" President Trump responded: "I have to see. Look, you—I have to see. No, I'm not going to just say yes. I'm not going to say no, and I didn't last time either."[36]

On September 23, 2020, a reporter asked President Trump if he would commit to a "peaceful transferal of power after the election." The President refused, saying, "we're going to have to see what happens."[37] The President claimed, "the ballots are disaster," adding that if he could "get rid of the ballots…we'll have a very peaceful—there won't be a transfer, frankly; there'll be a continuation."[38] That is, according to President Trump, there would be a "continuation" of his presidency.

The following day, September 24, another reporter followed up by asking if the election would be legitimate only if President Trump won. The President again suggested there was something suspect about mail-in ballots, adding that he was "not sure" the election could be an honest one.[39]

## 1.4 PRESIDENT TRUMP'S LAUNCH OF THE BIG LIE

Consistent with the pre-election narrative planted by President Trump, within hours of polls closing, President Trump began pushing the claim that late-reported vote tallies were illegitimate.[40] Even though he had been reminded by his Campaign Manager that very day that a large number of mail-in ballots would not be counted for several hours or days,[41] President Trump claimed that Democrats were going to "find…ballots at four o'clock in the morning and add them to the list."[42] He also suggested that Democrats were continuing to vote after the polls had closed.[43]

Indeed, this is exactly what Steve Bannon described when he said President Trump would "take advantage" of the Democrats' "natural disadvantage" on election night.[44]

In the ensuing days and weeks, President Trump often referred to "dumps" of votes that were injected into the counting process.[45] His supporters latched onto these false claims.[46] There were no "dumps" of votes—just tallies of absentee ballots as they were reported by jurisdictions throughout the country in a fully transparent process.[47] These batches of ballots included votes for both Trump and Biden. The late-reported votes favored the former Vice President, just as President Trump's campaign advisors said they would, particularly in primarily Democratic cities.[48]

Attorney General Bill Barr recognized immediately that the "Red Mirage" was the basis for President Trump's erroneous claim of fraud. "[R]ight out of the box on election night, the President claimed that there was major fraud underway," Barr said. "I mean, this happened, as far as I could tell, before there was actually any potential of looking at evidence."[49] President Trump's claim "seemed to be based on the dynamic that, at the end of the evening, a lot of Democratic votes came in which changed the vote counts in certain states, and that seemed to be the basis for this broad claim that there was major fraud."[50]

President Trump knew about the Red Mirage. He chose to lie about it repeatedly—even after being directly informed that his claims were false. This was often the case in the post-election period. The President consciously disregarded facts that did not support his Big Lie.

### 1.5 POST-ELECTION: PRESIDENT TRUMP REPLACES HIS CAMPAIGN TEAM

President Trump's campaign leadership, including Bill Stepien (the campaign's manager) and Justin Clark (the campaign's deputy manager), supported President Trump, and were willing to pursue recounts and other standard post-election litigation, but they were not willing to promote baseless conspiracy theories.[51] Stepien and others characterized this group as "Team Normal."[52]

Less than two weeks after the election, President Trump pushed "Team Normal" aside because its members didn't tell him what he wanted to hear. In their place, Trump promoted Rudy Giuliani and his associates, men and women who spread baseless and extreme claims of election fraud. Giuliani, the former mayor of New York City, recruited several investigators and lawyers to assist him.[53] Giuliani's team included Jenna Ellis, Bernard Kerik, Boris Epshteyn, Katherine Friess, and Christina Bobb.[54] Ellis functioned as

Giuliani's deputy on the new Trump Campaign legal team.[55] Kerik, the former commissioner of the New York Police Department and a pardoned felon, served as Giuliani's chief investigator.[56] Other attorneys who collaborated with Giuliani's legal team included Sidney Powell, Cleta Mitchell, and John Eastman. As discussed elsewhere in this report, Eastman became a key player in President Trump's efforts to overturn the election.

## 1.6 PRESIDENT TRUMP'S CAMPAIGN TEAM TOLD HIM HE LOST THE ELECTION AND THERE WAS NO SIGNIFICANT FRAUD

President Trump's campaign team quickly realized that none of the significant fraud claims were real. Bill Stepien testified that, as of November 5th, the Trump Campaign had not found any proof of fraudulent activity. There were "allegations and reports," but "nothing hard [and] fast" that drew the results of the election into question.[57]

The Trump Campaign continued to investigate claims of fraud into the second week after the election. According to Stepien, as people shared "wild allegations" with the President, the campaign team was forced to review the facts and then serve as a "truth telling squad" to the President regarding why the claims "didn't prove to be true."[58] For example, Stepien recalled someone alleging that thousands of illegal votes had been cast in Arizona. That wasn't true. The votes had been submitted by overseas voters (such as military deployed or stationed abroad) who were obviously eligible to participate in the election.[59]

Alex Cannon was a lawyer for the Trump Campaign and previously worked for the Trump Organization. After the election, Cannon was tasked with looking into allegations of voter fraud in the 2020 election—including the claim that thousands of ineligible votes had been cast in Arizona.[60] Cannon recalled that Vice President Pence asked him what he was finding. "And I said that I didn't believe we were finding it, or I was not personally finding anything sufficient to alter the results of the election," Cannon responded. Vice President Pence thanked him.[61]

Cannon reported his assessment to Mark Meadows, the White House Chief of Staff, as well. In mid to late-November 2020, Meadows asked Cannon what his investigation had turned up. "And I remember sharing with him that we weren't finding anything that would be sufficient to change the results in any of the key states," Cannon told Meadows. "So there is no there, there?" Meadows replied.[62]

Jason Miller, a senior advisor to the Trump Campaign, pushed claims of election fraud in public. In private, however, Miller says that he told President Trump a different story, informing him numerous times that there was not enough election fraud to have changed the election:

Miller: My understanding is that I think there are still very valid questions and concerns with the rules that were changed under the guise of COVID, but, specific to election day fraud and irregularities, there were not enough to overturn the election.

Committee Staff: And did you give your opinion on that to the President?

Miller: Yes.

Committee Staff: What was his reaction when you told him that?

Miller: "You haven't seen or heard"—I'm paraphrasing, but—"you haven't seen or heard all the different concerns and questions that have been raised."

Committee Staff: How many times did you have this conversation with the President?

Miller: Several. I couldn't put a specific number on it, though.

Committee Staff: But more than one?

Miller: Correct.[63]

Matthew Morgan, the Trump Campaign's top lawyer, came to a similar conclusion. Nearly two months after the election, on January 2nd, Morgan met with the Vice President's staff. According to Morgan, the consensus in the room was that even if all the claims of fraud and irregularities were "aggregated and read most favorably to the campaign...it was not sufficient to be outcome determinative."[64]

As far as the Trump Campaign's professional leadership was concerned, there was no evidence that the election had been "stolen" from President Trump. To the contrary, they had seen ample evidence that President Trump simply lost—and told the President so.

On November 6th, Jared Kushner arranged for the senior campaign staff to brief President Trump in the Oval Office on the state of the race.[65] Since election day, Matt Oczkowski, the Campaign's leading data expert, had tracked voting returns in the swing States to analyze the campaign's odds of success.[66] Miller texted such updates on data from key States to Meadows.[67] The Trump Campaign's data did not add up to victory. Oczkowski "delivered to the President in pretty blunt terms that he was going to lose" the election.[68] There were not enough outstanding votes in the battle-ground States for President Trump to overcome Biden's lead. President Trump disagreed and insisted that he would still prevail through legal challenges.[69]

But the data did not lie.

On November 7th, the *Associated Press* called Pennsylvania and the overall presidential election for former Vice President Biden.[70] At that point, a small team of the President's campaign advisors including Stepien met with the President and told him that his path to victory was virtually non-existent.[71] The campaign team conveyed to the President that his chance of success was only "5, maybe 10 percent," which Stepien explained to the Committee was a "very, very, very bleak" assessment.[72]

In retrospect, the campaign's estimate of a 5 to 10 percent chance of winning, as of November 7th, was far *too optimistic.* In one of the most favorable possible scenarios, for example, President Trump and his team would need to win recounts in Arizona and Georgia, while also prevailing in litigation challenging absentee or vote by mail ballots in Wisconsin, or possibly Michigan or Pennsylvania.[73] But the election wasn't even close enough to trigger automatic recounts in Arizona or Georgia.

The narrowest margin of total votes between the two candidates was in Arizona, where former Vice President Biden won by more than 10,000 votes. This may seem like a small number of votes, but it was more than enough to avoid an automatic recount. As Benjamin Ginsberg, a longtime Republican elections lawyer, explained to the Select Committee, "the 2020 election was not close." [74] Previous campaigns had successfully challenged vote differentials in the hundreds—not thousands—of votes. [75] Ginsberg explained, "you just don't make up those sorts of numbers in recounts." [76] Georgia performed a hand recount of all the ballots anyway, confirming within weeks of the election that Biden had won the State. [77] Also, by January 6th, Arizona and New Mexico had conducted statutory post-election audits of voting machines or randomly-selected, representative samples of ballots at the State- or county-level that affirmed the accuracy of their election results. [78]

Chris Stirewalt, who led the elections desk at Fox News at the time, concurred with Ginsberg's analysis. Asked what President Trump's odds of victory were as of November 7th, Stirewalt replied: "None." [79]

Meanwhile, the Trump Campaign continued to crunch the numbers. On the morning of November 12th, Oczkowski circulated among top campaign advisors a presentation describing what happened in each of the battleground States the campaign was monitoring. [80] This analysis by the data team examined the turnout and margins on a county-by-county basis in a dozen States while also analyzing demographic changes that impacted the results. [81] Among the States were Arizona, Georgia, Michigan, Pennsylvania, Nevada, and Wisconsin. [82] Oczkowski's team determined that President Trump lost each of those six States because Biden had performed better than President Trump in certain areas like population centers or suburbs. [83] Yet, in the weeks that followed, President Trump and his new legal team— the "clown car"—went to great lengths to challenge the results of the election in these six states, spreading multiple conspiracy theories.

The voting data told a clear story: President Trump lost. But, regardless of the facts, the President had no intention of conceding defeat.

On election night, President Trump and Rudy Giuliani agreed that the President should just declare victory—even though he had no basis for doing so. Giuliani also told the Select Committee that President Trump asked him on November 4th to take over his campaign's legal operation. [84] Giuliani thought the only way that it would work would be for the President to call the existing campaign team to announce Giuliani's takeover because, in Giuliani's words, "they are going to be extraordinarily resentful, because they don't like me already, and I don't trust them." [85] He said that the President agreed. [86]

Although Giuliani wouldn't assume leadership of the Campaign's legal operations until mid-November, the former New York City mayor quickly began to butt heads with "Team Normal."

On November 6th, Giuliani and his team met with the Trump Campaign's leadership at its headquarters in Arlington, Virginia.[87]

"Team Normal" was not impressed. Stepien told the Select Committee the campaign team was concerned that Giuliani would be a distraction to them and to President Trump.[88] When Giuliani suggested traveling to Pennsylvania to assist in the campaign's efforts, the campaign team "didn't dissuade him from doing so."[89] After just 10 to 15 minutes in the conference room, Stepien and other staffers left the meeting.[90]

That same day, President Trump discussed the Campaign's legal strategy in the Oval Office with Giuliani, Clark, and Matt Morgan, the Trump Campaign's General Counsel.[91] Prior to the election, Morgan was responsible for the Campaign's litigation strategy.[92] Morgan and his team filed lawsuits challenging the changes States made to voting practices during the coronavirus pandemic.[93] Morgan also studied previous elections to determine the types of cases that were likely to succeed.[94] Clark described how the Campaign's original legal strategy was based on his general theory for election cases: "to look at what do you think, what do you know, and what can you prove" and then determine which cases to file from there.[95]

Giuliani had other ideas and advocated to President Trump that he be put in charge of the Campaign's legal operation so that he could pursue his preferred strategy.[96] "Mr. Giuliani didn't seem bound by those cases or by those precedents. He felt he could press forward on anything that he thought was wrong with the election and bring a strategy around that," Morgan explained.[97] "Rudy was just chasing ghosts," Clark said.[98] Morgan and Clark excused themselves from the meeting because it "was going nowhere."[99]

The next day, November 7th, Giuliani held a press conference at Four Seasons Total Landscaping in Philadelphia, Pennsylvania. He immediately began making outlandish claims, arguing that the Democrats had conspired to steal the election. "As you know from the very beginning, mail-in ballots were a source of some degree of skepticism, if not a lot of skepticism, as being innately prone to fraud," Giuliani said. "Those mail-in ballots could have been written the day before by the Democratic Party hacks that were all over the Convention Center."[100] Giuliani offered no evidence to support his shocking and baseless allegation. Echoes of President Trump's relentless campaign against mail-in balloting, and his decision to exploit the Red Mirage, were easy to hear.

Photo by Chris McGrath/Getty Images

On November 10th, Giuliani and Kerik met with President Trump in the Oval Office to discuss their investigation into voter fraud. White House Counsel Pat Cipollone and White House Senior Advisor Eric Herschmann were also in attendance. After Giuliani's presentation, President Trump asked Cipollone whether he had spoken to Attorney General Barr about the allegations of fraud.[101] One day before, Barr had issued a memorandum outlining a shift in DOJ policy that allowed Federal prosecutors to investigate claims of voting irregularities without waiting for the results to be certified.[102] President Trump's question was an early indication that he was going to pressure the DOJ to endorse his phony fraud claims.

Days later, Giuliani and Justin Clark engaged in a screaming match during a meeting in the Oval Office.[103] Giuliani was urging President Trump to file a lawsuit in Georgia, but Clark pointed out that a hand recount was already being conducted and argued it was better to wait.[104] Giuliani told President Trump that Clark was lying to him.[105] A formal changing of the guard would follow.

On November 14th, President Trump announced on Twitter that Giuliani was now the head of his campaign's legal team.[106] "Team Normal" saw drastic changes to their roles on the newly-structured campaign team—some self-imposed—and many outside law firms that had signed up to support the campaign's legal efforts disengaged completely.[107]

"I didn't think what was happening was necessarily honest or professional at that point in time," Stepien explained. "This wasn't a fight that I was comfortable with," he added.[108]

On the day the leadership change was announced, Giuliani participated in a "surrogate" briefing to coordinate messaging by Trump loyalists during their media appearances.[109] Giuliani announced that the messaging strategy should be "to go hard on Dominion/Smartmatic, bringing up Chavez and Maduro."[110] Giuliani claimed that additional lawsuits would soon be filed "to invalidate upwards of 1M ballots."[111]

Consistent with the messaging advanced by the new campaign team, President Trump in mid-November remained dug-in, still refusing to concede defeat. President Trump continued to insist that he was cheated out of victory, endorsing one wild conspiracy theory after another to deny the simple fact that he lost.

## 1.7 PRESIDENT TRUMP HAD HIS DAY IN COURT

"We've proven" the election was stolen, but "no judge, including the Supreme Court of the United States, has had the courage to allow it to be heard."[112] That was how President Trump described efforts to overturn the election in court one day before the electoral college met on December 14, 2020. That was false.

Judges across the nation *did* evaluate President Trump's claims that the election was stolen. As longtime Republican election attorney Benjamin Ginsberg testified before the Select Committee, the President's camp "did have their day in court," it's just that "in no instance did a court find that the charges of fraud were real."[113] In total, the Trump Campaign and allies of President Trump filed 62 separate lawsuits between November 4, 2020, and January 6, 2021, calling into question or seeking to overturn the election results.[114] Out of 62 cases, only one case resulted in a victory for the President Trump or his allies, which affected relatively few votes, did not vindicate any underlying claims of fraud, and would not have changed the outcome in Pennsylvania.[115] Thirty of the cases were dismissed by a judge *after* a hearing on the merits.[116]

In every State in which claims were brought, one or more judges specifically explained as part of their dismissal orders that they had evaluated the plaintiffs' allegations or supposed proof of widespread election fraud or other irregularities, and found the claims to be entirely unconvincing. In

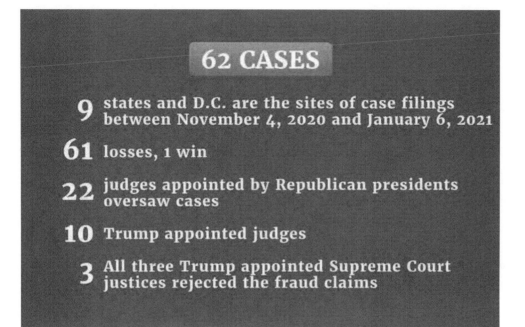

## 62 CASES

**9** states and D.C. are the sites of case filings between November 4, 2020 and January 6, 2021

**61** losses, 1 win

**22** judges appointed by Republican presidents oversaw cases

**10** Trump appointed judges

**3** All three Trump appointed Supreme Court justices rejected the fraud claims

Arizona, for example, the plaintiffs in *Bowyer v. Ducey* alleged that the election was tainted by the introduction of "hundreds of thousands of illegal, ineligible, duplicate or purely fictitious ballots."[117] A Federal judge dismissed their suit, finding it "void of plausible allegations" and "sorely wanting of relevant or reliable evidence."[118] Likewise, in *Ward v. Jackson*, an Arizona State-court judge dismissed a lawsuit by the State GOP chair following a two-day trial, finding no evidence of misconduct, fraud, or illegal votes.[119] This ruling was unanimously upheld by the State supreme court, where all seven justices were appointed by GOP governors.[120]

In Georgia, a State court dismissed *Boland v. Raffensperger*, which alleged that tens of thousands of illegal ballots were cast by out-of-State voters or with invalid signature matches.[121] The judge found that "the Complaint's factual allegations . . . rest on speculation rather than duly pled facts" and "do not support . . . a conclusion that sufficient illegal votes were cast to change or place in doubt the result of the election."[122] The judge who issued this decision had been appointed by a Republican governor, as had seven of the eight justices of the State supreme court who upheld her ruling.[123] Likewise, a Federal judge denied relief to the plaintiff in *Wood v. Raffensperger*, which alleged that new procedures for checking absentee ballot signatures spoiled the result by making it harder to reject illegal ballots, finding "no basis in fact or law to grant him the relief he seeks."[124]

The judge wrote that "[t]his argument is belied by the record" because absentee ballots were actually rejected for signature issues at the same rate as in 2018.[125]

In Michigan, a Federal judge found in *King v. Whitmer* that the plaintiffs' claims of "massive election fraud" were based on "nothing but speculation and conjecture that votes for President Trump were destroyed, discarded or switched to votes for Vice President Biden...."[126] Similarly, a State-court judge rejected plaintiffs' claims in two cases brought against Detroit and the surrounding county that accused them of systematic fraud in how absentee ballots were counted; the judge found that one group of plaintiffs "...offered no evidence to support their assertions,"[127] and that the other group's "interpretation of events is incorrect" and "decidedly contradicted" by "highly-respected" election experts.[128]

In Nevada, a State-court judge rejected a litany of claims of systematic election fraud in *Law v. Whitmer*, ruling that plaintiffs "did not prove under any standard of proof that illegal votes were cast and counted, or legal votes were not counted at all, due to voter fraud" or "for any other improper or illegal reason."[129] The ruling was unanimously upheld by the Nevada Supreme Court.[130]

In Pennsylvania, a Federal judge dismissed *Donald Trump for President v. Boockvar*, finding that the Trump Campaign had presented nothing but "strained legal arguments without merit and speculative accusations unpled in the operative complaint and unsupported by evidence."[131] The dismissal was upheld by the United States Court of Appeals for the Third Circuit, which held: "[C]alling an election unfair does not make it so. Charges require specific allegations and then proof. We have neither here."[132] That opinion was authored by another Trump appointee.[133]

Lastly, in Wisconsin, another judge dismissed a lawsuit accusing the Wisconsin Elections Commission of "constitutional violations" that "likely tainted more than 50,000 ballots."[134] The judge ruled: "This Court has allowed plaintiff the chance to make his case and he has lost on the merits," failing to show that the outcome was affected by Commission rules about drop boxes, ballot addresses, or individuals who claimed "indefinitely confined" status to vote from home.[135] The ruling was upheld by a three-judge panel of the United States Court of Appeals for the Seventh Circuit, all of whom were Republican appointees, including one appointed by President Trump himself.[136]

In all, the judges who heard these post-election cases included 22 Federal judges appointed by Republican presidents.[137]

President Trump and his lawyers were well-aware that courts were consistently rejecting his claims. During a December 18th meeting in the

Oval Office with President Trump, Sidney Powell and others, White House Senior Advisor Eric Herschmann pointed out that President Trump's lawyers had their opportunity to prove their case in court, and failed. Powell fired back that "the judges are corrupt." Herschmann responded: "Every one? Every single case that you've done in the country you guys lost, every one of them is corrupt, even the ones we appointed?"[138]

President Trump was faced with another choice after having his day in court. He could accept that there was no real evidence of voter fraud, or he could continue to amplify conspiracy theories and lies. He chose the latter.

## 1.8  PRESIDENT TRUMP REPEATEDLY PROMOTED CONSPIRACY THEORIES

Instead of accepting his defeat, President Trump attempted to justify his Big Lie with a series of increasingly preposterous claims. The President was not simply led astray by those around him. The opposite was true. He actively promoted conspiracy theories and false election fraud claims even after being informed they were baseless. Millions of President Trump's supporters believed the election was stolen from him. Many of them still do, but President Trump knew the truth and chose to lie about it.

The power of the President's bully pulpit should not be underestimated, especially in the digital age.[139] President Trump's relentless lying sowed seeds of distrust in America's election system. Researchers who studied this election-denial phenomenon have noted: "President Trump didn't just prime his audience to be receptive to false narratives of election fraud—he inspired them to produce those narratives and then echoed those false claims back to them."[140] Social media played a prominent role in amplifying erroneous claims of election fraud. Shortly after election day, the "Stop the Steal" campaign, discussed more fully in Chapter 6, went viral. "Stop the Steal" influencers echoed President Trump's premature declaration of victory, asserting that he won the election, the Democrats stole it from him, and it was the responsibility of American "patriots" to combat this supposed injustice.[141]

This resulted in what Attorney General Barr has described as an "avalanche" of false claims, as President Trump's supporters attempted to justify his "Big Lie."[142] The post-election allegations of fraud or other malfeasance were "completely bogus," "silly" and "usually based on complete misinformation," Barr explained.[143] Nonetheless, many of President Trump's supporters wanted to believe them. The stolen election narrative has proven to be remarkably durable precisely because it is a matter of belief—not evidence, or reason. Each time a claim was debunked, more

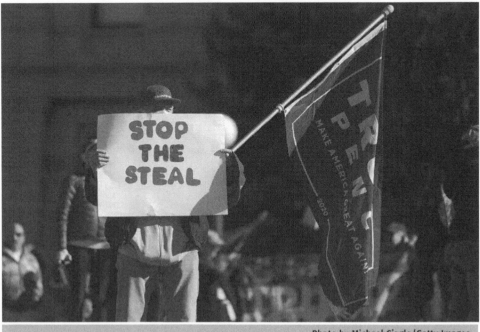

claims emerged in its place. Barr later complained that this dynamic forced him and others to play "whack-a-mole." [144]

The United States Department of Justice, under Barr's leadership and then Acting Attorney General Jeffrey Rosen, was forced to knock down one lie after another. As discussed in Chapter 4, Barr took unprecedented steps to investigate the "avalanche" of lies. Claims of election fraud were referred to United States Attorney's offices and the FBI for investigation. Deputy Attorney General Richard Donoghue tracked dozens of investigations. None of them were found to have merit.[145] The top officials in President Trump's Justice Department personally told the President that the claims he was promoting were false. But that did not matter to the President. As Barr told the Select Committee, President Trump never showed any "indication of interest in what the actual facts were." [146]

For example, on December 27th, Rosen and Donoghue spent approximately two hours on the phone with President Trump. They debunked a litany of claims regarding the election, explaining that each had been investigated and found to be baseless.[147] According to Donoghue, President Trump "had this arsenal of allegations that he wanted to rely on." Donoghue thought it was necessary to explain to the President "based on actual investigations, actual witness interviews, actual reviews of documents, that these allegations simply had no merit." Donoghue wanted "to cut through the noise" and be "very blunt" with the President, making it clear "these allegations were simply not true."[148]

During their December 27th conversation with President Trump, Rosen and Donoghue rebutted false claims regarding: suitcases of ballots in Georgia, Dominion's voting machines in Antrim County, a truckload of ballots in Pennsylvania, ballots being scanned multiple times, people voting more than once, dead people voting, Native Americans being paid to vote, and more votes than voters in particular jurisdictions.[149] As the officials debunked each claim, President Trump "would just roll on to another one."[150] Donoghue told President Trump that Federal law enforcement officials had conducted dozens of investigations and hundreds of interviews, and they had concluded that the major allegations were not supported by the evidence developed.[151] Donoghue and Rosen told President Trump "flat out" that "much of the information he [was] getting [was] false and/or just not supported by the evidence."[152] President Trump responded: "You guys may not be following the internet the way I do."[153]

The Department of Justice was not alone in trying to contain the President's conspiracy-mongering. President Trump's lies were often debunked in real-time by State authorities, judges, experts, journalists, Federal officials, and even members of his own legal team. As discussed above, the President's campaign team found that there was no significant fraud in the election. So, the President pushed them aside. The courts rejected nearly every claim brought by the President's legal team. Even though courts rejected the claims as speculative, unsupported and meritless, President Trump, Rudy Giuliani, and others continued to assert them as truth to Trump's followers in speeches, tweets, and podcasts.[154]

The burden of refuting the false claims made by President Trump and his surrogates often fell on State and local officials. For example, in Michigan, the Secretary of State's office posted thorough and prompt responses to the claims of election fraud on a "Fact Check" page on its website.[155] In Georgia, the Secretary of State's office issued news releases and held frequent press conferences in the weeks following the election to respond to claims of fraud.[156] County clerks in the contested States also spoke out publicly to refute allegations. Even as the President undermined the public's confidence in how votes are cast and counted, these clerks assured voters that their elections were secure and they could have confidence in the results.[157] Outside experts also publicly denounced and dismantled the claims being raised and amplified by President Trump. This was done in the context of litigation, congressional hearings, and press releases.[158] President Trump simply ignored these authoritative sources and continued to promote false claims that had been soundly discredited.

Below, the Select Committee presents two case studies demonstrating how President Trump and his surrogates lied in the face of overwhelming evidence. The first case study deals with Dominion Voting Systems. President Trump repeatedly claimed that Dominion's software "switched votes" and "rigged" the election well after the leaders of campaign and Justice Department officials told him that these claims were baseless. The President's smear of Dominion was central to his "Big Lie."

The second case study examines video footage recorded in Fulton County on election night. President Trump and his representatives concocted a fictional narrative based on a deceptively edited version of the footage. After these two case studies, the Select Committee examines a variety of other claims the President repeatedly made. Once again, these claims had no basis in truth.

### DOMINION VOTING SYSTEMS

Between election day and January 6th, President Trump repeatedly spread conspiracy theories about Dominion voting machines. The President tweeted or retweeted false claims about Dominion more than 30 times.[159] He also repeatedly lied about the company's software during his post-election speeches and interviews.[160] President Trump's own campaign staff, administration officials, and State officials, all told him the claims had no merit. Hand recounts confirmed the fidelity of the machines. But none of this overwhelming evidence mattered. President Trump demonstrated a conscious disregard for the facts and continued to maliciously smear Dominion.

President Trump's allies began spreading false claims regarding Dominion within days of the election. On November 8th, the day after networks called the election for Joe Biden, Sidney Powell claimed on Fox News that Dominion machines "were flipping votes in the computer system or adding votes that did not exist."[161] On November 12th, Rudy Giuliani appeared on Fox News to claim that Dominion was connected to Venezuelan dictator Hugo Chavez and its software was created "in order to fix elections."[162] The same day, President Trump retweeted a "REPORT" claiming that Dominion had "DELETED 2.7 MILLION TRUMP VOTES NATIONWIDE" and switched hundreds of thousands of votes in key swing states.[163]

By that time, the Trump Campaign team had looked into allegations regarding Dominion and its software and concluded that the claims were false. An internal campaign memo, dated November 12, said that Dominion's software "did not lead to improper vote counts" and cited reports concluding that, among other things, Dominion machines "Did Not Affect The Final Vote Count."[164] The memo also addressed various claims of foreign influence regarding Dominion.[165] Jason Miller told the Select Committee that by November 12th he had told President Trump the results of the analysis of the Dominion claims by the campaign's internal research team, specifically telling him "that the international allegations for Dominion were not valid."[166] Emails and text messages show that this same analysis was shared with Mark Meadows, President Trump's chief of staff.[167] White House Press Secretary Kayleigh McEnany told the Select Committee that she found herself "waving [President Trump] off of the Dominion theory," encouraging him to use more "fact-driven" arguments.[168] But it was to no avail.

Even though members of the Trump Campaign team reported that the result of the election was not compromised by any problems with Dominion machines, the President continued to assail Dominion on Twitter in the days that followed, for example retweeting a false claim that Dominion's machines were "engineered by China, Venezuela, [and] Cuba" and claiming that Dominion had "[r]igged" the election.[169]

Officials in the Trump administration also worked to debunk the false rumors about vote manipulation. The United States Department of Homeland Security's Cybersecurity & Infrastructure Security Agency (CISA) released a joint statement of election security officials on November 12, reassuring voters that the election was "the most secure in American history." CISA emphasized: "There is no evidence that any voting system deleted or lost votes, changed votes, or was in any way compromised."[170]

This was another decision point for the President. He could choose to endorse the findings of his administration's own cyber security experts, or he could continue to promote baseless fictions about Dominion. President Trump chose the lies. The President and his supporters never did produce any evidence showing that Dominion's machines affected the results of the election. But President Trump was undeterred by the facts. Indeed, the President and his supporters seized upon a simple human error in a small Michigan county as their initial pretense for these allegations as well as to keep the Dominion conspiracy theory alive.

During the early-morning hours of November 4th, Sheryl Guy, a clerk in Antrim County, Michigan, reported the *unofficial* results of the vote count.[171] Guy's online report was odd. It showed that former Vice President Biden had somehow won Antrim, a county that is majority-Republican and President Trump was expected to easily win. Trump's supporters quickly pointed to Biden's improbable win as evidence that Dominion had tampered with the votes.[172] That wasn't true. Guy had made a mistake in updating the election counting software after a late addition of a local candidate to the ballot in some of the county's precincts, which caused her unofficial counts to be off when she tallied the votes reported by the various precincts.[173] Guy, a Republican, was informed of the odd result and began to investigate immediately. The result was corrected, and President Trump won Antrim just as was expected.[174]

Within days, local and State officials in Michigan explained to the public what had happened. On November 7th, the Michigan Secretary of State's office issued a detailed description of Guy's error and assured the public that the *official* results were not impacted.[175] The Michigan Senate's Committee on Oversight, led by Republican Senator Ed McBroom, conducted its own comprehensive review of the claims related to Antrim County and confirmed that the initial reporting error was entirely attributable to an honest mistake by the county clerk.[176]

The mix-up in Antrim County was quickly corrected. A human erred— not the voting machines. But President Trump used it as a pretext to continue lying about Dominion.

On November 12th, the same day CISA released its statement on election security, President Trump asked Tim Walberg, a Republican Congressman from Michigan, to "check with key leadership in Michigan's Legislature as to how supportive they could be in regards to pushing back on election irregularities and potential fraud." [177] That night, President Trump asked his Acting Secretary of Homeland Security, Chad Wolf, to look into allegations of election irregularities in Michigan.[178] The next day, President Trump's assistant sent Wolf a letter from Michigan State legislators raising claims about the election, including an incorrect claim that flawed Dominion software had caused votes to be counted for the wrong candidate.[179]

Administration officials quickly knocked down the Dominion claim. Wolf forwarded the allegations to the leadership of CISA, including CISA Director Christopher Krebs.[180] Krebs provided Wolf with a press release from the Michigan Secretary of State that debunked the false claim about Antrim County and Dominion's software in detail.[181] Wolf shared an update about the information he received from Krebs with White House Chief of Staff Mark Meadows.[182]

On November 17th, Krebs tweeted out a statement issued by the nation's leading election scientists that dismissed claims that election systems had been manipulated as either "unsubstantiated" or "technically incoherent." [183] President Trump fired Krebs that same day.[184] President Trump claimed the statement released by Krebs was "highly inaccurate, in that there were massive improprieties and fraud." [185] The President had no evidence for his claim.

On November 19th, Rudy Giuliani, Sidney Powell, and Jenna Ellis held a press conference at the Republican National Committee (RNC) headquarters in Washington, DC. Powell asserted that there was "massive influence of communist money through Venezuela, Cuba, and likely China in the interference with our elections here in the United States."[186] She pointed a finger at Dominion, claiming its software was "created in Venezuela at the direction of Hugo Chavez to make sure he never lost an election," and Giuliani echoed her claims.[187]

Hope Hicks told the Select Committee how that press conference was received in the White House. The day after the press conference, President Trump spoke by phone with Sidney Powell from the Oval Office. During the call, Powell repeated the same claims of foreign interference in the election she had made at the press conference. While she was speaking, the President muted his speakerphone and laughed at Powell, telling the others in the room, "This does sound crazy, doesn't it?"[188]

A few days later, the Trump Campaign issued a statement claiming Powell was not part of the Trump Campaign's legal team.[189] But Powell's outlandish claims were no different from those President Trump was making himself. On November 19th, the same day as Powell's appearance at the RNC, President Trump tweeted and retweeted a link to a segment on One America News Network (OAN) that was captioned, "Dominion-izing the Vote."[190] The segment claimed that Dominion had switched votes from Trump to Biden. OAN featured a supposed cyber expert, Ron Watkins, a key figure in the QAnon conspiracy movement.[191] On his own Twitter account, Watkins celebrated and thanked his supporters just minutes after President Trump tweeted the clip, and President Trump went on to share the clip again several times in the days that followed.[192]

Officials inside the Trump administration continued to debunk the Dominion conspiracy theory, including during in-person meetings with President Trump. Attorney General Bill Barr met with President Trump face-to-face on three occasions after the election.[193] Barr told the Select Committee, "every time I was with the President, I raised the machines as sort of Exhibit A of how irresponsible this was."[194] During the first of these meetings, on November 23rd, Barr explained to the President that the conspiracy theory about Dominion's voting machines had "zero basis," and was "one of the most disturbing allegations." Barr stressed that this was "crazy stuff" and was poisoning Americans' confidence in the voting system for no reason. This "complete nonsense" was "doing [a] great, great disservice to the country," Barr said.[195]

President Trump ignored Barr's grave concerns. On November 29th, President Trump was interviewed by Fox News' Maria Bartiromo. It was the

President's first interview since he lost his bid for reelection. He claimed the election was "rigged" and rife with "theft" and "a total fraud."[196] He repeated various conspiracy theories, leading with the claim that Dominion's voting machines had "glitches," which he alleged moved "thousands of votes from my account to Biden's account."[197] He claimed that there had been "big, massive dumps" of votes—a reference to the Red Mirage.[198] He rambled off various other, spurious allegations, including that dead people voted in significant numbers.[199] None of it was true.

On December 1st, Attorney General Barr met again with President Trump and told him that "the stuff his people were shoveling out to the public was bullshit."[200] Attorney General Barr specifically told President Trump that the claims about Dominion voting machines were "idiotic claims."[201] President Trump was still not dissuaded from continuing the lie. The day after his meeting with the Attorney General, President Trump released a video in which he repeated several claims of election fraud, including a claim that "votes had been wrongly switched from Trump to Biden" using Dominion voting machines.[202]

By early-December, courts had assessed and rejected claims that Dominion machines were manipulated to affect the outcome of the 2020 election. In Michigan, a Federal judge found that claims, including those related to fraud due to the use of Dominion voting machines, were based on "nothing but speculation and conjecture that votes were destroyed, discarded or switched...."[203] In Arizona, a Federal judge dismissed claims that Dominion machines had deleted, switched, or changed votes.[204] But President Trump and his supporters refused to accept denunciations of the fabricated Dominion claims.

Through December, President Trump and his legal team tried to echo the Dominion conspiracy theory by claiming to have found evidence that votes were switched in Antrim County. The clerk's unintentional error was fixed weeks earlier and there was no evidence showing that Dominion had altered the vote tally in Antrim, or anywhere else.[205] But President Trump's legal team used a case challenging a local marijuana ordinance that had passed by one vote to gain access to Dominion's voting machines. An Antrim County judge issued an order granting the plaintiff's experts access to the county's computer, Dominion voting machines, thumb drives and memory cards.[206] Although the purpose of the order was to allow the plaintiff to seek evidence related to his ordinance challenge, it soon became clear that President Trump's legal team was behind the effort.[207]

An organization named Allied Security Operations Group ("ASOG"), led by Russell Ramsland, conducted an analysis of Antrim County's voting machines and related systems. On December 13th, ASOG released a report on its findings. The inspection yielded no evidence of vote manipulation. Still, the report included an unsubstantiated assertion that the Dominion voting machines used in Antrim County and throughout Michigan were "purposefully designed with inherent error to create systemic fraud and influence election results" and that a malicious algorithm was used to manipulate the results of the 2020 election.[208] Documents obtained by the Select Committee show that President Trump and Vice President Mike Pence were briefed on ASOG's findings by Giuliani's team.[209] On December 14th, President Trump widely disseminated the ASOG report and accompanying talking points prepared by Giuliani's team.[210] He also trumpeted the report on Twitter, writing on December 14th: "WOW. This report shows massive fraud. Election changing result!"[211]

During a meeting with Attorney General Bill Barr that day, President Trump claimed the ASOG report was "absolute proof that the Dominion machines were rigged" and meant he was "going to have a second term."[212] Barr told the Select Committee that he believed the ASOG report was "very amateurish," its authors lacked "any real qualifications," and it failed to provide any supporting information for its sweeping conclusions about Dominion.[213] Barr told President Trump he would look into the report, but that the DOJ already had a good idea of what happened in Antrim County and it was human error, not a problem with the machines.[214] In any event, Barr promised President Trump they would have a definitive answer within a couple of days because a hand recount was being conducted.[215]

In the ensuing days, as Barr predicted, the ASOG report was swiftly and soundly criticized by experts within and outside the Trump Administration, including the Department of Justice and the Department of Homeland Security.[216] The initial analysis of election security experts at the Department of Homeland Security was that the ASOG report was "false and misleading" and "demonstrates a callous misunderstanding of the actual current voting certification process."[217] Subsequent analyses of the ASOG report and the underlying data from Antrim County were even more critical.[218] These thorough assessments of the Antrim County data and the ASOG report demonstrate that virtually every one of the claims that President Trump and his surrogates made about the report was false.[219] ASOG's inspection did not reveal any malicious software or algorithms or any other evidence that the voting machines had been compromised.[220]

Most importantly, as Attorney General Barr had promised President Trump, within days of the release of the ASOG report, a full hand recount of every ballot cast in Antrim County confirmed the results reported by the Dominion machines and refuted ASOG's assertion that an algorithm has manipulated the vote count.[221] Giuliani's chief investigator, Bernie Kerik, acknowledged that his team was not able to find any proof that a Dominion voting machine improperly switched, deleted, or injected votes during the 2020 election.[222]

President Trump was not swayed by these basic facts. The President continued to promote the ASOG report, hounding DOJ to investigate the matter further. He returned to ASOG's claims during a December 27th call with Acting Attorney General Rosen and Acting Deputy Attorney General Donoghue, citing the report's claimed error rate of 68 percent in Antrim County. Donoghue pointed out to the President that the difference between the computer and hand count was only one vote and that he "cannot and should not be relying on" ASOG's fraudulent claim, because it was simply "not true." [223]

President Trump's fixation on Dominion's voting machines and the baseless theory that the machines had manipulated votes led to a concerted effort to gain access to voting machines in States where President Trump was claiming election fraud. On the evening of December 18th, Powell, Lt. Gen. Michael Flynn (ret.) and Patrick Byrne met with the President at the White House. Over several hours, they argued that President Trump had the authority, under a 2018 executive order, to seize voting machines. Several administration officials joined the meeting and forcefully rejected this extreme proposal.[224] Multiple lawyers in the White House, including Eric Herschmann, Derek Lyons, and White House Counsel Pat Cipollone "pushed back strongly" against the idea of seizing voting machines. Cipollone told the Select Committee it was a "horrible idea," which had "no legal basis," [225] and he emphasized that he had "seen no evidence of massive fraud in the election." [226] White House advisor Eric Herschmann similarly told the Select Committee that he "never saw any evidence whatsoever" to sustain the allegations against Dominion.[227] National Security Adviser Robert O'Brien phoned into the December 18th meeting and was asked if he had seen "any evidence of election fraud in the voting machines or foreign interference in our voting machines." O'Brien responded that his team had "looked into that, and there's no evidence of it." [228]

Around the same time, President Trump, Mark Meadows, and Rudy Giuliani were repeatedly asking the leadership of DHS whether the agency had authority to seize voting machines, and they were repeatedly told that DHS has no such unilateral authority.[229] Giuliani and Powell were also engaged in efforts to access voting machines in multiple States with the assistance of sympathetic local election officials.[230] Those efforts turned up no evidence of any vote manipulation by any Dominion machine, but President Trump continued to press this bogus claim.

On January 2, 2021, President Trump had a lengthy phone call with Georgia Secretary of State Brad Raffensperger. The President repeatedly brought up Dominion's voting machines, alleging that they were at the heart of a conspiracy against him.[231] Raffensperger was incredulous. "I don't believe that you're really questioning the Dominion machines," Raffensperger said. "Because we did a hand re-tally, a 100 percent re-tally of all the ballots, and compared them to what the machines said and came up with virtually the same result. Then we did the recount, and we got virtually the same result."[232] In other words, the story in Georgia was the same as the story in Antrim County, Michigan: Officials performed a hand recount to put to rest any allegations that Dominion's machines had manipulated the vote. But once again, President Trump consciously disregarded these basic facts and persisted with his lies.

During a January 4, 2021, speech in Dalton, Georgia, President Trump chose to ignore Secretary Raffensperger's straightforward observations. The President rhetorically attacked Dominion once again, claiming that a "crime" had been "committed in this state" and it was "immeasurable."[233] The President called for an "immediate forensic audit of an appropriate sampling of Dominion's voting machines and related equipment."[234] His allegations were both false and nonsensical. Georgia had already performed a statewide hand recount of all ballots.

President Trump and his allies have never provided any evidence showing that Dominion's voting software altered votes in the 2020 presidential election. In fact, some of the most vocal proponents of the Dominion claims harbored their own misgivings about the claims they were making in public. For example, Rudy Giuliani repeatedly claimed in public that Dominion voting machines stole the election, and that foreign countries had interfered in the election, but the evidence uncovered by the Select Committee reveals that he did not believe either of those things to be true. Giuliani testified that he did not believe that voting machines stole the election.[235] He also acknowledged that he had seen no evidence that foreign countries had interfered in the election or manipulated votes.[236]

This testimony is consistent with his lead investigator Bernie Kerik's acknowledgment that he had not come across proof that voting machines were used to switch, delete, or inject votes improperly.[237] Christina Bobb, an attorney who worked with Giuliani, similarly could not point to any evidence of wrongdoing by Dominion.[238] Even Sidney Powell, perhaps the most committed proponent of the Dominion falsehoods, was unable to provide the Select Committee with any evidence or expert report that demonstrated that the 2020 election outcome in any State had been altered through manipulation of voting machines.[239] And Powell defended herself in a defamation suit brought by Dominion by claiming that "no reasonable person would conclude that her statements were truly statements of fact." [240]

By January 6, 2021, President Trump's claims regarding Dominion had been debunked time and again. The President knew, or should have known, that he had no basis for alleging that Dominion's voting machines had cost him the election.

### THE STATE FARM ARENA VIDEO

President Trump also recklessly promoted allegations that video footage from a ballot counting center in Fulton County, Georgia, was proof of major election fraud. He was repeatedly informed that these allegations were false, but he pressed them anyway.

On December 3rd, Rudy Giuliani presented State legislators with selectively edited footage of ballots being counted on Election Night at Fulton County's State Farm Arena. [241] Giuliani misrepresented the video as "a smoking gun" proving election fraud. [242] The President repeatedly claimed that he would have won Georgia, if not for a supposed conspiracy that unfolded on election night. President Trump and some of his supporters alleged that political operatives faked a water main rupture to expel Republican poll watchers. [243] These same operatives then supposedly took illegal ballots from suitcases hidden under tables and added those ballots to the official count multiple times over by scanning them more than once. [244] Not one of these allegations was true.

In a speech on December 5th, President Trump made the false claim about the State Farm Arena and claimed that "if you just take the crime of what those Democrat workers were doing...[t]hat's 10 times more than I need to win this state." [245] During a December 22nd speech, he played the same deceptive footage presented by Giuliani several weeks earlier. [246] President Trump also repeatedly scapegoated one of these Fulton County election workers during his January 2nd phone call with Georgia's Secretary of State, repeatedly referencing her by name and calling her "a professional vote scammer and hustler." [247] It was a malicious smear.

President Trump was directly notified *at least* four different times that the allegations he was making were false. On December 15th, then–Deputy Attorney General Jeffrey Rosen told him: "It wasn't a suitcase. It was a bin. That's what they use when they're counting ballots. It's benign." [248] Rosen's deputy, Richard Donoghue, also debunked this claim, including on a phone call on December 27th and in a meeting in the Oval Office on December 31st: "I told the President myself...several times, in several conversations, that these allegations about ballots being smuggled in in a suitcase and run through the machines several times, it was not true, that we had looked at it, we looked at the video, we interviewed the witnesses, and it was not true." [249]

Likewise, Georgia Secretary of State Brad Raffensperger told President Trump that his allegations about the video were false. During his January 2nd call with the President, Raffensperger explained that Giuliani's team "sliced and diced that video and took it out of context" and that "the events that transpired are nowhere near what was projected" once one looks at more complete footage. [250] Raffensperger also explained to the President that his team "did an audit of that, and we proved conclusively that they were not scanned three times." [251] Yet, when Raffensperger said he would send President Trump a link to the television segment, the President refused: "I don't care about the link. I don't need it." [252]

The actual evidence contradicted all of President Trump's claims about what the Fulton County video depicted. For example, the chief investigator for Raffensperger's office explained in a December 6th court filing that "there were no mystery ballots that were brought in from an unknown location and hidden under tables...." [253] As the investigator noted, the security footage showed there was nothing under the table when it was brought into the room. Hours later, with reporters and observers present, the "video shows ballots that had already been opened but not counted placed in the boxes, sealed up, [and] stored under the table." [254] This finding was affirmed by the FBI, DOJ, and the Georgia Bureau of Investigation, which interviewed witnesses and reviewed the full video footage and machine data from the site. [255]

The ballots in question were not double counted. This was confirmed by a full hand recount in November, as well as a subsequent review by investigators. [256] They found that although one of the workers was shown in the video scanning certain batches multiple times, this was for a valid reason: her scanner kept jamming. The investigators confirmed from scanner logs, as well as the footage, that she only hit the "accept" button once per batch. [257] Investigators also found that staff likely did not tell the observers to leave, let alone forcefully eject them from the facility. [258]

Despite this conclusive evidence and testimony, President Trump continued to point to the Fulton County video as evidence of a grand conspiracy. On January 5th, for instance, President Trump's executive assistant emailed a document "from POTUS" to Senator Josh Hawley (R-MO), Senator Ted Cruz (R-TX), and Representative Jim Jordan (R-OH) that cited "Suitcase Gate" among the "worst fraud incidents" in Georgia. [259]

During his January 6th speech, President Trump told the crowd that "in Fulton County, Republican poll watchers were ejected, in some cases, physically from the room under the false pretense of a pipe burst." The President continued:

> …then election officials pull boxes, Democrats, and suitcases of ballots out from under a table. You all saw it on television, totally fraudulent. And illegally scanned them for nearly two hours, totally unsupervised. Tens of thousands of votes. This act coincided with a mysterious vote dump of up to 100,000 votes for Joe Biden, almost none for Donald Trump.[260]

No part of President Trump's story was true. He had already been informed that it was false.

In June 2021, when Giuliani's law license was revoked by a New York State appellate court, the court's ruling cited his statements about supposed suitcases of ballots in Georgia as one of its reasons for doing so. "If, as respondent claims, he reviewed the entire video, he could not have reasonably reached a conclusion that illegal votes were being counted," the court's ruling reads.[261]

President Trump's conspiracy-mongering endangered innocent public servants around the country, including in Fulton County. For example, during a December 10, 2020, appearance in Georgia, Giuliani falsely accused Ruby Freeman and Shaye Moss, two Black public servants shown in the Fulton County video, of "surreptitiously passing around USB ports as if they're vials of heroin or cocaine."[262] In fact, Moss had been given a ginger mint by her mother, Freeman.[263] As described in Chapter 2, baseless accusations like these forever changed the lives of election workers like Freeman and Moss. All in service of President Trump's Big Lie.

### THE FAKE BALLOT MYTH

The Trump Campaign's distortion of the State Farm Arena video is just one example of the "fake ballots" lie. President Trump frequently claimed that "fake ballots" for Biden were injected into the vote-counting process. To hear the President tell it, there were truckloads of ballots delivered in the middle of the night to vote-counting centers and millions more votes were cast than there were registered voters. Judges, Trump administration officials, State authorities, and independent election experts found each iteration of the "fake ballot" claim to be just that: fake. The Trump Campaign and its surrogates brought nine cases that raised some version of a "fake ballots" claim. Every one of those cases was promptly dismissed.[264] For example, in *Costantino v. City of Detroit*, a Michigan court ruled that the plaintiff's claims regarding forged, backdated and double-counted votes in

Detroit were "incorrect and not credible" and "rife with speculation and guess-work about sinister motives."[265]

Many of the fake ballot claims were publicly raised and repeated by President Trump, but never included in any lawsuit. For example, a truck driver for the U.S. Postal Service claimed that he delivered hundreds of thousands of completed ballots from Bethpage, New York to Lancaster, Pennsylvania.[266] President Trump repeated this allegation numerous times.[267] The DOJ and FBI interviewed the relevant witnesses, including the truck driver, and reviewed the loading manifests. They determined that the allegation was not true.[268] Both Attorney General Barr and his successor, Jeffrey Rosen, told President Trump this claim was false. But that didn't stop the President from repeating it.

Another alleged "truckload of ballots" was supposedly delivered to the Detroit counting center at 4:30 a.m. on election night. This truck allegedly carried 100,000 ballots in garbage cans, wastepaper bins, cardboard boxes, and shopping baskets.[269] A widely circulated video purportedly showed an unmarked van dropping off ballots, which were then wheeled into the counting center on a wagon.[270] In fact, the only ballot delivery in Detroit after midnight on election night was an official delivery of 16,000 ballots, stacked in 45 well-organized trays of approximately 350 ballots each.[271] The wagon depicted in the video contained camera equipment being pulled by a reporter.[272] The claim of 100,000 fake ballots being smuggled into the counting center in the middle of the night is even more ridiculous in light of the fact that only 174,384 absent voter ballots were recorded in the City of Detroit in the 2020 election.[273] The addition of 100,000 fake ballots to approximately 74,000 legitimate ballots would certainly have been obvious to election officials.[274]

President Trump also repeatedly claimed that more votes were cast than there were registered voters in certain States, cities, or precincts. It was easy to fact-check these allegations and demonstrate they were false.

For example, in Pennsylvania, approximately nine million people were registered to vote and approximately 6.8 million votes were cast in the 2020 presidential election.[275] Nevertheless, President Trump and his allies made numerous "more votes than voters" claims in Pennsylvania. Citing 2020 mail-in voting data tweeted by Pennsylvania State Senator Doug Mastriano, President Trump claimed that 1.1 million ballots had been "created" and counted improperly.[276] In fact, there was no discrepancy in the actual numbers—Mastriano erroneously compared the 2.6 million mail-in ballots cast *in the November general* election to the 1.5 million ballots that were returned *in the June primary* election.[277]

President Trump also promoted a false claim by a different Pennsylvania legislator that Pennsylvania had 205,000 more votes than voters.[278] This claim was based on a flawed comparison by State Representative Frank Ryan of the votes recorded by State election authorities as having been cast and those reflected in a separate State registry.[279] In fact, the discrepancy was a result of some counties not yet uploading their official results to the registry.[280] In late-December 2020, Acting Deputy Attorney General Donoghue told President Trump that this allegation was baseless.[281] President Trump kept repeating it anyway.[282]

The President and his surrogates made similar false claims concerning excess votes in Michigan. Many of those claims originated with a grossly inaccurate affidavit submitted by Russell Ramsland, the person behind the "very amateurish" and "false and misleading" ASOG report regarding Dominion voting machines in Antrim County.[283] Ramsland claimed in a similar affidavit filed in Federal court in Georgia that 3,276 precincts in Michigan had turnout of between 84% and 350%, with 19 precincts reporting turnout in excess of 100%.[284] Ramsland's affidavit was widely ridiculed, in part, because he relied on data for dozens of precincts that are located in Minnesota, not Michigan.[285] Even after he corrected his affidavit to remove the Minnesota townships, his Michigan data remained wildly off-base.[286]

### THE "MULTIPLE COUNTING OF BALLOTS" FICTION

The President and his surrogates repeatedly claimed that ballots for former Vice President Biden were counted multiple times.[287] These claims originated when some noticed election officials re-running stacks of ballots through counting machines. But the allegation is based on a fundamental misunderstanding of the vote-counting process—it is routine and appropriate for election officials to re-scan ballots if they are not properly scanned and tabulated in the initial effort. In *Costantino v. City of Detroit*, the court rejected the "incorrect and not credible" affidavits speculating that ballots were run through scanners and counted multiple times in favor of the "more accurate and persuasive explanation of activity" put forward by the "highly-respected" election official with 40 years of experience.[288]

As with other misguided claims of election fraud, the claim that ballots were counted multiple times disregards the safeguards in the voting process. In particular, as noted above, it would certainly have been apparent in the canvassing process if hundreds of ballots were counted multiple times in Detroit because the total number of ballots would greatly exceed the number of voters who voted. But that was not the case.

## THE IMAGINARY "DEAD" AND "INELIGIBLE" VOTERS

In addition to their false claims regarding fake ballots, President Trump and his surrogates also relentlessly asserted that tens of thousands of ballots were cast by dead or otherwise ineligible voters. For example, President Trump and Giuliani frequently alleged that more than 66,000 unregistered juveniles voted in Georgia.[289] In fact, no underage people voted in Georgia.[290] Giuliani offered several different made-up figures of the number of non-citizens who supposedly voted in Arizona, but provided no evidence to substantiate his claims.[291] In fact, Arizona requires every new voter to provide proof of citizenship in order to register to vote—or to complete a Federal voter registration form that requires the individual to sign an attestation to citizenship status under penalty of perjury—and no person can vote without being registered.[292] By mid-November, Trump Campaign staff determined this allegation that thousands of non-citizens voted in Arizona was based on "highly unreliable" information, and it is one of the false claims that led to Giuliani losing his New York law license.[293] These "ineligible" voters did not exist.

Nor were thousands of votes cast in the names of dead Americans.

During his January 2nd, call with Georgia Secretary of State Raffensperger, the President claimed that "close to about 5,000 [dead] voters" cast ballots in the election. Raffensperger quickly informed the President this wasn't true.[294] But the "dead voter" lie wasn't limited to Georgia. President Trump wanted Americans to believe that "dead voters" contributed to his defeat in several battleground States.[295]

But even the Trump Campaign and its lawyers recognized early on that the claims regarding "dead voters" were grossly exaggerated, to say the least. By early November, Trump lawyers discovered that many people listed by the campaign as having died were actually alive and well.[296] In early December, Eric Herschmann advised Chief of Staff Meadows by text message that the Trump legal team had determined that the claim of more than 10,000 dead people voting in Georgia was not accurate.[297] The ensuing exchange makes clear that both men knew that Giuliani's claims were absurd:

> Herschmann: Just an FYI. Alex Cannon and his team verified that the 10k+ supposed dead people voting in GA is not accurate
>
> Meadows: I didn't hear that claim. It is not accurate. I think I found 22 if I remember correctly. Two of them died just days before the general
>
> Herschmann: It was alleged in Rudy's hearing today. Your number is much closer to what we can prove. I think it's 12

Meadows: My son found 12 obituaries and 6 other possibles depending on the Voter roll acuracy [sic]

Herschmann: That sounds more like it. Maybe he can help Rudy find the other 10k ??

Meadows: lol [298]

Shortly thereafter, a Georgia court dismissed the claim that there were tens of thousands of votes cast by ineligible voters, noting the claims "rest on speculation rather than duly pled facts." [299]

The Trump Campaign's own expert on the supposed "dead voters" admitted that the Campaign lacked the necessary data to make any conclusions about whether any (or how many) votes were cast in the name of a deceased person. [300] State officials *did* have such data, however, and were able to conduct the type of matching analysis required. These State authorities determined that there were only a handful of cases in which people voted on behalf of deceased individuals. [301]

Even in those cases where the person who voted actually did die, President Trump's lawyers knew that the vast majority of the voters included on their list of dead voters actually cast their votes before they passed. [302] In early-January 2021, just days before January 6th, Republican Senator Lindsey Graham asked several Trump lawyers to provide evidence to support the Campaign's claims regarding dead voters. [303] As Giuliani's team investigated, they concluded that they could not find evidence of dead voters anywhere near the number that Giuliani and President Trump were claiming publicly. After noting the shortcomings in their evidence, Katherine Friess, a lawyer working with the Giuliani legal team, warned that Senator Graham would "push back" on their evidence. [304] As predicted by Friess, Senator Graham was not impressed by the information provided by Giuliani's team. In his speech on the Senate floor on January 6th, Graham explained why he would not object to the certification of electoral votes. Senator Graham referred to the failure of the Trump attorneys to provide the evidence he requested:

> They said there's 66,000 people in Georgia under 18 voted. How many people believe that? I asked, 'Give me 10.' Hadn't had one. They said 8,000 felons in prison in Arizona voted. Give me 10. Hadn't gotten one. Does that say there's—There's problems in every election. I don't buy this. Enough's enough. We've got to end it. [305]

Documents obtained by the Select Committee reveal that President Trump and his lawyers knew that the claims being made in court about dead or ineligible voters in Georgia were inaccurate, and the lawyers were concerned that if the President vouched for those claims in another court pleading he might be criminally prosecuted. On December 31st, as the lawyers rushed to file a Federal lawsuit in Georgia, some of the lawyers raised concerns about the President signing a "verification" under oath that the allegations regarding voter fraud in Georgia, including claims regarding dead people voting, were true. As Eastman noted in an email to his colleagues on December 31st:

> Although the President signed a verification [regarding the Georgia claims] back on Dec. 1, he has since been made aware that some of the allegations (and evidence proffered by the experts) has been inaccurate. For him to sign a new verification with that knowledge…would not be accurate. And I have no doubt that an aggressive DA or US Atty someplace will go after both the President and his lawyers once all the dust settles on this.[306]

Despite these concerns, President Trump and his attorneys filed a complaint that incorporated the same inaccurate numbers, and President Trump signed a verification swearing under oath that the inaccurate numbers were "true and correct" or "believed to be true and correct" to the best of his knowledge and belief.[307] A Federal judge reviewing the relevant emails and pleadings recently concluded:

> The emails show that President Trump knew that the specific numbers of voter fraud were wrong but continued to tout those numbers, both in court and to the public. The Court finds that these emails are sufficiently related to and in furtherance of a conspiracy to defraud the United States.[308]

## 1.9 PRESIDENT TRUMP'S JANUARY 6TH SPEECH

At noon on January 6, 2021, President Trump addressed thousands of his supporters at a rally just south of the White House. The election had been decided two months earlier. The courts found there was no evidence of significant fraud. The States certified their votes by mid-December. It was over—President Trump lost. But that's not what the President told those in attendance. He delivered an incendiary speech from beginning to end, arguing that nothing less than the fate of America was at stake.

"Our country has had enough," President Trump said. "We will not take it anymore and that's what this is all about."[309] He claimed that his followers had descended on Washington to "save our democracy" and "stop the

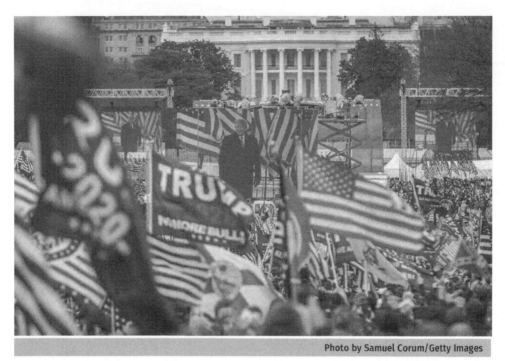

Photo by Samuel Corum/Getty Images

steal." [310] He refused, once again, to concede. And he proclaimed that "[t]oday I will lay out just some of the evidence proving that we won this election and we won it by a landslide." [311]

For months, President Trump had relentlessly promoted his Big Lie.[312] He and his associates manufactured one tale after another to justify it. For more than an hour on January 6th, the President wove these conspiracy theories and lies together.[313]

By the Select Committee's assessment, there were more than 100 times during his speech in which President Trump falsely claimed that either the election had been stolen from him, or falsely claimed that votes had been compromised by some specific act of fraud or major procedural violations. That day, President Trump repeated many of the same lies he had told for months—even after being informed that many of these claims were false. He lied about Dominion voting machines in Michigan, suitcases of ballots in Georgia, more votes than voters in Pennsylvania, votes cast by non-citizens in Arizona, and dozens of other false claims of election fraud.[314] None of those claims were true.

As explained in the chapters that follow, the Big Lie was central to President Trump's plan to stay in power. He used the Big Lie to pressure

State and local officials to undo the will of the people. His campaign convened fake electors on the baseless pretense that former Vice President Biden won several States due to fraud or other malfeasance. The President tried to subvert the Department of Justice by browbeating its leadership to endorse his election lies. And when the DOJ's senior personnel did not acquiesce, President Trump sought to install a loyalist who would.

When all those efforts failed, President Trump betrayed his own Vice President. He pressured Vice President Pence to obstruct the joint session of Congress on January 6th, falsely claiming that he had the power to refuse to count certain electoral votes. President Trump knew this was illegal but attempted to justify it with lies about the election.

On December 19, 2020, President Trump summoned a mob to Washington, DC on the same day that Congress was set to certify former Vice President Biden's victory by claiming the election was stolen and promising a "wild" protest.[315]

And the bogus stolen election claim was the focus of President Trump's speech on January 6th. The litany of lies he told riled up a mob that would march to the U.S. Capitol to intimidate Vice President Pence and Members of Congress.

"And we fight. We fight like hell. And if you don't fight like hell, you're not going to have a country anymore," President Trump told the crowd.[316] He incited them with these words just after praising his own election night lie—the Big Lie.

President Trump told his followers to "fight" to "save" their country from a bogus specter of supposed election fraud.[317] And many of them did.

## 2

## "I JUST WANT TO FIND 11,780 VOTES"

In a now infamous telephone call on January 2, 2021, President Trump pressured Georgia Secretary of State Brad Raffensperger for more than an hour. The President confronted him with multiple conspiracy theories about the election—none of which were true. Raffensperger and other Georgia officials debunked these allegations, one after another, during their call. Under Raffensperger's leadership, Georgia had, by that time, already conducted a statewide hand recount of all ballots. That recount and other post-election reviews proved that there was no widespread fraud, and that voting machines didn't alter the outcome of the election.[1] This should have put President Trump's allegations to rest. But, undeterred by the facts, the President badgered Raffensperger to overturn the Georgia results.

President Trump insisted that "the ballots are corrupt" and someone was "shredding" them.[2] He issued a thinly veiled threat, telling Raffensperger, "it is more illegal for you than it is for them because you know what they did and you're not reporting it."[3] Of course, the Georgia officials weren't doing anything "illegal," and there was nothing to "report." Even so, President Trump suggested that both Raffensperger and his general counsel, Ryan Germany, could face criminal jeopardy.[4] "That's a criminal, that's a criminal offense. And you can't let that happen," the President said.[5] "That's a big risk to you and to Ryan, your lawyer . . . I'm notifying you that you're letting it happen."[6]

And then the President made his demand. "So look. All I want to do is this. I just want to find 11,780 votes, which is one more than we have," President Trump told Raffensperger.[7]

It was a stunning moment. The President of the United States was asking a State's chief election officer to "find" enough votes to declare him the winner of an election he lost.

Raffensperger saw the President's warning to him on January 2nd as a threat. "I felt then—and I still believe today—that this was a threat," Raffensperger wrote in his book.[8] And this threat was multifaceted: first, the President "notifying" Raffensperger and his team of criminal activity could be understood as directing the law-enforcement power of the Federal Government against them. While Raffensperger did not know for certain whether President Trump was threatening such an investigation, he knew Trump had "positional power" as President and appeared to be promising to "make [my] life miserable." [9]

But the threat was also of a more insidious kind. As Raffensperger wrote in his book: "Others obviously thought [it was a threat], too, because some of Trump's more radical followers have responded as if it was their duty to carry out this threat." [10] Raffensperger's deputy held a press conference and publicly warned all Americans, including President Trump, that President Trump's rhetoric endangered innocent officials and private citizens, and fueled death threats against Georgia election workers, sexualized threats directed towards Raffensperger's wife, and harassment at the homes of Georgia election officials.[11] The January 2nd call promised more of the same. The upshot of President Trump's message to Raffensperger was: do what I ask, or you will pay.

President Trump's phone call with Secretary Raffensperger received widespread coverage after it was leaked. But Georgia was not the only State targeted by President Trump and his allies. The call was one element of a larger and more comprehensive effort—much of it unseen by and unknown to the general public—to overturn the votes cast by millions of American citizens across several States.

As Chapter 1 explained, the root of this effort was the "Big Lie": President Trump and his allies publicly claiming that the election was rife with fraud that could have changed the result, even though the President's own advisors, and the Department of Justice, told the President time and time again that this was not the case.[12] But in parallel with this strategy, President Trump and his allies zeroed in on key battleground States the President had lost, leaning on Republican State officials to overrule voters, disregard valid vote counts, and deliver the States' electoral votes to the losing candidate. Had this scheme worked, President Trump could have, for the first time in American history, subverted the results of a lawful election to stay in power. His was a deeply anti-democratic plan: to co-opt State legislatures—through appeals to debunked theories of election fraud, or pure partisan politics—to replace Biden electors with Trump electors, so President Trump would win the electoral vote count in the joint session of Congress on January 6th.

Had enough State officials gone along with President Trump's plot, his attempt to stay in power might have worked. It is fortunate that a critical mass of honorable officials withstood President Trump's pressure to participate in this scheme. They and others who stood up to him closed off avenues for thwarting the election so that, by noon on January 6th, President Trump was left with one desperate, final gambit for holding on to power: sending his armed, angry supporters to the U.S. Capitol.

## 2.1 THE ELECTORAL COLLEGE, AND PRESIDENT TRUMP'S ATTEMPT TO SUBVERT IT

When Americans vote for a presidential candidate on election day, they are actually casting votes for that candidate's proposed presidential electors to participate in the electoral college. After a State certifies its election results and announces a winner, it also issues a "certificate of ascertainment," which contains the names of the duly chosen electoral college electors. The electors whose names appear as having received the most votes on the certificate of ascertainment will go on to participate in the electoral college, while a losing candidate's proposed electors have no role to play and no standing to participate in the electoral college. This happens after every Presidential election, in each of the fifty States and the District of Columbia.

This process comes from a clause in the U.S. Constitution that gives States the power to choose electoral college electors according to State law.[13] That clause says that each State "shall appoint" electoral college electors "in such [m]anner as the Legislature thereof may direct." All 50 States have decreed that electors will be selected by popular vote.

Tuesday, November 3rd, was the day established by Federal law as election day in 2020. Each State's rules had been set—and courts had weighed in when certain rules were challenged. Polls opened around the country and votes came in, whether in person or via the mail, according to each State's laws.

Over 154 million voters cast votes according to the rules in place on election day.[14] President Trump lost. He and his supporters went to court, filing long-shot legal challenges to the election, but they failed in courts around the country, before judges appointed by executives of both parties (including President Trump himself), and, for those judges who were elected, that are members of both parties.

Rather than abiding by the rule of law and accepting the courts' rulings, President Trump and his advisors tried every which way to reverse the outcome at the State level. They pressured local and State elections officials to stop counting votes once it became clear that former Vice President Joseph Biden would prevail in the final count. They pressured Governors, secretaries of State, and local officials not to certify the popular vote in several swing States that former Vice-President Biden had won. And, when that did not work, they pressured State legislators to disregard the vote counts and instead appoint Trump electors to vote in the electoral college.

This fundamentally anti-democratic effort was premised on the incorrect theory that, because the Constitution assigns to State legislatures the role of directing how electoral college electors are chosen (which every State legislature had done *before* the election, giving that power to the people at the ballot boxes) then the State legislatures could simply choose Trump/Pence electors *after* seeing the election results. In effect, President Trump and his advisors pushed for the rules to be changed after the election—even if it meant disenfranchising millions of Americans.

## 2.2 THE PLAN EMERGES

More than a month before the Presidential election, the media reported that the Trump Campaign was already developing a fallback plan that would focus on overturning certain election results at the State level. An article published on September 23, 2020, in *The Atlantic* explained, "[a]ccording to sources in the Republican Party at the State and national levels, the Trump Campaign is discussing contingency plans to bypass election results and appoint loyal electors in battleground States where Republicans hold the legislative majority." [15] Ominously, the same reporting predicted, almost exactly, what would later come to pass: "With a justification based on claims of rampant fraud, Trump would ask State legislators to set aside the popular vote and exercise their power to choose a slate of electors directly." [16]

Numerous senior Trump Campaign advisors—including Campaign Manager William Stepien, Deputy Campaign Manager and Senior Counsel Justin Clark, and President Trump's lead attorney Rudolph Giuliani—all told the Select Committee that there was, indeed, a State-focused "strategy" or "track" to challenge the outcome of the election, which included pressing State legislators to challenge results in key States and to appoint new electoral college electors. [17]

"You know, in the days after election day, later in that first week, bleeding into the second, as our numbers and data looked bleaker, internally we knew that," Stepien told the Select Committee. [18] "As the AP [Associated Press] called the race, I think some surrounding the President were looking for different avenues to pursue." That's when Stepien remembered the concept first coming up. [19]

Those around President Trump were pushing this idea, and pushing it hard.

Just two days after the election, President Trump's son, Donald Trump, Jr., forwarded to White House Chief of Staff Mark Meadows a suggestion that "State Assemblies can step in and vote to put forward the electoral slate[,] Republicans control Pennsylvania, Wisconsin, Michigan, North Carolina, etc. we get Trump electors" and so "we either have a vote WE control and WE win OR it gets kicked to Congress 6 January . . ." [20] Chief of Staff Meadows responded: "Working on this for pa, ga and nc already." [21]

Within one week after the election, Meadows had also sent or received several other similar messages:

"The state legislature can take over the electoral process"—Mark Meadows's text to Georgia State Senator Marty Harbin.[22]

"Agreed"—Mark Meadows's text to a different sender, who suggested that the Trump Administration "should get that out there" if they were "seriously considering the state legislature strategy." [23]

"I will tell him"—Mark Meadows's text to a sender who suggested President Trump "[s]tart building momentum for the state legislatures." [24]

"I love it"—Mark Meadows's text to Representative Andy Biggs, who relayed what he acknowledged as a "highly controversial" idea to have "Republican legislature's (sic)" "appoint a look doors (sic) [electors]." [25]

". . . Why can't the states of GA NC PENN and other R controlled state houses declare this is BS (where conflicts and election not called that night) and just send their own electors . . . I wonder if POTUS knows this . . ."—former Secretary of Energy Rick Perry to Mark Meadows.[26]

Another White House official exploring such a plan less than a week after the election was Vince Haley, Deputy Assistant to the President for Policy, Strategy and Speechwriting. He suggested:

". . . Imagine if every red state legislature slated zero electors. It would reveal that we are a red country. To do this we would have to jack this to the nth degree as a battle of tribes . . . ." [27]

Haley pushed this strategy in several texts and emails, including to Assistant to the President and Director of Presidential Personnel Johnny McEntee,[28] an individual Haley characterized as "a very trusted lieutenant" for President Trump, "a direct conveyor to Boss with ideas," and "[a]t his side almost all the time." [29]

For Haley, however, purported election fraud was a way to justify President Trump-friendly legislatures changing the outcome of the election, but there were other reasons for doing so, too. Election fraud was "only one rationale for slating Trump electors," Haley told McEntee, and "[w]e should baldly assert" that State legislators "have the constitutional right to substitute their judgment for a certified majority of their constituents" if that prevents socialism.[30] Haley added, "[i]ndependent of the fraud—or really along with that argument—Harrisburg [Pennsylvania], Madison [Wisconsin], and Lansing [Michigan] do not have to sit idly by and submit themselves to rule by Beijing and Paris," proposing that radio hosts "rally the grassroots to apply pressure to the weak kneed legislators in those states . . ."[31]

McEntee replied "Yes!" and then: "Let's find the contact info for all these people now."[32] Hours later, Haley sent him names and—in most cases—cell phone numbers for top GOP legislators in six States, suggesting ". . . for POTUS to invite them down for a WH meeting . . ."[33] The President would later call several named in that message, including Rusty Bowers and Karen Fann in Arizona; Lee Chatfield and Mike Shirkey in Michigan; and Jake Corman in Pennsylvania.[34]

Others weighed in with the President about a State-focused plan, too. Some were already looking ahead to January 6th.

On November 8th, former Speaker of the House Newt Gingrich met President Trump at the White House.[35] Two days later, he sent a follow-up note to the President's executive assistant titled "please give to POTUS[,] newt."[36] It suggested that "[t]he only way Trump loses is rigged system" and added that President Trump could encourage "GOP legislatures elect not to send in electors," forcing a House vote by State delegations on January 6th that Gingrich expected President Trump would win.[37] Meadows replied: "Thanks Speaker."[38]

Newsmax CEO Christopher Ruddy had President Trump's ear and reportedly spoke with him by phone at least four times before December.[39] He forwarded a memo to other close advisors of the President recommending that the Trump team persuade one or more Republican-led chambers in Arizona, Georgia, Michigan, Pennsylvania, Wisconsin, and even Minnesota to "pick a separate competitive State slate of Electors," which the memo predicted might turn January 6th into "a cat-fight in Congress wherein VP Pence is Presiding."[40]

Attorney and conservative activist Cleta Mitchell was recruited by Mark Meadows immediately after the election to assist the Trump Campaign's legal work.[41] By November 5th, she emailed Dr. John Eastman of Chapman University,[42] who would later play an outsized role pushing a theory about

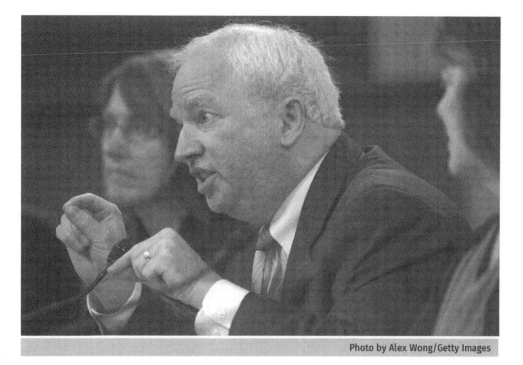

Photo by Alex Wong/Getty Images

what Vice President Pence could or couldn't do during the January 6th joint session of Congress that is detailed in Chapter 5 of this Report. In her email, Mitchell asked Eastman to write a memo justifying an idea that State legislators "reclaim" the power to pick electors and asked, rhetorically, "Am I crazy?"[43] Dr. Eastman wrote the memo, entitled "The Constitutional Authority of State Legislatures to Choose Electors," and sent it along for sharing "widely."[44]

According to the Office of Presidential Scheduling, President Trump was scheduled to meet in the Oval Office on November 10th with Morgan Warstler and John Robison, Texas entrepreneurs close to former Governor Rick Perry.[45] The next day, Warstler tweeted that he "[w]as in Oval yesterday,"[46] and months later wrote that "I told whole Trump team in Oval" that "State legislatures can choose the electors–no matter what current state law OR state courts say."[47]

After this apparent meeting, John Robison sent the White House an email entitled "URGENT follow up to our Tuesday Meeting with POTUS," that he asked be printed out for the President to "explain the move forward plan for what was discussed."[48] The email stated that "[President Trump] liked the plan we presented to use a parallel path of state legislators," and the attached memo proposed hundreds of briefings for State lawmakers by

President Trump's surrogates and members of the Freedom Caucus.[49] The email envisioned President Trump hosting "4+ MONSTER RALLY-TRIALS" with "[t]ens of thousands of Trump voters staring up at the GOP state legislators from their districts who ALONE control which slate of electors their state will submit," a proposal that seemed to foreshadow the State hearings that Rudolph Giuliani and President Trump championed less than a month later.[50]

Deputy White House Chief of Staff Dan Scavino called Robison's message "Bat. Shit. Crazy," but the President's executive assistant, who was asked to print it for the President, wrote "Printed," and may have shared it with the President anyway.[51]

By then, President Trump was engaged. According to Stepien, his Campaign Manager, the State-focused strategy came up in a November 11th meeting among close advisors as "something to consider."[52] At that point, the election had been called, but the President "was very interested in keeping pathways to victory open, so [Stepien] believe[d] [the President] found the concept intriguing."[53] Then, the plan "just started happening" even though it was something Stepien, "honestly, kind of dismissed at hand," characterizing it as one "of the crazy, crazier ideas that w[as] thrown out, in and around that time."[54]

But not everyone was convinced. On November 19th, the prior Republican Presidential nominee, Senator Mitt Romney (R-UT), issued a harsh public condemnation of President Trump's open and notorious efforts to overturn the election:

> Having failed to make even a plausible case of widespread fraud or conspiracy before a court of law, the President has now resorted to overt pressure on state and local officials to subvert the will of the people and overturn the election. It is difficult to imagine a worse, more undemocratic action by a sitting American President.[55]

Senator Romney was right to identify and decry President Trump's actions. And yet, in hindsight, it is clear that the effort to pressure State and local officials by the Trump team was only just getting started.

## 2.3 OUTREACH AND IMPLEMENTATION OF THE PLAN

Just one day after the State-focused plan came up in the Oval Office with the President and his top lieutenants, President Trump started taking concrete steps aimed at State legislators. And in the weeks that followed, the

President spearheaded outreach aimed at numerous officials in States he lost but that had GOP-led legislatures, including in Michigan, Pennsylvania, Georgia, and Arizona.

The Select Committee estimates that in the two months between the November election and the January 6th insurrection, President Trump or his inner circle engaged in at least 200 apparent acts of public or private outreach, pressure, or condemnation, targeting either State legislators or State or local election administrators, to overturn State election results. This included at least:

- 68 meetings, attempted or connected phone calls, or text messages, each aimed at one or more State or local officials;
- 18 instances of prominent public remarks, with language targeting one or more such officials;[56] and
- 125 social media posts by President Trump or senior aides targeting one or more such officials, either explicitly or implicitly, and mostly from his own account.[57]

Furthermore, these efforts by President Trump's team also involved two other initiatives that tried to enlist support from large numbers of State legislators all at once:

- The Trump Campaign contacted, or attempted to contact, nearly 200 State legislators from battleground States between November 30, 2020 and December 3, 2020, to solicit backing for possible Statehouse resolutions to overturn the election. At least some messages said they were "on behalf of the president."[58]
- Nearly 300 State legislators from battleground States reportedly participated in a private briefing with President Trump, Rudolph Giuliani, John Eastman, and others on January 2nd. The President reportedly urged them to exercise what he called "the real power" to choose electoral votes before January 6th, because, as President Trump said on the call, "I don't think the country is going to take it."[59]

It may be impossible to document each and every meeting, phone call, text message, or other contact that President Trump and his allies had with State and local officials in various battleground States. What follows is a summary that focuses on four States and that demonstrates the lengths to which President Trump would go in order to stay in power based on lies—the Big Lie—about the election.

## PRESIDENT TRUMP'S EARLY PRESSURE ON PUBLIC SERVANTS

To carry out his plan, President Trump, Rudolph Giuliani, and other surrogates of President Trump publicly and privately sought assistance from State and local officials whom they assumed would help as Republicans on the same team with the "same goal." [60] Some helped. Others didn't.

On November 12th, U.S. Representative Tim Walberg (R-MI) sent an email to President Trump's Executive Assistant Molly Michael, describing a request he had received earlier that day:

> During my conversation with the President this morning he asked me to check with key leadership in Michigan's Legislature as to how supportive they could be in regards to pushing back on election irregularities and potential fraud. He wanted me to gauge their willingness to talk with him about efforts to bring about transparency and integrity in Michigan's election and report back to him. [61]

Representative Walberg added that he had already acted on this request: "I've had conversations with [Michigan] Speaker Lee Chatfield, Senate Majority Leader Mike Shirkey, and Senate President Pro Tempore Aric Nesbitt. They all assured me they would look forward to speaking with the President to report on their continuing efforts" related to overseeing the election "and receiving any suggestions from President Trump." [62] The President would soon host Chatfield, Shirkey, Nesbitt, and four other Michigan State lawmakers at the White House. [63]

In Arizona, on November 13, 2020, the day after officials finished counting ballots cast in Maricopa County, Chairwoman Kelli Ward, of the Arizona Republican Party, texted Mark Meadows that she had "[j]ust talked to POTUS" and that "[h]e may call the Chairman of the Maricopa Board of Supervisors," Clint Hickman. [64] Ward also left a message for Hickman that said, "I just talked to President Trump, and he would like me to talk to you and also see if he needs to give you a call to discuss what's happening on the ground in Maricopa. Give me a call back when you can." [65] According to Hickman, Ward was unusually active after the election, even for a party chair, and was the first person to pressure him. One of her first messages to Hickman before trying to connect him with President Trump was: "We need you to stop the counting." [66]

In Georgia, the President initially took a more public approach. After the Associated Press called the race there on November 12th, President Trump tweeted harsh criticisms of Governor Brian Kemp and Secretary of State Brad Raffensperger. [67] Often these tweets called for them to take specific actions that would have shifted the election results in his favor, such as rejecting a court settlement (which he referred to as a consent decree) that dictated the procedures for verifying signatures on absentee ballots. And he was relentless.

In November alone, President Trump tweeted that Raffensperger was "a so-called Republican (RINO)" and asked "Where is @BrianKempGA," [68] before suggesting that "They knew they were going to cheat." [69] He called to "Break the unconstitutional Consent Decree!" [70] and urged stricter signature matches with a demand to "Get it done! @BrianKempGA." [71] He called Kemp "hapless" and asked why he wouldn't use emergency powers to overrule Raffensperger on the signature-verification procedures, declaring that "Georgia Republicans are angry." [72] President Trump also retweeted posts asking, "Who needs Democrats when you have Republicans like Brian Kemp," and "why bother voting for Republicans if what you get is Ducey and Kemp?" [73]

Pennsylvania was an early, but not unique, example of how President Trump's State-pressure campaign affected the lives of the public servants running this country's elections.

On November 7th, Rudy Giuliani headlined a Philadelphia press conference in front of a landscaping business called Four Seasons Total Landscaping, near a crematorium and down the street from a sex shop.[74]

Standing in front of former New York Police Commissioner and recently-pardoned convicted felon, Bernard Kerik, Giuliani gave opening remarks and handed the podium over to his first supposed eyewitness to election fraud, who turned out to be a convicted sex offender.[75] Giuliani claimed "at least 600,000 ballots are in question" in Pennsylvania and falsely suggested that large numbers of ballots in the State had been cast for dead people, including boxer Joe Frazier and actor Will Smith's father.[76]

Within days, Republican Philadelphia City Commissioner Al Schmidt and others publicly debunked Giuliani's specific allegations of election fraud, including the claims about dead people voting in Pennsylvania elections.[77] In reaction, President Trump tweeted on the morning of November 11th that "[a] guy named Al Schmidt, a Philadelphia Commissioner and so-called Republican (RINO), is being used big time by the Fake News Media to explain how honest things were with respect to the Election in Philadelphia. He refuses to look at a mountain of corruption & dishonesty. We win!" [78]

That statement targeting Schmidt led to a deluge of threatening and harassing phone calls and emails by people who heard President Trump and falsely held out hope that Schmidt or someone else could overturn the results of Pennsylvania's election.[79]

As a public official, Schmidt was no stranger to threats. But being targeted by the President of the United States was different. In Schmidt's public testimony to the Select Committee, he described why. "[P]rior to that the threats were pretty general in nature. 'Corrupt election officials in Philadelphia are going to get what's coming to them'" and other similar threats.[80] "After the President tweeted at me by name, calling me out the way that he did," Schmidt explained, "the threats became much more specific, much more graphic, and included not just me by name but included members of my family by name, their ages, our address, pictures of our home. Just every bit of detail that you could imagine."[81]

As the President continued to push the Big Lie and vilify public officials, such threats multiplied.

### EFFORTS TO PREVENT STATE AND LOCAL OFFICIALS FROM CERTIFYING THE ELECTION

Some of President Trump's early outreach was part of an effort to prevent State and local officials from certifying his loss. One example comes from Michigan, and the other from Arizona.

Wayne County, Michigan, includes Detroit and its surrounding areas. On November 17th, the county's Board of Canvassers met to certify election results, a process the Michigan Supreme Court described over a century ago as ministerial and clerical.[82]

The meeting started at 6:00 p.m. and lasted over three hours.[83] Its two Republican members, Board Chair Monica Palmer and Board Member William Hartmann, first voted to block the certification of the election.[84] After a brief break, Palmer and Hartmann returned, changed their votes, and certified the election results.[85] Just over twenty minutes later, Palmer and Hartmann received a call from President Trump and RNC Chair Ronna McDaniel.[86]

Palmer claimed that the call "was not pressure." Rather, she said, "[i]t was genuine concern for my safety" and "there were general comments about different States, but we really didn't discuss the details of the certification."[87]

The Select Committee doesn't know exactly what President Trump privately said on that phone call.[88] By the next evening, however, Palmer and Hartmann had each issued signed affidavits reassuming their earlier position that Wayne County's results should not be certified.[89] Palmer's affidavit even declared that "I rescind my prior vote," though rescinding wasn't possible and her statement had no legal effect.[90] And, President Trump apparently knew before it was public that Hartmann and Palmer would try to change their votes; almost eight hours *before* either of these affidavits were publicly released, President Trump tweeted that these "two harassed patriot Canvassers refuse to sign the papers!"[91]

Republicans in Arizona experienced similar treatment. In the most populous and electorally significant county in Arizona, Maricopa County's Board of Supervisors met on November 20th to certify the county's election results. Their Board, made up of four Republicans and one Democrat, carefully reviewed the official canvass, asked questions for approximately two hours, then unanimously voted to certify the results.[92]

Earlier that day, Kelli Ward contacted two of the board's members, Jack Sellers and Bill Gates, and asked them to delay the certification on the basis of supposed improprieties.[93] According to Sellers and Gates, however, Arizona law required certification that day and they had no information (neither then, nor ever) to doubt the county's election results.[94]

When Arizona certified its 2020 statewide election results on November 30th, it fell to Governor Doug Ducey, a Republican, to sign the certification. While on camera during the signing ceremony, Governor Ducey's phone played a ringtone for the song "Hail to the Chief," which he immediately silenced.[95]

The Governor later confirmed it had been President Trump calling and that he returned the President's call shortly afterwards, but declined to say what the two discussed other than saying that President Trump did not ask him to withhold certification.[96] The Select Committee does not know whether that is true, but that evening President Trump blasted Ducey on Twitter, accusing him of "rushing to put a Democrat in office," and warning that "Republicans will long remember!"[97] The President also retweeted posts bashing Ducey and his Georgia counterpart Brian Kemp, which asked "Who needs Democrats when you have Republicans like Brian Kemp and Doug Ducey?", "why bother voting for Republicans if what you get is Ducey and Kemp?", and "Brian Kemp: 'My state ran the most corrupt election in American history.' Doug Ducey: 'Hold my beer.'"[98] President Trump even commented "TRUE!" when retweeting a post that "Gov Ducey has betrayed the people of Arizona."[99]

Governor Ducey pushed back, writing on Twitter that, "I've been pretty outspoken about Arizona's election system, and bragged about it quite a bit, including in the Oval Office . . . In Arizona, we have some of the strongest election laws in the country . . . The problems that exist in other states simply don't apply here."[100] Governor Ducey explained the law for certifying elections in Arizona and pointed out that the certification now triggered a "5-day window for any elector to bring a credible challenge to the election results in court. If you want to contest the results, now is the time. Bring your challenges."[101] And, Governor Ducey referenced his oath of office:

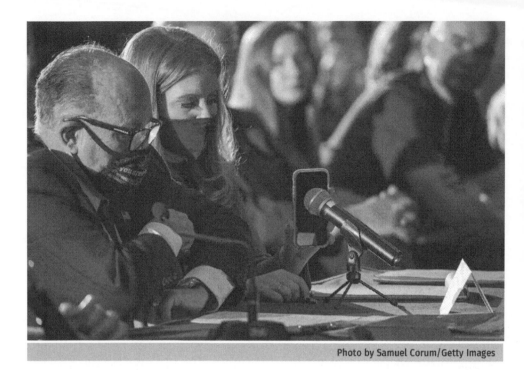

"That's the law. I've sworn an oath to uphold it, and I take my responsibility seriously." [102] President Trump and his allies never brought a credible challenge and, instead, lost every case they brought challenging the results in Arizona.

### EFFORTS TO REPLACE ELECTORAL COLLEGE ELECTORS AND OVERTURN THE ELECTION

Once counties and States certified the election, or when it was nearly certain that they would, President Trump and his team's focus largely shifted. President Trump and his team encouraged State legislators to meet in special sessions, if necessary, and choose electoral college electors who would vote for the Trump/Pence ticket. Ultimately, no State legislature took that step, but it was the basis for pressuring State officials from November through January 6, 2021.

### MEETINGS WITH STATE LEGISLATORS—THE "HEARINGS"

The concept of State legislators appointing their own electors featured prominently in a series of hastily arranged official and unofficial "hearings" with State legislators that the Trump team announced on November 24, 2020.[103]

On November 25th, President Trump called in to an unofficial meeting with legislators in Gettysburg, Pennsylvania.[104] The meeting was set up to appear like an official hearing, but it was not. It took place in a hotel ballroom, and those presenting arguments or purported evidence, like Giuliani, Jenna Ellis, and others, were not placed under oath.[105] According to President *Pro Tempore* of the Pennsylvania Senate Jake Corman, he had initially been asked by State Senator Doug Mastriano to hold a hearing about the election. Corman responded that any formal hearing should be official, with sworn testimony, and open to both parties.[106] That was not what Senator Mastriano ultimately convened.

President Trump had originally made plans to attend the Pennsylvania gathering in person, but he cancelled after several advisors tested positive for COVID–19.[107] When President Trump called in and spoke to those gathered in the hotel ballroom, his false claims were met with cheers, and he made his purpose clear: "this election has to be turned around . . . Why wouldn't they overturn an election? Certainly overturn it in your State . . . We have to turn the election over." [108]

President Trump made the ask and Giuliani told the legislators how to carry it out. Giuliani told the assembled legislators that it was their "power" and "responsibility" to pick Pennsylvania's presidential electors and that "[they] have to convince the rest of [their] members, Republican and Democrat, they owe that to the people of" Pennsylvania.[109] Jenna Ellis told them that although Pennsylvania law dictates that electors are chosen by popular vote, "[y]ou can take that power back at any time. You don't need a court to tell you that." [110]

President Trump invited some of the lawmakers to come meet him at the White House that evening and, according to Giuliani, it was "a large group" that went.[111] Special Assistant to the President Cassidy Hutchinson's text messages with Kerik included the guest list and descriptions of the vehicles that would need access to the White House grounds.[112] Pennsylvania State Senator Doug Mastriano drove one car, a hired driver drove a van with most of the State legislators, and Kerik drove an SUV with attorney Katherine Friess and election-conspiracy proponent Phil Waldron.[113] Hutchinson estimated that at least 29 visitors traveled from Pennsylvania to the White House that day, and she explained that their conversation with the President touched on holding a special session of the State legislature to appoint Trump electors.[114]

Just a few days later, on November 30, 2020, President Trump also called into another one of Giuliani and Jenna Ellis's hotel "hearings," this time in Arizona. Several Arizona State lawmakers hosted the meeting at a Hyatt Regency in Phoenix after they did not receive permission to organize an official hearing at the State Capitol.[115] Before the hearing started, State GOP Representative Mark Finchem "promised information to show that the state's 11 electoral votes should not go to Democrat Joe Biden," and argued that "the U.S. Constitution empowers lawmakers to decide, on their own, whether the election was valid and, if not, to select the electors of their choice." [116]

Giuliani told the assembled legislators that the officials certifying Arizona's election results "have made no effort to find out" if the results of the election were accurate, "which seems to me gives the state legislature a perfect reason to take over the conduct of this election because it's being conducted irresponsibly and unfairly." [117] Likewise, Jenna Ellis said that it was "not just the choice, but the actual duty and obligation of the legislature to step in and to make sure that you don't certify false results." [118] During a recess, she also took to Twitter, writing, "[t]he certification of Arizona's FALSE results is unethical and knowingly participating in the corruption that has disenfranchised AZ voters. BUT, this in no way impacts the state legislature's ability to take back the proper selection of delegates." [119]

When it was President Trump's turn to address this handful of lawmakers over the phone, he called them "legends for taking this on," and used the opportunity to criticize Governor Ducey: "you'll have to figure out what's that all about with Ducey. He couldn't [certify] fast enough" and "Arizona will not forget what Ducey just did. We're not gonna forget." [120] That night Giuliani joined President Trump in criticizing Governor Ducey, while at the same time making baseless allegations about voting machines in Arizona and calling for a special legislative session to change the outcome of the election: "Governor Ducey of Arizona refuses to meet with me. He doesn't want to explain that he selected a foreign corrupt Voting Machine company to count the vote. I understand his reluctance, but [sic] just call a special session. Let's find out how crooked your election really was?" [121]

Michigan was next. Giuliani's team announced that the Michigan legislature would hold a hearing on December 1st, but the relevant committee chair excluded Giuliani because it was only open to witnesses "with first hand knowledge." [122] That chairman, Michigan State Senator Edward McBroom (R-Vulcan), had already held Senate Oversight hearings by then in an actual effort to evaluate claims of fraud in the 2020 election, which ultimately resulted in a comprehensive report that concluded that the Republican-led committee "found no evidence of widespread or systematic fraud" in Michigan's election. [123]

Michigan's House Oversight Committee, however, did allow Giuliani to testify in a hearing on December 2nd. Before the hearing, Giuliani joined the State's GOP chairwoman to give what was billed as a legal briefing. In the online presentation, Giuliani told the audience there's "nothing wrong with putting pressure on your state legislators" [124] to pick new electors and that "you have got to get them to remember that their oath to the Constitution sometimes requires being criticized. Sometimes it even requires being threatened." [125]

When Giuliani appeared for the hearing in Michigan, he was not placed under oath, used his time to refer to Michigan's election as a "con job," and urged legislators to "have the courage to say that certification that was done by your state is a complete phony." [126] The information presented was baseless—and sometimes racist—conspiracy theories. One witness brought to criticize Michigan's voter verification even said: "I think Chinese all look alike. So how would you tell? If some Chow shows up, you can be anybody and you can vote." [127] And, as he had promised in the legal briefing the day before, Giuliani then called on the legislators to do what the Trump Campaign had reportedly been discussing since before election day. He said that the State legislature could still singlehandedly decide the election result "anytime you want to. Anytime. You can take it back tonight. You can take it back the day before the electors go down to Washington." [128] Jenna Ellis also participated, insisting "no honest person can hear these citizens of your own state today . . . and can let this proceed. What the Constitution obligates you to do is to take back your plenary power." [129]

Finally, Georgia. There, Giuliani and others appeared in multiple hearings, the first of which was held on December 3, 2020. In that hearing, Giuliani was direct and called on Georgia legislators to overturn the election results—"you are the final arbiter of who the electors should be"—based on the false premise that "there is more than ample evidence to conclude that this election was a sham." [130] Then, at a separate hearing on December 10th, he told State legislators that Georgia's Governor, Lieutenant Governor, and secretary of State were engaged in a "cover up" of "a crime in plain sight," and that it fell to "the state legislature [ ] to vindicate the honor of the state." [131] And, Giuliani used yet another appearance, on December 30th, to call the 2020 election "the most crooked election, the most manipulated election in American history," and implore the Republican legislators to hold a special session to vote on appointing new electors, something he said that they could do "right up until the last moment" before January 6th.[132]

More perniciously, Giuliani also used these hearings to advance conspiracy theories that falsely accused Fulton County election workers of rigging Georgia's election results. His delegation to the December 3rd hearing played clips of election-night surveillance footage from the State Farm

Arena that showed election workers scanning ballots, sometimes after partisan poll watchers had gone home.[133] Although the poll watchers should have been there the entire time while election workers counted the votes, there was nothing nefarious about the circumstances and no question about the end result. In fact, the FBI, Department of Justice, and Georgia Bureau of Investigation would determine that these ballots were legitimate ballots, that observers were not illegally ejected, and that the ballots were scanned and counted properly, contrary to claims by President Trump and his attorneys.[134] And yet Giuliani baselessly declared at the December 3rd hearing that, to him, the video was a "powerful smoking gun" proving that "those votes are not legitimate votes."[135]

But Giuliani's claims took a more ominous turn during the December 10th hearing. There, he publicly named two of the election workers shown in the video, Ruby Freeman and her daughter, Wandrea ArShaye "Shaye" Moss, and accused them of vote-tampering and engaging in criminal conduct.[136] He seized on a clip of Freeman passing Moss a ginger mint, claiming that the two women, both Black, were smuggling USB drives "as if they're vials of heroin or cocaine." He also suggested that Freeman and Moss should be jailed and that they deserved to have their homes searched.[137] Not only were Giuliani's claims about Freeman and Moss reckless, racist, and false, they had real-world consequences that turned both women's lives upside down. And further heightening the personal impact of these baseless attacks, President Trump supported, and even repeated, them, as described later.

In the end, the hearings were widely panned. In Michigan alone, current and former Republican lawmakers publicly questioned the hearings and implored President Trump and his team to stop. U.S. Representative Paul Mitchell (R-Mich.) implored on Twitter "Please JUST STOP!" and "wondered why Republican leaders allowed testimony he said was 'driving the party into this ditch.'"[138] Similarly, former Michigan lawmaker Martin Howrylak (R-Oakland) said that he was "embarrassed" by the hearing, and former Michigan Senator Ken Sikkema (R-Grand Rapids) said that "the way the committee was run was atrocious."[139] Later, the President promoted a tweet calling a Democratic lawmaker a "#pos" for speaking out at the Michigan hearing.[140] Months later, Giuliani's license to practice law in New York was suspended for, among other reasons, the "false claims" he made on various dates, including during the hearings in Michigan, Pennsylvania, Arizona, and Georgia.[141]

## THE TRUMP CAMPAIGN'S BARRAGE OF PHONE CALLS TO STATE LEGISLATORS

Not only was replacing electors a theme during the official and unofficial State hearings, it was also a critical component of President Trump's plan both before and after the hearings took place.

In fact, while the hearings were happening, the Trump Campaign set up an operation to contact hundreds of State legislators and ask them to support an effort to appoint electoral college electors for the Trump/Pence ticket in States that President Trump had lost.

On the same day as Giuliani's hearing in Michigan, Trump Campaign staff contacted dozens of Republicans in Michigan's State legislature. A Trump Campaign supervisor sent text messages to his team, directing them to reach out to lawmakers "to explain the process for legislative redress and tell them how to send representative[s] to th[e] electoral college." [142] He added: "We're gonna be lobbyists. Woot." [143]

According to a Campaign staffer's spreadsheet produced to the Select Committee, the Trump Campaign apparently tried contacting over 190 Republican State legislators in Arizona, Georgia, and Michigan, alone.[144]

One voicemail left as part of this initiative was leaked to the press on December 1, 2020. In it, a Trump Campaign staffer said, "I did want to personally reach out to you on behalf of the President." [145] Her main point came later in the message: "we want to know when there is a resolution in the House to appoint electors for Trump if the President can count on you to join in support." [146] Another message from this effort that reached reporters made the same ask and claimed that, "[a]fter a roundtable with the President, he asked us to reach out to you individually" to whip support for a "joint resolution from the State House and Senate" that would "allow Michigan to send electors for Donald J. Trump to the Electoral College and save our country." [147]

Soon after the voicemail leaked, the Campaign staffer who left this voicemail got a text message from one of her supervisors, who wrote: "Honest to god I'm so proud of this" because "[t]hey unwittingly just got your message out there." [148] He elaborated: "you used the awesome power of the presidency to scare a state rep into getting a statewide newspaper to deliver your talking points." [149]

## OUTREACH BY PRESIDENT TRUMP AND SENIOR AIDES

While Campaign aides blanketed State officials with these calls, some State officials received more personalized outreach directly from President Trump, Giuliani, and their allies throughout the post-election period about this issue.

**Michigan.** As discussed earlier, Rep. Walberg reached out to State legislators in Michigan at the President's request in mid-November, including Senate Majority Leader Mike Shirkey and House Speaker Lee Chatfield. By November 18th, President Trump called Chatfield and Shirkey to invite them to what would become a meeting for a group of Michigan lawmakers in the Oval Office.[150] Although President Trump didn't tell Shirkey what the meeting would be about, the President was focused on the election and asked Shirkey what he and others were doing to investigate election fraud.[151] The meeting happened on November 20th.[152]

In Shirkey's words, there "wasn't a mystery" about why the group was at the White House once the meeting started.[153] When the President mentioned several baseless claims of election fraud in Wayne County, Shirkey told the President that he had lost the election and that it had nothing to do with Wayne County, where he had actually performed better than he had in 2016.[154]

From the President's body language, Shirkey concluded that wasn't what he wanted to hear. But the meeting continued, and the President dialed in Giuliani, who delivered a "long monologue," reciting a "litany" of allegations about supposed fraud that was short on substance.[155] Shirkey challenged Giuliani, asking "when are you going to . . . file a lawsuit in Michigan," which he said Giuliani did not answer.[156] Although Shirkey says he did not recall the President making any precise "ask," Chatfield recalled President Trump's more generic directive for the group to "have some backbone and do the right thing." [157] Chatfield understood that to mean they should investigate claims of fraud and overturn the election by naming electors for President Trump.[158] Shirkey told the President that he was not going to do anything that would violate Michigan law.[159]

After the meeting ended, Shirkey and Chatfield issued a joint statement: "We have not yet been made aware of any information that would change the outcome of the election in Michigan and as legislative leaders, we will follow the law and follow the normal process regarding Michigan's electors, just as we have said throughout this election." [160]

That was not the end, however. Chatfield and Shirkey received numerous calls from the President in the weeks following the election. Chatfield told the Select Committee that he received approximately five to ten phone calls from President Trump after the election, during which the President would usually ask him about various allegations of voter fraud.[161] Chatfield said that he repeatedly looked into the President's claims but never found anything persuasive that could have changed the outcome of the election.[162]

President Trump's calls were not enough, so he turned to the public. On January 3, 2021, the Trump Campaign posted a tweet that urged supporters

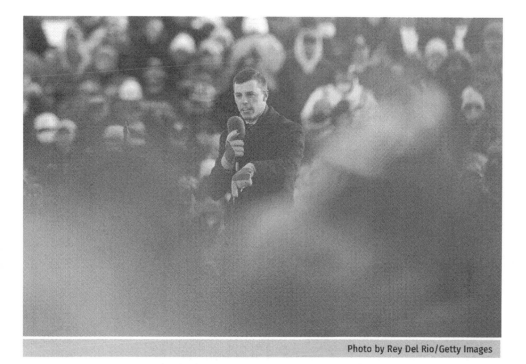

Photo by Rey Del Rio/Getty Images

to "Contact Speaker Lee Chatfield & Senate Majority Leader Mike Shirkey" to "Demand [a] vote on decertification."[163] Why President Trump thought the Michigan legislature would convene to decertify the election in a matter of hours when it had refused to do so since early November is not clear. But that didn't stop the President from making things personal. The President's January 3rd tweet included Shirkey's personal cellphone number as well as a number for Chatfield that turned out to be wrong. As a result, Shirkey said he received nearly 4,000 text messages, and another private citizen reported being inundated with calls and texts intended for Chatfield.[164]

**Pennsylvania.** On November 21st, Mark Meadows texted a number apparently belonging to Representative Scott Perry (R–PA) and asked: "Can you send me the number for the speaker and the leader of the PA Legislature. POTUS wants to chat with them."[165] Hours later, Meadows received a response of "Yes sir."[166] At the time, the leader of the Pennsylvania Senate was Jake Corman and the Speaker of the Pennsylvania House was Bryan Cutler.

Corman told the Select Committee that he received a call on Thanksgiving Day 2020 from Giuliani, urging him to call the legislature into a special session to replace Biden electors with Trump electors.[167] This idea wasn't new to Corman. President Trump and his allies had gone public about their intentions before then, including during the Pennsylvania hotel hearing, but Corman had braced himself for this even before the election. Before election day in 2020, a reporter from *The Atlantic* interviewed Corman and other prominent Republicans in Pennsylvania about the possibility that President Trump would try to circumvent the popular vote in swing States by asking the legislatures to appoint Trump/Pence electors. After the article, Corman drafted an op-ed, making it clear that the Pennsylvania legislature did not have the legal authority to appoint Trump/Pence electors in contravention of the popular vote, a position that he would generally maintain through the 2020 Presidential election cycle.[168]

During that call, Giuliani first tried "pumping [Corman] up as a patriot" before asking the Senator to call the Pennsylvania legislature into a special session. Corman told Giuliani that he did not have the authority to do that, a position with which his own lawyers agreed.[169] Giuliani's reply was that Corman must have bad lawyers. Corman said he offered to connect Giuliani with his legal team. His legal team spoke with Giuliani and a lawyer working with him, Jenna Ellis, the following day, reiterating their view that such a move by the legislature would be illegal.[170] That same day, or possibly the next, Giuliani and Ellis called him back to renew their request for a special legislative session and to demean Corman's attorneys, calling them "terrible," "bad," and "wrong."[171] Corman, however, held his ground and ended the call.[172]

While packing to return to Pennsylvania from his Thanksgiving visit to Florida, Corman says he received a call from an unknown number with a Washington, DC area code, which he let go to voicemail.[173] It turned out to be a White House operator calling on behalf of President Trump.[174]

Corman called back and spoke to President Trump, who insisted that he had won the election in Pennsylvania and said something to the effect of, "Jake, this is a big issue. We need your help."[175] Corman told the President that he couldn't do what the Trump team was asking; President Trump replied, "I'm not sure your attorneys are very good."[176] Corman wanted to end the call and offered to have his lawyers speak again with President Trump's, but they never had another call with the President's lawyers.[177]

Pennsylvania House Speaker Bryan Cutler was another main target for the President's team. He received voicemails in late November for four days in a row from Giuliani and/or Jenna Ellis, which he provided to the Select Committee.[178] Cutler explained that he did not feel comfortable talking with the President's team in case he ended up having to preside over a legislative session about the election, and he had his attorneys relay that to the President's team.[179] Giuliani received the message but continued to call Speaker Cutler nonetheless.[180]

In the first of these voicemails, on November 26th, Giuliani asked to "get together, quietly" to discuss "the amount of fraud that went on in your State," and said that Giuliani and Ellis had also just spoken to Pennsylvania House Majority Leader Kerry Benninghoff.[181] On November 27th, Ellis called and said in a second voicemail that they had just talked to Pennsylvania House Member Russ Diamond and were "very grateful" to the State's legislature "for doing your Article II duty."[182] On November 28th, Giuliani left a third voicemail and claimed to have "something important" that "really changes things," and said that "the president wanted me to make sure I got it to you."[183] And then on November 29th, Giuliani left a fourth message and said, "I understand that you don't want to talk to me now" but still sought "the courtesy of being able to talk to you as the president's lawyer" and a "fellow Republican" because "you're certifying what is a blatantly false statement . . . I can't imagine how that's in your interests or in the interests of our party."[184]

Giuliani and Ellis didn't get through, but the President did. "[I]f we wanted to do something, what were the options[?]" the President asked Cutler.[185] Cutler explained to President Trump that he could file a legal challenge contesting the election, and asked the President why his team had never requested a statewide recount.[186] Cutler was also clear about the "constitutional peculiarities" of Pennsylvania, where the State constitution specifically prohibits retroactive changes to how electors are chosen.[187]

Practically, President Trump's call achieved nothing. The President wasn't getting what he wanted in his calls to leaders in Pennsylvania: a special session of the legislature to appoint Trump/Pence electors.

Seemingly undeterred, President Trump invited several leaders of the Pennsylvania legislature to the White House for Christmas gatherings.[188] Senator Corman decided not to go, although Speaker Cutler did. President Trump spoke with Cutler on December 3rd, while Cutler, his chief of staff, and their wives were at that White House Christmas tour.[189] The issue of overturning the results of Pennsylvania's election came up again, as did the possibility of a special session of the State legislature to appoint Trump electors.[190] Cutler told the President that the State legislature could not reconvene without an order from the Governor and a petition from a supermajority of legislators, neither of which was likely to happen.[191] Cutler also told the President that they could not appoint new electors without a court order. In Cutler's opinion, President Trump "seemed to understand. And that was—that was clear."[192] The President's apparent understanding, however, did not result in any meaningful changes to his public rhetoric.

On December 3rd, the same day that Cutler met with President Trump, Cutler, Corman, House Majority Leader Benninghoff, and Senate Majority

Leader Kim Ward issued a three-page single-spaced joint statement asserting, in no uncertain terms, that Pennsylvania's General Assembly "lacks the authority . . . to overturn the popular vote and appoint our own slate of electors," since "[d]oing so would violate our Election Code and Constitution, particularly a provision that prohibits us from changing the rules for election contests of the President after the election."[193] In response, President Trump retweeted a December 4th post by Bernard Kerik, which tagged all four of these State legislators with the hashtag "Traitors," and declared that "These are the four cowardice[sic] Pennsylvania legislators that intend to allow the Democrat machine to #StealtheVote! #Cowards #Liars #Traitors."[194]

But five days later, President Trump publicly thanked Cutler for signing onto a December 4th letter that encouraged Members of Congress from Pennsylvania to object to their State's electoral votes on January 6th. The President tweeted: "Thank you to Speaker Cutler and all others in Pennsylvania and elsewhere who fully understand what went on in the 2020 election. It's called total corruption!"[195] When the Select Committee asked Cutler about this apparent change in his position, he said that he signed on to this letter not because of concerns that fraud or corruption meant the results of the election Pennsylvania were wrong, but rather because of concerns about "programmatic changes or areas for improvement" related to the election.[196] In fact, Cutler reiterated to the Committee that he "was not personally aware of" any widespread election fraud that would have changed the result of the election.[197]

The pressure facing State legislators during this period was significant. On December 9th, the *New York Times* quoted Pennsylvania's Senate Majority Leader Kim Ward, revealing that she too had received a call from President Trump in which he pushed his election fraud narrative.[198] Ward told the *Times* that she hadn't been given enough time to sign the same December 4th letter that Cutler did, but commented that if she had taken a stand against it, "I'd get my house bombed tonight."[199]

**Arizona.** In late November, Arizona House Speaker Russell "Rusty" Bowers, a longtime Republican who served 17 years in the State legislature, received a call from President Trump and Giuliani.[200] Giuliani alleged that Arizona's election results were skewed by illicit ballots, cast by non-citizens or on behalf of dead people.[201] Bowers demanded proof for these audacious claims on the call and President Trump told Giuliani to comply, but the evidence never came.[202] The point of the call, however, was different. Like in Michigan and Pennsylvania, President Trump and his allies were working the phones to get something. They wanted Bowers to hold a public hearing

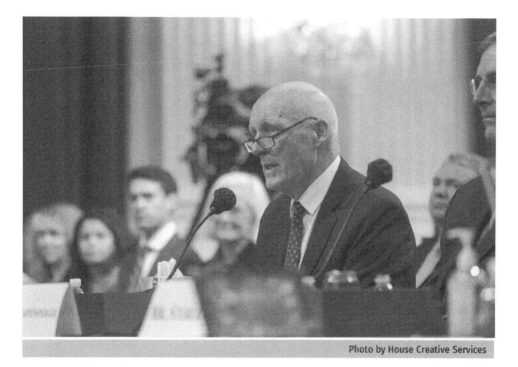

with the ultimate aim of replacing Presidential electors for former Vice President Joe Biden with electors for President Trump.[203]

Bowers had never heard of anything like that before, and Giuliani acknowledged that it had never been done. Where President Trump and Giuliani saw a potential opportunity, however, Bowers saw a fundamental problem.

As Bowers explained it, what they wanted him to do was "counter to my oath when I swore to the Constitution to uphold it." [204] And he said that to the President and Giuliani: "you are asking me to do something against my oath, and I will not break my oath." [205] Giuliani replied: "aren't we all Republicans here? I mean, I would think you would listen a little more open to my suggestions, that we're all Republicans." [206]

The pressure didn't stop with that call. On December 1st, Giuliani and Ellis got an audience with some of the most powerful Republican lawmakers in Arizona, including Bowers, Senate President Karen Fann, Senate President Pro Tempore Vince Leach, House Majority Leader and Senator-Elect Warren Petersen, Senate Majority Whip Sonny Borrelli, Senator Michelle Ugenti-Rita, and others.[207] The Select Committee was unable to get Giuliani and Ellis' perspective on this outreach because Giuliani claimed that his communications with Bowers—who was not his client nor part of his legal team—were "privileged," while Ellis invoked her Fifth Amendment rights against self-incrimination.[208]

Bowers, on the other hand, told the Select Committee that Giuliani and Ellis asked the lawmakers to deliver Arizona's electors for President Trump, despite the certified popular vote count.[209] To bolster their request, Giuliani and Ellis raised numerous allegations of election fraud at the meeting, though they never produced evidence in support of their claims. In live testimony before the Committee, Bowers recalled Giuliani saying in this meeting that "we've got lots of theories, we just don't have the evidence." [210] At the time, Bowers didn't know whether it was a gaffe or an example of Giuliani not thinking through what he had just said.[211] In any event, Bowers said he and others in his group made particular note of that comment.[212] And it was borne out; Bowers testified that "No one provided me, ever, such evidence." [213]

In late December, in another phone call with President Trump, Bowers reiterated that he would not do anything illegal for him.[214] Afterward, John Eastman joined the chorus of Trump allies attempting to change his mind. In a call on January 4th that included the Speaker's chief counsel as well as Arizona House Majority Leader-Elect Ben Toma, Eastman urged Bowers to hold a vote to decertify Arizona's Presidential electors.[215] When Bowers told Eastman he couldn't unilaterally reconvene the legislature, Eastman urged him to "just do it and let the court sort it out." [216] Bowers refused and the Arizona legislature took no such action.

Many of President Trump's efforts in Arizona focused on State officials, but his team also continued to reach out to the Board of Supervisors for Maricopa County even after it certified the election. One focus was voting machines. According to the *Arizona Republic*, Giuliani left a voicemail in mid- to late-December for Board Member Steve Chucri that "I see we're gonna get a chance to take a good look at those machines . . . give me a call as soon as you get a chance. The president also wanted me to pass on a few things to you, too." [217] On December 4th, Giuliani also left a message for the Board's Chairman Clint Hickman: "I was very happy to see that there's gonna be a forensic audit of the machines. And I really wanted to talk to you about it a bit. The President wanted me to give you a call. All right? Thank you. Give me a call back." [218] Hickman chose not to call back.[219]

Then, on Christmas Eve, Giuliani left voicemails for Board Members Bill Gates and Jack Sellers, asking them to call him back. In his message for Gates, Giuliani said:

> It's Giuliani, President Trump's lawyer. If you get a chance, would you please give me a call? I have a few things I'd like to talk over with you. Maybe we can get this thing fixed up. You know, I really

think it's a shame that Republicans sort of are both in this, kind of, situation. And I think there may be a nice way to resolve this for everybody.[220]

In his message for Sellers, Giuliani said "I'd like to see if there is a way that we can resolve this so that it comes out well for everyone. We're all Republicans, I think we all have the same goal. Let's see if . . . we can get this done outside of the court."[221] Like Hickman, neither Gates nor Sellers returned Giuliani's calls.[222]

So President Trump made the call himself. On December 31st, Board Chair Clint Hickman received a voicemail from the White House switchboard, asking him to call back for President Trump. Hickman said that he did not return the call, in part because the county was still facing litigation over the election.[223] Another call from the White House came through on January 3rd with a request that Hickman call back for the President. But, by then, the President's call with Georgia Secretary of State Brad Raffensperger, described below, had leaked, and Hickman "didn't want to walk into that space."[224]

**Georgia.** On December 5th, President Trump traveled to Georgia to headline a rally and mobilize voters in advance of a January Senate runoff. But the President's day started with a morning call to Governor Brian Kemp during which they discussed reconvening the legislature in a special session.[225] After the call, Kemp took to Twitter. He acknowledged that he had spoken to the President and that he told the President that he supported the idea of, and had already called for, a signature audit in Georgia.[226] President Trump responded later that night by complaining that Georgia had not yet done a signature-verification audit and instead insisted that the Governor should "[a]t least immediately ask for a Special Session of the Legislature."[227] The following day, Governor Kemp and Lieutenant Governor Geoff Duncan issued a definitive statement rejecting President Trump and his allies' calls to overturn the results in Georgia:

> While we understand four members of the Georgia Senate are requesting the convening of a special session of the General Assembly, doing this in order to select a separate slate of presidential electors is not an option that is allowed under state or federal law.

> State law is clear: the legislature could only direct an alternative method for choosing presidential electors if the election was not able to be held on the date set by federal law. In the 1960s, the General Assembly decided that Georgia's presidential electors will be determined by the winner of the State's popular vote. Any attempt

by the legislature to retroactively change that process for the November 3rd election would be unconstitutional and immediately enjoined by the courts, resulting in a long legal dispute and no short-term resolution.[228]

President Trump responded by directing his ire at Georgia officials and, throughout the month of December, President Trump grew even more relentless in his social media attacks against Kemp than he had been the previous month. He retweeted attorney Lin Wood calling on Georgians to call and urge the FBI to focus more on election fraud and "[t]ell them to also investigate @BrianKempGA @GeoffDuncanGA & @GaSecofState."[229] And he retweeted another post by Lin Wood that depicted Governor Kemp and Secretary Raffensperger wearing masks digitally altered to show the Chinese flag, and warned that they "will soon be going to jail."[230] Even without his many retweets, President Trump posted an average of about one tweet per day in December 2020 either criticizing Governor Kemp or pressuring him explicitly or implicitly to take actions to help overturn the election.[231]

President Trump seemed consumed with his plans to overturn the election and, based on documents obtained by the Select Committee, it appears that the President received input from many outside donors or advisors who had access to his staff's email addresses. On December 7th, a Trump donor named Bill White emailed senior Trump advisors, including Dan Scavino and Rudolph Giuliani, to say that he "[j]ust spoke to [Georgia State] Senator [William Burton] Jones [who] asked if Potus can R[e]T[weet] this now pls," along with a tweet by Senator Jones that read: "Georgia Patriot Call to Action... call your state Senate & House Reps & ask them to sign the petition for a special session."[232] President Trump and Giuliani each retweeted Senator Jones's tweet an hour later.[233]

Bill White also emailed Molly Michael, Dan Scavino, and Giuliani, on December 8th with information that he said "POTUS asked me last night" to send right away.[234] He recommended a Presidential tweet criticizing Georgia's Lt. Gov. Duncan as well as tweets to put pressure on Senate Majority Leader Mike Dugan and Senate President Pro Tempore Butch Miller.[235] He wrote that President Trump would be calling Dugan and Miller "to ask them to call special session and strategize with them why they are keeping this from happening."[236] Dugan later confirmed that he had received a call from President Trump's office but that the two of them were not able to connect.[237] And the following day, Steve Bannon revealed on his podcast that President Trump spoke to Georgia House Speaker Ralston and Speaker Pro Tempore Jan Jones.[238] Speaker Ralston confirmed that he spoke to President Trump on December 7th about the election, during which he told the President that Georgia law made a special legislative session "very much an uphill battle."[239]

## 2.4  AN OUTRIGHT REQUEST FOR VICTORY

Beyond asking State officials to not certify, to decertify, or to appoint Trump electors for consideration during the joint session, President Trump and some of his closest advisors inserted themselves directly into the counting of ballots and asked, outright, for enough votes to win.

White House Chief of Staff Mark Meadows did this. Not only did he place calls on behalf of the President to election officials in Georgia, Meadows traveled there to personally visit election officials and volunteers, coordinated with Members of Congress, and even suggested that the President send election workers Trump memorabilia like presidential challenge coins and autographed MAGA hats, a suggestion that his assistant Cassidy Hutchinson thought could be problematic and, ultimately, did not act on.[240]

When Meadows made a visit on short notice to examine the audit of absentee ballots in Cobb County, Georgia, he spoke to Deputy Secretary of State Jordan Fuchs and Frances Watson, the Secretary of State's chief investigator. Ultimately, Meadows connected Watson with the President, who claimed that he had won the election and pressed her to say that he had won. The Select Committee obtained a copy of their recorded call, which is detailed below.

The President told Watson that he had "won Georgia . . . by a lot," told her, "you have the most important job in the country right now," and suggested, "when the right answer comes out you'll be praised."[241] Four days later, Meadows texted Deputy Secretary of State Fuchs, in which he asked, "[i]s there a way to speed up Fulton county signature verification in order to have results before Jan 6 if the trump campaign assist[s] financially."[242] Fuchs wrote in response that she "Will answer ASAP."[243]

Meadows also played a central role in the lead up to the President's January 2, 2021, call with Georgia Secretary of State Brad Raffensperger. In fact, it was Meadows who originally sent text messages to Raffensperger and requested to speak: On November 19th, he texted "Mr Secretary. Mark Meadows here. If you could give me a brief call at your convenience. Thank you".[244] And on December 5th, Meadows texted, "mr Secretary. Can you call the White House switchboard at [phone number]. For a call. Your voicemail is full."[245] Then, on December 11th, Meadows texted, "Thanks so much" to a number that apparently belongs to United States Representative

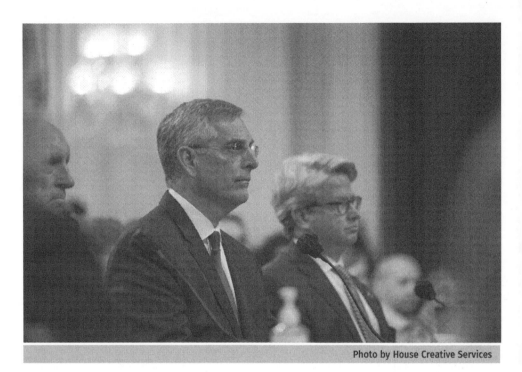

Jody Hice (R-GA) after Rep. Hice told him that he had just made a statement "regarding a recall on Raffensperger. If this is something Potus wants
to know and help push. . . ." [246]

All of that led to the remarkable January 2nd call between President
Trump and his advisors on one side, and Secretary of State Brad Raffensperger and his advisors on the other. By January 2nd, the President had
tried to speak by phone with Raffensperger at least 18 times.[247] Raffensperger, for his part, had avoided talking to the President because of ongoing
litigation with the President's Campaign.[248] Despite Raffensperger's reluctance, the two spoke, with their respective lawyers on the line. During the
call, President Trump went through his litany of false election-fraud claims
and then asked Raffensperger to deliver him a second term by "finding"
just enough votes to ensure victory. The President said, "I just want to find
11,780 votes, which is one more than we have because we won the
State." [249] He reiterated it several different ways: "fellas, I need 11,000
votes. Give me a break. You know, we have that in spades already. Or we can
keep going, but that's not fair to the voters of Georgia because they're
going to see what happened." [250]

When it was clear that Raffensperger and his advisors would not agree to the President's request, the President ramped up the pressure by accusing them of committing crimes: "the ballots are corrupt. And you are going to find that they are—which is totally illegal—it is more illegal for you than it is for them because, you know, what they did and you're not reporting it. That's a criminal, that's a criminal offense. And you can't let that happen. That's a big risk to you and to Ryan, your lawyer . . . I'm notifying you that you're letting it happen." [251]

The President would stop at nothing to win Georgia. Separate from asking Raffensperger to alter, without justification, the election results in Georgia, he also attacked election workers. In that call, President Trump mentioned Ruby Freeman's name 18 times, referred to her daughter Shaye Moss several of those times, and accused them of crimes.[252] Raffensperger and his aides rebutted President Trump's false claims of fraud on the call and explained why they were wrong, but they did not deliver the one thing President Trump wanted most: the 11,780 votes he asked for.[253]

The next day, President Trump tweeted about his phone call with Raffensperger, falsely claiming that "[Secretary Raffensperger] was unwilling, or unable, to answer questions such as the 'ballots under table' scam. . . . He has no clue!" [254] He added that Raffensperger, Governor Kemp, and Lt. Governor Duncan "are a disgrace" and "have done less than nothing" about rampant political corruption.[255]

Even though Raffensperger and his team repeatedly told the President why his specific allegations of election fraud in Georgia were wrong,[256] President Trump met the next day with the top leadership of the Justice Department in an effort to convince them to send a letter falsely claiming that the Department had "identified significant concerns" affecting the election results in Georgia and calling on Governor Kemp, Speaker Ralston, and Senate President Pro Tempore Miller to convene a special session.[257] It was only after a showdown in the Oval Office, described in Chapter 4 during which the White House Counsel and others threatened to resign that President Trump decided against replacing Department of Justice leadership and issuing that letter.

## 2.5  SOME OFFICIALS EAGERLY ASSISTED PRESIDENT TRUMP WITH HIS PLANS

While many State officials resisted President Trump's demands, some eagerly joined the President's efforts.

President Trump routinely coordinated with Pennsylvania State Senator Doug Mastriano, whose request led to the November 25, 2020, hotel "hearing" in Gettysburg, and who traveled to Washington to meet with the

President afterward.[258] Senator Mastriano, who would later charter and pay for buses to Washington for the President's "Stop the Steal" rally on January 6th and was near the Capitol during the attack, quickly rose to favor with the President.[259]

On November 30th, President Trump called Mastriano, interrupting him during a radio interview and telling listeners that "Doug is the absolute hero" and people are "really angry in Pennsylvania." [260]

On December 5th, Senator Mastriano sent an email to President Trump's executive assistant, Molly Michael, with a Supreme Court Amicus Brief for the President that the pair "discussed yesterday," related to a case brought by Representative Mike Kelly (R–PA) against his own State, which the Supreme Court rejected just a few days later.[261]

On December 14th, President Trump's executive assistant sent Mastriano an email "From POTUS" with talking points promoting a conspiracy theory about election machines.[262]

And on December 21st, Mastriano sent another email for President Trump, in which he wrote: "Dear Mr. President—attached please find the 'killer letter' on the Pennsylvania election that we discussed last night" that "I only just completed." [263] This letter recapped the Gettysburg hotel hearing on November 25th, and claimed that "there is rampant election fraud in Pennsylvania that must be investigated, remedied and rectified." [264] President Trump sent that letter to John Eastman, Acting Attorney General Jeffrey Rosen, Acting Deputy Attorney General Richard Donoghue, Rush Limbaugh, former Florida Attorney General Pam Bondi, Lou Dobbs, and others. [265]

As January 6th approached, Senator Mastriano's involvement in attempts to overturn the election only grew. On December 23rd, he led a second group of Pennsylvania State senators for a meeting with President Trump in the Oval Office, which Giuliani claimed "swayed about 20" of them. [266] Neither Speaker Cutler nor Senate President Corman participated.

Mastriano also sent emails indicating that he spoke with President Trump on December 27th, 28th, and 30th, along with files that President Trump had requested or that he had promised to him. [267] One of these was a pair of letters from State senators asking U.S. Senate Majority Leader Mitch McConnell and House Minority Leader Kevin McCarthy to reject Pennsylvania's electoral votes on January 6th. [268] President Trump's executive assistant notified the White House's Director of Legislative Affairs that "[t]he President would like the below attached letters to be sent to Mitch and Kevin and all GOP house and senate members," but was told in reply, "[g]iven the political nature of the letters, would you mind sending them?" [269]

On January 5th, President Trump spoke again with Mastriano and then notified the White House operator that Mastriano "will be calling in for the Vice President" soon. [270] That evening Senator Mastriano sent two more emails for the President. One was a letter addressed to Vice President Pence on behalf of nearly 100 legislators from various States; the other was a letter directed to McConnell and McCarthy from Pennsylvania lawmakers, this time asking Congress to postpone acting on the 6th. [271] President Trump tweeted the letter that night, captioning it "BIG NEWS IN PENNSYLVANIA!" and, after midnight, he retweeted that "Pennsylvania is going to Trump. The legislators have spoken." [272] As described elsewhere in this report, that letter, and letters like it, were used in the effort to convince Vice President Pence that he could and should affect the outcome of the joint session of Congress on January 6th.

The Select Committee subpoenaed Senator Mastriano to testify about these interactions with President Trump and his advisors, among other matters. Unlike numerous other witnesses who complied with subpoenas and provided deposition testimony to the Select Committee, Mastriano did not; he logged in to a virtual deposition at the appointed time but logged out before answering any substantive questions or even taking the oath to the tell the truth. [273]

The President apparently got what he wanted in State officials like Senator Mastriano, but not those who dared question or outright reject his anti-democratic efforts to overturn the election. In some cases, those who questioned him made the President and his advisors dig in and push harder. On January 1st, Campaign Senior Advisor Jason Miller asked for a "blast text and Twitter blast out" that would urge President Trump's supporters to "Contact House Speaker Bryan Cutler & Senate President Pro Tem Jake Corman!" to "Demand a vote on certification." [274] Senior Campaign attorneys, however, replied that this might violate Pennsylvania's "very stringent" lobbying laws and get them prosecuted or fined.[275] Instead, they agreed on a similar call to action aimed at Arizona Governor Doug Ducey and Arizona House Speaker Rusty Bowers rather than Speaker Cutler and President *Pro Tempore* Corman in Pennsylvania.[276]

## 2.6 THE FINAL OUTREACH TO STATE LEGISLATORS

The efforts to overturn the election through State legislatures continued throughout the final two weeks before the joint session of Congress on January 6th. Based on actual events and documents obtained by the Select Committee, President Trump's Campaign team, outside advisors, and motivated volunteers generally acted in accord with what was written down in a "Strategic Communications Plan" when engaging with, and sometimes demonizing, State officials. Activities that occurred thereafter were in accord with the plan.

The "Plan" was explained in a document that was presented to the White House.[277] The plan contemplated pressuring Republican legislators both in Congress and in six key swing States. The document itself purports to be the product of the "GIULIANI PRESIDENTIAL LEGAL DEFENSE TEAM" and declared that "We Have 10 Days to Execute This Plan & Certify President Trump!" [278]

Kerik told the Select Committee that pieces of the plan had been in place for some period of time before the document was actually created, and that he thought that the "catalyst" for actually memorializing the plan was the approaching deadline of January 6th.[279] In fact, the 10-day plan to help "certify president Trump" had been the subject of "continual discussions" for "6 weeks" and was "being discussed every day at some point prior to the 10 days that we're talking about. So it was a continuous thing that went on." [280]

Ultimately, the Giuliani team shared the Strategic Communications Plan and urged its implementation. Kerik sent the plan to Mark Meadows via email on December 28th with this note, in part:

There is only one thing that's going to move the needle and force the legislators to do what their [sic] constitutionally obligated to do, and that is apply pressure . . . . We can do all the investigations we want later, but if the president plans on winning, it's the legislators that have to be moved, and this will do just that. We're just running out of time.[281]

Neither Giuliani nor Kerik told the Select Committee that they recalled officially implementing the plan, and Giuliani said that he thought Meadows even rejected it, but there is no doubt that President Trump's team took certain actions consistent with it.[282]

The document described its goal as a "[n]ationwide communications outreach campaign to educate the public on the fraud numbers, and inspire citizens to call upon legislators and Members of Congress to disregard the fraudulent vote count and certify the duly-elected President Trump."[283] The "FOCUS of CAMPAIGN" was "SWING STATE REPUBLICAN SENATORS" in Arizona, Georgia, Michigan, Nevada, Pennsylvania, and Wisconsin, "REPULBICAN [sic] MEMBERS OF THE HOUSE" and "REPUBLICAN MEMBERS OF THE SENATE."[284] Among the steps that it recommended were "RALLIES AND PROTESTS" in six key swing States, including protests at "Governor's Mansions," "Lt. Governor's home[s]," "Secretary of State's homes," and "weak Members' homes."[285]

Although the plan did not mention specific individuals by name, an apparently related document produced to the Select Committee by Giuliani did, naming State legislative leaders as "TARGETS" under a header of "KEY TARGET STATE POINTS," including Arizona House Speaker Rusty Bowers, Arizona Senate President Karen Fann (incorrectly described as the State Senate's majority leader), Georgia House Speaker David Ralston, Georgia Senate Majority Leader Mike Dugan, Georgia Senate President Pro Tempore Butch Miller as a possible back up, Michigan House Speaker Lee Chatfield, Michigan Senate Majority leader Mike Shirkey, Pennsylvania House Speaker Brian Cutler, Pennsylvania House Majority Leader Kerry Benninghoff, Pennsylvania Senate President Pro Tempore Jake Corman, Pennsylvania Senate Majority Leader Kim Ward, Wisconsin State Assembly Speaker Robin Vos, and Wisconsin Senate Majority Leader Scott Fitzgerald.[286]

Consistent with these proposals, Giuliani appeared as a guest on Steve Bannon's podcast on New Year's Eve and told him that "we have a weak element to our party . . . a cowardly element"[287] and, "[n]ow I think every Republican knows—maybe this is worse—this election was stolen. Now the question is: can they live up to their oath of office? . . . We gotta start working on the leadership."[288] Giuliani also described President Trump's objective in this effort: "For the president, the way forward is really it's in the hands of the leaders of those legislatures and the Members of Congress, and what our people can do is let them know what they think, and that they're not gonna get away with pushing this aside. That the consequences of turning your back on a massive voter fraud are gonna be dire for them, and historically these people are gonna become enemies of the country." [289]

A key component of this plan was to call out Republican officials who rejected President Trump and his team's efforts or claims of fraud. Kerik and numerous other members of the Campaign's legal team did just that. On December 27th, Kerik suggested that Senator Pat Toomey (R–PA) was "corrupt" and said that "for any Pennsylvania official to certify their vote, it's malfeasance and criminal." [290] That was entirely consistent with Kerik's past tweets about the election, one of which apparently called public officials "who betrayed" President Trump "spineless disloyal maggots." [291] It wasn't just rhetoric, however, because, as described below, people showed up outside certain officials' home—sometimes menacingly—and, of course, showed up at the Capitol on January 6th.

The pressure in those final days did not stop with the types of activities outlined in the Strategic Communications Plan. January 2, 2021, was a busy day for a Saturday at the Trump White House. That was the day President Trump called on Georgia Secretary of State Raffensperger to find enough votes for victory in Georgia and participated in a call with Lindsay Graham and Members of the Freedom Caucus to plan for the joint session on January 6th. [292]

It was also the day that the President joined in a virtual briefing for nearly 300 Republican legislators from swing States. [293] The event was hosted by a short-lived organization called "Got Freedom?" that listed Jenna Ellis among its leadership team, [294] and included Giuliani, John Eastman, and Peter Navarro as the program's "featured speakers." [295] A press release by Got Freedom? said that the meeting was hosted by Phillip Kline, a former attorney general of Kansas, who was disbarred in 2013. [296] It indicated that purported proof of voter fraud "should serve as an important resource for state legislators as they make calls for state legislatures to meet to investigate the election and consider decertifying their state election results." [297]

According to the *Washington Examiner*, when President Trump joined the call he told the participants: "You know that we won the election, and you were also given false numbers to certify." It quoted him saying "[y]ou are the real power" because "[y]ou're more important than the courts. You're more important than anything because the courts keep referring to you, and you're the ones that are going to make the decision." When asked about that quote, specifically, Giuliani, who was on the call, said he didn't recall the exact words that the President used but told the Select Committee "that would be the sum or substance of what he had been saying and what he believed." [298] During the call, the President reportedly "referenced the planned protests in Washington" just days later on January 6th, and told the group "I don't think the country is going to take it." [299]

When reporting on the call, the *Washington Examiner* also provided details about what Giuliani told the assembled State legislators. Consistent with his team's "Strategic Communications Plan," Giuliani said, "[w]e need you to put excessive pressure on your leadership where the real weakness and cowardice is mostly located," and the report quoted Navarro telling them that "Your job, I believe, is to take action, action, action." [300] That evening, Navarro stated on *Fox News* that "these legislators—they are hot, they're angry, they want action," and "we explained exactly how the Democrat Party as a matter of strategy stole this election from Donald J. Trump." [301]

Organizers from Got Freedom? sent a follow-up email that evening to participants on behalf of Phill Kline, in which they described the event as "an important briefing for legislators who hold the power to decertify the results of their state elections." [302] It emphasized the following:

As elected officials in the House and Senate of your respective States, Professor Eastman laid out the Constitutional imperatives for you:
- Assert your plenary power
- Demand that your laws be followed as written
- Decertify tainted results unless and until your laws are followed
- Insist on enough time to properly meet, investigate, and properly certify results to ensure that all lawful votes (but only lawful votes) are counted. [303]

The email also recommended that they ". . . sign on to a joint letter from state legislators to Vice President Mike Pence to demand that he call for a 12-day delay on ratifying the election . . ." on January 6th. [304] The letter ultimately garnered more than 100 signatures by State legislators from Arizona, Georgia, Michigan, Pennsylvania, and Wisconsin. [305] Doug Mastriano forwarded a copy of the letter via email to President Trump's executive assistant, and the National Archives produced to the Select Committee a printed version with a stamp at the top indicating, "THE PRESIDENT HAS SEEN." [306]

But this plan would fail to sway its intended audience. As discussed in Chapter 5, the Vice President rejected this and numerous other attempts to convince him to act unlawfully on January 6th. The election had been decided and certified by the States. It was the Vice President and Congress's job to open and count the legitimate electoral college votes.

And in the early morning hours of January 7th, after a day unlike any seen in American history, when a mob of angry insurrectionists attempted to violently upend a Presidential election, the Vice President and Members of Congress, shaken but steady, delayed but resolute, regrouped and reconvened and did their Constitutional duty to certify Joseph R. Biden as the next President of the United States.

President Trump's plot to pressure State legislators to overturn the vote of the electoral college failed—but only barely. Even so, the consequences of President Trump's efforts to overturn State election results were significant.

## 2.7 THE HARM CAUSED BY DEMONIZING PUBLIC SERVANTS

Many of the people who refused to be pushed into manipulating election results—governors, secretaries of State, State legislators, State and local election officials, and frontline election workers just doing their jobs—found themselves subjected to public demonization and subsequent spamming, doxing, harassment, intimidation, and violent threats. Some of the threats were sexualized or racist in nature and targeted family members. President Trump never discouraged or condemned these tactics, and in fact he was an active participant in directing his supporters, through tweets and speeches, to apply pressure to public servants who would not comply.

President Trump and his team were not above using incendiary rhetoric or threats to achieve their goal of overturning the election. Giuliani said so before the purported hearing in Michigan in December. Recall that he told an online audience, there's "nothin' wrong with putting pressure on your state legislators"[307] and "you have got to get them to remember that their oath to the Constitution sometimes requires being criticized. Sometimes it even requires being threatened."[308]

That pressure came privately and publicly in the post-election period.

Privately, for example, President Trump called Michigan Senate Majority Leader Mike Shirkey three times after their White House meeting: November 21st, November 25th, and December 14th.[309] Shirkey did not recall many specifics of those calls and claimed he did not remember the President applying any specific pressure.[310] The day after one of those calls, however, Shirkey tweeted that "our election process MUST be free of intimidation and threats," and "it's inappropriate for anyone to exert pressure on them."[311] From this and other public statements, it is clear that Shirkey was sensitive to outside forces pressuring people with roles in the election. In fact, the same day that the electoral college met and voted former Vice President Joe Biden as the winner of the 2020 Presidential election, Shirkey received another call from President Trump and issued another public statement. Shirkey's statement that day, December 14, 2020, read: "Michigan's Democratic slate of electors should be able to proceed with their duty, free from threats of violence and intimidation" and "[i]t is our responsibility as leaders to follow the law . . . ."[312]

Publicly, President Trump used both Twitter posts and paid social media and cable television ads to advance his pressure campaign.

In Arizona, for example, President Trump used social media to both praise and criticize legislators. When Speaker Bowers and Senate President Karen Fann requested an audit of Maricopa County's election software and equipment, President Trump publicly commended them, retweeting a press release about their announcement and commenting: "Thank you to Senate President Karen Fann and House Speaker Russell Bowers—and all, for what you are doing in Arizona. A fast check of signatures will easily give us the state."[313] But just days later, President Trump assailed Bowers for opposing a special session to appoint new electors. He retweeted a post by Campaign lawyer Christina Bobb that accused Bowers of "intentionally misleading the people of Arizona" and that included a demand by Stop-the-Steal organizer Ali Alexander for 50,000 phone calls to Rusty Bowers "[r]ight the heck now" to threaten him with a primary challenge.[314]

And, as his efforts to change the outcome of the election continued to meet resistance, President Trump personally approved a series of advertisements that the Campaign ran on cable television and social media in several important States. One advertisement in Arizona called for pressure on Governor Ducey in particular, alleging, "The evidence is overwhelming. Call Governor Ducey and your legislators. Demand they inspect the machines and hear the evidence."[315] Another claimed that "illegal aliens voted, and here in Arizona Trump votes were discarded. It's an outrage. Call Governor Ducey and your legislators at 602–542–4331. Demand they inspect the machines and hear the evidence. Call Governor Ducey, at 602–542–4331. Stand up for President Trump. Call today. Paid for by Donald J. Trump for President, Inc."[316]

Several days earlier, Trump Campaign Senior Advisor Jason Miller had explained the intention for this round of advertisements in an email. He wrote that, "the President and Mayor Giuliani want to get back up on TV ASAP, and Jared [Kushner] has approved in budgetary concept, so here's the gameplan" in order to "motivate the GOP base to put pressure on the Republican Governors of Georgia and Arizona and the Republican-controlled State legislatures in Wisconsin and Michigan to hear evidence of voter fraud before January 6th." [317] Miller anticipated a budget of $5 million and asked for the messaging to follow an earlier round of advertisements, "but the endings need to be changed to include phone numbers and directions to call the local Governor or state legislature." [318] On December 22nd, Jason Miller texted Jared Kushner that "POTUS has approved the buy." [319]

References to anger and fighting were featured in some of the President's remarks during that period. After the Georgia Secretary of State's Chief Operating Officer, Gabriel Sterling, made an impassioned public plea and accurately warned that someone would die as a result of the threatening election-related rhetoric that President Trump failed to condemn, President Trump dismissively tweeted in response: "Rigged Election. Show signatures and envelopes. Expose the massive voter fraud in Georgia. What is Secretary of State and @BrianKempGA afraid of. They know what we'll find!!!" [320] The President also tweeted that, between Governor Ducey in Arizona and Governor Kemp in Georgia, "the Democrat Party could not be happier" because these Republicans "fight harder against us than do the Radical Left" and were singlehandedly responsible for losing him both States, something that "Republicans will NEVER forget[.]" [321] Regarding Kemp, he asked "What's wrong with this guy? What is he hiding?" [322] and he alleged that "RINOs" Governor Kemp, Lieutenant Governor Geoff Duncan, and Secretary Raffensperger "will be solely responsible" for Senators Loeffler and Perdue losing their senate runoff because they "[w]on't call a Special Session or check for Signature Verification! People are ANGRY!" [323]

President Trump's spoken remarks were not much different. After the President wrapped up a November 26th public phone call to wish U.S. service members a happy Thanksgiving, he answered a reporter's question about election integrity in Georgia by lashing out at Secretary Raffensperger in particular. President Trump made several baseless claims of election fraud in Georgia, declared that Raffensperger himself appeared to be complicit, and labeled the Georgia Secretary of State "an enemy of the people." [324]

President Trump and his team's practice of naming and viciously criticizing people had real consequences. Philadelphia City Commissioner Al Schmidt's story, recounted earlier, is just one of many examples. And the consequences weren't just limited to high-profile public figures. Schmidt's deputy, for example, Seth Bluestein faced threats after being demonized by a surrogate for President Trump, and many of the threats he received were anti-Semitic in nature. He received a Facebook message telling him that "EVERYONE WITH A GUN IS GOING TO BE AT YOUR HOUSE- AMERICANS LOOK AT THE NAME- ANOTHER JEW CAUGHT UP IN UNITED STATES

VOTER FRAUD." [325] Bluestein got a security detail at his home, and the experience gave his three-year-old daughter nightmares. [326]

Similarly, after President Trump promoted online accusations that Arizona House Speaker Rusty Bowers had been "intentionally misleading the people of Arizona . . ." [327] Bowers's personal cell phone and home address were published, [328] leading demonstrators to congregate at his home, honk horns and shout insults until police arrived. [329] Bowers told the Select Committee this was the first of at least nine protests at his home, sometimes with protesters shouting into bullhorns and calling him a pedophile. [330] One protestor who showed up at his home was armed and believed to be a member of an extremist militia. [331]

Sadly, those were not isolated incidents. Stories similar to Schmidt's and Bowers' proliferated after President Trump's loss in the election. Examples from each of the States discussed in this chapter are documented below, but this list is by no means exhaustive:

- *Arizona*: After Secretary of State Katie Hobbs's home address and son's phone number were publicly released, demonstrators congregated outside her home chanting "we are watching you." [332] A social media user at the time recommended: "Let's burn her house down and kill her family and teach these fraudsters a lesson." [333] Secretary Hobbs has continued to receive threats since then, reporting over 100 threats to the FBI in mid-2022, including a September 2021 voicemail message that "you should be hunted" and "will never be safe in Arizona again." [334]

- *Arizona*: Maricopa County Recorder Adrian Fontes testified before Congress that his family had "go-bags" packed in case they needed to evacuate and that, because of the threats, he had moved his children "out of the family home at least once for three days in the wake of serious threats to [his] family's safety." [335]

- *Arizona*: Paul Boyer, a Republican State senator, had to evacuate his family, get police protection, and change his phone number after he voted against jailing Maricopa's County Supervisors over election disputes. [336]

- *Arizona*: On January 5, 2021, a comment on a blog suggested some members of the Maricopa County Board of Supervisors "have earned a good old fashioned neck tie party" as "punishment for Treason." [337] According to Board member Clint Hickman, "the threats never abated." [338] And on January 6th, police convinced Hickman and his family to leave their home. [339]

- *Michigan*: Secretary of State Jocelyn Benson and her family were driven out of their home for several days after dozens of protestors with bullhorns and firearms congregated outside "shouting obscenities and graphic threats into bullhorns"[340] while she spent time with her son and got him ready for bed.[341] Secretary Benson said that she only feels safe "sometimes" as a result of continuing threats.[342]

- *Michigan:* Several members of the Wayne County Board of Canvassers received threats, as did Aaron Van Langevelde, a Republican member of the State Board of Canvassers.[343] Van Langevelde was bombarded with communications and people began showing up at his family's home, forcing police to ensure his and his family's safety and escort him across the State after he voted to certify Michigan's election.[344]

- *Michigan:* Detroit City Clerk Janice Winfrey, a Democrat, and Rochester Hills City Clerk Tina Barton, a Republican, were both targeted. Barton had never before received a death threat in over a decade of work as an election official but, as a result of the 2020 Presidential election, was subject to "a torrent of threats and harassment," such as an anonymous caller who "repeatedly threatened to kill her and her family."[345] Winfrey was confronted outside her home by a man who indicated he had been surveilling her and that "You are going to pay dearly for your actions in this election!"[346] She started carrying a firearm because death threats against her continued.[347]

- *Michigan:* Michigan House Speaker Lee Chatfield confirmed that "I and my family have received numerous threats, along with members on both sides of the aisle."[348] This included the top Democrat on Michigan's House Oversight Committee, Rep. Cynthia Johnson, who was threatened with lynching after she challenged the witnesses that Giuliani offered to her committee.[349] One caller who allegedly threatened to kill Rep. Johnson and wipe out her family in December 2020 called the Capitol again on the morning of January 7, 2021, and said that "everyone better get out of the building because it'll fucking explode."[350]

- *Pennsylvania:* Secretary of the Commonwealth Kathy Boockvar said she received so many threats "I didn't feel comfortable walking the dog on the street."[351] This included a message in November 2020 threatening to murder her in her home at night, forcing her and her husband to flee for a week.[352] Another voicemail she received after certifying Pennsylvania's election results threatened: "You crooked f***ing bitch. You're done."[353]

- *Pennsylvania:* House Speaker Bryan Cutler told the Select Committee there were at least three protests outside either his district office or his home, and that his then-15-year-old son was home by himself for the first one.[354] Senate Jake Corman's spokesperson revealed in December 2020 that he, too, was being subjected to violent threats,[355] something

Senate Majority Leader Kim Ward also received.[356]

- *Pennsylvania*: Philadelphia City Commissioner Omar Sabir, spent several nights evacuated from his home and continued to receive death threats a year after the 2020 election, reflecting that, "I feel anxiety every time I walk outside of the house." [357] Commissioner Lisa Deeley, another City Commission colleague, also received death threats and said she suffers occasional anxiety attacks as a result.[358]
- *Georgia*: After Georgia Secretary of State Brad Raffensperger's email and phone number were published, he said that he and his wife received frequent hostile messages, some of which "typically came in sexualized attacks." [359] As a result, the Secretary's wife cancelled visits from their grandchildren out of fear for the kids' safety.[360] That was not an overreaction as that came after police found self-identified members of the Oath Keepers outside their home and after someone broke into their daughter-in-law's house.[361]
- *Georgia*: On January 5, 2021, Governor Kemp and Secretary Raffensperger were reportedly named in a Craigslist post encouraging people to "put an end to the lives of these traitors." [362]
- *Georgia*: Fulton County Elections Director Richard Barron was named and depicted on screen in the video President Trump played at his December 5th rally. He said that this incident led to a spike in death threats targeted at election workers, including himself.[363] His team's registration chief, Ralph Jones, received death threats following the election including one calling him a "n[igger] who should be shot," and another threatening "to kill him by dragging his body around with a truck." [364]
- *Georgia*: Election offices in ten Georgia counties received emailed threats of bombings that would "make the Boston bombings look like child's play" and that the "death and destruction" would continue "[u]ntil Trump is guaranteed to be POTUS . . . ." [365]

One of the most striking examples of the terror that President Trump and his allies caused came in Georgia, where election workers Ruby Freeman and Shaye Moss, mother and daughter, were besieged by incessant, terrifying harassment and threats that often evoked racial violence and lynching, instigated and incited by the President of the United States.

As described earlier, in a State legislative hearing in Georgia, Giuliani publicly—and baselessly—accused Freeman and Moss of engaging in criminal conduct. He showed a video of Freeman passing Moss a ginger mint before claiming that the two women, both Black, were smuggling USB drives "as if they're vials of heroin or cocaine." [366]

Photo by Kevin Dietsch/Getty Images

President Trump seemed fixated on Freeman and Moss, too. He played surveillance video showing them inside the State Farm Arena at a December 5th rally in Georgia,[367] and mentioned Freeman by name 18 times during the January 2nd call to Secretary of State Raffensperger in which he asked the Secretary to simply "find" enough votes to ensure victory.[368]

Freeman's and Moss's lives were forever changed. After their contact information was published, they were besieged by the President's supporters. In early December 2020, Freeman "told police she had received hundreds of threats at her home."[369] Moss's son also started receiving threatening phone calls, including one stating he "should hang alongside [his] nigger momma."[370]

In the wake of President Trump's December 5, 2020, rally, Freeman called 911 because strangers had come to her home trying to lure her out, sending threatening emails and text messages.[371] She pleaded with the 911 dispatcher for help after hearing loud banging on her door just before 10 p.m. "Lord Jesus, where's the police?" she asked the dispatcher. "I don't know who keeps coming to my door." "Please help me!"[372]

Ultimately, Freeman fled from her own home based on advice from the FBI.[373] She would not move back for months.[374]

In her testimony to the Select Committee, Freeman recounted how she had received "hundreds of racist, threatening, horrible calls and messages" and that now "[t]here is nowhere I feel safe—nowhere." [375] But it's not just a sense of security that the President and his followers took from Freeman. She told the Select Committee that she also lost her name and reputation:

My name is Ruby Freeman. I've always believed it when God says that he'll make your name great, but this is not the way it was supposed to be. I could have never imagined the events that followed the Presidential election in 2020. For my entire professional life, I was Lady Ruby. My community in Georgia where I was born and lived my whole life knew me as Lady Ruby. . . . Now I won't even introduce myself by my name anymore. I get nervous when I bump into someone I know in the grocery store who says my name. I'm worried about who's listening. I get nervous when I have to give my name for food orders. I'm always concerned of who's around me. I've lost my name, and I've lost my reputation.

I've lost my sense of security—all because a group of people, starting with Number 45 and his ally Rudy Giuliani, decided to scapegoat me and my daughter Shaye to push their own lies about how the presidential election was stolen. [376]

Freeman's sense of dread is well-founded. According to Federal prosecutors, a member of the Oath Keepers militia convicted of multiple offenses for his role in the January 6th insurrection had a document in his residence with the words "DEATH LIST" written across the top. [377]

His death list contained just two names: Ruby Freeman and Shaye Moss. [378]

Georgia Electors cast their Electoral College votes at the Georgia State Capitol on December 14, 2020.

Photo by Jessica McGowan/Getty Images

# 3

# FAKE ELECTORS AND THE "THE PRESIDENT OF THE SENATE STRATEGY"

On the morning of January 6th, in his speech at the Ellipse, President Trump exhorted his thousands of assembled supporters to march to the U.S. Capitol, explaining that "[w]e have come to demand that Congress do the right thing and only count the electors who have been lawfully slated, lawfully slated."[1] This was no off-the-cuff remark; it was the culmination of a carefully planned scheme many weeks in the making. This plea by the President turned the truth on its head. There was only one legitimate slate of electors from the battleground States of Arizona, Georgia, Michigan, Nevada, New Mexico, Pennsylvania, and Wisconsin, and Trump wanted them rejected. This scheme involved lawyers, such as Kenneth Chesebro and Rudy Giuliani, as well as Mark Meadows. It also was aided at key points by Chairwoman of the Republican National Committee Ronna McDaniel, Members of Congress, and Republican leaders across seven States—some of whom did not know exactly what they were being asked to do. President Trump oversaw it himself.

President Trump and his allies prepared their own fake slates of electoral college electors in seven States that President Trump lost: Arizona, Georgia, Michigan, Nevada, New Mexico, Pennsylvania, and Wisconsin. And on December 14, 2020—the date when true, certified electors were meeting to cast their electoral votes for the candidate who had won the popular vote in each of those States—these fake electors also met, ostensibly casting electoral votes for President Trump, the candidate who had lost.

There was no legitimate reason for Trump electors to meet, vote, and produce fake slates on December 14th in States that former Vice President Biden won. Instead, this effort was aimed directly at the President of the Senate (which, under the Constitution, is the Vice President) in his role at the joint session of Congress on January 6th. President Trump and his advisors wanted Vice President Pence to disregard real electoral college votes for former Vice President Biden, in favor of these fake competing electoral slates.

But there never were real, competing slates of electors. By the time the fake Trump electors met on December 14th, appropriate government officials in each of the seven States had already certified their State's official election results for former Vice President Biden. No court had issued an order reversing or calling into question those results, and most election-related litigation was over. And as detailed in Chapter 2, despite the illicit efforts of President Trump and his allies, no State legislature had agreed to the President's request to reverse the result of the election by appointing a different slate of electors.

Given all of this, these groups of Trump backers who called themselves Presidential electors were never actually electors, and the votes they purported to cast on December 14th were not valid. They were fake. They had no legal standing, and their fake votes could not have been used by Vice President Pence to disregard the real votes of electors chosen by the voters.

By January 6th, President Trump had been discouraged by his top lawyers from following through on this plan. The Trump Campaign's senior staff attorneys had concerns,[2] and several days before the joint session, the Acting Attorney General and the Deputy Attorney General blocked the sending of a letter indicating that there were "competing slates" of electors, including "in Georgia and several other States."[3] But this reasoning did nothing to change President Trump's rhetoric or plan. He continued to assert that there were "competing" or "dual" slates of electors to create an opportunity to stay in office on January 6th.[4]

These lawyers were right: President Trump's plan was illegal. In his June 7, 2022, opinion, Federal District Judge David Carter wrote that this initiative to "certify alternate slates of electors for President Trump" constituted a "critical objective of the January 6 plan."[5] This followed Judge Carter's earlier determination in March that "[t]he illegality of the plan was obvious," and "[e]very American—and certainly the President of the United States—knows that in a democracy, leaders are elected, not installed. With a plan this 'BOLD,' President Trump knowingly tried to subvert this fundamental principle. Based on the evidence the Court finds it more likely than not that President Trump corruptly attempted to obstruct the Joint Session of Congress on January 6, 2021."[6]

The fake elector effort was an unlawful, unprecedented and destructive break from the electoral college process that our country has used to select its President for generations.[7] It led directly to the violence that occurred on January 6th. To address the damage that it caused, it is important to understand how it transpired.

### 3.1 LAYING THE GROUNDWORK FOR THE FAKE ELECTOR PLAN: THE CHESEBRO MEMOS

The fake elector plan emerged from a series of legal memoranda written by an outside legal advisor to the Trump Campaign: Kenneth Chesebro. Although John Eastman would have a more prominent role in advising President Trump in the days immediately before January 6th, Chesebro—an attorney based in Boston and New York recruited to assist the Trump Campaign as a volunteer legal advisor—was central to the creation of the plan.[8] Memos by Chesebro on November 18th, December 9th, and December 13th, as discussed below, laid the plan's foundation.

Chesebro's first memo on November 18th suggested that the Trump Campaign could gain a few extra weeks for litigation to challenge Wisconsin's election results, so long as a Wisconsin slate of Republican nominees to the electoral college met on December 14th to cast placeholder electoral college votes on a contingent basis.[9] This memo acknowledged that "[i]t may seem odd that the electors pledged to Trump and Pence might meet and cast their votes on December 14 even if, at that juncture, the Trump-Pence ticket is behind in the vote count, and no certificate of election has been issued in favor of Trump and Pence."[10] However, Chesebro argued that if such a slate of alternate electors gathered to cast electoral votes on a contingent basis, this would preserve the Trump Campaign's options so "a court decision (or, perhaps, a state legislative determination) rendered after December 14 in favor of the Trump-Pence slate of electors should be timely."[11]

On December 9th, Chesebro penned a second memo, which suggested another purpose for fake electoral college votes on January 6th. It stated that unauthorized Trump electors in these States could be retroactively recognized "by a court, the state legislature, *or Congress.*"[12] Under this theory, there would be no need for a court to decide that the election had been decided in error; instead, Congress itself could choose among dueling slates of purported electoral votes—and thereby decide the Presidential election—even though Article II of the Constitution grants that power to the electoral college via the States.[13]

Chesebro's contemporaneous communications make clear that the goal was having Congress act on the fake electoral votes. He emailed an organizer of the fake electors in Nevada that "the purpose of having the electoral votes sent in to Congress is to provide the opportunity to debate the election irregularities in Congress, and to keep alive the possibility that the votes could be flipped to Trump..."[14] And a legal advisor to the Arizona GOP reportedly described being told by Chesebro around this time that their supposed electors "would just be sending in 'fake' electoral votes to Pence so that 'someone' in Congress can make an objection when they start counting votes, and start arguing that the 'fake' votes should be counted."[15]

Many of the States contested by the Trump team had laws that specified requirements for electors to validly cast and transmit their votes—and the December 9, 2020, memo recognized that some of these criteria would be difficult, if not impossible, for the fake electors to fulfill. (As described later, most were not fulfilled.) For example, Nevada State law required that the secretary of state preside when Presidential electors meet,[16] and Nevada Secretary of State Barbara Cegavske, a Republican, had already signed a certificate ascertaining the Biden/Harris electors as the authorized, winning slate.[17] Several States also had rules requiring electors to cast their votes in the State capitol building, or rules governing the process for approving substitutes if any original proposed electors from the November ballot were unavailable. As a result, Chesebro's December 9, 2020, memo advised the Trump Campaign to abide by such rules, when possible, but also recognized that these slates could be "slightly problematic in Michigan," "somewhat dicey in Georgia and Pennsylvania," and "very problematic in Nevada."[18]

On December 13th, the fake elector scheme became even clearer in an email sent by Chesebro to Giuliani. His message was entitled "Brief notes on 'President of the Senate' strategy." It addressed how the fake electors meeting the next day, December 14th, could be exploited during the joint session of Congress on January 6th by the President of the Senate—a role that the Constitution grants to the Vice President of the United States.[19] Chesebro argued that, on January 6th, the President of the Senate could:

> ...firmly take the position that he, and he alone, is charged with the constitutional responsibility not just to open the votes, but to count them—including making judgments about what to do if there are conflicting votes...[20]

Chesebro's email suggested that the President of the Senate (which under the Constitution, is the Vice President) could toss out former Vice President Biden's actual electoral votes for any State where the Trump Campaign organized fake electors, simply "because there are two slates of votes."[21] Of course, there were never two slates of electoral votes, so this premise itself was fundamentally wrong. But he was arguing that even if votes by fake electors were never retroactively ratified under State law, their mere submission to Congress would be enough to allow the presiding officer to disregard valid votes for former Vice President Biden.[22] Chesebro suggested this might result in a second term for President Trump, or, at minimum, it would force a debate about purported election fraud—neither of which was a lawful, legitimate reason to organize and convene fake electors.[23]

As discussed below and in Chapter 5, John Eastman worked with Chesebro as January 6th approached and wrote two additional memos that built upon, and extended, the plan to use the fake electoral votes during the joint session.[24]

### 3.2  PRESIDENT TRUMP AND THE CAMPAIGN ADOPT THE FAKE ELECTOR SCHEME

In early December, the highest levels of the Trump Campaign took note of Chesebro's fake elector plan and began to operationalize it. On December 6th, White House Chief of Staff Mark Meadows forwarded a copy of Chesebro's November 18, 2020, memo to Trump Campaign Senior Advisor Jason Miller writing, "Let's have a discussion about this tomorrow."[25] Miller replied that he just engaged with reporters on the subject, to which Meadows wrote: "If you are on it then never mind the meeting. *We just need to have someone coordinating the electors for states.*"[26] Miller clarified that he had only been "working the PR angle" and they should still meet, to which Meadows answered: "Got it."[27] Later that week, Miller sent Meadows a spreadsheet that the Trump Campaign had compiled.[28] It listed contact information for nearly all of the 79 GOP nominees to the electoral college on the November ballot for Arizona, Georgia, Michigan, Nevada, Pennsylvania, and Wisconsin.[29] And on December 8th, Meadows received a text message from a former State legislator in Louisiana recommending that the proposed "Trump electors from AR [sic] MI GA PA WI NV all meet next Monday at their state capitols[,] [c]all themselves to order, elect officers, and cast their votes for the President.... Then they certify their votes and transmit that certificate to Washington."[30] Meadows replied: "We are."[31]

Cassidy Hutchinson, a Special Assistant to the President and an assistant to Chief of Staff Mark Meadows, confirmed Meadows's significant involvement in the plan. Hutchinson told the Select Committee that Meadows followed the progress of the fake elector effort closely and that she "remember[ed] him frequently having calls, meetings, and outreach with individuals and this just being a prominent topic of discussion in our office." When asked how many of his calls or meetings it came up in, she estimated "[d]ozens." [32]

The evidence indicates that by December 7th or 8th, President Trump had decided to pursue the fake elector plan and was driving it. Trump Campaign Associate General Counsel Joshua Findlay was tasked by the campaign's general counsel, Matthew Morgan, around December 7th or 8th with exploring the feasibility of assembling unrecognized slates of Trump electors in a handful of the States that President Trump had lost.[33] Findlay told the Select Committee "it was my understanding that the President made this decision...." [34] As recounted by Findlay, Morgan conveyed that the client—President Trump—directed the campaign lawyers to "look into electors in these potential litigation States[.]" [35]

President Trump personally called RNC Chairwoman Ronna Romney McDaniel days before December 14th to enlist the RNC's assistance in the scheme.[36] President Trump opened the call by introducing McDaniel to John Eastman, who described "the importance of the RNC helping the campaign to gather these contingent electors in case any of the legal challenges that were ongoing changed the results in any of the States." [37] According to McDaniel, she called President Trump back soon after the call ended, letting him know that she agreed to his request and that some RNC staffers were already assisting.[38]

On December 13th and 14th, President Trump worked with Rudolph Giuliani on the plan's implementation. On the 13th, Miller texted some of his colleagues to check in about the fake elector meetings scheduled for the following day. He let them know that Giuliani had told him "POTUS was aware" that they would be filing litigation in four States just "to keep the effort going"—which the Select Committee believes was to create a pretext to claim that it was still possible for the fake electors to be authorized retroactively.[39] (In subsequent litigation, a Federal district court found that President Trump "filed certain lawsuits not to obtain legal relief, but to disrupt or delay the January 6th congressional proceedings through the courts." [40]) The next day, Miller sent an email asking whether they were going to issue a press release about electors, and he was told the "Mayor [is] going to discuss with POTUS." [41]

### 3.3 THE CAMPAIGN LEGAL TEAM BOWS OUT, AND GIULIANI STEPS IN

Not everyone on the campaign was eager to pursue the fake elector plan. On December 11th, the U.S. Supreme Court rejected a high-profile lawsuit filed by the State of Texas challenging the election results in Pennsylvania,

Ronna McDaniel at the Republican National Convention on August 24, 2020.
(Photo by Chip Somodevilla/Getty Images)

Georgia, Michigan, and Wisconsin.[42] After that decision, the Trump Campaign's senior legal staffers said that they reduced their involvement in the fake elector effort, apparently because there was no longer a feasible scenario in which a court would determine that President Trump actually won

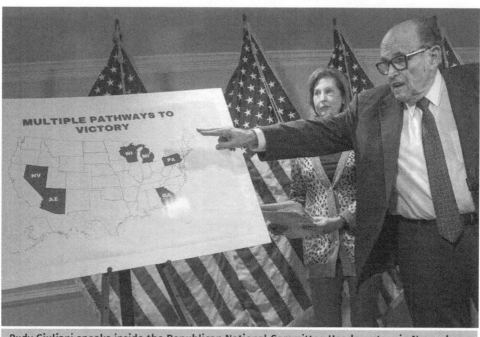

Rudy Giuliani speaks inside the Republican National Committee Headquarters in November about various lawsuits related to the 2020 election.

(Photo by Drew Angerer/Getty Images)

any of the States he contested.[43] Justin Clark, who oversaw the Trump Campaign's general counsel's office, said that he basically conveyed, "I'm out," and encouraged his colleagues on the legal team to do the same.[44] Findlay told the Select Committee that "we backed out of this thing," and Morgan, his boss, said he had Findlay pass off responsibility for the electors as "my way of taking that responsibility to zero."[45]

Clark told the Select Committee that "it never sat right with me that there was no...contingency whereby these votes would count."[46] "I had real problems with the process," Clark said, because "it morphed into something I didn't agree with."[47] In his view, the fake electors were "not necessarily duly nominated electors" despite being presented as such.[48] He said he believed he warned his colleagues that "unless we have litigation pending like in these States, like I don't think this is appropriate or, you know, this isn't the right thing to do."[49]

Morgan told the Select Committee that he saw no value in pushing slates of purported electors if they were not authorized by a State government's certificate of ascertainment. As he put it, "[M]y view was, as long as you didn't have a certificate of ascertainment, then the electors were, for lack of a better way of saying it, no good or not—not valid."[50] Findlay confirmed that Morgan told him after the Supreme Court ruling on December 11th that "there's not really anything left for us to do on this project" and that "it doesn't seem like a good idea for us to be involved in it."[51]

Campaign lawyers were not the only ones who doubted the legality of the fake elector plan. The Office of White House Counsel appears to have expressed concerns about it as well. In his testimony to the Select Committee, White House Counsel Pat Cipollone acknowledged his view that by mid-December, the electoral process was "done." Cipollone told the Select Committee that the White House Counsel's office "probably" had discussions about the electors plan and that his Deputy, Pat Philbin, would have been involved in evaluating the electors issue.[52] In an informal Committee interview, Philbin described the fake elector scheme as one of the "bad theories" that were like "Whac-A-Mole" in the White House during this period.[53] Mr. Cipollone agreed with this characterization.[54]

In her testimony, Cassidy Hutchinson testified that she heard at least one member of the White House Counsel's Office say that the plan was not legal:

> Committee Staff: … to be clear, did you hear the White House Counsel's Office say that this plan to have alternate electors meet and cast votes for Donald Trump in States that he had lost was not legally sound?
>
> Hutchinson: Yes, sir.[55]

She also recalled a meeting that took place in or before mid-December during which this view was relayed to Giuliani and members of his team by lawyers in the White House Counsel's Office.[56]

By December 11th, Findlay emailed his main points of contact in six battleground States to say "[t]hank you for your work on the presidential elector project" and, in order to pass off his responsibilities, let them know that "Rudy's team has designated Kenneth Chesebro as the point person for the legal documents" going forward.[57]

While the campaign's core legal team stepped back from the fake elector effort on December 11th, it nonetheless went forward because "Rudy was in charge of [it]" and "[t]his is what he wanted to do," according to Findlay.[58] When Findlay was asked if this decision to let the effort proceed under Giuliani's direction "was coming from your client, the President," Findlay responded: "Yes, I believe so. I mean, he had made it clear that Rudy was in charge of this and that Rudy was executing what he wanted."[59] Findlay also recalled being told that Chesebro's elector memos had become "the justification for why Rudy and Ken were going to keep going forward with this stuff." [60] He explained that Giuliani "really bought into Ken's theory on this," and that the two of them "were kind of the main ones driving this" from that point forward.[61] Clark told the Select Committee that "...my understanding of who was driving the process...was Mayor Giuliani and his team." [62] On December 10th, when Kenneth Chesebro emailed one of the State party officials involved in organizing the fake elector effort in Nevada, he reported that "I spoke this evening with Mayor Guiliani [sic], who is focused on doing everything possible to ensure that that [sic] all the Trump-Pence electors vote on Dec. 14." [63]

In the days that followed this handoff, Chesebro would draft and distribute documents intended for use in the Trump team's fake elector ceremonies that were then shared with key contacts in Arizona,[64] Georgia,[65] Michigan,[66] Nevada,[67] New Mexico,[68] Pennsylvania,[69] and Wisconsin.[70] He also gave some of the groups step-by-step logistical guidance, such as when and where they should convene, how many copies each person would need to sign, and to send their fake votes to Congress via registered mail.[71] "Pretty Simple!" he commented in some of these emails.[72]

A campaign operative named Michael Roman was also tapped for a major operational role in the fake elector effort. When Findlay sent his email handing off certain responsibilities for the initiative, he also wrote that Giuliani's team had designated Roman "as the lead for executing the voting on Monday" December 14th.[73] Roman was the Trump Campaign's Director of Election Day Operations (EDO), with team members who specialized in political outreach and mobilization in battleground States where the Trump team now urgently needed the fake electors to meet on December 14th.

With help from his EDO staff, as well as Giuliani's team and RNC staffers working alongside the Campaign as part of the Trump Victory Committee, Roman ran an improvised "Electors Whip Operation." [74] For example, Roman sent an email on December 12th directing an aide to create "a tracker for the electors" with tabs for Arizona, Georgia, Michigan, Nevada, Pennsylvania, and Wisconsin, listing contact information, whether they had been contacted, whether they agreed to attend on December 14th, and names of "[s]ubstitute electors" to replace any reticent or unavailable participants as needed.[75] Roman referred to others on this email as the "WHIP TEAM" and directed them to fill out the spreadsheet, to update him on "what you have and what you need," and to plan on a call that evening.[76]

In the days that followed, this group focused on tracking which Republicans previously named as President Trump's nominees to the electoral college would be willing to show up for fake elector ceremonies, finding adequate substitutes for those who refused to attend, and actually coordinating the unrecognized elector signing ceremonies in seven States on December 14th.[77] In all seven States, these efforts to mobilize fake electors benefitted from support from the RNC, as well as the State Republican parties.[78] However, it was the Trump team who drove the process from start to finish, as one of the fake electors and later co-chair of the Michigan Republican party, Meshawn Maddock, told an audience in January 2022: "We fought to seat the electors. The Trump campaign asked us to do that."[79]

### 3.4 SOME OF THE PROPOSED FAKE ELECTORS EXPRESS CONCERNS ABOUT THE PLAN

The Trump team's fake elector plan raised concerns not just for several senior officials but also for some of the Republican activists being recruited to be the fake electors. Findlay told the Select Committee that "there were definitely electors in probably most of the States that had concerns about this process."[80] After being tasked with reaching out to the potential fake electors, Findlay notified his colleagues on December 10th that "a lot of questions are arising" from them.[81] He also noted that an RNC staffer seconded to the Trump Victory Committee "requested a call with the PA electors and/or leadership to address concerns," which "may be necessary to get people to appear."[82]

The Republican Party of Pennsylvania's general counsel relayed several specific concerns to the Trump Campaign via email on December 13th. Warning that "[w]e're all getting call [sic] from concerned Electors," he elaborated as follows:

> I'm told that on the call with the Electors they were told that the Ballot form would be conditioned upon ultimate certification by the Governor, indemnification by the campaign if someone gets sued or worse, (charged with something by the AG or someone else), and the receipt by the Electors of a legal opinion by a national firm and certified to be accurate by a Pa. lawyer.

> What was sent was a "memo" by Chesebro not addressed to the Electors, and no certification by a Pa. lawyer. To make it worse, Chesebro describes the Pa. plan as "dicey". And there's no indication by anyone with authority that there's any indemnification authorized by the campaign.[83]

Pennsylvania GOP Chairman Lawrence Tabas informed the Select Committee that his State's fake electors never were indemnified by the Trump Campaign.[84]

When Wisconsin Republican Party Chairman Andrew Hitt was notified in late November that "the campaign wants to [sic] list of electors," he texted his executive director that "I am def concerned about their inquiry" and that "I hope they are not planning on asking us to do anything like try and say we are only the proper electors." [85] On December 12th, after Hitt received a message about a phone call with Giuliani to discuss the fake elector issue, he texted a colleague: "These guys are up to no good and its [sic] gonna fail miserably." [86] Despite such concerns, Hitt and many other fake electors participated anyway.[87]

Even so, 14 of the original Republicans who had been listed as electoral college nominees on the November ballot bowed out when the fake Trump electors gathered in December.[88] Former Michigan Secretary of State Terri Lynn Land declined to attend, which the State's GOP chair, Laura Cox, told the Select Committee was because "I think she just said she was uncomfortable with the whole thing" and that she "has her own beliefs." [89] A senior advisor for the Pennsylvania GOP said that Chairman Tabas "did not serve as an elector because Joe Biden won the election and it was Biden's electors that were certified." [90] Former U.S. Representative Tom Marino (R-PA) said he backed out because "I'm a constitutionalist," and "as a former prosecutor, when the attorney general says that he's not finding anything there, that's good enough for me." [91] The other eleven dropouts included a Georgia State lawmaker, a former State party chair from New Mexico, two former State party chairs from Pennsylvania, and Pennsylvania's RNC national committeewoman.[92]

Other participants asserted that they would have had much greater concerns if the Trump team had been more forthcoming about how the fake electoral votes would be used.[93] The Trump Campaign's director of election day operations in Georgia told the Select Committee that "I absolutely would not have" wanted to participate in organizing the Trump team's fake electors in Georgia "had I known that the three main lawyers for the campaign that I'd spoken to in the past and were leading up were not on board." [94] He said he felt "angry" because "no one really cared if—if people were potentially putting themselves in jeopardy" by doing this, and "we were just...useful idiots or rubes at that point." [95]

### 3.5 ON DECEMBER 14TH, THE FAKE ELECTORS MEET AND VOTE

On December 14th, using instructions provided by Chesebro, the fake Trump electors gathered and participated in signing ceremonies in all seven States. In five of these States—Arizona, Georgia, Michigan, Nevada, and Wisconsin—the certificates they signed used the language that falsely

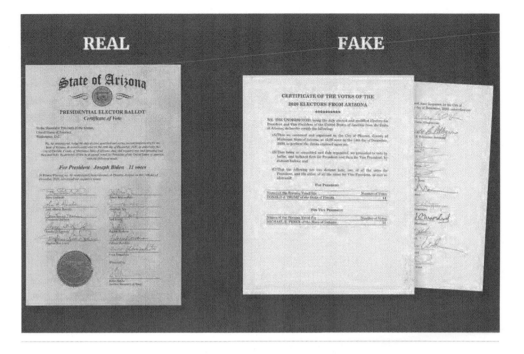

REAL

FAKE

declared themselves to be "the duly elected and qualified Electors" from their State.[96] This declaration was false because none of the signatories had been granted that official status by their State government in the form of a certificate of ascertainment.

The paperwork signed by the fake Trump electors in two other States contained partial caveats. In New Mexico, the document they signed made clear that they were participating "on the understanding that it might later be determined that we are the duly elected and qualified Electors...."[97] In Pennsylvania, the document they signed indicated that they were participating "on the understanding that if, as a result of a final non-appealable Court Order or other proceeding prescribed by law, we are ultimately recognized as being the duly elected and qualified Electors...."[98]

All seven of these invalid sets of electoral votes were then transmitted to Washington, DC. Roman's team member in Georgia, for example, sent him an email on the afternoon of December 14th that affirmed the following: "All votes cast, paperwork complete, being mailed now. Ran pretty smoothly."[99] Likewise, Findlay updated Campaign Manager Bill Stepien and his bosses on the legal team that the Trump team's slate in Georgia was not able to satisfy all provisions of State law but still "voted as legally as possible under the circumstances" before transmitting their fake votes to Washington, DC, by mail.[100]

On the evening of December 14th, RNC Chairwoman McDaniel provided an update for President Trump on the status of the fake elector effort. She forwarded President Trump's executive assistant an "Elector Recap" email, which conveyed that "President Trump's electors voted" not just in "the states that he won" but also in six "contested states" (specifically, Arizona, Georgia, Michigan, Nevada, Pennsylvania, and Wisconsin).[101] Minutes later, President Trump's executive assistant replied: "It's in front of him!"[102]

The Trump team and the fake electors also engaged in acts of subterfuge to carry out their plans on December 14th. For instance, a campaign staffer notified the Georgia participants via email that he "must ask for your complete discretion."[103] He explained that their efforts required "complete secrecy," and told them to arrive at the State capitol building and "please state to the guards that you are attending a meeting with either Senator Brandon Beach or Senator Burt Jones."[104] Indeed, Greg Bluestein of the *Atlanta Journal-Constitution* reported that he tried to enter this group's meeting room but "[a] guy at the door called it an 'education meeting' and scrambled when I tried to walk in."[105]

Former Michigan GOP Chair Laura Cox told the Select Committee that an attorney who "said he was working with the President's Campaign" informed her that the Michigan slate for President Trump was "planning to meet in the capit[o]l and hide overnight so that they could fulfill the role of casting their vote in, per law, in the Michigan chambers."[106] She said that she "told him in no uncertain terms that that was insane and inappropriate," and that she warned Michigan's senate majority leader as a precaution.[107] Instead, the group of fake electors in Michigan signed their paperwork in the State GOP headquarters, where staff told them not to bring phones inside.[108]

### 3.6 THE FALLOUT FROM THE FAKE ELECTOR PLAN

In spite of the Trump Campaign's efforts to give the fake electors' votes the sheen of authenticity, they failed. The U.S. Senate Parliamentarian noted in correspondence by January 3rd that materials from the Trump team's supposed electors in Arizona, Georgia, Nevada, New Mexico, and Pennsylvania had "no seal of the state" and "no evidence votes were delivered by the executive of the state for signature by electors,"[109] and, as a result, these materials failed to meet requirements of federal law. Similarly, the Senate Parliamentarian noted that the Trump team's slates from Georgia, New Mexico, and Pennsylvania appeared to violate another statute which requires the approval of the Governor for the substitution of electors.[110]

Meanwhile, the documents from Michigan and Wisconsin did not even arrive to Congress on time, so they also had missed the required statutory deadline.[111]

Several of the Trump team's fake electoral slates also failed to follow State rules specifying where they were required to meet. In Georgia and Wisconsin, State lawmakers or their staff appear to have helped participants gather inside their State capitols.[112] But in Michigan, the fake Trump electors were blocked from entering the State capitol building.[113] Despite this, they still signed documents attesting that they "convened and organized in the State Capitol, in the City of Lansing, Michigan, and at 2:00 p.m.... performed the duties enjoined upon us." [114] That document had been signed earlier in the day off-site, and one of the signatories even told the Committee she didn't join their march to the State capitol building because she "didn't see a need to go." [115]

If the entire premise of the fake votes was not enough, these infirmities also meant that they had no legal relevance. In no way could they ever have been used by the Vice President to disregard the real votes of electors chosen by the voters.

In the weeks between December 14th and January 6th, President Trump's team continued to embrace the idea that the fake electoral votes had a purpose. Although Giuliani and White House speechwriter Stephen Miller made public comments on December 14th suggesting that the uncertified Trump votes were merely contingent, that pretense was dropped in short order.[116]

For example, on December 17th, White House Press Secretary Kayleigh McEnany said on Fox News that in numerous States "there has been an alternate slate of electors voted upon that Congress will decide in January." [117] On December 21st, President Trump and Vice President Pence each joined parts of a White House meeting in which Members of Congress from the Freedom Caucus encouraged the Vice President to reject Biden electors from one or more of the seven contested States.[118] And days later, Eastman cited the existence of the fake votes in an email to Boris Epshteyn, a member of the Giuliani legal team, writing, "[t]he fact that we have multiple slates of electors demonstrate[s] the uncertainty of either. That should be enough." [119]

As discussed further in Chapter 5, that email contained Eastman's 2-page memo proposing a strategy for January 6th based on the incorrect legal theory that Vice President Pence could assert some authority as President of the Senate to prevent or delay the election of former Vice President Biden during the joint session. Eastman's memo relied on the fake votes, which the memo featured in the very first line: "7 states have transmitted dual slates of electors." [120] When Eastman submitted his memo to Epshteyn, he also copied Chesebro, who had edited the memo and called it "[r]eally awesome." [121]

By that point, Chesebro and Eastman were coordinating their arguments about the fake-elector votes and how they should be used. On January 1, 2021, Chesebro sent an email to Eastman and Epshteyn that recommended that Vice President Pence derail the joint session of Congress. In it, he raised the idea of Vice President Pence declaring "that there are two competing slates of electoral votes" in several States, and taking the position that only he, or possibly Congress, could "resolve any disputes concerning them." [122]

Two days later, Eastman completed his second major memo advising President Trump and his team on strategies for January 6th, again arguing that there were "dual slates of electors from 7 states," and calling for Vice President Pence to assert power to act "[a]s the ultimate arbiter" to take steps that could overturn the election, either by sending the election back to State legislatures to reassess or by rejecting Biden's certified electoral votes from States in which there were also fake Trump electors. [123]

By early January, most of the fake elector votes had arrived in Washington, except those from Michigan and Wisconsin. [124] Undeterred, the Trump team arranged to fly them to Washington and hand deliver them to Congress for the Vice President himself. "Freaking trump idiots want someone to fly original elector papers to the senate President..." Wisconsin Republican Party official Mark Jefferson wrote to Party Chairman Hitt on January 4th. [125] Hitt responded, "Ok I see I have a missed call from [Mike] Roman and a text from someone else. Did you talk to them already? This is just nuts...." [126]

The next day, Trump Campaign Deputy Director for Election Day Operations G. Michael Brown sent a text message to other campaign staff suggesting that he was the person who delivered the fake votes to Congress. [127] After sending the group a photo of his face with the Capitol in the background, Brown said, "This has got to be the cover a book I write one day" and "I should probably buy [Mike] [R]oman a tie or something for sending me on this one. Hasn't been done since 1876 and it was only 3 states that did it." [128] The reference to 1876 alludes to a controversy during that election about certain States' electoral college votes. [129]

President Trump and his Campaign apparently had assistance from allies on Capitol Hill for this effort, including Senator Ron Johnson, his chief of staff, and the chief of staff to Representative Mike Kelly, although Senator Johnson has said that "[his] involvement in that attempt to

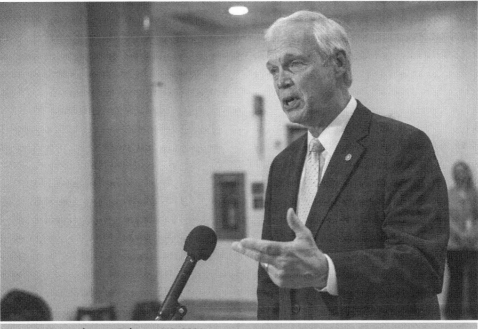
Senator Ron Johnson, February 12, 2021.

(Photo by Samuel Corum/Getty Images)

deliver" fake elector paperwork "spanned the course of a couple seconds." [130] On the morning of January 6th, Representative Kelly's then-chief of staff texted an aide to the Vice President, Chris Hodgson, about hand-delivering the fake elector votes to the Vice President's team before the joint session, a message that Hodgson ignored: "Just following up-any chance you or someone from your team can meet to take the Michigan and Wisconsin packets." [131]

According to the office of Senator Ron Johnson, Representative Kelly's chief of staff then had a phone call with Senator Johnson's chief of staff at 11:58 a.m. "about how Kelly's office could get us the electors [sic] because they had it." [132] Shortly after 11:30 a.m., the Trump Campaign's lead attorney in Wisconsin had texted Senator Johnson expressing a "[n]eed to get a document on Wisconsin electors to you [for] the VP immediately. Is there a staff person I can talk to immediately." [133] Senator Johnson then put his chief of staff in touch with the campaign to handle the issue.[134]

Shortly afterwards, Senator Johnson's chief of staff texted Hodgson: "[Sen.] Johnson needs to hand something to VPOTUS please advise." [135] When Hodgson asked what it was, the response he got was, "Alternate slate of electors for MI and WI because archivist didn't receive them." [136] Hodgson did not mince words: "Do not give that to him [the Vice President].

Senator Mike Lee, April 28, 2016.

(Photo by Leigh Vogel/Getty Images)

He's about to walk over to preside over the joint session, those were supposed to come in through the mail."[137]

Those fake electoral votes, which the Trump team tried for weeks to
manufacture and deliver, never made it to the Vice President. But they
would have been invalid even if they did arrive on time. The Trump team's
activities were based on the false pretense that these fake electoral votes
had a decisive role to play at the joint session of Congress. And yet any such
role that they could have played would have helped unlawfully obstruct an
official proceeding that determines how our Nation carries out the peaceful
transfer of power between Presidents.

Indeed, as the joint session approached, Senator Mike Lee had
expressed grave concerns about the fake elector effort in a series of text
messages to one of the Trump team's senior legal advisors. Although Senator Lee had spent a month encouraging the idea of having State legislatures
endorse competing electors for Trump, he grew alarmed as it became clear
that the Trump team wanted the fake electors' votes to be considered on
January 6th even without authorization from any State government body.[138]

On December 30th, Senator Lee texted Trump advisor Cleta Mitchell
that January 6th was "a dangerous idea," including "for the republic
itself."[139] He explained that, "I don't think we have any valid basis for

objecting to the electors" because "it cannot be true that we can object to any state's presidential electors simply because we don't think they handled their election well or suspect illegal activity."[140] Senator Lee even questioned her about the plan's dangerous long-term consequences: "[w]ill you please explain to me how this doesn't create a slippery slope problem for all future presidential elections?"[141]

# 4

# "JUST CALL IT CORRUPT AND LEAVE THE REST TO ME"

### 4.1  THE DOJ FOUND NO SIGNIFICANT EVIDENCE OF FRAUD

U.S. Attorney General William Barr knew there would be trouble before all the votes had been counted. "So, right out of the box on election night, the President claimed that there was major fraud underway," Barr explained. "I mean, this happened, as far as I could tell, before there was actually any potential of looking at evidence." [1] President Trump was quick to claim, "there was major fraud" based solely on the phenomenon known as the "Red Mirage." [2]

As explained elsewhere in this report, Democrats were more inclined to vote via mail-in ballot during the 2020 Presidential election than Republicans, who were more likely to vote in-person on election day. This was widely known, and partly a result of, President Trump's own public statements criticizing mail-in balloting. It also created a gap in the timing of how votes were tallied. The early vote tally favored Republicans on election night because the mail-in ballots, which skewed toward Democrats, were not yet fully counted. This occurred not just in 2020, but also in previous elections. [3] The President knew of this phenomenon but exploited it on election night, nonetheless, as he and his allies had planned to do. [4]

President Trump exploited this timing gap and used it as "the basis for this broad claim that there was major fraud," Barr said. [5] But the Attorney General "didn't think much of that." People "had been talking for weeks and everyone understood for weeks that that was going to be what happened on election night," Barr explained. [6] Cities with Democratic majorities in the battleground States wouldn't have their votes fully counted until "the end of the cycle," with "a lot of Democratic votes coming in at the end." [7] This was not some well-guarded secret, as "everyone understood that the dynamic of election night in many States would be whether or not the Democratic votes at the end of the day would overcome the election day votes." [8]

Within days of the election, the President made an "avalanche" of fraud allegations. It "was like playing Whac-A-Mole," Barr explained, "because something would come out one day and the next day it would be another issue." [9] Barr told his "staff very soon after the election" that he "didn't think the President would ever admit that he lost the election, and he would blame it on fraud, and then he would blame the actions and evidence on the Department of Justice." [10]

Barr soon took steps to investigate claims of fraud in the 2020 Presidential election, even in the absence of evidence. The Department of Justice's (DOJ) longstanding policy had been to avoid any substantive investigations until after the election's results were certified. [11] As the country's premier Federal law enforcement agency, DOJ is justifiably concerned that its substantial power can influence the outcome of an election, and it has enacted policies to mitigate this possibility. [12]

On November 7, 2020, the media declared former Vice President Biden the winner of the Presidential election. Two days later, on November 9th, Attorney General Barr authorized wider investigations into claims of election fraud. [13] Barr instructed DOJ and FBI personnel "to pursue substantial allegations of voting and vote tabulation irregularities prior to the certification of elections in your jurisdictions in certain cases." [14] Barr noted that nothing in his memo "should be taken as any indication that the Department has concluded that voting irregularities have impacted the outcome of any election." [15]

## 4.2 NOVEMBER 23, 2020: BARR CHALLENGES PRESIDENT TRUMP'S ELECTION LIES

As Barr predicted, the President did call on him for information about alleged election fraud. Trump challenged him with a blizzard of conspiracy theories in three face-to-face meetings after the election. The first such meeting occurred on November 23, 2020.

On November 23rd, the Attorney General spoke with White House Counsel Pat Cipollone, who said that it was important for him come to the White House and speak to President Trump. [16] Barr had not seen the President since before the election in late October, and the White House counsel believed that it was important that the Attorney General explain what the Department of Justice was doing related to claims of election fraud. [17]

"The President said there had been major fraud and that, as soon as the facts were out, the results of the election would be reversed," Barr recalled.

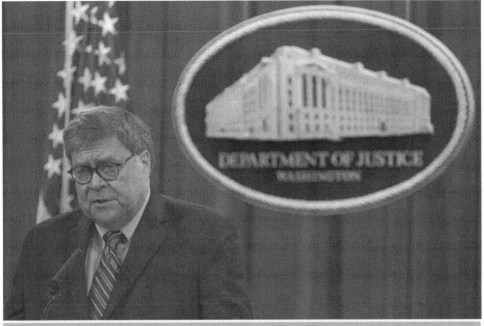

U.S. Attorney General William Barr at the Department of Justice on December 21, 2020.
(Photo by Michael Reynolds-Pool/Getty Images)

Trump continued "for quite a while," and Barr was "expecting" what came next.[18] President Trump alleged that "the Department of Justice doesn't think it has a role looking into these fraud claims."[19] Barr anticipated this line of attack because the President's counsel, Rudolph Giuliani, was making all sorts of wild, unsubstantiated claims.[20] And Giuliani wanted to blame DOJ for the fact that no one had come up with any real evidence of fraud.[21] Of course, by the time of this meeting, U.S. Attorneys' Offices had been explicitly authorized to investigate substantial claims for 2 weeks and had yet to find any evidence of significant voter fraud.[22]

Barr explained to the President why he was wrong. DOJ, was willing to investigate any "specific and credible allegations of fraud."[23] The fact of the matter was that the claims being made were "just not meritorious" and were "not panning out."[24] Barr emphasized to the President that DOJ "doesn't take sides in elections" and "is not an extension of your legal team."[25]

During the November 23rd meeting, Barr also challenged one of President Trump's central lies. He "specifically raised the Dominion voting machines, which I found to be one of the most disturbing allegations."[26] "Disturbing," Barr explained, because there was "absolutely zero basis for the allegations," which were being "made in such a sensational way that they obviously were influencing a lot of people, members of the public."[27] Americans were being deceived into thinking "that there was this systematic corruption in the system and that their votes didn't count and that these machines, controlled by somebody else, were actually determining it, which was complete nonsense."[28] Barr stressed to the President that this was "crazy stuff," arguing that not only was the conspiracy theory a waste of time, but it was also "doing [a] great, great disservice to the country."[29]

As Attorney General Barr left the meeting, he talked with Mark Meadows, the White House Chief of Staff, and Jared Kushner, President Trump's son-in-law.[30] "I think he's become more realistic and knows that there's a limit to how far he can take this," Meadows said, according to Barr.[31] Kushner reassured Barr, "we're working on this, we're working on it."[32] Barr was hopeful that the President was beginning to accept reality.[33] The opposite happened.

"I felt that things continued to deteriorate between the 23rd and the weekend of the 29th," Barr recalled.[34] Barr was concerned because President Trump began meeting with delegations of State legislators, and it appeared to him that "there was maneuvering going on."[35] Barr had "no problem" with challenging an election "through the appropriate process," but "worried" that he "didn't have any visibility into what was going on" and that the "President was digging in."[36]

### 4.3  DECEMBER 1, 2020: PRESIDENT TRUMP IS IRATE AFTER BARR SAYS THERE IS NO SIGNIFICANT FRAUD

Attorney General Barr had been clear that DOJ was investigating claims of fraud. The Department simply was not turning up any real evidence of malfeasance, and certainly nothing that would overturn the election. Just as Barr feared, the President turned on DOJ anyway.

On November 29, 2020, Fox News's Maria Bartiromo interviewed President Trump. It was his first TV interview since he lost his bid for reelection. The President claimed the election was "rigged" and rife with "fraud."[37] President Trump repeated various conspiracy theories, leading with the claim that Dominion's voting machines had "glitches," which moved "thousands of votes from my account to Biden's account."[38] President Trump pointed to "dumps of votes,"a reference to the batches of mail-in ballots that had been tabulated later in the counting process.[39] He rambled off various other, spurious allegations, including that dead people voted in significant numbers.[40]

"This is total fraud," the President said.[41] "And how the FBI and Department of Justice—I don't know—maybe they're involved, but how people are getting away with this stuff—it's unbelievable. This election was rigged. This election was a total fraud."[42]

"Where is the DOJ and the FBI in all of this, Mr. President?" Bartiromo asked.[43] "You have laid out some serious charges here. Shouldn't this be something that the FBI is investigating? Are they? Is the DOJ investigating?" Bartiromo asked incredulously.[44]

"Missing in action," the President replied, "can't tell you where they are."[45] He conceded that when he asked if DOJ and FBI were investigating, "everyone says yes, they're looking at it."[46] But he didn't leave it there. "You would think if you're in the FBI or Department of Justice, this is, this is the biggest thing you could be looking at," President Trump said. "Where are they? I've not seen anything. I mean, just keep moving along. They go onto the next President."[47] He claimed the FBI was not even investigating Dominion, adding that votes processed in its machines "are counted in foreign countries."[48]

None of this was true. Just 6 days earlier, Attorney General Barr had explained to President Trump how DOJ and FBI were investigating fraud claims. Barr also made it a point to emphasize that the Dominion claims were nonsense. The President simply lied. The "crazy stuff," as Barr put it, was all Trump could cite.

Attorney General Barr then decided to speak out. He invited Michael Balsamo, an *Associated Press (AP)* reporter, to lunch on December 1st. Barr told the journalist that "to date, we have not seen fraud on a scale that could have effected a different outcome in the election."[49]

That made the President irate.

Later that evening, Attorney General Barr met with President Trump at the White House. It was their second face-to-face meeting after the November election.[50] At first, President Trump didn't even look at Attorney General Barr.[51] The President "was as mad as I've ever seen him, and he was trying to control himself," Barr said.[52] The President finally "shoved a newspaper" with the *AP* quote in Barr's face.[53]

"Well, this is, you know, killing me. You didn't have to say this. You must've said this because you hate Trump—you hate Trump," Barr remembered him saying.[54] "No, I don't hate you, Mr. President," Barr replied. "You know, I came in at a low time in your administration. I've tried to help your administration. I certainly don't hate you."[55]

President Trump peppered him with unsupported conspiracy theories.[56] Because he had authorized DOJ and FBI to investigate fraud claims, Attorney General Barr was familiar with the conspiracy theories raised by the President. The "big ones" he investigated included claims such as: Dominion voting machines switched votes, votes had been "dumped at the end of the night in Milwaukee and Detroit," non-residents voted in Nevada, the number of ballots counted in Pennsylvania exceeded the number of votes cast, as well as a story about a truck driver supposedly driving thousands of pre-filled ballots from New York to Pennsylvania, among others.[57] Under Attorney General Barr, DOJ would also investigate a false claim that a video feed in Fulton County captured multiple runs of ballots for former Vice President Biden. As explained in detail in Chapter 1 of this report, there was no truth to any of these allegations, but that didn't stop President Trump from repeatedly citing these fictional accounts.

"And I told him that the stuff that his people were shoveling out to the public was bullshit, I mean, that the claims of fraud were bullshit," Barr recalled about the December 1st meeting.[58] "And, you know, he was indignant about that. And I reiterated that they wasted a whole month of these claims on the Dominion voting machines and they were idiotic claims."[59]

President Trump repeated that there had been a "big vote dump" in Detroit.[60] But Attorney General Barr quickly parried this claim.[61] There was nothing suspicious in how the votes flowed into a central location, Barr explained, because that is how votes are always counted in Wayne County.[62] Moreover, Barr pointed out that the President performed *better* in Detroit in 2020 than he had in 2016. "I mean, there's no indication of fraud in Detroit," Barr said.[63] Barr explained that the "thing about the truck driver is complete, you know, nonsense."[64] DOJ and FBI had investigated the matter, including by interviewing the relevant witnesses.[65] There was no truck filled with ballots.

Nothing that Attorney General Barr said during that meeting could satisfy President Trump. So, the President shifted the focus to Barr. He complained that the Attorney General hadn't indicted former FBI Director James Comey and that U.S. Attorney John Durham's investigation into the origins of the FBI's Crossfire Hurricane investigation hadn't made more progress.[66] "Look, I know that you're dissatisfied with me," Barr said, "and I'm glad to offer my resignation."[67] President Trump pounded the table in front of him with his fist and said, "Accepted."[68]

White House lawyers Pat Cipollone and Eric Herschmann tracked Barr down in the parking lot after he left.[69] They convinced Barr to stay in the administration.[70] But his days as Attorney General were numbered. President Trump was not going to stop spreading conspiracy theories. Nor would the President cease in his effort to co-opt DOJ for his own corrupt political purposes.

President Trump released a video on Facebook the very next day.[71] He repeated many of the same lies, including the conspiracy theory about Dominion voting machines switching votes. The President also offered charts, falsely claiming that fraudulent "vote dumps" had swung the election against him.[72] Among the examples he cited was the supposed "vote dump" in Detroit, Michigan.[73] In fact, Barr had already debunked this and other claims.

On December 3, 2020, Rudolph Giuliani appeared before the Georgia Senate Government Oversight Committee to allege that massive cheating had occurred during the election.[74] Giuliani offered a video recorded on election night at the State Farm Arena in Atlanta, Georgia, as a key piece of evidence.[75] Giuliani alleged that the video showed a secret suitcase of ballots being double- and triple-counted after Republican poll watchers had been inappropriately dismissed.[76] The video was selectively edited and showed nothing of the sort. The Georgia Secretary of State's Office investigated and immediately debunked the claim, finding that the secret suitcase was just a secure box and nothing nefarious had occurred.[77] President Trump, Giuliani and others continued to push the lie anyway.

On December 4th, Attorney General Barr asked Byung J. ("BJay") Pak, who was then the U.S. Attorney for the Northern District of Georgia, to independently investigate the State Farm claim. Barr told Pak that this was a "priority," because "he was going to go to the White House for a meeting" and the "issue might come up." Barr asked Pak to "try to substantiate the allegation made by Mr. Giuliani."[78]

Pak watched the video from State Farm Arena and asked the FBI to investigate the matter further. Pak told the Select Committee that FBI agents "interviewed the individuals" shown in the video who were supposedly "double, triple counting" the ballots, and "determined that nothing irregular happened in the counting and the allegations made by Mr. Giuliani were false."[79] And, as noted above, the supposed "suitcase" was a secure storage container used to store ballots. With this evidence in hand, Pak told Attorney General Barr that there was no substance to the allegations.[80]

## 4.4 DECEMBER 14, 2020: BARR SUBMITS HIS RESIGNATION

Finally, Attorney General Barr had had enough. He submitted his resignation on December 14, 2020.[81] During an interview with the Select Committee, former Attorney General Barr reflected on his face-to-face encounters with President Trump in November and December 2020:

> And, in that context, I made clear I did not agree with the idea of saying the election was stolen and putting out this stuff which I told the President was bullshit. And, you know, I didn't want to be part of it. And that's one of the reasons that went into me deciding to leave when I did.

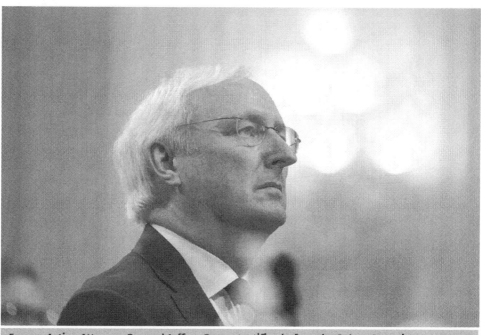

Former Acting Attorney General Jeffrey Rosen testifies before the Select Committee on June 23, 2022.

(Photo by House Creative Services)

I observed, I think it was on December 1st, that—you know, I believe you can't live in a world where the incumbent administration stays in power based on its view, unsupported by specific evidence, that the election—that there was fraud in the election.[82]

Around mid-day on December 14th, Attorney General Barr met with President Trump and Meadows in the Oval Office to discuss his resignation.[83] When he arrived, and even before Barr could mention his resignation, President Trump began speaking at length about the recently released Allied Security Operations Group (ASOG) report on Dominion voting machines in Antrim County, Michigan.[84] While the Attorney General had been briefed on the allegations in Antrim County and did not find them credible, he promised the President that he would have DOJ investigate them.[85] The Attorney General then told President Trump that he had come for a separate reason and wished to speak to the President privately, so Meadows left.[86]

Barr told President Trump that it was clear the President was dissatisfied with him as Attorney General and that he had decided to resign.[87] President Trump accepted his resignation and asked Barr who would replace him; Attorney General Barr recommended Jeffrey A. Rosen as Acting Attorney General and Richard Donoghue as his deputy.[88] Although President Trump called Donoghue to discuss the possibility of appointing him Acting Attorney General, Donoghue advised that normal procedures be followed and Rosen be named Acting Attorney General.[89] President Trump followed this advice, and upon Barr's departure, Rosen became Acting Attorney General while Donoghue would function as his deputy.

## 4.5  ACTING ATTORNEY GENERAL JEFFREY ROSEN AND ACTING DEPUTY ATTORNEY GENERAL RICHARD DONOGHUE HOLD THE LINE

Barr felt that he was leaving the Department in the hands of two trusted lieutenants. But President Trump immediately began to pressure Rosen and Donoghue, just as he had Barr.

On December 14, 2020, the day Barr resigned, Molly Michael, Special Assistant to the President and Oval Office Coordinator, sent an email to Acting Attorney General Jeffrey Rosen. The email had two documents attached, both of which were labeled "From POTUS." [90] The first was a set of talking points focused on false allegations of voter fraud in Antrim County, Michigan. The second document was the same ASOG report the President had given Barr.[91]

The next day, President Trump held a meeting in the White House with Acting Attorney General Rosen, Acting Deputy Attorney Donoghue, Cipollone, Meadows, Acting Deputy Secretary of Homeland Security Ken Cuccinelli, and Acting General Counsel of the Department of Homeland Security Chad Mizelle.[92] Barr did not attend, even though he was not scheduled to leave DOJ until the following week. The timing of the meeting was notable, as the previous day the electoral college had met and cast their votes in favor of former Vice President Biden.

During testimony before the Select Committee, Donoghue explained that the December 15th, meeting "was largely focused on" the ASOG report.[93] According to Donoghue, the President "was adamant that the report must be accurate, that it proved that the election was defective, that he in fact won the election, and the [D]epartment should be using that report to basically tell the American people that the results were not trustworthy." [94] President Trump discussed "other theories as well," including erroneous allegations of voter fraud in Georgia and Pennsylvania, but "the bulk of that conversation on December 15th focused on Antrim County, Michigan." [95] President Trump asked why DOJ wasn't "doing more to look at this" and whether the Department was "going to do its job." [96]

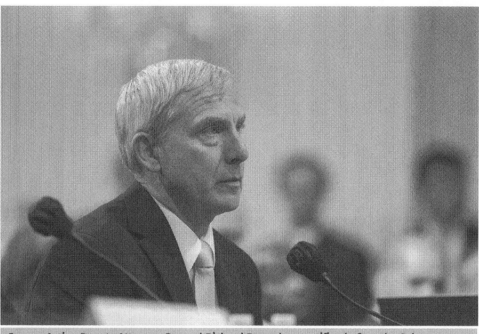

Former Acting Deputy Attorney General Richard Donoghue testifies before the Select Committee on June 23, 2022.

(Photo by House Creative Services)

The Department of Justice *was* doing its job. In fact, Attorney General Barr had ordered unprecedented investigations into the many specious claims of voter fraud. The President simply didn't want to hear the truth—that DOJ found that not one of the bogus claims was true. As explained in Chapter 1, the original vote totals in Antrim County were the result of a human error that had since been corrected, not the result of any problem with Dominion machines or software. There was no evidence of fraud.

## 4.6 PRESIDENT TRUMP IS INTRODUCED TO JEFFREY CLARK

On December 21, 2020, 11 House Republicans met with President Trump at the White House to discuss their plans for objecting to the certification of the electoral college vote on January 6th.[97] After the meeting, Mark Meadows tweeted: "Several members of Congress just finished a meeting in the Oval Office with @realDonaldTrump preparing to fight back against mounting evidence of voter fraud. Stay tuned." [98] Among those in attendance was Congressman Scott Perry, a Republican from Pennsylvania.[99]

By the next day, Representative Perry had introduced a little-known DOJ official named Jeffrey Clark to the President.[100] At the time, Clark was

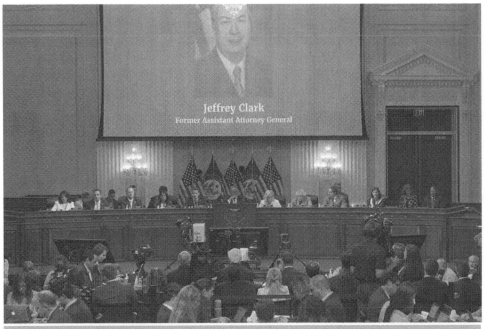

Former Assistant Attorney General Jeffrey Clark appears on a screen during a Select Committee hearing on June 23, 2022.

(Photo by Mandel Ngan-Pool/Getty Images)

the Acting Head of the Civil Division and Head of the Environmental and Natural Resources Division at the Department of Justice.[101] Clark had no experience in, or responsibilities related to, investigating allegations of election fraud.

President Trump called Acting Attorney General Rosen "virtually every day" between December 23rd and January 3rd.[102] The President usually discussed his "dissatisfaction" with DOJ, claiming the Department was not doing enough to investigate election fraud.[103] On Christmas Eve, Trump brought up Jeffrey Clark's name. Rosen found it "peculiar," telling the Select Committee: "I was quizzical as to how does the President even know Mr. Clark?"[104]

Rosen then spoke directly with Clark on December 26th.[105] Clark revealed that he had met with the President in the Oval Office several days prior.[106] Clark had told the President that if he were to change the leadership at the Department of Justice, "then the Department might be able to do more" to support the President's claims that the election had been stolen from him.[107]

In his discussion with Acting Attorney General Rosen, Clark was "defensive" and "apologetic," claiming that the meeting with President

Trump was "inadvertent and it would not happen again, and that if anyone asked him to go to such a meeting, he would notify Rich Donoghue and me [Rosen]." [108] Of course, Clark had good reasons to be defensive. His meeting with President Trump and Representative Perry on December 22nd was a clear violation of Department policy, which limits interactions between the White House and the Department's staff. As Steven Engel, former Assistant Attorney General for the Office of Legal Counsel, explained to the Select Committee, "it's critical that the Department of Justice conducts its criminal investigations free from either the reality or any appearance of political interference." [109] For that reason, the Department has longstanding polices in place, across administrations, to "keep these communications as infrequent and at the highest levels as possible, just to make sure that people who are less careful about it, who don't really understand these implications, such as Mr. Clark, don't run afoul of the of those contact policies." [110] Rosen added that only the Attorney General or Deputy Attorney General "can have conversations about criminal matters with the White House," or they can "authorize" someone from within DOJ to do so.[111] Clark had no such authorization.

Representative Perry continued to advocate on Clark's behalf. The Congressman texted Meadows on December 26th, writing: "Mark, just checking in as time continues to count down. 11 days to 1/6 and 25 days to inauguration. We gotta get going!" [112] Representative Perry followed up: "Mark, you should call Jeff. I just got off the phone with him and he explained to me why the principal deputy [position] won't work especially with the FBI. They will view it as not having the authority to enforce what needs to be done." [113] Meadows responded: "I got it. I think I understand. Let me work on the deputy position." [114] Representative Perry then sent additional texts: "Roger. Just sent you something on Signal", "Just sent you an updated file", and "Did you call Jeff Clark?" [115]

## 4.7 DECEMBER 27TH PHONE CALL

On December 27, 2020, President Trump called Acting Attorney General Rosen once again. At some point during the lengthy call, Rosen asked that Acting Deputy Attorney General Donoghue be conferenced in.[116] According to Donoghue's contemporaneous notes, Trump referenced three Republican politicians, all of whom had supported the President's election lies and the "Stop the Steal" campaign.[117] One was Representative Scott Perry. Another was Doug Mastriano, a State senator from Pennsylvania who would later be on the grounds of the U.S. Capitol during the January 6th attack.[118] President Trump also referenced Representative Jim Jordan from Ohio, praising him as a "fighter."[119] Representatives Perry and Jordan had often teamed up to spread lies about the election. The two spoke at a "Stop the Steal" rally in front of the Pennsylvania State capitol in Harrisburg, just days after the November election.[120] The pair also pressed their conspiratorial case during interviews with friendly media outlets.[121]

President Trump made a "stream of allegations" during the December 27th call.[122] As reflected in his notes, Donoghue considered the call to be an "escalation of the earlier conversations," with the President becoming more adamant that "we weren't doing our job."[123] President Trump trafficked in "conspiracy theories" he had heard from others, and Donoghue sought to "make it clear to the President these allegations were simply not true."[124] Donoghue sought to "correct" President Trump "in a serial fashion as he moved from one theory to another."[125]

The President returned to the discredited ASOG report, which former Attorney General Barr had already dismissed as complete nonsense. ASOG had claimed—based on no evidence—that the Dominion voting machines in Antrim County, Michigan had suffered from a 68 percent error rate. As noted above and in Chapter 1, that was not close to being true.

Bipartisan election officials in Antrim County completed a hand recount of all machine-processed ballots on December 17, 2020, which should have ended the lies about Dominion's voting machines.[126] The net difference between the machine count and the hand recount was only 12 out of 15,718 total votes.[127] The machines counted just one vote more for former Vice President Biden than was tallied during the hand recount.[128] Donoghue informed the President that he "cannot and should not be relying on" ASOG's claim, because it was "simply not true."[129] This did not stop the President from later repeating the debunked allegation multiple times, including during his January 6th speech at the Ellipse.[130]

Acting Deputy Attorney General Donoghue debunked a "series" of other conspiracy theories offered by President Trump during the December 27th call as well. One story involved a truck driver "who claimed to have moved an entire tractor trailer of ballots from New York to Pennsylvania."[131] There was no truth to the story. The FBI "interviewed witnesses at the front end and the back end of" the truck's transit route, "looked at loading manifests," questioned the truck driver, and concluded that there were no ballots in the truck.[132]

President Trump then returned to the conspiracy theory about voting in Detroit. Former Attorney General Barr had already debunked the claim that a massive number of illegal votes had been dumped during the middle of the night, but the President would not let it go. President Trump alleged that someone "threw the poll watchers out," and "you don't even need to look at the illegal aliens voting—don't need to. It's so obvious."[133] The President complained that the "FBI will always say there's nothing there," because while the Special Agents ("the line guys") supported him, the Bureau's leadership supposedly did not.[134] This was inconsistent with Donoghue's view.[135] But President Trump complained that he had "made some bad decisions on leadership" at the FBI.[136]

President Trump also "wanted to talk a great deal about Georgia, [and] the State Farm Arena video," claiming it was "fraud staring you right in the face."[137] President Trump smeared Ruby Freeman, a Georgia election worker who was merely doing her job, as a "Huckster" and an "Election scammer."[138] President Trump said the "networks," meaning the television networks, had "magnified the tape and saw them running them [ballots] through repeatedly."[139] The President repeated the lie that Democrats had "[c]losed the facility and then came back with hidden ballots under the table."[140] He suggested that both Rosen and Donoghue "go to Fulton County and do a signature verification." They would "see how illegal it is" and "find tens of thousands" of illegal ballots.[141]

President Trump "kept fixating" on the supposed suitcase in the video.[142] But Acting Deputy Attorney General Donoghue debunked the President's obsession. "There is no suitcase," Donoghue made clear.[143] Donoghue explained that the DOJ had looked at the video and interviewed multiple witnesses. The "suitcase" was an official lock box filled with genuine votes.[144] And election workers simply did not scan ballots for former Vice President Biden multiple times.[145] All of this was recorded by security cameras.[146]

In response to what President Trump was saying during the conversation, Rosen and Donoghue tried to make clear that the claims the President made weren't supported by the evidence. "You guys must not be following the internet the way I do," the President remarked.[147] But President Trump was not finished peddling wild conspiracy theories.

The President pushed the claim that Pennsylvania had reported 205,000 more votes than there were voters in the state.[148] "We'll look at whether we have more ballots in Pennsylvania than registered voters," Acting Attorney General Rosen replied, according to Donoghue. They "[s]hould be able to check that out quickly."[149] But Rosen wanted President Trump to "understand that the DOJ can't and won't snap its fingers and change the outcome of the election. It doesn't work that way."[150]

"I don't expect you to do that," President Trump responded. "Just say the election was corrupt and leave the rest to me and the Republican Congressmen."[151]

Donoghue explained this "is an exact quote from the President."[152]

"We have an obligation to tell people that this was an illegal, corrupt election," President Trump told the DOJ team at another point in the call.[153] President Trump insisted this was DOJ's "obligation," even though Rosen and Donoghue kept telling him there was no evidence of fraud sufficient to overturn the outcome of the election. "We are doing our job," Donoghue informed the President. "Much of the info you're getting is false."[154]

The call on December 27th was contentious for additional reasons. President Trump did not want to accept that the Department of Justice was not an arm of his election campaign. He wanted to know why the Department did not assist in his campaign's civil suits against States. There was a simple answer: There was no evidence to support the campaign's claims of fraud.[155]

Donoghue and Rosen also "tried to explain to the President on this occasion and on several other occasions that the Justice Department has a very important, very specific, but very limited role in these elections."[156] The States "run their elections" and DOJ is not "quality control for the States."[157] DOJ has "a mission that relates to criminal conduct in relation to federal elections" and also has "related civil rights responsibilities."[158] But DOJ cannot simply intervene to alter the outcome of an election or support a civil suit.[159]

When President Trump made these demands on December 27th, it was already crystal clear that the Department of Justice had found no evidence of systemic fraud.[160] The Department simply had no reason to assert that the 2020 Presidential contest was "an illegal corrupt election."[161]

"People tell me Jeff Clark is great" and that "I should put him in," President Trump said on the call. "People want me to replace the DOJ leadership."[162] Donoghue responded "[S]ir, that's fine, you should have the leadership you want, but understand, changing the leadership in the Department won't change anything."[163]

The President did not really care what facts had been uncovered by the Department of Justice. President Trump just wanted the Department to say the election was corrupt, so he and the Republican Congressmen could exploit the statement in the days to come, including on January 6th. And when Rosen and Donoghue resisted the President's entreaties, he openly mused about replacing Rosen with someone who would do the President's bidding.

## 4.8  CONGRESSMAN SCOTT PERRY CALLS DONOGHUE

Toward the end of the December 27th call, President Trump asked Donoghue for his cell number.[164] Later that day, Representative Perry called

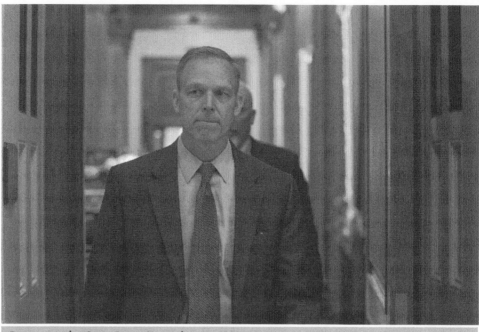

Representative Scott Perry, November 14, 2022.

(Photo by Anna Moneymaker/Getty Images)

Donoghue to press the President's case.[165] Representative Perry was one of President Trump's key congressional allies in the effort to overturn the election's results. Representative Perry was an early supporter of the "Stop the Steal" campaign and, as noted above, addressed the crowd at one such event outside the Pennsylvania State capitol in Harrisburg on November 5, 2020.[166] Representative Perry was also one of 27 Republican Congressmen who signed a letter requesting that President Trump "direct Attorney General Barr to appoint a Special Counsel to investigate irregularities in the 2020 election." The letter was dated December 9, 2020—more than 1 week after Barr told the press there was no evidence of significant fraud.[167] There was no reason to think that a Special Counsel was warranted. Representative Perry and the other congressmen advocated for one to be appointed anyway.

Representative Perry attended the December 21st Oval Office meeting along with at least 10 other congressional Republicans to discuss the strategy for objecting to the electoral college votes on January 6th. Along with 125 other Republican Members of Congress. Representative Perry also supported Texas's lawsuit against Pennsylvania and three other states.[168] That is, Representative Perry supported Texas's effort to nullify the certified electoral college vote from four states, including his own home state.

Donoghue took notes during his conversation with Representative Perry and provided those notes to the Select Committee.[169] The notes reflect that when Representative Perry called Donoghue on December 27th, Representative Perry explained that President Trump asked him to call and that he, Representative Perry, did not think DOJ had been doing its job on the election.[170] Representative Perry brought up other, unrelated matters and argued that the "FBI doesn't always do the right thing in all instances."[171] Representative Perry also brought up Jeff Clark. He said he liked him and thought that Clark "would do something about this," meaning the election fraud allegations.[172]

On the evening of December 27th, Representative Perry emailed Donoghue a set of documents alleging significant voting fraud had occurred in Pennsylvania.[173] One document asserted that election authorities had counted 205,000 more votes than had been cast.[174] Representative Perry also shared this same claim on Twitter the following day.[175] President Trump kept raising the same claim. Sometimes there was an alleged discrepancy of 205,000 votes, other times it was supposedly 250,000 votes.[176] Either way, it was not true.

Acting Deputy Attorney General Donoghue forwarded Representative Perry's email to Scott Brady, who was the U.S. Attorney for the Western District of Pennsylvania at the time.[177] As Brady soon discovered, there was no discrepancy.[178] President Trump's supporters came up with the claim by comparing the Pennsylvania Secretary of State's website, which reported the total number of votes as 5.25 million, to a separate State election registry, which showed only 5 million votes cast.[179] The problem was simple: Pennsylvania's election site had not been updated.[180] The totals for four counties had not yet been reported on the election site. Once those votes were counted on the site, the totals matched. This was simply not an example of fraud, as President Trump, Representative Perry and others would have it.

## 4.9 DECEMBER 28, 2020: THE CLARK LETTER

On December 28, 2020, Clark sent a 5-page draft letter to Donoghue and Rosen.[181] The letter was addressed to three Georgia State officials: Governor Brian Kemp, Speaker of the House David Ralston, and President *Pro Tempore* of the Senate Butch Miller. It contained places for Rosen and Donoghue to affix their signatures, which they steadfastly refused to do.[182] The letter, if signed and sent, may very well have provoked a constitutional crisis.[183]

The letter was attached to an email from Clark, in which he requested authorization to attend a classified briefing by the Office of the Director of

National Intelligence (ODNI) "led by DNI Ratcliffe on foreign election interference issues."[184] ODNI did not find any foreign interference in the voting process or counting,[185] but Clark apparently believed some of the conspiracy theories that had been floated. Specifically, Clark claimed that "hackers have evidence (in the public domain) that a Dominion machine accessed the internet through a smart thermostat with a net connection trail leading back to China." Clark added: "ODNI may have additional classified evidence."[186] This crackpot claim had been shared by other Trump officials and associates as well.[187] Ultimately, after Clark received the ODNI briefing, "he acknowledged [to Donoghue] that there was nothing in that briefing that would have supported his earlier suspicion about foreign involvement."[188]

Clark intended to send the letter to officials in Georgia and several other contested States that President Trump needed to flip if he was going to overturn the election results. "The Department of Justice is investigating various irregularities in the 2020 election for President of the United States," Clark wrote.[189] Clark continued: "The Department will update you as we are able on investigatory progress, but at this time we have identified significant concerns that may have impacted the outcome of the election in multiple States, including the State of Georgia."[190]

Clark continued by arguing that Georgia's State legislature should call a special session. "In light of these developments, the Department recommends that the Georgia General Assembly should convene in special session so that its legislators are in a special position to take additional testimony, receive new evidence, and deliberate on the matter consistent with its duties under the U.S. Constitution," Clark wrote.[191] Clark referenced the fake electors that the President and his campaign organized and argued that there were two competing slates of electors, both of which were legitimate.[192] "The Department believes that in Georgia and several other States, both a slate of electors supporting Joseph R. Biden, Jr., and a separate slate of electors supporting Donald J. Trump, gathered on [December 14, 2020] at the proper location to cast their ballots, and that both sets of those ballots have been transmitted to Washington, D.C., to be opened by Vice President Pence," Clark wrote.[193]

The letter was a lie. Senior DOJ officials—Barr, Rosen and Donoghue— had repeatedly stated the opposite. They found no evidence of fraud that would have impacted the election's results—none. But since mid-November, the Trump Campaign's legal team under Giuliani attempted to execute its dual-track strategy of both filing lawsuits and convincing state legislatures in contested states to appoint separate slates of Presidential electors for President Trump.[194] By late December, however, the dual-track approach had largely failed, and no legislatures had sent a second lawful slate of electors for Trump to Congress. Clearly, President Trump and his campaign team could not get the job done. So, the President and those around him sought to use the hefty imprimatur of the U.S. Department of Justice to achieve the same thing. No doubt, a letter coming from the Department of Justice is different from a meandering call from Giuliani or one of his associates. And, because it was December 28th and there was little more than a week until the January 6th joint session of Congress, President Trump needed more, and soon. Clark's letter, which laid out a plan that was almost identical to what President Trump and his team had pressured State officials to carry out virtually since election day, could have been just what President Trump needed.

Several examples demonstrate the parallels between President Trump's and Rudolph Giuliani's approach to overturning the election in November and December, and what Clark proposed in this letter. First, the letter sought to have the Georgia State legislature convene a special session to focus on allegations of fraud in the election.[195] Giuliani and his team had been making calls to State legislatures and telling them in both official and unofficial State legislature committee hearings that State legislatures should convene in special sessions.[196] They also argued that State legislatures had the authority to convene a special session themselves, despite limitations in State law requiring such a session to be convened by the governor.[197] Clark included the same argument in his draft letter.[198]

Additionally, the draft letter recommended that the Georgia legislature consider choosing the alternate—fake—slate of electoral college electors that sent fake electoral college votes to Congress and Vice President Pence.[199] Having State legislatures choose Trump electors in States where President Trump lost was one of the Trump team's early goals immediately after the election, but it didn't work.[200] When no State legislature appointed its own set of electors before December 14th, the Trump Campaign arranged for electors to meet in contested States anyway and cast fake electoral college votes.[201] This letter, with the Department of Justice seal at the top, was just one more way that President Trump and those close to him could pressure State officials to send competing electoral college votes to Congress for consideration during the joint session, despite former Vice President Biden's certified victory in each of the contested States.

Despite the similarities between the requests in Clark's proposed letter and the requests that President Trump and his team made to State officials for nearly 2 months, the extent to which Clark directly coordinated his actions with the Trump Campaign and its outside advisors is unclear. Clark asserted his Fifth Amendment rights and various other privileges to avoid answering the Select Committee's questions about these and other topics.[202] When Giuliani was asked during his Select Committee deposition whether he remembered discussing DOJ issuing a letter like Clark's, Giuliani refused to answer because it implicated attorney-client privilege with President Trump, but when asked if he recalled ever recommending that Clark be given election-related responsibilities at DOJ, Giuliani said, "I do recall saying to people that somebody should be put in charge of the Justice Department who isn't frightened of what's going to be done to their reputation, because the Justice Department was filled with people like that."[203] And the investigation has also revealed that Clark and John Eastman were in communication throughout this period.[204]

One person who had worked with Eastman and others in his circle was a lawyer installed to work with Clark at the Department of Justice in mid-December—the final weeks of the Trump administration—named Ken Klukowski.[205] Klukowski was a Trump administration political appointee serving as a senior counsel under Clark in DOJ's Civil Division.[206] After serving as a lawyer in the Office and Management and Budget (OMB) for more than a year and volunteering as a lawyer for the Trump Campaign after election day, Klukowski only joined the Department when the administration's personnel staff "expedite[d]" his appointment because the White House's Presidential Personnel Office "want[ed] him in soon."[207]

On the morning of December 28th, Clark asked Klukowski to draft the Georgia letter for him.[208] Clark dictated the substantive key points of the letter to Klukowski and told him exactly what to include.[209] After several meetings with Clark throughout the day to update him on progress, Klukowski turned in his assignment and gave the letter to Clark, which Clark sent along to Acting Attorney General Rosen and Acting Deputy Attorney General Donoghue, as described above.[210]

Donoghue quickly responded to Clark's email, stating "there is no chance that I would sign this letter or anything remotely like this."[211] The plan set forth by Clark was "not even within the realm of possibility."[212] Donoghue warned that if they sent Clark's letter, it "would be a grave step for the Department to take and it could have tremendous Constitutional, political and social ramifications for the country."[213] Contrary to President Trump's and Clark's wild claims about the election, Donoghue stressed that DOJ's ongoing investigations related to matters of such a "small scale that they simply would not impact the outcome of the Presidential Election."[214] Clark's assertion to the contrary was baseless.

Donoghue and Rosen reaffirmed their strong opposition to the draft letter in a "contentious" meeting with Clark on December 28th.[215] "What you are doing is nothing less than the United States Justice Department meddling in the outcome of a presidential election," Donoghue admonished Clark, to which Clark indignantly responded, "I think a lot of people have meddled in this election."[216]

Under questioning by Rosen and Donoghue, Clark eventually also revealed that he had been in a meeting in the Oval Office with President Trump. Donoghue demanded to know, "Why the hell are we hearing your name from the President of the United States and a Congressman?"[217] When Clark was reminded that meeting the President without authorization or informing his superiors was a clear violation of the White House contacts policy, he retorted, "It's a policy, there's a lot more at stake here than a policy."[218] In fact, the contacts policy was designed for situations just like this where political figures might try to influence criminal investigations or legal actions taken by the Department of Justice, as President Trump attempting to do.[219]

In the days that followed, Clark called witnesses, got a briefing from ODNI and pursued his own investigations. Acting Deputy Attorney General Donoghue was "shocked" to learn that Clark did not cease his efforts even after learning there was "no foreign interference."[220] Instead of adhering to the facts, Clark "doubled down." During a follow-up meeting on January 2nd, Clark acknowledged he had received the ODNI briefing, and he acknowledged that there was nothing in the briefing that would have supported his earlier suspicion about foreign involvement, but he nevertheless "spewed out some of these theories, some of which we'd heard from the President, but others which were floating around the internet and media, and just kept insisting that the Department needed to act and needed to send those letters."[221]

## 4.10  DECEMBER 29TH MEETING

The next day, Rosen, Donoghue, and Engel had a meeting with Mark Meadows, Pat Cipollone, and Cipollone's deputy, Pat Philbin, in the White House Chief of Staff's office.[222] While the meeting dealt primarily with the Presidential transition, the group discussed a draft civil complaint modeled after *Texas v. Pennsylvania* that the President wanted the Department of Justice to file challenging the results of the Presidential election, tentatively called *United States v. Pennsylvania*.[223] The DOJ officials said that they had not had time to thoroughly review the proposed suit, but initially indicated that it appeared to be flawed and did not seem "viable" for DOJ to file.[224] Meadows suggested that the DOJ leadership meet with William Olson and Kurt Olsen, the two attorneys affiliated with the Trump Campaign that had been working on the proposed suit, and added that Eastman and a retired judge from North Carolina named Mark Martin both had views about the lawsuit.[225]

In this meeting, Meadows also raised a new and outrageous allegation of election fraud: that an Italian company had been involved in changing votes in the Presidential election.[226] According to Meadows, there was a man, whom Donoghue later learned was in an Italian prison, who claimed to have information supporting the allegation and that CIA officers stationed in Rome were either aware of the plot to interfere in the election or had participated in it.[227] Donoghue described how it was apparent that Meadows was not clear on the specifics of the allegation but passed them along to DOJ to investigate, nonetheless.[228] Following the meeting Donoghue provided the information to the FBI, which quickly determined that the allegations were not credible.[229] Meadows and other senior officials in the Trump administration, however, pressed DOJ to investigate every allegation of fraud regardless of how absurd or specious.

In the days after the December 29th meeting with Meadows, the senior DOJ officials more closely examined the proposed *United States v. Pennsylvania* lawsuit and determined that DOJ could not file it.[230] Engel was principally tasked with examining the veracity of the suit and summarized his analysis in a series of talking points that he provided to Donoghue on December 31st.[231] Engel concluded that for multiple reasons, the proposed lawsuit lacked merit. First, the U.S. Government did not have standing to challenge how a State administered its election.[232] Such a challenge could only be brought by President Trump as a candidate and his campaign, or, possibly, an aggrieved electoral college elector.[233] Second, there was no identified precedent in the history of the Supreme Court establishing that such a lawsuit could be filed by the U.S. Government.[234] Third, by late December, States had already certified the results of their elections and the electoral college had met, so suing States by this point would not impact the results of the election.[235] Finally, unlike *Texas* v. *Pennsylvania*, which was one State suing another State, this lawsuit would not automatically be heard by the Supreme Court, so it should have been filed in a Federal district court months prior—if at all—to have any possibility of impacting the outcome of the election.[236]

When asked about it during his interview with the Select Committee, Engel described *United States* v. *Pennsylvania* as "a meritless lawsuit" and said, "there was never a question" about whether "the Department was going to file" it.[237] As senior DOJ officials had already explained to President Trump multiple times in November and December 2020, the Department of Justice was strictly limited in what election-related actions it could

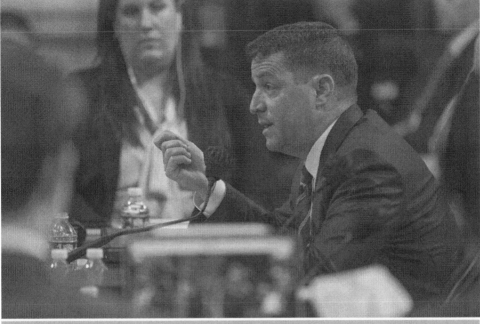
Steven Engel testifies before the Select Committee on June 23, 2022.
(Photo by House Creative Services)

take. It could not oversee States' actions in administering their elections, and it could not support litigation filed by President Trump's campaign.[238] Nonetheless, President Trump continued to push DOJ to file this lawsuit over the following days and essentially act as an arm of his political campaign.

### 4.11 ROSEN'S DECEMBER 30TH CALL WITH PRESIDENT TRUMP

Even after the December 29th meeting, President Trump and those working on his behalf still wanted DOJ leadership to file *United States* v. *Pennsylvania*. On December 30th, Acting Attorney General Rosen had a phone call with President Trump that included a discussion about the lawsuit.[239] During the call, Rosen clearly explained to the President that DOJ could not file the lawsuit.[240] Rosen said, "This doesn't work. There's multiple problems with it. And the Department of Justice is not going to be able to do it." [241] According to Rosen, President Trump accepted what he said without argument.[242] Yet President Trump and his allies continued pressuring the Department to file the lawsuit.

On December 31st, 2020, President Trump suddenly returned to Washington, DC, from Florida, where he had been celebrating Christmas. Shortly after Air Force One landed, Rosen and Donoghue were summoned to the Oval Office once again. They met with the President that afternoon. President Trump "was a little more agitated than he had been in the meeting on the 15th," according to Donoghue.[243] The President remained "adamant that the election has been stolen, that he won, that the American people were being harmed by fraud, and that he believed the Justice Department should be doing something about it."[244]

The President once again raised the prospect of naming Clark the Acting Attorney General.[245] Donoghue and Rosen repeated what they had told the President previously—that he "should have the leaders that" he wanted, "but it's really not going to change anything."[246]

President Trump again asked why DOJ would not file a complaint with the Supreme Court, alleging that the election was fraudulent. Rosen and Donoghue explained, once more, that the DOJ did not have standing.[247] DOJ represents the Federal government, not the American people. President Trump was incredulous and became "very animated."[248] The President kept repeating the same questions, "How is that possible? How can that possibly be?"[249]

President Trump also floated the prospect of naming a special counsel, suggesting Ken Cuccinelli from the Department of Homeland Security as a possible candidate.[250] "This sounds like the kind of thing that would warrant appointment of a special counsel," Donoghue recalled the President saying.[251] The President did not order the DOJ to name a special counsel, but he was clearly still thinking about it. Donoghue and Rosen "didn't say a lot" in response, but simply pointed out that there was no evidence to support the many individual allegations that had been made, so there was "no evidence that would warrant appointing a special counsel."[252]

President Trump again raised the Antrim County, Michigan allegations.[253] As mentioned above, bipartisan election officials in Antrim County completed a hand recount of all ballots on December 17th.[254] This should have resolved the matter once and for all. There was simply no evidence that Dominion's machines had manipulated the result. But President Trump would not accept this reality.

During the December 31st meeting, the President also raised the prospect of seizing the voting machines. "Why don't you guys seize machines?" he asked.[255] "You guys should seize machines because there will be evidence," Donoghue recalled President Trump saying.[256] Rosen pushed back, saying the DOJ had no basis to seize voting machines from the States. They needed a search warrant, but there was no evidence to justify one.[257] Rosen explained to President Trump again that the DOJ has no responsibility for oversight, as the States conduct the elections. Rosen added that to the extent that any Federal agency is involved, it is the Department of Homeland Security, which ensures "software selection and quality control."[258] At that point, the President called Ken Cuccinelli.[259] Donoghue recalled the President saying something along the lines of, "Ken, the Acting Attorney General is telling me it's your job to seize machines."[260] Rosen had said nothing of the sort, but Cuccinelli quickly shot down the President's line of inquiry, making it clear that the Department of Homeland Security had no such authority.[261] White House Counsel Pat Cipollone was also in attendance and supported the DOJ leadership throughout the meeting.[262]

When Rosen spoke to Clark by phone on December 31st or January 1st, Clark revealed that he had spoken to the President again, despite previously promising Rosen and Donoghue that he would inform them of any other contact that he received from the White House.[263] Clark told Rosen that President Trump had offered Clark the position of Acting Attorney General and asked him to respond by Monday, January 4th. Clark, however, said that he needed to do some "due diligence" related to claims of election fraud before deciding whether he would accept the President's offer.[264]

### 4.13   JANUARY 2, 2021: ROSEN AND DONOGHUE CONFRONT CLARK AGAIN

On Saturday, January 2nd, Rosen and Donoghue attempted, once again, to persuade Clark to stand down. The two reiterated that Clark should stop meeting with the President.[265] Donoghue reprimanded Clark, emphasizing that he was the boss and that Clark's ongoing contacts with the President were a violation of DOJ's White House contact policy.[266] Clark acknowledged that he had been briefed by the ODNI, as he had requested, and "that there was nothing in that briefing that would have supported his earlier suspicion about foreign involvement."[267] Nevertheless, Clark still wanted to send his letter to Georgia and other contested States alleging voter fraud.[268]

During the conversation, Clark confirmed President Trump had offered him the position of Acting Attorney General.[269] Clark told Rosen that he would decline the offer—if Rosen and Donoghue signed his dishonest letter to officials in Georgia.[270] The two refused once again, making it clear "that there was no way we were going to sign that letter."[271] Rosen reiterated his decision in an email on the night of January 2nd, writing: "I confirmed again today that I am not prepared to sign such a letter."[272]

That same day, President Trump attempted to coerce Georgia Secretary of State Brad Raffensperger into manufacturing enough votes to steal the election in that State. That call is discussed in Chapter 2 of this report. But one part of it deserves mention here. During that same call, President Trump brought up BJay Pak, whom President Trump had appointed as the U.S. Attorney for the Northern District of Georgia. President Trump referred to Pak as "your never-Trumper U.S. attorney there." [273] The implication was that Pak was not doing enough to validate President Trump's fictitious claims of voter fraud. President Trump's mention of Pak proved to be ominous.

### 4.14   JANUARY 3, 2021: CLARK INFORMS DOJ LEADERSHIP THAT HE WILL ACCEPT PRESIDENT TRUMP'S OFFER

On January 3rd, Clark informed Rosen that he had decided to accept the President's offer to serve as the Acting Attorney General. Clark offered Rosen the position of his deputy.[274] Rosen thought that Clark's offer was "preposterous" and "nonsensical." [275] Rosen told the Select Committee that "there was no universe where I was going to do that to stay on and support someone else doing things that were not consistent with what I thought should be done." [276] Donoghue believed it was a done deal, and Clark would become the head of DOJ. But Pat Cipollone told Rosen that it was "not a done deal and that we should fight this out at the White House." [277]

White House call logs from January 3rd show that President Trump and Clark spoke four times that day starting at 6:59 a.m.[278] The first three calls of the day, two in the morning and one in the early afternoon, show that the President spoke with "Mr. Jeffrey Clark." [279] The final call between the two of them, from 4:19 to 4:22 p.m., however, shows that President Trump spoke to "Acting Attorney General Jeffrey Clark," suggesting that Clark had, in fact, accepted the President's offer.[280]

Acting Attorney General Rosen told the Select Committee that he would have felt comfortable being replaced by either Donoghue or Engel, but he did not "want for the Department of Justice to be put in a posture where it would be doing things that were not consistent with the truth, were not consistent with its own appropriate role, or were not consistent with the Constitution." [281]

As a result, Rosen took four immediate steps to try and prevent Clark's ascension to Attorney General. First, he called Meadows and asked him to set up a meeting for that evening with President Trump.[282] Second, he

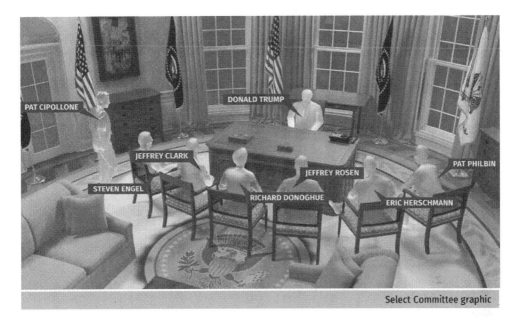

Select Committee graphic

spoke to Cipollone, who told Rosen that Clark's appointment was not inevitable and that he would also be at the meeting that evening to support Rosen and Donoghue.[283] Third, Rosen called Engel and asked him to come to DOJ headquarters so he could attend the White House meeting.[284] Finally, Rosen asked Donoghue and another senior Department attorney named Patrick Hovakimian to convene a meeting of the rest of the Department's leadership to describe the situation to them and hear how they would react to Clark's appointment.[285]

Hovakimian set up a conference call. Although some of the Assistant Attorneys General were not able to participate in the call, all of those who did agreed that they would resign if Rosen were removed from office.[286] Pat Hovakimian drafted a resignation letter that read:

> This evening, after Acting Attorney General Jeff Rosen over the course of the last week repeatedly refused the President's direct instructions to utilize the Department of Justice's law enforcement powers for improper ends, the President removed Jeff from the Department. PADAG Rich Donoghue and I resign from the Department, effectively immediately.[287]

Hovakimian never sent the letter because the threat of mass resignations dissuaded President Trump from replacing Rosen. Regardless, the letter stated a plain truth: President Trump was trying to use DOJ for his own "improper ends."

## THE JANUARY 3, 2021, OVAL OFFICE MEETING

At Rosen's request, White House Chief of Staff Mark Meadows arranged a meeting with the President at 6:15 p.m. that evening.[288]

We should pause to reflect on the timing and purpose of the meeting. Congress was set to meet in a joint session in less than 72 hours. The States had already certified their electors. Former Vice President Biden was going to be certified as the winner of the 2020 Presidential election. There was no material dispute over Biden's victory. Trump and his lawyers had not produced any evidence of significant fraud. Instead, they presented one nonsensical conspiracy theory after another. The DOJ and FBI were forced to debunk these claims—and they did.

None of this stopped President Trump's effort to subvert DOJ. Quite the opposite. The President pushed forward with a plan to install Jeff Clark as the Acting Attorney General, apparently to attempt to interfere with the certification of the electoral college vote on January 6th. It is for this reason Rosen requested an emergency meeting on January 3rd.

Before heading into the Oval Office, Rosen and Donoghue discussed the possible leadership change with Cipollone and Pat Philbin. "They were completely opposed to it," Donoghue explained.[289] In fact, no one who attended the Oval Office meeting supported the leadership change—other than Jeff Clark.[290] Donoghue didn't initially join the meeting, but the President soon called him in.[291]

During the meeting, Clark attempted to defend the last-minute move to make him Acting Attorney General. Clark said he would "conduct real investigations that would, in his view, uncover widespread fraud."[292] Clark declared that this was the "last opportunity to sort of set things straight with this defective election," and he had the "intelligence," the "will," and "desire" to "pursue these matters in the way that the President thought most appropriate."[293] Everyone else quickly disagreed.[294]

President Trump asked Donoghue and Engel what they would do, and both confirmed they would resign.[295] Donoghue added that theirs would not be the only resignations. "You should understand that your entire Department leadership will resign," Donoghue recalled saying.[296] This included every Assistant Attorney General. "Mr. President, these aren't bureaucratic leftovers from another administration," Donoghue continued.[297] "You picked them. This is your leadership team. You sent every one of them to the Senate; you got them confirmed."[298] Donoghue argued that the President would look bad in the wake of the mass resignations. "What is that going to say about you, when we all walk out at the same time?"[299] Donoghue recalled asking the President. "And what happens if, within 48 hours, we have hundreds of resignations from your Justice Department because of your actions? What does that say about your leadership?"[300] Steve Engel reinforced Donoghue's point, saying that Clark would be leading a "graveyard."[301]

White House Counsel Pat Cipollone threatened to resign as well, describing Clark's letter as a "murder-suicide pact."[302] Cipollone warned that the letter would "damage everyone who touches it" and no one should have anything to do with it.[303]

Some of the participants in the meeting argued that Clark was the wrong person for the job of Attorney General. Clark attempted to defend his credentials, arguing that he had been involved in complicated civil and environmental litigation.[304] "That's right. You're an environmental lawyer," Donoghue fired back.[305] "How about you go back to your office, and we'll call you when there's an oil spill."[306]

The meeting lasted approximately 3 hours.[307] Only toward the end of the contentious affair did President Trump decide to reverse his earlier decision to make Clark the Acting Assistant Attorney General. Donoghue recalled President Trump addressing Clark along the following lines:

> I appreciate your willingness to do it. I appreciate you being willing to suffer the abuse. But the reality is, you're not going to get anything done. These guys are going to quit. Everyone else is going to resign. It's going to be a disaster. The bureaucracy will eat you alive. And no matter how you want to get things done in the next few weeks, you won't be able to get it done, and it's not going to be worth the breakage.[308]

Clark tried to change President Trump's mind, saying "history is calling, this our opportunity" and "we can get this done."[309] But the President was clearly rattled by the threat of mass defections and reiterated that the change would not happen. President Trump then wondered what would happen to Clark, and if Donoghue was going to fire him. Donoghue explained that only the President had that authority. That was the end of the matter. "And we all got up and walked out of the Oval Office," Donoghue recalled.[310]

But for one DOJ employee, the matter was not entirely settled. During the January 3rd meeting in the Oval Office, President Trump complained bitterly about BJay Pak, the U.S. Attorney for the Northern District of Georgia.[311] Barr had tasked Pak with investigating the State Farm Arena video in early December 2020. Like the FBI and Georgia State officials, Pak concluded that nothing nefarious had occurred. President Trump was dissatisfied.[312]

"No wonder nothing's been found in Atlanta, because the U.S. attorney there is a Never Trumper," Donoghue recalled the President saying.[313]

Donoghue objected, saying Pak had "been doing his job."[314] But the President insisted, pointing out that Pak criticized him years earlier. "This guy is a Never Trumper," the President reiterated.[315] "He should never have been in my administration to begin with. How did this guy end up in my administration?"[316] The President threatened to fire Pak.[317] When Donoghue pointed out that Pak was already planning to resign the next day, a Monday, President Trump insisted that it be Pak's last day on the job.[318] Pak later confirmed to Donoghue that he would be leaving the next day.[319]

President Trump asked if those in attendance at the Oval Office meeting knew Bobby Christine, who was the U.S. Attorney for the Southern District of Georgia.[320] Even though Pak had a first assistant, who was next in line for Pak's job upon his resignation, President Trump wanted Christine to take the role.[321] Christine did take over for Pak, but he did not find any evidence of fraud either. It was Donoghue's impression that Christine "concluded that the election matters...were handled appropriately."[322]

Later in the evening of January 3rd, President Trump called Donoghue to pass along yet another conspiracy theory.[323] The President had heard that an ICE agent outside of Atlanta was in custody of a truck filled with shredded ballots.[324] Donoghue explained that ICE agents are part of the Department of Homeland Security, so the matter would be under that Department's purview. President Trump asked Donoghue to inform Ken Cuccinelli.[325] That story—like all the others—turned out to be fiction when DOJ investigators evaluated the claim. The truck *was* carrying shredded ballots, but they were from a *previous* election. The old ballots had been shredded to make room for storing ballots from the 2020 election.[326]

### 4.15  PRESIDENT TRUMP'S UNPRECEDENTED ATTEMPT TO SUBVERT THE DOJ

The most senior DOJ officials at the end of President Trump's term stopped him from co-opting America's leading law enforcement agency for his own corrupt purposes. Recall that Attorney General Barr commented "you can't live in a world where the incumbent administration stays in power based on its view, unsupported by specific evidence, that the election—that there was fraud in the election.[327]

Richard Donoghue concluded that Jeffrey Clark's letter "may very well have spiraled us into a constitutional crisis."[328]

Jeffrey Rosen summed up his short time as the Acting Attorney General like this:

[D]uring my tenure, we appointed no special prosecutors, we sent no letters to States or State legislators disputing the election outcome; we made no public statements saying the election was corrupt and should be overturned; we initiated no Supreme Court actions, nor filed or joined any other lawsuits calling into question the legitimacy of our election and institutions.[329]

President Trump attempted to get DOJ to do each of those things.

# 5

# "A COUP IN SEARCH OF A LEGAL THEORY"

On the morning of January 6, 2021, Vice President Michael R. Pence gathered his staff to pray. Vice President Pence and his closest advisors knew the day ahead "would be a challenging one."[1] They asked God for "guidance and wisdom" in the hours to come.[2] No Republican had been more loyal to President Donald J. Trump throughout his turbulent presidency than Vice President Pence. The Vice President rarely, if ever, criticized his boss. But as January 6th approached, President Trump turned on his own Vice President.

President Trump was desperate. As described in the previous chapters, the President was searching for a way to stay in power. He had lost the election to former Vice President Biden. He had run out of legal options to overturn the election weeks earlier, when his lawyers lost nearly every court challenge they filed.

The President pursued other means as well. President Trump and his lawyers tried to convince State and local officials to overturn the election, but they met resistance. Those same officials would not break the law or violate their oath to the Constitution. President Trump and his associates tried to convince State legislatures to replace the legitimate electors won by former Vice President Biden with Trump electors. The Trump Campaign even convened their own fake electors who submitted false electoral votes to Washington. But those efforts failed, too.

President Trump also attempted to use the Department of Justice (DOJ) for his own corrupt political purposes. President Trump offered the job of Acting Attorney General to a loyalist. He wanted this same DOJ official, Jeffrey Clark, to send a letter to several States suggesting that they should certify the fake electors convened by the Trump Campaign. President Trump's effort to subvert the DOJ came to a head on January 3rd, when the Department's senior personnel and lawyers in the White House Counsel's Office threatened mass resignations if Clark was installed.

At that point, theories about a role the Vice President could play at the joint session had been circulating in certain corners of the internet and among Trump-supporting attorneys.[3] President Trump focused his attention on the man who had loyally served by his side for four years.

On January 4, 2021, President Trump summoned Vice President Pence to a meeting in the Oval Office with John Eastman, a law professor representing President Trump in litigation challenging the election result. Eastman argued, on President Trump's behalf, that the Vice President could take matters into his own hands during the joint session on January 6th. Eastman offered Vice President Pence two options. First, the Vice President could unilaterally reject the certified electors from several States won by former Vice President Biden, thereby handing the presidency to President Trump. Or, according to Eastman, Vice President Pence could delay the joint session to give State legislatures the opportunity to certify new electors loyal to the President. Eastman admitted, in front of the president, that both options violated the Electoral Count Act of 1887, the statute that sets forth the process for counting and disputing electoral votes during the joint session.[4] Eastman admitted as much in a subsequent conversation with the Vice President's staff as well.[5]

Therefore, President Trump knew, or should have known, that this scheme was illegal—in fact, it violated the Electoral Count Act and the U.S. Constitution. President Trump repeatedly demanded that Vice President Pence go through with it anyway.

Vice President Pence rejected President Trump's demands "many times" on January 4th and in the days that followed.[6] Vice President Pence correctly pointed out that he had no power to take any action other than counting the certified electoral votes. America's founders could not possibly have contemplated a scenario in which the Vice President could unilaterally reject electoral votes and decide the outcome of a Presidential election. However, instead of backing down, President Trump ratcheted up the pressure even further, relentlessly harassing Vice President Pence both in public and in private.

President Trump used his bully pulpit, at rallies and on Twitter, to lie to his supporters. President Trump told them that Vice President Pence had the power to deliver another 4 years in the White House. It was not true. President Trump's campaign of coercion became so intense that Marc Short, Vice President Pence's Chief of Staff, alerted the head of the Vice President's Secret Service detail to the impending danger. On January 5th, Short warned that as the "disagreements" between President Trump and Vice President Pence "became more public, that the president would lash out in some way."[7]

Indeed, President Trump did. And those around him recognized that his lashing out at the Vice President could have disastrous consequences. On the morning of January 6th, an agent in the Secret Service's intelligence division was alerted to online chatter "regarding the VP being a dead man walking if he doesn't do the right thing."[8] A few minutes later, another agent made a comment that turned out to be an ominous prediction: "I saw several other alerts saying they will storm the [C]apitol if he [the Vice President] doesn't do the right thing etc."[9]

During his speech at the Ellipse on January 6th, President Trump repeatedly pointed his finger at Vice President Pence. President Trump insisted that "if Mike Pence does the right thing, we win the election."[10] President Trump added: "And Mike Pence is going to have to come through for us, and if he doesn't, that will be a, a sad day for our country because you're sworn to uphold our Constitution."[11]

President Trump's scheme required Vice President Pence to *break* his oath to the Constitution, not uphold it. By the time President Trump spoke at the Ellipse, he also knew that Vice President Pence had no intention of overturning the election.

President Trump then sent a mob to the U.S. Capitol. He did so even after being informed by the Secret Service that people in the crowd possessed weapons. He wanted his supporters to intimidate Vice President Pence and any other Republican who refused his demands. The President told the crowd assembled before him to march down Pennsylvania Avenue, to "our Republicans, the weak ones" at the U.S. Capitol, "to try and give them the kind of pride and boldness that they need to take back our country."[12]

The mob overran the U.S. Capitol in short order. At 2:24 p.m., while the attack was well underway, President Trump tweeted:

> *Mike Pence didn't have the courage to do what should have been done to protect our Country and our Constitution, giving States a chance to certify a corrected set of facts, not the fraudulent or inaccurate ones which they were asked to previously certify. USA demands the truth!*[13]

Again, the opposite was true. Vice President Pence showed courage on January 6th. The Vice President refused to be intimidated by President Trump's mob, even as chants of "Hang Mike Pence!" echoed throughout the halls of the U.S. Capitol and a makeshift gallows was constructed on the Capitol grounds.[14]

It is no mystery why the mob turned on Vice President Pence. President Trump told his supporters that the election was stolen, and that Vice President Pence had the power, but lacked the courage, to fix it. None of this was true.

President Trump and Vice President Pence have both reflected on the events of January 6th in the months since then. Vice President Pence has described President Trump's demands as "un-American."[15] President Trump has since insisted that Vice President Pence "could have overturned the Election!"[16] Asked about the calls to hang the Vice President, President Trump said it was "common sense."[17]

In early 2022, U.S. District Judge David Carter evaluated the Trump-Eastman scheme to pressure the Vice President. Judge Carter described it as "a campaign to overturn a democratic election, an action unprecedented in American history."[18] It was "a coup in search of a legal theory," Judge Carter found, that likely violated at least two Federal laws.[19] The Trump-Eastman scheme was not a feature of the U.S. Constitution, as President Trump told his supporters. Instead, it "would have permanently ended the peaceful transition of power, undermining American democracy and the Constitution."[20]

And it all began because President Trump refused to accept the result of the election, expressed through the votes of 81 million Americans.

## 5.1 PRESIDENT TRUMP AND HIS ALLIES EMBARK ON A DESPERATE GAMBIT TO BLOCK CERTIFICATION OF THE 2020 PRESIDENTIAL ELECTION.

**THE INTELLECTUAL FRAMEWORK FOR THE THEORY THAT THE VICE PRESIDENT COULD CHANGE THE OUTCOME OF THE ELECTION AT THE JOINT SESSION EMERGED FROM DISCUSSIONS AMONG THE LAWYERS WORKING WITH THE TRUMP CAMPAIGN AFTER THE 2020 ELECTION.**

When the electoral college met to cast votes for the certified winner in each State on December 14, 2020, any possibility of President Trump reversing his defeat came to an end. The contest was decided well before then, but December 14th marked what should have been the formal end of the Trump campaign. Former Vice President Biden had won the election and his victory was cemented by the States' electoral votes. Instead of bowing to this reality, some pro-Trump lawyers had already begun scheming ways to deny the inevitable. Over the course of the post-election period, as their other plans each failed, the importance of January 6th and the need to pressure Vice President Pence increased. These same lawyers concluded that the Vice President could help President Trump subvert the election on January 6th, but they would need Vice President Pence to set aside history and the law to do so. They'd need him to violate the Electoral Count Act of 1887 ("the ECA"). The ECA had governed the joint session for 130 years, but it was an inconvenient barrier for President Trump's plan to stay in office.

**KENNETH CHESEBRO ARTICULATED A "PRESIDENT OF THE SENATE" STRATEGY IN EARLY DECEMBER, WHEN THE TRUMP CAMPAIGN WAS CONVENING "ALTERNATE" ELECTORS IN KEY STATES PRESIDENT TRUMP LOST.**

On December 13, 2020, Kenneth Chesebro, a pro-Trump lawyer, sent a memo to Rudolph Giuliani, the President's lead outside counsel, upon request from Trump Campaign official Boris Epshteyn.[21] Chesebro laid out a "'President of the Senate' strategy," arguing that the "President of the Senate" ("he, and he alone") is charged with "making judgments about what to do if there are conflicting votes."[22] Chesebro argued that when the joint session met on January 6th, the President of the Senate should not count Arizona's electoral college votes for former Vice President Biden, "[b]ecause there are two slates of votes."[23] Of course, there were not two legitimate "slates of votes" from Arizona. There were the official electors, certified by the State, and a group of fake electors convened by the Trump campaign.

Chesebro's memo set President Trump's pressure campaign on a course to target the Vice President on January 6.[24] Judge Carter found that the "draft memo pushed a strategy that knowingly violated the Electoral Count Act" and "is both intimately related to and clearly advanced the plan to obstruct the Joint Session of Congress on January 6, 2021."[25] That plan was also advanced by John Eastman.[26]

**ON DECEMBER 23, JOHN EASTMAN DRAFTED THE FIRST OF HIS TWO "JANUARY 6TH SCENARIO" MEMOS, ARTICULATING THE ARGUMENT THAT UNDER THE CONSTITUTION THE VICE PRESIDENT IS THE "ULTIMATE ARBITER."**

On December 23, 2020, Eastman wrote a two-page memo summarizing ways to ensure that "President Trump is re-elected."[27] Eastman suggested that Vice President Pence could refuse to count the electoral college votes from seven States: Arizona, Georgia, Michigan, Nevada, New Mexico, Pennsylvania, and Wisconsin. According to Eastman, Vice President Pence could simply reject these States' electoral college votes. At that point, President Trump would have 232 electoral college votes compared to former Vice President Biden's 222. This was sufficient, in Eastman's view, to guarantee President Trump's victory, because he would have a majority of the electoral college votes. "Pence then gavels President Trump as re-elected," Eastman wrote.

Eastman considered the possibility that Democrats in Congress would object, stating the plain truth that 270 electoral college votes are necessary to win. In that event, according to Eastman, the election could be sent to the House of Representatives.[28] The Republican-majority of delegations in the House would then re-elect Trump as president. Eastman concluded: "The main thing here is that Pence should do this without asking for permission—either from a vote of the joint session or from the Court.... The fact is that the Constitution assigns this power to the Vice President as the ultimate arbiter. We should take all of our actions with that in mind." [29]

From the start, President Trump was looped in on Eastman's proposal. The same day Eastman started preparing the memo, he sent an email to President Trump's assistant Molly Michael, at 1:32 p.m.: "Is the President available for a very quick call today at some point? Just want to update him on our overall strategic thinking." [30] Only five minutes later, Eastman received a call from the White House switchboard; according to his phone records, the conversation lasted for almost 23 minutes. [31]

## EASTMAN CHANGED HIS EVALUATION OF THE 12TH AMENDMENT, AND THE ROLE OF THE VICE PRESIDENT, AFTER PRESIDENT TRUMP LOST THE ELECTION.

In Eastman's theory, which was the foundation of President Trump's January 6th plot, the Vice President of the United States is the "ultimate arbiter" and could unilaterally decide the victor of the 2020 Presidential election. [32] However, just before the 2020 presidential election, Eastman had acknowledged in writing that the Vice President had no such expansive power.

In the course of a lengthy exchange of ideas and emails throughout the pre- and post-election period with an individual named Bruce Colbert, Eastman provided comments on a letter Colbert was drafting to President Trump. [33] The draft letter purported to provide recommendations of "crucial legal actions" for the Trump Campaign to take "to help secure your election victory as President of the United States." [34] One of the draft letter's recommendations was that "the President of the Senate decides authoritatively what 'certificates' from the states to 'open.'" In response, Eastman wrote on October 17, 2020, "I don't agree with this" and continued, "[t]he 12th Amendment only says that the President of the Senate opens the ballots in the joint session and then, in the passive voice, that the votes shall then be counted. 3 USC § 12 says merely that he is the presiding officer, and then it spells out specific procedures, presumptions, and default rules for which slates will be counted. *Nowhere does it suggest that the President of the Senate gets to make the determination on his own.* §15 doesn't, either." [35]

By the first week of December, Eastman's correspondence with this same individual illustrates that he was open to advocating for the very point he had rejected before the election—that is, that "the 12th Amendment confers dispositive authority on the President of the Senate to decide which slate to count." [36] And on December 5, 2020, Eastman wrote to Colbert, "I have spoken directly with folks at the top of the chain of command on this. They are now aware of the issues." [37]

The emails also signaled another idea that Eastman would continue to repeat in the coming weeks: that the Vice President could act without getting permission from a court. Specifically, he argued that they could take the position that the Vice President's authority was a "non-justiciable political question"—in other words, that Vice President Pence could just act, and no court would have jurisdiction to rule on the issue.[38] As Eastman's emails later in the month make clear, he thought there was an important reason to keep this issue out of the courts—they would rule that the theory was unlawful.

### EASTMAN'S "JANUARY 6 SCENARIO" CLEARLY REQUIRED THE VICE PRESIDENT TO VIOLATE THE ELECTORAL COUNT ACT, THE FEDERAL LAW GOVERNING THE CERTIFICATION OF PRESIDENTIAL ELECTIONS.

There are other parts of Eastman's two-page December 23rd memo worthy of attention. Eastman wrote that Vice President Pence could recuse himself from presiding over the joint session of Congress on January 6th. In that event, the session would be overseen by the Senate President *Pro Tempore*, Senator Charles Grassley. Eastman was clearly arguing that Vice President Pence (or Senator Grassley) *should violate the Electoral Count Act.* "When he gets to Arizona, he announces that he has multiple slates of electors, and so is going to defer decision on that until finishing the other States," Eastman wrote.[39] "This would be the first break with the procedure set out in the Act."[40] This "break" with "procedure" that Eastman's memo was openly advocating for was in other words the Vice President breaking the law. When Chesebro read Eastman's memo, he commented favorably, declaring it "[r]eally awesome."[41]

At this point, Eastman continued, Congress would likely follow the "process" set forth in the Electoral Count Act, and "the two houses [would] break into their separate chambers" for debate.[42] But Eastman advised "we should not allow the Electoral Count Act constraint on debate to control" and the Trump team "should demand normal rules (which includes the filibuster)."[43] Eastman thought this would create a "stalemate," giving "the state legislatures more time to weigh in to formally support the alternate slate of electors, if they had not already done so."[44] As discussed previously in this report, at the time he drafted this memo—and throughout the post-election period—Eastman, Giuliani, President Trump and others were simultaneously working to replace certified electors for former Vice President Biden in certain States. Eastman, Giuliani, and President Trump all pressured State legislators to name their own separate electors or to certify the campaign's fake electors.

**EASTMAN'S THEORY WAS—IN THE WORDS OF PRESIDENT TRUMP'S SENIOR WHITE HOUSE AND CAMPAIGN OFFICIALS—"INSANE," "CRAZY," "NUTTY" AND IT WOULD NEVER PRACTICALLY WORK.**

Eric Herschmann, an attorney working for President Trump in the White House, met with Eastman to discuss his memo. Herschmann thought Eastman's plan was "crazy." Herschmann summarized the conversation to the Select Committee:

> And I said to him, hold on a second, I want to understand what you're saying. You're saying you believe the Vice President, acting as President of the Senate, can be the sole decisionmaker as to, under your theory, who becomes the next President of the United States? And he said, yes. And I said, are you out of your F'ing mind, right? And that was pretty blunt. I said, you're completely crazy. You're going to turn around and tell 78 plus million people in this country that your theory is, this is how you're going to invalidate their votes because you think the election was stolen? I said, they're not going to tolerate that. I said, you're going to cause riots in the streets. And he said words to the effect of there's been violence in this history of our country to protect the democracy or to protect the [R]epublic.[45]

As recounted by Herschmann, Eastman was shockingly unconcerned with the prospect of violence should Vice President Pence follow his and President Trump's recommended course.

Herschmann asked a straightforward question—if the States wanted to recertify their electors, then why weren't they doing it themselves? "Why aren't they already coming into session and saying, we want to change the [S]tates, and why do you need the VP to go down this path[?]"[46] Eastman had no response. In addition to being "crazy," Herschmann "didn't think there was any chance in the world" that Eastman's plan "could work."[47]

Herschmann pressed Eastman further, asking if he had "any precedent at all for the VP or anyone acting in the capacity as the President of the Senate declaring some statute invalid."[48] Eastman replied "no," but argued that "these are unprecedented times."[49] Herschmann was unimpressed, calling this a "ridiculous" answer.[50]

White House Counsel Pasquale Anthony "Pat" Cipollone thought the Eastman plan was "nutty."[51] Trump Campaign official Jason Miller testified that the Campaign's General Counsel, Matt Morgan, and Deputy Campaign Manager, Justin Clark, thought Eastman was "crazy," understood that there was "no validity to [his theory] in any way, shape, or form," and shared their views with "anyone who would listen."[52]

## THE VICE PRESIDENT'S CONCLUSION THAT HE DID NOT HAVE THE ABILITY TO AFFECT THE OUTCOME OF THE ELECTION

Vice President Pence's counsel, Greg Jacob, was simultaneously researching the role of the Vice President during the joint session. The Office of the Vice President produced a preliminary staff memo on the subject on October 26, 2020.[53] Jacob then discussed the matter with Marc Short on election day or the day before.

This wasn't the first time Jacob would be required to write a memo about the Vice President's role in the electoral process. Before the election, Short explained to him that some in the White House were encouraging President Trump to prematurely declare victory on election night.[54] Of course, that is exactly what President Trump did. Jacob and Short wanted to avoid the Vice President getting drawn in to any such declarations, and Jacob pointed to his role in presiding over the counting of the electoral votes on January 6th as a reason not to. Jacob sent a memo to Short on election day reflecting this advice.[55]

Then, on December 7, 2020, the Lincoln Project aired a provocative ad taunting President Trump, saying that Vice President Pence "Will Put the Nail in Your Political Coffin" during the joint session on January 6th.[56] This prompted a discussion between Jacob and Vice President Pence.[57] Jacob authored another memo, dated December 8, 2020.[58] Jacob continued researching the Vice President's role during the joint session into early January. Jacob told the Select Committee that his view of the matter was not fully formed until then.[59]

Jacob did extensive research on and historical analysis of both the Electoral Count Act of 1887 and the 12th Amendment to the U.S. Constitution.[60] The 12th Amendment contains a single relevant line: "The President of the Senate shall, in the Presence of the Senate and House of Representatives, open all the Certificates, and the Votes shall then be counted."[61] Though Jacob concluded that this line was "inartfully drafted," it said nothing about resolving disputes over electoral votes.[62]

Jacob concluded that the Vice President must adhere to the Electoral Count Act.[63] The ECA has been followed for 130 years and "every single time that there has been any objection to electors, it has been resolved in accordance with the Electoral Count Act procedures," Jacob testified.[64] After reviewing the history and relevant cases, Jacob found that "[t]here is no justifiable basis to conclude that the Vice President has that kind of authority" to affect the outcome of the presidential election.[65] Jacob stated that his "review of text, history, and, frankly, just common sense" all confirmed that the Vice President had no such power.[66]

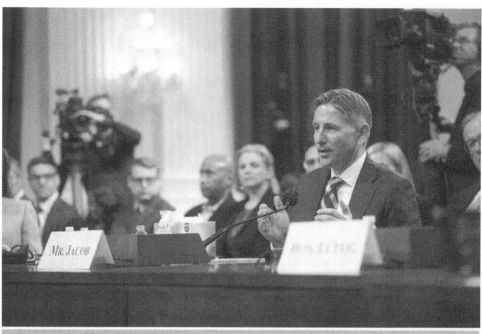

Greg Jacob testifies before the Select Committee on June 16, 2022.

Photo by House Creative Services

**PRESIDENT TRUMP'S ALLIES FILED LAWSUITS SEEKING A COURT ORDER DIRECTING VICE PRESIDENT PENCE NOT TO COUNT CERTAIN ELECTORAL VOTES.**

One of President Trump's congressional allies, Representative Louie Gohmert (R–TX), pushed a version of Eastman's theory in the courts. On December 27, 2020, Representative Gohmert and several of the Trump Campaign's fake electors for the State of Arizona (including Republican Party Chair Kelli Ward) filed suit against Vice President Pence in the U.S. District Court for the Eastern District of Texas.[67] As Ward explained to Marc Short in a phone call the day the suit was filed, President Trump was aware of the lawsuit and had signed off on it: "We wouldn't have done that without the president telling us it was okay," she told him.[68]

In the suit, the Plaintiffs alleged that there were "competing slates" of electors from five States.[69] They asked the court to rule that portions of the Electoral Count Act of 1887 were unconstitutional and that "the Twelfth Amendment contains the exclusive dispute resolution mechanisms" for determining an objection raised by a Member of Congress to the electors submitted by any State.[70] Essentially, Representative Gohmert was asking the court to tell Vice President Pence that he was prohibited from following the procedures set forth in the Electoral Count Act. Much like Eastman's

Representative Louie Gohmert outside the Capitol on March 17, 2021.
(Photo by Chip Somodevilla/Getty Images)

theory, the *Gohmert* plaintiffs asserted that the Vice President has the "exclusive authority and sole discretion" to determine which electoral votes to count.[71]

Although the *Gohmert* suit was premised on the same theory Eastman advocated, Eastman did not agree with the decision to file suit. Eastman argued that filing a suit against the Vice President had "close[ ] to zero" chance of succeeding, and there was a "very high" risk that the court would issue an opinion stating that "Pence has no authority to reject the Biden-certified ballots."[72] As highlighted by Judge Carter, Eastman's theory was that Vice President Pence should take this action "without asking for permission" from Congress or the courts.[73] Another attorney, Bill Olson, stated that getting a judicial determination "that Pence is constrained by [the Electoral Count Act]" could "completely tank the January 6 strategy."[74] Those who were advocating to press on with the Eastman scheme did not want to bring it before a Federal judge because of the high risk that a court's determination that the scheme was illegal would stop the plan to overturn the election dead in its tracks.

Eastman himself pushed this cavalier attitude towards the courts and compliance with the law during a call with Arizona House Speaker Rusty

John McEntee, February 28, 2020.

(Photo by Alex Wong/Getty Images)

Bowers on January 4th. During this call, just two days before the joint session, Eastman pressed Speaker Bowers to bring the Arizona House into session to certify Trump electors or decertify the Biden electors.[75] Speaker Bowers responded as he had previously responded to similar entreaties by Giuliani and President Trump: by explaining that doing so would require him to violate his oaths to the U.S. and Arizona Constitutions and that he "wasn't going to take such an action."[76] Undeterred, Eastman still pushed Speaker Bowers to "just do it and let the courts sort it through."[77]

Ultimately, Representative Gohmert's legal gambit failed; a U.S. district judge dismissed the case quickly.[78] The judge's ruling was upheld by the Supreme Court, which rejected Gohmert's appeal without further consideration.[79]

## OTHER INDIVIDUALS ADVISING PRESIDENT TRUMP AND HIS CAMPAIGN ALSO ADVOCATED FOR A ROLE FOR THE VICE PRESIDENT AT THE JOINT SESSION.

Other individuals inside and outside the White House also advanced versions of the theory that the Vice President had agency in the joint session. The issue of Vice President Pence's role came up during a December meeting in the Oval Office. Either President Trump or his chief of staff, Mark Meadows, tasked John McEntee, the director of the Presidential Personnel Office, with researching the matter further.[80] Though McEntee was one of President Trump's close advisors, he was not a lawyer and had no relevant experience. Yet, he wrote a one-page memo claiming that "the VP has substantial discretion to address issues with the electoral process."[81]

This wasn't the only one-page analysis drafted by McEntee before January 6th.[82] He later proposed a "middle path" in which he envisioned the Vice President accepting *only half* the electoral votes from six disputed States (specifically, Wisconsin, Michigan, Pennsylvania, Georgia, Arizona and Nevada).[83] McEntee portrayed this as a way to avoid "disenfranchis-[ing]" States while still achieving the desired result: delivering a second term to President Trump. McEntee conveyed this memo to the President with a cover note reading, "This is probably our only realistic option because it would give Pence an out."[84] McEntee told the Select Committee that this judgment was based on his assessment that "it was, like, pretty obvious [the Vice President] wasn't going to just reject…the electors or whatever was being asked of him at that time."[85]

Another advocate of a plan for the Vice President to play a role in the joint session was Jenna Ellis, a lawyer working for the Trump Campaign. She argued in two memos that Vice President Pence had the power to delay the counting of certified electoral votes. In the first memo, addressed to President Trump and dated December 31, 2020, Ellis advised that Vice President Pence should "not open any of the votes" from six States that "currently have electoral delegates in dispute."[86] Ellis asserted that this "dispute" provided "sufficient rational and legal basis to question whether the [S]tate law and Constitution was followed." Ellis proposed a delay of ten days, as the Vice President and Congress awaited a "response from the [S]tate legislatures, which would then need to meet in an emergency electoral session." If any of the State legislatures "fails to provide a timely response, no electoral votes can be opened and counted from that [S]tate." Ellis claimed that Vice President Pence would not be "exercising discretion nor establishing new precedent," but instead "simply asking for clarification from the constitutionally appointed authority."[87]

Ellis sent the substance of this memorandum in an email to Fox News host Jeanine Pirro on January 1, 2021, under the subject line "Constitutional

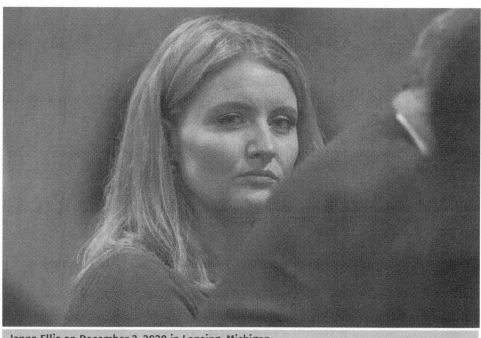

Jenna Ellis on December 2, 2020 in Lansing, Michigan.

(Photo by Rey Del Rio/Getty Images)

option."[88] And, on January 4, 2021, she sent the same substance to Fox News contributor John Solomon under the subject line "Pence option."[89]

Ellis addressed a second memo, dated January 5, 2021, to Jay Sekulow, an outside attorney who represented President Trump during his first impeachment proceedings and in other litigation.[90] Ellis again claimed that Vice President Pence had the power to delay the certification of the vote. Ellis recommended that the Vice President should, when he arrived at the first contested State (Arizona), "simply stop the count" on the basis that the States had not made a "final determination of ascertainment of electors." "The [S]tates would therefore have to act."[91]

Sekulow clearly disagreed. "Some have speculated that the Vice President could simply say, 'I'm not going to accept these electors,' that he has the authority to do that under the Constitution," Sekulow said during an episode of his radio show.[92] "I actually don't think that's what the Constitution has in mind." Sekulow added that the Vice President serves a merely "ministerial, procedural function."[93]

In addition, Herschmann discussed this memo with Sekulow. They agreed that Ellis did not have the "qualifications or the experience to be giving advice on this" or to be "litigating the challenges" that President

Trump's team was filing in court.[94] Herschmann did not think that Sekulow shared the memo with the President.[95]

## 5.2 PRESIDENT TRUMP AND HIS ALLIES EXERT INTENSE PUBLIC AND PRIVATE PRESSURE ON THE VICE PRESIDENT IN ADVANCE OF THE JOINT SESSION OF CONGRESS ON JANUARY 6TH

### JANUARY 2, 2021: THE VICE PRESIDENT MEETS WITH HIS ADVISORS, CEMENTING HIS INTENDED PATH FOR THE JOINT SESSION.

On January 2, 2021, Vice President Pence met with his counsel Greg Jacob, Chief of Staff Marc Short, and Matt Morgan to discuss the joint session.[96] Morgan was the Trump Campaign's General Counsel and had previously served as counsel to Vice President Pence. At this point, the Vice President already had a clear understanding of what his role would be in the electoral count.[97] Vice President Pence was concerned that most people did not understand how the certification of the electoral votes worked. So Jacob began drafting a statement for the Vice President to issue on January 6th. The statement was intended to provide a "civic education" on the joint session, explaining to the American people his actions, including why the Vice President "didn't have the authorities that others had suggested that he might."[98]

The men discussed the various points of pressure being applied to the Vice President, including Eastman's theories, the *Gohmert* suit, Ellis's arguments, as well as how the electoral count process should work. They also discussed allegations of irregularities and maladministration of the election, concluding that none of the allegations raised was sufficient to reverse President Trump's defeat.[99]

While Vice President Pence recognized Congress's authority under the Electoral Count Act to raise objections to the certification, neither he nor his staff were aware of any evidence of fraud that would have had a material effect on the outcome of the election in any State.[100] Because of President Trump's repetition of election fraud allegations, Jacob and the Vice President's staff conducted their own evaluation of these claims. Jacob asked Morgan to send the campaign's best evidence of election "fraud, maladministration, irregularities, [and] abuses in the system."[101] The Vice President's legal staff memorialized the review they conducted of these materials in a memo to Vice President Pence, which concluded: "most allegations of substantive voter fraud—defined to mean the casting of illegal ballots in violation of prevailing election laws—are either relatively small in number, or cannot be verified."[102]

Vice President Pence also discussed the Trump Campaign's fake electors with his advisors. Both Jacob and Morgan assured Vice President Pence that there were not dual slates of electors. The electors organized by the Trump Campaign were not valid.[103] Morgan had already written a memo on the topic in December, concluding that the "alternate" electors—that is, fake—lacked a certificate of ascertainment issued by the State.[104] Without such an ascertainment, the Trump Campaign's fake electors had no standing during the joint session. Jacob had also prepared a "flow chart" memo outlining each of the legal provisions implicated in the joint session on January 6th.[105] Jacob advised Vice President Pence that "none of the slates that had been sent in would qualify as an alternate slate within the meaning of the Electoral Count Act."[106] Vice President Pence was still worried that the fake elector issue was sowing confusion, so he wanted his statement on January 6th to be as transparent as possible.[107]

That same day, January 2nd, Marc Short released a brief statement on behalf of the Vice President. "Vice President Pence shares the concerns of millions of Americans about voter fraud and irregularities in the last election," the statement read. "The vice president welcomes the efforts of members of the House and Senate to use the authority they have under the law to raise objections and bring forward evidence before the Congress and the American people on January 6th."[108] Short testified that the statement was consistent with the Vice President's view that he did not have the power to reject electors.[109] Short issued this statement because of the "swirl" regarding the question of "where [Vice President Pence] stood."[110]

Steve Bannon's podcast, *War Room: Pandemic*, was one of the primary sources of this swirl.

### JANUARY 2, 2021: EASTMAN AND BANNON QUESTION THE "COURAGE AND SPINE" OF VICE PRESIDENT PENCE.

Steve Bannon's podcast, *War Room: Pandemic*, was one of the primary sources of this swirl. Eastman was a guest on a January 2nd episode of Bannon's show. Much of their conversation focused on Vice President Pence, and the belief that he had the power to overturn the election.

"[W]e are entering into one of the most, um, important constitutional crisis [sic] the country's ever had," Bannon said.[111] Bannon complained that Vice President Pence had "spit the bit," meaning he had given up on efforts to keep President Trump in power.[112] Eastman claimed that the election had been "illegally conducted," and so the certified votes now "devolved back to the [S]tate legislature[s], and the only other place where it devolved back to is to Congress and particularly the Vice President, who will sit in presiding over a Joint Session of Congress beginning on January 6 to count the ballots."[113] Eastman claimed that the Vice President (and Congress) had the power to reject the certified electors from several States out-of-hand. "[T]hey've got multiple slates of ballots from seven states," Eastman said. "And they've gotta decide [ ] which is the valid slate to count...I think they have that authority to make that determination on their own."[114]

Bannon claimed the Vice President of the United States is "hardwired in," and an "actual decisionmaker."[115] The Vice President's role is not "ministerial," Bannon declared.[116] Eastman agreed.[117] "Are we to assume that this is going to be a climactic battle that's going to take place this week about the very question of the constitutionality of the Electoral Count Act of 1887?" Bannon asked.[118]

Eastman replied, "I think a lot of that depends on the courage and the spine of the individuals involved." Bannon asked Eastman if he meant Vice President Mike Pence. "Yes," Eastman answered.[119]

**JANUARY 3, 2021: EASTMAN DRAFTS ANOTHER "JANUARY 6 SCENARIO" MEMO "WAR GAMING" THE WAYS THAT VICE PRESIDENT PENCE COULD CHANGE THE OUTCOME OF THE ELECTION.**

The next day, January 3, 2021, Eastman drafted a six-page memo that imagined several scenarios for January 6th, only some of which led to President Trump's victory.[120] In a section titled, "War Gaming the Alternatives," Eastman set forth the ways he thought President Trump could remain in power.[121] Importantly, Eastman concluded that President Trump could remain president if—and only if—Vice President Pence followed Eastman's illegal advice and determined which electoral college ballots were "valid."[122] In another scenario, Eastman imagined that President Trump may somehow win re-election in January 2021 if Vice President Pence remanded the electoral votes to State legislatures, such that they could have ten days to investigate President Trump's baseless claims of fraud. In that case, Eastman allowed that former Vice President Biden may still win, should the State legislatures determine that the evidence was "insufficient to alter the results of the election."[123]

**Eastman Knew that there Were No Valid "Alternate" Slates, But He Nonetheless Predicated His Advice to the Vice President and President on this Claim.** In his six-page memo, consistent with the earlier two-page memo, Eastman states that "the Trump electors" met and transmitted votes, finding that "[t]here are thus dual slates of electors from 7 [S]tates."[124] Even since January 6th, Eastman has continued to affirm and defend his assertion that there were dual slates of electors, writing: "Trump electors from seven [S]tates in which election challenges were still pending met (albeit of their own accord) on the date designated by Congress, cast their votes, and transmitted those votes to Congress."[125]

Eastman used these slates as a premise for his argument that the result of the election was disputed. However, Eastman acknowledged on multiple occasions—both before and after January 6th—that these "dual slates" had no legal significance. In an email sent on December 19, 2020, Eastman wrote that the seven Trump/Pence slates of electors "will be dead on arrival in Congress" "unless those electors get a certification from their State Legislators." [126] Of course, this certification never came and there was no basis for any action on the "dual slates." [127]

Nevertheless, on December 23, 2020, Eastman used the existence of these slates as a justification for the Vice President to act, in an email to Boris Epshteyn, a Trump Campaign lawyer. "The fact that we have multiple slates of electors demonstrates the uncertainty of either. That should be enough." [128]

Again after January 6th, Eastman acknowledged in an email that the fake electors' documents were invalid and irrelevant.[129] "Alas," he said, "[T]hey had no authority" because "[n]o legislature certified them." [130]

Eastman concluded his memo by asserting that his plan was "BOLD, Certainly," but he attempted to justify it, arguing that "this Election was Stolen by a strategic Democrat plan to systematically flout existing election laws for partisan advantage; we're no longer playing by Queensbury Rules, therefore." [131]

Eastman repeated what he wrote in his earlier, shorter memo, claiming that Vice President Pence should act "without asking for permission— either from a vote of the joint session or from the Court." [132] Eastman claimed "that the Constitution assigns this power to the Vice President as the ultimate arbiter." [133] Eastman ended on an especially hyperbolic note. If the election's results were not upended, "then the sovereign people no longer control the direction of their government, and we will have ceased to be a self-governing people. The stakes could not be higher." [134]

*January 4, 2021: President Trump and Eastman Meet with Pence and His Staff in the Oval Office.*

**Eastman Argues in an Oval Office Meeting that the Vice President can Reject Electoral Votes or that He Can Delay the Certification, Sending the Electoral Votes Back to the States.** Late in the afternoon of January 4, 2021, President Trump summoned Vice President Pence to the Oval Office for a showdown.[135] President Trump and Eastman sought to convince the Vice President that he had the power to refuse to count the certified electors from several States won by former Vice President Biden.

Short and Jacob attended with the Vice President.[136] Trump's chief of staff, Mark Meadows, was only briefly present, leaving as the meeting started.[137]

**The White House Counsel is Excluded from the Meeting.** One key lawyer was conspicuously absent: Pat Cipollone, the White House Counsel. Cipollone and his deputy, Pat Philbin, were shooting down a series of "terrible" proposals at the time.[138] Philbin told the Select Committee that he considered resigning every day from approximately November 15 until the end of the administration.[139] Philbin had researched the Vice President's role in the January 6th joint session and concluded that Vice President Pence had no power to affect the outcome.[140] Cipollone agreed and informed Short and Jacob that this was the opinion of White House Counsel's Office.[141]

Mark Meadows invited Cipollone to speak with Eastman prior to the Oval Office meeting.[142] Cipollone told Eastman that his scheme was "not something that is consistent with the appropriate reading of the law." [143] After delivering this assessment directly to Eastman in Meadows' office, Cipollone walked to the Oval Office with the intent to attend the meeting. However, by the time the Vice President and his staff arrived, Cipollone was gone.[144]

Cipollone declined to testify as to what he told President Trump or why he did not attend the Oval Office meeting, but he was clear that he didn't end up attending the meeting because of something that happened after he walked into the Oval Office.[145] Whatever happened, Cipollone maintained, was protected by executive privilege, suggesting that he was asked to leave by the President.[146] What is clear, however, is that Cipollone had already shared his view directly with Meadows and Eastman, i.e., that the proposal President Trump and Eastman were about to advocate to the Vice President was illegal.[147]

**During this Oval Office Meeting, Eastman Admits that Both Paths are Based on the Same Legal Theory and Concedes His Plan Violates the Electoral Count Act.** During the Oval Office meeting, Eastman claimed that there were two legally viable options.[148] First, Vice President Pence could reject outright the certified electors submitted by several States, and second, he could suspend the joint session and send the "disputed" electoral votes back to the States.[149] Eastman advised that the Vice President had the "raw authority to determine objections himself," according to Jacob.[150] However, by the end of the meeting Eastman was emphasizing the second option that he argued would be "more politically palatable" than the "more aggressive" option of the Vice President rejecting electoral votes outright.[151] If Vice President Pence did not want to reject the electors, Eastman claimed, then the Vice President could send the certified electoral votes back to the States for further deliberation.

Eastman later conceded that both actions were based on the same underlying legal theory of the Vice President's power.[152] Eastman also

January 6th Committee Interview

Well, again,
I was the White House Counsel.

Pat Cipollone
Former White House Counsel

Pat Cipollone is seen on a screen during a Select Committee hearing on July 12, 2022.
(Photo by Sarah Silbiger-Pool/Getty Images)

admitted—during this meeting with the President and Vice President—that his proposal violated the Electoral Count Act.[153] Moreover, Eastman eventually acknowledged that the concept of the Vice President unilaterally rejecting electors was not supported by precedent and that the Supreme Court would never endorse it.[154]

Jacob recorded his reflections on the January 4th meeting in a contemporaneous memo to the Vice President.[155] Jacob's memo confirms that Eastman admitted that his proposal violated the law in the presence of President Trump.

First, Jacob wrote, Eastman acknowledged that "his proposal violates several provisions of statutory law"—namely, the Electoral Count Act of 1887.[156] Jacob's memo explains that the Electoral Count Act calls for all vote certificates to be "acted upon," and any objections to a State's certificates be "finally disposed of." However, as Jacob wrote, Eastman was proposing instead that "no action be taken" on the certificates from the States Eastman asserted were "contested." And, according to the Electoral Count Act, the Vice President (as President of the Senate) is to "call for objections." But Eastman did not want the Vice President to "call for objections" for these States. As Jacob noted, this would have deprived Congress of the ability under the Act to make, debate, and vote on objections.[157]

Additionally, the Electoral Count Act contains a provision that requires any "competing slates of electors" to be "submitted to the Senate and House for debate and disposition." As Jacob noted, Eastman conceded that the "alternate" (fake) electors' votes were not proper. But Eastman's proposal still would have refused to count the real electors' votes from those States and instead referred both the real and fake electors' votes to State legislatures "for disposition." Finally, in order for State legislatures to take action to determine which of the slates should be counted, Eastman's proposal called for "an extended recess of the joint session." But this too would have violated the Electoral Count Act, which provides only for very short delays.[158]

There was another foundational problem with Eastman's plan. There were no legitimate "competing" or "alternate" slates of electors. President Trump, Eastman and others had manufactured the conditions they needed in order to claim that the election result was "disputed" by convening fake electors who sent fake documents to Washington before January 6th. And their efforts to convince State legislatures to certify Trump electors had already failed.

Jacob noted in his memo that in the Oval Office meeting, Eastman conceded "no legislature has appointed or certified any alternate slate of electors" and that the purported "alternate slates" (fake electors) were illegitimate without what Jacob described as "the imprimatur of approval by a State legislature." [159] Moreover, Eastman acknowledged that "no Republican-controlled legislative majority in any disputed States has expressed an intention to designate an alternate slate of electors." [160] In other words, Eastman acknowledged that the fake votes were invalid, that no State legislature had approved them, and no State legislature *would* approve them.[161] But President Trump and Eastman still pressed this unlawful scheme on the Vice President. Although Eastman started the January 4th Oval Office meeting maintaining that Vice President Pence had unilateral authority to reject electors, by the end of the meeting he conceded that he would "not recommend that the Vice President assert that he has the authority unilaterally to decide which of the competing slates of electors should be counted." [162]

Jacob ended his memo with a scathing summary. "If the Vice President implemented Professor Eastman's proposal, he would likely lose in court," Jacob wrote. "In a best-case scenario in which the courts refused to get involved, the Vice President would likely find himself in an isolated standoff against both houses of Congress, as well as most or all of the applicable State legislatures, with no neutral arbiter to break the impasse." [163]

Following the Oval Office meeting, during the evening of January 4, 2021, Jacob invited Eastman to send along "any written materials on electoral vote counting issues," including a law review article by Laurence Tribe that Eastman had cited in the Oval Office meeting that day, for Jacob to review on the Vice President's behalf.[164] Jacob reviewed everything that Eastman submitted; nothing changed the analysis he had already done for the Vice President, indeed much of it did not even support Eastman's own arguments.[165]

**The Vice President was Not Persuaded by Eastman's Theory and Remained Convinced That His Role at the Joint Session would be Merely Ceremonial.** Pence did not relent on January 4th, or at any point during the harrowing two days that followed. "[F]rom my very first conversation with the Vice President on the subject, his immediate instinct was that there is no way that one person could be entrusted by the Framers to exercise that authority," Jacob testified. "And never once did I see him budge from that view, and the legal advice that I provided him merely reinforced it. So, everything that he said or did during [the January 4th meeting in the Oval Office] was consistent with his first instincts on this question." [166]

### JANUARY 4, 2021: PRESIDENT TRUMP PUBLICLY PRESSURES THE VICE PRESIDENT DURING A RALLY SPEECH IN GEORGIA.

President Trump did not relent either. His instinct was to increase public pressure on Vice President Pence, despite the Vice President's consistent message to President Trump about the limits of his authority. That evening, during a Senate campaign rally in Dalton, Georgia, President Trump made it seem as if the Presidential election hadn't already been decided and projected his unhinged ambitions onto his opponents.[167] President Trump claimed that "there's nothing the radical Democrats will not do to get power that they so desperately crave," including "the outright stealing of elections, like they're trying to do with us." [168]

"We're not going to let it happen," President Trump said, adding, "I hope Mike Pence comes through for us, I have to tell you." President Trump called Vice President Pence a "great vice president," a "great guy," as well as a "wonderful" and "smart man." But he alluded to the Vice President's role, "he's going to have a lot to say about it," and added an ominous note. "Of course, if he doesn't come through, I won't like him quite as much," President Trump said.[169]

### JANUARY 5, 2021: EASTMAN PRESSURES PENCE'S STAFF IN A PRIVATE MEETING WHILE PRESIDENT TRUMP TWEETS.

**In a Reversal of Where the Oval Office Meeting Ended the Day Before, Eastman Argues that Pence Should Reject Electors Outright.** Eastman met with Jacob and Short again the following day.[170] During the Oval Office meeting the Vice President had made clear that he would not unilaterally reject electors, and, by pivoting to recommend the Vice President send the electors back to the States, Eastman seemed to recognize this. But the following morning, Eastman returned to pressing for the more "aggressive" path.[171]

Jacob recorded Eastman's request on January 5, 2021, in a handwritten note: "Requesting VP reject." [172] Jacob later summarized Eastman's remarks as follows: "I'm here asking you to reject the electors." [173] This overnight reversal surprised Jacob because Eastman was returning to the more aggressive position he had seemed to abandon in the Oval Office meeting the day before.[174] President Trump's tweets that morning may explain Eastman's reversal. While Eastman was meeting with the Vice President's staff, his client, President Trump, was pressing the argument publicly.

At 11:06 a.m. on the morning of January 5th, President Trump tweeted: "The Vice President has the power to reject fraudulently chosen electors." As his tweet made clear, President Trump would not be persuaded by reason—or the law. The President made this public statement despite the Vice President's clear and consistent rejection of this theory including during an in-person meeting the day before. During that same meeting, Eastman conceded that this "aggressive" path of rejecting electors was not advisable.

Herschmann briefly participated in the January 5th meeting, seeing it as "an opportunity...to just chew [Eastman] out." [175] Herschmann had already pushed back "brutal[ly]" on Eastman's theory regarding the Vice

President. In this conversation, he emphasized the need to fact check dubious claims of election fraud.[176] Herschmann told Eastman that "someone better make sure" that the allegations Eastman provided to members of Congress were accurate before they objected to the certification of the vote the next day.[177] "[N]othing should come out of someone's mouth that [isn't] independently verified and [ ] reliable."[178]

**At the End of the Morning Meeting, Eastman Concedes to Pence's Counsel That His Theory Has No Historical Support.** Jacob then had his own "Socratic" debate with Eastman over the legal merits of his position. According to Jacob, Eastman conceded much ground by the end of the session. Eastman "all but admitted that it [his plan] didn't work."[179]

For example, Eastman had previously claimed to have found historical support in the actions of John Adams and Thomas Jefferson, who both presided over the counting of electoral votes when they were Vice President. Not so. Jacob told the Select Committee that Eastman conceded in private that the cases of Jefferson and Adams did not serve "as examples for the proposition that he was trying to support of a Vice Presidential assertion of authority to decide disputes[,] because no dispute was raised in either case during the joint session." Jacob added: "And, moreover, there was no [question] as to the outcomes in those States."[180]

Eastman conceded that there was no historical support for the role that he and President Trump were pushing Vice President Pence to play. No Vice President—before or after the adoption of the Electoral Count Act—had ever exercised such authority. This included then–Vice President Richard Nixon's handling of the electoral votes of Hawaii following the 1960 election. Though Eastman and other Trump lawyers used this Hawaii example to justify the theory that the Vice President could unilaterally choose which electors to count, Eastman admitted to Jacob that Vice President Nixon had not in fact done what Eastman was recommending Vice President Pence do.[181]

Eastman also admitted that he would not grant the expansive powers he advocated for Vice President Pence to any other Vice President. Eastman did not think that Vice President Kamala Harris should have such power in 2025, nor did he think that Vice President Al Gore should have had such authority in 2001.[182] He also acknowledged that his theory would lose 9-0 at the Supreme Court.[183]

According to Jacob, Eastman "acknowledged by the end that, first of all, no reasonable person would actually want that clause [of the 12th Amendment] read that way because if indeed it did mean that the Vice President

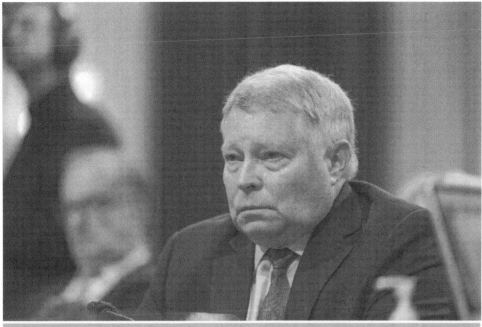

Judge J. Michael Luttig testifies before the Select Committee on June 16, 2022.
Photo by House Creative Services

had such authority, you could never have a party switch thereafter." If politicians followed Eastman's advice, "[y]ou would just have the same party win continuously if indeed a Vice President had the authority to just declare the winner of every State." [184]

The Vice President's office was unmoved by Eastman's specious reasoning. As he left Marc Short's office, Eastman was thinking of his client's reaction. "They're going to be really disappointed that I wasn't able to persuade you," Eastman said.[185]

**Former Republican Officials with Executive, Legislative, and Judicial Experience All Agreed with Vice President Pence's Conclusion about His Limited Role at the Joint Session.** As President Trump's pressure campaign intensified, the Vice President's outside counsel, Richard Cullen, turned for support to John Michael Luttig, a conservative former judge of the U.S. Court of Appeals for the Fourth Circuit.[186] Eastman had clerked for Luttig—a man with impeccable legal and conservative credentials—more than two decades prior. Luttig rejected Eastman's so-called legal analysis of the Vice President's role in no uncertain terms. In a series of tweets, posted at 9:53 a.m. on January 5th, Luttig set forth his legal conclusions.

"The only responsibility and power of the Vice President under the Constitution is to faithfully count the electoral college votes as they have been cast," Judge Luttig wrote. "The Constitution does not empower the Vice President to alter in any way the votes that have been cast, either by rejecting certain of them or otherwise." [187]

Confusion in the media about where the Vice President stood on this issue prompted former Speaker of the House Paul Ryan to reach out to the Vice President to share his belief that the Vice President had no unilateral authority.[188] Short also spoke with former Speaker Ryan and as he testified to the Select Committee, "I said to him, Mr. Speaker, you know Mike...you know he recognizes that. And we sort of laughed about it, and he said, I get it." [189]

The Vice President also consulted with former Vice President Dan Quayle, who reinforced and affirmed Vice President Pence's consistent understanding of his role.[190]

### JANUARY 5, 2021: PRESIDENT TRUMP AGAIN PRESSURES VICE PRESIDENT PENCE IN A ONE-ON-ONE MEETING AT THE WHITE HOUSE AND ANOTHER PHONE CALL WITH EASTMAN.

President Trump demanded to see Vice President Pence again that same day. Vice President Pence had canceled a planned lunch with President Trump, intending to work on the statement he planned to issue on January 6th to explain publicly why he wouldn't bow to the President's pressure.[191] But Pence couldn't avoid Trump. Vice President Pence had to delay a Coronavirus Task Force meeting later that same day when he was called to the Oval Office to meet with the President.[192]

The two men met alone, without staff present. While we have not developed direct evidence of what was discussed during this one-on-one meeting between the President and Vice President, it did not change the fundamental disagreement between them about the limits of the Vice President's authority during the joint session. Jacob said the Vice President left the meeting "determined." [193] Vice President Pence did tell Marc Short what transpired during the meeting, but Short refused to tell the Select Committee what was said.[194] Short described Vice President Pence's demeanor as "steady." [195] Short testified that the below excerpt from the book *Peril* may have been sensationalized but was generally consistent with Short's understanding of the discussion:

> "If these people say you have the power, wouldn't you want to?" Trump asked.

> "I wouldn't want any one person to have that authority," Pence said.

*"But wouldn't it almost be cool to have that power?" Trump asked.*

*"No," Pence said. "Look, I've read this, and I don't see a way to do it. We've exhausted every option. I've done everything I could and then some to find a way around this. It's simply not possible. My interpretation is: No....*

*"No, no, no!" Trump shouted. "You don't understand, Mike. You can do this. I don't want to be your friend anymore if you don't do this."*[196]

Later that day, Jacob and Short were both present for a call between President Trump and Vice President Pence.[197] Eastman and at least one other lawyer were with President Trump on the call as well.[198]

Eastman recognized that Vice President Pence was not going to change his mind on rejecting electors outright, but he still asked if the Vice President would consider sending the electors back to the States.[199] "I don't see it," Vice President Pence responded, "but my counsel will hear out whatever Mr. Eastman has to say."[200]

Jacob received other calls from Eastman on January 5th.[201] Jacob told the Select Committee that he had a detailed discussion with Eastman concerning the ways his proposal would violate the Electoral Count Act.[202] Eastman resorted to a ridiculous argument—comparing their current situation to the crisis that faced President Abraham Lincoln during the Civil War. Eastman invoked President Lincoln's suspension of the writ of habeas corpus.[203] He also told Jacob to "stay tuned" because "we" were trying to get some letters from State legislators indicating that they were interested in the Vice President sending the electors back to the States.[204]

**JANUARY 5, 2021: AN ACCURATE NEW YORK TIMES ARTICLE ABOUT THE VICE PRESIDENT PROMPTS A FALSE STATEMENT IN RESPONSE BY PRESIDENT TRUMP.**

On the evening of January 5th, *The New York Times* published an article titled, "Pence Said to Have Told Trump He Lacks Power to Change Election Result."[205] The *Times* reported on the tension brewing within the White House, citing "people briefed on the conversation" between President Trump and Vice President Pence that had taken place in the Oval Office the previous day. "Vice President Mike Pence told President Trump on Tuesday [January 4th] that he did not believe he had the power to block congressional certification of Joseph R. Biden, Jr.'s victory in the presidential election despite Mr. Trump's baseless insistence that he did," the *Times* reported.[206]

The *Times*' report was published at approximately 7:36 that evening.[207] Jason Miller called President Trump to make sure he had seen it.[208] President Trump spoke to Miller at least twice, once at 8:18 p.m. and a second time at 9:22 p.m.[209] Immediately after concluding his second call with Jason

Miller, President Trump asked to speak to the Vice President; President Trump and Vice President Pence spoke from 9:33 to 9:41 p.m.[210] President Trump also spoke with Steve Bannon and Eastman, among others.[211]

At 9:58 p.m. on January 5th, President Trump issued a statement that he had dictated to Jason Miller disputing the *Times'* account.[212] President Trump lied—repeatedly—in his short statement.[213] The President claimed the article was "fake news." It wasn't. President Trump claimed he and Vice President Pence were "in total agreement that the Vice President has the power to act." They weren't. President Trump claimed the election "was illegal." It wasn't. President Trump then laid out Vice President Pence's options for the next day, summarizing Eastman's theory:

> Our Vice President has several options under the U.S. Constitution. He can decertify the results or send them back to the [S]tates for change and certification. He can also decertify the illegal and corrupt results and send them to the House of Representatives for the one vote for one [S]tate tabulation.[214]

This was also a blatant attempt to mischaracterize the Vice President's position in the hope that public opinion would somehow sway the resolute Vice President. President Trump knew full well at the time that he and Vice President Pence were *not* "in total agreement." The Vice President's counsel, Greg Jacob, was shocked by the statement.[215] "[T]he Vice President was not in agreement that the Vice President had the power to take the actions that were being asked of him that day," Jacob later told the Select Committee.[216] Marc Short was furious as well and called Jason Miller to forcefully "express [his] displeasure that a statement could have gone out that misrepresented the Vice President's viewpoint without consultation." [217]

The Vice President was "obviously irritated that a statement putting words in his mouth" was issued by the President and considered issuing his own statement contradicting President Trump's.[218] Ultimately, Pence and Short concluded that it was not worthwhile since it was already late in the evening and they expected the question to be resolved by Vice President Pence's "Dear Colleague" letter the next day.[219]

### JANUARY 5, 2021: BANNON PUBLICLY AMPLIFIES THE PRESSURE ON VICE PRESIDENT PENCE.

While President Trump misrepresented the Vice President's agreement with Eastman's theory, his on-again, off-again political advisor, Steve Bannon, pressed President Trump's campaign against Vice President Pence in public. Bannon echoed the public pressure on Pence that the President continued to propagate by talking about his purported authority. The Select Committee learned from phone records that Bannon spoke to President Trump at least twice on January 5th.[220]

During a January 5, 2021, episode of *War Room: Pandemic*, Bannon and his guests openly berated Vice President Pence. Bannon cited an erroneous news report claiming that Senator Grassley would preside over the certification of the electoral college vote—instead of Vice President Pence.[221] Bannon's cohost, Raheem Kassam, took credit for the public pressure placed on Vice President Pence. "I want to remind people who has been sitting here, saying 'Light Pence Up' for the last couple of weeks. Right? That would be Raheem Kassam." They then discussed President Trump's speech in Georgia the previous evening. "I think the President of the United States took your advice last night, wrote a line in there," Bannon said. To which Kasseem responded: "…and yours…hold the line."

Jack Posobiec, an alt-right personality with a large Twitter following, chimed in quoting a member of their audience as saying that "Pence will betray Donald Trump."[222] In response, Bannon stated: "Call the play. Run the play."[223]

The "play" was Bannon's version of the "Green Bay Sweep"—a plan to subvert the transfer of power on January 6th named for a brutally effective power running play developed in the National Football League (NFL) in the 1960's. Steve Bannon's political version of the sweep was intended to undermine the legitimate results of the 2020 presidential election.

One account of Bannon's "Green Bay Sweep" comes from Peter Navarro, Director of the White House Office of Trade and Manufacturing Policy. Navarro refused to cooperate with the Select Committee and was subsequently indicted for contempt of Congress. Although he doesn't fully explain in his book, *In Trump Time: A Journal of America's Plague Year*, how Bannon's sweep was intended to work, Navarro writes that Vice President Pence was envisioned as the "quarterback" who would "assert his constitutional power" to delay certification.[224] Navarro writes that his own role was to "carefully document the fraud and myriad election irregularities," while Bannon's "role was to figure out how to use this information—what he called the 'receipts.'"[225]

Navarro's account helps explain why Trump and his loyalists became so fixated on Vice President Pence. They saw Vice President Pence as their last hope for keeping President Trump in office. Navarro writes of Pence's supposed "betrayal."[226] In a telling sentence, Navarro likens Vice President Pence to Brutus, a Roman politician and the most famous assassin of Julius Caesar. Navarro writes:

*On this cold, momentous day, I shiver as I think to myself, "January 6 will be either Mike Pence's finest hour or the traitorous 'Et tu, Brute?' end of both his and Donald Trump's political careers."* [227]

The goal of these Trump allies was clear: to overturn the election result.[228] Statements by participants in this effort indicate there were several different endgame strategies in mind. One was to get the Vice President to unilaterally reject the Electoral College votes of Arizona, Georgia, Pennsylvania, and other States, then simply declare that Trump had won a majority of the electors actually submitted. The other major possibility was to reject or "return" the Electoral College votes of these States and then declare there was no majority in the Electoral College process, thereby triggering a so-called contingent election under the 12th Amendment.[229] This would have meant that the House of Representatives had chosen the president not on the basis of one-member-one-vote, but on the basis of one-State-one-vote, pursuant to the 12th Amendment. Donald Trump's strategists emphasized repeatedly that the GOP had a 27-to-22 margin in control of the States' Congressional delegations, with Pennsylvania being tied at 9-to-9, therefore presumably a non-factor.

### 5.3 PRESIDENT TRUMP AND HIS ALLIES CONTINUE TO PRESSURE THE VICE PRESIDENT ON JANUARY 6TH, THREATENING HIS LIFE AND OUR DEMOCRACY.

**JANUARY 6, 2021: PRESIDENT TRUMP CONTINUED TO FALSELY ASSERT IN MULTIPLE TWEETS POSTED THE MORNING OF JANUARY 6TH THAT THE VICE PRESIDENT HAD A ROLE TO PLAY IN THE OUTCOME OF THE ELECTION.**

Despite the public pressure initiated by the President and amplified by Bannon, Navarro and others, there was no ambiguity in the Vice President's decision. By January 6th, President Trump had been told multiple times that Vice President Pence was not going to reject the certified electors from any State. Nor was Vice President Pence going to move for a delay and send the electors back to the States. Either move would have been illegal, requiring Vice President Pence to break the law, violating his oath to the U.S. Constitution. Pence made his decision clear "[m]any times" to President Trump, and he was "very consistent" in rejecting the President's demands.[230] President Trump continued to publicly pressure the Vice President anyway.

At 1:00 a.m. on January 6th, President Trump tweeted:

If Vice President @Mike_Pence comes through for us, we will win the Presidency. Many States want to decertify the mistake they made in certifying incorrect & even fraudulent numbers in a process NOT approved by their State Legislatures (which it must be). Mike can send it back![231]

Later that morning, at 8:17 a.m., President Trump tweeted again:

States want to correct their votes, which they now know were based on irregularities and fraud, plus corrupt process never received legislative approval. All Mike Pence has to do is send them back to the States, AND WE WIN. Do it Mike, this is a time for extreme courage![232]

And, at 8:22 a.m., President Trump tweeted again, making a pitch for Congress to choose him, as if people's votes on election day and the electoral college didn't matter:

THE REPUBLICAN PARTY AND, MORE IMPORTANTLY, OUR COUNTRY, NEEDS THE PRESIDENCY MORE THAN EVER BEFORE—THE POWER OF THE VETO. STAY STRONG![233]

President Trump's tweets made it clear that he thought the Republican State legislatures would simply deliver him victory. President Trump emphasized this point, writing twice that if Vice President Pence gave in, "we win." However, there was no sign of a change in the Vice President's position. A moment of truth was looming.

**January 6, 2021: President Trump Has a "[H]eated" Conversation with Vice President Pence Before his Rally on the Ellipse.** President Trump tried to reach Vice President Pence by phone early that morning.[234] He finally talked to his Vice President at approximately 11:20 a.m.[235] The exchange quickly became contentious.

Eric Herschmann, a lawyer in the White House Counsel's Office, overheard the conversation. Members of President Trump's family and other White House officials were present as well.[236] Herschmann recalled that "it started off as a calmer tone, everything, and then it became heated."[237] Ivanka Trump also described the call as "pretty heated."[238] Ivanka Trump elaborated: "It was a different tone than I'd heard him take with the Vice President before."[239] Ivanka Trump told her Chief of Staff, Julie Radford, that "her dad had just had an upsetting conversation with the Vice President."[240] President Trump had even called Vice President Pence the "P Word."[241]

Nick Luna, President Trump's personal assistant (commonly known as the "body man"), was also in the Oval Office during the conversation. Luna told the Select Committee that President Trump called Vice President Pence

**President Trump on the phone in the Oval Office.**
Photo provided to the Select Committee by the National Archives and Records Administration.

a "wimp" on the call, with President Trump adding that he "made the wrong decision" in choosing Pence as his running mate.[242]

Keith Kellogg, Vice President Pence's National Security Advisor, also heard the conversation. President Trump "told the Vice President that, you know, he has legal authority to send these folks [the electors] back to the respective States," Kellogg told the Select Committee.[243] President Trump insisted that Vice President Pence had the "constitutional authority to" reject certain electoral college votes.[244] When Vice President Pence would not budge, President Trump told him "you're not tough enough to make the call."[245]

But Vice President Pence would not be bullied. The Vice President, who was at his residence at the time, had been meeting with Greg Jacob to final-ize the statement he would be releasing later that day. When the President called, Pence stepped away to answer the phone. According to Jacob, when Pence returned, he did not say anything about the call—but he looked "steely, determined, [and] grim," as he reentered the room.[246]

**c. January 6, 2021: Trump, Eastman and Giuliani Continue to Pressure Vice President Pence at the Ellipse Rally.** Despite the Vice President's unwavering stance, the President and his outside counsel continued to turn up the heat of public pressure.

At President Trump's urging, thousands had gathered on the morning of January 6th to hear the President and others speak at a rally held at the Ellipse, a park just south of the White House. Before President Trump spoke, Eastman took the stage alongside Giuliani. Both would further amplify the President's public pressure on the Vice President, but when Giuliani spoke on the Ellipse, he already knew that what Eastman had outlined would never practically happen.

At 9:31 a.m. that morning, Giuliani called Eric Herschmann "out of the blue" to ask him for his view and analysis of the practical implications of Eastman's theory.[247] According to Herschmann, after an "intellectual discussion about...the VP's role," Giuliani agreed that the "practical implication of [what Eastman had proposed] would be almost impossible."[248] Immediately after this 5½ minute conversation with Herschmann, Giuliani had two calls with the White House, at 9:41 a.m. and 9:53 a.m.[249]

Giuliani recognized Eastman who joined him on stage, claiming that he was "one of the preeminent constitutional scholars in the United States."[250]

Giuliani said Vice President Pence could either "decide on the validity of these crooked ballots, or he can send it back to the legislat[ures], give them five to 10 days to finally finish the work."[251] He added that that they had "letters from five legislat[ures] begging us to do that."[252] This was not true. At most, what Giuliani, Eastman and other allies of President Trump had managed to procure were letters from individual State legislators or groups of State legislators. None of the letters came from a majority of any State's legislative chamber, let alone a majority of an entire State legislature.[253]

For instance, a letter that Eastman described to Jacob as a "[m]ajor new development" on the evening of January 5th contained the signatures of 21 members of the Pennsylvania Senate.[254] Eastman claimed that it "now looks like PA Legislature will vote to recertify its electors if Vice President Pence implements the plan we discussed," but the letter asked only for a "delay" in certification to "allow for due process."[255] The Select Committee learned from the most senior Pennsylvania Senate Republican that he signed the letter because of pressure he was feeling due to the voluminous post-election outreach from President Trump, Trump allies, and the public.[256] And, he only agreed to sign a letter directed to Congressional leaders—not the Vice President—after raising in a conversation with Vice President Pence's brother, Congressman Greg Pence, his desire to avoid pressuring the Vice President.[257]

Moreover, as Jacob explained, "what any of the State legislatures said they did or did not want to do had no impact on the legal analysis of what the Vice President's authorities were."[258] There was simply no legal path to send any votes back to the States on January 6th.

On the stage at the President's rally on the Ellipse, Giuliani repeated a conspiracy theory about the "crooked Dominion machines...deliberately" changing votes via an algorithm.[259] He explained that the 10-day delay in the certification would be used "to see the machines that are crooked" and "to find criminality there"—demonstrating that his repeated assertions of a stolen election were not based on any real proof, or even evidence, of actual widespread fraud or criminality.[260]

"Let's have trial by combat," Giuliani told the crowd.[261]

Eastman came to the microphone following Giuliani, and he proceeded to repeat proven falsehoods regarding voting machines. He then issued his "demand":

> And all we are demanding of Vice President Pence is this afternoon, at 1:00, he let the legislatures of the state look into this so we get to the bottom of it, and the American people know whether we have control of the direction of our government, or not. We no longer live in a self-governing republic if we can't get the answer to this question. This is bigger than President Trump. It is a very essence of our republican form of government, and it has to be done. And anybody that is not willing to stand up to do it, does not deserve to be in the office. It is that simple.[262]

Eastman told the assembled crowd that nothing less than the fate of the American Republic was in Vice President Pence's hands.

President Trump Directs the Angry Mob at the Capitol to Pressure Vice President Pence.

When President Trump later took the stage at the Ellipse, he heaped praise on Giuliani and Eastman. "He's got guts, unlike a lot of people in the Republican Party," President Trump said of Giuliani. "He's got guts. He fights, he fights."[263] President Trump described Eastman as "one of the most brilliant lawyers in the country."[264] President Trump claimed that Eastman had looked at the election and said, "What an absolute disgrace that this can be happening to our Constitution."[265] Trump falsely argued that the keys to the election were in Vice President Pence's hands, saying:

*And he [Eastman] looked at Mike Pence, and I hope Mike is going to do the right thing. I hope so. I hope so. Because if Mike Pence does the right thing, we win the election.... [T]his is from the number one, or certainly one of the top, Constitutional lawyers in our country. He has the absolute right to do it.[266]*

President Trump repeatedly lied, claiming that several States wanted to overturn former Vice President Biden's victory:

*States want to revote. The States got defrauded. They were given false information. They voted on it. Now they want to recertify. They want it back. All Vice President Pence has to do is send it back to the States to recertify and we become president and you are the happiest people.[267]*

Contrary to the statement President Trump dictated the night before, he all but admitted that Vice President Pence did not agree with him:

*And I actually, I just spoke to Mike. I said: "Mike, that doesn't take courage. What takes courage is to do nothing. That takes courage." And then we're stuck with a president who lost the election by a lot and we have to live with that for four more years. We're just not going to let that happen.[268]*

Later in his speech at the Ellipse, President Trump repeated:

*So, I hope Mike has the courage to do what he has to do. And I hope he doesn't listen to the RINOs and the stupid people that he's listening to.[269]*

This was nothing less than a direct appeal to the large angry crowd to pressure Vice President Mike Pence to change his settled and oft-repeated conclusion about the limits of his authority. It was a shocking attempt to use public opinion to change the Vice President's position. President Trump launched a mob toward the Capitol with the false hope that there was a scenario in which Vice President Pence would do what Eastman and President Trump had asked him to do, preventing the transfer of authority to President-elect Biden.

### VICE PRESIDENT PENCE FULFILLED HIS DUTY ON JANUARY 6TH

**The Vice President Waited to Release His Statement Out of Deference to President Trump, Who Was Still Speaking on the Ellipse, and Ultimately Released It Just Minutes Before the Joint Session Convened at 1:00 p.m.** President Trump's speech began late and ran long. He didn't finish speaking until approximately 1:10 p.m.—after the joint session had begun at 1:00 p.m. Minutes before he gaveled the joint session into order, Vice President Mike Pence released the "Dear Colleague" letter he had been working on for days with his staff.[270] There was never any ambiguity in Vice President Pence's understanding of his role and authority, but he wanted to make it clear for everyone to see. "This may be the most important thing I ever say," Vice President Pence remarked.[271]

"Today it will be my duty to preside when the Congress convenes in Joint Session to count the votes of the Electoral College, and I will do so to the best of my ability," Vice President Pence wrote. Vice President Pence explained that his "role as presiding officer is largely ceremonial" and dismissed the arguments that he could take unilateral action as contrary to his oath to support and defend the Constitution:

> As a student of history who loves the Constitution and reveres its Framers, I do not believe that the Founders of our country intended to invest the Vice President with unilateral authority to decide which electoral votes should be counted during the Joint Session of Congress, and no Vice President in American history has ever asserted such authority. Instead, Vice Presidents presiding over Joint Sessions have uniformly followed the Electoral Count Act, conducting the proceedings in an orderly manner even where the count resulted in the defeat of their party or their own candidacy.[272]

**Vice President Pence Adheres to the U.S. Constitution and Complies with the Law Governing the Certification of the Presidential Election.** When Vice President Pence gaveled the opening of the joint session, he knew that many of his Republican colleagues planned to challenge the election's results based on fictitious claims of fraud. The Vice President took steps to ensure that those objections adhered to the process set forth in the Electoral Count Act.

Every four years, on January 6th, vice presidents read from a script that remains essentially unchanged. Eastman's theory of the Vice President's power and the Trump Campaign's scheme to convene and submit the slates of "alternate" (fake) electors motivated Vice President Pence and his advisors to alter the script and to make sure they were prepared to respond to any unexpected actions in the joint session.[273]

Vice President Pence met with the Senate Parliamentarian on January 3rd to discuss the joint session and revised the joint session scripts in consultation with her office.[274] Vice President Pence and the Parliamentarian agreed that the Vice President's role is ministerial.[275]

The Vice President knew that the fake slates of electors organized by the Trump Campaign were not certified by the States and thus were not valid; he revised the script for the joint session to be transparent with the American people about what the Vice President would—and wouldn't—be doing during the joint session.[276]

Vice President Pence during the Joint Session of Congress.

One of the most noticeable and important changes to the script was directed specifically at thwarting the fake electors scheme. The Vice President knew, informed by the research and analysis of his staff, that absent certification of the electoral votes by a State authority, the purported "alternate" slates were "not consequential" and would play no role in the certification of the Presidential election at the joint session.[277] The Senate Parliamentarian confirmed this understanding.[278]

For decades, Vice Presidents read a similar simple passage concerning the ascertainment of the vote. Most recently, Vice President Joseph Biden read this passage aloud in 2017, as did his most recent predecessors:

> After ascertainment has been had that the certificates are authentic and correct in form, the tellers will count and make a list of the votes cast by the electors of the several States.

On January 6, 2021, Vice President Pence read from a revised script (emphasis added):

> After ascertaining that the certificates are regular in form and authentic, tellers will announce the votes cast by the electors for each state, beginning with Alabama, which the parliamentarians

advise me is the only certificate of vote from that State and purports to be a return from the State that has annexed to it a certificate from an authority of that State purporting to appoint or ascertain electors.[279]

Vice President Pence used the same phrasing for each of the 50 States counted.

The Vice President's attention to this issue was warranted. Trump's allies pushed the fake electors scheme until the very end. Although the Trump Campaign had taken pains to direct the fake electors to send their documents to the appropriate authorities immediately after voting on December 14th, and though the Senate Parliamentarian's and Vice President's offices had been tracking the receipt by mail of both the legitimate and fake certificates, the Trump Campaign apparently became concerned that two States' documents had not been received before the joint session.[280]

On January 4th, the Trump campaign asked Republican Party officials in Wisconsin to fly their fake electors' documents to Washington, DC.[281] Shortly after, staffers for Representative Mike Kelly (R–PA) and Senator Ron Johnson (R–WI) reached out to Vice President Pence's Director of Legislative Affairs, apparently seeking to deliver the fake certificates.[282] A message from Senator Johnson's staffer was sent just minutes before the beginning of the joint session. This staffer stated that Senator Johnson wished to hand-deliver to the Vice President the fake electors' certificates from Michigan and Wisconsin. The Vice President's aide unambiguously turned him away.[283]

Vice President Pence made certain to call for objections as well, in compliance with the Electoral Count Act. After the tellers read off the votes cast for each State, he asked: "Are there any objections to counting the certificate of vote of the state . . . that the teller has verified, appears to be regular in form and authentic?" [284]

For most States, there were no objections. Republicans only rose to object to the States that President Trump contested. The first such state was Arizona. At approximately 1:46 p.m., Congressman Paul Gosar (R–AZ) announced his objection.[285] "I rise for myself and 60 of my colleagues to object to the counting of the electoral ballots from Arizona," Gosar said.[286]

Vice President Pence then asked: "Is the objection in writing and Signed by a senator?" It was. Senator Ted Cruz endorsed the unfounded challenge to Arizona's electoral votes.[287] Because the objections complied with the law, Vice President Pence directed the House and Senate to withdraw from the joint session so that the House and Senate could separately debate and vote on the objection.[288]

When the joint session finally resumed after the attack on the Capitol, the clerks announced the results of each chamber's vote. Just six U.S. Senators voted for the objection to the counting of Arizona's electoral college votes. The objection was also defeated in the House, though 121 Republican Members voted to reject Arizona's legitimate electors.[289] Pennsylvania was the only other State the chambers debated, after the House's objection was signed by Senator Josh Hawley (R—Mo.).[290]

## 5.4 PRESIDENT TRUMP ENDANGERS PENCE'S LIFE, CAUSING THE VICE PRESIDENT, HIS FAMILY, AND STAFF TO NARROWLY MISS THE RIOTERS AS THEY FLEE THE MOB ATTACKING THE CAPITOL.

As the debate over Arizona's legitimate electors took place on the Senate floor, the Vice President's staff could see trouble brewing outside.[291] From inside the Vice President's ceremonial office, staffers witnessed the crowds swelling on the east side of the Capitol. Then, the rioters broke through security barriers.[292] Jacob told young staffers that they should stand back from the windows, because the Vice President's office was not "the most popular office on the block right now."[293]

The Vice President was presiding over the Senate debate on the Arizona objection when the noise from the rioters became audible and those in the Senate Chamber realized the rioters had entered the Capitol.[294] The Secret Service evacuated Vice President Pence from the Senate floor at 2:12 p.m.[295] Twelve minutes later, at 2:24 p.m., President Trump tweeted that Vice President Pence "didn't have the courage to do what should have been done to protect our country and our Constitution."[296] By that time, the Secret Service had moved the Vice President to his ceremonial office across the hall.[297] But the situation was spiraling out of control—and they wouldn't stay there long. As Sarah Matthews, the Deputy White House Press Secretary, later explained: President Trump's tweet was like "pouring gasoline on the fire."[298]

Thirty seconds after President Trump's tweet, rioters who were already inside the Capitol opened the East Rotunda door just down the hall. A mere thirty seconds later, rioters breached the crypt one floor below the Vice President.

Though the Vice President refused the Secret Service's first two attempts to evacuate him from his ceremonial office, the situation quickly became untenable and the Vice President was told that the Secret Service could no longer protect him in this office in the Capitol that was quickly being overrun.[299] Marc Short recalls Tim Giebels, the head of the Vice President's Secret Service protective detail, saying, "At this point, I can't protect you behind these glass doors, and so I need to move you." [300] This time, the third, the Secret Service was not asking the Vice President to move; they were stating the fact that the Vice President must be moved. [301] At 2:20 p.m., NSC staff monitoring radio communications reported that the second floor of the Capitol and the door to the Senate Chamber "ha[ve] now been breached." [302]

At 2:25 p.m., the Secret Service rushed the Vice President, his family, and his senior staff down a flight of stairs, through a series of hallways and tunnels to a secure location. [303] The Vice President and his team stayed in that same location for the next four and a half hours.

The angry mob had come within 40 feet of the Vice President as he was evacuated. [304] President Trump never called to check on Vice President Pence's safety, so Marc Short called Mark Meadows to tell him they were safe and secure. [305] Short himself became *persona non grata* with President Trump. The President directed staff to revoke Short's access to the White House after Vice President Pence refused to betray his oath to the Constitution. [306] Marc Short never spoke with President Trump again. [307]

After arriving at the secure location, the head of the Vice President's Secret Service detail wanted to move the Vice President away from the Capitol, and staff hurried into the waiting vehicles. But the Vice President refused to get in the car. [308] As Greg Jacob explained in his testimony to the Select Committee:

> The Vice President wouldn't get in his car.... [H]e was determined that unless there was imminent danger to bodily safety that he was not going to abandon the Capitol and let the rioters have a victory of having made the Vice President flee or made it difficult to restart the process later that day. [309]

It was an unprecedented scene in American history. The President of the United States had riled up a mob that hunted his own Vice President.

The Vice President's staff came to believe that the theory "pushed and sold" to the public that the Vice President had a role to play in the joint session was a cause of the attack on the Capitol. "The reason that the Capitol was assaulted was that the people who were breaching the Capitol believed that...the election [outcome] had not yet been determined, and, instead, there was some action that was supposed to take place in Washington, D.C., to determine it," Jacob said. [310] "I do think [the violence] was the result of that position being continuously pushed and sold to people who ended up believing that with all their hearts." [311] The people had been "told that the Vice President had the authority" to determine the outcome of the election during the joint session. [312]

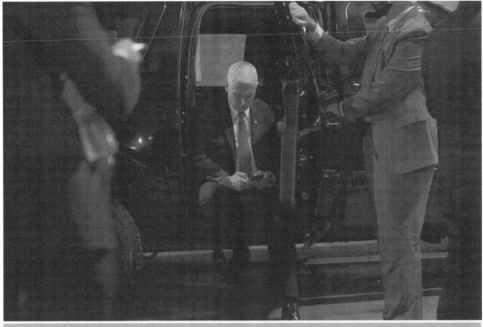

Of course, that was President Trump's and John Eastman's plan all along—to convince people that the election had been stolen, and that Vice President Pence could take action to change the outcome during the joint session on January 6th.

Jacob was writing an email to Eastman when the Capitol was breached.[313] At 2:14 p.m., just before being evacuated, Jacob hurriedly hit send on his email, but not before adding the following: "thanks to your bullshit, we are now under siege." [314]

Eastman quickly replied to Jacob's email and, incredibly, blamed Vice President Pence and Jacob for the attack. "The 'siege' is because YOU and your boss did not do what was necessary to allow this to be aired in a public way so the American people can see for themselves what happened," Eastman wrote.[315] Naturally, Jacob was "somewhere between aghast and livid." [316] It was "ridiculous" to blame Vice President Pence for the attack, when he simply followed the law.[317]

### THE JOINT SESSION RECONVENES: "LET'S GET BACK TO WORK."
The Senate reconvened at approximately 8:06 p.m.[318] Congressional leadership and the Vice President insisted on finishing the work of the people. "Today was a dark day in the history of the United States Capitol," Vice President Pence said. "But thanks to the swift efforts of U.S. Capitol Police,

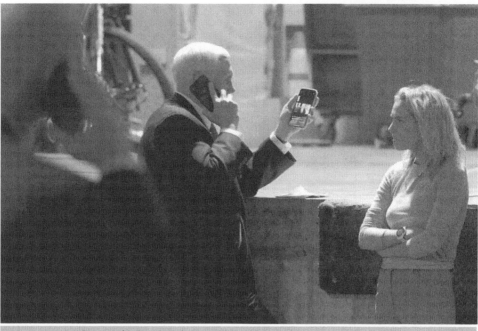

federal, state and local law enforcement, the violence was quelled. The Capitol is secured, and the people's work continues." The Vice President addressed "those who wreaked havoc in our Capitol today," saying "you did not win." Vice President Pence continued:

*Violence never wins. Freedom wins. And this is still the people's house. And as we reconvene in this chamber, the world will again witness the resilience and strength of our democracy, for even in the wake of unprecedented violence and vandalism at this Capitol, the elected repre- sentatives of the people of the United States have assembled again on the very same day to support and defend the Constitution of the United States.*

"Let's get back to work," Vice President Pence concluded.[319]

Despite the violence that had unfolded at the Capitol, Eastman kept agi- tating for further delay. At 11:44 p.m. on January 6th, Eastman sent yet another email to Greg Jacob.[320] In a shockingly tone-deaf manner, Eastman claimed that the Electoral Count Act had been violated already, by allowing debate beyond two hours, so—he argued—Vice President Pence should no longer be concerned that what President Trump and Eastman had pressured him to do also would violate it.[321] "Of course," as Jacob pointed out, the debate couldn't have been completed in two hours due to the "intervening riot of several hours." [322]

Eastman argued that Vice President Pence should "adjourn for 10 days to allow the legislatures to finish their investigations, as well as to allow a full forensic audit of the massive amount of illegal activity that has occurred here." [323] Eastman described this—a delay in the certification of the vote and the peaceful transfer of power with no legal or historical precedent or support, based on entirely specious and disproven allegations of election fraud, following on a violent attack on the seat of American democracy—as a "relatively minor violation." [324]

Vice President Pence later described Eastman's email as "rubber room stuff," meaning it was certifiably crazy.[325]

## 5.5 AFTERMATH OF THE ATTACK.

Eastman called Herschmann on January 7th to discuss litigation on behalf of the Trump Campaign in Georgia.[326] This gave Herschmann another opportunity to lay into Eastman. "[Are] you out of your F'ing mind?" Herschmann asked. "I only want to hear two words coming out of your mouth from now on: orderly transition." Herschmann said. After some berating, Eastman repeated after Herschmann: "Orderly transition." "Now I'm going to give you the best free legal advice you're ever getting in your life," Herschmann said. "Get a great F'ing criminal defense lawyer, you're going to need it." [327] Days afterward, Eastman sent an email to Giuliani, making a request that tacitly acknowledged just how much trouble he was in: "I've decided that I should be on the pardon list, if that is still in the works." [328]

Vice President Pence and his team never bowed to President Trump's relentless pressure. They began January 6, 2021, with a prayer. The attack on the U.S. Capitol delayed the peaceful transfer of power. The joint session did not end until early in the morning on January 7th.

At 3:50 a.m. that morning, Short texted Vice President Pence a passage from Second Timothy, chapter 4, verse 7: "I fought the good fight. I finished the race. I have kept the faith." [329]

**Donald J. Trump** ✔
@realDonaldTrump

Peter Navarro releases 36-page report alleging election fraud 'more than sufficient' to swing victory to Trump washex.am/3nwaBCe. A great report by Peter. Statistically impossible to have lost the 2020 Election. Big protest in D.C. on January 6th. Be there, will be wild!

ⓘ This claim about election fraud is disputed

Peter Navarro releases 36-page report alleging election fraud 'more than sufficie...
Director of the Office of Trade and Manufacturing Policy Peter Navarro published a lengthy report Thursday outlining several examples of voting irregularities that a...
🔗 washingtonexaminer.com

1:42 AM · Dec 19, 2020 · Twitter for iPhone

# 6

## "BE THERE, WILL BE WILD!"

On December 14, 2020, electors around the country met to cast their Electoral College votes. Their vote ensured former Vice President Joe Biden's victory and cemented President Donald J. Trump's defeat. The people, and the States, had spoken. Members of President Trump's own Cabinet knew the election was over. Attorney General William Barr viewed it as "the end of the matter."[1] Secretary of State Mike Pompeo and Secretary of Labor Eugene Scalia concurred.[2] That same day, Scalia told President Trump directly that he should concede defeat.[3]

President Trump had no intention of conceding. As he plotted ways to stay in power, the President summoned a mob for help.

At 1:42 a.m., on December 19th, President Trump tweeted: "Big protest in D.C. on January 6th. Be there, will be wild!"[4]

The President's tweet galvanized tens of thousands of his supporters around the country. President Trump had been lying to them since election day, claiming he won, and that the Democrats had stolen victory from him. Now, with a single tweet, the President focused his supporters' anger on the joint session of Congress in Washington, DC on January 6th.

Anika Navaroli, the longest-tenured member of Twitter's Trust and Safety Policy team, monitored the reaction to President Trump's "be wild" tweet. She told the Select Committee that the President was "essentially staking a flag in DC ... for his supporters to come and rally."[5] The tweet created a "fire hose" of calls to overthrow the U.S. Government. President Trump's supporters had a new sense of urgency because they felt "as if their Commander in Chief" had summoned them.[6]

For many extremists and conspiracy theorists, the President's announcement was a call to arms.[7]

For the Proud Boys—described in more detail below—and their leader, Henry "Enrique" Tarrio, President Trump's tweet set in motion a chain of events that led directly to the attack on the U.S. Capitol. In the days that followed, the Proud Boys reorganized their hierarchy, imposed a stricter

Tarrio's video appears on a screen during a Select Committee hearing on June 09, 2022.
Photo by Drew Angerer/Getty Images

chain-of-command, and instructed followers to go "incognito" on January 6th.[8] The Proud Boys had made their presence known at previous pro-Trump events, including "Stop the Steal" rallies, where they brandished their black and yellow apparel and engaged in street brawls.[9] Suddenly, they did not want to stand out from the crowd. They wanted to blend in. They were planning something big.[10]

Tarrio allegedly used encrypted messages to plot the January 6, 2021, attack. On January 4, 2021, Tarrio told his men that they should "storm the Capitol."[11] While the attack was underway, Tarrio claimed credit in a private chat, writing: "We did this."[12] And on the evening of January 6th, Tarrio released a video of a man, presumably Tarrio himself, dressed in an odd costume standing in front of the U.S. Capitol. The eerie production had been recorded prior to the events of that day. Tarrio—who was not in Washington, DC on January 6th[13]—titled it, "Premonition."[14]

The Oath Keepers, a far-right, anti-government militia movement—also described in more detail below—began planning for January 6th after the President's tweet as well. Stewart Rhodes, the group's leader, had agitated against the U.S. Government for years.[15] Immediately following the 2020 presidential election, Rhodes and others schemed to stop the peaceful transfer of power. They stored weapons outside of Washington, DC,[16] hoping that President Trump would deputize them as his own militia.[17] An Oath Keeper leader, Kelly Meggs, read President Trump's December 19th tweet and commented in a Facebook message: "He called us all to the Capitol and wants us to make it wild!!! Sir Yes Sir!!!"[18] The Oath Keepers formed two military "stacks" and marched up the steps of the U.S. Capitol on January 6th. Meggs led one of them.[19]

Members of both the Proud Boys and Oath Keepers have been charged with "seditious conspiracy" and other serious crimes, including conspiracy to interfere with a Federal proceeding; some, including Stewart Rhodes, have been convicted.[20] U.S. law defines seditious conspiracy as plotting "to overthrow," or "to oppose by force," or to use "force to prevent, hinder, or delay the execution of any law of the United States."[21] Some of the two groups' members have already admitted that this is what they intended to do.[22]

Other extremists and conspiracy theorists mobilized after President Trump's tweet as well. These movements are described in more detail in subsequent sections. Three Percenter militias—another far-right, anti-government movement—shared "#OccupyCongress" memes[23] and planned for violence at the U.S. Capitol.[24] Nick Fuentes, leader of the white nationalist "Groypers," rallied his followers for January 6th.[25] Fuentes bragged afterwards that the "Capitol siege was fucking awesome."[26] Users on TheDonald.win, a website populated by some of President Trump's most ardent fans, openly discussed surrounding and occupying the U.S. Capitol.[27]

Adherents of QAnon, a bizarre and dangerous conspiracy cult, believed January 6th would bring the prophesied "Storm"—a violent purge of Democrats and government officials promised by the mysterious online personality known only as "Q."[28] QAnon's devotees flocked to Washington, DC because of the President's tweet and subsequent rhetoric. They shared a digital banner, "Operation Occupy the Capitol," which depicted the U.S. Capitol being torn in two.[29]

One especially notorious conspiracy theorist, Alex Jones, repeatedly told his *InfoWars'* viewers that January 6th would be a day of reckoning.[30] Jones is known for his outlandish conspiracy-mongering, including his baseless claim that the massacre of school children at Sandy Hook Elementary School was really a "false flag" operation staged by the U.S. Government. Of course, his vicious lie was disproven in court, but Jones is obsessed with "deep state" conspiracy theories and often propagates them.[31] After the 2020 presidential election, Jones argued that President Trump should use the power of the Government to impose martial law on American citizens.[32] Along with his *InfoWars* co-hosts, Jones amplified President Trump's "Big

Lie" and relentlessly promoted President Trump's "wild" protest. One of Jones' co-hosts floated the idea of "storming right into the Capitol." [33] Jones himself marched to the Capitol January 6th. [34]

Jones's influence helped shape the planning for January 6th behind the scenes as well. The Select Committee investigated how event organizers and the White House staff planned President Trump's rally at the Ellipse, a park south of the White House. This event was intended to rile up the President's supporters just prior to the joint session of Congress. A wealthy heiress paid for the event after listening to Jones' *InfoWars* rant about the importance of President Trump's tweet. She spent $3 million with the goal to "get as many people there as possible." [35] It worked—Americans who believed the election was stolen flocked to the Nation's capital.

By January 5th, President Trump's supporters—a large, angry crowd ready for instructions—had assembled in Washington. That evening, he could hear his raucous supporters at a rally not far from the White House. The President knew his supporters were "angry," [36] and he planned to call on them to march on the U.S. Capitol. [37] He even wanted to join them on the march. [38] It was all part of President Trump's plan to intimidate officials and obstruct the joint session of Congress.

"We fight like hell," President Trump told the crowd assembled at the Ellipse on January 6, 2021. "And if you don't fight like hell, you're not going to have a country anymore." [39] Some of those in attendance, as well as elsewhere in Washington that day, were already prepared to fight. They had begun preparing two and a half weeks earlier—when President Trump told them it would "be wild!"

## 6.1 HOW FAR-RIGHT EXTREMISTS AND CONSPIRACY THEORISTS PLANNED FOR JANUARY 6TH

### THE "STOP THE STEAL" COALITION

President Trump's "be wild" tweet immediately mobilized extremists and conspiracy theorists in the "Stop the Steal" coalition. The phrase "Stop the Steal" was originally coined in early 2016 by President Trump's longtime political advisor, Roger Stone. [40] At the time, Stone alleged first that Candidate Trump's Republican rivals were attempting to steal Candidate Trump's nomination. [41] After Trump became the nominee, Stone repurposed the saying to claim that former Secretary of State Hillary Clinton would steal the presidency. [42] When President Trump won the 2016 election, "Stop the Steal" was rendered moot—and did not become a significant political movement until President Trump's defeat on election night in 2020. [43] As early as November 5, 2020, Stone advised associates that he intended to reconstitute "Stop the Steal" by building an army of lawyers and suing "like there's no tomorrow." [44]

Ali Alexander, a rightwing provocateur who has worked closely with Stone,[45] quickly organized a new "Stop the Steal" campaign. On November 10, 2020, Alexander established "Stop the Steal" as an entity incorporated in Alabama.[46] Alexander added a bank account and various websites.[47]

One of Alexander's key allies in the "Stop the Steal" movement was Alex Jones. Prior to January 6th, Jones riled up crowds both in-person and online with incendiary rhetoric about the election. Jones' *InfoWars* was also a platform for others in the election-denial coalition. For instance, both Enrique Tarrio and Stewart Rhodes made multiple appearances on *InfoWars*, including between election day 2020 and January 6, 2021.[48]

Another frequent guest on *InfoWars* was Roger Stone—a nexus character in the "Stop the Steal" coalition.[49] Stone recommended that then Presidential Candidate Donald Trump appear on Jones's show in December 2015.[50] Trump accepted the invitation and praised Jones at length during his appearance.[51] The significance of Trump's interview with Jones should not be underestimated. Donald Trump was a leading presidential contender at the time and would go on to win the election. His appearance with Jones normalized *InfoWars*, welcoming its conspiracy-minded audience into Trump's base.[52] Trump did not appear on *InfoWars* again. However, Stone continued to make regular guest appearances.[53]

After election day 2020, Alexander Jones, and other "Stop the Steal" organizers, held rallies around the country to protest fictional claims of voter fraud. These events provided an opportunity for radicals and extremists to coalesce. The Proud Boys, Oath Keepers, and Three Percenters were all attendees. QAnon adherents were well-represented. So, too, were the white nationalist Groypers and their leader, Nick Fuentes.

"Stop the Steal" events and other protests throughout 2020 helped build the momentum for January 6th. The Select Committee collected data on 85 right-wing events between January 1, 2020, and January 20, 2021, which were inspired by opposition to COVID-19 lockdown measures, racial justice protests, and, later, the perceived theft of President Trump's victory.[54] Far-right extremists protested at or inside State capitols, or at other government buildings, in at least 68 instances.[55] Of those, 49 occurred during the period after the election through January 6th.[56] In the year leading up to January 6th, there were at least nine events at which far-right actors entered State capitols.[57] At least four of these capitol incursions—in Michigan,[58] Idaho,[59] Arizona,[60] and Oregon[61]—involved identifiable individuals who later participated in the attack on the U.S. Capitol.

Alex Jones and Ali Alexander inside the Georgia State Capitol during a "Stop the Steal" rally on November 18, 2020 in Atlanta, Georgia.

Photo by Elijah Nouvelage/Getty Images

Consider, for example, the protests held in Atlanta between November 18 and 21, 2020. Leaders and rank-and-file members of the Proud Boys, Oath Keepers, and Groypers, gathered outside the State capitol and the governor's mansion for nonstop events, including armed protests. Enrique Tarrio[62] and Stewart Rhodes[63] personally led contingents of the Proud Boys and Oath Keepers, respectively.

Jones first announced the Atlanta events on InfoWars on November 16th. In his announcement, Jones teased that he would be joined by Roger Stone and also called on listeners to "surround the governor's mansion" in order to prevent the election results from being certified.[64] Fuentes advertised that he would be speaking at the capitol every day at noon.[65] In fiery speeches across Atlanta, Fuentes spread election lies as well as wink-and-nod hints at intimidation and violence.[66]

Alexander, standing alongside Jones and Fuentes outside the State capitol on November 18th, exhorted the crowd to "storm the capitol" with them.[67] The three men led a crowd into the State capitol building. On November 20th, Roger Stone gave a speech outside the Georgia capitol. Speaking through a telephone held up by Alexander, Stone advanced election lies, and finished with a provocative rallying cry: "Victory or death!"[68]

That same day, Fuentes told the crowd, "Look, we've been in front of the State capitol, maybe we've been trying the wrong approach." [69] Days earlier, at a nighttime event outside the governor's mansion, Alexander, again flanked by Jones and Fuentes, goaded the crowd: "We'll light the whole shit on fire." [70]

While the crowd did not turn violent, the "Stop the Steal" protests in Atlanta, Georgia, prefigured January 6th in important respects. "Stop the Steal" organizers tried to use the mob they had assembled—including extremists from the Proud Boys, Oath Keepers, Three Percenters and Groypers—to intimidate lawmakers and overturn the election results in Georgia, which was required to certify former Vice President Biden's victory in the State by the end of that week. [71] They implored their followers to "storm the capitol." [72] As discussed in Chapter 8, this same coalition of radicals did just that on January 6, 2021.

Other "Stop the Steal" events helped pave the way for the events of January 6th. Two rallies in Washington D.C.—on November 14 and December 12, 2020—were critically important. Alexander's "Stop the Steal" was not the only protest organization present at these events. Both were called "Million MAGA Marches" and drew in other rally organizers. One of these other protests was called the "Jericho March" prayer rally. [73] Regardless, the same constellation of actors that appeared in Atlanta also incited Trump supporters in Washington.

For instance, during the Jericho March rally on December 12th, Stewart Rhodes called on President Trump to invoke the Insurrection Act as part of a desperate gambit to remain in power. In Rhodes' vision, he would lead militiamen on behalf of President Trump when others tried to remove him from office. [74] If President Trump did not invoke the Insurrection Act, Rhodes warned the crowd, then they would be forced to wage a "much more desperate [and] much more bloody war." Alex Jones also gave an incendiary speech at the Jericho March event, declaring: "I don't know who is going to the White House in 38 days, but I sure know this, Joe Biden is a globalist, and Joe Biden will be removed, one way or another!" [75]

As the crowds gathered in Washington on December 12th, President Trump was publicly lobbying the Supreme Court to hear his fictious claims of election fraud. The President assailed the Supreme Court on Twitter throughout the day. [76] The "Stop the Steal" coalition was eager to help. After the Jericho March event ended, Jones, his InfoWars co-host Owen Shroyer, and Ali Alexander led a march on the Supreme Court. Once there, the crowd chanted slogans such as "Stop the Steal!"; "1776!!"; "Our revolution!"; and "The fight has just begun!!" [77]

"Million MAGA March" protest on November 14, 2020 in Washington, DC.
Photo by Tasos Katopodis/Getty Images

President Trump made sure to let the protestors in Washington know that he personally approved of their mission. During the November rally, President Trump waved to the crowd from his presidential motorcade.[78] Then, on the morning of December 12th, President Trump tweeted: "Wow! Thousands of people forming in Washington (D.C.) for Stop the Steal. Didn't know about this, but I'll be seeing them! #MAGA."[79] Later that day, President Trump flew over the protestors in Marine One.[80]

When President Trump tweeted one week later that there would be a "wild" protest in Washington on January 6th, the "Stop the Steal" coalition immediately began to mobilize. Jones posted an article on the *InfoWars* website asking readers if they would "answer President Trump's call to defend the Republic?"[81] The next day, December 20th, Jones devoted much of his *InfoWars* show to the President's announcement. Jones told his audience several times that if 10 million Americans came to Washington, DC on January 6th, Congress would have to listen to them.[82] He repeated this idea over the course of the episode, saying things such as, "He's calling *you*, he needs your help, we need your help, we need 10 million people there," "[w]e need martial law and have to prevent the police state of foreigners from taking over." Jones added: "It's literally in our hands. It's literally up to us."[83]

Other *InfoWars* hosts promoted the "wild" protest as well. In late December, Matt Bracken told InfoWars viewers that it may be necessary to storm the U.S. Capitol. "We're going to only be saved by millions of Americans moving to Washington, occupying the entire area, if—if necessary storming right into the Capitol," Bracken said. "You know, they're—we know the rules of engagement. If you have enough people, you can push down any kind of a fence or a wall." [84]

Far-right extremists planned to do just that.

## 6.2  THE PROUD BOYS: "[Y]OU WANT TO STORM THE CAPITOL"

From the Proud Boys' founding in 2016, violence was intrinsic to their mission. "We will kill you. That's the Proud Boys in a nutshell," their founder said.[85] New recruits pledge an oath, established in the group's bylaws, identifying themselves as unapologetic "Western chauvinists," [86] promoting an exclusionary, hyper-masculine interpretation of Western culture.[87] They find common ground in an embrace of misogyny and hate for their perceived enemies.[88] The group is somewhat ethnically diverse, but their public and private messages fester with toxic white supremacist, xenophobic, and anti-Semitic slurs.[89]

The Proud Boys have participated in, or instigated, protests since their founding.[90] They've long been known as street brawlers looking for a fight.[91] But 2020 was a watershed year for the group. As protests spread around the country, the Proud Boys deputized themselves as agents of law and order—vigilantes against perceived threats.[92] More often, they played the role of instigators.[93] They portrayed themselves as counter-protestors and identified their targets as Black Lives Matter and Antifa—though they were hard-pressed to define their organizational enemies.[94]

During the presidential debate on September 29, 2020, President Trump was asked to disavow far-right extremists, including the Proud Boys. The President did not explicitly condemn the group. Instead, he seemingly endorsed their mission. "Stand back and stand by," President Trump told the Proud Boys, before adding, "but I'll tell you what … somebody's got to do something about Antifa and the left." [95] The President's words electrified the group, injecting new life into their recruitment and activities. According to Nick Quested, a filmmaker who spent significant time with the group and testified before the Select Committee, the Proud Boys had found their "savior" in President Trump.[96]

Joseph Biggs, a senior Proud Boy, immediately trumpeted President Trump's debate statement on Parler,[97] a fringe social media platform. Biggs made it clear that the Proud Boys were ready to fight Antifa.[98] The group's

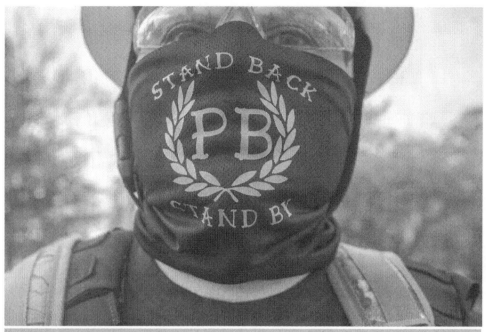

A Proud Boy during a "Stop the Steal" rally on November 7, 2020 in Salem, Oregon.
Photo by Nathan Howard/Getty Images

size "tripled" in response to President Trump's apparent endorsement, according to Jeremy Bertino, a Proud Boys leader who has pleaded guilty to seditious conspiracy in relation to January 6th.[99] Similarly, Enrique Tarrio and another Proud Boys member, George Meza, testified to the Select Committee that the President's comment was a pivotal, energizing moment.[100] The group started selling merchandise with their new "stand back and stand by" slogan the very same night.[101]

As the presidential votes were tallied, the Proud Boys became agitated at the prospect that President Trump would lose. On November 5, 2020, Biggs posted on social media, "It's time for fucking war if they steal this shit."[102] As former Vice President Joe Biden's victory became apparent, Proud Boys leaders directed their ire toward others in the Government. Biggs, speaking on a Proud Boys livestream show with Tarrio and others, warned that government officials are "evil scum, and they all deserve to die a traitor's death." Ethan Nordean—another Proud Boys leader who allegedly helped lead the attack at the Capitol—responded, "Yup, Day of the Rope,"[103] referring to a day of mass lynching of "race traitors" in the white supremacist novel *The Turner Diaries*.[104]

## THE PROUD BOYS IN WASHINGTON PRIOR TO JANUARY 6TH

Within days of the election, dozens of "Stop the Steal" protests were organized around the country.[105] The Proud Boys participated alongside other right-wing extremist groups in some of them, including a November 7, 2020, protest outside of the Pennsylvania State capitol in Harrisburg.[106] The two events in Washington, DC—on November 14, 2020, and the other on December 12, 2020—proved to be especially important for the group's evolution.

The daytime events on both dates passed by without violence or major unrest, but as the sun set, bouts of violence erupted,[107] driven by clashes between far-right extremist groups—chiefly the Proud Boys—and counter-protestors.[108] Among far-right extremists, the Proud Boys had the largest showing in both November and December,[109] with roughly 200 to 300 Proud Boys at the November 14th rally, and the same number or more in December.[110] As discussed in Chapter 8, they mustered about the same contingent for the attack on the U.S. Capitol.

The gathering on November 14th provided a chance for Tarrio to socialize with rally leaders and far-right celebrities. In fact, his travel to DC by private jet appears to have been paid for by Patrick Byrne, a businessman who had President Trump's ear in the last weeks of his presidency and encouraged the President to authorize the seizure of voting machines in a December 18th meeting.[111] Tarrio's testimony and photographs from the day show that he met with "Stop the Steal" organizer Ali Alexander that evening, and the pair toasted each other.[112] Tarrio described the event as a "historic" meeting of Trump supporters and celebrated the opportunity to share that platform with Alexander, Jones, and Jones' *InfoWars* co-host, Owen Shroyer.[113] Shroyer would later be charged with crimes committed during the January 6th attack.[114]

A month later, the Proud Boys returned to the Nation's capital. On the evening of December 11th, hundreds of Proud Boys and friends gathered in downtown Washington, DC to listen to an impromptu bullhorn speech by Tarrio and Nordean, along with Roger Stone and Shroyer.[115] Stone implored the crowd to "fight to the bitter end." [116]

The next day, as the Proud Boys marched in force on the streets, Tarrio teased in a social media post that he had a meeting in the White House.[117] The visit, which was only a public White House tour, appears to have been facilitated by a friend, Bianca Gracia, the head of Latinos for Trump.[118] As the rallies concluded the next day, the Proud Boys took to the streets again. Two key events occurred that evening.

First, members of the Proud Boys tore down a Black Lives Matter banner from a historically Black church in downtown Washington, DC.[119] They filmed themselves burning it.[120] Tarrio was eventually charged with destruction of property.[121] He was arrested on January 4, 2021, and banned from Washington, DC, barring him from joining the group at the Capitol.[122] As explained in Chapter 8, however, Tarrio's arrest did not stop him from conspiring with his men on January 6th.

Minutes after the flag burning, a man wearing black clothes walked into a crowd of Proud Boys.[123] Assuming he was associated with Antifa, they began pushing and harassing him, and he drew a knife in response.[124] In the ensuing melee, four Proud Boys suffered stab wounds, including Bertino, a confidant to Tarrio.[125] Bertino's wounds were severe and life-threatening, preventing him from joining the group on January 6th.[126]

### STORMING THE WINTER PALACE

The Proud Boys began to reorient and formalize their operations to focus on January 6th after President Trump's December 19th tweet. Inspired, in part, by Bertino's stabbing, the Proud Boys centered their new hierarchy in group chats that used terms such as "Ministry of Self Defense" (MOSD).[127] However, the words "Self Defense" were misleading: Enrique Tarrio and others would soon go on the offense. And the MOSD served as their organizational scaffolding for the January 6, 2021, attack.

On December 20, 2020, Tarrio established a "national rally planning committee" and created an encrypted MOSD chat to organize their activities.[128] Tarrio added Proud Boys leaders from across the country, including several who played lead roles in the violence on January 6th.[129] In the ensuing weeks, the Proud Boys traded equipment recommendations, shared maps marked with law enforcement positions, and established command and control structures.[130] A separate encrypted chat, named "Boots on the Ground," was established for foot soldiers who would be in Washington, DC on January 6th.[131]

The Proud Boys' planning for January 6th was a significant step in the group's evolution. Previously, they were loosely organized. The MOSD was created to enforce a "top down structure" with a defined leadership.[132] Tarrio stressed the command structure by telling members that they needed to "[f]it in [] or fuck off."[133]

From the start, it was clear that MOSD chat members were intensely interested in disrupting the electoral count on January 6th. On December 20, 2020, one MOSD leader stated, "I assume most of the protest will be at the capital [sic] building given what's going on inside."[134] On December 29, 2020, in a group message to the MOSD, a member wrote, "I know most of the events will be centered around freedom plaza...." Tarrio responded, "Negative. They're centered around the Capitol."[135]

On December 30, 2020, Tarrio received an intriguing document titled, "1776 Returns."[136] The document was apparently sent to him by cryptocurrency investors in South Florida.[137] The file's author(s) divided their plan into five parts, "Infiltrate, Execution, Distract, Occupy and Sit-In," with the goal of overrunning several Federal buildings around the U.S. Capitol. The plan specifically mentioned House and Senate office buildings, setting forth steps for occupying them. The author(s) called for "the masses to rush the building[s]," distract law enforcement in the area by pulling fire alarms around the city, target specific Senators' offices, and disguise participants' identities with COVID masks.[138]

One proposal mentioned in the document is titled, "Storm the Winter Palace."[139] This is a reference to a dramatic reenactment of the 1917 Bolshevik Revolution, during which Vladimir Lenin ordered his forces to take over the Romanovs' residence in Petrograd. The "Winter Palace" was the seat of the provisional government, which had held out against the Bolshevik revolutionaries. The Proud Boys would frame their actions on January 6th as part of the American Revolution. But the "1776 Returns" document shows their inspiration came at least in part from the Communist Revolution, which led to 70-plus years of totalitarian rule. No historical event has been less American.

The Proud Boys did not adopt the "1776 Returns" plan in full. Several Proud Boys testified that they were unaware of the document before it became public.[140] But the document does appear to have been significantly edited while in the Proud Boys' hands.[141] The person who sent it to Tarrio—his ex-girlfriend, Eryka Gemma Flores—commented, "The revolution is [more] important than anything." To which Tarrio responded: "That's what every waking moment consists of ... I'm not playing games."[142]

On January 3rd, Tarrio posted a conspicuous question on Telegram: "What if we invade it?" The first response to his post read: "January 6th is D day [sic] in America."[143] In private, on the Proud Boys' leadership group message, planning continued. One MOSD leader, John Stewart, floated a plan that centered around "the front entrance to the Capitol building."[144] At 7:10 p.m. on January 3rd, Stewart wrote to the MOSD leaders:

> I mean the main operating theater should be out in front of the house of representatives. It should be out in front of the Capitol building. That's where the vote is taking place and all of the objections. So, we can ignore the rest of these stages and all that shit and plan the operations based around the front entrance to the Capitol building. I strongly recommend you use the national mall and not Pennsylvania avenue though. It's wide-open space, you can see everything coming from all angles.[145]

Early the next morning, on January 4th, Tarrio sent a voice memo to the same group of MOSD leaders stating, "I didn't hear this voice until now, you want to storm the Capitol." [146]

One of Tarrio's comrades in the Proud Boys' leadership, Charles Donohoe—who pleaded guilty to conspiracy to obstruct an official proceeding and assaulting, resisting, or impeding certain officers[147]—later told authorities that by January 4th he "was aware that members of MOSD leadership were discussing the possibility of storming the Capitol." [148] Donohoe "believed that storming the Capitol would achieve the group's goal of stopping the government from carrying out the transfer of presidential power" and "understood that storming the Capitol would be illegal." [149] By the following evening, January 5th, Tarrio was discussing with other Proud Boy leaders a "tactical plan" for the following day. Their "objective" was "to obstruct, impede, or interfere with the certification of the Electoral College vote." [150] Moreover, Donohoe understood that the Proud Boys "would pursue this through the use of force and violence, in order to show Congress that 'we the people' were in charge." [151] On January 6th, Charles Donohoe understood that two of his fellow Proud Boys' leaders—Ethan Nordean and Joe Biggs—"were searching for an opportunity to storm the Capitol." [152]

Jeremy Bertino, the Proud Boys leader who was stabbed on the night of December 12th, later told authorities that his fellow extremists plotted to stop the peaceful transfer of power. In October 2022, Bertino pleaded guilty to "seditious conspiracy" and other crimes.[153] Bertino admitted that the Proud Boys traveled to Washington, DC on January 6, 2021, "to stop the certification of the Electoral College Vote." They "were willing to do whatever it would take, including using force against police and others, to achieve that objective." [154]

In testimony before the Select Committee, Bertino recalled a telling text exchange with Tarrio on the evening of January 6th. "I was like, 'holy shit,' or something like that I said to him," Bertino recalled. "And I was like, 'I can't believe this is happening,' or something like that, and '1776.' " [155]

Tarrio replied to Bertino: "Winter Palace." [156]

### 6.3 THE OATH KEEPERS: "HE CALLED US ALL TO THE CAPITOL AND WANTS US TO MAKE IT WILD!!!"

The Oath Keepers, founded in 2009 by Elmer Stewart Rhodes, is a far-right anti-government organization. The group targets former and current military and law enforcement for recruitment. Their name refers to the oath taken by public servants to support and defend the U.S. Constitution. The Oath Keepers' claimed fealty to the U.S. Constitution is belied by their obsession with conspiracy theories about alleged evil-intentioned elites in the Government.[157] Rhodes has often spouted these conspiracy theories on *InfoWars*.[158]

Over the summer of 2020, the Oath Keepers organized armed groups, ostensibly to serve as volunteer, self-appointed security at protests around the country. The Oath Keepers used the protests to draw in new recruits.[159] They also built muscle memory by coordinating for these events. For example, the Oath Keepers hired Michael Greene, who later coordinated Oath Keepers' activities on January 5th and 6th, to lead security operations in multiple cities around the country.[160] In the early part of 2020, protests against COVID-related lockdowns served as additional growth and networking opportunities. Kellye SoRelle, a lawyer for the Oath Keepers, met the Oath Keepers at a lockdown protest in Austin, Texas in early 2020. SoRelle saw these COVID events as a "coalescing moment" for different far-right groups.[161]

The "Stop the Steal" movement created another opportunity for the Oath Keepers to grow their influence. Rhodes repeatedly amplified the stolen election conspiracy theory. On November 10, 2020, he posted a "Call to Action!" on the Oath Keepers website, alleging the election was "stolen" and exhorting his followers to "refuse to EVER recognize this as a legitimate election, and refuse to recognize Biden as a legitimate winner."[162] Under a section entitled "What We the People Must Do," Rhodes quoted a "patriot from Serbia, who also loves America." The Serbian author described how his fellow countrymen fomented a political revolution. Parts of the statement presaged the attack on the U.S. Capitol:

> ... Millions gathered in our capital [*sic*]. There were no barricades strong enough to stop them, nor the police determined enough to stop them. Police and Military aligned with the people after few hours of fist-fight [*sic*]. We stormed the Parliament. And burned down fake state Television! WE WON![163]

The Oath Keepers were obsessed with the Insurrection Act—seeing it as a way for President Trump to cling to power. Rhodes believed that the President could empower militias like the Oath Keepers to enforce law and order after other Americans refused to accept President Trump's rule.[164] Indeed, President Trump had been intensely interested in the Insurrection Act as a potential tool to quell the protests in summer 2020.[165] Rhodes wished the Act had been invoked then, but he did not give up on the fantasy.[166] As mentioned above, Rhodes called for President Trump to invoke the Insurrection Act during his speech in Washington on December 12, 2020.[167]

That day, Rhodes also coordinated with Jericho March organizers to provide security.[168] He coordinated with a paramilitary group known as 1st

Amendment Praetorian (1AP), to guard VIPs, including retired Lieutenant General Michael Flynn and Patrick Byrne.[169] Rhodes indicated that the Oath Keepers would be "working closely" with them for the event.[170]

The Oath Keepers continued to call for President Trump to invoke the Insurrection Act throughout December 2020, arguing that the President needed to do so to "Stop the Steal."[171] This fantasy reflected a warped sense of reality. Rhodes testified that President Trump could have mobilized "unorganized militia," including the Oath Keepers, to suppress an insurrection if he attempted to stay in power after losing the election.[172] But the Oath Keepers themselves were the ones contemplating insurrection. On December 10, 2020, Rhodes messaged others: "Either Trump gets off his ass and uses the Insurrection Act to defeat the Chicom puppet coup or we will have to rise up in insurrection (rebellion) against the ChiCom puppet Biden. Take your pick."[173] Rhodes was blunt in other messages to the Oath Keepers, writing: "We need to push Tump [sic] to do his duty. If he doesn't, we will do ours. Declare Independence. Defy[,] Resist[,] Defend[,] Conquer or Die. This needs to be our attitude."[174]

### 6.4 "TRUMP SAID IT'S GONNA BE WILD!!!!!!! IT'S GONNA BE WILD!!!!!!!"

As the Proud Boys began their plans for January 6th, Kelly Meggs, the leader of the Florida chapter of the Oath Keepers, reached out. In the past, the Proud Boys and the Oath Keepers had their differences, deriding each other's tactics and ethos during the summer 2020 protests.[175] But President Trump's tweet on December 19th conveyed a sense of urgency which provided the two extremist rivals the opportunity to work together for a common goal.

After President Trump's tweet, Meggs called Enrique Tarrio. They spoke for 3 minutes and 26 seconds.[176] Meggs also sent a message on Facebook, bragging about an alliance he had formed among the Oath Keepers, the Florida Three Percenters, and the Proud Boys: "We have decided to work together and shut this shit down."[177] The Oath Keepers were making plans of their own, too.

"Oath Keepers president [Rhodes] is pretty disheartened," Roberto Minuta, one of Rhodes' men, messaged someone on December 19th. "He feels like it's go time, the time for peaceful protest is over in his eyes. I was talking with him last night."[178] Minuta has been charged with "seditious conspiracy" and other crimes.[179]

In the days that followed, the Oath Keepers planned for violence. They used encrypted chats on Signal to discuss travel plans, trade tips on tactical equipment to bring, and develop their plans for once they were on the ground in the DC area.[180] On December 21st, 2020, Joshua James messaged the group, stating, "SE region is creating a NATIONAL CALL TO ACTION FOR DC JAN 6TH. ... 4 states are mobilizing[.]"[181] Meggs, Rhodes, and others created several different chat groups to coordinate for January 6th.[182]

On December 22nd, Meggs echoed President Trump's tweet in a Facebook message to someone else:

> Trump said It's gonna be wild!!!!!!! It's gonna be wild!!!!!!! He wants us to make it WILD that's what he's saying. He called us all to the Capitol and wants us to make it wild!!! Sir Yes Sir!!! Gentlemen we are heading to DC pack your shit!!"[183]

Meggs also wrote that the Oath Keepers would have 50–100 members in Washington, DC on January 6th.[184]

The Oath Keepers hosted periodic group video meetings to discuss plans for January 6th. Richard Dockery, a former Oath Keepers member, testified to the Select Committee about a video call that took place around December 31st, and related specifically to planning for January 6th.[185] During the call, Oath Keepers' leadership announced plans to provide security for far-right celebrities like Roger Stone.[186] If there were any problems while they were providing security, "there was a quick reaction force in Virginia that would come help them out ... and that they would have firearms."[187]

Rhodes announced during an episode of *InfoWars* in November 2020 that the Oath Keepers had established a "Quick Reaction Force" (QRF) outside of Washington, DC.[188] After President Trump announced the "wild" protest, the group's advanced coordination largely focused on planning related to their QRF, as well as the various security details for VIPs and stage areas on January 5th and 6th.[189] Oath Keepers from North Carolina, Florida, South Carolina, and Arizona converged on the Comfort Inn in Ballston, Virginia, and used the location to store their cache of weapons for January 6th.[190] Oath Keepers leaders communicated actively about the QRF for January 6th.[191] Rhodes and another contingent of Oath Keepers stayed at the Hilton Garden Inn in Vienna, Virginia, and stored weapons there as well.[192]

Rhodes amassed an arsenal of military-grade assault weapons and equipment in the days leading up to January 6th. On December 30th, Rhodes spent approximately $7,000 on two night-vision devices and a weapon sight and shipped them to Marsha Lessard, a rally organizer who lived near Washington, DC and who had previously been in contact with the organizers of the Ellipse rally.[193] On January 1st and 2nd, Rhodes purchased additional weapons and accessories at a cost of approximately $5,000.[194] The following day, January 3rd, Rhodes and Kellye SoRelle departed Texas for Washington, DC. While traveling, Rhodes spent an additional $6,000 on an AR-style rifle and firearms attachments.[195] Making one final shopping trip in Mississippi, Rhodes purchased $4,500 of firearms equipment including more sights, magazines, and weapons parts on January 4th.[196]

On the morning of January 6th, with weapons stockpiled, Rhodes messaged the Signal group of Oath Keepers leaders:

> We have several well equipped [sic] QRFs outside DC. And there are many, many others, from other groups, who will be watching and waiting on the outside in case of worst case [sic] scenarios.[197]

## 6.5 "READY TO STEP IN AND DO WHAT IS NEEDED"

Stewart Rhodes's and Oath Keepers' lawyer Kellye SoRelle arrived in Washington on the afternoon of January 5th.[198] They immediately went to Freedom Plaza, where President Trump had instructed rally organizers to give some of his most extreme supporters time to speak.[199] As a small group of Oath Keepers patrolled Freedom Plaza, they were able to see the results of President Trump's call to mobilize.[200] SoRelle testified that there were Oath Keepers, Proud Boys, and "Alex Jones people" mingling together in the crowd, with "just a small distinction between them."[201]

The Oath Keepers later found themselves at the Phoenix Park Hotel,[202] where they ate and drank with a motley coalition of far-right political activists who were united in their shared belief in President Trump's Big Lie.[203] Among them were: Proud Boys-linked Bianca Gracia of Latinos for Trump; Joshua Macias, leader of Vets for Trump;[204] and Amanda Chase, a Virginia State senator.[205] In a livestream discussion moderated by Chase, they promoted false election fraud claims. Macias and Rhodes encouraged President Trump to invoke the Insurrection Act and call up combat veterans who are "ready to step in and do what is needed."[206]

SoRelle later told the Select Committee that there was discussion of going to "storm the Capitol," although she claimed that this was "normal" discussion and supposedly did not indicate violence or "any of that type of stuff."[207]

That same evening, Gracia asked SoRelle and Rhodes to follow her to a garage where she was supposed to meet Proud Boys leader Enrique Tarrio,[208] who had just been released from custody and ordered to leave the DC area.[209] Instead of immediately leaving Washington, DC, Tarrio instead made his way to a garage near the hotel where the others gathered.[210] Portions of the ensuing meeting were captured on video by documentary filmmaker Nick Quested and his camera crew. SoRelle claims that she was asked to attend to discuss Tarrio's legal woes,[211] but there is evidence indicating that the conversation turned tactical.

Tarrio discussed the court's order, informing the group he was going north to Maryland, so he could "stay close just to make sure my guys are ok."[212] Tarrio discussed his confiscated phone with Gracia. He told her that "they couldn't get in there," apparently referencing the two-factor authentication enabled on his phone.[213] Tarrio also appeared familiar with another attendee, Vets for Trump leader Macias, who rested his hand on Tarrio's shoulder at various points.[214] Rhodes and Tarrio shook hands.[215]

Much of the substantive conversation between Rhodes, Tarrio, and the others cannot be heard because Tarrio asked Quested's camera crew to stop recording.[216] However, some of the conversation is audible from afar and Rhodes can be heard telling Tarrio that he "has three groups in Tyson's Corner,"[217] a reference to the QRFs that he had mustered in the event that President Trump called the Oath Keepers into service.

Tarrio later expressed appreciation for Rhodes's presence at the garage meeting and underscored that their two organizations needed to stand together on January 6th. Tarrio explained that the Proud Boys and Oath Keepers are "just two different groups" and that he and Rhodes "don't get along," but said that "for situations like this where there is a need to unite regardless of our differences ... what he did today was commendable."[218] Tarrio added that Rhodes's presence at the garage meeting was "thoughtful" because Rhodes had "quickly provided security" for the meeting and "seemed concerned" about Tarrio's legal situation.[219] In a likely nod to prior coordination between Proud Boys and Oath Keepers at other post-election events, Tarrio further explained that "my guys have helped him [Rhodes] out in the past," and that he and Rhodes have "mutual respect" for one another.[220] Tarrio then traveled north to a hotel near Baltimore, Maryland, where he stayed through the events of the next day.[221]

## 6.6 "FRIENDS OF STONE"

As explained above, a constellation of far-right characters came together in late 2020 as part of the "Stop the Steal" cause. Among them was Roger Stone, a right-wing political operative whose career as a self-trumpeted dirty trickster stretched back decades. Stone is arguably President Trump's oldest political advisor.[222] For example, he worked for Donald Trump's independent presidential bid during the 2000 campaign.[223] In addition to his political connections, Stone cultivated relationships with far-right extremists, including the two groups charged with seditious conspiracy: the Oath Keepers and the Proud Boys.

The Select Committee found that at least seven members of the Oath Keepers provided security for Stone, or were seen with him, in the weeks

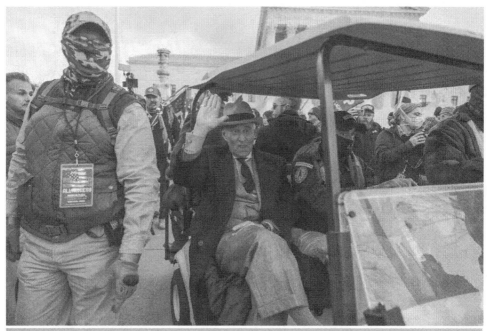

Roger Stone in front of the Supreme Court on January 5, 2021 in Washington, DC.
Photo by Tasos Katopodis/Getty Images

immediately preceding the attack on the U.S. Capitol.[224] Text messages released by Edward Vallejo, an Oath Keeper charged with seditious conspiracy and other crimes, show that Stewart Rhodes and Kelly Meggs discussed providing security for Stone.[225] Some of these Oath Keepers guarded Stone during an event at Freedom Plaza in Washington, DC on the night of January 5th.[226] Stone was also flanked by Oath Keepers outside of the Willard Hotel on the morning of January 6th.[227] One of the Oath Keepers who provided security for Stone was Joshua James, who pleaded guilty to seditious conspiracy, obstruction of Congress and other charges in March 2022.[228] James was also reportedly seen in Stone's hotel room at the Willard hours before the attack on the U.S. Capitol.[229]

Stone has a longstanding, close relationship with the Proud Boys. Stone has taken the Proud Boys oath[230] and repeatedly defended the group.[231] Danish documentarians filmed him working with Proud Boys for years.[232] In one scene, filmed in 2019, Stone warmly greets Joe Biggs, a Proud Boys leader central to the Capitol violence. Stone says of Biggs: "My guy, right here."[233] In a 2019 court case, Stone identified Enrique Tarrio as one of his volunteers, explaining that Tarrio had access to his phone and could post to Stone's Instagram account from it.[234]

As mentioned above, Stone, Tarrio and another Proud Boy leader, Ethan Nordean, addressed an impromptu rally in Washington, DC on the night of December 11, 2020. Owen Shroyer, an *InfoWars* host, was also with them.[235] "We will fight to the bitter end for an honest count of the 2020 election," Stone told the crowd. "Never give up, never quit, never surrender, and fight for America!"[236] A few weeks later, on January 2, 2021, Tarrio led a Proud Boys protest outside of Senator Marco Rubio's home in Florida. The Proud Boys wanted to convince Rubio to vote against certification of the vote on January 6th.[237] Stone reportedly called into the event to speak to Tarrio's crowd.[238]

One way in which Stone maintained these contacts was through a Signal chat group named "F.O.S."—or Friends of Stone.[239] Two days after the election, Stone sent a text: "We provide information several times a day. So please monitor the F.O.S. feed so you can act in a timely fashion."[240] Ali Alexander and Stone continued to coordinate about Stop the Steal strategy and events between the election and January 6th.[241] In addition to Alexander, Stone's "Friends" on the Signal chat included Rhodes and Tarrio.[242]

In July 2020, President Trump granted Stone clemency after he was convicted of lying to Congress and other charges.[243] Then, on December 23rd, President Trump pardoned Stone.[244] Several days later, at a dinner on the evening of December 27th, Stone thanked President Trump. In a post on Parler, Stone wrote that he "thanked President Trump in person tonight for pardoning me" and also recommended to the President that he "appoint a special counsel" to stop "those who are attempting to steal the 2020 election through voter fraud." Stone also wrote that he wanted "to ensure that Donald Trump continues as our president."[245] Finally, he added: "#StopTheSteal" and "#rogerstonedidnothingwrong."[246] The Select Committee has learned that Stone discussed the January 6th event with the President, likely at this same dinner on December 27th.[247] The President told Stone he "was thinking of speaking."[248]

The Select Committee sought to question Roger Stone about his relationships with President Trump and far-right extremists, as well as other issues. During his deposition, Stone invoked his Fifth Amendment right nearly 90 times.[249] Stone has publicly stated that he committed no wrongdoing and that he encouraged a peaceful protest.[250]

## 6.7  WHITE NATIONALISTS: "THE CAPITOL SIEGE WAS FUCKING AWESOME..."

Nick Fuentes is an online provocateur who leads a white nationalist movement known as "America First," or the "Groypers." Fuentes immediately responded to President Trump's "be wild" tweet. On December 19, 2020,

Fuentes wrote on Twitter: "I will return to Washington DC to rally for President Trump on January 6th!" [251] Fuentes and his Groypers did return to Washington, DC for the joint session. As the attack was underway, Fuentes incited followers from his perch immediately outside of the U.S. Capitol. Some of his followers joined the attack inside, with one even sitting in Vice President Pence's seat on the Senate dais. [252]

Fuentes and a fellow Groyper leader, Patrick Casey, rose to prominence in 2017 after rallying at the Charlottesville "Unite the Right" event. [253] For years, the Groypers have repeatedly promoted white supremacist and Christian nationalist beliefs, often cloaked in wink-and-nod humor, puns, or religion, and they regularly gin up public opposition to other right-wing organizations or politicians whom they deem insufficiently conservative. [254]

Fuentes was a key voice for "Stop the Steal" conspiracy theories leading up to January 6th. He spent 2 months leading rallies in State capitals across the country, [255] spreading the Big Lie and livestreaming coded calls to violence. [256] He also used his livestream to raise significant funds between November 2020 and January 2021. [257]

On November 9, 2020, Fuentes promised, "GROYPERS ARE GOING TO STOP THIS COUP!" [258] Two days later, Fuentes organized a "Stop the Steal" rally at the Michigan State Capitol. He told the crowd that they should be "more feral" in their tactics to overturn the election, suggesting that they target lawmakers in their homes. [259] On November 14th, Fuentes rallied a crowd of his followers at the Million MAGA March in Washington, DC, pushing "Stop the Steal" conspiracies, calling for President Trump to rule for life, and exhorting his followers to "storm every State capitol until January 20, 2021, until President Trump is inaugurated for 4 more years." [260]

As discussed above, Fuentes was a prominent figure at the "Stop the Steal" rally in Atlanta, Georgia, in November 2020. [261] He promoted election conspiracies, criticized the Republican Party, joked about the Holocaust, and denounced former Vice President Biden as illegitimate. [262] Fuentes also suggested his followers intimidate politicians in their homes. [263]

On December 12th, Fuentes again rallied a crowd of supporters at the "Stop the Steal" events in Washington, DC, calling for the destruction of the Republican Party because it had failed to overturn the election. [264] As others spoke at the Jericho March rally, Fuentes headlined a "Stop the Steal" protest just a few blocks away. [265]

On January 4th, Fuentes suggested that his followers kill State legislators who don't support efforts to overturn the 2020 election. As discussed in Chapter 2, President Trump and his surrogates were pressuring State legislators at the time to do just that. Fuentes complained that his side "had no leverage." Fuentes then asked: "What can you and I do to a state legisla-tor, besides kill them?" He then quickly added: "Although we should not do that. I am not advising that, but I mean, what else can you do, right?[266]

On January 5th, Casey advertised the marches in Washington, DC on his Telegram channel and provided repeated updates on the logistics of getting into the city. Casey also spoke to his followers about the next day's rally on a livestream on DLive.[267] As discussed in Chapter 8, the Groypers clearly played a role in the January 6th attack. They even planted their flag in the inner chambers of the U.S. Capitol.[268] Fuentes crowed about the attack the day after, tweeting: "The Capitol Siege was fucking awesome and I'm not going to pretend it wasn't." [269] In another tweet on January 7th, Fuentes wrote: "For a brief time yesterday the US Capital [sic] was once again occu-pied by The American People, before the regime wrested back control." [270]

Despite his boasts on Twitter, Fuentes exercised his Fifth Amendment privilege against self-incrimination and refused to provide information about his organizing activities to the Select Committee.[271]

## 6.8  THE THREE (III%) PERCENTERS: "#OCCUPYCONGRESS"

The Oath Keepers were not the only anti-government extremists who viewed President Trump's December 19th, tweet as a call to arms. Militias around the country were similarly inspired to act. "People were retweeting it right and left. ... I saw people retweeting it, talking about, yeah, it's going to be crazy, going to be a huge crowd," Michael Lee Wells, a militia leader in North Carolina, told the Select Committee.[272] Members of militias known as the "Three Percenters" were electrified.

The Three Percenters believe that three percent of American colonists successfully overthrew the British during the American Revolution.[273] This is not true. Far more than a tiny fraction of the colonial population fought in or supported the Revolutionary War.[274] Regardless, this ahistorical belief has become an organizing myth for militias around modern-day America.

As with the Oath Keepers, many Three Percenters have turned against the U.S. Government, such that they equate it with the British monarchy and believe it should be overthrown.[275] The movement does not have one, centralized hierarchy. Instead, semi-autonomous branches organize and run themselves.[276] The Three Percenter cause was growing prior to the attack on the U.S. Capitol. Jeremy Liggett, a militia leader in Florida, told the Select Committee it was "trendy" in far-right circles to identify with the Three Percenter movement in the months leading up to January 6th.[277]

President Trump tapped into this well of anti-government extremism. The President's repeated insistence that the election had been stolen reso-nated with militia members who were already inclined to believe in shady political conspiracies. The President's December 19th tweet mobilized Three Percenters around the country. Suddenly, they had a focal point for their anti-government beliefs: the joint session of Congress on January 6th. Court filings and other evidence reveal that Three Percenters immediately began planning for violence after President Trump's "be wild" announcement.

For example, Lucas Denney and Donald Hazard led a militia affiliated with the Three Percenter movement called the "Patriot Boys of North Texas." Both Denney and Hazard were charged with assaulting officers on January 6th.[278] Denney pleaded guilty and has been sentenced to 52 months in prison.[279] After President Trump's tweet, they discussed travel plans, as well as the need to procure body armor, helmets, knuckle gloves and pepper spray.[280] But they did not plan to act alone. Instead, they saw themselves as part of a coalition. In multiple messages, both Denney and Hazard claimed they were also affiliated with Proud Boys and intended to work with them on or before January 6th.[281]

Denney repeatedly cited President Trump's tweet. "Trump himself is calling for a big protest in DC on January 6th. I'm not going to miss this one," Denney told Hazard on December 21st.[282] On December 30th, Denney wrote in a Facebook message:

> Trump has called this himself. For everyone to come. It's the day the electoral college is suppose to be certified by congress to officially elect Biden. But, Pence is in charge of this and he's going to throw out all the votes from States that were proved to have fraud. There's so much more going on behind the scenes though. That's why he's called this rally for support. ... Trump will stay President ... [283]

As this message indicates, Denney was well-aware of President Trump's multi-part plan to disrupt the transfer of power. He thought that Vice President Pence had the power to "throw out" electoral votes, just as the President demanded. In other messages, Denney claimed that President Trump wanted militias to descend on Washington, DC so they could serve as a security force against a perceived threat from Antifa and Black Lives Matter on January 6th.[284]

Additional messages between the two reveal their intent to march on the U.S. Capitol. For instance, Denney attempted to post two banners on Facebook that advertised events on January 6th.[285] Both banners contained the hashtag "#OccupyCongress." The pictures contained images of the U.S. Capitol and referenced "The Great Betrayal." One of them read "If They Won't Hear Us" and "They Will Fear Us." In another post, Denney wrote: "I can't wait to be in the middle of it on the front line on the 6th."[286]

Curiously, Denney had also heard a "rumor" that President Trump would march with them. On January 4, 2021, he stated in a Facebook message:

> Things are going to be happening here. Trump is going to be speaking to everyone Wed [January 6] before everyone marches to the capital [sic]. Rumour [sic] has it that he may march with us. I'll tell you more when you get here on where to be wed and what time so you have the best seats.[287]

On or about January 6th, Denney sent another message via Facebook, writing: "Trump speaking to us around 11 am then we march to the capital and after that we have special plans that I can't say right now over Facebook. But keep an eye out for live feed tomorrow from me. Tomorrow will be historic."[288] Later on January 6th, during the attack, Hazard was captured on video bragging: "We have stormed our nation's capitol."[289]

The Patriot Boys of North Texas were not the only Three Percenter group that mobilized after President Trump's tweet. The Department of Justice has alleged that multiple other cadres of Three Percenter militiamen prepared for violence on January 6th and then took part in the attack on the U.S. Capitol.

In Florida, a Three Percenter organization known as the "Guardians of Freedom" established a "B-squad" for January 6th because they allegedly wanted to avoid being called a "militia."[290] These men were led by Jeremy Liggett, mentioned above.[291]

On December 24, 2020, the B-squad sent out a flyer, "CALLING ALL PATRIOTS!" to Washington, D.C.[292] The flyer read: "The Guardians of Freedom III% are responding to the call from President Donald J. Trump to assist in the security, protection, and support of the people as we all protest the fraudulent election and re-establish liberty for our nation. JOIN US & Thousands of other Patriots!"[293] The B-Squad claimed it was the "right & duty of the people to alter or to abolish" the Government.[294] Its members discussed bringing tactical gear to Washington, DC.[295]

On December 30th, Liggett posted a meme to Facebook stating that "3% Will Show In Record Numbers In DC."[296] When the Select Committee asked about this post, Liggett downplayed its significance or disclaimed any knowledge about other Three Percenter groups that might "show in record numbers."[297] However, on January 3, 2021, Liggett posted a "safety video" on Facebook in which he and others dressed in military gear. Liggett instructed listeners about self-defense and the tools they (like him) could bring to Washington, DC, including "an expandable metal baton, a walking cane and a folding knife."[298] He advised "all of you Patriots going to

Washington, D.C. ... to support Trump," and to "keep up the fight." [299] Several "B-squad" members have been charged with civil disorder and disorderly and disruptive conduct, which took place while rioters nearby were assaulting officers in the tunnel area of the Capitol's Lower West Terrace on January 6th. [300]

In California, another group of men associated with the Three Percenter movement quickly began plotting their next moves after President Trump's tweet. Alan Hostetter and Russell Taylor ran a non-profit known as the American Phoenix Project, which protested COVID-19 lockdowns and the 2020 election results, while also promoting violence ahead of January 6th. [301] Ahead of the joint session, Hostetter and Taylor organized a small group in an encrypted chat they named "The California Patriots—DC Brigade." [302]

On December 19th, Taylor linked to President Trump's "will be wild" tweet and asked members of the chat "Who is going?" [303] The same day, Hostetter posted a message to his Instagram account, explaining he was traveling to Washington, DC on January 6th because President Trump "tweeted that all patriots should descend on Washington DC" and that day "is the date of the Joint Session of Congress in which they will either accept or reject the fake/phony/stolen electoral college votes." [304] The next day, Taylor renamed the Telegram chat as "The California Patriots-Answer the Call Jan 6." [305] On December 29th, Taylor posted to that chat: "I personally want to be on the front steps and be one of the first ones to breach the doors!" [306]

Between December 19th and January 6th, Hostetter, Taylor and their alleged co-conspirators exchanged messages about bringing weapons, such as hatchets, bats, or large metal flashlights, as well as possibly firearms, with them to Washington, DC. [307] They were "ready and willing to fight." [308] In one message, Hostetter predicted that January 6th would be similar to the "War of Independence" because "[t]here will likely be 3% of us again that will commit fully to this battle, but just as in 1776 patriots will prevail." [309]

There are additional examples of how President Trump's "be wild" tweet led Three Percenters to descend on the U.S. Capitol. One Three Percenter group issued an open letter on December 16, 2020, announcing that they "stand ready and are standing by to answer the call from our President should the need arise that We The People are needed to take back our country from the pure evil that is conspiring to steal our country away from the American people.... We will not act unless we are told to." [310] In late December, after the President's tweet, The Three Percenters Original (TTPO) issued a letter to its members announcing that "this organization will be answering that call!" [311]

There is also additional evidence showing that militia groups like the Three Percenters coordinated with other groups both before and on January 6th. Josh Ellis, the owner of the MyMilitia website, testified that he used Zello (a walkie-talkie app) when he was in Washington, DC on January 6th. The Proud Boys, Oath Keepers, other militia members, and "regular patriots" all used these Zello channels in the leadup to January 6th and in response to President Trump's December 19th tweet. They used these channels to share intelligence.[312]

### 6.9 QANON: "OPERATION OCCUPY THE CAPITOL"

Shortly after the January 6th attack, a video of a bearded man in a "Q" shirt chasing U.S. Capitol Police Officer Ryan Goodman through the halls of the U.S. Capitol went viral.[313] That man was Doug Jensen, a QAnon believer.[314] After Jensen's arrest, FBI agents asked him why he traveled from Iowa to Washington, DC in the first place. "Trump posted make sure you're there, January 6 for the rally in Washington, D.C.," Jensen responded.[315]

Jensen was not the only QAnon believer to attack the U.S. Capitol on January 6th. The letter "Q" and related slogans, such as "Where We Go One, We Go All," were ubiquitous among the rioters. They were visible on shirts, signs, and flags throughout the crowd. What was once a marginal digital movement had become a bricks-and-mortar force powerful enough to help obstruct a joint session of Congress.

QAnon is a bizarre and dangerous cult that gained popularity in 2017, when a person known only as "Q" began posting on 4chan, an anonymous message board.[316] The poster supposedly held a "Q" security clearance at the Department of Energy. QAnon adherents believe that President Trump is a messianic figure battling the forces of the "deep state" and a Satanic pedophile ring operated by leading Democrats and the American elite.[317] Q's first post in October 2017 predicted that former Secretary of State Hillary Clinton would be arrested in short order.[318] Although that prophecy did not come to pass, the conspiracy theory evolved and grew over time, spreading across social media platforms and eventually finding a home in 8kun, another anonymous message board known for trafficking in conspiracy theories and hate.[319]

President Trump was given multiple opportunities to disavow QAnon. Instead, he essentially endorsed its core tenets. During an August 19, 2020, press briefing, President Trump was asked what he thought about the QAnon belief that he was fighting a Satanic cabal. "I mean, you know, if I can help save the world from problems, I'm willing to do it. I'm willing to put myself out there," he replied.[320] During a townhall on NBC News two weeks prior to the election, President Trump first claimed he "knew nothing" about QAnon, but he then praised its believers for being "very strongly against pedophilia." The President emphasized: "And I agree with that. I mean, I do agree with that." [321]

In 2020, QAnon played a significant role in spreading various election conspiracy theories. After the election, QAnon accounts amplified the claim that Dominion Voting System's software had altered votes.[322] On November 19th, President Trump tweeted and retweeted a link to a segment on One America News Network (OAN) that was captioned, "Dominion-izing the Vote." [323] The segment claimed that Dominion had switched votes from President Trump to former Vice President Biden. OAN featured a supposed cyber expert, Ron Watkins, a key figure in the QAnon conspiracy movement.[324] Watkins's father, Jim, owned the 8kun site that "Q" called home, and Ron helped oversee its message boards.[325]

After promoting the OAN segment, President Trump retweeted Ron Watkins's account on several other occasions. On December 15, 2020, President Trump retweeted a post in which Watkins spread false claims of foreign influence in the election.[326] Then, on January 3rd, President Trump retweeted Ron Watkins's account four more times.[327]

QAnon's adherents were clearly paying attention to President Trump's words—and tweets. The President's "be wild" tweet was widely heard as a clarion call. Jim Watkins told the Select Committee that "thousands and thousands of people probably" agreed that the President's December 19th tweet was a call for them to come to Washington, DC.[328] Jim Watkins himself marched in Washington, DC on January 6th because of the President's call, but he has not been charged with any crime.[329]

Other QAnon adherents flocked to Washington, DC in response to the President's call to action. "POTUS HAS REQUESTED YOUR ATTENDANCE Washington DC JANUARY 6TH 2021," Thomas Munn, a QAnon believer, posted on Facebook. Munn added: "Our President has only asked two things from us, so far...#1 Vote #2 January 6, 2021." [330] Jacob Chansley, better known as the QAnon Shaman, told the FBI that he traveled from Arizona because President Trump had requested that all "patriots" come to Washington, DC on January 6th.[331]

During the investigation, the Select Committee learned that the QAnon conspiracy theory often overlaps with other extremist beliefs. Stewart Rhodes of the Oath Keepers testified to the Select Committee that he's "not a Q-tard" and "not a follower of Q at all." [332] However, Rhodes cynically exploited QAnon for his own purposes. The Oath Keepers' website and text messages were littered with QAnon phrases.[333] Nick Quested, a filmmaker who shadowed the Proud Boys, often heard QAnon themes in the Proud Boys' private discussions.[334]

As January 6th drew closer, multiple posts on the QAnon-linked website 8kun indicated that violence was imminent. "You can go to Washington on Jan 6 and help storm the Capitol," one user wrote. This same user continued: "As many Patriots as can be. We will storm the government buildings, kill cops, kill security guards, kill federal employees and agents, and demand a recount."[335] Other posts on 8kun debated the politicians that users should target once they got inside the Capitol.[336]

A QAnon-inspired banner was also widely shared by groups planning events for January 5th and 6th. The top of the image read: "Operation Occupy the Capitol." The central image showed the U.S. Capitol being torn in two. In the lower left corner, there appeared a QAnon phrase: "#WeAreTheStorm."[337]

## 6.10  THEDONALD.WIN: "OCCUPY THE CAPITOL"

Within three minutes of President Trump's tweet, a user on TheDonald.win message board posted: "Trump Tweet. Daddy Says Be In DC on Jan. 6th."[338] Moderators pinned the post to the top of the board from December 19th until January 6th. It garnered nearly 6,000 comments and more than 24,000 upvotes during that time.[339] Many of the site's users quickly interpreted President Trump's tweet as a call for violence. For example, one user wrote, "[Trump] can't exactly openly tell you to revolt. This is the closest he'll ever get."[340] Jody Williams, the site's then-owner, testified that while users had been talking about traveling to Washington, DC since the election, after the tweet "anything else was kind of shut out, and it just was going to be the 6th."[341]

In the days that followed, users on TheDonald.win discussed: surrounding and occupying the U.S. Capitol; cutting off access tunnels used by Members of Congress; the types of weapons they should bring; and even how to build a hangman's gallows.[342] The parallels to what transpired on January 6th are obvious.

TheDonald.win and its predecessor site was a website for some of its namesake's most ardent fans. Even before President Trump was elected, his social media team monitored and interacted with the site's users. In the summer of 2016, then-candidate Trump himself engaged in a written question and answer session on TheDonald, which at the time was a forum on Reddit.[343] This online community, which had upwards of 790,000 users, was banned by Reddit in mid-2020.[344] However, the site's users migrated to another online location, becoming TheDonald.win.[345]

Dan Scavino, the President's social media guru, amplified content from this website. During the 2016 presidential campaign, "a team in the war

White House social media director Dan Scavino Jr.

room at Trump Tower was monitoring social media trends, including TheDonald subreddit ... and privately communicating with the most active users to seed new trends."[346] "Campaign staffers monitored Twitter and TheDonald subreddit, and pushed any promising trends up to social media director Dan Scavino, who might give them a boost with a tweet."[347] In 2017, President Trump tweeted a video of himself attacking CNN.[348] The video had appeared on The Donald four days earlier.[349] In 2019, *Politico* reported that Scavino "regularly monitors Reddit, with a particular focus on the pro-Trump /r/The_Donald channel."[350]

The Select Committee sought to question Scavino about how he and others on President Trump's social media team interacted with The Donald subreddit and then TheDonald.win. But Scavino refused to cooperate with the committee's subpoena.[351]

After President Trump's December 19th tweet, users on the site posted simple maps of the U.S. Capitol and telegraphed their intent to invade the building.[352] "If we occupy the capitol building, there will be no vote," one user wrote.[353] "The media will call us evil if we have to occupy the Capitol Building on January 6th. Let them," another post read.[354] One user argued the goal should be to "surround the enemy" and "create [a] perimeter" around the Capitol on January 6th, such that no one was allowed to leave until President Trump was "re-admitted for another 4 years." [355] This same user posted a diagram of the U.S. Capitol's perimeter with arrows indicating where the "Capitol Access Tunnels" were located.

On January 5th, another user on TheDonald.win encouraged President Trump's supporters to "be prepared to secure the capitol building," claiming that "there will be plenty of ex military to guide you." [356] Multiple other posts made it clear that the U.S. Capitol was the target on January 6th, with one poster writing that people should bring "handcuffs and zip ties to DC," so they could enact "citizen's arrests" of those officials who certified the election's results. [357] Another post highlighted the "most important map for January 6th. Form a TRUE LINE around the Capitol and the tunnels." [358] That "post included a detailed schematic of Capitol Hill with the tunnels surrounding the complex highlighted." [359]

Other posts on TheDonald.win included specific plans to build gallows outside the U.S. Capitol. "Gallows are simpler and more cost effective, plus they're an American old west tradition too," one user wrote on December 22, 2020. [360] A week later, another wrote: "Let's construct a Gallows outside the Capitol building next Wednesday so the Congressmen watching from their office windows shit their pants." [361] Another said that "building a hanging platform in front of Congress on the 6 should send a strong message." [362] The site hosted a diagram showing how to tie a hangman's knot, [363] with one site member writing that they should build gallows "so the traitors know the stakes." [364] On January 5, 2021, hours before the attack began, a user posted an image of gallows and titled it, "Election Fraud Repair Kit." [365]

Text messages between Trump Campaign Senior Advisor Jason Miller and White House Chief of Staff Mark Meadows show that these kinds of posts reached deep into the President's inner circle. Miller sent Meadows a text on December 30th, declaring, "I got the base FIRED UP." [366] The thread contained a link to a TheDonald.win comment thread filled with reactions to a post by Miller promoting January 6th. [367] Users in the thread made comments such as "gallows don't require electricity," and that millions will "bust in through the doors if they try to stop Pence from declaring Trump the winner," all in response to Miller. [368]

On December 19, 2020, the same day President Trump posted his inflammatory "be wild" tweet, he also tweeted a noteworthy video. The short clip was titled, "FIGHT FOR TRUMP!—SAVE AMERICA—SAVE THE WORLD." [369] The video reportedly appeared on TheDonald.win two days earlier. [370] As with so much else on TheDonald.win, this refrain featured prominently on the day of the attack on the Capitol. During his speech at the Ellipse south of the White House on January 6th, the crowd broke out into a chant of "Fight for Trump! Fight for Trump!" President Trump thanked those in attendance. [371]

In the two and a half weeks since he first announced the January 6th "protest," extremists and conspiracy theorists plotted to make the unprecedented, presidentially announced protest against the peaceful transfer of power "wild" indeed. Meanwhile, event organizers and White House staffers prepared for the final rally of President Trump's term.

## 6.11  HOW THE WHITE HOUSE AND RALLY ORGANIZERS PREPARED FOR JANUARY 6TH

In the days following President Trump's tweet, rally organizers secured permits for about one dozen events in Washington, DC on January 5th and 6th.[372] At 7:12 a.m., not even 6 hours after President Trump's tweet, Cindy Chafian, an executive at Women for America First (WFAF), emailed the National Park Service (NPS) about an event that had been planned to coincide with President-elect Biden's inauguration on January 20, 2021.[373] Chafian's ask was simple: "Can I change the date to January 6th?"[374]

WFAF was founded in 2019 by Amy and Kylie Kremer, a mother-daughter pair who were longtime supporters of the President.[375] WFAF became a significant player in the "Stop the Steal" movement.[376] The Kremers started a "Stop the Steal" Facebook group that gathered some 365,000 members in less than 24 hours.[377] Their online organizing coincided with their on-the-ground mobilization activities. The Kremers organized a bus tour to promote the Big Lie, in addition to events in Washington, DC on November 14, 2020, and December 12, 2020.[378] After President Trump's December 19th tweet, the Kremers focused on January 6th. Kylie Kremer proudly declared their support on Twitter: "The calvary [sic] is coming, President! JANUARY 6th | Washington, DC TrumpMarch.com #MarchForTrump #StopTheSteal."[379] After the date of their permit was revised, WFAF ultimately provided President Trump the stage on the Ellipse where he would direct the crowd to march on the Capitol.[380]

The Kremers were not alone in responding quickly to the President's tweet. Ali Alexander, the founder of Stop the Steal, LLC,[381] was eager to get ahead of other organizers. On the morning of December 19th, Alexander told his event planner, "Everyone is trying to get the jump on us so I'd like to get the court side of the capitol (lawn) and I'd like to get capitol steps and court."[382] Alexander told his event planner to "grab whatever we can. All of it."[383] Alexander's team did just that: they registered and launched a new website, WildProtest.com,[384] which advertised planned events for January 6th under a banner that read: "President Trump Wants You in DC January 6."[385]

Still other organizers were quick to seize on the President's tweet. Arina Grossu and Robert Weaver, co-founders of the self-proclaimed "Judeo-Christian" Jericho March organization,[386] held a rally in Washington, DC on

December 12, 2020. Oath Keepers leader Stewart Rhodes, Flynn, Jones, Alexander, and others shared a stage at that event.[387] Grossu and Weaver exchanged emails just a few hours after President Trump's first mention of January 6th. In an email on the morning of December 19th, Weaver told Grossu to "enjoy the peace before the storm" and said, "Trump has called for a protest on 1/6, FYI." [388] The Jericho March's website used President Trump's "Be there, will be wild!" language to advertise additional events between January 2nd and January 6, 2021.[389]

Marsha Lessard, the leader of a vaccine-skeptic group, Virginia Freedom Keepers, worked to stage an event with Bianca Gracia, the leader of Latinos for Trump on January 6th.[390] The women had ties to the Oath Keepers[391] and Proud Boys,[392] respectively—two groups central to the violence on January 6. Latinos for Trump reportedly advertised their January 6th event with the same QAnon-inspired banner, "Operation Occupy the Capitol." [393] Another conservative group, Moms for America, worked with Alexander before securing a permit for an event on January 5th.[394]

### 6.12 "HE'S CALLING ON *YOU*, HE NEEDS YOUR HELP"

As discussed above, Alex Jones was one of the loudest supporters of the "Stop the Steal" movement. Jones dedicated much of the December 20th episode of his *InfoWars* show to President Trump's "be wild" tweet, telling his listeners that nothing less than the fate of the American Republic was at stake. "He's calling *you*, he needs your help, we need your help," Jones told his audience.[395] The Select Committee has learned that, between the time of the President's tweet and Jones's December 20th show, Jones's staff had several calls with Chafian, who had just procured a new permit for WFAF's event on the Ellipse.[396] The two parties apparently discussed whether this newly hatched January 6th event was an opportunity to work together.[397]

Jones's broadcast also led to an influx of funds for the January 6th event at the Ellipse. Julie Fancelli is the billionaire heiress to the Publix supermarket fortune and a longtime supporter of President Trump.[398] Fancelli had recently become a donor to Jones's *InfoWars* site.[399] She listened to Jones's December 20th show,[400] and decided she wanted to back the cause.

Inspired by Jones and the fervor that continued to surround the President's tweet, Fancelli called Caroline Wren, a Republican fundraiser linked to the Trump Campaign, the next day.[401] According to Wren, Fancelli said that "she wanted to see a lot of people there in DC, so how much would that cost?" [402] Fancelli spoke with Jones's staff and they recommended that she connect with Chafian, who was organizing the Ellipse rally.[403] In the waning days of 2020, Fancelli and Jones spoke several times.[404]

Fancelli worked with Wren to create a multimillion-dollar budget to convene as many supporters of President Trump as possible.[405] To ensure that Fancelli's dollars made maximum impact, Wren contacted some of the major players who were rallying supporters for January 6th. Wren emailed Kylie Kremer[406] and exchanged texts with Jones[407] and Chafian.[408] Fancelli's goal was clear: she wanted to spend $3 million to "get as many people there as possible."[409] The resulting budget allocated $500,000 to a busing program and a centralized ad campaign by the Tea Party Express to promote the event.[410] Another $500,000 went to assisting WFAF and Jones in their organizational efforts.[411]

Caroline Wren also connected with Ali Alexander. On December 29th, Wren told the Stop the Steal leader, "I can pay for the buses and I have my team looking for available companies, so let me know what cities you need them in!"[412] Wren's offer came in response to a tweet from Alexander earlier that day: "Coalition of us working on 25 new charter buses to bring people FOR FREE to #JAN6 #STOPTHESTEAL for President Trump. If you have money for more buses or have a company, let me know. We will list our buses sometime in the next 72 hours. STAND BACK & STAND BY!"[413]

The final words of Alexander's tweet directly echoed President Trump's command to the Proud Boys during the September 29, 2020, presidential debate.[414] Alexander's word choice was apt. The Proud Boys were already planning to show up in force, and to ensure that the crowd would be "wild."

### 6.13 "TRUMP IS SUPPOSED TO ORDER US TO THE CAPITOL"

On the evening of December 27th, President Trump boosted the upcoming event on Twitter: "See you in Washington, DC, on January 6th. Don't miss it. Information to follow!"[415] The Select Committee learned that this tweet came after the White House spoke with a former Trump staffer, Justin Caporale, who was asked to help produce the Ellipse rally.[416] That same evening, the President had dinner with Donald Trump, Jr., and his girlfriend Kimberly Guilfoyle,[417] who spoke with rally organizer Caroline Wren during the meal.[418] Wren also texted Guilfoyle talking points that described her ambitions for the event, saying that "buses of people are coming in from all over the country to support you. It's going to be huge, we are also adding in programming the night of January 5th."[419]

After Guilfoyle's call with Wren, there was a series of calls among the senior White House staff,[420] likely underscoring the seriousness of the White House's interest in the event.

Within a few days, the White House began to take a more direct role in coordinating the rally at the Ellipse.[421] In a December 29th text to Wren, Caporale wrote that after the President's planned speech there "maybe [*sic*] a call to action to march to the [C]apitol and make noise."[422]

This is the earliest indication uncovered by the Select Committee that the President planned to call on his supporters to march on the U.S. Capitol. But it wasn't the last. On January 2nd, rally organizer Katrina Pierson informed Wren that President Trump's Chief of Staff, Mark Meadows, had said the President was going to "call on everyone to march to the [C]apitol."[423]

Inside the White House, the President's intent was well-known. Cassidy Hutchinson, an aide to Meadows, recalled in her testimony that she overheard discussions to this effect toward the end of December or early January. One such discussion included an exchange between Meadows and Rudolph Giuliani that occurred on January 2nd.[424] Hutchinson understood that President Trump wanted to have a crowd at the Capitol in connection with what was happening inside—the certification of the electoral count.[425] Hutchinson also recalled that President Trump's allies in Congress were aware of the plan. During a call with members of the House Freedom Caucus, the idea of telling people to go to the Capitol was discussed as a way to encourage Congress to delay the electoral college certification and send it back to the States.[426]

On January 4th, WFAF's Kylie Kremer informed Mike Lindell, the CEO of MyPillow and an ally of President Trump, that "POTUS is going to have us march there [the Supreme Court]/the Capitol" but emphasized that the plan "stays only between us."[427]

The "Stop the Steal" coalition was aware of the President's intent. On January 5th, Ali Alexander sent a text to a journalist saying: "Ellipse then US capitol [*sic*]. Trump is supposed to order us to the capitol [*sic*] at the end of his speech but we will see."[428]

## 6.14 "WELL, I SHOULD WALK WITH THE PEOPLE."

President Trump wanted to personally accompany his supporters on the march from the Ellipse to the U.S. Capitol. During a January 4th meeting with staffers and event organizer Katrina Pierson, President Trump emphasized his desire to march with his supporters.[429] "Well, I should walk with the people," Pierson recalled President Trump saying.[430] Though Pierson said that she did not take him "seriously," she knew that "he would absolutely want to be with the people."[431] Pierson pointed out that President Trump "did the drive-by the first time and the flyover the second time"—a reference to the November and December 2020 protests in Washington, DC.[432] During these previous events, President Trump made cameo appearances to fire up his supporters. Now, as January 6th approached, the President again wanted to be there, on the ground, as his supporters marched on the U.S. Capitol.

The President's advisors tried to talk him out of it. White House Senior Advisor Max Miller "shot it down immediately" because of concerns about the President's safety.[433] Pierson agreed.[434] But President Trump was persistent, and he floated the idea of having 10,000 National Guardsmen deployed to protect him and his supporters from any supposed threats by leftwing counter-protestors.[435] Miller again rejected the President's idea, saying that the National Guard was not necessary for the event. Miller testified that there was no further conversation on the matter.[436] After the meeting, Miller texted Pierson, "Just glad we killed the national guard and a procession." [437] That is, President Trump briefly considered having the National Guard oversee his procession to the U.S. Capitol. The President did not order the National Guard to protect the U.S. Capitol, or to secure the joint session proceedings.

Although his advisors tried to talk the President out of personally going, they understood that his supporters would be marching.[438] Pierson's agenda for the meeting reflected the President's plan for protestors to go to the U.S. Capitol after the rally.[439] But President Trump did not give up on the idea of personally joining his supporters on their march, as discussed further in Chapter 7.

### 6.15 "POTUS...LIKES THE CRAZIES."

As Katrina Pierson helped plan the Ellipse rally, she faced another complication. The "Stop the Steal" movement played an outsized role in promoting January 6th. And now, as the day approached, its leading voices wanted prime speaking gigs—perhaps even on the same stage as President Trump. Roger Stone, Alex Jones and Ali Alexander were all angling for significant stage time. Pierson knew they were trouble.

In her testimony before the Select Committee, Pierson cited several concerns, including that Jones and Alexander had played a prominent role in the November 2020 protest in Atlanta, Georgia. This was no ordinary protest. Jones and Alexander "had gone into the Georgia Capitol with some inflammatory rhetoric," Pierson explained.[440] When Pierson was asked if Jones and Alexander "surrounding the governor's mansion" and "going into the Capitol" were the "kind of thing" that gave her pause, she responded: "Absolutely." [441] After the Georgia protest, Pierson explained,

Photos of Roger Stone, Alex Jones and Ali Alexander appear on a screen during a Select Committee hearing on July 12, 2022.

Photo by Anna Moneymaker/Getty Images

the Kremers—who had helped organize "Stop the Steal" activities—distanced themselves from Jones and Alexander.[442]

But there was an additional problem. President Trump wanted to include the "Stop the Steal" leaders in the January 6th event. As Pierson put it in a text message to Kylie Kremer: "POTUS ... likes the crazies."[443] Pierson said that she believed this was the case because President Trump "loved people who viciously defended him in public."[444] But their "vicious" defenses of the President clearly troubled Pierson.

Pierson tried to trim the speaker lineup—which still included the "Stop the Steal" trio of Stone, Jones, and Alexander. She was initially vetoed by the White House after Deputy Chief of Staff for Communications Dan Scavino,[445] who had approved the "original psycho list."[446] At one point, she texted Scavino's boss, Mark Meadows, saying: "Things have gotten crazy and I desperately need some direction."[447] She was concerned by the possibility of "crazy people" being included in the event, their incendiary role in Georgia, and the fact that people coming to Washington, DC were planning to protest at the U.S. Capitol.[448]

Meadows told Pierson that she should take control of the situation and remove the possibility of controversial speakers.[449] Pierson agreed to do so.[450] But the President remained an obstacle. During their January 4th meeting, Pierson tried to convince President Trump to minimize the role of these potentially explosive figures at the Ellipse. She offered to place them at a planned event the night before in Freedom Plaza or on other stages in DC on January 6th. She told the President to "[k]eep the fringe on the fringe"[451] and advised him to "[e]liminate convicted felons that could damage other speakers."[452]

President Trump was still unwilling to remove them from the lineup entirely. The President instructed Pierson to give Stone a speaking slot on January 5th and asked for more information about Ali Alexander.[453] After discussing the matter with Scavino, President Trump also requested that Alexander be given a speaking slot. President Trump "brought up Ali [Alexander] ... just keep him on stage not associated with POTUS or main event," Scavino wrote.[454]

In the end, the "Stop the Steal" leaders—Stone, Jones and Alexander — did not appear on the stage at the Ellipse on January 6th, although they did speak at other planned events, consistent with the President's request about Alexander. "POTUS expectations are [to have something] intimate and then send everyone over to the Capitol," Pierson explained in a text message to Justin Caporale and Taylor Budowich.[455] Caporale redacted this text and others in his early production of documents to the Select Committee, and he only revealed them after they had already been produced by other witnesses.[456]

However, other incendiary voices—in addition to President Trump's — were given time on the Ellipse stage. The Select Committee learned that President Trump's aides warned him against the inclusion of figures like John Eastman[457] and Rudolph Giuliani,[458] given their false claims about election fraud.[459] Both men, of course, ended up sharing a stage with him on January 6th.[460] Meadows himself directed that they be allowed to speak.[461]

### 6.16  JANUARY 5, 2021: "FORT TRUMP"

While the "Stop the Steal" coalition was not given speaking slots on the Ellipse stage on January 6th, its leaders had plenty of opportunities to speak the day before. And they used their platforms to rile up the crowd in Washington, DC in advance of the joint session.

Ali Alexander spoke at an event sponsored by Moms for America in front of the U.S. Capitol. Alexander claimed that he was honored to be sharing the same stage with President Trump the following day, even though behind the scenes his appearance had been nixed.[462]

"We must rebel," Alexander told rallygoers. "I'm not even sure if I'm going to leave D.C. We might make this 'Fort Trump,' right?" Alexander said, while standing in front of the U.S. Capitol. "We're going to keep fighting for you, Mr. President."[463] On his Twitter account, Alexander also spread the idea that President Trump's supporters should occupy areas of Washington, DC, using the phrases and hashtags such as "Fort Trump" and "#OccupyDC".[464]

Alex Jones and Roger Stone spoke at a separate event hosted by Virginia Women for Trump in front of the Supreme Court.[465] The event, named the "One Nation Under God" prayer rally, was cohosted by the American Phoenix Project—the Three Percenter-linked group run by Alan Hostetter and Russel Taylor, discussed above, which is charged with conspiracy to obstruct an official proceeding.[466]

Jones repeated his claims about the election being stolen, claiming that those in attendance stood against a "Satanic world government."[467] Stone led a "Stop the Steal" chant, claiming the "evidence of election fraud is not only growing, it is overwhelming, and it is compelling." President Trump "won the majority of the legal votes cast" and President Trump "won this election," Stone said. Nothing less than the fate of Western Civilization was at stake, according to Stone:

Let's be very clear. This is not fight between Republicans and Democrats. This is not a fight between liberals and conservatives. This is a fight for the future the United States of America. It is a fight for the future of Western Civilization as we know it. It's a fight between dark and light. It's a fight between the godly and the godless. It's a fight between good and evil. And we dare not fail, or we will step out into one thousand years of darkness.[468]

Stone claimed that they "renounce violence" and those on "the left … are the violent ones." But he insisted that "nothing is over until we say it is," and "Victory will be ours."[469]

Both Taylor and Hostetter spoke as well. Hostetter told the crowd, "We are at war."[470] Taylor promised to "fight" and "bleed," vowing that "Patriot[s]" would "not return to our peaceful way of life until this election is made right."[471]

A long rally was also hosted at Freedom Plaza, an open-air space on Pennsylvania Avenue in Washington, DC. It is a symbolic protest site, standing in the direct line between the White House and the U.S. Capitol. Stone, Jones and Alexander all appeared at Freedom Plaza on the evening of January 5th. Their remarks were incendiary.

Stone repeated his apocalyptic language from earlier in the day, claiming that rallygoers were embroiled in "an epic struggle for the future of this country between dark and light."[472] "I want them to know that 1776 is always an option," Ali Alexander said. "These degenerates in the deep state are going to give us what we want, or we are going to shut this country down."[473] When Alex Jones took to the stage, he screamed at the crowd: "*It's 1776!*"[474]

Another speaker that evening was Lt. Gen. Michael Flynn (ret.). "Tomorrow, tomorrow, trust me, the American people that are standing on the soil that we are standing on tonight, and they're going to be standing on this soil tomorrow, this is soil that we have fought over, fought for, and we will fight for in the future," Flynn also told the crowd. Flynn addressed Members of Congress, saying "those of you who are feeling weak tonight, those of you that don't have the moral fiber in your body, get some tonight because tomorrow, we the people are going to be here, and we want you to know that we will not stand for a lie. We will not stand for a lie."[475]

### 6.17 "TOGETHER, WE WILL STOP THE STEAL."

On the evening of January 5th, the President edited the speech he would deliver the next day at the Ellipse. The President's speechwriting team had only started working on his remarks the day before.[476] Despite concerns from the speechwriting team, unfounded claims coming from Giuliani and others made their way into the draft.[477]

The initial draft circulated on January 5th emphasized that the crowd would march to the U.S. Capitol.[478] Based on what they had heard from others in the White House, the speechwriting team expected President Trump to use his address to tell people to go to the Capitol.[479]

That evening, President Trump convened an impromptu gathering in the Oval Office with members of his staff, primarily his press team[480] and White House Deputy Chief of Staff Dan Scavino, who was in charge of President Trump's personal Twitter account.[481] Despite the bitter cold, the President ordered his staff to keep the door to the Rose Garden open so he could hear the music and cheering from his supporters at Freedom Plaza.[482] The music playing at Freedom Plaza was so loud "you could feel it shaking in the Oval."[483]

As President Trump listened, he was tweeting, at one point telling his supporters he could hear them from the Oval Office.[484] His speechwriters incorporated those tweets into a second draft of the speech that was circulated later that evening.[485] The following appeared in both tweet form[486] and was adapted into the speech:

> "All of us here today do not want to see our election victory stolen by emboldened Radical Left Democrats. Our Country has had enough, they won't take it anymore! Together, we will STOP THE STEAL."[487]

President Trump and members of his staff in the Oval Office on the evening of January 5, 2021.

Photo provided to the Select Committee by the National Archives and Records Administration.

In speaking with staff, he still seemed optimistic that "Congress would take some sort of action in his favor."[488] The White House photographer, who was also in attendance, recalled that President Trump again remarked that he should go to the Capitol the next day, and even asked about the best route to get there.[489] The President peppered staff for ideas concerning how "we could make the RINOs do the right thing" and make the next day "big."[490] Deputy Press Secretary Sarah Matthews, who was present in the Oval Office that evening, understood that President Trump wanted to get Republican Members of Congress to send the electoral votes back to the States, rather than certify the election.[491] Matthews recalled that initially no one spoke up in response, since they were trying to "process" what he had said.[492]

Eventually, Deere suggested that President Trump should focus his speech on his administration's accomplishments, rather than on his claim that the election had been stolen.[493] But the President told Deere that while they had accomplished a lot, the crowd was going to be "fired up" and "angry" the next day because they believed the election had been stolen and was rigged.[494] President Trump knew the crowd was angry because he could hear them.[495] Of course, President Trump was responsible, more than any other party, for ginning up their anger.

President Trump ended the evening by asking an aide how many people were going to be at the rally. The aide responded that he was not sure but told President Trump that he saw videos on Twitter of "pro-trump people chanting on planes heading to DC," which he asked to be shared with Scavino.[496]

"We will not let them silence your voices," the President told the crowd from the podium at the Ellipse. "We're not going to let it happen, I'm not going to let it happen."[497] His supporters started chanting, "fight for Trump!" The President thanked them.[498]

President Trump knew not only that his supporters were angry, but also that some of them were armed.[499] At times, he ad-libbed, deliberately stoking their rage even more. At one point he said: "And we fight. We fight like hell. And if you don't fight like hell, you're not going to have a country anymore."[500] The word "fight," or a variation thereof, appeared only twice in the prepared text.[501] President Trump would go on to utter the word twenty times during his speech at the Ellipse.[502]

President Trump had summoned a mob, including armed extremists and conspiracy theorists, to Washington, DC on the day the joint session of Congress was to meet. He then told that same mob to march on the U.S. Capitol and "fight." They clearly got the message.

President Trump speaks at the January 6th Ellipse rally.

# 7

# 187 MINUTES OF DERELICTION

At 1:10 p.m. on January 6th, President Trump concluded his speech at the Ellipse. By that time, the attack on the U.S. Capitol had already begun. But it was about to get much worse. The President told thousands of people in attendance to march down Pennsylvania Avenue to the Capitol. He told them to "fight like hell" because if they didn't, they were "not going to have a country anymore." Not everyone who left the Ellipse did as the Commander-in-Chief ordered, but many of them did. The fighting intensified during the hours that followed.[1]

By 1:21 p.m., President Trump was informed that the Capitol was under attack. He could have interceded immediately. But the President chose not to do so. It was not until 4:17 p.m. that President Trump finally tweeted a video in which he told the rioters to go home.

The 187 minutes between the end of President Trump's speech and when he finally told the mob to leave the U.S. Capitol was a dereliction of duty. In the U.S. military, a service member is deemed to be "derelict in the performance of duties when that person willfully or negligently fails to perform that person's duties or when that person performs them in a culpably inefficient manner."[2] As Commander-in-Chief, President Trump had the power—more than any other American—to muster the U.S. Government's resources and end the attack on the U.S. Capitol. He willfully remained idle even as others, including his own Vice President, acted.

President Trump could have called top officials at the Department of Justice, the Department of Homeland Security, the Department of Defense, the F.B.I., the Capitol Police Department, or the DC Mayor's Office to ensure that they quelled the violence. He made no such calls. Instead, President Trump reached out to Rudolph Giuliani and friendly Members of Congress, seeking their assistance in delaying the joint session of Congress. And the President tweeted at 2:24 p.m., at the height of the violence, that his own Vice President lacked the "courage" to act—a statement that could only further enrage the mob. Meanwhile, Vice President Michael Pence assumed the duties of the President, requesting the assistance of top officials, even though he was not in the chain of command and had no constitutional power to issue orders.

In testimony before the Select Committee, Chairman of the Joint Chiefs of Staff General Mark Milley explained that President Trump did "[n]othing," "[z]ero" to marshal the Government's resources during the assault on the U.S. Capitol.[3] In contrast, Vice President Pence had "two or three calls" with General Milley and other military officials—even as the mob hunted him. During those calls, Vice President Pence was "very animated" and "issued very explicit, very direct, unambiguous orders." The Vice President told Acting Secretary of Defense Chris Miller to "get the military down here, get the [National] [G]uard down here," and "put down this situation."[4] President Trump could have made those same demands. He chose not to do so—a damning fact that President Trump's own Chief of Staff, Mark Meadows, quickly tried to cover up.

"We have to kill the narrative that the Vice President is making all the decisions," General Milley recalled Meadows as saying. "We need to establish the narrative, you know, that the President is still in charge and that things are steady or stable," Meadows said, which General Milley described as a "[r]ed flag."[5] In his testimony, General Milley also reflected on what it meant for a President not to be taking action in a time of crisis:

> You know, you're the Commander in Chief. You've got an assault going on on the Capitol of the United States of America, and there's nothing? No call? Nothing? Zero? And it's not my place to, you know, pass judgment or—I'm the, you know—but no attempt to call the Secretary of Defense? No attempt to call the Vice President of the United States of America, who's down on the scene? To my knowledge, it wasn't—I just noted it.[6]

President Trump's closest advisors—both inside and out of the White House—implored him to act sooner. Earlier in the week, two of the President's most trusted aides, Eric Herschmann and Hope Hicks, both wanted President Trump to emphasize that January 6th would be a peaceful protest. President Trump refused.[7]

On the 6th, as the riot began to escalate, a colleague texted Hicks and wrote, "Hey, I know you're seeing this. But he really should tweet something about Being NON-violent."[8] "I'm not there," Hicks replied. "I suggested it several times Monday and Tuesday and he refused."[9]

Once the attack was underway, President Trump initially ignored the counsel of his own family, members of his administration, Republican elected officials, and friendly Fox News personalities. Both Ivanka Trump and Donald Trump, Jr. wanted their father to tell the rioters to go home sooner. The President delayed. At 2:38 p.m., President Trump sent this tweet: "Please support our Capitol Police and Law Enforcement. They are truly on the side of our Country. Stay peaceful!"[10] Sarah Matthews, the White House Deputy Press Secretary, told the Select Committee that President Trump resisted using the word "peaceful." The President added the words "Stay peaceful!" only after Ivanka Trump suggested the phrase.[11] Trump, Jr. quickly recognized that his father's tweet was insufficient. "He's got to condem [sic] this shit. Asap. The captiol [sic] police tweet is not enough," Trump, Jr. wrote in a text to White House Chief of Staff Mark Meadows.[12] President Trump did not tell the rioters to disperse in either his 2:38 p.m. tweet, or another tweet at 3:13 p.m.[13]

Multiple witnesses told the Select Committee that Minority Leader Kevin McCarthy contacted the President and others around him, desperately trying to get him to act. McCarthy's entreaties led nowhere. "I guess they're just more upset about the election theft than you are," President Trump told McCarthy.[14] Top lawyers in the White House Counsel's Office attempted to intercede. Two Fox News primetime personalities, always so obsequious, begged those around the President to get him to do more. But President Trump was unmoved.

There's no question that President Trump had the power to end the insurrection. He was not only the Commander-in-Chief of the U.S. military, but also of the rioters.

One member of the mob, Stephen Ayres, told the Select Committee that he and others quickly complied as soon as President Trump finally told them to go home. "[W]e literally left right after [President Trump's 4:17 p.m. video] come out. You know, to me if he would have done that earlier in the day, 1:30 [p.m.] . . . maybe we wouldn't be in this bad of a situation or something," Ayres said.[15] Another rioter, Jacob Chansley, commonly referred to as the "QAnon Shaman," was one of the first 30 rioters to enter the U.S. Capitol. Chansley told a reporter that he left the building because "Trump asked everybody to go home."[16] At 4:25 p.m., just eight minutes after President Trump tweeted his video, an Oath Keeper named Ed Vallejo messaged other members of his group, a fair number of whom were at the Capitol: "Gentleman [sic], Our Commander-in-Chief has just ordered us to go home. Comments?"[17]

Even then, President Trump did not disavow the rioters. He endorsed their cause, openly sympathized with them, and repeated his Big Lie once again. "I know your pain, I know you're hurt. We had an election that was stolen from us," President Trump said at the beginning of his 4:17 p.m. video. "It was a landslide election, and everyone knows it, especially the other side. But you have to go home now. We have to have peace. We have

President Trump appears on a monitor in the White House briefing room depicting a video he released instructing rioters to go home.

(Photo by Joshua Roberts/Getty Images)

to have law and order. We have to respect our great people in law and order. We don't want anybody hurt." The President portrayed the violence as something his political foes would use against him, saying: "This was a fraudulent election, but we can't play into the hands of these people."[18]

The President concluded his short video by again praising the men and women who had overrun the U.S. Capitol. "We have to have peace. So go home. We love you. You're very special," President Trump said. "You've seen what happens. You see the way others are treated that are so bad and so evil. I know how you feel, but go home, and go home in peace."[19]

Just after 6:00 p.m. on January 6th, President Trump issued his final tweet of the day, again lauding the rioters and justifying their cause. President Trump made excuses for the riot, saying this is what happens "when a sacred landslide election victory is so unceremoniously & viciously stripped away from great patriots who have been badly & unfairly treated for so long." The President added: "Go home with love & in peace. Remember this day forever!"[20]

The following day, President Trump's advisors encouraged him to deliver a short speech denouncing the attack on the U.S. Capitol. The President struggled to deliver his prepared remarks. According to Cassidy

Hutchinson, President Trump wanted to say that he would pardon the rioters. Lawyers in the White House Counsel's Office objected, so this language was not included.[21] John McEntee, the Director of the White House Presidential Personnel Office, also testified that in the days following the attack, he heard President Trump mention the possibility of a "blanket pardon" for all those involved in the events of January 6th.[22]

President Trump never did give up on the prospect. Since leaving office, the now former President has said he would consider "full pardons with an apology to many" of the January 6th defendants if he is reelected.[23]

## 7.1 "REINSERT THE MIKE PENCE LINES"

President Trump tweeted three times on the morning of January 6th, repeating a false claim of election fraud at 8:06 a.m.,[24] pressuring Vice President Pence to delay the electoral count at 8:17 a.m.,[25] and urging Republican party officials to do the same at 8:22 a.m.[26] He made calls to his Republican allies in Congress, many of whom were already committed to objecting to the electoral count.[27] And he dialed his lawyers and advisors—including Steve Bannon and Rudolph Giuliani (twice), both of whom had been counseling the President on how to stay in power.[28]

There was one person—critical to his plan—whom President Trump tried to reach but couldn't. At 9:02 a.m., he asked the switchboard operator to call his Vice President. Vice President Pence did not answer the call.[29]

Instead, between 9:52 a.m. and 10:18 a.m., the President spoke with his speechwriter, Stephen Miller, about the words he would deliver at the Save America Rally just hours later.[30] The former President's speech had come together over the course of 36 hours, going from a screed aimed at encouraging congressional objections to one that would ultimately incite mob violence.[31]

Only four minutes after the call concluded, at 10:22 a.m., Miller emailed revisions to the speechwriters, instructing them to "[s]tart inputting these changes asap" that included "red highlights marking POTUS edits."[32] The President had made some cosmetic additions, like peppering in the word "corrupt" throughout,[33] but there was one substantive edit—a new target—that would focus the crowd's anger on one man.

None of the preceding drafts mentioned Vice President Pence whatsoever. But now, at the very last minute, President Trump slipped in the following sentences calling the Vice President out by name:

> Today, we will see whether Republicans stand strong for the integrity of our elections. And we will see whether Mike Pence enters history as a truly great and courageous leader. All he has to do is

President Trump speaks with speechwriter Stephen Miller about his Ellipse speech in the Oval Office on the morning of January 6, 2021.
(Photo provided to the Select Committee by the National Archives and Records Administration)

refer the illegally-submitted electoral votes back to the states that were given false and fraudulent information where they want to recertify. With only 3 of the 7 states in question we win and become President and have the power of the veto.[34]

No one on the speechwriting team could explain why President Trump added these lines just 30 minutes before he was originally scheduled to speak at 11:00 a.m.[35] But by 10:49 a.m., Vincent Haley, a speechwriter who was helping load the teleprompter at the Ellipse, was told to hold off and delete the mention of the Vice President—for now.[36] Miller said that Eric Herschmann, a lawyer who was one of the President's senior advisors, asked him in a "brief sidebar" that morning to omit reference to the Vice President and his role in the certification process because he "didn't concur with the legal analysis" and that it "wouldn't advance the ball" but would be "counterproductive" instead.[37] As detailed in Chapter 5, Herschmann and others in the White House were vocal critics of Dr. John Eastman's theory, which claimed that the Vice President had the unilateral power to reject electors during the joint session of Congress. President Trump repeatedly pressured Pence to either reject certified electors, or delay the

President Trump on a phone call with Vice President Mike Pence in the Oval Office on the morning of January 6, 2021.
(Photo provided to the Select Committee by the National Archives and Records Administration)

electoral count based on Eastman's unconstitutional and illegal theory. Vice President Pence would not budge. The Vice President consistently rejected President Trump's demands.

After tweeting four more times that morning—all of them spreading lies about the election[38]—the President apparently thought he had one last chance to convince his number two to overrule the will of the American people.

As recounted in Chapter 5, President Trump called Vice President Pence at 11:17 a.m.[39] The call between the two men—during which the President soon grew "frustrat[ed] or heated,"[40] visibly upset,[41] and "angry"[42]—lasted nearly 20 minutes.[43] And President Trump insulted Vice President Pence when he refused to obstruct or delay the joint session.

After that call, General Keith Kellogg said that the people in the room immediately went back to editing the Ellipse speech.[44] At 11:30 a.m., Miller emailed his assistant, Robert Gabriel, with no text in the body but the subject line: "insert—stand by for phone call."[45] At 11:33 a.m., Gabriel emailed the speechwriting team: "REINSERT THE MIKE PENCE LINES. Confirm receipt."[46] One minute later, speechwriter Ross Worthington confirmed

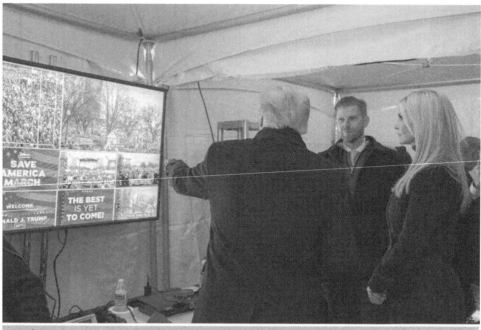

President Trump looks backstage at the crowd gathered at the Ellipse.
(Photo provided to the Select Committee by the National Archives and Records Administration)

that he had reached Vincent Haley by phone.[47] Haley corroborated that he added one "tough sentence about the Vice President" while he was at the teleprompter.[48]

The final written draft had the following Pence reference: "And we will see whether Mike Pence enters history as a truly great and courageous leader."[49] Haley wasn't confident that line was what he reinserted, but email traffic and teleprompter drafts produced by the National Archives and Records Administration (NARA) indicate that he was mistaken.[50]

After defying President Trump's pressure, Vice President Pence—and the ire of the President he inspired—was back in the speech.

After the heated call, President Trump's personal assistant Nicholas Luna handed him a message on White House card stock and the President departed for the Ellipse to give his speech.[51] Preserved by NARA, the message read: "THEY ARE READY FOR YOU WHEN YOU ARE."[52] When it finally came time for him to speak, President Trump repeatedly directed his anger at Vice President Pence—often ad-libbing lines that were not included in the draft text.

## 7.2 "I'LL BE THERE WITH YOU"

From a tent backstage at the Ellipse, President Trump looked out at the crowd of approximately 53,000 supporters and became enraged. Just under half of those gathered—a sizeable stretch of about 25,000 people[53]—refused to walk through the magnetometers and be screened for weapons,[54] leaving the venue looking half-empty to the television audience at home.

According to testimony received by the Committee, earlier that morning at the White House, the President was told that the onlookers were unwilling to pass through the magnetometers because they were armed. "We have enough space, sir. They don't want to come in right now," Deputy Chief of Staff Tony Ornato reportedly told President Trump. "They have weapons that they don't want confiscated by the Secret Service."[55]

So, when President Trump got to the rally site and could see the crowd for himself, "[h]e was fucking furious," as Cassidy Hutchinson later texted Ornato.[56] Hutchinson testified that just minutes before addressing the crowd, President Trump shouted to his advance team: "I don't [fucking] care that they have weapons. They're not here to hurt *me*. Take the [fucking] mags away. Let my people in. They can march to the Capitol from here. Take the [fucking] mags away."[57]

By noon, President Trump took to the stage at the Ellipse.[58] The President wanted all of those in attendance, including those who hadn't passed through the magnetometers, to come closer to the stage. "And I'd love to have if those tens of thousands of people would be allowed," President Trump said. "But I'd love it if they could be allowed to come up here with us. Is that possible? Can you just let [them] come up, please?"[59]

President Trump repeatedly made it clear to those around him in the days before January 6th that he wanted to march to the Capitol alongside his supporters. That is, President Trump wanted to join his supporters in what the Secret Service refers to as an "off-the-record" movement (OTR).

While the President spoke, Hutchinson texted Ornato, "He also kept mentioning OTR to Capitol before he took the stage."[60] Minutes before the President stepped out, Chief of Staff Mark Meadows assured the President he was working on it.[61]

President Trump's plan to march appeared once in an early draft of the script, then a later revision was made to add the word "building" after "Capitol," making it clear exactly where the crowd should go.[62] And the President repeatedly told the crowd that he would join them.

"[A]fter this, we're going to walk down, and I'll be there with you, we're going to walk down, we're going to walk down," he said to the crowd. "[W]e're going to walk down to the Capitol, and we're going to cheer on our brave senators and congressmen and women, and we're probably not going to be cheering so much for some of them." [63]

President Trump used the phrase scripted for him by his White House speechwriters, "peacefully and patriotically" once, about 20 minutes into his speech. [64] Then he spent the next 50-or-so minutes amping up his crowd with lies about the election, attacking his own Vice President and Republican Members of Congress, and exhorting the crowd to fight. "And we fight. We fight like hell" the President said to a crowd that had already spent the day chanting, "Fight for Trump! Fight for Trump!," and that would keep up the chorus when storming the Capitol. [65]

Finally, he told the crowd where to go to "take back our country": "So we're going to, we're going to walk down Pennsylvania Avenue. I love Pennsylvania Avenue. And we're going to the Capitol, and we're going to try and give . . . we're going to try and give our Republicans, the weak ones because the strong ones don't need any of our help. We're going to try and give them the kind of pride and boldness that they need to take back our country. So let's walk down Pennsylvania Avenue." [66]

When the President announced his intentions from the microphone, people listened.

House Republican Leader Representative. Kevin McCarthy called Hutchinson mid-speech: [67]

"Do you guys think you're coming to my office[?]" he asked her. [68]
She assured him that they weren't coming at all. [69]

"Figure it out. Don't come up here," he replied. [70]

The announcement from the stage put the Secret Service on alert, prompting agents to designate over email a last-minute response team "to filter in with the crowds" on the President's "walk/motorcade over" to the Capitol and establish an emergency plan "if things go south." [71] White House security officials were monitoring the situation in real time, remarking that President Trump was "going to the Capitol" and that "they are finding the best route now." [72] Nonetheless, these staffers were in "a state of shock," [73] because they knew—particularly if the President joined—this would "no longer [be] a rally." [74]

"[W]e all knew . . . that this was going to move to something else if he physically walked to the Capitol," an employee said. "I don't know if you want to use the word 'insurrection,' 'coup,' whatever. We all knew that this would move from a normal democratic . . . public event into something else." [75]

But the logistics made the move all but impossible.

It was complicated for the Secret Service to coordinate a presidential movement even on a normal day. But today was not a normal day. Tens of thousands of President Trump's supporters had flooded into downtown DC in the days before the rally, and the Secret Service would have to account for that unpredictability. By the end of the President's speech, it was clear that the crowd at the Capitol was growing violent.

At 1:19 p.m., a Secret Service agent wrote to Bobby Engel, the head of President Trump's Secret Service detail: "FYSA . . . [Capitol Police] having serious challenges securing [the Capitol]. Nine priority breach attempts at this time. OTR to anywhere near there is not advisable. Give me a call when free. Front Office concerned about OTR to [the Capitol]." [76]

### 7.3 THE PRESIDENT'S ANGER WHEN HE COULD NOT MARCH TO THE CAPITOL

President Trump concluded his remarks at 1:10 p.m. Luna heard the President mention his intention to join the march to the Capitol "after he finished his remarks." [77] Just before the President got into his vehicle, Meadows told him, "We're going to work on it, sir." [78] President Trump was seated in his motorcade vehicle by 1:17 p.m. [79]

The Committee received information informally from current and former members of the Secret Service and former White House staff relevant to what happened next—what a number of witnesses have described as an "angry," "irate," or "furious" interaction in the Presidential vehicle between the President and the Secret Service. [80] That initial information, received informally, shaped the Committee's questioning of witnesses. The Committee's principal concern was that the President *actually intended* to participate personally in the January 6th efforts at the Capitol, leading the effort to overturn the election either from inside the Chamber or from a stage outside the Capitol. The Committee regarded those facts as important because they are relevant to President Trump's intent on January 6th. But a book published by Mark Meadows in November 2021 made the categorical claim that the President *never* intended to travel to the Capitol that day. [81] Because the Meadows book conflicted sharply with information that was being received by the Committee, the Committee became increasingly wary that witnesses might intentionally conceal what happened.

In our initial informal discussion with the lead of the President's detail, Robert Engel confirmed that President Trump did wish to travel to the Capitol from the Ellipse, but stated that he did not recall many other details. [82] But the Committee also received information from Kayleigh McEnany and Cassidy Hutchinson that also directly contradicted Mark Meadows's book and provided considerably more detail. McEnany testified that

President Trump did indeed wish to travel to the Capitol on January 6th, and continued to have that goal even after returning from the Ellipse to the White House.[83] McEnany, who spoke with President Trump shortly after he returned to the White House, recalls him expressing a desire to go to the Capitol: "I recall him . . . saying that he wanted to physically walk and be a part of the march and then saying that he would ride the Beast if he needed to, ride in the Presidential limo."[84] When asked, McEnany confirmed that "yes, he did seem sincere about wanting to do that."[85] Hutchinson's testimony was generally consistent with the information the Select Committee was receiving informally. Like McEnany, Hutchinson confirmed that the President did ask to be transported to Capitol Hill.[86] Many other White House witnesses would ultimately confirm that President Trump wished to travel to the Capitol on January 6th, comprehensively rebutting the false statements in Meadows's book.[87]

Part of Hutchinson's account was a second-hand description of what occurred in the Presidential vehicle, which built upon and was consistent with information the Committee has received informally.

Hutchinson testified that, when she returned from the Ellipse, Ornato was standing outside his office door when he "waved me down," Hutchinson said. The two of them walked into Ornato's office, and he shut the door behind them.[88] Engel was already there, sitting in a chair "looking down, kind of looking a little lost and kind of discombobulated."[89]

According to Hutchinson, Ornato then recounted a struggle in the President's car.[90] At no point during Ornato's telling—or at any point thereafter—did Engel indicate that what Ornato relayed was untrue.[91]

Another witness, a White House employee with national security responsibilities, provided the Committee with a similar description: Ornato related the "irate" interaction in the presidential vehicle to this individual in Ornato's White House office with Engel present.[92] And just as Hutchinson testified, this employee told the Select Committee that Engel listened to Ornato's retelling of the episode and did not dispute it: "I don't remember his specific body language, but . . . [h]e did not deny the fact that the President was irate."[93] Engel testified that he does not recall either the conversation with Hutchinson or the similar conversation with the White House employee with national security responsibilities.[94]

The Committee regarded both Hutchinson and the corroborating testimony by the White House employee with national security responsibilities national security official as earnest and has no reason to conclude that either had a reason to invent their accounts. A different Secret Service

Cassidy Hutchinson describes a story relayed to her by Tony Ornato about President Trump's desire to go to the Capitol after the Ellipse speech on January 6th during a January 6th Select Committee hearing.

(Photo by Brandon Bell/Getty Images)

agent, who served on a protective detail at the White House and was present in the presidential motorcade at the Ellipse, provided this view:

> Committee Staff: Just a couple of additional questions. Ms. Hutchinson has suggested to the Committee that you sympathized with her after her testimony, and believed her account. Is that accurate?

> Witness: I have no—yeah, that's accurate. I have no reason—I mean, we—we became friends. We worked—I worked every day with her for 6 months. Yeah, she became a friend of mine. We had a good working relationship. I have no reason—she's never done me wrong. She's never lied that I know of. I don't have any reason—I don't—I don't distrust Ms. Hutchinson.[95]

Also, the White House employee with national security responsibilities indicated that knowledge of the angry altercation in the Presidential vehicle was known within the White House—and was "[water] cooler talk."[96] In addition, Hutchinson has provided testimony to the Committee about efforts by her prior counsel, who was apparently paid by a Trump-funded organization, to suggest that Hutchinson did not need to testify about the issue in the presidential vehicle, could suggest that she "did not recall" it, or should downplay it.[97]

To further corroborate the accounts received of President Trump's intent to travel to the Capitol, the Committee interviewed a member of the Metropolitan Police who was also present in the motorcade, Officer Mark Robinson. Officer Robinson confirmed that he was aware contemporaneously of the "heated discussion" that took place in the Presidential vehicle:

> Committee Staff: And was there any description of what was occurring in the car?
>
> Mr. Robinson: No. Only that—the only description I received was that the President was upset and that he was adamant about going to the Capitol, and there was a heated discussion about that.
>
> Committee Staff: When you say "heated," is that your word, or is that the word that was described by the TS agent?
>
> Mr. Robinson: No. The word described by the TS agent meaning that the President was upset, and he was saying there was a heated argument or discussion about going to the Capitol.
>
> . . . .
>
> Mr. Schiff: So about how many times would you say you've been part of that motorcade with the President?
>
> Mr. Robinson: Probably over a hundred times.
>
> Mr. Schiff: And, in that hundred times, have you ever witnessed another discussion of an argument or a heated discussion with the President where the President was contradicting where he was supposed to go or what the Secret Service believed was safe?
>
> Mr. Robinson: No.[98]

The Committee also interviewed the Secret Service agent who was in the same car as Officer Robinson. That person shared a similar account, and confirmed that he did not take issue with Officer Robinson's testimony: "[The driver of the Presidential car] said something to the effect of, 'The President is pretty adamant that he wants to go to the Capitol,'" the agent said, recalling what he had heard on the 6th.[99]

In addition, the Committee interviewed the USSS Press Secretary, who communicated with both Engel and with the driver in the presidential vehicle after Hutchinson appeared publicly. That witness indicated that Engel's account of the events confirmed that the President was indeed angry, or furious.[100] In fact, when asked about a reporter's tweet indicating that sources within the Secret Service confirmed that "Trump was furious about not being [able] to go to [the] Capitol with his supporters," the Press Secretary said he "certainly corroborated it" with the reporter because "that's what I had been told, you know, that [the President] was upset, he was agitated, about not being able to go[.]"[101]

In addition to the testimony above, the Committee has reviewed hundreds of thousands of new Secret Service documents, including many demonstrating that the Secret Service had been informed of potential violence at the Capitol before the Ellipse rally on January 6th. (These documents were critical to our understanding of what the Secret Service and White House knew about the threat to the Capitol on January 6th.) The Committee has also more recently conducted additional interviews with Engel and Ornato, and has also interviewed the driver of the Presidential vehicle.

Both Engel and the driver[102] testified that, within 30 seconds of getting into the vehicle, the President asked if he could travel to the Capitol.[103] This again is directly inconsistent with the account of events in Meadows's book. According to Engel, he told the President immediately that the move wasn't happening.[104] The President was unhappy with Engel's response and began "pushing pretty hard to go."[105] The President repeatedly asked why he could not go to the Capitol.[106] Engel replied that the Secret Service "didn't have any people at the Capitol" to provide the President with appropriate security.[107] The President responded angrily, telling Engel and the driver "I'm the President and I'll decide where I get to go."[108] He reassured Engel that "it would essentially be fine and that the people there [meaning the people who were marching from the Ellipse to the Capitol at President Trump's instruction] were [Trump] supporters or something to that effect,"[109] According to the Secret Service agent driving the vehicle, the President was "animated and irritated" about not going to the Capitol.[110]

According to Mr. Engel, he ultimately told the President that they would "assess what our options were and wait until we can get a plan in place before we went down there."[111] We note that the driver's account acknowledged President Trump's anger to a greater degree than either Engel's initial account in Spring 2022, or his more recent account in November 2022. Engel did not characterize the exchange in the vehicle the way Hutchinson described the account she heard from Ornato, and indicated that he did not recall President Trump gesturing toward him.[112] Engel did not recall being present when Ornato gave either Hutchinson or the White House employee with national security responsibilities an accounting of the events.[113] The driver testified that he did not recall seeing what President Trump was doing and did not recall whether there was movement.[114]

The Select Committee has great respect for the men and women of the Secret Service. That said, it is difficult to fully reconcile the accounts of several of the witnesses who provided information with what we heard from Engel and Ornato.[115] But the principal factual point here is clear and undisputed: President Trump specifically and repeatedly requested to be taken to the Capitol. He was insistent and angry, and continued to push to travel to the Capitol even after returning to the White House.

The motorcade didn't disband upon arriving to the White House, as they usually do. Instead, they were instructed to stand by in case the President's move to the Capitol did indeed happen.[116] The Select Committee received a document from the Secret Service that reflects that at 1:25 p.m., "PPD IS ADVISING THAT [THE PRESIDENT] IS PLANNING ON HOLDING AT THE WHITE HOUSE FOR THE NEXT APPROXIMATE TWO HOURS, THEN MOVING TO THE CAPITOL."[117] "They had not made a decision whether or not we were going to transport the President to the Capitol," Robinson was told.[118]

Engel testified that he went to Ornato's office when he returned to the West Wing in order to discuss a possible move to the Capitol by President Trump.[119] Given the deteriorating security conditions at the Capitol, it was quickly determined that they could not safely transport the President there.[120] The motorcade waited on West Executive Drive approximately 40 minutes before finally receiving word from the Secret Service that the move had been officially nixed. Internal Secret Service communications bear this out: Not until 1:55 p.m. did Engel notify other agents via email that "[w]e are not doing an OTR to [the Capitol]."[121]

### 7.4 "WE'RE GOING TO TRY TO GET THE PRESIDENT TO PUT OUT A STATEMENT"

Minutes after arriving back at the White House, the President ran into a member of the White House staff and asked whether he or she watched his speech on television.[122]

"Sir, they cut it off because they're rioting down at the Capitol," the employee said.

The President asked what he or she meant by that.

"[T]hey're rioting down there at the Capitol," the employee repeated.

"Oh really?" the President asked. "All right, let's go see."[123]

A photograph taken by the White House photographer—the last one permitted until later in the day—captures the moment the President heard the news from the employee at 1:21 p.m.[124] By that time, if not sooner, he had been made aware of the violent riot at the Capitol.

President Trump walked through the corridor from the Oval Office into the Presidential Dining Room and sat down at the table with the television remote and a Diet Coke close at hand.[125] For the rest of the afternoon—as his country faced an hours-long attack—he hunkered down in or around the dining room, watching television.[126] He left only for a few minutes—from 4:03 p.m. to 4:07 p.m.—to film a video in the Rose Garden, only a few steps away, after hours of arm-twisting.[127] But otherwise, the President remained in the dining room until 6:27 p.m., when he returned to his private residence.[128]

What happened during the 187 minutes from 1:10 p.m. to 4:17 p.m., when President Trump finally told the rioters to go home, is—from an official standpoint—undocumented.

For instance, the Presidential Daily Diary—the schedule that tracks every meeting and phone call in which the President partakes—is inexplicably blank between 1:21 p.m. and 4:03 p.m.[129] When asked to explain the gap in record-keeping on and around January 6th, White House officials in charge of its maintenance provided no credible explanation, including: "I don't recall a specific reason."[130]

The men who spent most of the afternoon in that room with the President, Mark Meadows and Dan Scavino, both refused to comply with lawful subpoenas from the Select Committee.[131] Others in the dining room appeared before the Select Committee but cited executive privilege to avoid answering questions about their direct communications with President Trump.[132] Others who worked just outside of the Oval Office, like the President's personal secretaries Molly Michael and Austin Ferrer Piran Basauldo, claimed not to remember nearly anything from one of the most memorable days in recent American history.[133]

The White House photographer, Shealah Craighead, had been granted access to photograph the President during his January 6th speech, but once she got to the White House—and it became clear that an attack was unfolding on the Capitol's steps—she was turned away.[134]

"The President [didn't] want any photos," she was told.[135]

Here's what President Trump did during the 187 minutes between the end of his speech and when he finally told rioters to go home: For hours, he watched the attack from his TV screen.[136] His channel of choice was Fox News.[137] He issued a few tweets, some on his own inclination and some only at the repeated behest of his daughter and other trusted advisors.[138] He made several phone calls, some to his personal lawyer Rudolph Giuliani, some to Members of Congress about continuing their objections to the electoral certification, even though the attack was well underway.[139]

Here's what President Trump did not do: He did not call any relevant law enforcement agency to ensure they were working to quell the violence. He did not call the Secretary of Defense; he did not call the Attorney General; he did not call the Secretary of Homeland Security.[140] And for hours on end, he refused the repeated requests—from nearly everyone who talked to him—to simply tell the mob to go home.[141]

Throughout the afternoon, senior staff regularly entered the room to give him updates on what was happening at the Capitol.[142] And, of course, President Trump used Twitter, where information is shared on an instantaneous basis.

Shortly after President Trump entered the dining room, White House Press Secretary Kayleigh McEnany swung by to "check in with him" about the letter Vice President Pence released around 1:00 p.m. announcing that he would not, in fact, overturn the will of the voters.

The President, once again, brought up going to the Capitol.[143] McEnany recorded what he said in her notes, certain of which she later produced to the Select Committee: "POTUS wanted to walk to [sic] capital. Physically walk. He said fine ride beast," referring to the nickname for the presidential vehicle. "Meadows said not safe enough[.]"[144]

Meadows told Hutchinson at some point in the day that "the President wasn't happy that Bobby [Engel] didn't pull it off for him," meaning the trip to the Capitol, "and that Mark didn't work hard enough to get the movement on the books."[145]

Despite the turmoil just outside its walls, the proceedings in the joint session—which had begun at 1:00 p.m.—were still ongoing, and the President was watching them on the television.[146] He was eager to know which senators were lodging objections on his behalf.[147] "Back there and he wants list of senators," McEnany's notes read. "Who [sic] objecting to what. He's calling them one by one."[148]

The Select Committee subpoenaed several Members of Congress who reportedly spoke with President Trump during the afternoon.[149] None of them complied.[150]

Cellular records obtained by the Select Committee suggest that President Trump was on the phone with his lawyer Rudolph Giuliani at least twice during this period. Giuliani's phone connected with the White House switchboard for 3 minutes and 53 seconds at 1:39 p.m. and again for more than 8 minutes at 2:03 p.m.[151] Between the two calls, at 1:49 p.m., President Trump tweeted a link to a video of his speech from the Ellipse.[152]

Before 1:57 p.m., Herschmann phoned Senior Advisor to the President Jared Kushner—who was on a plane travelling home from overseas—advising him that "people are trying to break into the Capitol" and that "this is getting pretty ugly." [153]

"We're going to see what we can do here," Herschmann said. "We're going to try to get the President to put out a statement." [154]

## 7.5 "HE DOESN'T WANT TO DO ANYTHING"

Throughout the afternoon, the President's advisors tried to get him to tell the mob to leave the Capitol, but to no avail.

Ben Williamson, the White House Acting Director of Communications, watched on the news as officers and rioters pepper sprayed each other and crowds used bicycle barricades to push against officers holding the line. [155] He and Sarah Matthews, the Deputy Press Secretary, devised a plan: He would go to Meadows and she would go to McEnany to urge that the President issue a statement. [156] Williamson first texted Meadows:

"Would recommend POTUS put out a tweet about respecting the police over at the Capitol." [157]

Minutes later, around 2:05 p.m., Hutchinson found Meadows seated in his office on the couch, absorbed by his cell phone screen. [158]

"Are you watching the TV, chief?" she asked. He indicated he was.

"Have you talked to the President?" she asked.

"No," he replied. "He wants to be alone right now." [159]

Rioters broke into the west side of the Capitol building around 2:13 p.m. [160] Just a few minutes later, Hutchinson saw Cipollone "barreling down the hallway" and—after looking at Hutchinson and shaking his head—opened the door to Meadows's office unannounced. [161] Meadows was right where she left him, "still sitting on his phone." [162]

"The rioters have gotten to the Capitol, Mark. We need to go down and see the President now," she heard Cipollone say. [163] Cipollone would not confirm or deny any of this exchange, citing executive privilege. [164]

"He doesn't want to do anything, Pat," Meadows said, peering up from his phone. [165]

"Mark something needs to be done, or people are going to die and the blood's gonna be on your [fucking] hands," Cipollone said. "This is getting out of control. I'm going down there." [166]

Meadows finally stood up from the couch and walked with Cipollone toward the dining room to meet with the President. [167]

At exactly 2:24 p.m., President Trump made his first public statement during the attack on the Capitol by tweet. It read nothing like the statement his advisors had envisioned. It read:

> Mike Pence didn't have the courage to do what should have been done to protect our Country and our Constitution, giving States a chance to certify a corrected set of facts, not the fraudulent or inaccurate ones which they were asked to previously certify. USA demands the truth![168]

Minutes later, Meadows and Cipollone returned from their talk with the President.[169] No statement was forthcoming.

"Mark, we need to do something more. They're literally calling for the Vice President to be [fucking] hung," Hutchinson heard Cipollone say.[170]

"You heard him, Pat," Meadows replied. "He thinks Mike deserves it. He doesn't think they're doing anything wrong."[171]

"This is [fucking] crazy. We need to be doing something more," Cipollone said.[172]

Cipollone told the Select Committee that "there needed to be an immediate and forceful response, statement, public statement, that people need to leave the Capitol now."[173] He said he was "pretty clear" about his view in the White House that day, and he made that view known as soon as he became aware of the unrest.[174] He would not comment on how the President responded, or on this conversation with Meadows, citing executive privilege.[175] He did indicate that everyone in the White House—except President Trump—agreed that people needed to leave the Capitol:

> Vice Chair Cheney: And who on the staff did not want people to leave the Capitol?
>
> Mr. Cipollone: On the staff?
>
> Vice Chair Cheney: In the White House.
>
> Mr. Cipollone: I can't think of anybody on that day who didn't want people to get out of the Capitol once the—particularly once the violence started. No. I mean—
>
> Mr. Schiff: What about the President?
>
> Vice Chair Cheney: Yeah.
>
> Mr. Cipollone: Well, she said the staff. So I answered.
>
> Vice Chair Cheney: No. I said in the White House.

**Noose set up outside of the Capitol on January 6, 2021.**

Mr. Cipollone: Oh, I'm sorry. I apologize. I thought you said who else on the staff. [*Pauses to confer with counsel*] Yeah. I can't reveal communications. But obviously I think, you know—yeah.[176]

What the President *did* tweet—a broadside at his Vice President—enlarged the target on Vice President Pence's back. A Secret Service agent in the Protective Intelligence Division, tasked with monitoring threats against protectees in part by scouring social media, told his colleagues the tweet was "probably not going to be good for Pence."[177]

A second agent in reply noted that it had garnered "[o]ver 24K likes in under 2 mins."[178]

### 7.7 "I GUESS THEY'RE JUST MORE UPSET ABOUT THE ELECTION THEFT THAN YOU ARE"

Minutes after drawing increased attention to his besieged Vice President, the President called newly elected Senator Tommy Tuberville of Alabama at 2:26 p.m.[179] He misdialed, calling Senator Mike Lee of Utah instead, but one passed the phone to the other in short order.[180]

President Trump wanted to talk objections to the electoral count. But Senator Tuberville—along with every other elected official trapped and surrounded in the building—had other things on his mind.[181]

"I said, 'Mr. President, they've taken the Vice President out. They want me to get off the phone, I gotta go,'" Senator Tuberville told reporters.[182] "'[W]e're not doing much work here right now.'"[183]

In the next half hour, between 2:26 p.m. and 3:06 p.m., President Trump spoke with House Leader Kevin McCarthy.[184]

Leader McCarthy told the public in a live interview with CBS News, while he and his colleagues were sheltering at a secure location,[185] that he was "very clear" in telling President Trump "to talk to the nation to tell them to stop this."[186]

Leader McCarthy later recounted his conversation to a number of people, including Representative Jaime Herrera Beutler, a Republican congresswoman from Washington State.[187] "You have got to get on TV, you've got to get on Twitter, you've got to call these people off," he said he told the President.[188]

"[These] aren't my people, you know, these are—these are Antifa," President Trump insisted, against all evidence.[189] "They're your people. They literally just came through my office windows, and my staff are running for cover. I mean, they're running for their lives. You need to call them off," Leader McCarthy told him.[190]

What President Trump said next was "chilling," in Representative Herrera Beutler's words.[191]

"Well, Kevin, I guess they're just more upset about the election theft than you are," the President said.[192]

The call then devolved into a swearing match.[193]

Mick Mulvaney, former Chief of Staff to President Trump, had a similar call with Leader McCarthy in the days after the attack. McCarthy told Mulvaney that he urged the President to get the rioters to stop, and the President replied, "Kevin, maybe these people are just more angry about this than you are."[194]

Marc Short, the Vice President's Chief of Staff, spoke with Leader McCarthy later that afternoon.[195] Leader McCarthy told Short that he had spoken with President Trump and that he was "frustrat[ed]" that the White House was "not taking the circumstance as seriously as they should at that moment."[196] The administration was demonstrating a "lack of response or lack of responsibility," Leader McCarthy told Short.[197]

At 2:49 p.m.—as the violence escalated—President Trump's speechwriter Gabriel Robert texted someone: "Potus im sure is loving this."[198]

## 7.8 "STAY PEACEFUL!"

No one was getting through to the President.

So Herschmann went to Ivanka Trump's office, hoping she would come to the dining room and be "a calming influence" on her father.[199] Herschmann "just sort of barged in" and told her to turn on the television.[200] After taking in a few of the violent scenes together, Herschmann and Ivanka Trump left the room and walked to the dining room, where her father was holed up.[201]

At 2:38 p.m., the President issued a tweet: [202]

> Please support our Capitol Police and Law Enforcement. They are truly on the side of our Country. Stay peaceful! [203]

Ivanka Trump told the Select Committee that the President "did not push back on [her] suggestion" to issue the tweet, and that it was either she or President Trump himself who suggested the last line, "Stay peaceful!" [204] She confirmed there may have been some tweaking of the wording.[205] McEnany, who was in the room at the time, wrote in her notes that "I say add 'we support PEACEFUL protest.' Ivanka add stay peaceful! Instead." [206] To the Select Committee, McEnany echoed Ivanka Trump that the President wasn't resistant in any way to putting out the message.[207]

But in private, McEnany told a different story to her deputy Sarah Matthews.

Back in the White House press office, Matthews told McEnany that the tweet did not go far enough in condemning the violence.[208] McEnany—noting that other staffers in the room were distracted—said "in a hushed tone . . . that the President did not want to include any sort of mention of peace in that tweet." [209]

That took "some convincing on their part," McEnany said, and "it wasn't until Ivanka Trump suggested the phrase 'Stay peaceful!' that he finally agreed to include it." [210]

Ivanka Trump repeatedly returned to the dining room to counsel her father throughout the day. It has been reported that each time Ivanka Trump "thought she had made headway" with her father, Meadows would call her "to say the [P]resident still needed more persuading"—a cycle that repeated itself over "several hours" that afternoon.[211] After one such trip, Ivanka Trump told the Select Committee she went to her husband's office next door because she needed to "regroup" and collect herself.[212]

Several witnesses corroborated pieces of this account. General Kellogg said he saw Ivanka Trump coming and going from the dining room at least twice that afternoon.[213] Hutchinson said that it was "several times." [214] Once, Ivanka Trump reportedly left her father with a look on her face as if

Sarah Matthews testifies at a January 6th Select Committee hearing.
(Photo by House Creative Services)

"[s]he had just had a tough conversation."²¹⁵ Radford, Ivanka Trump's Chief of Staff, saw that she was "[v]isibly upset" but continued going "down there when people were asking her to be down there and trying to get action taken."²¹⁶

Radford told the Select Committee that Ivanka Trump believed that "[s]omething should be said or put out that was even stronger."²¹⁷

Hutchinson, too, recalled Ivanka Trump dropping by Meadows's office alongside Cipollone and talking about trying to convince her father to say something "more direct than he had wanted to at that time and throughout the afternoon."²¹⁸

"I remember her saying at various points," Hutchinson said, "she wanted her dad to send them home. She wanted her dad to tell them to go home peacefully, and she wanted to include language that he necessarily wasn't on board with at the time."²¹⁹

### 7.9 "THE PRESIDENT NEEDS TO STOP THIS ASAP"

President Trump's 2:38 p.m. tweet did not condemn the violence at the Capitol. It did not tell rioters to leave the building.

Testimony footage of former White House Press Secretary Kayleigh McEnany is played during a January 6th Select Committee hearing.

(Photo by Pool/Getty Images)

In the minutes before the tweet, Fox News—on the President's screen—relayed that the Capitol was on lockdown;[220] that Capitol police officers were injured; that rioters were in the building and "just feet from the House chamber."[221] In the minutes afterward, networks would report there was tear gas in the Capitol, forcing Members of Congress to evacuate in protective masks.[222] At 2:39 p.m., Secret Service agents reported that "[m]ore just got in."[223]

"I don't know how they're gonna retake the Capitol building back at this point," one agent wrote to others two minutes later.[224]

At 2:44 p.m., a Capitol police officer shot a rioter named Ashli Babbitt.[225] A handwritten note—dashed off onto a White House pocket card and preserved by the National Archives—read: "1x civilian gunshot wound to chest @ door of House cha[m]ber."[226] One White House employee saw the note on the dining table in front of President Trump.[227]

A barrage of text messages inundated Meadows's phone with a consistent plea.[228] Everyone from conservative media personalities to Republican allies in Congress—and even the President's own family—urged the President to do more:

<u>Representative Marjorie Taylor Greene, 2:28 p.m.:</u> "Mark I was just told there is an active shooter on the first floor of the Capitol Please tell the President to calm people[.] This isn't the way to solve anything." [229]

<u>Laura Ingraham, 2:32 p.m.:</u> "Hey Mark, The [sic] president needs to tell people in the Capitol to go home." "This is hurting all of us." "He is destroying his legacy and playing into every stereotype . . . we lose all credibility against the BLM/Antifa crowd if things go South." "You can tell him I said this." [230]

<u>Mick Mulvaney, 2:35 p.m.:</u> "Mark: he needs to stop this, now. Can I do anything to help?" [231]

<u>Representative Barry Loudermilk, 2:44 p.m.:</u> "It's really bad up here on the hill." "They have breached the Capitol." [232] At 2:48 p.m., Meadows responded: "POTUS is engaging." [233] At 2:49 p.m., Loudermilk responded: "Thanks. This doesn't help our cause." [234]

<u>Representative William Timmons, 2:46 p.m.:</u> "The president needs to stop this ASAP." [235] At 2:49 p.m., Meadows responded: "We are doing it." [236]

<u>Donald Trump, Jr., 2:53 p.m.:</u> "He's got to condem [sic] this shit. Asap. The captiol [sic] police tweet is not enough." [237] Meadows responded: "I am pushing it hard. I agree." [238] Later, Trump, Jr., continued: "This his [sic] one you go to the mattresses on. They will try to fuck his entire legacy on this if it gets worse." [239]

White House staff discussed issuing yet another, stronger statement to address the ongoing—and escalating—violence. Around 3:00 p.m., one proposal was written in block capital letters on a pocket card from the chief of staff's office:

ANYONE WHO ENTERED THE CAPITOL ~~ILLEGALLY~~ WITHOUT PROPER AUTHORITY SHOULD LEAVE IMMEDIATELY[.] [240]

The handwriting appears to have been scrawled quickly and somewhat messily. Hutchinson recalled Meadows returning from the dining room with the note in hand and placing it on her desk. [241] The word "illegally" had been newly crossed out. [242]

But there would be no further action, Meadows told her. [243]

At 3:13 p.m., 35 minutes after his last tweet, the President issued another tweet. Rather than coming out with a stronger statement, the 3:13 p.m. tweet largely parroted the one preceding it:

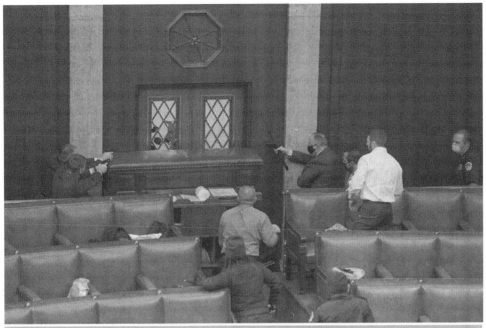

**Guns are drawn in the House Chamber on January 6th as rioters attempt to break in.**
(Photo by Drew Angerer/Getty Images)

I am asking for everyone at the U.S. Capitol to remain peaceful. No violence! Remember, WE are the Party of Law & Order—respect the Law and our great men and women in Blue. Thank you![244]

Ivanka Trump—who was in the room when her father published the message—told the Select Committee that "the gravity of the situation" made her feel "that it would be helpful to tweet again."[245] "The [earlier] tweet didn't stop the violence," Herschmann said.[246]

This tweet—like the last one—didn't tell the rioters to go home. It suggested that they "remain" at the Capitol, albeit peacefully.

### 7.10 "WE LOVE YOU. YOU'RE VERY SPECIAL"

The President's tweets were not tamping down on the violence, and White House staff knew it.[247] By 3:17 p.m., Fox News was reporting gunshots on Capitol Hill. Law enforcement officers could be seen in the House chamber, pointing guns over the barricaded door: The chyron blared "Guns Drawn on House Floor."[248] Between 3:29 p.m. and 3:42 p.m., the network was flashing images of a protestor in the presiding officer's chair, right where Vice

President Pence had been sitting 90 minutes earlier.[249] Other images showed Members of Congress trapped in the House gallery, crouching below the balcony for cover.[250]

Allies continued to text Meadows, begging the President to order the mob to go home and indicating that it was time the American people hear from the President directly:

Unknown, 3:04 p.m.: "Are you with potus right now? Hearing he is in the dining room watching this on TV . . ." "Is he going to say anything to de-escalate apart from that Tweet?"[251]

Reince Priebus, 3:09 p.m.: "TELL THEM TO GO HOME !!!"[252]

Unknown, 3:13 p.m.: "POTUS should go on air and defuse this. Extremely important."[253]

Alyssa Farah, 3:13 p.m.: "Potus has to come out firmly and tell protestors to dissipate. Someone is going to get killed . . ."[254]

Representative Chip Roy, 3:25 p.m.: "Fix this now."[255] Meadows responded: "We are."[256]

Sean Hannity (Fox News), 3:31 p.m.: "Can he make a statement. I saw the tweet. Ask people to peacefully leave the capital [sic]."[257] Meadows responded: "On it."[258]

Katrina Pierson, 3:40 p.m.: "Note: I was able to keep the crazies off the stage. I stripped all branding of those nutty groups and removed videos of all of the psychos. Glad it [sic] fought it."[259]

Unknown, 3:42 p.m.: "Pls have POTUS call this off at the Capitol. Urge rioters to disperse. I pray to you."[260]

Unknown, 3:57 p.m.: "Is he coming out?" "He has to right?"[261]

Brian Kilmeade, 3:58 p.m. (Fox News): "Please get him on tv. Destroying every thing you guys have accomplished."[262]

Donald Trump, Jr., 4:05 p.m.: "We need an oval address. He has to lead now. It's gone too far and gotten out of hand."[263]

At any moment in the afternoon, it would have been easy for President Trump to get before cameras and call off the attack. The White House Press Briefing Room is just down the hallway from the Oval Office, past the Cabinet Room and around the corner to the right. It would have taken less than 60 seconds for the President to get there.[264] The space, moreover, is outfitted with cameras that are constantly "hot," meaning that they are on and ready to go live at a moment's notice.[265] The White House press corps is

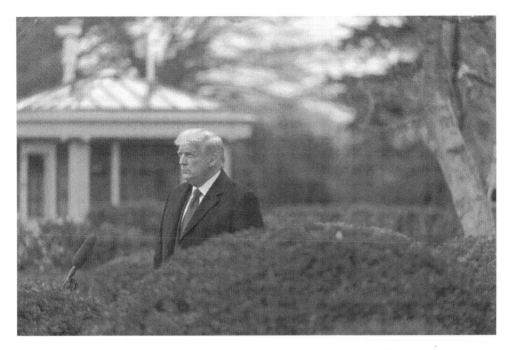

also situated in the West Wing, right by the briefing room.[266] The whole affair could have been assembled in minutes.[267]

However, it was not until nearly 3 hours after the violence began that President Trump finally agreed to tell the mob to go home.[268]

The Presidential Daily Diary notes that President Trump left the dining room to shoot the video at 4:03 p.m.[269] By this point—per Fox News coverage playing continually in the dining room—more law enforcement officers had arrived at the Capitol to resist the violent mob.[270]

The video shoot took place in the Rose Garden, the outdoor space that borders the Oval Office and the West Wing.[271] The setup was not ornate, just a camera and a microphone. Luna made sure that the background and lighting looked good, and that President Trump's hair and tie were in place.[272] President Trump delivered his remarks in one take, more or less, although he stopped and restarted at one point.[273] In all, the video took less than 4 minutes to shoot, and the President was back in the dining room by 4:07 p.m.[274]

"I would stick to this script . . . ," McEnany told President Trump before he stepped out to film.[275]

He didn't.

Kushner and others had drafted a statement, but President Trump spoke entirely off the cuff.[276] Here's what he said:

> I know your pain. I know you're hurt. We had an election that was stolen from us. It was a landslide election and everyone knows it, especially the other side. But you have to go home now. We have to have peace. We have to have law and order. We have to respect our great people in law and order. We don't want anybody hurt. It's a very tough period of time. There's never been a time like this where such a thing happened where they could take it away from all of us, from me, from you, from our country. This was a fraudulent election. But we can't play into the hands of these people. We have to have peace. So go home, we love you. You're very special. You've seen what happens. You see the way others are treated that are so bad and so evil. I know how you feel, but go home and go home in peace.[277]

A photo obtained from the National Archives shows President Trump and Herschmann huddled next to each other, watching a completed take through the monitor on the video camera.[278]

"There needs to be a more direct statement" telling the rioters to leave the Capitol, Luna heard Herschmann—yet again—tell the President.[279] Herschmann testified that he did not recall this exchange.[280]

But according to Luna, President Trump rejected the note.

"These people are in pain," he said in reply.[281]

Down at the Capitol, the video began streaming onto rioters' phones, and by all accounts including video footage taken by other rioters, they listened to President Trump's command.

"Donald Trump has asked everybody to go home," one rioter shouted as he "deliver[ed] the President's message." "That's our order," another rioter responded. Others watching the video responded: "He says, go home."[282]

The crowd afterward began to disperse.[283] The video made clear what had been evident to many, including those closest to him: The President could have called off the rioters far earlier and at any point that day.[284] But he chose not to do so.[285]

It was not until it was obvious that the riot would fail to stop the certification of the vote that the President finally relented and released a video statement made public at 4:17 p.m.[286]

President Trump huddles with aides, watching a completed take of a video through the monitor of the video camera.
(Photo provided to the Select Committee by the National Archives and Records Administration)

### 7.11 "REMEMBER THIS DAY FOREVER!"

After leaving the Rose Garden, the President returned to the dining room. At 6:01 p.m., he issued another tweet, the last of the day:

> These are the things and events that happen when a sacred land-slide election victory is so unceremoniously & viciously stripped away from great patriots who have been badly & unfairly treated for so long. Go home with love & in peace. Remember this day for-ever! [287]

He retired to his residence for the evening at 6:27 p.m.[288] A White House photographer captured the President walking back to the residence with an employee in tow, carrying personal items President Trump wished to bring home with him for the night.[289] In the employee's hands are the gloves the President was wearing while addressing the crowd at the Ellipse.[290]

The President had one parting comment to the employee—the thing that was evidently occupying his mind even after an afternoon of violence—before he retired to his home.

"Mike Pence let me down," the President concluded.[291]

Even after President Trump finally told the rioters to go home, he and his lead attorney, Rudolph Giuliani, continued to seek to delay the joint session of Congress.

Giuliani began frantically calling the White House line the very minute that the President's video went up on Twitter.[292] Failing to get through, he called back, once every minute—4:17 p.m., 4:18 p.m., 4:19 p.m., 4:20 p.m.[293] He managed to get through, briefly, to Mark Meadows at 4:21 p.m., and then kept calling the White House line: at 4:22 p.m., three times on two different phones at 4:23 p.m., 4:24 p.m., and once more at 5:05 p.m.[294] He finally managed to speak with President Trump at 5:07 p.m., and the two spoke for almost 12 minutes.[295]

After he spoke with President Trump, Giuliani's phone calls went nearly without fail to Members of Congress: Senator Marsha Blackburn, and then Senator Mike Lee.[296] He made three calls to Senator Bill Hagerty, then two to Representative Jim Jordan.[297] He called Senator Lindsey Graham,[298] Senator Josh Hawley,[299] and Senator Ted Cruz.[300] Giuliani had two calls with Senator Dan Sullivan over the course of the evening.[301] There were another three calls to Representative Jordan, none of which connected.[302] After 8:06 p.m., when the joint session resumed, the calls to Members of Congress finally stopped.[303] Shortly afterward, at 8:39 p.m., Giuliani had one final call of 9 minutes with the President.[304]

When asked about these calls during his deposition before the Select Committee, Giuliani initially refused to answer. Giuliani insisted his calls to Members of Congress—none of whom were his client—were all attorney-client privileged.[305] But Giuliani eventually relented.

"I was probably calling to see any—if anything could be done," he said. "About the vote—the vote." [306]

We know definitively what Giuliani was up to because he left a voice message for Senator Tuberville—inadvertently on Senator Lee's phone—recording his request.[307] He wanted for "you, our Republican friends to try to just slow it down," referring to the electoral count, and delay the joint session.[308] Here are his own words:

> The only strategy we can follow is to object to numerous States and raise issues so that we get ourselves into tomorrow—ideally until the end of tomorrow. So if you could object to every State and, along with a congressman, get a hearing for every State, I know we would delay you a lot, but it would give us the opportunity to get the legislators who are very, very close to pulling their vote.[309]

Mike Pence reopens the joint session of Congress and resumes counting electoral votes.
(Photo by Will McNamee/Getty Images)

The President, too, was at home, but he remained focused on his goal. Between 6:54 p.m. and 11:23 p.m., he spoke with 13 people, some more than once.[310] Of the 13, six ignored or expressly refused to comply with Select Committee requests for their testimony.[311] Two agreed to appear but refused to answer questions about their phone calls with the President, citing executive privilege.[312] Two more refused to answer questions, claiming attorney-client privilege.[313]

Of the 13, five were President Trump's attorneys or lawyers who worked with him on efforts to reverse the outcome of the election. With one exception, each of these calls took place before 8:06 p.m., when Vice President Pence reopened the joint session of Congress and resumed counting the electoral votes.[314] The President spoke with White House Counsel Pat Cipollone for 7 minutes at 7:01 p.m.[315] He spoke with Kurt Olsen and Mark Martin, lawyers who both advised him on the Vice President's role in the joint session:[316] He spoke with Martin for 9 minutes at 7:30 p.m., and Olsen twice, for 11 minutes at 7:17 p.m. and for another 10 minutes at 7:40 p.m.[317] He spoke with Cleta Mitchell, the lawyer leading his election challenges in Georgia, for 2 minutes at 7:53 p.m.[318] The President spoke with Herschmann for 5 minutes at 10:50 p.m.[319]

Another five of the people who spoke with President Trump that night were employees or outside advisors who counseled him on communications issues. These calls, by contrast, predominantly took place after the joint session resumed.[320] He spoke with his communications director, Scavino, twice: for 7 minutes at 7:08 p.m. and for 15 minutes at 9:55 p.m.[321] He spoke with McEnany for 11 minutes at 9:42 p.m.[322] He took calls from Steve Bannon, for 7 minutes at 10:19 p.m., and Sean Hannity, for 8 minutes at 11:08 p.m.[323]

At 9:23 p.m., President Trump spoke with Jason Miller, his Campaign Communications Director, for 18 minutes.[324]

Of his own initiative, Miller had drafted a statement for the President assuring the nation that the transfer of power—despite the day's events—would, indeed, take place.[325] On their call, the President pushed back on the phrasing.

The President wanted the statement to promise a "peaceful transition" of power, rather than just an "orderly" one.[326]

Miller rejected the change and told him why rather bluntly.

"[T]hat ship's kind of already sailed," he said, "so we're going to say 'orderly transition.' "[327]

## 7.13  HE "JUST DIDN'T WANT TO TALK ABOUT IT ANYMORE"

The President did not, by any account, express grief or regret for what happened at the Capitol. Neither did he appear to grasp the gravity of what he had set in motion.

In his last phone call of the night, the President spoke with Johnny McEntee, his Director of Personnel.[328]

"[T]his is a crazy day," the President told him. McEntee said his tone was one of "[l]ike, wow, can you believe this shit . . .?"[329]

Did he express sadness over the violence visited upon the Capitol?

"No," McEntee said. "I mean, I think he was shocked by, you know, it getting a little out of control, but I don't remember sadness, specifically."[330]

President Trump didn't make any other phone calls for the rest of the night.[331] The President didn't call Vice President Pence. In fact, President Trump never called to check on his Vice President's safety that day. He didn't call the heads of any of the Federal law enforcement agencies. He didn't call the leadership—neither Republican nor Democrat—of the legislative branch of government that had just been overrun by a mob.[332]

Only two days after the riot, by January 8th, the President was over the whole thing.

He "just didn't want to talk about it anymore," he told his press aides. "[H]e was tired of talking about it." [333]

Ivanka Trump claimed to the Select Committee that her father was "disappointed and surprised" by the attack, but she could not name a specific instance of him expressly saying it.

"He—I just felt that," she said. "I know him really well." [334]

Here's what she could definitively say:

Committee Staff: Has he ever expressed to you any sentiment that he did or did not do the right thing in how he responded on the day of the 6th?

Ms. Trump: No.

Committee Staff: Has he ever expressed any sentiment about something that he wished he had done on the day of the 6th?

Ms. Trump: No.

Committee Staff: Has he ever said anything to you about the people who were injured or who died that day?

Ms. Trump: No.

Committee Staff: Has he ever said anything to you about whether he should or should not continue to talk about the 2020 Presidential election after the events on the 6th?

Ms. Trump: No. [335]

## 7.14 PRESIDENT TRUMP'S "RHETORIC KILLED SOMEONE"

The President may not have expressed regret over his behavior, but some of his most loyal supporters made the connection between his words and the violence.

A member of the speechwriting team, Patrick MacDonnell, conceded the next day in a text that "maybe the rhetoric could have been better." [336] As the riot was in full throttle, even steadfast supporter Ali Alexander of "Stop the Steal" texted, "POTUS is not ignorant of what his words will do." [337]

"We all look like domestic terrorists now," Hope Hicks texted Julie Radford. [338]

Separately, Hicks texted Herschmann, "So predictable and so sad."

"I know," he replied. "Tragic."

"I'm so upset. Everything we worked for wiped away," she continued.

"I agree. Totally self-inflicted," he wrote. [339]

Brad Parscale, Trump's Former Campaign Manager, texted Katrina Pierson at 7:21 p.m. on January 6th, saying the day's events were the result of a "sitting president asking for civil war." [340]

"This week I feel guilty for helping him win . . . a woman is dead," Parscale added.

"You do realize this was going to happen," Pierson answered.

"Yeah. If I was trump [sic] and knew my rhetoric killed someone," he said.

"It wasn't the rhetoric," she said.

Parscale's reply: "Yes it was." [341]

**8**

# ANALYSIS OF THE ATTACK

Late in the evening on January 6, 2021, Henry "Enrique" Tarrio, the head of the Proud Boys, posted a video on his Parler account. The brief footage showed a masked man, wearing a black cape, standing in front of the U.S. Capitol Building. Tarrio titled the 18-second video, set to ominous music, "Premonition." He offered no further explanation. The clear implication of the brief footage, recorded sometime prior to January 6th, was that Tarrio had foreknowledge of the events that transpired earlier that same day.[1]

Indeed, Tarrio cheered on his fellow Proud Boys as they attacked the U.S. Capitol. He had been arrested and ordered to leave Washington, DC two days earlier. Although Tarrio was not physically present, he continued to monitor and communicate with his men via encrypted chats and social media. At 2:36 p.m. on January 6th, Tarrio wrote on Parler that he was "enjoying the show," adding: "Do what must be done" and "#WeThePeople."[2] Two minutes later, Tarrio wrote: "Don't fucking leave." Several minutes after that, Tarrio messaged his Proud Boys: "Make no mistake..." and "We did this..."[3]

Law enforcement officials subsequently uncovered significant evidence showing that Tarrio and his lieutenants planned to storm the U.S. Capitol. In June 2022, Tarrio and four other Proud Boys were charged with seditious conspiracy and other crimes related to their alleged responsibility for the assault.[4] The U.S. Department of Justice (DOJ) has alleged that they "conspired to prevent, hinder and delay the certification of the Electoral College vote, and to oppose by force the authority of the government of the United States."[5] On January 6, 2021, the Proud Boys "directed, mobilized and led members of the crowd onto the Capitol grounds and into the Capitol, leading to dismantling of metal barricades, destruction of property, breaching of the Capitol building, and assaults on law enforcement."[6]

The Select Committee's analysis corroborates the DOJ's findings and allegations. The Select Committee reviewed extensive footage of the attack, including that recorded by the U.S. Capitol Police's (USCP) surveillance cameras, the Metropolitan Police Department's (MPD) body-worn cameras, publicly available videos, as well as on-the-ground film produced by an embedded documentarian. The Select Committee interviewed rioters, law enforcement officers, and witnesses that were present on January 6th, while also consulting thousands of court filings. Using these sources of information, the Select Committee developed a timeline of events to understand how the unprecedented attack on the U.S. Capitol unfolded.

As explained below, the Proud Boys marched from the Washington Monument to the U.S. Capitol on the morning of January 6th. While tens of thousands of President Trump's supporters gathered at a rally at the Ellipse near the White House, the Proud Boys prepared to attack. Shortly before the joint session of Congress was set to begin at 1:00 p.m., the Proud Boys instigated an assault on outmanned law enforcement at the Peace Circle, a key location. They quickly overran security barriers and made their way onto the U.S. Capitol's restricted grounds. Throughout the next several hours, members of the Proud Boys led the attack at key breach points, preventing law enforcement from gaining crowd control and inciting others to press forward.

President Trump finished his speech at the Ellipse at approximately 1:10 p.m. Toward the end of his remarks, the President directed his supporters to march down Pennsylvania Avenue to the Capitol. Their natural path took them through the Peace Circle, which had already been cleared out by the Proud Boys and their associates. Thousands of rioters and protestors streamed onto the Capitol's restricted grounds in short order.

The Proud Boys were not solely responsible for attacking the U.S. Capitol. As explained in Chapter 6, other far-right extremists and conspiracy theorists prepared for violence after President Trump summoned them to Washington for a "wild" protest on January 6th. And they joined in the assault as well. Three Percenters, QAnon adherents, and other radicals were on the frontlines, pressing the charge. The Oath Keepers attacked the Capitol, forming two military-style "stacks" to push their way into the building. The white nationalist Groypers were present as their leader gave an inflammatory speech from the same Peace Circle where the attack was launched. Like members of the Proud Boys, Oath Keepers, and Three Percenters, some of the Groypers have been charged for their actions on January 6th.

Unaffiliated Americans enraged by President Trump's lies rioted as well. The January 6th, attack has often been described as a riot—and that is partly true. Some of those who trespassed on the Capitol's grounds or entered the building did not plan to do so beforehand. But it is also true that extremists, conspiracy theorists and others were prepared to fight. That is

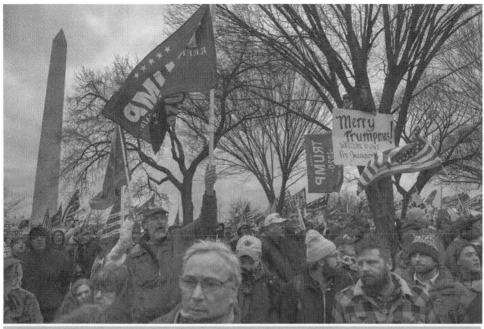

Trump supporters from around the country gather at the Washington Monument on the morning of January 6, 2021.

Photo by Brent Stirton/Getty Images

an insurrection. They answered President Trump's call to action. Some, like the Proud Boys, deliberately harnessed the mob's anger to overrun the Capitol.

### 8.1 THE MOB ASSEMBLES IN WASHINGTON

During the early morning hours of January 6th, tens of thousands of Americans from around the country began to gather at the Ellipse and the Washington Monument. They had come to hear President Trump speak and, more importantly, for his "wild" protest.

Nick Quested, a documentary filmmaker, captured the mood that morning. Jacob Chansley (a.k.a. the QAnon Shaman) proclaimed "this is our 1776," vowing "Joe Biden is never getting in." [7] An unnamed woman from Georgia, who said she hosted a podcast dedicated to a new so-called Patriot Party, also proclaimed January 6th to be the new 1776. She added an ominous warning. "I'm not allowed to say what's going to happen today because everyone's just going to have to watch. Something's gonna happen, one way or the other." [8]

The Secret Service set up magnetometers to screen for weapons and other contraband, but many rally-goers chose to avoid the screening altogether.

At 6:29 a.m., Stewart Rhodes, the leader of the Oath Keepers, reminded his group's members that DC prohibited blades over "3 inches" and encouraged them to "[k]eep [the knives] low profile." [9] Others were thinking along the same lines. At 7:25 a.m., the National Park Service reported that a significant number of attendees ditched their bags in trees, rather than have them inspected.[10] Cassidy Hutchinson told the Select Committee she heard that thousands of people refused to walk through magnetometers to enter the Ellipse because they did not want to be screened for weapons.[11] According to Hutchinson, the Deputy Chief of Staff for Operations whose responsibilities included security-related issues, Tony Ornato, told the President that the onlookers "don't want to come in right now. They—they have weapons that they don't want confiscated by the Secret Service." [12] When he arrived at the Ellipse that morning, President Trump angrily said: "I don't [fucking] care that they have weapons. They're not here to hurt *me*. They can march to the Capitol from here." [13]

Approximately 28,000 rally-goers did pass through the magnetometers. The Secret Service confiscated a significant number of prohibited items from these people, including: 269 knives or blades, 242 cannisters of pepper spray, 18 brass knuckles, 18 tasers, 6 pieces of body armor, 3 gas masks, 30 batons or blunt instruments, and 17 miscellaneous items like scissors, needles, or screwdrivers.[14]

At 8:07 a.m., Secret Service countersurveillance agents reported that "members of the crowd are wearing ballistic helmets, body armor and carrying radio equipment and military grade backpacks." [15] By 9:45 a.m., the Secret Service noted people openly carrying pepper spray as they strolled the streets.[16]

President Trump's mob was itching for a fight. National Park Service officers arrested a man who had entered the restricted area around the Washington Monument. Immediately, about 100 people started forming a circle around the officer, "threaten[ing] law enforcement," as the officer later recounted.[17] The officer retreated into the Washington Monument with the man in custody.[18] The crowd responded angrily, punching the Monument's glass windows and continuing to threaten officers.[19] Law enforcement around the Washington Monument felt so unsafe that they "locked themselves in a security box by the mall." [20] Rioters nevertheless "scaled the sides of the security box and climbed on top of the structure." [21] It was a harbinger of things to come.

MPD monitored and responded to a stream of threats that morning. Three men in fatigues from Broward County, Florida brandished AR-15s in front of MPD officers on 14th Street and Independence Avenue.[22] MPD advised over the radio that one individual was possibly armed with a "Glock" at Fourteenth Street and Constitution Avenue, and another was possibly armed with a "rifle" at Fifteenth Street and Constitution Avenue around 11:23 a.m.[23] The National Park Service detained an individual with a rifle between 12:00 and 1:00 p.m.[24]

Far-right extremists brought guns into Washington or the surrounding area. Christopher Kuehne, a member of the Proud Boys, met up with friends on January 5th to discuss their plans for the following day. One person in attendance said he did not travel to Washington just to "march around" and asked, "do we have patriots here willing to take it by force?"[25] Kuehne told them he had guns, and he was ready to go.[26] During the attack, Kuehne helped prop open Capitol blast doors as besieged law enforcement retreated inside.[27] Guy Reffitt, a Three Percenter from Texas, attended the rally at the Ellipse, and then carried a loaded firearm onto Capitol grounds.[28] Jerod Thomas Bargar lost his gun—that he'd carried from the Ellipse in a 'We the People' holster[29]—while scuffling with police on the west side of the Capitol around 2:30 p.m.[30] Bargar wanted to be armed, he said, when he went into the "belly of the beast." [31]

Mark Andre Mazza drove from Indiana, bringing a Taurus revolver, a .45-caliber weapon that he loaded with both shotgun and hollow-point rounds.[32] After assaulting a police officer, he lost the weapon,[33] dropping it or losing it on the steps of the lower West Plaza leading to the Capitol's West Front Terrace.[34] The Select Committee reviewed Mazza's social media accounts before they were taken down, finding that he shared multiple conspiracy theories, including QAnon material.[35] Mazza later indicated that he intended to target House Speaker Nancy Pelosi, telling authorities that "you'd be here for another reason" if he had found the Speaker inside the Capitol.[36]

Lonnie Leroy Coffman from Falkville, Alabama, parked by the Capitol building before walking nearly 2 miles to the Ellipse to hear the President speak.[37] In his car, he had stocked a handgun, a rifle, a shotgun, hundreds of rounds of ammunition, large-capacity ammunition-feeding devices, machetes, camouflage smoke devices, a bow and arrow, and 11 Mason jars filled with gasoline and styrofoam, as well as rags and a lighter (tools needed to make Molotov cocktails).[38] Police found two more handguns on Coffman when he was arrested later that day.[39]

Many in attendance were aware of Washington's prohibition on carrying a concealed weapon and made plans accordingly. The Oath Keepers left their guns stowed away in their cars or across State lines for easy access should they be needed.[40] The group staged a "quick reaction force" across the river in Virginia, amassing an arsenal to come to DC "by land" or "by sea," as Florida State-chapter lead—and defendant convicted of seditious conspiracy—Kelly Meggs said.[41] Oath Keeper Jason Dolan testified at the seditious conspiracy trial that the "quick reaction force [was] ready to go get our firearms in order to stop the election from being certified within Congress."[42] Dolan further testified that the Oath Keepers came to Washington, DC "to stop the certification of the election....[b]y any means necessary. That's why we brought our firearms."[43]

Garret Miller—a January 6th defendant who traveled from Richardson, Texas—posted on Facebook that "he was bringing guns with him but 'might just keep 1 hidden one and store the rest in Virginia'" after learning about the DC law.[44] He also threatened to assassinate Congresswoman Alexandria Ocasio-Cortez and predicted a "civil war could start."[45]

Many members of the crowd decided against bringing firearms into the nation's capital, and armed themselves in other ways. Alex Kirk Harkrider from Carthage, Texas, and his co-defendant, Ryan Nichols, left guns in a parked car just outside the district before attending the rally.[46] Harkrider still brought a tomahawk axe.[47] During the march to the Capitol, he yelled "[c]ut their fucking heads off!"[48] One rioter told the Select Committee he saw another carrying a "pitchfork."[49]

Members of the mob carried flags and turned the flagpoles into weapons. Michael Foy, from Wixom, Michigan, carried a hockey stick to the Ellipse—he draped a Trump flag over it.[50] Just hours later, Foy used that hockey stick to repeatedly beat police officers at the inaugural tunnel.[51] Former New York City police officer Thomas Webster carried a Marine flag, which he later used to attack an officer holding the rioters back at the lower West Plaza.[52] Another individual, Danny Hamilton, carried a flag with a sharpened tip, which he said was "for a certain person," to which Trevor Hallgren(who had traveled with Hamilton to Washington, DC) responded: "it has begun." Later, Hallgren commented that "[t]here's no escape Pelosi, Schumer, Nadler. We're coming for you....Even you AOC. We're coming to take you out. To pull you out by your hairs." On January 5th, Hallgren took a tour of the Capitol with Representative Barry Loudermilk, during which he took pictures of hallways and staircases.[53]

The mob President Trump summoned to Washington, DC, on January 6th, was prepared to fight.

## 8.2 MARCH OF THE PROUD BOYS

While tens of thousands of President Trump's supporters attended the rally at the Ellipse, the Proud Boys had other plans. On the morning of January

6th, they gathered at the Washington Monument. At 10:30 a.m., the Proud Boys started their march down the National Mall towards the U.S. Capitol. In total, there were approximately 200–300 Proud Boys, as well as their associates, in the group.[54]

Enrique Tarrio, the chairman of the Proud Boys, was not in attendance. As explained in Chapter 6, Tarrio had been arrested two days earlier and ordered to leave Washington. However, Tarrio continued to monitor events remotely from Baltimore, communicating with his men throughout the day. With Tarrio offsite, the Proud Boys were led by three other senior members of the group: Ethan Nordean, Joseph Biggs, and Zachary Rehl.

Ethan Nordean (a.k.a. "Rufio Panman") was a member of the Proud Boys' Elders chapter and president of his local chapter in Seattle, Washington.[55] Nordean was regarded as the leader for January 6th after Tarrio was arrested.[56] In the days leading up to January 6th, Nordean made ominous comments on social media. In conversations with his fellow Proud Boys, he argued that the Presidential election was tainted by fraud and violence was a necessary remedy. For example, on January 4th, Nordean posted a video on social media with the title: "Let them remember the day they decided to make war with us."[57] In another social media post on January 5th, Nordean warned "we are coming for them."[58] He added a telling line: "You've chosen your side, black and yellow teamed with red, white and blue against everyone else."[59] The "black and yellow" is a reference to the Proud Boys. And when Nordean wrote the "red, white and blue," he likely meant the Trump supporters who would be in attendance for January 6th.

Joseph Biggs (a.k.a. "Sergeant Biggs") was a senior Proud Boys member and served as an event "organizer" for the group.[60] Biggs previously worked with Alex Jones and InfoWars.[61] In late December 2020, Biggs posted a message on Parler in which he explained that the Proud Boys "will not be attending DC in colors."[62] That is, unlike at previous events, the Proud Boys would not wear their branded, black and yellow clothing, but instead seek to be inconspicuous. Biggs continued:

> We will be blending in as one of you. You won't see us. You'll even think we are you…We are going to smell like you, move like you, and look like you. The only thing we'll do that's us is think like us! Jan 6th is gonna be epic.[63]

Tarrio posted a similar message, saying the Proud Boys would go "incognito" on January 6th.[64] Consistent with this decision, Biggs was dressed in a plaid shirt, glasses, and dark hat as he led the march from the Washington Monument.[65] Other Proud Boys dressed in a similar fashion.

Protestors, including a group of Proud Boys, gather at the Capitol on January 6, 2021.
Photo by Jon Cherry/Getty Images

Zachary Rehl (a.k.a. "Captain Trump") was president of the local Philadelphia, Pennsylvania Proud Boys chapter.[66] Like his comrades, Rehl believed President Trump's Big Lie about the 2020 Presidential election.[67] He raised more than $5,500 in funds for January 6th. Like Nordean, Biggs and others, Rehl was dressed "incognito" as he helped lead the group from the Washington Monument.[68]

Shortly after 11:00 a.m., the Proud Boys arrived at the west side of the Capitol, near a reflecting pool. From there, they marched to the east front of the Capitol. Surveillance footage shows the Proud Boys passing Garfield Circle on the southwest corner of the Capitol at 11:15 a.m.[69] They walked north towards the Peace Circle next, and surveillance cameras captured them on video there at approximately 11:21 a.m.[70] There was just one USCP officer standing guard at the Peace Circle fence at the time.[71]

As the Proud Boys paraded around the Capitol grounds, Nick Quested, a documentary filmmaker who spent time with the group, recalled them taunting USCP officers. One Proud Boy told the officers to "[r]emember your oath," "[c]hoose a side," and "[b]e on the right side of history." [72] By 11:41 a.m., the Proud Boys made their way around to the east side of the Capitol, crossing along Constitution Avenue.[73] While on the east front, they posed for pictures with members of their Arizona delegation, who were clearly identifiable by their orange caps.[74] They then walked back across the north side of the Capitol towards the National Mall, where they stopped to eat at food trucks.[75] The Proud Boys stayed by the food trucks until they returned to the Peace Circle at approximately 12:49 p.m.[76]

## 8.3  THE INITIAL ATTACK

Within minutes of arriving at the Peace Circle, the Proud Boys and their associates launched the attack on the U.S. Capitol. The circle is the site of the Peace Monument, a statue erected from 1877 to 1878 to commemorate naval deaths at sea during the Civil War with "two classically robed" women—one woman representing "grief," covering her face, and the other woman representing "history." The woman standing in for "history" holds a tablet that reads, "They died that their country might live." [77]

The Peace Circle's geographical location is crucially important for understanding how the January 6th, attack unfolded. It sits at the end of Pennsylvania Avenue, just in front of the U.S. Capitol. At the conclusion of his speech at the Ellipse, President Trump directed rally attendees to march down Pennsylvania Avenue to the U.S. Capitol. Their shortest natural path would lead them right to the Peace Circle and to the northwest side of the Capitol grounds, also known as the West Plaza. By the time rally-goers arrived, the Proud Boys and their allies had already removed the fencing that stood in the crowd's way. As a result, thousands of people streamed into the restricted Capitol grounds with relative ease.

When the Proud Boys arrived back at the Peace Circle at 12:49 p.m., they still had about 200 to 300 members and many other protestors had joined them.[78] Shortly after arriving, the Proud Boys incited the crowd with antagonistic chants such as "1776."[79] Officer Caroline Edwards, who was standing guard, explained to the Select Committee that the Proud Boys asked her and the other USCP officers if they could walk past the fencing and talk to the officers. "No," she replied. The Proud Boys and others immediately turned on Edwards and her fellow officers, referring to them as "Nancy Pelosi's dogs" and shouting.[80]

At approximately 12:51 p.m., Quested captured a rioter named Ryan Samsel with his arm around Proud Boys leader Joe Biggs, who led the chants.[81] Samsel subsequently claimed that Biggs encouraged him to push through the barricades and, when Samsel hesitated to follow through, Biggs "flashed a gun, questioned his manhood and repeated his demand" to move to the front and "challenge the police." [82] Biggs has contested Samsel's version of events.[83] After speaking with Biggs, Samsel breached the outer fencing of the Peace Circle at 12:53 p.m.[84] The first set of fencing at the

Peace Circle was staged on 1st Street Northwest, with the second set of fencing not far behind. Once Samsel breached the outer fencing, USCP officers, including Officer Edwards, moved from their posts to meet Samsel and other rioters.[85]

In less than a minute, at 12:54 p.m., the rioters pushed USCP officers to the ground, removed the fencing, and quickly stormed east towards the U.S. Capitol building.[86] Officer Edwards was thrown to the ground, causing her to hit her head on concrete steps.[87]

Two Proud Boys from New York, Dominic Pezzola and William Pepe, were among those leading the march to the next line of security barriers.[88] Pepe, an employee of the Metropolitan Transportation Authority in upstate New York, took sick leave to travel to Washington for the January 6th events.[89] Pepe dragged part of the fence away at the next security barrier, ensuring that USCP officers were left defenseless.[90] The Proud Boys' actions were not spontaneous. Jeffrey Finley, a Proud Boys leader from West Virginia, later admitted "there appeared to be a coordinated effort to pull the barricades apart."[91] Proud Boy Jeremy Bertino admitted to similar facts when pleading guilty to seditious conspiracy, stating stated that he "believed...that the purpose of traveling to Washington, DC, on January 6, 2021, was to stop the certification of the Electoral College Vote, and that the MOSD leaders were willing to do whatever it would take, including using force against police and others, to achieve that objective." Based on discussions he and other Proud Boys leaders had in the leadup to January 6th, he "believed that storming the Capitol would achieve the group's goal of stopping Congress from certifying the Electoral College Vote. Bertino understood that storming the Capitol or its grounds would be illegal and would require using force against police or other government officials."[92]

Parallel to the Peace Circle, at the Garfield Circle walkway located at the southeast corner of the Capitol grounds, rioters breached the fencing at 12:55 p.m. and began rushing the West Plaza where they would converge with others from the Peace Circle.[93]

By 12:58 p.m., the crowd filled the lower West Plaza of the Capitol just below the inauguration stage that had been built for the ceremony scheduled two weeks later. After the initial breaches, the USCP was able to deploy enough officers to stop the rioters from advancing past the base of the inauguration stage. More importantly, rioter momentum was further halted when the first group of MPD officers arrived on scene at 1:11 p.m.,[94] almost precisely as President Trump finished his Ellipse speech. The MPD officers initially pushed back the rioters on the West Plaza, slowing them down before they would later breach the Capitol.[95]

A stalemate ensued on the West Plaza before rioters were able to make any further progress. Rally-goers arriving from the Ellipse provided crucial momentum.

## 8.4 PRESIDENT TRUMP'S MOB DESCENDS ON THE U.S. CAPITOL

Toward the end of his speech at the Ellipse, President Trump made sure an already angry crowd of his supporters stayed enraged. "We fight like hell[,] and if you don't fight like hell, you're not going to have a country anymore," the President told the tens of thousands of people who had assembled at the Ellipse, or in the vicinity. About one minute later, President Trump directed those in attendance "to walk down Pennsylvania Avenue ... to the Capitol." The President told the people they were "going to try and give" Republicans, including his own Vice President, "the kind of pride and boldness that they need to take back our country." [96]

"There's enough people here to storm the Capitol," a member of the crowd said at 1:06 p.m., just as the President was concluding his remarks.[97] Ronald Sandlin, who pleaded guilty to and has been sentenced for felonies committed on January 6th, including telling officers in the Capitol that "[y]ou're going to die," watched the President's speech from a nearby restaurant and live-streamed a video in which he encouraged "other patriots" to "take the Capitol." [98] Sandlin repeated the phrase "freedom is paid for with blood" several times during his video.[99]

"We're getting ready to go march on Capitol Hill. We're gonna go fuck some shit up," Cody Mattice, another January 6th defendant who pleaded guilty and has been sentenced,[100] said while walking to the Capitol. Mattice later added: "We're getting up front, and we're taking this shit." [101] Ryan Nichols, who was charged with eight felonies, livestreamed a diatribe as he marched towards the Capitol at 1:40 p.m. Nichols echoed the President's unconstitutional claim that Vice President Pence had the power to decide the election himself. "I'm hearing that Pence just caved.... I'm telling you if Pence caved, we're gonna drag motherfuckers through the streets," Nichols said.[102] "Cut their heads off!" Nichols yelled with his codefendant Harkrider, before encouraging others to join "Republican protestors [who] are trying to enter the House right now." [103]

On the way to the Capitol, Oath Keeper Jessica Watkins chatted with others in a Zello group named "Stop the Steal J6." Watkins said that "100%" of the Ellipse crowd was "marching on the Capitol," because "it has spread like wildfire that Pence has betrayed us." [104] As she approached the Capitol with a contingent of Oath Keepers, Watkins said: "I'm probably gonna go silent when I get there 'cause I'm a be a little busy.[105] Donald

Hazard, a Three Percenter from Texas who claimed to be allied with Proud Boys on January 6th, told a *Washington Post* reporter that he wanted his face recorded on video as he marched to the Capitol. "I want the enemy to know exactly who is coming after them," Hazard explained.[106]

Leaders of the "Stop the Steal" movement continued to incite the crowd during the march as well. Alex Jones of InfoWars arrived at the Ellipse shortly before 9:00 a.m. on the morning of January 6th.[107] After some initial difficulty gaining access to the event area, Jones was seated in the VIP section.[108] While Jones stayed to listen to a portion of President Trump's speech, planning for the crowd's march to the Capitol was already under-way and Jones intended to leave the Ellipse early to lead the march. The origins of the plan to have Jones lead the march are unclear. Jones has pub-licly stated that "the White House told me three days before, we are going to have you lead the March."[109] Stop the Steal's Ali Alexander also believed "the White House" wanted him to lead a march to the Capitol.[110] It is likely that both got that idea from Caroline Wren, a Republican fundraiser who helped organize the Ellipse event.[111] Jones texted Wren at 12:27 p.m., asking when he should leave the Ellipse and begin the march.[112]

While Wren originally expected Jones, Roger Stone, and retired Lt. Gen. Michael Flynn to march to the Capitol, Stone did not attend the Ellipse rally and so he was not present to accompany Jones on the march as planned.[113] Additionally, while President Trump was delivering his speech, Wren asked Flynn if he was going to march with Jones. Flynn responded, "Hell, no. It's freezing."[114]

While Stone and Flynn did not march, Jones and Alexander led others to the Capitol, though it is not clear how many people followed them.[115] Jones and Alexander gathered with Jones's camera and security crew just outside the event perimeter, near Freedom Plaza, to discuss their plans.[116] The dis-cussion, recorded by Alex Jones's film crew, sheds some light on what Jones and Alexander knew about the President's plans and what they intended for the march. The group, which included InfoWars host Owen Shroyer, huddled outside the Ellipse security perimeter to discuss how best to pro-ceed. They tried to predict the Presidential motorcade's route to the Capitol. The video shows Alex Jones telling his crew, "I think the Wren lady, where's she at? She knows what they said they were going to do. Everything she's said has been accurate, so we need to call her real quick."[117] They then decided to walk down Pennsylvania Avenue, as the President had directed in his speech.

Shroyer recommended the group wait for President Trump to finish speaking, and they agreed to at least delay their departure from Freedom Plaza to allow Jones to gather a crowd.[118] Jones began speaking from his

Alex Jones uses a bullhorn to speak to crowd on January 6, 2021.

bullhorn, imploring people to gather and walk down Pennsylvania Avenue.[119] While using the bullhorn, Jones told the crowd that they were experiencing "the second American revolution,"[120] and stated, "[l]et's go take our country back. Trump is only minutes away. Let's start marching to the Capitol, peacefully."[121]

Proud Boys were among the crowd Jones gathered during his march. Matthew Walter, president of a Tennessee chapter of the organization,[122] was near the National Mall with two other Proud Boys from Tennessee and decided to join Jones.[123] Other, more prominent members of the Proud Boys appear to have been in contact with Jones and Shroyer about the events of January 6th and on that day. Records for Enrique Tarrio's phone show that while the attack on the Capitol was ongoing, he texted with Jones three times and Shroyer five times.[124] Ethan Nordean's phone records reflect that he exchanged 23 text messages with Shroyer between January 4th and 5th, and that he had one call with him on each of those days.[125] Records of Joseph Biggs's communications show that he texted with Shroyer eight times on January 4th and called him at approximately 11:15 a.m. on January 6th, while Biggs and his fellow Proud Boys were marching at and around the Capitol.[126]

Once they had marched the length of Pennsylvania Avenue and reached the west side of the Capitol, Jones and Alexander used a bullhorn to continue directing those around them to the east side, making further references to President Trump's alleged imminent arrival. A video recorded by a rallygoer at 1:51 p.m. shows Jones and Alexander standing together as Jones encourages the crowd to proceed to the east side of the Capitol. He tells those listening that "we've got a permit on the other side, it's great that this happened, but Trump's not going to come when we've taken this over. We are not Antifa, we are not BLM." [127]

Jones has repeatedly claimed that he tried to calm the crowd, but his actions also coincided with two police line breaches and one breach of the Capitol building itself. At 1:57 p.m., minutes after Jones encouraged rally goers to move east, newly arrived protestors breached the bike rack fencing used to keep the crowd away from the east side steps.[128] After the breach, police retreated to the base of the large set of steps behind them and the crowd moved forward to meet the newly established police line.[129]

Jones followed shortly behind the crowd that led the initial east fence breach, and his arrival coincided with the next breach up the east stairs. Publicly available video shows Jones already departed from the west side, rounding the north side of the Capitol on the way to the east side at 2:00 p.m.[130] As he was walking, Jones told his group, "those fucking cops need to fucking back off man." [131] He was then asked about Vice President Pence, to which Jones responded: "he floundered and was neutral, he passed the ball." [132] At the conclusion of the video, one of Jones's camera crew can be heard saying, "let's take a break here. Let me talk to this cop to see if I can get Alex up there to deescalate the situation." Other video released by Jones shows one of his camera crew interacting with USCP officers and asking how Jones can help deescalate the situation.[133] The Select Committee's review of the evidence showed that Jones simultaneously called on the crowd to "fight" and start a "revolution," while occasionally peppering his rhetoric with the word "peacefully."

Minutes after Jones's arrival on the scene, at approximately 2:06 p.m., rioters breached the new police line and stormed up the stairs towards the Columbus Doors (also known as the Rotunda Doors).[134] The crowd's cheers and celebration as they move up the steps can be heard while Jones's camera crew negotiates with USCP officers nearby.[135] As explained below, the rioters broke through another key breach point with Jones and Alexander on the scene just minutes later.

Rioters clash with police at the Capitol on January 6, 2021.

## 8.5 THE MOB SURGES

Far-right extremists continued to lead the charge as protestors streamed onto the U.S. Capitol's restricted grounds. On the north side of the West Plaza, there was a scaffold with stairs used by construction workers to build the inauguration stage. Law enforcement officers were stationed at the base of the stairs, preventing rioters from climbing to the upper West Plaza, where doors to the Capitol building itself were located. At 1:49 p.m., MPD declared a riot at the Capitol.[136]

Shortly before 1:50 p.m., rioters gathered in front of this scaffold on the northwest corner of the Capitol. The rioters included Proud Boys and other extremists. One rioter, Guy Reffitt, belonged to a Three Percenter group from Texas.[137] By approximately 1:50 p.m., he stood at the front of the pack near the scaffold, carrying a pistol and flexicuffs.[138] He wore body armor under a blue jacket and a helmet with a mounted body camera.[139]

Reffitt advanced on the police line, absorbing rubber bullets and pushing through chemical spray.[140] As he recounted shortly after the attack, Reffitt got "everything started moving forward."[141] He "started the fire" and the presence of law enforcement was not going to prevent Reffitt's advance.[142] According to Reffitt:

> [T]here was no reason for me to give up because I had come so far to do what I wanted, what we wanted and needed to do. And I had a mindset. I didn't mean to actually be the first guy up there. I didn't even mean to do that. I just, the adrenaline and knowing that I can't let my country fall.[143]

Reffitt had indeed planned for violence on January 6th, noting on December 28, 2020, that he would "be in full battle rattle."[144] While driving to Washington, DC on January 5th, Reffitt expressed his desire to "drag[ ] those people out of the Capitol by their ankles" and "install[ ] a new government."[145] On the morning of January 6th, Reffitt clarified the target, telling "other members of his militia group and those gathered around him" at the Ellipse that "I'm taking the Capitol with everybody fucking else"and that "[w]e're all going to drag them mother fuckers out kicking and screaming....I just want to see Pelosi's head hit every fucking stair on the way out...And Mitch McConnell too. Fuck' em all."[146] Reffitt was convicted and ultimately sentenced to 7 years in prison for his conduct.[147]

A member of the Proud Boys, Daniel Scott, helped lead the charge up the scaffolding stairs.[148] Scott, also known as Milkshake, had marched with the Proud Boys from the Washington Monument to the Capitol. During the march, Scott was recorded in a video yelling, "Let's take the fucking Capitol!"[149] Someone else responded, "Let's not fucking yell that, alright?" And then Nordean added: "It was Milkshake, man, you know...idiot." Scott had apparently blurted out the Proud Boys' plan. At the scaffolding, Scott then helped others "take" the U.S. Capitol. While wearing a blue cap with white lettering that read, "Gods, Guns & Trump," he pushed police officers backwards, clearing a path for the rioters. Another Proud Boy, Chris Worrell, was also nearby.[150] As rioters massed under the scaffold, Worrell sprayed officers with OC (or pepper) spray.[151] Other Proud Boys were present at the scaffold, including Micajah Jackson[152] and Matthew Greene.[153]

The attack at and in the vicinity of the scaffolding cleared a path for a wave of rioters who forced their way up the stairs and to the U.S. Capitol building itself.[154] As the rioters rushed up the stairs, another January 6th defendant, Ryan Kelley, climbed up the scaffolding around 1:51 p.m.[155] In the ensuing minutes he waved people on, encouraging them to follow.[156] Kelley—who ran in the Republican primary to be the governor of Michigan in 2022—denied to the Select Committee that he had climbed the scaffolding to wave people on.[157] The FBI arrested Kelley a few months after his deposition.[158]

By 2:00 p.m., rioters at the top of the scaffolding stairs were only feet away from Capitol building doors and windows.

## 8.6   THE UNITED STATES CAPITOL IS BREACHED

Incited by President Trump, over the course of the next hour, extremists, conspiracy theorists and others breached the U.S. Capitol building at several locations. They probed for weaknesses in the building's defenses, battling law enforcement personnel who stood in their way. Once again, the Proud Boys and other extremists played conspicuous roles.

### THE SENATE WING IS BREACHED AT 2:13 P.M.

At 2:13 p.m., Dominic Pezzola, a Proud Boy from New York, smashed a window on the Senate wing.[159] This was the first breach of the Capitol building. Pezzola used a riot shield he stole from a law enforcement officer to break through the window. After climbing through, rioters were able to easily open a nearby Senate wing door from the inside—giving them unfettered passage into the building at 2:14 p.m. Two minutes later, at approximately 2:16 p.m., rioters pushed opened a second door, the Senate fire door, from the inside.[160] Just as the building was being breached, Vice President Pence and Speaker Pelosi were ushered off the Senate and House floors, respectively.[161]

The first person to enter the Capitol building was a Kentucky native named Michael Sparks. Sparks had expressed his desire to kill people after watching protests in the summer of 2020.[162] Following one of President Trump's calls to Washington, DC on December 30, 2020, Sparks answered that he would "be there."[163]

As Pezzola entered the building, he was joined by other noteworthy extremists and conspiracy theorists. Robert Gieswein, an individual from Colorado affiliated with Three Percenters who espoused conspiracy beliefs, climbed through the Senate wing window.[164] Doug Jensen, a QAnon adherent, was part of this first cadre of people to enter the Capitol as well.[165] Jensen wore a brazen "Q" shirt. Jensen later told authorities that he "intentionally positioned himself to be among the first people inside the United States Capitol because . . . he wanted to have his t-shirt seen on video so that 'Q' could 'get the credit.'"[166] Another prominent QAnon believer, Jacob Chansley (a.k.a. the "QAnon Shaman"), also entered through the Senate wing door at approximately 2:14 p.m.[167]

White supremacists and Confederate-sympathizers were among the first rioters to enter the U.S. Capitol. Kevin Seefried and his son, Hunter, entered the building at approximately 2:13 p.m. through the Senate wing window smashed by Proud Boy Dominic Pezzola.[168] Kevin Seefried carried a

Doug Jensen and rioters confront police after storming the Capitol.
(Photo by Win McNamee/Getty Images)

Confederate Battle Flag with him and unfurled it inside the building. According to some historians, while the Confederate Flag has appeared in the building before, it was the first time that an insurrectionist ever carried the banner inside the U.S. Capitol.[169] According to court filings, Hunter Seefried helped punch out the Senate wing window and then clear the broken glass before he, his father and others entered the Capitol.[170] Kevin Seefried was found guilty of obstructing an official proceeding, which is a felony offense, as well as four misdemeanors.[171] The Department of Justice has alleged that at 2:16 p.m., just 3 minutes after the Senate wing was first breached, five individuals associated with the Nick Fuentes's white nationalist "America First" movement entered the U.S. Capitol.[172] The five, all of whom are in their 20s, have been identified as: Joseph Brody, Thomas Carey, Gabriel Chase, Jon Lizak, and Paul Lovley.[173] Four of the five "initially met at an America First event and attended subsequent events together."[174] Nick Fuentes and other America First leaders espouse "a belief that they are defending against the demographic and cultural changes in America."[175] Online researchers say that Brody is the masked man seen in a photo wearing a MAGA hat and holding a rifle in front of a Nazi flag.[176] (The photo was not taken on January 6th.) As discussed in Chapter 6, members of the America First movement, commonly known as

"Groypers," were well-represented at "Stop the Steal" events in late 2020 and these rallies helped pave the road to January 6th. Indeed, at least three members of the group—Lovley, Lizak and Chase—attended the "Stop the Steal, March for Trump" rally in Washington, DC on November 14, 2020.[177]

On January 6th, Brody and his America First associates made their way to various points inside and outside of the Capitol after the initial breach, including House Speaker Nancy Pelosi's conference room and office, as well as the U.S. Senate Chamber.[178] After exiting the Capitol, the group went to the north side of the building. One of the five, Brody, and another rioter allegedly used a "metal barricade" to assault a law enforcement officer who was defending the North Door.[179] (The attack on the North Door is discussed below.) Brody and Chase also allegedly helped others destroy media equipment.[180] Still another America First associate, Riley Williams, directed rioters up a staircase to Speaker Pelosi's office and was accused of aiding and abetting the theft of a laptop found there.[181] Other white supremacists were among the first rioters to enter the U.S. Capitol. Timothy Hale-Cusanelli, an Army Reservist from New Jersey who was identified by a confidential source to law enforcement as an "an avowed white supremacist and Nazi sympathizer," entered through the Senate wing breach around 2:14 p.m.[182] Hale-Cusanelli "[u]sed tactical hand signals" to direct other members of the mob, and he commanded them to "'advance' on the Capitol."[183] Afterwards, he bragged to a friend that January 6th was "exhilarating," that he hoped "for a 'civil war,'" and that the 'tree of liberty must be refreshed with the blood of patriots and tyrants.'"[184] Robert Packer was also among the first rioters to enter the Capitol, and he made his way into the Crypt by 2:25 p.m.[185] Packer was wearing a "Camp Auschwitz" sweatshirt, a "symbol of Nazi hate ideology," at the time.[186]

After breaking in, some of the first rioters headed north toward the Senate chambers.[187] Officer Eugene Goodman, a USCP officer, intercepted them before they headed up the stairs leading to the chambers. Immediately after entering, a rioter asked Officer Goodman, "Where are the [M]embers at?" and "where are they counting the votes?"[188] Jensen, Gieswein, Sparks, and others stalked Officer Goodman through the halls of the Senate.[189] Jensen demanded that Officer Goodman and other USCP officers arrest Vice President Pence.[190] Sparks chanted, "This is our America!"[191] Other rioters who entered through the Senate wing door clashed with police offices at the Senate carriage door located on the northeast side of the Capitol.[192] When the rioters followed Officer Goodman up the stairs to the Senate Chamber, they were stopped by a line of USCP officers outside the Ohio Clock Tower.[193]

Joe Biggs of the Proud Boys entered the Capitol shortly after the first breach. At 2:14 p.m., Biggs walked through the senate wing door and moved north. Part of his route was captured in videos posted on Parler, a right-wing social media site.[194] Someone recorded the Proud Boys leader shortly after he entered the Capitol and asked him, "Hey Biggs what do you gotta say?"[195] Smiling, Biggs replied: "this is awesome!"[196] Other Proud Boys were seen with Biggs, or near him, as he entered the Capitol. One of them is Paul Rae, a Proud Boys member from Florida, who appears to have communicated directly with Biggs after they entered through the door.[197] Another Proud Boy from Florida, Arthur Jackman, was seen with his hand on Biggs's right shoulder. Jackman "became involved in the Proud Boys to support Donald Trump," was in Washington on January 6th "to support President Trump and to stop the steal" and "believe[d] the election was stolen." Still another, Joshua Pruitt, who was clad in a Punisher shirt, entered the Capitol through the Senate wing door around this time.[198] At approximately 2:17 p.m., 3 minutes after entering the U.S. Capitol for the first time, Biggs exited through another door.[199]

At 2:43 p.m., law enforcement was able to regain control of the Senate wing door, forcing all the rioters out. But their success lasted for only 5 minutes. At 2:48 p.m., rioters again breached the Senate wing door, pushing law enforcement out of the way.[200] The second breach was one of the more violent breaches of the day, with the mob forcefully pushing law enforcement backwards until the pathway was clear for them to enter.

### THE COLUMBUS DOORS (EAST ROTUNDA DOORS) ARE BREACHED AT 2:24 P.M. AND 2:38 P.M.

While the Proud Boys and other extremists were overwhelming law enforcement at the West Plaza scaffolding, another group led the attack on security barriers on the East Plaza. At 2:06 p.m., a crowd broke through security barriers and charged a set of doors just outside the Rotunda.[201] The mob's surge occurred just minutes after Alex Jones arrived on the scene.[202] The crowd's cheers and celebration as they move up the steps can be heard while Jones's camera crew negotiates with USCP officers nearby.[203]

Once rioters had filled the Rotunda stairs, Jones and his team, along with the Proud Boy Walter, ascended the stairs. They moved into the thick of the crowd at the top of the stairs, where Jones began calling for peace but also revolution, leading the crowd in chants of "1776" and other bellicose rhetoric.[204] Publicly available video shows that Jones reached the top of the stairs at 2:18 p.m.[205] Walter told the Select Committee that he thought Jones was successful in getting some people down, "but I also think that may have created enough space for people to be able to move, whereas before you couldn't move."[206] Apparently, Jones's security team also realized he was not successfully controlling the crowd, as one of his security guards reportedly told him, "Alex, they're going to blame this all on you, we got to get out of here as fast as possible."[207] By approximately 2:21 p.m., Jones began descending the stairs.[208] Despite claiming to make attempts to calm the crowd, Jones further incited the mob as he departed, loudly proclaiming "we will never submit to the new world order" and then leading the crowd in the chant "fight for Trump."[209]

At 2:24 p.m., rioters gained entrance to the Capitol through the doors leading into the Rotunda,[210] an entrance that was only a few feet directly behind Jones as he was speaking. As the Rotunda was breached by rioters, Jones and Alexander left the area and decided to leave the Capitol complex area altogether.[211]

Law enforcement officials were able to thwart the initial breach of the doors leading into the Rotunda. By 2:28 p.m., they temporarily regained control and stopped rioters from entering.[212] But their success was short-lived. Within ten minutes, the doors were breached once again.[213] And two members of the Proud Boys—Ronald Loehrke and James Haffner—helped lead the attack.[214]

Loehrke was allegedly recruited by Nordean, the Proud Boys leader, for January 6th. In late December 2020, Nordean asked Loehrke via text message if he was coming to "DC."[215] After Loehrke indicated he was, Nordean said he wanted Loehrke "on the front line" with him.[216] Loehrke replied, "Sounds good man."[217] Loehrke and Haffner marched with the Proud Boys from the Washington Monument to the Capitol grounds and were present during the breach at the Peace Circle.[218] The pair made their way to the east side of the Capitol, where they began removing the security barriers and resisting USCP officers.[219] Other members of the crowd joined. Eventually, the rioters breached these barriers too, allowing them to reach the doors of the Rotunda.

When the rioters reached the Columbus Doors, they were again stopped by USCP officers. But as the officers explained to the Select Committee, the rioters pushed them against the doors and sprayed them with OC spray (commonly known as pepper spray), making it impossible to defend the Capitol.[220] James Haffner was one of the rioters who allegedly sprayed the officers.[221]

Shortly after Haffner and others assaulted the USCP officers, they were able to breach the Columbus Doors at approximately 2:38 p.m. A Proud Boys contingent—including Haffner, Loehrke, and Joe Biggs—then entered the Capitol.[222] It was the second time that Biggs entered the U.S. Capitol that day.

A military-style "stack" of Oath Keepers entered through the Columbus Doors as well. The Oath Keeper members attended the Ellipse rally, where they were provided personal security details for VIPs in attendance.[223] Afterwards, they marched to the Capitol, as directed by President Trump.

Stewart Rhodes, the leader of the Oath Keepers, monitored the attack on the Capitol from just outside, including during the assault on the Columbus Doors. At 2:28 p.m., Rhodes texted members of the F.O.S., or Friends of Stone, (FOS) Signal chat—which included Roger Stone, the Proud Boys' Enrique Tarrio, Ali Alexander, Alex Jones, and others[224]—that he was at the "Back door of the U.S. Capitol." [225] Rhodes followed up at 2:30 p.m. by texting members of another chat that there was "Pounding on the doors" of the Capitol.[226]

At 2:32 p.m., Rhodes held a three-way call with two other Oath Keepers, Kelly Meggs and Michael Green.[227] Three minutes later, Meggs's group ("Stack 1") started pushing through the rioters amassed on the East Plaza steps in a military-stack formation, with each person placing a hand on the shoulder of the person in front.[228] This stack entered the Capitol around 2:40 p.m.[229]

One minute later, Rhodes was caught on camera on the Upper West Terrace responding to a rioter who said the Members of Congress must be "shitting their pants inside." Rhodes replied: "Amen They need to shit their fucking pants. Sic semper tyrannis." [230]

Once inside, Stack 1 moved through the Rotunda. At 2:44 p.m., Stack 1 pushed into the Senate hallway, which was filled with officers blocking the way. "Push, push, push. Get in there. They can't hold us," Watkins implored the others. However, the officers repelled their attack, pushing them back into the Rotunda.[231]

Other Oath Keepers made their way to the Capitol as Stack 1 tried to advance. Joshua James and another group of Oath Keepers ("Stack 2") pushed through the Columbus Doors at approximately 3:15 p.m.[232] "This is my fucking Capitol. This is not yours. This is my building," James shouted at officers inside the Rotunda who were trying to push the rioters out of the Capitol.[233]

**ADDITIONAL BREACH POINTS**

In addition to the breaches discussed above, rioters opened other entry points into the U.S. Capitol. The Upper West Terrace door, which leads directly into the Rotunda, was breached at 2:33 p.m. when rioters opened it from the inside.[234]

Inside the Capitol, rioters broke through the police lines, such as in the Crypt, a space located directly underneath the Rotunda. The Crypt is anchored by a marble "compass stone," marking the center of the building, and is lined with 13 statues representing the original American colonies.[235] The rioters quickly moved towards the House Chambers and, by 2:40 p.m., started to crowd the main doors outside the Chambers, moving to the east side near the Speaker's lobby. As they moved to the east side, rioters opened the east House doors from the inside at 2:41 p.m., allowing rioters from the northeast side of the Capitol to enter.[236]

The north doors were the last Capitol doors breached. At 3:10 p.m., rioters entered through the north doors where they were quickly met by USCP.[237] Within a minute, the hallway just inside the doors was filled with rioters. At 3:12 p.m., a combination of USCP and MPD officers forcefully pushed the rioters out of the doors.[238] However, rioters continued to attack just outside the north doors throughout the afternoon and evening.

The north doors have an outer entranceway that is separated by a vestibule from a set of inner doors that lead directly into the Capitol. Rioters threw bricks at the doors and forcefully tried to stop police officers from clearing the area.[239] Law enforcement officers briefly opened the inner doors to spray a chemical irritant that was intended to disperse the mob.[240] But the rioters continued to fight. For instance, as the crowd held the outer doors open, John Thomas Gordon of West Virginia repeatedly threw a heavy projectile at the inner doors, while swearing at the officers.[241] Another rioter gave Gordon, who came to Washington to attend the "Stop the Steal" rally, a pair of goggles so he would withstand the chemical spray. Gordon kicked the inner doors as he and others desperately tried to enter the Capitol.[242] Law enforcement held the doors, withstanding the mob's best efforts to break in.

As law enforcement officers started to clear the building, rioters continued to fight police officers at the tunnel on the West Plaza. Rioters violently struck officers, including MPD Officer Daniel Hodges, and sprayed them with OC spray. Although rioters did not break through the police line at the tunnel, they were able to successfully break a window just north of it. There is no surveillance coverage for this area, so Select Committee staff was unable to determine the precise time of the breach. According to open-source videos, however, the breach appears to occur at approximately 4:15 p.m.[243]

## 8.7 PRESIDENT TRUMP POURS FUEL ON THE FIRE

After Dominic Pezzola and others breached the Capitol at 2:13 p.m., a mob quickly entered and headed towards the Senate and House Chambers, where Members were meeting.[244] As the crowd moved through the Capitol, they chanted "Fight for Trump" and "Stop the Steal!" They also chanted

"Nancy, Nancy" as they searched for Speaker Pelosi.[245] At 2:18 p.m., the House went into recess as hundreds of rioters confronted USCP officers inside the Crypt, which is a short distance from the first breach point.[246]

USCP officers formed a line across the Crypt in an attempt to stop the mob's advance.[247] By 2:21 p.m., the rioters had tried to break through police lines, but they were temporarily unsuccessful.[248]

As USCP officers held the line inside the Crypt, President Trump poured fuel on the fire, tweeting at 2:24 p.m.:

> "Mike Pence didn't have the courage to do what should have been done to protect our Country and our Constitution, giving states a chance to certify a corrected set of facts, not the fraudulent or inaccurate ones which they were asked to previously certify. USA demands the truth!" [249]

One minute later, the mob violently pushed through the USCP officers in the Crypt and continued moving south towards the House Chamber.[250] Joshua Pruitt, the Proud Boy dressed in a Punisher shirt, was at the front of the line as rioters broke through in the Crypt.[251] Officer David Millard told the Select Committee that rioters in the Crypt claimed they were in the Capitol because their "boss" told them to be there—meaning President Trump.[252] Officer Millard also recalled members of the mob telling him they were there to stop the steal.[253]

After breaking through the police line in the Crypt, the mob pursued USCP officers as they retreated to the U.S. Capitol Visitor's Center (CVC). Pruitt was among the rioters who advanced into the CVC, where he came close to Senator Chuck Schumer.[254] When the USCP officers attempted to lower metal barriers to halt the crowd's momentum, another small group of Proud Boys immediately interceded to prevent the barricades from coming down.[255] The Proud Boy contingent included three men from the Kansas City, Kansas area: William Chrestman,[256] Chris Kuehne,[257] and Louis Colon.[258] Felicia Konold and Cory Konold, two Proud Boy associates from Arizona, joined the Kansas City group while marching from the Washington Monument to the Capitol earlier in the day and were on the scene.[259] Two other Proud Boys, Nicholas Ochs and Nicholas DeCarlo, filmed the incident.[260]

Surveillance footage shows Chrestman using a wooden club, or modified axe handle, to prevent the barrier from being lowered to the floor.[261] Colon later admitted to authorities that he purchased and modified an axe handle "to be used as both a walking stick and an improvised weapon" on January 6th.[262] Colon also told authorities that he attended a meeting with Chrestman and others on the night of January 5th, during which someone

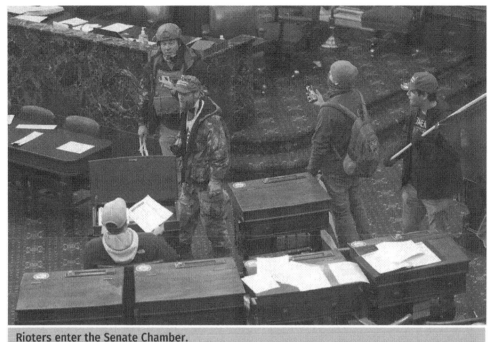

Rioters enter the Senate Chamber.

Photo by Win McNamee/Getty Images

asked, "do we have patriots here willing to take it by force?" Colon under-stood that the individual meant that they should use "force against the government." This same individual commented that they should "go in there and take over." [263]

At 2:36 p.m., the mob pushed through a line of USCP officers guarding the House Chamber.[264] Rioters also entered the Senate Chamber.[265] Within minutes, Jacob Chansley (a.k.a. the QAnon Shaman) entered the Senate Chamber, making his way to the Senate dais, where Vice President Pence had been presiding over the joint session. An officer asked Chansley to vacate the dais, but instead he shouted, "Mike Pence is a fucking traitor." Chansley also left a note that read: "It's Only a Matter of Time. Justice is Coming!" [266] Surrounded by others, Chansley held a conspiracy-laden prayer session, saying: "Thank you for allowing the United States of America to be reborn. Thank you for allowing us to get rid of the commu-nists, the globalists, and the traitors within our government." [267] Other extremists, including at least one associate of the white nationalist "America First" movement, also sat in the Vice President's seat.[268]

While law enforcement fought to contain the mob inside the Capitol, the fighting raged outside as well. Key agitators continued to fire up the crowd. Nick Fuentes, the leader of the "America First" movement, amplified President Trump's rhetoric aimed at Vice President Pence, including the President's 2:24 p.m. tweet.[269] Speaking through a bullhorn while standing on the Peace Monument, Fuentes shouted:

> We just heard that Mike Pence is not going to reject any fraudulent elector votes! That's right, you heard it here first: Mike Pence has betrayed the United States of America. Mike Pence has betrayed the President and he has betrayed the people of the United States of America—and we will never ever forget![270]

As rioters flowed through the halls and offices inside the Capitol, others broke through the defensive lines of USCP and MPD officers on the lower West Plaza at 2:28 p.m., allowing them to take over the inauguration stage.[271] According to MPD Officer Michael Fanone, MPD officers were then forced to conduct the "first fighting withdrawal" in the history of the force, with law enforcement seeking to "reestablish defensive lines" to prevent the "crowd that had swelled to approximately 20,000 from storming the U.S. Capitol."[272]

After surging through the West Plaza, rioters quickly headed towards the West Plaza tunnel. The violence that escalated at 2:28 p.m. on the lower West Plaza continued as rioters reached the tunnel. By 2:41 p.m., law enforcement retreated inside the tunnel, allowing rioters to slowly fill in.[273] Just ten minutes later, the mob jammed the tunnel, desperately trying to break through the police lines.[274] The fighting in and immediately outside of the tunnel raged for over two hours.[275]

Throughout the afternoon, members of the mob struck officers with weapons, shot them with OC (or pepper) spray, and dragged officers from the tunnel into the crowd. Lucas Denney, a Three Percenter from Texas who carried a baton on January 6th, pushed a riot shield into and on top of police officers at the tunnel. The crowd chanted "heave-ho!" as Denney did so.[276] Jeffrey Scott Brown sprayed a chemical or pepper spray at officers and pushed the front of the line in the tunnel.[277] Kyle Young, a January 6th defendant with a long prior criminal history, participated in multiple assaults and violence at the tunnel, including using a pole to jab at police officers.

Young's 16-year-old son was present during the fighting.[278] Robert Morss, a former Army Ranger who wore a military-style vest, participated in a heave-ho effort in the tunnel where he and rioters had created a shield wall.[279] Peter Schwartz and another rioter passed a large cannister of spray back and forth before Schwartz's companion sprayed officers and then the two joined in the heave-ho.[280]

Rioters assault police officers at a tunnel to the Capitol.

One of the most brutal attacks of the day occurred outside the tunnel when rioters dragged MPD Officer Michael Fanone into the crowd, and then tased, beat, and robbed him while a Blue Lives Matter flag fluttered above him. Albuquerque Head, a rioter from Tennessee, grabbed Officer Fanone around the neck and pulled him into the mob.[281] "I got one!" Head shouted.[282] Lucas Denney, the Three Percenter, "swung his arm and fist" at Officer Fanone, grabbed him, and pulled him down the stairs.[283] Daniel Rodriguez then tased him in the neck. Kyle Young lunged towards Officer Fanone, restraining the officer's wrist.[284] While Young held him, still another rioter, Thomas Sibick, reached towards him and forcibly removed his police badge and radio.[285] Officer Fanone feared they were after his gun. Members of the crowd yelled: "Kill him!," "Get his gun!" and "Kill him with his own gun!"[286]

In an interview with FBI agents, Daniel Rodriguez admitted his role in the attack on Officer Fanone.[287] During that same interview, Rodriguez discussed the influences that led him down the path to January 6th. Rodriguez was a fan of Alex Jones's InfoWars and told FBI agents that he became active at rallies after watching the conspiracy show.[288] Rodriguez was motivated by Jones's decision to support then candidate Trump in 2015.[289] He also began to affiliate himself with the Three Percenter movement, which he learned about by watching InfoWars.[290] And when President Trump called for a "wild" protest in Washington on January 6th, Rodriguez thought it was necessary to respond. "Trump called us. Trump called us to DC," Rodriguez told interviewing agents.[291] "If he's the commander in chief and the leader of our country, and he's calling for help—I thought he was calling for help," Rodriguez explained. "I thought he was—I thought we were doing the right thing."[292]

Rodriguez and another January 6th defendant, Edward Badalian, began preparing for violence after President Trump's December 19th tweet. They gathered weapons and tactical gear[293] and discussed their plans in a Signal chat named, "Patriots 45 MAGA Gang."

"Congress can hang. I'll do it," Rodriguez posted to the chat. Please let us get these people dear God."[294]

Badalian also posted a flyer titled "MAGA_CAVALRY," which showed rally points for "patriot caravans" to connect with the "Stop The Steal" movement in DC.[295] The same flyer was popular among Three Percenters and other self-described "patriot" groups. It also garnered the attention of law enforcement. The FBI's Norfolk, Virginia division noted in a January 5th intelligence assessment that the flyer was accompanied by another image, titled "Create Perimeter," which depicted the U.S. Capitol and other buildings being surrounded by the same caravans.[296]

## 8.8 THE EVACUATION

When rioters surrounded the perimeter of the Capitol, and reached the Senate and House Chambers, Members were forced to evacuate for safety. USCP officers responded to both Chambers and served as escorts. By the time the Capitol was breached, the Senate and House had split from the joint session, with Senators returning to their Chamber to debate the objection to Arizona's electoral vote. The House remained in its Chamber to debate the objection.[297]

Starting in the Senate, Vice President Pence was escorted off the floor at 2:12 p.m. and was taken to his Senate office. Between 2:12 p.m. and 2:25 p.m., Secret Service agents worked to identify potential threats and a route that could be used to transport Vice President Pence.[298] One of the issues for Vice President Pence's evacuation was that the rioters were outside the Ohio Clock Tower, which was just feet away from the staircase that Vice President Pence could descend to evacuate.[299] Eventually, after the mob started filling the entire Capitol, the Secret Service made the decision to move Vice President Pence, and he was escorted from the Senate at 2:25 p.m.[300] By 2:27 p.m., the Vice President can be seen moving toward a secure

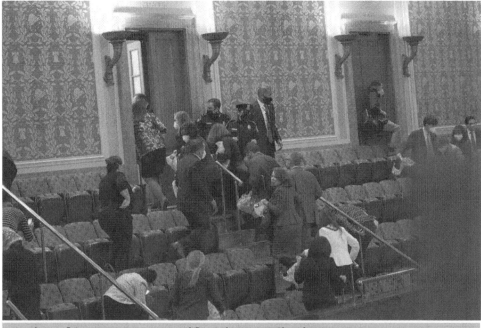

Members of Congress are evacuated from the House Chamber.
(Photo by Drew Angerer/Getty Images)

location connected to the Capitol. The Vice President arrived at the secure location at 2:29 p.m.[301] Following the Vice President's evacuation, Senators were evacuated at 2:30 p.m.[302]

On the House side, Speaker Pelosi, House Majority Leader Steny Hoyer, and House Majority Whip James Clyburn were removed from the House floor at the same time as Vice President Pence. By 2:18 p.m., USCP surveillance showed Speaker Pelosi in the basement hallway headed towards the garage.[303] The surveillance footage also showed Leader Hoyer and Whip Clyburn in the same basement as Speaker Pelosi. At 2:23 p.m., Speaker Pelosi and Whip Clyburn were moved to an undisclosed location.[304]

Minority Leader Kevin McCarthy was evacuated just after Speaker Pelosi left the Capitol. At 2:25 p.m., as rioters were moving through the Crypt and breaking through the east Rotunda door, Leader McCarthy and his staff hurriedly evacuated his office.[305] At approximately 2:38 p.m., the Members of Congress on the House floor began their evacuation.[306] Members of Congress can be seen evacuating through the Speaker's Lobby when a USCP officer fatally shot Ashli Babbitt at 2:44 p.m.[307] Members and staffers were just feet away when Babbitt attempted to climb through a shattered glass door. USCP officers had barricaded the door with furniture to prevent the rioters from gaining direct access to elected officials.

The congressional Members in the House Gallery were evacuated after the Members on the House floor. Congressional Members in the Gallery had to wait to be evacuated because rioters were still roaming the hallways right outside the Chamber. At 2:49 p.m., as Members were trying to evacuate the House Gallery, the USCP emergency response team cleared the hallways with long rifles so that the Members could be escorted to safety.[308] USCP surveillance footage shows several rioters lying on the ground, with long rifles pointed at them, as Members evacuate in the background.[309] By 3:00 p.m., the area had been cleared and Members were evacuated from the House gallery to a secure location. [310]

## 8.9 CLEARING THE U.S. CAPITOL BUILDING AND RESTRICTED GROUNDS

Shortly after law enforcement officers evacuated the House and Senate Members, they started to clear rioters out of the Capitol and off the grounds. Starting before 3:00 p.m., law enforcement spent approximately three hours pushing rioters out of the Capitol building and off the East and West Plazas. In general, law enforcement cleared rioters out of the Capitol through three doors: (1) the House side door located on the northeast side of the Capitol; (2) the Columbus Doors (East Rotunda Doors); and (3) the Senate wing door, which was next to the first breach point. As discussed above, the Proud Boys and other extremists led the charge at the latter two locations during the early stages of the attack.

Outside the Capitol, law enforcement pushed the mob from the upper West Plaza towards the East Plaza, crossing the north doors. Eventually, these rioters were forced to exit the Capitol grounds on the east side. The last point where rioters were removed was the lower West Plaza—the scene of some of the most intense hand-to-hand fighting that day. After law enforcement cleared the tunnel, where violence had raged for hours, police officers corralled rioters to the west and away from the Capitol building.[311]

After rioters first breached the Senate wing door on the first floor, they immediately moved south towards the House Chamber. This route took them to the Crypt—with the mob filling this room by 2:24 p.m. This was also one of the first rooms that law enforcement cleared as they started to secure the building. By 2:49 p.m., law enforcement officers cleared the Crypt by pushing towards the Senate wing door and up the stairs to the Rotunda.[312]

Around the same time that police officers cleared the Crypt, they also removed rioters from hallways immediately adjacent to the House and Senate Chambers. On the House side, rioters were pushed out shortly before 3:00 p.m. The House hallway immediately in front of the House Chamber's door was cleared at 2:56 p.m.[313] The mob outside of the Speaker's lobby was pushed out of the House side door at 2:57 p.m.[314]

USCP officers were able to quickly clear out the Senate Chamber, which was initially breached at 2:42 p.m.[315] Rioters were cleared from the hallways outside the Senate by 3:09 p.m.[316] Surveillance shows officers checking the Senate Gallery and hallways for rioters; there are no people on camera by this time.[317]

The Rotunda served as a key point where the mob settled during the Capitol attack. For example, at 2:45 p.m., hundreds of people can be seen standing in the Rotunda.[318] It appears law enforcement officers funneled rioters from other parts of the Capitol into the Rotunda. Once they had President Trump's supporters herded there, law enforcement started to push them towards the east doors shortly after 3:00 p.m. At 3:25 p.m., law enforcement successfully pushed rioters out of the Rotunda and closed the doors so that the room could remain secure.[319] By 3:43 p.m., just 18 minutes after the Rotunda doors were closed, law enforcement successfully pushed the rioters out of the east doors of the Capitol.[320]

The last rioters in the Capitol building were cleared out of the Senate wing door—the same location where rioters first breached the building at 2:13 p.m. Like the other locations inside the Capitol, law enforcement began forcing rioters out of the Senate wing door after 3:00 p.m. By 3:40 p.m., law enforcement had successfully pushed many of the rioters out of the door and onto the upper West Plaza.[321] However, officers were unable to close the doors because some rioters remained in the doorway and attempted to re-enter the building. At 4:23 p.m., a combination of USCP and MPD officers forced these people out of the doorway and successfully secured the door.[322]

After clearing the inside of the Capitol, law enforcement officers proceeded to sweep the perimeter adjacent to the building, starting with the upper West Plaza. After pushing the last rioter out of the Senate wing door, officers started to clear the upper West Plaza, which is located just outside this same doorway. Law enforcement officers in riot gear formed a line and marshalled the crowd north from the upper West Plaza. By 4:31 p.m., 8 minutes after closing the Senate wing door, rioters were cleared from the upper West Plaza.[323]

Many of these same officers started to secure the north side of the Capitol as they pushed rioters from the upper West Plaza towards the East Plaza. By approximately 4:32 p.m., law enforcement officers walked out of the North Doors, forming additional lines to push rioters eastward. As discussed earlier, the North Doors had been the location of violent fighting throughout much of the afternoon. By 4:46 p.m., law enforcement had

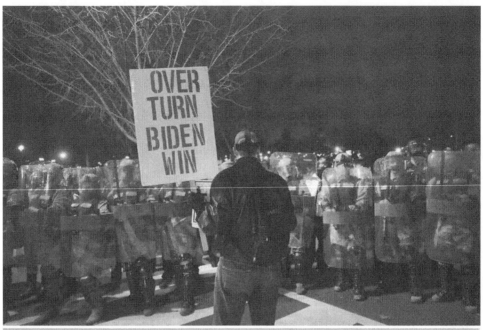

Police officers form line to push rioters away from the Capitol building.
(Photo by Spencer Platt/Getty Images)

successfully pushed the rioters from the north side of the Capitol to the East Plaza.[324]

Law enforcement cleared the East Plaza next. By 4:59 p.m., officers had swept all the remaining rioters from the east stairs of the Capitol.[325] At this point, the mob that had overrun the upper West Plaza, the north side of the Capitol, and the East Plaza had been moved off the grounds adjacent to the Capitol.

The last areas of the Capitol grounds to get cleared were the tunnel and the lower West Plaza. Thousands of rioters had packed into the West Plaza just after the initial invasion, led by the Proud Boys and their associates. The tunnel was the location of the day's most violent fighting and the conflict extended until late in the day.

After 5:00 p.m., it appears that law enforcement directed their attention to clearing the lower West Plaza, including the tunnel. At 5:04 p.m., police officers in the tunnel shot smoke bombs to get the remaining rioters to back away from the doors.[326] By 5:05 p.m., the rioters had all retreated and the police officers inside the tunnel moved out and started clearing out the area.[327]

At 5:13 p.m., on the opposite side of the lower West Plaza, officers pushed the mob down the scaffold stairs and to the lower West Plaza.[328]

Vice President Pence and Speaker Pelosi preside over the joint session of Congress.
Photo by Erin Schaff—Pool/Getty Images

These are the same stairs that rioters, led by the Proud Boys and other extremists, had previously climbed before reaching the Senate wing door.

Once the rioters from the tunnel and the scaffold were all situated on the lower West Plaza, officers formed another line and started walking the mob back towards the grass—which was away from the actual Capitol building. The line appears to have been fully formed at 5:19 p.m., and the officers started their sweep at 5:30 p.m.[329] By 5:37 p.m., police officers pushed rioters back to the grassy area away from the Capitol. It was at this time that in or around the Capitol building.[330] At 6:56 p.m., a little more than an hour after the Capitol grounds were cleared, Vice President Pence returned to the Capitol from the loading dock.[331] Vice President Pence walked up the stairs in the basement of the Capitol to his office in the Senate at 7:00 p.m.[332]

Shortly after 8:00 p.m., the joint session of Congress resumed, with Vice President Pence saying: "Let's get back to work."[333] At 3:32 a.m., the Congress completed the counting of the votes and certified the election of Joseph R. Biden, Jr. as the 46th President of the United States.

## 1. Electoral Count Act.

As our Report describes, Donald J. Trump, John Eastman, and others corruptly attempted to violate the Electoral Count Act of 1887 in an effort to overturn the 2020 Presidential Election. To deter other future attempts to overturn Presidential Elections, the House of Representatives has passed H.R. 8873, "The Presidential Election Reform Act," and the Senate should act promptly to send a bill with these principles to the President. H.R. 8873 reaffirms that a Vice President has no authority or discretion to reject an official electoral slate submitted by the Governor of a state. It also reforms Congress's counting rules to help ensure that objections in the joint session conform to Congress's narrow constitutional role under Article II and the Twelfth Amendment. It provides that presidential candidates may sue in federal court to ensure that Congress receives the state's lawful certification, and leaves no doubt that the manner for selecting presidential electors cannot be changed retroactively after the election is over.

## 2. Accountability.

The Select Committee has made criminal referrals to the Department of Justice, and both the Department of Justice and other prosecutorial authorities will now make their determinations on whether to prosecute individuals involved in the events resulting in an attack on the United States Congress on January 6, 2021. Additional steps may also be appropriate to ensure criminal or civil accountability for anyone engaging in misconduct described in this Report. Those courts and bar disciplinary bodies responsible for overseeing the legal profession in the states and the District of Columbia should continue to evaluate the conduct of attorneys described in this Report. Attorneys should not have the discretion to use their law licenses to undermine the constitutional and statutory process for peacefully transferring power in our government. The Department of Justice should also take appropriate action to prevent its attorneys from participating in campaign-related activities, or (as described in this report) activities aimed at subverting the rule of law and overturning a lawful election. This report also identifies specific attorney conflicts of interest for the Department to evaluate.

## 3. Violent Extremism.

Federal Agencies with intelligence and security missions, including the Secret Service, should (a) move forward on whole-of-government strategies to combat the threat of violent activity posed by all extremist groups, including white nationalist groups and violent anti-government groups while respecting the civil rights and First Amendment civil liberties of all citizens; and (b) review their intelligence sharing protocols to ensure that threat intelligence is properly prioritized and shared with other responsible intelligence and security agencies on a timely basis in order to combat the threat of violent activity targeting legislative institutions, government operations, and minority groups.

### 4. Fourteenth Amendment, Section 3.

Under Section 3 of the Constitution's Fourteenth Amendment, an individual who previously took an oath to support the Constitution of the United States, but who has "engaged in an insurrection" against the same, or given "aid or comfort to the enemies of the Constitution" can be disqualified from holding future federal or state office. The Select Committee has referred Donald Trump and others for possible prosecution under 18 U.S.C. 2383, including for assisting and providing aid and comfort to an insurrection. The Committee also notes that Donald J. Trump was impeached by a majority of the House of Representatives for Incitement of an Insurrection, and there were 57 votes in the Senate for his conviction. Congressional committees of jurisdiction should consider creating a formal mechanism for evaluating whether to bar those individuals identified in this Report under Section 3 of the 14th Amendment from holding future federal or state office. The Committee believes that those who took an oath to protect and defend the Constitution and then, on January 6th, engaged in insurrection can appropriately be disqualified and barred from holding government office—whether federal or state, civilian or military—absent at least two-thirds of Congress acting to remove the disability pursuant to Section 3 of the Fourteenth Amendment. The Committee notes that Ms. Wasserman Schultz and Mr. Raskin have introduced H. Con. Res. 93 to declare the January 6 assault an insurrection and H.R. 7906 to establish specific procedures and standards for disqualification under section 3 of the Fourteenth Amendment in the United States district court for the District of Columbia.

### 5. National Special Security Event.

Until January 6th, 2021, the joint session of Congress for counting electoral votes was not understood to pose the same types of security risks as other major events on Capitol Hill. Both the inaugural and the State of the Union have long been designated as National Special Security Events, requiring specific security measures and significant advance planning and preparation. Given what occurred in 2021, Congress and the Executive Branch should work together to designate the joint session of Congress occurring on January 6th as a National Special Security Event.

**6. To the extent needed, consider reforming certain criminal statutes, including to add more severe penalties.**

As indicated in the Report, the Committee believes that 18 U.S.C. § 1512(c)2 and other existing provisions of law can be applied to efforts to obstruct, influence, or impede the joint session on January 6th, including to related planning efforts to overturn the lawful election results on that date. To the extent that any court or any other prosecutorial authorities ultimately reach any differing conclusion, Congress should amend those statutes to cover such conduct. Congress should also consider whether the severity of penalties under those statutes is sufficient to deter unlawful conduct threatening the peaceful transfer of power.

**7. House of Representatives Civil Subpoena Enforcement Authority.**

The current authority of the House of Representatives to enforce its subpoenas through civil litigation is unclear. Congressional committees of jurisdiction should develop legislation to create a cause of action for the House of Representatives to enforce its subpoenas in federal court, either following the statutory authority that exists for the Senate in 2 U.S.C. § 288d and 28 U.S.C. § 1365 or adopting a broad approach to facilitate timely oversight of the executive branch.

**8. Threats to Election Workers.**

Congressional committees of jurisdiction should consider enhancing federal penalties for certain types of threats against persons involved in the election process and expanding protections for personally identifiable information of election workers.

**9. Capitol Police Oversight.**

Congressional committees of jurisdiction should continue regular and rigorous oversight of the United States Capitol Police as it improves its planning, training, equipping, and intelligence processes and practices its critical incident response protocols, both internally and with law enforcement partners. Joint hearings with testimony from the Capitol Police Board should take place. Full funding for critical security measures should be assured.[1]

**10. Role of the Media.**

The Committee's investigation has identified many individuals involved in January 6th who were provoked to act by false information about the 2020 election repeatedly reinforced by legacy and social media. The Committee agrees that individuals remain responsible for their own actions, including their own criminal actions. But congressional committees of jurisdiction should continue to evaluate policies of media companies that have had the effect of radicalizing their consumers, including by pro-voking people to attack their own country.

## 11. Discussion of the Insurrection Act.

The Committee has been troubled by evidence that President Trump's possible use of the Insurrection Act was discussed by individuals identified in this Report. Congressional Committees of jurisdiction should further evaluate all such evidence, and consider risks posed for future elections.

# GOVERNMENT AGENCY PREPARATION FOR AND RESPONSE TO JANUARY 6TH

## INTRODUCTION

The Select Committee investigated the facts relating to law enforcement entities' preparation for, and response to, the January 6th events at the Capitol, including the character of the intelligence prior to the insurrection. This appendix does not address the cause of the attack, which resulted from then President Trump's multi-pronged effort to overturn the 2020 presidential election.

Prior to January 6th, numerous government agencies received intelligence that those descending on The Mall for a rally organized by the President were armed and that their target may be the Capitol. The intelligence community and law enforcement agencies detected the planning for potential violence directed at the joint session of Congress.

That intelligence included information about specific planning by the Proud Boys and Oath Keepers militia groups who ultimately led the attack on the Capitol. By contrast, the intelligence did not support a conclusion that Antifa or other left-wing groups would likely engage in a violent counterdemonstration, or attack President Trump's supporters on January 6th. Indeed, intelligence from January 5th indicated that some left-wing groups were instructing their members to "stay at home" and not attend on January 6th.[1]

As January 6th approached, some of the intelligence about the potential for violence was shared within the executive branch, including the Secret Service and the President's National Security Council. That intelligence should have been sufficient for President Trump, or others at the White House, to cancel the Ellipse speech, and for President Trump to cancel plans to instruct his supporters to march to the Capitol. Few in law enforcement predicted the full extent of the violence at the Capitol, or that the President of the United States would incite a mob attack on the Capitol, that he would send them to stop the joint session knowing they were armed and dangerous, that he would further incite them against his own vice President while the attack was underway, or that he would do nothing to stop the assault for hours.

Nevertheless, as explained below, and in multiple hearings by the Committee on House Administration, there are additional steps that should have been taken to address the potential for violence on that day.

## DISCUSSION

### INTELLIGENCE RECEIVED BY GOVERNMENT AGENCIES

On December 19, 2020, President Trump tweeted: "Big protest in D.C. on January 6th. Be there, will be wild!"[2] Following President Trump's tweet, an analyst at the National Capital Region Threat Intelligence Consortium (NTIC) noticed a tenfold uptick in violent online rhetoric targeting Congress and law enforcement.[3] The analyst also noticed that violent right-wing groups that had not previously been aligned had begun coordinating their efforts.[4] These indications reached the head of the D.C. Homeland Security and Emergency Management Agency (HSEMA), Christopher Rodriguez, as well as incoming Chief of D.C. Metropolitan Police Department (MPD) Robert Contee.[5] Chief Contee remembered that the information prompted the DC Police to "change the way that we were going to deploy for January the 6th."[6]

Following President Trump's "be there, will be wild!" tweet, Director Rodriguez arranged a briefing to provide the DC Mayor Muriel Bowser the latest threat intelligence about January 6th, outline the potential for violence, and "make operational recommendations," including that the Mayor request assistance from the DC National Guard.[7] During the briefing, the Mayor was told that "there is greater negative sentiment motivating conversation than the last two events in November and December of 2020," and that "others are calling to 'peacefully' storm the Capitol and occupy the building to halt the vote."[8]

As early as December 30th, in its intelligence briefing entitled, "March for Trump," the U.S. Secret Service (USSS) highlighted the President's "will be wild!" tweet alongside hashtags #WeAreTheStorm, #1776Rebel, and #OccupyCapitols, and wrote, "President Trump supporters have proposed a movement to occupy Capitol Hill."[9] It added that promoters of the January 6th rally on social media had borrowed the President's phrase and were marketing the January 6th rally as the "WildProtest."[10]

Other law enforcement entities were receiving similar indications from both government and private entities. By December 21st, the U.S. Capitol Police (USCP) had learned of a surge in viewers of online maps of the Capitol complex's underground tunnels, which were attracting increased attention on www.thedonald.win, alongside violent rhetoric supporting the President.[11] By the late afternoon of January 5, 2021, Capitol Police Assistant Chief for Intelligence Yogananda Pittman urged Capitol Police Chief Steven Sund to convene a "brief call" to discuss "a significant uptick in groups wanting to block perimeter access to the Capitol tomorrow starting as early as 0600 hours."[12] Chief Sund remembered discussing those indications and the preparations Capitol Police already had "in place, and [that] everybody seemed fine with utilizing the resources we had." [13] Chief Sund added that, by that time, he had already deployed "all the available resources." [14]

The Federal Bureau of Intelligence (FBI) and the U.S. Department of Homeland Security's Office of Intelligence and Analysis (DHS I&A) were also aware of the increased online interest in the Capitol tunnels. The FBI's special agent in charge of the intelligence division at the Washington Field Office, Jennifer Moore, pointed out that there was nothing illegal about discussing the tunnels. Without a very specific discussion of violence, it was a matter of ensuring that the appropriate law enforcement partner agencies were aware of the uptick, ensuring that the Capitol Police were aware.[15] "People's First Amendment rights, obviously, are protected. We cannot troll—can['t] just troll the internet looking for things that's out there," Moore said.[16] "So it would have to be with such specificity and such planning and such detail that we would be able to open a case, immediately seek authority for an undercover, have enough probable cause for that undercover off of one tip would be tough." [17]

Other agencies were also surfacing indications and receiving tips. On December 26, 2020, the Secret Service received a tip about the Proud Boys detailing plans of having "a large enough group to march into DC armed and will outnumber the police so they can't be stopped." [18] It stressed, "Their plan is to literally kill people....Please please take this tip seriously and investigate further." [19] On December 24th, the Secret Service received a compilation of social media posts from "SITE," a private intelligence group. One of them urged that protesters "march into the chambers." [20] Another, referring to President Trump's December 19th "will be wild!" post, wrote that Trump "can't exactly openly tell you to revolt," so the December 19th post was "the closest he'll ever get." [21] Another understood the President's tweet to be urging his supporters to come to Washington "armed." [22] Others were to the same effect ("there is not enough cops in DC to stop what is coming," [23] "make sure they know who to fear," [24] and "waiting for Trump to say the word" [25]).

By December 28th, that compilation had reached the newly installed head of the Capitol Police intelligence unit, Jack Donohue.[26] The same day, a self-styled "internet expert" who had been "tracking online far right extremism for years" sent an email to the Capitol Police public information inbox warning of "countless tweets from Trump supporters saying they will be armed," and of tweets "from people organizing to 'storm the Capitol' on January 6th." [27] She added, "January 6th will be the day most of these people realize there's no chance left for Trump. They'll be pushed to what they feel is the edge," noting that many would be armed and that she was, for the first time, "truly worried." [28] Other senior Capitol Police officers do not recall seeing that email before the January 6th attack.[29] The next day,

Secret Service agents forwarded to Capitol Police warnings that pro-Trump demonstrators were being urged to "occupy federal building[s]," "march into the capital building [sic] and make them quake in their shoes by our mere presence." [30]

In addition, on January 1, 2021, a lieutenant in the intelligence branch of the MPD forwarded to the Capitol Police intelligence unit a tip—later forwarded to USCP Deputy Chief Sean Gallagher—that he had "found a website planning terroristic behavior on Jan 6th, during the rally." [31] The source included a link to www.thedonald.win site, describing a "detailed plan on [s]torming the capitol in DC on Jan 6th." [32] On January 2, 2021, the FBI saved in its system a social media post stating, "This is not a rally and it's no longer a protest. This is a final stand...many are ready to die to take back #USA....And don't be surprised if we take the #capital building [sic]." [33] On January 3rd, FBI and Capitol Police received a Parler post that "after weds we are going to need a new congress," and "Jan 6 may actually be their last day in Congress." [34]

On January 4th, Jack Donoghue, head of USCP's intelligence unit, and his assistant director, Julie Farnam, briefed Capitol Police leadership, including Chief Gallagher and Chief Pittman (but not Chief Sund), about the January 3rd Threat Assessment, which highlighted that Congress itself was the target of potential violence on January 6th. Assistant Director Farnam explicitly warned the group:

> Supporters see this as the last opportunity to overturn the election. There was disappointment and desperation amongst the protestors, and this could be an incentive to become violent, because they have nothing left to lose. The targets are not the counter protestors; the target is Congress. The protests are heavily publicized. Stop the Steal has a propensity for attracting White supremacists, militia groups, groups like the Proud Boys. There are multiple social media posts saying that people are going to be coming armed, and it's potentially a very dangerous situation.[35]

On January 5, 2021, at 12:19 p.m., the Architect of the Capitol head of security, Valerie Hasberry, forwarded an alert to Capitol Police incident command that an individual was calling on thousands to "go to Washington Jan 6 and help storm the Capital [sic]," adding "we will storm the government buildings, kill cops, kill security guards, kill federal employees and agents." [36] "There is now chatter on Parler about storming the Capitol," Ms. Hasberry wrote to her AOC employee working at the USCP.[37] "Please let me know if there are any updates to credible threats." [38] Within an hour, she was advised by her staff that "[t]here is no talk about any credible threats or storming the Capitol." That same day, representatives from DHS,

FBI, HSEMA, Secret Service, DC Police, and Capitol Police shared notice of a website, Red State Secession, that urged its visitors to post the home and work addresses of Democratic Members of Congress and "political enemies" under the title, "Why the Second American Revolution Starts Jan 6." [39] It asked for their routes to and from the January 6th congressional certification because "the crowd will be looking for enemies." [40]

The FBI was uploading to, and tagging in, its system incoming information from all FBI field offices about January 6th under the label, "CERTUNREST2021." While the incoming information was reviewed on a regular basis by the Washington Field Office, "unified monitoring" of the items in the aggregate didn't begin until January 5th. [41] That same day, the FBI captured a January 6th-related threat that warned a "Quick Reaction Force" of Trump supporters was preparing for January 6th in Virginia with weapons and prepared "to respond to 'calls for help'" in the event that "protesters believed the police were not doing their job," and a "Situation Incident Report" from FBI's Norfolk Field Office warned of a "war" on January 6th. [42] While Capitol Police leadership received neither warning until after the attack, [43] Assistant Director Farnam, USCP intelligence unit, warned that Congress would be the target on January 6th. She noted that a "sense of desperation and disappointment may lead to more of an incentive to become violent. Unlike previous post-election protests, Congress itself is the target on the 6th." [44] The Chairman of the Joint Chiefs of Staff, General Mark Milley, remembers Deputy Secretary of Defense David Norquist expressing a similar view based on the social media traffic in early January 2021: "Norquist says...[t]he greatest threat is a direct assault on the Capitol. I'll never forget it." [45]

### DISCUSSION OF THE POTENTIAL FOR VIOLENCE

Federal and local agencies agreed that there was a potential for violence on January 6th. As noted above, the intelligence leading up to January 6th did not support a conclusion that Antifa or other left-wing groups would likely engage in a violent counter-demonstration, or attack President Trump's supporters on January 6th. In fact, none of these groups was involved to any material extent with the attack on the Capitol on January 6th.

That said, certain witnesses testified that they believed that there would be violence with Antifa or similar counter protest groups. President Trump's National Security Advisor, Robert O'Brien, said the White House saw a risk of violence from counter-protesters. [46] Then Acting DHS Secretary Chad Wolfe said that his "main concern [...] at the time was what we had seen throughout the summer and throughout the fall, which was you were going to have groups on either side, and so you were going to have counterprotests. And usually where those counterprotests interacted was where you had the violence." [47]

General Milley said the potential for violence was clear to all: "Everyone knew. I can't imagine anybody in those calls that didn't realize that on the 6th was going to be the certification of an intensely contested election, and there were large crowds coming into town, and they were coming into protest. And everybody knew there was a probability, more than a possibility, a probability of violence." [48] He expected "street fights when the sun went down," while [Deputy Secretary] Norquist said the most dangerous thing was assault on the Capitol.[49] Director of DHS Special Operations Christopher Tomney remembered, "[T]here was broad discussion/acknowledgment that folks were calling for bringing weapons into the city on that day, so there was no surprise, there was no—you know, no one disagreed that there was going to be the high likelihood that there could be some violence on January 6." [50]

Acting Deputy Attorney General Richard Donoghue described the discussion about the threat landscape as "generally about left-wing, right wing, or Pro-Trump, anti-Trump groups coming to the Capitol. It didn't really matter what they called themselves. It was a matter of they're upset, they're coming to the Capitol, and there's a potential for violence." [51] Donoghue added: "Everyone knew what everyone else was doing. Everyone knew that there was a danger of violence. Everyone knew that the Capitol and other facilities were potential targets. And I think we all felt comfortable that we were aware what the situation was, and we had the resources in place to address it." [52]

### OPERATIONALIZATION OF JANUARY 6-RELATED INTELLIGENCE

Preparing for January 6th required coordination among the several local and Federal law enforcement agencies that have distinct authorities and jurisdiction over adjacent areas in the Washington, DC, area. These range from the MPD, United States Park Police (USPP), and USSS to the USCP.

### DC GOVERNMENT PREPARATION

**December 30, 2020, HSEMA briefing.** Following the DC HSEMA's December 30th intelligence briefing, Mayor Bowser, anticipating that President Trump's December 19th "will be wild!" tweet would have a big effect on the number of people coming into the District,[53] agreed with HSEMA Director Rodriguez, who thought "the intelligence was showing that we needed to posture ourselves, we needed to brace ourselves, and we needed additional resources in the city particularly the DC National Guard." [54] MPD Chief Contee, who attended the December 30th briefing and was seeing similar intelligence, concurred with the request for the DC National Guard.[55]

In light of the upcoming holiday weekend, HSEMA Director Rodriguez wanted to expedite the DC request for National Guard assistance.[56] On December 31st, Mayor Bowser requested the assistance of the DC National

Guard to assist the MPD at traffic points within the city.[57] Mayor Bowser's request explicitly limited National Guard assistance to "non-law enforcement activities" so that the MPD could focus on the civil protests and specified that Guard troops should not be armed.[58]Army Secretary Ryan McCarthy approved Mayor Bowser's request.[59] By this time, DC HSEMA Director Rodriguez had fully activated HSEMA and coordinated with Federal, State and local partners, to deal with "consequence management."[60]

On January 4th, Mayor Bowser held a press conference and invited the MPD, USCP, and USPP.[61] Mayor Bowser announced that she had activated the DC Fire and Emergency Management Services (DC FEMS) in preparation of the January 6th event and that the DC National Guard would assist MPD at traffic points and with crowd control. Mayor Bowser urged DC residents to stay out of downtown on January 5th and 6th, acknowledging the possibility of violence. She stated that, while "[p]eople are allowed to come into our city to participate in First Amendment activities," DC officials would "not allow people to incite violence, intimidate our residents, or cause destruction in our city."[62]

The next day, Mayor Bowser sent a letter requesting that Federal agencies coordinate with the Mayor's office and the MPD in their response on January 6th.[63] The letter plainly stated that it was intended to ensure coordination among the agencies involved. DC HSEMA Director Rodriguez testified that there was a concern, in light of the Federal response to the previous summer's civil justice protests, "that in the event that activities on the street escalated, the city could once again become...militarized and that armed military and Federal law enforcement personnel could be brought into the District," perhaps intimidating residents.[64]

### DC FEMS PREPARATION

Mayor Bowser also activated DC FEMS (Fire and Emergency Medical Service Department), several days before January 6th.[65] DC FEMS focused most of its attention on the event at the Ellipse since the permits indicated it would be the largest event of the day, with an estimated 5,000 people attending. Other DC and Federal agencies believed the number would likely be closer to 35,000. This led DC FEMS to establish an area command for the Ellipse, including a Mobile Command Unit, six ambulances, four engine companies, and a first aid tent staffed by George Washington University medical staff.[66]

### MPD PREPARATION

After the DC HSEMA's December 30th intelligence briefing, MPD Chief Contee ordered full deployment of the Department, cancelling previously scheduled days off, fully deploying the Civil Disturbance Unit, and contacting police departments in Montgomery and Prince George's Counties in Maryland so that their forces would be pre-staged at certain locations.

Chief Contee also staged police at the White House and Lafayette Park. Chief Contee said that although the MPD "are normally not fully deployed for civil disturbance for counting votes at the U.S. Capitol," [67] "obviously, as we got closer from the time of the initial [December 19th Trump] tweet leading up, *with all of the rhetoric that's out there on social media, you know, people were going to bring guns*, were going to do this and that and so forth, that caused us obviously to change the way that we were going to deploy for January the 6th." [68] Because of the numerous social media posts about guns, MPD also posted signs on the National Mall indicating that possession of firearms in Washington, D.C., was illegal and would be prosecuted. [69]

### U.S. CAPITOL POLICE PREPARATION

On January 3rd, the same day Capitol Police's Intelligence and Interagency Coordination Division (IICD) issued a threat assessment indicating that "Congress itself is a target," Chief Sund called House Sergeant-at-Arms Paul D. Irving to discuss requesting the DC National Guard to assist in policing the Capitol's perimeter. [70] Chief Sund needed approval from the Capitol Police Board, which consisted of Irving, Senate Sergeant-at-Arms Michael C. Stenger, and the Architect of the Capitol J. Brett Blanton. Chief Sund remembers that Irving responded immediately that he did not "like the optics" and that the intelligence did not support the request. [71] Irving, however, remembers Chief Sund calling him to say the DC National Guard had offered 125 unarmed National Guardsmen to the USCP and MPD. [72] He also remembered that, during a conference call, Chief Sund told Stenger and him that the National Guard would be utilized in similar fashion to the assistance provided to the DC police, namely, staffing intersections, and for traffic control to free up officers, but then could be used for crowd control, although he acknowledged that the Capitol campus does not have many intersections in need of staffing. [73]

The Capitol Police Board, including Chief Sund, later agreed that a request for the DC National Guard would not be necessary, particularly if the USCP was in an "all hands on deck" posture. [74] Chief Sund agreed with Stenger and Irving that the intelligence did not support a request for DC National Guard assistance. [75] According to Irving, Chief Sund did not believe the National Guard would add much to the USCP security plan for January 6th. [76] Chief Sund briefed the Capitol Police Board on the USCP's enhanced security plan, and "all hands on deck posture"—including 1,200-plus officers, added Civil Disturbance Units (CDU), an enhanced Containment Emergency Response Team ("CERT"), and an expanded perimeter. [77] Chief Sund did not believe, based on the intelligence he had, that it was then necessary to cancel officers' days off. [78]

USCP leadership did not create a department-wide plan for the January 6th event. [79] In retrospect Chief Sund believed "there should have been a plan for the joint session of Congress inside the Capitol to reflect all the planning and all the coordination that goes on inside the Capitol." [80]

## GOVERNMENT AGENCY PREPARATION

**Interagency Coordination.** In the appendix on Deployment of the National Guard, we describe certain reasons why the deployment of the National Guard was delayed, highlighting the activity of Secretary of the Army McCarthy and how he understood an order given by Acting Secretary of Defense Christopher Miller. In our interviews with Department of Defense (DoD) officials, they testified that they had asked the Department of Justice to serve the role of "lead Federal agency," meaning to lead the coordination and the response on January 6th. The Justice Department does not command National Guard units. Department of Defense, Department of Justice (DOJ), and Department of Homeland Security (DHS) officials testified from each agency's perspective about the discussions concerning which department would serve as a lead Federal agency. Notably, these discussions occurred at the same time President Trump was offering the Acting Attorney General position to Jeffrey Clark, replacing then Acting Attorney General Jeffrey Rosen. Had Clark ultimately been appointed, and had he been placed in charge of the Federal security response to the violence on January 6th, the situation could have been materially worse.

**January 3rd Coordination Call.** Realizing that there had not yet been a coordination call among the Federal agencies engaged in planning for the January 6th events and related contingencies, Acting Secretary Miller convened one for January 3rd, because "nobody else was doing it." [81] In addition to DoD officials including General Milley, DOJ, DHS, Department of the Interior (DOI) officials participated. Acting Secretary Miller's objectives were to ensure that "everyone had the same perception of the threat and then figure out how to synchronize, coordinate." He also wanted to make sure that DoD was prepared for any additional requests for support. [82]

Director of DHS Special Operations Tomney remembered that participants discussed the threat outlook and estimated crowd [83] of up to 30,000—not large for the District. [84] The consensus was that 8,000 to 10,000 police officers would be available on January 6th, a force regarded as appropriate for up to a million protesters. General Milley asked the police participants on the call whether they needed any other assistance from the Department of Defense. [85] General Milley and Secretary Miller expressed concern about the number of groups requesting permits and the attendance of groups like the Proud Boys and Oath Keepers who, as Secretary Miller explained, had "conducted acts of violence in the past." [86] General Milley asked whether requests for permits could be declined, canceled, or permits revoked.[87] Participants from the Department of the Interior responded that "that wasn't an option."[88]

According to Director Tomney, DHS felt confident in the United States Secret Service's ability to protect the White House and Vice President, the Federal Protective Service's (FPS) ability to protect potentially affected Federal buildings, as well as the Immigration and Customs Enforcement and Customs and Border Protection's ability to augment FPS, if needed.[89] General Milley and the other DoD participants left the call reassured that the law enforcement agencies involved were prepared for January 6th.[90]

During the January 3rd call, the DoD also raised the issue of a lead Federal agency. General Milley noted the desirability of a law enforcement lead for coordinating the interagency planning and response effort, given the "potpourri of jurisdictions" and diversity of agency authorities.[91] Secretary Miller testified that he believed he and Acting Attorney General Jeffrey Rosen were in agreement that the DOJ should lead interagency coordination for January 6th,[92] although when asked during the call, Rosen did not confirm that the DOJ would play that role.[93] The question of a lead Federal agency remained "an open, unanswered question" at the end of the January 3rd call.[94] The same day, Rosen was attempting to secure a White House meeting with President Trump regarding the imminent appointment of Clark in his stead.[95]

### DELIBERATION ON AGENCY ROLES

On a January 4th inter-agency call with the same group, Acting Deputy Attorney General Donoghue made the DOJ's role clear: it would take the lead in *certain areas* of responsibility, although he stressed that the DOJ was never designated lead Federal agency and could not serve in that capacity.[96] On the evening of January 4th, the FBI established a Strategic Information Operations Center ("SIOC") at FBI headquarters, which became operational on January 5th.[97] Unlike the previous summer's civil protests, DoD did not have a representative at the SIOC. All the DoD officials who were interviewed by the Select Committee, however, believe that the DOJ agreed to take—and may have been assigned by the White House—the lead coordinating role.[98] Director Tomney, however, remembered that the DOJ participants neither agreed to, nor explicitly declined, the lead agency role.[99]

During the January 3rd and 4th calls, General Milley, according to Donoghue, noted that "[t]here should be plenty of police forces available without using Federal military troops," so he was adamant that no active-duty troops would be deployed on January 6th.[100] During this call, participants also discussed whether there was a need for a police-based quick reaction force and concluded that the size of the MPD and USCP police forces made that unnecessary.[101]

According to Donoghue, at the end of the January 4th call, "[i]t was clear that everyone understood what everyone else's responsibility was, and everyone understood what was available to them if they needed more resources to meet their responsibilities."[102] The calls had also given local and Federal law enforcement entities the chance to "voice any issues, concerns, or requests for Department of Defense support if they felt that they were incapable of handling at their level. So, institutionally, there was agreement on the threat assessment and the plan going forward."[103] The DoD's leading role during the January 3rd and 4th calls had, in fact, left Acting DHS Secretary Chad Wolf with the impression that DoD was the lead agency, as they were "coordinating phone calls, they were setting agendas for phone calls, and they were calling out different people, okay, what do you need… So they were quarterbacking the situation and the response."[104]

## AGENCY ACTIONS ON PERMITTING

Three organizations in the National Capitol Region handle permits for organized activities depending on where the planned activity is to occur. The USSS issues permits for the Ellipse, while the DC MPD issues permits for the area around the Ellipse. The USCP handles permitting for activities on the Capitol campus. All three entities, as well as other law enforcement agencies, communicate about applications for permits and the expected number of attendees. They are reluctant to deny permits for what appears to be First Amendment–protected protests.[105] The USCP received, evaluated, and approved six group permit requests for January 5th and 6th activity on Capitol Grounds.[106]

On December 19th, the day of President Trump's "will be wild!" tweet, Cindy Chafian, spokesperson from the "Eighty Percent Coalition," applied to the MPD and USCP for a permit to hold a rally.[107] On December 29th, Chafian applied to USPP for a permit for a January 5th rally in Freedom Plaza.[108] The next day, Kylie Kremer filed for a permit for "Women for America First" to hold a rally for up to 5,000 people on the Ellipse.[109] On December 31st, the National Park Service (NPS) held two meetings with Chafian as well as the MPD and USCP.[110] Then, on January 1st, the USSS confirmed that President Trump would attend the January 6th rally at the Ellipse, prompting USPP to provide additional support for the rally.[111]

On January 4th, "Women for America First" requested that the NPS increase the authorized attendance at its rally to 20,000 from the 5,000 in the original application. The same day, reacting to the USPP briefing that 5,000 people were expected, Joseph Roth, the USSS site lead, commented that he found it "funny that this permit says 5,000 people when they have said 30k repeatedly."[112] On January 5th, the NPS issued a permit for 30,000 participants for the Ellipse event.[113] At no point was any permit granted for a march from the Ellipse to the Capitol. The President planned to announce that march "spontaneously."[114]

At the White House, the increased crowd estimate concerned Bobby Peede, Director of Presidential Advance, who emailed White House Deputy Chief of Operations Anthony Ornato, noting that the USSS was planning on using only 12 magnetometers. Peede added that "the mag issue is a pretty major problem if the expected crowd shows up." Secret Service documents reveal internal discussion of an initial USSS assessment that 17 magnetometers would be needed. On January 6th, only 10 magnetometers were initially assigned to the Ellipse.[115]

### AGENCY PREPARATIONS FOR JANUARY 6TH

**January 5th Congressional Briefing by Chief Sund and Paul Irving.** On January 5th, Chief Sund briefed the Chairperson of the Committee on House Administration (CHA), Representative Zoe Lofgren, along with numerous staff, as well as House Sergeant-at-Arms Paul Irving. Given CHA's oversight of the Capitol Police, this was "an opportunity for the chair of the committee to hear from the security professionals on the security plan."[116] Chair Lofgren's staff director described it as a "topline" briefing that covered various aspects of the security plan, including Chief Sund's direction of "all hands on deck," his focus on the prospect of counter protesters, as well as Chair Lofgren's concern that Members of Congress speaking at the Ellipse that day could incite protesters.[117] After the briefing, the CHA staff director specifically asked about the availability of the National Guard in case it was needed. "Chief Sund said that the Guard could be activated with an emergency declaration from the [Capitol Police] board, but they are here. They are a phone call away, and if we need them, they are ready to go."[118]

Speaker Pelosi did not receive a similar briefing, but her chief of staff was given a readout of Chief Sund's briefing to Chairperson Lofgren. On that basis, as well as the assurances Chief Sund provided, the Speaker's chief of staff said, "So I believed and the Speaker believed the security professionals were in charge of the security and they were prepared. We were told that there was a plan."[119]

### FEDERAL AGENCY RESPONSE ON JANUARY 6TH

Although intelligence was available suggesting potential violence at the Capitol, it was not apparent exactly what President Trump would do to provoke the crowd at the January 6th Ellipse rally. Chief Sund, for example, drove into work on January 6th believing that preparations for the day's events were sound and that there was no extraordinary risk or threat. "You know, on my way in, I called Inspector Glover with MPD just to get a read. He said he was actually parked over by the Ellipse. Asked him, Hey, how are things going over there? He said, there's big crowds, lots of people in line, but right now he wasn't seeing any concern with the folks that we had. So that was my initial take," Sund told the Select Committee.[120]

Throughout the morning, Robert Engel, the special agent in charge of the President's Secret Service detail, received updates from the event at the Ellipse. At 10:35 a.m., an update informed Engel that 20,000 attendees had been processed and outside of the magnetometers, but that there were "several thousand on the mall watching but not in line."[121] An hour later, Engel forwarded an update to White House Deputy Chief of Operations Ornato, informing him that 30,000 attendees had been processed.[122]

Acting Attorney General Rosen met with FBI leadership for a briefing that morning.[123] He remembered this briefing, unlike previous ones, as "more of a situational update," adding that the DOJ was "going to hope for the best, prepare for the worst."[124] At 10:43 a.m., Acting Deputy Attorney General Donoghue received an email from Matt Blue, Acting Chief of the Counterterrorism Section, stating "[t]here are no credible threats as of the 10:00 brief."[125] Twelve minutes later, Rosen spoke to White House Counsel Pat Cipollone via phone.[126] Acting Attorney General Rosen admits that "in hindsight" no one at the Department contemplated "how bad that afternoon turned out to be."[127] Nobody in the DOJ leadership could have predicted President Trump's actions that day.

The President's speech at the Ellipse began just before noon. David Torres,[128] head of the USSS's Protective Intelligence Division (PID), insisted that the Secret Service was not listening to the President's speech, however PID agents monitored the speech throughout.[129] At 12:20 p.m., Faron Paramore, assistant director of Strategic Intel & Information (SII), sent an email to USSS leadership that "POTUS just said that he is going up to the U.S. Capitol to 'watch' the vote" and asked whether this is true. Secret Service executive Kimberly Cheatle responded "[h]e said it, but not going, to our knowledge."[130] Minutes later, the USSS PIOC warned that "Mogul just mentioned in his speech that he would accompany the protesters to the Capitol," with a note that "DAD Torres requested this be sent for awareness."[131] At 1:14 p.m., the USSS Joint Operations Center (JOC) sent an email designating a response team to accompany the President in his march to the Capitol, "per [his] announcement" at the Ellipse. The JOC notes: "Multiple reports of armed individuals with various weapons and malicious intent. Be on your guard."[132]

At 12:24 p.m., while the President was speaking, the Vice President, with his USSS detail, departed the Vice President's Residence for the Capitol.[133] After being routed to the Senate side due to the protests, the Vice President's detail arrived at the Capitol at 12:38 p.m. and was inside the Senate Chamber at 12:54 p.m.[134]

Around 1 p.m., Chief Contee notified Mayor Bowser about the discovery of a pipe bomb at the Republican National Committee and of the Capitol perimeter breach.[135] Within minutes, Mayor Bowser was at the Joint Operations Center with Chief Contee.[136] They tried to contact Chief Sund and sent command officials to Capitol Police headquarters.[137] At approximately 12:59 p.m., once the violence had begun, Chief Sund first called Deputy Chief Jeff Carroll of the MPD, which provided almost immediate reinforcements.[138] Approximately 10 minutes later, MPD officers arrived at the West Front balcony to assist the USCP officers. Chief Sund's next call was to the House and Senate Sergeants-at-Arms to request National Guard resources.[139]

As the violence at the Capitol escalated, DC FEMS realized that they were facing an "expanding incident with the potential for mass casualties, fires, active shooter, and hazardous materials incidents that would exceed the resources at hand."[140] As violence escalated at the West Front, non-lethal grenadiers began launching chemical munitions at the crowd.[141] Around the same time, the USCP discovered a nearby truck containing firearms and Molotov cocktails,[142] as well as a second explosive device at the Democratic National Headquarters at 1:07 p.m., while Vice President-elect Kamala Harris was inside. Responding to these incidents required a commitment of significant USCP resources for mitigation and to evacuate nearby buildings, preventing their deployment to the Capitol to help secure the building.

Chief Gallagher recalled that "it started to really unfold into an investigative—heavy on the investigation of let's pull up the cameras. Let's try to get an image of the pipe bombs. Let's get the images to our law enforcement partners. Let's try to play back the cameras and see if we can identify anybody that placed these pipe bombs. Let's get the owner of the vehicle, run the vehicle information for that suspicious vehicle. So we were coordinating all of that type of response that was from our Investigations Division.... We also had our IICD team trying to run down as much information, working with our Investigations Division as they could, on the suspicious vehicle, the tags of the vehicle, stuff of that nature."[143] Not including those in the command center, the incidents would require the response of 34 USCP personnel, with additional assistance provided by the FBI and ATF. USCP's senior leadership at the Command Center and in the intelligence division also divided their time between the escalating threat to their officers at the Capitol and the explosive devices elsewhere on campus.

The next update to the DOJ was at 1:17 p.m., after President Trump had finished speaking at the Ellipse. After several attempts, Acting Attorney General Rosen got in touch with Acting U.S. Attorney for the District of Columbia Michael Sherwin, who was at the Ellipse. Rosen admits he was not very concerned with the situation at the time, because "[i]t was early, but at least the initial report was: Crowd size doesn't appear to be unexpected, and the conduct so far is okay."[144] He had only watched the end of the President's speech.[145] It was early afternoon before the DOJ's senior leadership began to realize the extent of what was occurring. Acting Deputy Attorney General Donoghue remembered hearing protesters outside the Department of Justice "marching down Constitution, going from the Ellipse toward the Capitol" in the late morning, early afternoon, but wasn't specifically monitoring the protests as "there were a million things going on."[146]

At the same time, the President was pressing his request to go to the Capitol. According to Robert Engel, the head of his Secret Service detail, President Trump asked to go to the Capitol once they had gotten into the Presidential SUV.[147] Engel denied the President's request and returned to the White House.[148] The Committee has significant evidence regarding this period of time.[149]

President Trump, nevertheless, persisted in his request to go to the Capitol. A 1:35 p.m. entry in the USSS Civil Disturbance Unit's time log shows that the plan was to hold at the White House for the next 2 hours and then move the President to the Capitol.[150] Soon after, Engel emailed USSS leadership from the West Wing to say they were "discussing options and setting expectations."[151] Minutes later, after receiving an email from USSS leadership saying that it would not be advisable for the President to go "anywhere near" the Capitol, Engel responded, "[w]e are not doing an OTR to Punch Bowl."[152]

Mayor Bowser also spoke directly with Army Secretary Ryan McCarthy who informed her that they had not gotten a request for National Guard assistance from the USCP. Mayor Bowser informed Secretary McCarthy that she did not have the authority to re-direct the 340 DC National Guard troops at traffic points across the city, but that she had already deployed the DC MPD and FEMs to the Capitol. Because she and Chief Sund had not connected, Mayor Bowser concluded that the security of the Capitol was "now our responsibility" and requested National Guard assistance. At the end of this call, Mayor Bowser believed that Secretary McCarthy was "running [her request] up his chain of command."[153]

USCP Chief Sund was concerned when the explosive device was discovered near RNC Headquarters but did not then believe there was a need to change the USCP's operational posture. Minutes later, when a large group of rioters approached the outer west perimeter of the Capitol, Chief Sund raised the alarm and began to reposition his officers: "When we looked up, and I saw them approaching the officers that were standing, you know, right there on the barrier, I looked over to Chief Thomas and I said, Chad, where's our—where's CDU? Get CDU down there now."[154]

The USCP timeline shows that at 12:55 p.m. all available officers were directed to the West Front of the Capitol. Then, at approximately 1:25 p.m., FBI Deputy Director David Bowdich received a report about the pipe bombs at the RNC and DNC.[155] Bowdich testified that the FBI considered the possibility that the DNC and RNC bombs were possible distractions.[156] At 1:28 p.m., USCP requested the AOC deliver 400 additional bike racks to the East Front to serve as protective barriers, even though rioters were using bike racks as weapons. The pipe bomb discovery at the DNC prevented the AOC from delivering them.[157]

Chief Gallagher was surprised that the violence had escalated so fast. "The amount of violence that immediately took place when that crowd of 30,000, 35,000, whatever the number that was estimated to come was, that did catch, I think, caught Capitol Police and all of our partners a little off guard with how violent they were and how quick they were."[158] At 1:49 p.m., DC MPD Commander Glover declared a riot on the West Front of the Capitol. "Cruiser 50, we're going to give riot warnings. We're going to give riot warnings. Going to try to get compliance, but this is now effectively a riot," Commander Glover yelled into his radio. "1349 hours. Declaring it a riot," the dispatcher responded, which allowed a change in the type of equipment the MPD could use in responding to the violence.[159]

While the violence continued to escalate at the Capitol, the USCP leadership focused on three things: (1) requesting support from local and Federal law enforcement agencies nearby; (2) planning for and coordinating with arriving reinforcements; and (3) protecting congressional leadership and other Members of Congress. Chief Sund was "still making other calls to other agencies for support—ATF, FBI, you name it, Secret Service."[160]

Yogananda Pittman, Gallagher's direct supervisor, told the Select Committee that she took roles that day beyond her responsibility as Assistant Chief of Police for Protective and Intelligence Operations. "So we started—so I started to take Protective Services Bureau resources, as well as the chief's staff, to set up operations adjacent to headquarters building, specifically lot 16, so that we could have a check-in procedure for those units so they could stage vehicles," Pittman said.[161] "Because like we know now, there were breaches on both sides of the buildings and these folks are inside of the Capitol. So you have to deploy them with your officers. They don't know the layout of the land. We're telling them to respond to north barricade. They don't know the north from the south."[162]

Just after 2 p.m., when the Capitol was breached, Assistant Chief Pittman turned her full attention to the protection of congressional leadership.[163] Meanwhile, the USCP officers at the West Front were overwhelmed. Commander Glover praised the actions of his fellow law enforcement officers that day but also noted a lack of leadership.[164] He observed that the

USCP officers he encountered when walking toward the Capitol's West Front seemed to be "very hectic and scattered, with no clear direction,...fighting for every inch on the line," capable, but "without a whole lot of command and control."[165]

When it became clear to him that securing the Capitol would require additional resources, Chief Sund requested the assistance of the DC National Guard.[166] During a 2:30 p.m. call set up by HSEMA Director Rodriguez, the USCP specified the support they needed from the Guard.[167] Mayor Bowser also made "two urgent requests of the President" that she communicated to Chief of Staff Mark Meadows.[168] One was for the National Guard's assistance.[169] The other was that the President make a statement asking "people to leave, to leave the building and to get out of the city, to stop."[170] At 2:56 p.m., Meadows told Mayor Bowser that the President "had approved the request" and was "going to make a statement."[171]

At the Justice Department, it had become clear by early afternoon that the situation was rapidly deteriorating. Donoghue first became aware of the Capitol breach when he walked into Rosen's office and saw on television that the rioters were in the Rotunda.[172] Rosen turned to him and said, "[D]o you see this, do you see what's going on, can you believe this?"[173]

At 2:14 p.m., the Vice President's detail had alerted Secret Service over their radio channel that the Capitol Building had been breached and that they were holding the Vice President in his Senate office.[174] About 5 minutes later, the detail reported that the rioters had gained access to the second floor and that they would need to relocate the Vice President,[175] despite the Vice President's objection.[176] Five to 7 minutes later, after confirming that the route was safe, the lead agent on the Vice President's Secret Service detail reasserted the need for the Vice President to leave his Senate office.[177] (At 2:24 p.m. President Trump tweeted, "Mike Pence didn't have the courage to do what should have been done.") At 2:25 p.m., the Vice President and his detail left for a secure location.[178] Vice President Pence refused to leave the Capitol for his residence and remained in the secure Capitol location until the Senate and House floors were cleared around 7 that evening.[179]

At 2:29 p.m., DC MPD Commander Glover transmitted an emergency radio message: "Cruiser 50. We lost the line. We've lost the line. All MPD, pull back. All MPD, pull back up to the upper deck ASAP. All MPD, pull back to the upper deck ASAP. All MPD, come back to the upper deck. Upper deck. Cruiser 50. We've been flanked. 10–33. I repeat, 10–33 West Front of the Capitol. We have been flanked, and we've lost the line."[180] Commander Glover later told the Select Committee that a "10–33" indicates an immediate need for "emergency assistance for any officer, life or death at that moment in time. That's when that line on the north side finally just broke and we just lost it, and we kind of got overrun behind us...[W]hen you hear that in general daily activity, it's like the radio stops and you're focused on getting to that officer, wherever they are, because you know it's that bad, that they're fighting for their life; something they're perceiving or seeing or realizing is that their life is in immediate danger." [181]

Donoghue left Rosen's office to go to the FBI's Strategic Information and Operations Center (SIOC) across the street at the FBI's Hoover Building.[182] Before he left, Donoghue remembers someone at SIOC telling him "Capitol Police say they don't need help at this point, they've got it covered." [183] When Donoghue arrived at the Washington Field Office, he found FBI Deputy Director Bowdich in a conference room by himself on the phone with a senior FBI official.[184] After a brief discussion, Donoghue and Bowdich agreed that they should both go to the Capitol to evaluate the situation firsthand.[185] Donoghue remembered that they arrived at the assembly area on D Street.[186] Donoghue called Rosen to say that he and Bowdich were going to the Capitol.[187]

Around this time, Bowdich says that he received a call from Senator Mark Warner, who said "[t]his is a mess, and we now have the vast majority of the Senate in one room." [188] Bowdich recalls the number being about 87 senators,[189] and that he directed the FBI's Baltimore team to "protect that room, recognizing you have almost the entire Senate in one room." [190] Bowdich also directed a SWAT team to Senator Mitch McConnell's office, in response to a call from McConnell's staff informing him that rioters were kicking in their door. On arriving, the SWAT team found that McConnell's staff had reached safety.[191]

At 3:25 p.m., Rosen spoke to Speaker Nancy Pelosi and Senator Chuck Schumer about the ongoing crisis. A video of the call shows Senator Schumer imploring Rosen, "get the President to tell them to leave the Capitol, Mr. Attorney General, in your law enforcement responsibility. A public statement that they should all leave." [192]

As the day's crisis unfolded, Mayor Bowser activated the DC mutual assistance compact with neighboring jurisdictions for law assistance support and spoke to the Governors of Maryland and Virginia to solicit additional National Guard support. At about 3:30 p.m., Mayor Bowser spoke to congressional leadership, including Speaker Pelosi and House Majority Leader Steny Hoyer.[193] Then, around 4 p.m., Mayor Bowser, MPD Chief Contee and Army Secretary McCarthy met in the Joint Operations Center at MPD headquarters.[194] At 4:30 p.m., Mayor Bowser held a press conference with DC HSEMA Director Rodriguez as well as Secretary McCarthy.[195] Mayor Bowser also declared a 6 p.m. curfew for the District.[196]

Vice President Pence, who remained inside the Capitol, called Acting Attorney General Rosen at 4:34 p.m. to ask what the DOJ was doing and what more the Department could do to help.[197] Vice President Pence told Rosen that the situation at the Capitol seemed then to be "improving." [198] The head of his USSS security detail recalls overhearing the Vice President asking USCP Chief Sund, over the phone, whether it would be possible to "go back to finish the business of the government this evening." [199] At 4:42 p.m., the head of the Vice President's detail emailed the USSS Office of Protective Operations that the Vice President was confirming with Chief Sund that it would "take days to sweep and reopen" the Capitol.[200]

Congressional leadership continued to push to return to the Capitol to continue certifying the electoral votes. Senior DOJ and FBI officials—including Rosen, Bowdich, and Donoghue—held two conference calls. Donoghue remembered that the first, at 6 p.m., was a "law enforcement-level call" with General Daniel R. Hokansen, chief of the National Guard Bureau, and focused on the role of the DC National Guard.[201] The second call, at approximately 7 p.m., included Speaker Pelosi, Leader McConnell, Leader Schumer, the Vice President, the Secretary of Defense, and General Milley, as well as other congressional leaders.[202] During that call, FBI and other law enforcement officials on the ground provided an updated timeline for clearing the Capitol to "hopefully get in an hour later." [203]

At 8:05 p.m., the U.S. Capitol Police announced that the Capitol Building was clear and that Congress could resume counting electoral votes.[204] Shortly after Members returned, Donoghue left the Capitol.[205]

DC FEMS statistics help describe the scope of the January 6th riot at the Capitol. Over the course of the day, DC FEMS reported 22 EMS responses, 14 EMS transports, including two cardiac arrests and two critical injury transports. There were an estimated 250 injured law enforcement officers from numerous agencies.[206] One hundred-fourteen USCP officers reported injuries.[207] Five police officers who were at the Capitol on January 6th died in the days following the riot.

Federal and local law enforcement authorities were in possession of multiple streams of intelligence predicting violence directed at the Capitol prior to January 6th. Although some of that intelligence was fragmentary, it should have been sufficient to warrant far more vigorous preparations for the security of the joint session. The failure to sufficiently share and act upon that intelligence jeopardized the lives of the police officers defending the Capitol and everyone in it.

While the danger to the Capitol posed by an armed and angry crowd was foreseeable, the fact that the President of the United States would be the catalyst of their fury and facilitate the attack was unprecedented in American history. If we lacked the imagination to suppose that a President would incite an attack on his own Government, urging his supporters to "fight like hell," we lack that insight no more. And the best defense against that danger will not come from law enforcement, but from an informed and active citizenry.

# DC NATIONAL GUARD PREPARATION FOR AND RESPONSE TO JANUARY 6TH

## INTRODUCTION

H. Res. 503 Section 4(a) directs the Select Committee to examine the "facts, circumstances, and causes relating to the domestic terrorist attack on the Capitol," including the "activities of intelligence agencies, law enforcement agencies, and the Armed Forces, including with respect to intelligence collection, analysis, and dissemination and information sharing among the branches and other instrumentalities of government." This appendix focuses on the activities of the DC National Guard in the days leading up to and on January 6, 2021.

In contrast to the National Guard units in 50 States and three territories, where deployment authority lies with the governor of those respective jurisdictions, the DC Guard falls directly under the command of the United States President. In the discussion section below, this appendix provides a narrative of the preparations for and eventual deployment of the DC Guard on January 6th, and the interaction between then-President Trump and the DC Guard in the relevant time period. It is based on the Select Committee's interviews of 24 witnesses and review of over 37,000 pages of documents.

## DISCUSSION

### A "GUT-WRENCHING" SUMMER

The approval process for the deployment of the DC National Guard is unique, unlike any of the 50 States or three territories across the country where ultimate authority rests in the hands of the governor.[1] In the nation's capital, where no governorship exists, the Guard is ultimately under the command of the President of the United States when acting in its militia capacity to support civil authorities.[2] By executive order, however, President Richard Nixon delegated the President's day-to-day control of the DC Guard to the Secretary of Defense and specified that its Commanding General should report to the Secretary of Defense or the Secretary's designee.[3] By memorandum, the Secretary of Defense, in turn, delegated day-to-day control of the DC Guard to the Secretary of the Army.[4] The commander of the DC Guard reported directly to the Secretary of the Army on January 6, 2021.[5]

During the 2020 summer protests in response to the murder of George Floyd,[6] the approval process for Guard deployment ran smoothly. "Very, very proactive," then-Commanding General of the DC Guard William

Walker said.[7] Secretary of the Army Ryan McCarthy "really wanted us out there."[8] Secretary McCarthy, with all his authorities, was physically beside Major General Walker throughout that summer. "[H]e was with me for all of it," Major General Walker said.[9] "He came to the [A]rmory every day. He brought his staff with him."[10] As has been widely reported, a number of President Trump's senior advisors, including Attorney General Bill Barr, resisted President Trump's requests to deploy the Guard or other troops in various states and cities where violence had occurred or was underway.[11]

In the summer of 2020, nothing was being written down; it "was just all verbal back and forth."[12] That approach sped up response times. But as the DC Guard footprint grew and controversies began plaguing the operation, Secretary McCarthy came away with the lesson that deliberative and by written order beat fast and by oral command.[13]

"What we learned in the process was we were not capturing a lot of the information in writing in the orders process, which is fundamental, foundational because of the stress of the situation and the speed of the situation," Secretary McCarthy said.[14]

While a concept of operations ("con-op") was developed at the lower level during the summer 2020 operations, it did not require approval or input at the secretary level.[15] That approach came to be seen as a mistake that should not be replicated the next time there was a civil disturbance crisis in the nation's capital. General Walter Piatt, director of the Army staff, explained: "That's where Secretary McCarthy put that restriction to say, I want a concept of the operation before we just send a force to do something."[16]

One of the most visible and highly criticized of the summer 2020 operations was the use of low-flying helicopters that appeared to be bearing down on protesters with the aim of dispersing them. On June 1st, as Guard presence tripled overnight, the use of helicopters meant for aerial surveillance[17] "somehow got translated to a very competent Army officer that 'I am to fly low and loud to deter looters,'" General Piatt said.[18] "[W]hat the investigation revealed was that we did not have good procedures in place to provide military support to a very serious civil disturbance ongoing. The—because—the pilot of that aircraft believed that was his mission."[19]

The "embarrass[ment]"[20] of the low-flying helicopter affected Secretary McCarthy. General Charles Flynn, then- deputy chief of staff for operations, plans, and training, told the Select Committee, "I know the Secretary was concerned."[21] He further explained: "I'm sure that affected his thinking."[22]

Secretary McCarthy became convinced that a concept of operations needed to be "explicit, tailored"[23] and—most importantly—that it needed to "come from [the] top down."[24] Secretary McCarthy told his staff,

"[W]hen we get a request next time, we have to be absolutely certain that we understand the mission clearly," [25] and that "no other civil authority could re-mission off that support without the approval of either the Secretary of the Army or, in certain circumstances, the Secretary of Defense." [26]

In mid-June 2020, then-Secretary of Defense Mark Esper, Secretary McCarthy, Chairman of the Joint Chiefs of Staff General Mark Milley, and Major General Walker huddled to talk about what went wrong in the preceding weeks. Senior defense officials then decided they would take a "more active" role in directing the force. [27] "[A]s a result, we all took a more active interest in what was happening down to the tactical level to make sure that we were, again, abiding by kind of the core principles of civil-military relations," former Secretary Esper said. [28]

Major General Walker said he was not told about that shift in perspective: "[I]f the Army thought different of how we respond to civil unrest, civil disturbance, I would hope . . . they would communicate that with the guy—with the person who is going to execute that change." [29]

In the words of General Milley, the summer of 2020 had been "a pretty gut-wrenching experience." [30] The Department of Defense was still recovering when it was faced with the decision of the manner and degree to which the DC Guard should provide assistance to law enforcement authorities planning, just seven months later, for the events anticipated in connection with Congressional certification of the electoral votes on January 6, 2021.

**A "Tailored" Request for Guard Resources.** On December 19, 2020, President Trump tweeted, "Big protest in DC on January 6th. Be there! Will be wild!" From that day forward, a rookie DC intelligence analyst saw a tenfold uptick in violent rhetoric targeting Congress and law enforcement. [31] Right-wing groups were sharing histories of violence and some not traditionally aligned had begun coordinating their efforts. [32] The analyst's report reached more senior DC leadership, including, eleven days later, Mayor Bowser. [33] In the course of the Committee's investigation, it received and reviewed a significant number of documents indicating that certain intelligence and law enforcement agencies understood that violence was possible or even likely on January 6th. The Committee received many of those materials from the U.S. Secret Service, but also from other agencies as well.

On Thursday, December 31, 2020, the day after the briefing, Mayor Bowser sent a letter to Major General Walker requesting Guard assistance for January 5 and 6, 2021. [34] A second letter specified the District's request as limited to two forms of assistance: crowd management at Metro stations and blocking vehicles at traffic posts. It did not request help with potential civil disturbance. [35]

General Piatt viewed the "limited request" [36] as a "pretty good, tailored mission," that was "not vague." [37] General James McConville, chief of staff of the Army, called the request appropriately "restricted" [38] with "a very low military signature." [39]

According to testimony by Defense Department witnesses, after a summer of perceived overreach, military leadership was grateful for the delineated parameters set by the city itself.

The substance of the request—limited to traffic and crowd control "so they could have more police officers to do police functions" [40]—was not seen as narrow by District officials. "I would say it's a specific request," Chief of DC Police (Metropolitan Police Department ("MPD")) Robert Contee said. [41] "[L]eave the unlawful stuff, leave that to the police to deal with." [42] Mayor Bowser said: "I don't know any law enforcement person who would suggest that urban disturbances aren't best handled by the police." [43]

"Civil disturbance was not something we requested at that time. Mostly also because the vast majority of the, if not all, of the permitted protests were taking place on Federal lands," said Director of the DC Homeland Security and Emergency Management Agency Christopher Rodriguez. [44] The District had no jurisdiction. "Mayor Bowser cannot make a request on behalf of the White House or on behalf of the Capitol for U.S. Capitol—for . . . DC National Guardsmen to deploy to those two entities. She can't," Chief Contee said. [45] At this time, it was well known that President Trump had planned a speech and rally on "Federal lands"—on the Ellipse south of the White House. It was not widely known that President Trump intended to "spontaneously" instruct the tens of thousands of supporters at that Ellipse rally to march down Pennsylvania Avenue to the Capitol. [46]

**Five Days of "Tremendous Resistance".** At first, Secretary McCarthy was not sold on involving the Guard at all. Major General Walker called Secretary McCarthy "instantly when I got the letters" from the District on Thursday, December 31st, and "initially I felt I must have caught him at a bad time." [47] Secretary McCarthy recalls it being a short conversation. "I said, 'okay, got it. Thank you.' You want to immediately flip it so that Secretary of Defense knows that we alerted his office," he said. [48]

According to Major General Walker's account of this call, the Secretary initially stated "'We're not doing it,'" [49] and then left the door open for further discussion. Major General Walker explained: "'I said, 'Well, sir, I think you should look at it.' And then he told me, 'Well, we'll talk about it, but we don't really want to do this, because the look it would give, the military out there interfering.' . . . He says, 'Well, we'll discuss it on Monday.'" [50]

On Sunday, January 3rd, Secretary McCarthy called Chief Contee, who had formally assumed the role of acting head of MPD just the day before.[51]

"I thought initially that . . . he is just calling me basically as a rubber stamp to say, . . . 'You asked for it, you got it.' . . . It didn't go that way," Chief Contee said.[52] "[H]e had concerns about deploying National Guard for this event. He talked about the optics of the event, having boots on the ground. . . . And I pushed back on that."[53]

In his interview with the Select Committee, Secretary McCarthy described evaluating the request on the evening of January 3rd. "I sat at home. I chewed on it," he said.[54] "You know, I'm not particularly inclined to support it, because my concern was really we didn't have a command-and-control architecture in place. We didn't really have all of the mechanisms to be successful, you know. . . . So it was a very tough decision for me."[55]

Over five days, from December 31st to January 4th, District officials faced what Major General Walker called "tremendous resistance."[56]

Both Chief Contee and Director Rodriguez recalled that five-day period on January 6th, when Chief Steven Sund, of the U.S. Capitol Police, was pleading for reinforcements.[57] Acting Defense Secretary Christopher Miller, "heard through the grapevine that [Secretary McCarthy] was inclined—I don't want to say inclined to disapprove, but, you know, looking at it carefully or whatever. So—but that's fine. He can do whatever he wants. I knew that I was going to honor [the mayor's] request . . . ."[58]

How close those Guard assets could go to the Capitol became a sticking point. Colonel Craig Hunter, the highest-ranking commander on the ground on January 6th, said the Army "really want[ed] to go through the concept of operations to see, okay, exactly—basically Metro stop by Metro stop, intersection by intersection, to see where will Guardsmen be exactly, you know, how close are you to the Capitol . . . ."[59] He said an initial request by MPD to post Guard troops at the South Capitol Metro station—like all other Metro stations—was denied.[60] In conference calls that "went back and forth,"[61] Major General Walker was told, "There was a concern about being too close, military uniforms too close to the Capitol."[62]

Major General Walker had a different perspective. He saw his people as "citizen soldiers," "your neighbors that are going to come to your aid and rescue when you need us,"[63]—not traditional boots on the ground. "[T]hat's where, to me, the vest came in. This was the National Guard, not the Army," he said.[64]

Military authorities determined that a geographical boundary would have to be established as a condition of approving the Guard's deployment to assist MPD. No servicemember could go east of Ninth Street. It wasn't made explicit to District officials, but they all knew what lay east. "[T]he

Capitol is east," Chief Contee said.[65] "[I]f you move them anywhere east of Ninth Street, they will be close to the Capitol. That was certainly the way I understood it."[66]

Director Rodriguez worried "that it constrained our ability to react quickly if the situation got out of hand."[67] Without the limitation, the District fully intended to post its resources farther east: "[W]e couldn't get as close to the Capitol as could have been helpful," Mayor Bowser said.[68] "[W]e would have had a broader traffic box."[69]

**Fears of Politicizing the Military in an Antidemocratic Manner.** Both Acting Secretary Miller and Secretary McCarthy were sensitive to the sight of troops near the site of the Congressional certification of electoral votes, because of President Trump's previous expression of interest in using Federal troops in civilian situations. Again, Attorney General Barr and other members of the Trump Administration had resisted President Trump's desire to deploy such troops. Secretary Esper said it "tended to be the case . . . that the President was inclined to use the military," contrary to longstanding principles of reserving the armed forces as a last resort.[70]

According to his testimony, Acting Secretary Miller's express first priority—after being installed with just two months left in the Trump administration—was "to make every effort to return the Department of Defense to a nonpoliticized entity," because previously, "the Department was being showcased too much."[71] In testimony to the U.S. House Committee on Oversight and Reform on May 12, 2021, he cited "fears that the President would invoke the Insurrection Act to politicize the military in an antidemocratic manner" as shaping his thinking.[72] "No such thing was going to occur on my watch," he wrote,[73] later adding that "if I would have put troops on Capitol Hill" before the attack and without a request from civil authorities, "that would have been seen as extremely provocative, if not supporting this crazy narrative that the military was going to try to overturn the election."[74]

Secretary McCarthy felt similar pressure. He had been taken aback when—as he was walking down the Pentagon's hallways—"one of the most seasoned reporters" asked him whether the Army was planning to seize ballot boxes.[75] It was "an incredibly tense period," according to Secretary McCarthy.[76] As our investigation has demonstrated, President Trump had considered proposals from Lt. General (ret.) Michael Flynn, Sidney Powell, and others that troops be utilized to seize ballot boxes in certain parts of the country.

On December 18, 2020—the same day as the contentious White House meeting with Flynn and others,—Secretary McCarthy issued a statement, "mirror[ing] what General Milley said about a month before,"[77] reiterating that "There is no role for the U.S. military in determining the outcome of an

American election." [78] Given the heat of the rhetoric, he thought, "[I]f we don't say anything, it's going to scare people." [79] Secretary McCarthy told the Select Committee he thought he would be fired after publicly stating that the military would not assist in a coup.[80] General McConville, who signed the statement alongside Secretary McCarthy's signature,[81] linked their words directly to the Ninth Street limitation: "[T]here was no plan to put any military anywhere near the Capitol because of what we had said, the military has no role in determining the outcome of elections." [82]

On January 1st, Executive Officer to Secretary McCarthy Colonel John Lubas wrote in an internal email that the Secretary "wants to clearly communicate that this request is NOT from the White House." [83] The email noted that the Secretary wanted to "aggressively message" that the request had come from District officials, not the President.[84]

"We wanted everybody to know that, because it would create confusion and even more tension of having soldiers on the street without a request and that they be near the Capitol with certification of an election, a contested election," Secretary McCarthy said.[85]

On January 3, 2021, 10 former Secretaries of Defense, including the recently fired, former Secretary Esper, published a joint op-ed warning that "[i]nvolving the military in election disputes would cross into dangerous territory." [86] Secretary McCarthy had himself worked for five of the 10 secretaries.[87] "I know all these [men]," he said.[88] "[T]hey were—everyone was telling us, be very conscious of your actions and how you—you know, what you're going to do that day. So we wanted to know where every soldier was by street corner." [89]

Was Secretary McCarthy concerned that President Trump might use the military to cling to power? "There was a lot of talk in the lead-up about martial law . . . and the employment of forces, and you know, that was something that we were all, you know, conscious of." [90] Our investigation suggests that those civilian and military officials who had considerable experience working directly with President Trump had genuine concerns about whether he would attempt to use the military to change the election results. Again, at this time, there is no evidence the Department of Defense understood exactly what President Trump and his associates planned for January 6th.

**"Very Strict on the Use of the Military" on January 6th.** By Monday, January 4th, with Secretary McCarthy now backing the operation, Acting Secretary Miller was briefed. He told the Select Committee that he "made the decision right there to honor the request." [91] That approval came with strings attached. The role of the DC Guard would be spelled out and tightly circumscribed in a memorandum that, as characterized by General Milley, was "very strict on the use of the military." [92] It decreed that without the Acting Secretary's "subsequent, personal authorization," the Guard would not be issued batons, helmets, or body armor; could not interact physically with protestors, except in self-defense; and that the Quick Reaction Force (QRF)—40 servicemembers staged in case of an emergency at Joint Base Andrews in Prince George's County, Maryland—could be deployed only as a last resort.[93]

Above the tactical level, changes in the mission of the Guard had to be approved by the Secretary of the Army and, in some cases—in order to "interact physically with protestors" or be issued batons—required running further up the chain to the Secretary of Defense.[94]

To District officials, that seemed new—and unnecessary. "[The Secretary told us,] if you send them to any other kind of mission, that has to get approval from me. And I just think that those were unnecessary restrictions . . ." Chief Contee said.[95]

What the QRF would be called upon to do, even in the case of an emergency, is a matter of debate. The letter and memorandum do not expressly note whether the QRF could be used to support the original mission of the Guard—traffic and crowd control—or a new mission helping contain sudden and out-of-hand civil disturbance.[96] The DC Guard official put in charge of the QRF for January 5th and 6th, Lieutenant Colonel David Reinke, said he had not been given much guidance as to their role.[97]

The Army and the DC Guard appear to have had different understandings. "[T]he intent of the quick reaction force was really to send these troops over to help if they had a problem at one of the traffic command posts," General McConville said.[98] "There never was an intent for a quick reaction force to go to the Capitol . . . ."[99] According to Army officials, without a con-op and a formal change in mission, the QRF could do traffic control and no more.

That was not how others imagined an emergency unit would or should operate. According to Major General Walker, "a quick reaction force, something's happening; do I have time to find you and call you and ask you?"[100] He called the preapproval language "highly unusual,"[101] particularly as their name "already implied that it's a last resort,"[102] their intended purpose was if "[u]nexpectedly, you have a spontaneous unrest,"[103] and if "I need to write a concept of operations for a quick reaction force? They're no longer quick. It's just a reaction force."[104]

**Capitol Police Board "Prepared" without Guard Help.** It wasn't clear to everyone involved in planning for the events anticipated on January 6th that all agencies, including the Capitol Police, were deploying all their resources ahead of that day. "We had had issues understanding, getting the full picture of U.S. Capitol Police's operational posture and what their planning was," Director Rodriguez said.[105]

Mayor Bowser was struck when—right before the press briefing that Monday, January 4th—the mayor asked the Capitol Police representative, "[W]here does your perimeter start? [And h]e gets up out of the room, calls somebody. And the next thing I know he can't participate in the conference." [106] She elaborated: "[T]hat should have been like a trigger to me. Like these people, they don't want to answer questions about their preparation." [107]

On the morning of January 3rd, Capitol Police Chief Steven Sund approached two of the members of the Capitol Police Board and purportedly requested—but concededly did not push for—Guard resources for the Capitol. [108] According to Chief Sund, in a minutes long meeting in the office of House Sergeant at Arms Paul Irving, Irving told Chief Sund he did not like the optics of asking for the Guard in advance and that the intelligence did not support it. [109] Chief Sund said he did not push back on either point. [110] In fact, he agreed that his reading of the intelligence—despite a forewarning put out by his own intelligence unit that "Congress was itself the target" on January 6th [111]—did not call for Guard support, [112] only that having more personnel on his perimeter would make him "more comfortable." [113] Irving suggested he talk to the Senate Sergeant at Arms, and then-chairman of the Capitol Police Board, Michael Stenger. [114] According to Irving, Stenger, in a meeting in his office, asked Chief Sund to reach out to the Guard and find out, if an emergency called for it, "how many people can [the commanding general] give us and how quickly can he give us those people?" [115] Chief Sund said he took their responses to mean "no," despite conceding that he was never told "you cannot have the National Guard" or anything to that effect. [116] "It was 100 percent a denial," he maintained. [117]

Irving recalled the matter coming up on a three-way phone conference during which "the consensus was that we didn't need" the Guard. [118] He did not consider it a request. [119] On the call, Chief Sund noted that the District planned to use the servicemembers to staff intersections, but the Capitol grounds had few of those, and it would not relieve many officers if they were used in a similar fashion. [120] "It was a combination of operationally the chief didn't feel that they would add much to his plan, and the intelligence really didn't speak for anything that we felt would justify the need for them," Irving said. [121] Irving doesn't recall taking the "optics" into consideration. [122] According to Irving, the conversation ended the same way Chief Sund said it had: "Why don't you just tell them to be on standby?" Stenger suggested. [123] It was never brought up again. [124]

The discussion about the use of the Guard remained within the Capitol Police Board and did not reach congressional leadership, including the Speaker of the House. That was normal. "[F]rom a tactical perspective, we would make decisions without the input from congressional leadership,"

Irving said.[125] "I always felt that I had full authority to implement security decisions as I deemed appropriate."[126] In fact, when the three men briefed congressional leaders on January 5th, Chief Sund conveyed the same optimistic outlook as he had with Major General Walker: "[We told them] we felt we were prepared based on the information we had, yes," he said.[127]

To keep these exchanges in perspective, we note again that we are aware of no evidence that these individuals were privy to President Trump's plans to instruct tens of thousands of his supporters to walk down Pennsylvania Avenue to the Capitol to help "take back" their country. Nor were they aware of how President Trump would suggest to his followers that Vice President Pence had the authority to change the outcome of the election, or how President Trump would behave in the hours that followed. Certain members of Congress, including those who met at the White House on December 21, 2020, may have had considerably more insight into President Trump's planning, but the Committee has no information suggesting that any of those members alerted the Capitol Police or other authorities of President Trump's plans.

**Soldiers Prepare for the Worst in Secret.** Guard reinforcements could draw from a pool of three groups already activated for the day: (1) the 40 members making up the QRF, staged in Maryland;[128] (2) the 90 members at the traffic control points, 24 at the Metro stations, and four as part of the command staff distributed throughout the city—but no farther east than Ninth Street—for a total of 118 representing the first shift;[129] and (3) the second shift of another 118 members,[130] preparing at the Armory in Southeast Washington, D.C, for a 3:00 p.m. shift takeover.[131] The Armory also housed a command-and-control squad that handled logistics at about 52 members strong, in addition to a Civil Support Team of about 20 members.[132] That gave Colonel Hunter a maximum limit of 348 activated servicemembers, eight more than the allotted 340—nearly all of whom reported directly to him on January 6th.[133]

The QRF was most prepared for responding to sudden and escalating civil unrest. At Joint Base Andrews, they were provisioned with full riot-control kits,[134] including a helmet with a face shield already attached, protective vest, shin guards, knee guards, shield, and baton.[135] The head of the QRF—himself provided little guidance on the contours of his mission—had his squad train for civil disturbance on January 5th and the morning of the 6th as they waited.[136] Not only had they trained, but they trained *together*, as a unit—a benefit military officials all agreed is ideal. Army leadership, all the way up to Secretary McCarthy,[137] had no idea that Lt. Col. Reinke had taken these initiatives. Secretary McCarthy agreed that had he known of their civil disturbance preparation, "it could have" affected the speed with which approval was ultimately given for their deployment.[138]

As to the second group of available resources—the servicemembers stationed at traffic control points since the early morning of January 6th—Army leadership held misconceptions about what equipment was available to them. Secretary McCarthy had agreed that some gear—expressly not batons—could remain stowed away in vehicle trunks.[139] Colonel Hunter had his troops put the gear into a white box truck instead and designated a rally point for the truck that would be central to all traffic control points.[140] On the night of January 5th, in anticipation of January 6th, Colonel Hunter had his troops move the civil disturbance gear—including the prohibited batons—into the individual vehicles themselves.[141] Captain Tarp, the head of the second shift, agreed that they were told to load the equipment into their vehicles "on the down low. Done so it wasn't visible, so it wouldn't look like we were escalating [our] role."[142]

The commanding general of the DC Guard was aware that the troops had all they needed in their trunks and—in the case of an emergency—would not need to return to the Armory to get it: "They already had it," Major General Walker said.[143]

But Army leadership did not know that. Although General Piatt said "We never asked, like, what was actually—I have no knowledge of what they [actually] had in" the vehicles,[144] the guidance from Secretary McCarthy's letter led him to believe that "weapons, ammunition, batons, shields, kneepads, other protection that we may be asked to do for civil disturbance, that was not [there]—because they were specifically told they would not participate in that mission . . . ."[145] Secretary McCarthy said, "The only thing I authorized General Walker to do was their ballistic helmets and body armor in the vehicle, not their shields or their riot batons."[146] He figured his orders had been followed.[147] When asked why he was not aware of the moves the Guard had made, Secretary McCarthy said, "I mean, I made a mistake. I think a local unit commander was anticipating more than what potentially we were prepared for."[148]

DC Guard leadership understood that loading this equipment flouted direct orders. "I wasn't going to have my soldiers unprepared," Major General Walker said.[149] The prohibition on batons, in particular, had been sent 54 minutes after the Guard had already begun their traffic control shifts on the morning of January 5th.[150]

The third group of available resources—the servicemembers awaiting at the Armory to take over as the second shift at the traffic control points—had equipment accessible to them at headquarters. Captain Tarp did note that it took time to ensure that the Armory equipment was in working order: repairing straps that were broken, wiping off dirt on the shields because "they were the same from the George Floyd protests," and affixing the helmet to the shields, which took upwards of 20 to 30 minutes.[151] In the three different locations where the Guard was stationed as the Capitol was being breached, all servicemembers had access to full civil disturbance gear right there with them.

Outside of the QRF, which had recently returned from two days of training together, there is debate as to how ready the rest of the Guard was to engage in civil disturbance response on January 6th. The notion that the military is not primed or naturally skilled to deal with civil disturbance appears to stand in tension with National Guard traditions, training, and doctrine. "They were not missioned, tasked, organized, equipped to do civil disturbance operations," General Flynn said.[152] Although General Piatt conceded that "[a]ll soldiers are trained in civil disturbance," he maintained that on "that day we were not postured to do civil disturbance operations." [153]

Major General Walker—who pointed out that the DC Guard shield, on Guard troop uniforms, features the Capitol building itself: "Protect the Capitol. That's why Thomas Jefferson created it" [154]—called civil disturbance "foundational" to what they do.[155]

**DC Ground Commander Takes Initiative.** On January 5th, as he led his forces in traffic control, Colonel Hunter did not observe activity that raised concerns.[156] But by the next morning—as thousands of out-of-towners invited by President Trump descended on the nation's capital—that all changed. "I could see like the Proud Boys," he said.[157] "I could see different people with Kevlars on, with bulletproof vests on. You know, they're all kitted up and they're wearing different patches and colors. And I said, 'Well, this crowd is definitely different . . . .' " [158] This, of course, was an indication of the potential for violence in the hours that followed.

Colonel Hunter, sitting at the intersection of 15th Street and Pennsylvania Avenue, saw crowds flowing past him and his soldiers toward the Capitol—walking as one, chanting as one. "Hey, is it that way to the Capitol? Where's the Capitol?" some asked.[159] Colonel Hunter got in his car and began writing an update report.[160]

He was interrupted by a soldier who had been watching CNN on his phone: "Hey, sir, I think there's been shots fired at the Capitol." [161] It was then that Colonel Hunter began to put a plan in place for the redeployment of the Guard. "So at that point in my mind I said, 'Okay, then they will be requesting the DC National Guard now, so we have to move." [162] The time was 2:12 p.m.[163]

The first thing he did was designate a rally point for DC Guard reinforcements.[164] Over the radio, he relayed the rally point to all 118 members currently spread across the city doing traffic control, and one by one, in order by their points, they called in to acknowledge where they would go once approval came down.[165] At 2:17 p.m., he called Lt. Col. Reinke, the head of the 40-strong QRF, and ordered his subordinate to "have all of your guys put their gear on and get on the bus."[166] "In my mind, this is about to happen really fast," he said.[167] "As soon as I make one call, I will get clearance to go and support. The United States Capitol was breached. I mean, this is unheard of."[168] Accordingly, he advised Lt. Col. Reinke that, "[W]e will be getting a call soon."[169]

He next tried to find the incident command post. He ran into the Assistant MPD Chief Jeffery Carroll, piled into a car and, sirens flipped on, sped off to U.S. Capitol Police headquarters.[170]

Once there, they got into the elevator, and "before the doors even closed," Assistant Chief Carroll asked him, "How many do you have coming right now?"[171] Colonel Hunter said, "I'm working on it. I need to make some calls, but we are—we're coming . . . . And I said, as soon as I start making these calls, I'm going to have so many National Guardsmen just flooding this way. I just need to have the location, have the plan set, be ready to receive them."[172]

No later than 2:50 p.m., Colonel Hunter had confirmed with Lt. Col. Reinke that the QRF was on the bus and ready.[173] The highest-ranking Guard official on the ground had sorted out all of the details and linked up with the law enforcement agencies that would lead them in support. At least 135 National Guard servicemembers—the 40 QRF members already in gear and on the bus and the 90 at traffic control posts awaiting word, with gear in their trunks to be donned at the rally point, along with four command staff plus Colonel Hunter himself—were ready to go. At 3:10 p.m., Colonel Hunter felt it was time to tell his superiors all that he had done and hopefully get fast approval.[174]

**3 Hours and 19 Minutes** At the Capitol, MPD Chief Contee was on the West Front, himself inhaling chemical agents—"you can smell it before you see it, felt it in my throat"[175]—as officers tried to resist rioters beating back the perimeter, having reached the stage built for the Inauguration set for two weeks later. "[T]he gas stuff and the spray, the mist that's in the air, I mean, it's real," he said.[176] "I'm trying to talk to the Mayor to give her a situational update, and the city administrator—I've got them both on the line. I'm coughing, trying to explain what's going on."[177] Chief Contee cut through the crowds of people around the Capitol to meet the mayor at MPD headquarters.[178]

Chief Sund said he reached out to House Sergeant at Arms Irving at 12:57 or 12:58 p.m., and told him, "We are getting overrun on the West Front by thousands. We need the National Guard now."[179] Irving recalled the call coming before a break in the electoral certification session just short of 1:30 p.m. and that the Chief said "that conditions were deteriorating outside and he *might* be making a request for the National Guard."[180]

Although Irving was firm in his stance that only the Capitol Police Board had the authority to request National Guard assistance, he nonetheless sought out the chief of staff to the Speaker to inform her of the impending request.[181] He did not need her to sign off, but "[a]ny change in security posture, given the time, I would give them a heads-up."[182]

The Speaker's chief of staff "immediately scribbled down a note" and went over to inform the Speaker—who was in the chair presiding over the floor debate on the Arizona objections—about the request for the National Guard.[183] "Absolutely. Go," Speaker Nancy Pelosi said.[184] Later, as they were evacuating the floor to an undisclosed location, the Speaker asked her, "Is the National Guard coming?"[185] The Speaker's chief of staff said, "Yes, we asked them."[186]

Irving said the formal request for Guard assistance came in a call after 2 p.m. from Chief Sund "and, of course, we said absolutely."[187] Chief Sund said he had made the request in that earlier 12:57 or 12:58 call and had been waiting for 71 minutes.[188] "I hung up the phone. I yelled across the command center, ['M]ark the time, 2:10, I finally got approval from the Capitol Police Board for the use of the National Guard,'" Chief Sund said.[189]

At around 2:30 p.m., Director Rodriguez patched Chief Contee—and a largely silent Mayor Bowser listening in[190]—into the conference call with Chief Sund and Major General Walker, who brought in General Piatt.[191] Major General Walker ordered his aide-de-camp on his second day on the job, Lt. Timothy Nick, to take handwritten notes of the call and the rest of the day.[192]

On the line at the Pentagon—gathered around the speaker of the Secretary of the Army's desk phone—were General Piatt, General McConville, and Secretary McCarthy.[193] According to Secretary McCarthy, it was during the call that he learned the Capitol had been breached,[194] watching it unfold in real time on television.[195] He didn't recall hearing Chief Sund's voice on the call, but said "we were trying to get . . . what we call the operational sight picture. What is going on? How big is the crowd? How violent is the crowd? . . . They started laying out really the—just how bad it was."[196] Secretary McCarthy resolved to run to the office of Acting Secretary of Defense Miller, leaving behind instructions to General Piatt to "find out the requirements," as he was "going to get the authority."[197] "[W]e go zipping down there," General McConville said.[198] As they were leaving, General Flynn showed up.[199]

General Flynn said, "when I came by the phone," he "heard voices screaming on the end."[200] He called the tones of their voices as "chaotic"[201] and that "[y]ou couldn't tell who was talking sometimes."[202] Chief Sund was pleading for help. "I want to say he even used the word, like, 'I am pleading,'" Chief Contee said.[203] Col. Matthews, listening in beside Major General Walker, said of Chief Sund: "His voice was cracking. He was almost crying."[204]

According to Chief Contee, the reaction to his pleas was "tepid."[205] "It was a very sluggish response," Chief Contee said.[206] "I remember just, you know, with all that was going on, not hearing a 'yes,' you know, just . . . what I would in my mind qualify as, like, excuses and not decisive action . . . I was hearing, like, all the reasons, you know, why we shouldn't be doing this."[207] Director Rodriguez called it a "kind of bureaucratic" response in the midst of "a rapidly evolving situation where literally the Capitol was being overrun."[208] He added: "I don't want to use the word disinterested, but more just, 'let's just hold on. Let's just wait. Let's just kind of calm down for a second while literally Rome is burning.'"[209]

For his part, General Flynn depicted General Piatt—the main interlocutor—as "the calming voice in an otherwise chaotic situation."[210] General McConville agreed: "I talked to some of my staff, and they said that General Piatt did an incredible job. He was like the—you know, in a very calm [voice], just saying, 'let's just settle . . . .'"[211]

But Major General Walker said he "just couldn't believe nobody was saying: 'Hey, go.'"[212] He asked the generals on the other line, "'Aren't you watching the news? Can't you see what's going on? We need to get there.' And [I was] cognizant of the fact that I'm talking to senior . . . people, but I could see what was happening . . . ."[213] Chief Sund was "perplexed" and "dumbfounded."[214] "It wasn't what I expected of, yeah, the cavalry's coming. It was a bunch of, round-the-house, oh, hey, let's do this, let's do that," he said.[215] "I was borderline getting pretty pissed off."[216]

Many participants on the call say General Piatt's stated concern was the optics of sending troops to the site of a democratic process.

"[T]he infamous talk about optics. That came up again. There was talk about boots on the ground again. You know, that's not good optics, having boots on the ground," Chief Contee said.[217] He recalled how Secretary McCarthy had vocalized the same hesitance during the five-day deliberation preceding January 6th.[218]

Director Rodriguez believed General Piatt replied to the request by saying, "[W]e don't like the optics of having military personnel at the Capitol against peaceful protesters."[219]

He recalls Chief Contee replying bluntly, "[W]ell, they're not peaceful anymore."[220]

Major General Walker heard one of the Army generals say it "wouldn't be their best military advice or guidance to suggest to the Secretary that we have uniformed presence at the Capitol."[221] He added: "They were concerned about how it would look, the optics."[222] Chief Sund heard the general use the word twice.[223] "General Piatt said—and I will never forget this—'Yeah, I don't know. I'm concerned about the optics of the National Guard standing a line with the Capitol in the background,'" Chief Sund said.[224] "[M]y officers are getting beaten, and they're worried about the optics of the National Guard."[225]

Although General Piatt denies explicitly using the word "optics"—"I don't recall ever saying that word on that phone call, because at the time it just wasn't important"[226]—he agreed that he said use of the Guard was "not my best military judgment or my best military advice."[227] He said he "made a couple of suggestions that were not well-received,"[228] including "if there was any other facility where we could go and relieve police . . . I think they took that as I was saying no, because they immediately came back and said, you're denying our request."[229]

General McConville—who wasn't present at the time—said he talked to people in the room about the use of the word "optics," and "some people said, 'No, it wasn't said.' And then some people said it was said."[230] Nonetheless, the sentiment behind it should not be a particularly controversial one, according to General McConville. "People like to use optics—I'm going to stay away because that's a political term in my eyes. But what type of signature do you want on the streets in Washington, DC? Do you want a police signature? Do you want a military signature? Do you want a Federal signature?" he said.[231] "[T]hat creates a reaction from the American people, and we need to think our way through that . . ."[232]

On the call, talk of needing a plan—the so-called con-op that had been a lesson learned from the summer—emerged. "[A]fter the optics, . . . then it was, you know, they wanted, like, specific information. There was something they were talking about, like, mission and . . . what exactly they're going to be doing when they get there," Chief Contee said.[233] Before running off, Secretary McCarthy had instructed General McConville to put together a plan: "My charter, my direction from him is to get a plan. We're gonna support; I just wanted to get something to support with."[234] But he acknowledged the impression nonetheless remained that he was "denying or pushing back."[235]

That impression was made explicit: "They said three times to me clearly, 'You're denying my request,'" General Piatt said.[236]

Chief Contee interrupted "Chief Sund mid-sentence" and said, "Wait a minute. Hold up. Let me make sure that I understand this correctly . . . [A]re you asking for support from the National Guard at the U.S. Capitol?"[237]

Chief Sund said, "Yes."[238]

Chief Contee then addressed the Army generals: "'Are you guys honoring his request?' I asked them that. And they didn't say 'no,' but they also didn't say 'yes.' "[239] Chief Sund recalled it the same way.[240]

General Piatt said he was "clear in my response, 'I don't have any authority to deny or approve. The Secretary is getting approval.' "[241]

"[T]he third time when they said, 'You're denying our request,' they also said, 'And we're going to go to the media,'" General Piatt said.[242] "[W]e were desperate. Everyone was desperate. So I'm not angry at that, but I just knew it wasn't helpful, so we told that to Secretary McCarthy."[243]

As for the threat to go public, Major General Walker said, "I remember that very clearly."[244] According to him, after the generals would not say yes or no, "Chief Contee says: 'I'm going to call the mayor and ask her to have a press conference saying that the Army is not going to allow the DC Guard to come and support.' "[245] General Piatt reportedly replied, "Please don't do that. I don't have the authority to authorize the National Guard to go. So please don't do that. Please don't hold the press conference."[246] Chief Contee doesn't recall saying that.[247] Mayor Bowser doesn't know if she was still on the line when the remark was made, but "it was certainly going to be something that I would do."[248]

In the end, "the call sort of ended very abruptly, . . . ."[249] The DC head of homeland security and emergency management left the call thinking "that help was not coming, and—at least [not] from the National Guard."[250] That was Chief Sund's belief, too. "[I]f a general says his troops are not coming, his troops aren't coming," he said.[251]

Before the call ended, General Flynn set up a video-conferencing bridge. General Piatt explained to the Select Committee that this was meant "to get the principals and the team together to start making a plan."[252] But Major General Walker—under whom "it was actually written . . . would maintain control of National Guard forces"[253]—said he was not privy to any planning while on the call.

"We were just told to hold," he said.[254]

How long did Major General Walker hold?

"Three hours and 19 minutes," he said.[255]

Major General Walker told the Select Committee regarding what occurred during this time. "[W]e all thought, it's in a minute, we're going to be told to go, in a minute. Then 5 minutes, then 10 minutes, then 15 minutes. We kept thinking, any minute now, somebody is going to say 'go,'" he said.[256] "And then an hour went by, then more time went by . . . . But we never thought it would take that long."[257] Col. Matthews confirmed that there were periods on the call when no one was talking.[258] At times, there was talk of securing buildings other than the Capitol.[259] He called the open channel essentially "a general officer chat line."[260]

What did Major General Walker think was happening in those 3 hours and 19 minutes?

"Delay." [261]

**An Absent Commander-in-Chief.** Vice President Mike Pence called several times to check in on the delayed response of the Guard. President Trump did not.

Vice President Pence called Acting Secretary Miller at least two times.[262] "He was very animated, and he issued very explicit, very direct, unambiguous orders. There was no question about that," General Milley said.[263] "And he said, 'Get the National Guard down here. Get them down here now, and clear the Capitol.' You know, and this is the Vice President of the United States. And there was other forceful language.' "[264]

Acting Secretary Miller clarified that "he did not order me," as "he's not in the chain of command," but he considered the talk with the Vice President "[h]yper professional" and "[v]ery focused," in which the secretary "highlighted that District of Columbia National Guard . . . was activated, and we were throwing every asset we could marshal to support law enforcement."[265]

In contrast, according to General Milley, Chief of Staff Meadows called and said, "'We have to kill the narrative that the Vice President is making all the decisions. We need to establish the narrative, you know, that the President is still in charge and that things are steady or stable,' or words to that effect. I immediately interpreted that as politics, politics, politics."[266]

President Trump himself did not call. As reports of Departments of Defense denials and delay were echoing in the media, no high-level Defense official—including Secretaries Miller[267] and McCarthy[268]—received a call from him that day.[269] At the time, General Milley thought that was "absolutely . . . highly unusual."[270]

"[Y]ou're the Commander in Chief. You've got an assault going on on the Capitol of the United States of America, and there's nothing? No call? Nothing? Zero?" he said.[271] "I grew up in an organization where commanders are responsible and take charge and they see situations unfolding and they issue orders and take charge."[272]

On January 3rd, at the end of a national security meeting concerning a foreign threat, the President asked "in passing" about January 6th preparations.[273] Acting Secretary Miller informed him they would be fulfilling Mayor Bowser's request for DC Guard support.[274] From then on, if not earlier, the secretary "felt like I had all the authorities I needed and did not need to discuss anything with the President regarding authorities."[275] The conversation lasted all of 30 seconds to a minute.[276] Secretary Miller testified that he never received any order at any time from President Trump to deploy the National Guard on January 6th. "There was no direct—there was no order from the President," he said.[277]

On January 5th, as demonstrators rallied in support of the President, Acting Secretary Miller received a call from the commander-in-chief.[278] The President asked him if he was watching the events on television.[279] The secretary told him he had caught some of the coverage.[280]

Unprompted, President Trump then said, "You're going to need 10,000 people" the following day, as in troops.[281] An email sent by Chief of Staff Meadows on January 5th explicitly noted that the DC Guard would be on hand to "protect pro Trump people."[282] The President and his staff appeared to be aware of the likelihood of violence on the day the election certification of his loss was slated to transpire. This communication from President Trump contemplated that the Guard could support and secure the safety of Trump supporters, not protect the Capitol. At that time, Secretary Miller apparently had no information on what President Trump planned for January 6th.

Acting Secretary Miller thought the 10,000 number was astronomical— "we expected 35,000 protesters . . . [and] even if there were more protesters than expected, [we thought] that local law enforcement could handle it"[283]—but, again, this was "no order from the President," just "President Trump banter that you all are familiar with."[284]

**Parallel Plans in the Midst of Crisis.** While the Army and the District engaged in the "heated"[285] 2:30 p.m. phone call, Secretary McCarthy was hurrying down the Pentagon hallways to Acting Secretary Miller's office. General Milley had been summoned there before Secretary McCarthy arrived with General McConville in tow,[286] "running down the hall, and he was actually winded when he showed up . . ."[287]

The next half hour was spent in "a quick, rapid fire meeting, [with] lots of quick questions."[288] Secretary McCarthy—out of breath—said he started by saying, "We've got to go. We've got to get something—we've got to put every capability we can up there."[289] The response he received was, "They were all kind of, like, 'Slow down. What's going on?' They wanted to get a sense of the situation."[290] Secretary McCarthy said it took about 15 to 20 minutes to "relay this," "laying out what I thought we needed to do."[291]

By 3:04 p.m., Acting Secretary Miller said he approved deployment of the DC Guard to assist law enforcement at the Capitol at that time.[292] Acting Secretary Miller did not understand why Major General Walker—if he felt the exigency demanded it—did not deploy troops as soon as his 3 p.m. order allowed it. "Why didn't he launch them? I'd love to know," he said.[293]

Secretary McCarthy agreed *"that's where we may have talked past each other in his office,"* because Secretary McCarthy thought he "had the authority as the Secretary of the Army" to conduct a mission analysis and send troops at *his* discretion, not that of Major General Walker.[294]

Major General Walker himself understood he had to wait for approval from Secretary McCarthy to deploy his forces. *But as he waited on that video call for hours, he did strongly consider sending them anyway.* He turned to his lawyer and said, "Hey, you know what? You know, we're going to go, and I'm just going to shoulder the responsibility."[295] According to Major General Walker, his lawyer responded, "What if you get sued?"[296] Colonel Mathews, that lawyer, "told him not to do that. Just hold on."[297] The Guard officials located with Major General Walker at the Armory all say he seriously contemplated aloud the possibility of breaking with the chain of command.

"Should we just deploy now and resign tomorrow?" was how Lieutenant Nick recalled Major General Walker bluntly putting it.[298]

"I would have done just that," Major General Walker said, "but not for those two letters"[299] from his superiors curtailing Guard redeployment.[300]

The man who signed one of the letters, however—himself a former member of the DC Guard[301]—now says Major General Walker should have moved forward regardless of whether he had proper authorization.

"I've launched QRF without approval more than once," Acting Secretary Miller said.[302] "If you're the person on the ground in the Army, and you realize that there's something that is unpredictable or unexpected and you have the ability to influence it, the culture, the training, the education, the expectation of you, the American people, is that you will execute and do what you can, even if it costs you your job."[303]

After authorization at 3:04 p.m., Secretary McCarthy said he gave Major General Walker a call. He told him to "[m]obilize the entire Guard, bring everybody in. . . . And I said, you know, move the QRF to the armory and get as many people as you can to the armory and configure them in a minimum of riot gear and batons. And then we're going to do a mission analysis of what we need to do with the police . . . ."[304] Major General Walker "categorically denies" that any such call took place.[305] In fact, Major General Walker said the two men did not talk at all until much later that night.[306] "Here's the bottom line. The Secretary was unavailable to me, and he never called me," Major General Walker said.[307]

Beginning around 3:00 p.m., 25 minutes of Secretary McCarthy's time was spent reassuring members of Congress that the Guard was indeed coming,[308] although he had not yet conveyed the order. That was time unspent on facilitating their actual coming. In addition to the alleged threat on the 2:30 p.m. call, a media tweet had gone out at 2:55 p.m. declaring that the Department of Defense had denied requests for Guard support.[309]

By 3:45 p.m., Secretary McCarthy was done with his calls and—after picking up some things from his office—headed down to the MPD headquarters to draft a con-op beside law enforcement.[310] Acting Secretary Miller arrived at 4:10 p.m.[311]

While he was waiting, Colonel Hunter decided he would keep the first shift handling traffic control out at their posts in case they were needed for re-mission by the MPD, relying instead only on the QRF and the second shift at the Armory to respond to the Capitol.[312] Those servicemembers ended up manning their traffic control posts up to 20 hours straight.[313] Army leadership never found out that the servicemembers at the traffic control posts didn't end up responding to the Capitol that night, incorrectly crediting some of the Guard's delay that day to their travel time.[314]

By 3:50 p.m., the QRF had arrived at the Armory, bringing their own equipment, given no new information upon making the extra pit stop there instead of the Capitol.[315] They were ready to go, steeped in "a lot of nerves."[316] The second shift of servicemembers originally missioned for traffic control had been told as early as 2:30 p.m. to expect a switch in mission to handling civil disturbance.[317] They rushed to gear up and prepare, but it was a lot of "hurry up and wait."[318] Not long afterward, "we're all ready. Now we're all donned. So go sit on the bleachers and wait . . . We were in a tight holding pattern until the time to deploy."[319]

At around the same time, at 3:49 p.m., Speaker Pelosi is heard in video footage from that day urging Acting Secretary Miller to hurry.

"Just pretend for a moment this was the Pentagon or the White House or some other entity that was under siege," she told him over the phone while she—and the rest of the Congressional leadership—were huddled in a secure location.[320] "Just get them there!"[321]

When Secretary McCarthy arrived at MPD headquarters, he joined Chief Contee, his Army Operations Director Brigadier General Chris LaNeve, and Assistant Chief Carroll by phone.[322]

In the next 20 minutes, Secretary McCarthy developed a con-op.

As Secretary McCarthy had decided after the summer, crafting a strategy was his job—"I was doing it with the Mayor, the police chief, and the deputy director of the FBI, my counterparts, and then ultimately wanted to understand what our role would be, the conditions"—and afterward, "we turned to [Major General Walker] to work the tactical details for that."[323]

But Major General Walker said, "If I need you to tell me how to execute a civil disturbance mission," he "[s]hould relieve me. Should fire me."[324]

It wasn't until later, post-January 6th, that Major General Walker said he found out that Secretary McCarthy, his boss, had been putting together a con-op—without him. "Then later they said they had to put together a plan for me to execute . . . which I found kind of disturbing," Major General Walker said.[325] "You're coming up with a plan without me being involved in the plan?"[326]

General McConville agreed that "usually[,] the Secretary of Army is not developing concepts for the employment, but because of the situation that wasn't done," so the secretary had to fill in the gap.[327] That, of course—given the preparations Colonel Hunter had laid out hours earlier—was not true. But Secretary McCarthy did not know that.[328]

He said Major General Walker never told him about how Colonel Hunter had prepared and that it was his responsibility to tell him.[329] "I don't talk to troop lead commanders, no," he said.[330]

Ultimately, no plan from Army leaders—strategic or tactical—made it to the troops.

"[I]f they came up with a plan, they never shared it with us," Major General Walker said.[331] *They claim they were putting a plan together. That's what took so long. I never saw a plan from the Department of Defense or the Department of the Army."*[332]

Colonel Hunter agreed that "[n]o one ever told me, because I already had the plan there, and no one ever informed me that there was a different plan or a different [con-op]."[333] He said to the extent a "hasty plan" was put into action on January 6th, it was his: "I created the concept of operation."[334] He added: "The [plan] that was actually used as far as which lot they would come into, who would meet them at the lot, and then who would lead them over to the Capitol. That was between myself and MPD and Capitol Police."[335]

After hours of wait, Major General Walker said, "The plan was executed just like we said it would be [from the start], get to the Capitol, take direction from the ranking police officers there . . . to help restore order."[336] Colonel Hunter passed the details of his hasty plan onto Lt. Col. Reinke—the highest ranking officer at the rally point—letting him know, "Hey, when you pull into this lot, they will meet you there. This is who is—you know, you're going with these personnel," exactly what Secretary McCarthy had just spent 20 minutes putting together.[337]

Although Lt. Col. Reinke said his QRF servicemembers were given rules of engagement before arriving at the rally point, he was not told more than report to Capitol Police and supplement and assist them.[338]

Captain Tarp, outranked by Lt. Col. Reinke but in charge of the second shift, was merely told by Brigadier General Ryan: "'You need to act like there's a fire now. You're going to [the] Capitol.' Those were his directions."[339]

*After an hour and a half spent in calls, travel, and making plans, Secretary McCarthy was prepared to green light the deployment of the Guard at 4:35 p.m.* But miscommunication led to another half-hour delay.

Secretary McCarthy relayed the "go" order to Major General Walker—with his subordinate Brigadier General LaNeve serving as the intermediary—in a conversation Major General Walker said never happened.

According to Secretary McCarthy, Brigadier General LaNeve "wasn't a junior aide."[340] In his role, "he can speak, once given the authority, delegated authority to speak as the Sec Army . . ."[341] He said that the first-star officer "was standing next to me,"[342] and General Piatt said that it was generally "not uncommon" for him to ask his staff to "transmit [the] communication from the Secretary to General Walker."[343]

For his part, Brigadier General LaNeve denies that he himself conveyed the "go" order.[344] He said he spoke with Major General Walker first at 4:25 p.m. to tell him that his forces should, "Get on the bus, do not leave."[345] On a second call at 4:35 p.m., Brigadier General LaNeve said he overheard Secretary McCarthy himself convey the "go" order to Major General Walker: He said something "to the effect of 'You're approved to provide support.'"[346] Secretary McCarthy, on his part, said he never spoke a word.[347]

Brigadier General LaNeve said the secretary then again handed him the phone to convey the details of "where to go and what officer to meet up with."[348] Those two details would be the full extent of the "con-op" allegedly communicated to Major General Walker.[349] He even recalled Major General Walker saying, "Roger," to acknowledge the plan.[350] But, Brigadier General LaNeve said, there was "mass confusion in that room," and he agreed that "[t]here were huge communications problems."[351]

Major General Walker said there was no such call, nor any like it.[352] He said he remained on the video conference line the whole time "with everybody else," he said.[353] He said he would not have taken an order from Brigadier General LaNeve anyhow. "[W]hy would I ever take directions from General LaNeve? Anybody? Brigadier General LaNeve, one-star," Major General Walker said.[354] "I mean, he's not a peer, it wouldn't be somebody that would convey that type of message to me. . . So my thinking wouldn't have been that he would have been speaking on behalf of the Secretary."[355]

Although his staff confirms they didn't see him field a call from Secretary McCarthy or Brigadier General LaNeve,[356] including never seeing him leave their conference room,[357] Major General Walker's own note taker appears to have jotted down at 4:37 p.m. the following: "advised to sent [sic] 150 to establish D st / 1st outer perimeter, General LaNeve," beside what appears to be his phone number.[358] That address is the rally point

Secretary McCarthy had asked General LaNeve to convey, the same one Colonel Hunter and law enforcement had already chosen earlier. Major General Walker said, "the only way [Lt. Nick] could have got it was listening to the VTC, which I was on." [359] He further said, "I never saw General LaNeve on the [video teleconference] . . . I didn't hear General LaNeve's voice." [360] Lt. Nick said he had it penned at much later—at 5:09 p.m.—"as the time they received the orders" to deploy. [361]

Major General Walker certainly did not *act* as if he had been given authority until, fortuitously, General McConville—who had heard about the 4:35 p.m. call—walked by the teleconference screen and was "surprised" to see the commanding general sitting idly at 5:09 p.m. [362]

Major General Walker agreed the first time he heard he had the authority was from the lips of the general: "General McConville came back into the call and said, Hey, you're a go." [363]

Lt. Col. Reinke's QRF and Captain Tarp's second shift got on the bus at 5:10 p.m. [364] They left at 5:15 p.m. [365] Lt. Col. Reinke said they didn't arrive at the Capitol Police parking lot until 5:55 p.m., [366] although official timing from the Army and Department of Defense put their arrival time at 5:40 p.m. and from the DC Guard at 5:20 p.m. [367] At the earliest, the troops arrived in the vicinity of the Capitol grounds at 5:29 p.m., when Lt. Col. Reinke texted Colonel Hunter: "Apparently we pulled into the wrong lot, trying to reroute to LOT 16 now." [368] He said they sat around for 20 minutes once they arrived, and then were sworn in, before relieving an entire line of officers. [369] Captain Tarp said they remained idle for 45 minutes waiting for Capitol Police to come "bus by bus to swear-in the officers. It was a long wait. Frustrating—we're sitting a mile from where we['re] going." [370]

Captain Tarp said, "By the time we got there, we were just holding back the people who remained past the curfew." [371] The height of the riot had passed.

Colonel Hunter estimated that—had his preparations been approved—the DC Guard could have arrived as early as an hour and a half earlier than they did.

"Within one hour, I'd say I could've had 135. So the [about 40] coming from Joint Base Andrews, if they would've headed directly to me at the Capitol, and then the 90 I had on the street and the 4 that were—including myself," he said. [372] "[S]o I arrived at the Capitol at 3:10. So, if I would've recalled everyone by 3:30, 3:40, we could've been—had gear on and walking towards the Capitol." [373]

He further stated: "I would give them another hour. So by 4:40 I should've had at least 250 coming from the Armory . . . That includes the second shift as well as full-timers." [374]

Presented with the plans Colonel Hunter had set in motion and the easy accessibility of their equipment, neither of which he had known about at the time, Secretary McCarthy conceded "you could have shaved minutes," [375] and the speed of deployment "could have" been pushed up, but "[i]t depends." [376]

When the Guard finally arrived at the Capitol, "pretty much all the other fighting, per se, had stopped on the Capitol complex," according to Robert Glover, head of the MPD Special Operations Division.[377] Then-Inspector Glover received the Guard troops when they arrived.[378] "[T]he bus just kind of showed up. It was my decision at that point, looking at their numbers and their capabilities at that moment in time and what was the most pressing activity—and that was to make the arrests," he said.[379] He had them create a secure "prisoner cordon" where they could stand guard as arrested individuals waited transport to jail.[380] "They were the freshest personnel that we had at that moment in time. And, again, they didn't have any significant numbers to really do much else at that moment in time either," he said.[381] "[T]heir orders were basically, support us in whatever we told them to do . . ." [382]

Secretary McCarthy said that it was possible that DOD and DC National Guard leaders had simply not been coordinating their planning.[383] He acknowledged that "a lot of things were probably missed. It was tremendously confusing," [384] and "that makes for a messy response." [385]

No one within the Department of Defense, Army, or Guard leveled accusations of an intentional delay. "I didn't see anybody trying to throw sand in the gearbox and slow things down," General Milley said.[386]

Major General Walker said the Army's reluctance to approve National Guard assistance to the Mayor during the planning for the anticipated January 6th events continued through January 6th itself.[387] "I don't know where the decision paralysis came from, but it was clearly there. The decision paralysis, decision avoidance," he said.[388]

## CONCLUSION

Former President Trump's eagerness to engage the U.S. military to play a visible role in addressing domestic unrest during the late spring and summer of 2020 does appear to have prompted senior military leadership to take precautions, in preparing for the joint session, against the possibility that the DC Guard might be ordered to deploy for an improper purpose. Those precautions seem to have been prudential as much as legal in nature.

What that entailed in the unprecedented circumstances of the January 6th attack on the Capitol is, however, harder to accept: a 3 hour and 19 minute lag-time in making a relatively small, but riot-trained and highly capable military unit available to conduct one of its statutory support missions.

While the delay seems unnecessary and unacceptable, it was the byproduct of military processes, institutional caution, and a revised deployment approval process. We have no evidence that the delay was intentional. Likewise, it appears that none of the individuals involved understood what President Trump planned for January 6th, and how he would behave during the violence. Imperfect inter-government and intra-military communications as the January 6th rally morphed, with President Trump's active encouragement, into a full-blown riot at the Capitol also help explain the time it took to deploy Guard troops to the Capitol after their assistance there was requested and approved. Post-hoc evaluation of real-time communications during an unprecedented and evolving crisis and limited tactical intelligence, nevertheless, carries the risk of a precision that was unrealistic at the time. It is also clear from testimony provided to the Select Committee that DoD and DC National Guard leaders have differing perspectives that are not reconcilable regarding the timing of deployment authorization.

Where the DC Guard's deployment on January 6th is concerned, then, the "lessons learned" at this juncture include: careful evaluation on the basis of limited information may take time; statutorily constrained inter-governmental requests for assistance and multi-level approval processes are complex and may be time-consuming; any visible military presence in the domestic setting is circumscribed by law and triggers considerable, constitutionally-driven sensitivities; and crisis communications are often imperfect, especially in unforeseen and rapidly evolving situations.

# THE BIG RIP-OFF: FOLLOW THE MONEY

## INTRODUCTION

This appendix will consider the extent to which President Trump's Campaign and related entities raised an unprecedented amount of political donations using inflammatory messaging alleging that the 2020 U.S. Presidential election was fraudulent or stolen. It will review what tools and methods were used to produce, transmit and optimize these fundraising solicitations; who drafted and approved the messaging and what they knew about the accuracy of the messaging; who ultimately benefitted from these donations; and the impact of these messages on their recipients.

The Select Committee's investigation demonstrates that President Trump's baseless claims of election fraud—the Big Lie—served a dual purpose, forming the foundation of his attempts to overturn the 2020 Presidential election and launching a fundraising effort to fund the former President's other endeavors and to enrich his associates—the Big Rip-off.

The false election fraud narrative embedded in fundraising emails and text messages amplified the Big Lie by perpetuating a belief that the 2020 election was stolen from President Trump and effectuated the Big Rip-off by misleading donors into thinking their donations could alter the election results.

At the same time, the Big Lie helped President Trump and the Republican National Committee (RNC) raise more than $250 million after the election, much of it from small-dollar donors who were promised their money would "Stop the Steal."

Despite what they told their supporters, however, most of their money was not used to stop any purported steal—it was diverted to accomplish the Big Rip-off. Millions of dollars that were raised ostensibly for "election defense" and "fighting voter fraud" were not spent that way at all.

Moreover, the Select Committee's investigation shows that the *RNC knew* that President Trump's claims about winning the election were baseless and that post-election donations would not help him secure an additional term in office. Yet, both the Trump Campaign and the RNC decided to continue fundraising after the election, *a decision that would have come from President Trump himself.*

In short, President Trump and his Campaign ripped off supporters by raising more than $250 million by claiming they wanted to fight fraud they knew did not exist and to challenge an election they knew he lost.

## DISCUSSION

### THE TRUMP CAMPAIGN FUNDRAISING TEAM

As detailed below, the Trump Campaign misled the American public and President Trump's donors on how they planned to use, and did use, the donated funds while bombarding supporters with hundreds of emails, as many as twenty-five emails per day, stating the election had been stolen. In those emails, they used inflammatory language accusing Democrats of trying to "steal the election," encouraged supporters to join the "Trump army"; "Defend" the election: and to "fight back" over, and over, and over again.[1] They sent these emails out because they knew they were effective at raising money.[2] This was made possible by the creation of a fundraising machine powered jointly by the Trump Campaign and the RNC.

### A. The TMAGAC Fundraising Machine

During the 2020 election cycle, President Trump operated a structure under which the Trump reelection campaign and the RNC merged programs and raised money jointly through the Trump Make America Great Again Committee (internally referred to by its acronym TMAGAC, which RNC officials pronounced "T-Magic").[3] TMAGAC was focused on raising money online through small-dollar donations.[4] Tim Murtaugh, the Trump Campaign's communications director, described the TMAGAC fundraising operation as "an entity unto itself within the campaign."[5]

The individual charged with leading the digital operation in 2020 was Gary Coby.[6] Coby first started working with the RNC in 2016 even before President Trump became the nominee.[7] Coby explained that, as digital director, his role during the 2020 Presidential election cycle was to "oversee the digital operation."[8] Similarly, senior staffers at the Trump Campaign and the RNC all made clear that Coby was the individual in charge of the TMAGAC digital team.[9] Both high-level staffers at the Trump Campaign and at the RNC confirmed that Coby had the trust of Jared Kushner, the President's son-in-law.[10]

Coby explained that during the 2020 Presidential election cycle, the TMAGAC digital team was a "big team with multiple organizations and vendor teams all working together as one, that include[d] RNC staff, [Donald J. Trump for President] staff, [and] maybe a half dozen vendor teams."[11] The RNC digital team, a subset of the TMAGAC digital team, was led operationally by Kevin Zambrano, Chief Digital Officer at the RNC. In 2020, members of the digital staff of both the RNC and Trump Campaign merged in an office building in Arlington, Virginia, with some suites jointly hosting RNC and Trump Campaign staff on the digital team, and other suites hosting third-party companies, such as Opn Sesame and Direct Persuasion.[12] Thereafter, Zambrano assisted Coby in managing the TMAGAC digital team.[13] Zambrano explained, "The majority of the staff was at the RNC doing both RNC and TMAGAC work."[14] This work was focused squarely on fundraising.[15]

The RNC digital team included Austin Boedigheimer, who, starting in January 2019, was the RNC's digital deputy director[16] and technically served as Zambrano's deputy.[17] In reality, Boedigheimer reported to both Zambrano and Coby.[18] Boedigheimer also led the TMAGAC digital fundraising team, which was comprised of all online fundraising efforts, including fundraising emails and text messages.[19] At the end of the 2020 cycle, that team had 20 or 30 people within smaller teams, such as the copy team, the text message team, the data team, the advertising team, and the graphics team.[20]

The RNC digital team also included a team of copywriters, who were responsible for writing the fundraising emails and text messages to solicit small-dollar donations through TMAGAC.[21] These copywriters reported to Hanna Allred, the RNC's Chief Copywriter.[22] By mid-2020, there were three copywriters who reported to Allred: Alex Murglin,[23] Ethan Katz,[24] and Alex Blinkoff.[25] Blinkoff and Katz worked in that role from June 2020 until they were fired approximately three weeks after the 2020 election, while Murglin remains a copywriter at the RNC.

Although the TMAGAC team consisted of both Trump Campaign and RNC staffers, TMAGAC operated as one entity working towards one goal—raising as much money as possible.[26]

## B. The Fundraising Assembly Line

The copywriting process worked like an assembly line, where different individuals performed a task and passed on the work product to someone else, including for internal approval.[27] To generate content for fundraising communications, Allred explained, the copywriting fundraising team was "watching the messaging coming out of the committee [RNC] and the campaign and from the President himself and what his family was talking about."[28] For example, in a November 2020 email, Boedigheimer stated to Allred, "Good to include lines like [']we need the resources to make sure they don't try to steal this election. We saw what happened on election night, we can't let them take the senate too.[']"[29]

It was evident that the copywriters "would draft a lot of the content based on…what the President was saying."[30] And there was no mistaking it, President Trump "was providing us [the copywriters] with a lot of content online."[31] Allred said Boedigheimer was encouraging her to use this language because it would cause President Trump's supporters to donate by "giving a purpose to their donation"[32] and that they used this repeatedly because it worked.[33] Boedigheimer did not dispute this, and reaffirmed that such language had been successful at fundraising.[34]

Further, the emails that were signed by President Trump or "Team Trump" were intentionally drafted to capture President Trump's voice, tone and messaging.[35] Boedigheimer explained, "[President Trump] obviously has a very aggressive[,] excitable tone, and we would try to incorporate that in our messaging as well."[36] The goal was to make the millions of recipients of aggressive, hyperbolic fundraising emails believe that the emails were coming from President Trump himself. In Zambrano's words, the purpose was to give recipients "red meat."[37]

## C. The Approvals Process

**The Structure.** Draft emails were submitted for approval to a designated group that handled approvals of all TMAGAC fundraising copy (the "Approvals Group").[38] Boedigheimer retained responsibility for ensuring that TMAGAC's fundraising copy was approved before being sent to the public.[39]

The Approvals Group consisted of three sets of stakeholders from the RNC and the Trump Campaign,[40] and included a variety of other interested staffers, including Zambrano, Boedigheimer, and Allred.[41] TMAGAC's fundraising copy could not be sent without approval from the legal, communications and research departments.[42]

**Perceived Responsibilities.** After election day, a small group of staffers in the Approvals Group actively reviewed and approved the numerous fundraising emails and text messages that spread false election fraud claims. These staffers included:

- **RNC Legal:** Justin Reimer, RNC Chief Counsel[43] and Jenna Kirsch, RNC Associate Counsel[44]
- **RNC Communications:** Cassie Docksey, Deputy Communications Director[45]
- **RNC Research:** Michael Reed, Deputy Chief of Staff for Communications[46]
- **Trump Campaign Legal:** Alex Cannon, Deputy General Counsel[47]
- **Trump Campaign Communications and Research:** Zach Parkinson, Deputy Director of Communications and Director of Research[48]

Boedigheimer, as head of the fundraising team handling the drafting and propagation of fundraising messaging, told the Select Committee his understanding of the role the three components of the Approvals Group (legal, communications, and research) performed when reviewing emails and text messages.

Regarding legal, Boedigheimer explained that he understood Alex Cannon's role, as the Trump Campaign's Deputy General Counsel, was to review the emails from a "legal perspective" by "essentially making sure that there's no legal issues with the content."[49]

Regarding communications, Boedigheimer stated that the communications staffers in the Approvals Group were reviewing the content and "[m]aking sure that it's on message and good from a comms perspective."[50]

Lastly, Boedigheimer explained that the research team was "looking for . . . things that are inaccurate."[51]

Although Boedigheimer provided only a vague explanation of the role of the Approvals Group, he emphasized that he had to "trust that the research, the comms, and the legal team are going to do their processes to make sure it's [the TMAGAC fundraising copy was] accurate."[52] He further noted, "[I]t was the approval chain's job to see what the accuracy of the email is and whether it's true or not. . . . We were sending information and then leaning on our approval chain to make sure that it's accurate."[53]

The Select Committee's investigation revealed that the Approvals Group did not operate that way, however. The Select Committee interviewed members of the Approvals Group handling the communications, research, and legal functions and confirmed that members of the Approvals Group typically engaged only in cursory reviews of the fundraising messages and did not review substantive claims of election fraud for accuracy.

Zach Parkinson, the Trump Campaign's Deputy Director of Communications and Research Director, represented the Trump Campaign's communications and research functions in the Approvals Group. Parkinson made clear, "Generally, our role when it came to fundraising emails and texts was to approve them for the communications team."[54] Parkinson noted that that he was typically the person who weighed in on behalf of the Trump Campaign's communications and research team.[55] He added, "we would review them for messaging consistency, sometimes we would review them for factual accuracy, and then we would provide the communications approval for those."[56]

Parkinson clarified that the scope of review for "factual accuracy" was limited. Specifically, his review of fundraising emails and text messages for accuracy was limited to questions concerning items such as time and location.[57]

Critically, Parkinson did not review statements regarding election fraud in the fundraising copy for accuracy because "most political text messages and fundraising emails are political rhetoric, and so a lot of them don't necessarily require fact checking."[58] He added that "political rhetoric," such as "Democrats are trying to steal the election," was not something he and his team were "necessarily tasked to say no to."[59] Parkinson made clear that he thought the legal department, namely Alex Cannon, would handle reviewing for accuracy, noting "I deferred to the legal team on the legitimacy and the ability to substantiate claims that were made that were put through these approvals and whether or not we could, again, substantiate them or they were in line with our legal efforts."[60] Parkinson, as the head of the research team, the very campaign team meant to fact-check and ensure accuracy in the Trump Campaign's statements, said he was "simply looking for messaging consistency."[61] Whether Democrats were engaged in fraud to steal the election was a "political argument" to Parkinson, which he did not review for accuracy.[62]

Like Parkinson, Michael Reed, then the RNC's Deputy Chief of Staff for Communications, was not reviewing the TMAGAC emails about election fraud for broader accuracy. Notably, Reed could not recall a single email that he researched to do a fact-check or follow up on to see if claims contained in the email were, in fact, true.[63]

Boedigheimer and the copywriters believed the research staffers were looking for messages that they believed were inaccurate, but they were doing no such thing.

Alex Cannon, the Trump Campaign's legal representative in the Approvals Group, was no different—the TMAGAC fundraisers thought he was doing far more than he was in fact doing. The Select Committee received a November 4, 2020, email from Nathan Groth, counsel for the Trump Campaign, to Alex Cannon. This email reflected that Cannon was not tasked with substantively reviewing fundraising emails like Boedigheimer thought. Groth wrote to Cannon, "Matt [Morgan, Trump Campaign's General Counsel] has instructed me to hand off all compliance matters, including approvals, to you."[64] Cannon confirmed, "I saw myself as doing exactly what I was instructed to do here, which is do what Nathan had previously been doing. So it's this. It's compliance issues like disclaimers and typos."[65] Therefore, when Cannon received emails that included claims such as "the Democrats are trying to steal the election," he viewed reviewing the veracity of this statement as "outside the purview of what [he] was tasked."[66] When asked, Cannon stated that he did not know who was tasked with ensuring that fundraising emails were true and accurate.[67]

Boedigheimer, and other members of the digital fundraising team he led, claimed to see the Approvals Group as a guardrail of sorts in the fundraising effort to protect from the dissemination of false messaging about the election, but the Approvals Group served no such role. The very staffers in the Approvals Group repeatedly told the Select Committee that they did not review the claims about election fraud to confirm whether they were even true.

When all was said and done, no one in the Trump Campaign claimed to be responsible for confirming the accuracy of President Trump's words, or other allegations of election fraud, before they were blasted to millions of Americans.[68]

Thus, after the election, the TMAGAC team drafted emails filled with inflammatory and unfounded claims, and the members of the Approvals Group tasked with fact checking these claims did no such thing—effectively, President Trump's claims were treated as true and blasted to millions of people with little to no scrutiny by those tasked with ensuring accuracy. This process was a fertile ground for the Big Lie to spread through hundreds of emails and text messages.

### D. Focus on Fundraising Metrics

Boedigheimer spoke with Coby and Zambrano often about how much money TMAGAC was raising, and they provided feedback regarding fund-raising goals.[69] Trump Campaign leadership was fully aware of post-election fundraising totals. According to Coby, President Trump's son-in-law and senior advisor Jared Kushner "had the most interest in the digital program" and "would just check in on [fundraising] results," and routinely received updates regarding fundraising from Coby.[70] Coby also made clear that Kushner was heavily involved in the Campaign's budget process[71] and that he updated Kushner on TMAGAC's post-election fundraising totals.[72]

The Select Committee received documents confirming Kushner's involvement. For example, on November 8, 2020, Kushner requested that a daily tracker be created showing the Trump Campaign's financial position from election day forward.[73] In an email, Kushner noted that the tracker would allow the Campaign to consider its cash flow ahead of the creation of "a new entity for POTUS['s] other political activities."[74] Just days after the election, and after the Campaign had three of its four best fundraising days ever on November 4th, 5th, and 6th,[75] Kushner was preparing for the launch of President Trump's new leadership PAC, Save America. Kushner stated that he needed this new daily tracker because the Trump Campaign was going to continue fundraising post-election.[76] Kushner continued to receive these detailed daily trackers, which included Save America's fund-raising hauls, through at least December 2020.[77]

### 2020 ELECTION: THE ROLE OF ELECTION FRAUD MESSAGING

### A. The Decision to Continue Fundraising after Election Day

Heading into election night of the 2020 Presidential race, as Americans across the country waited in line to vote on election day, the Trump Campaign and the RNC were planning what they would tell the American public about the results in the upcoming days. On election day, Boedigheimer and

Darren Centinello, a Trump Campaign staffer, discussed the three message options that the Trump Campaign had on the table.[78]

The first option was to send out copy claiming President Trump had won the 2020 election. But the Campaign knew this message was false, and Boedigheimer told Centinello that he could not get this messaging approved yet.[79] The Trump Campaign's second option was an email stating they were still waiting on the election results. This message would have been *the truth*. The Campaign rejected this option.

Instead, the Trump Campaign chose a third option. Boedigheimer confirmed that TMAGAC fundraisers had received approval for copy claiming that the Democrats are going to "try to steal the election" *before* election night.[80]

Zambrano confirmed that it would not surprise him that TMAGAC was immediately claiming that Democrats were trying to steal the election, because President Trump has been pushing that message.[81] Zambrano added, "That was the President's phrasing in the messaging that the team was sourcing from."[82] Importantly, Boedigheimer confirmed that the TMAGAC copywriting team did *not* base its use of the "trying to steal" language on any awareness of actual fraud.[83]

### B. Post-Election Fundraising Off the Big Lie

Both the Trump Campaign and the RNC directed TMAGAC to continue fundraising after the election.[84] Justin Clark, the deputy campaign manager, explained that the decision to continue fundraising after the election would have come from President Trump himself.[85]

Starting after the election and until January 6th, the Trump Campaign, along with the RNC, sent millions of emails to their supporters, with messaging such as claiming that the election was "RIGGED."[86] The Trump Campaign viewed the TMAGAC emails as another avenue to get out President Trump's post-election messaging about the alleged fraud.[87] These emails used false claims of voter fraud to create a sense of urgency that the election was being stolen. The Trump Campaign and the RNC told their supporters that their donations could stop Democrats from "trying to steal the election." They consistently encouraged donors to give money to continue "uncovering" fraud that had not occurred. These emails were sent out after being reviewed and approved by the Approvals Group.[88]

The TMAGAC fundraisers used inflammatory language and false election fraud claims after the election because it was both effective at fundraising and accurately captured President Trump's ongoing tone and messaging.[89] When the digital fundraising team drafted emails claiming, for example, that "Democrats are trying to steal the election," they did not bother to confirm whether or not those inflammatory statements were true, and instead they merely took President Trump's words and made an effective fundraising email.[90] As Zambrano stated, "the President issuing statements or tweets would be the genesis of the copy that would then go into the approval process for edits, for checks. That is why the approval process worked."[91] President Trump was the source of the lies. Not only was President Trump's fundraising driven by his daily deluge of lies about the election, but these lies were also able to go unchallenged before being spread because TMAGAC had an ineffective process when it came to scrutinizing and correcting those lies.

The TMAGAC fundraising machine continued to churn out hundreds of fundraising emails and text messages regardless of external developments. For example, Zambrano said that, after former Vice President Biden was widely declared the winner of the election, TMAGAC's fundraising efforts moved ahead the same way they had previously,[92] even though he "would say it wasn't looking good" as soon as one week after the election.[93]

### ALARMS RAISED ABOUT TMAGAC FUNDRAISING CONTENT

A number of individuals and entities associated with the TMAGAC fundraising campaign raised concerns about the dangerous and inflammatory language used in the emails issued for this campaign.

#### Concerns Raised in Internal RNC Review

Evidence obtained by the Select Committee shows that the RNC knew that President Trump's claims about winning the election were baseless and that additional donations would not help him secure an additional term in office. They walked as close to the line as they dared—making several changes to fundraising copy that seemingly protected the RNC from legal exposure while still spreading and relying on President Trump's known lies and misrepresentations.

The Select Committee did not interview a member of the RNC legal team due to concerns surrounding attorney-client privilege, but the Select Committee nonetheless got insight into their role from documents produced by Campaign and RNC staff, as well as interviews with staffers. As detailed below, the RNC lawyers were the only individuals who even attempted to walk back the fundraising emails.

Allred and Katz both received direction from the RNC's lawyers shortly after the election to not say "steal the election" and instead were told to use "try to steal the election."[94] Allred also recalled that, at some point, the RNC legal team directed the copywriters not to use the term "rigged."[95]

After the media called the election for former Vice President Joe Biden on Saturday, November 7, 2020, the RNC began to quietly pull back from definitive language about President Trump having won the election and instead used language of insinuation. For example, on November 10, 2020, Justin Reimer, RNC's then-chief counsel, revised a fundraising email sent to the Approvals Group to remove the sentence that "Joe Biden should not wrongfully claim the office of the President."[96] Instead, Reimer indicated the email should read, "Joe Biden does not get to decide when this election ends. Only LEGAL ballots must be counted and verified."[97] Both Alex Cannon and Zach Parkinson signed off on Reimer's edits.[98]

On November 11, 2020, Reimer again revised a fundraising email sent to the Approvals Group. This time, he revised a claim that "President Trump won this election by a lot" to instead state that "President Trump got 71 MILLION LEGAL votes."[99] Once again Cannon and Parkinson signed off on Reimer's edits.[100]

Also on November 11, 2020, Jenna Kirsch, associate counsel at the RNC, revised a fundraising email sent to the Approvals Group to, among other things, remove the request "to step up and contribute to our critical **Election Defense Fund** so that we can DEFEND the Election and secure FOUR MORE YEARS."[101] Instead of "secure FOUR MORE YEARS," Kirsch's revised version stated a contribution would "finish the fight."[102] Once again Cannon and Parkinson signed off on these edits for the Trump Campaign.[103] Regarding the change to finish the fight, Zambrano conceded, "I would say this a substantive change from the legal department."[104] Kirsch made numerous edits like this, in which she removed assertions about "four more years."[105] Such edits continued into late November 2020.

Further, Boedigheimer stated that he took questions to RNC legal in the post-election period about TMAGAC fundraisers using the "steal the election" language.[106] The RNC was clearly aware that President Trump's claims regarding the election were not true and tried to have it both ways.

The private split between the RNC and the Trump Campaign became even more pronounced when President Trump decided to double down on his false election fraud claims and chose Rudolph Giuliani to lead his legal efforts to overturn the election.[107] On November 19, 2020, Giuliani held a press conference at the RNC's headquarters in which he falsely suggested that the Biden Campaign orchestrated an elaborate nationwide voter-fraud scheme.[108] Cassie Docksey, a senior RNC staffer at the time, recalled that she spoke that day with Michael Ahrens, then the RNC's communications director, about the diverging from the Trump Campaign.[109] Ahrens told her that the RNC would no longer automatically amplify or replicate statements from the Trump Campaign or President Trump's legal team.[110] Docksey understood Ahrens to be relaying a decision made at the most senior levels of the RNC.[111]

Ahrens asserted that the RNC was unwilling to adopt the wide-ranging, baseless assertions President Trump's legal team was making and quietly decided to focus its communication strategy elsewhere.[112] Distancing the RNC from President Trump's false statements was a "regular course of the job before the election," and it "carried through after the election" in relation to President Trump's false claims about the election.[113] Starting at or before the November 19, 2020, press conference, the RNC senior leadership was in agreement that they would not claim that President Trump had won the election,[114] although the RNC "frequently" had to have internal discussions about President Trump's false statements about the election.[115]

According to Michael Reed, then the RNC's deputy chief of staff for communications, "there were conversations amongst [RNC] legal and comms and digital to ensure that anything that was being written by the digital team based off of something President Trump or the Campaign said was something we all were more comfortable with."[116] RNC Chairwoman McDaniel was a part of these conversations.[117]

RNC leadership knew that President Trump was lying to the American people. Yet, they did nothing to publicly distance themselves from his efforts to overturn the election. The RNC's response was merely to tinker around the edges of the fundraising copy but never to fundamentally challenge the one message that remained present in TMAGAC's post-election fundraising copy—President Trump's Big Lie.

In the end, multiple senior RNC staffers approved fundraising emails raising questions about the election results even though they did not know of any evidence about fraud impacting the winner of the 2020 Presidential election. For example, Cassie Docksey stated that she was not aware of any fraud that impacted the results of the Presidential election.[118] Ahrens conceded that "there was not evidence that we [the RNC] had seen that he [President Trump] won the election, that Biden had not won the election."[119]

Similarly, Justin Clark was "not aware of [fraudulent activity . . . to like defraud voters] by an individual or an entity that would have [changed the outcome of an election]."[120] Alex Cannon "did not find or see, in [his] limited ability as one individual . . . evidence that would be sufficient within the time period to change any sort of election results in any of the States."[121]

Nonetheless, the RNC and the Trump Campaign continued to send out hundreds of emails, spreading the Big Lie to and fundraising off of millions of supporters. Even though the RNC had closely held reservations about repeating the most extreme and unsupportable claims of fraud, the RNC stayed the course with a coordinated, single fundraising plan with the Trump Campaign. The RNC privately and quietly softened the most blatantly egregious claims written by its own copywriters but publicly stood shoulder to shoulder with President Trump and his Big Lie.

This is clearly evidenced by multiple TMAGAC emails in late December 2020 that asserted that former Vice President Joe Biden would be an "illegitimate President" when he took office.[122] These emails came after December 14, 2020, the day electors from each State met to cast their votes for President and Vice President. These emails came after Senate Majority Leader Mitch McConnell made it clear that he accepted the electoral college's certification of Biden's victory. These emails came after President Trump and his allies had lost all but one lawsuit challenging the election.[123] None of this made a difference to TMAGAC. When asked why TMAGAC would repeatedly send these emails stating that former Vice President Biden would be an illegitimate President, Hanna Allred, the chief copywriter, stated that it would be because the emails were "effective" for fundraising.[124]

### Trump Campaign Discussions

Alex Cannon was so bothered by the emails he was reviewing as a member of the Approvals Group that he took his concerns to Justin Clark, the campaign's deputy campaign manager. Cannon explained that he had discussions with Clark about the problematic tone of the post-election TMAGAC emails and noted to Clark that the emails "seemed a little over the top to [him]."[125] Cannon raised those concerns because, after spending weeks researching which fraud claims were verifiable and which were not, Cannon saw that the TMAGAC emails were inconsistent with the fact that systemic fraud did not exist.[126] Cannon also recalled that he may have expressed concern to Matt Morgan, the campaign's general counsel, regarding the difference between claims of election fraud made in the TMAGAC fundraising emails and his conclusion that there was not fraud that impacted the election results.[127] Cannon was not aware of any actions taken to address the concerns he had with this inconsistency.[128]

Justin Clark could not recall whether he looked at any fundraising emails after Cannon raised these concerns or whether Cannon spoke to Gary Coby about the substance of the fundraising emails.[129]

### Challenges From Within the Digital Team

In the days after the election, one junior copywriter presented senior Campaign staffers with a template for a more honest approach. Shortly after election night, Coby led a meeting of the entire Trump digital team, which included individuals from the Campaign, the RNC, Opn Sesame, Direct Persuasion, and others. In that meeting, as Coby addressed the staff and expressed that the digital team would continue to work, Ethan Katz, an RNC staffer in his early twenties, rose to ask a question:[130] How were staffers supposed to tell voters that the Trump Campaign wanted to keep counting votes in Arizona but stop counting votes in other States (like Pennsylvania, Georgia, and Michigan)?[131]

Katz said that Coby provided an answer without substance, which caused Katz to reiterate his question. His question made clear that the Campaign's position was wildly inconsistent.[132] Allred and Boedigheimer corroborated that Katz confronted leadership.[133]

Katz also recalled that, shortly after the election, Allred directed him to write an email declaring that President Trump had won the State of Pennsylvania before anyone had called Pennsylvania for either party.[134] Katz believed the Trump Campaign wanted to send this email out to preempt a potential call that was likely to be in former Vice President Biden's favor.[135] He refused to write the email. Allred was stunned, and instead assigned it to another copywriter.[136] Allred confirmed that Katz expressed discomfort at writing such an email and that she relied on another copywriter.[137] On November 4, 2020, the Trump Campaign sent out an email preemptively and falsely declaring that President Trump won Pennsylvania.[138]

Katz was fired approximately three weeks after the election.[139] In an interview with the Select Committee, when Allred was asked why Katz, her direct report, was fired, she explained that she was not sure why because TMAGAC was raising more money than ever after the election, but that the decision was not hers to make.[140]

### Concerns Raised by Trump Campaign Vendor Iterable

The Trump Campaign knew that emails that the Approvals Group had blessed were being rejected by another email service provider. After the election, the Trump Campaign attempted to expand the reach of their false voter fraud emails. The Trump Campaign formed a company named DataPier, owned by Cannon and Sean Dollman.[141] DataPier hired an outside company named Iterable to deliver its emails.[142] Cannon tried to send "toned-down RNC emails," through Iterable, but they still had to be "further toned [] down through [an] iterative process[.]"[143] For example, on November 7, 2020, Seth Charles, who was then Iterable's principal email deliverability and industry relations manager, said that there was an issue with the TMAGAC copy and offered line edits.[144] Two days later, Charles recommended to the Trump Campaign staffers that they look for "modified copy there [from TMAGAC emails] to be a little less threatening."[145] Charles claimed that some TMAGAC copy "obviously insinuates the so far unsubstantiated theory of voter fraud, as well as contributions and legal actions will result in some sort of different outcome."[146]

But Salesforce, TMAGAC's original email service provider, continued sending millions of Trump Campaign emails up until January 6th.

### Internal Complaints at Salesforce

The Trump Campaign knew that emails that the Approvals Group had blessed were being rejected by Iterable. However, the RNC continued to send millions of Trump Campaign emails through Salesforce, TMAGAC's original email service provider, up until January 6th. Evidence uncovered by the Select Committee shows that there were internal concerns at Salesforce regarding the content of the TMAGAC emails.

The Select Committee interviewed an individual ("J. Doe") who worked at Salesforce during the post-election period during which TMAGAC was sending out the fundraising emails concerning false election fraud claims.[147] Doe worked for Salesforce's privacy and abuse management team, colloquially known as the abuse desk.[148] An abuse desk is responsible for preventing fraud and abuse emanating from the provider's user or subscriber network.

Doe indicated to the Select Committee that, as soon as early 2020, they recalled issues arising with the RNC's use of Salesforce's services and that a "deluge of abuse would've started in June-ish."[149] Doe noted that Salesforce received a high number of complaints regarding the RNC's actions, which would have been primarily the fundraising efforts of TMAGAC.[150] In the latter half of 2020, Doe noticed that the emails coming from the RNC's account included more and more violent and inflammatory rhetoric in violation of Salesforce's Master Service Agreement ("MSA") with the RNC, which prohibited the use of violent content.[151] Doe stated that, near the time of the election, they contacted senior individuals at Salesforce to highlight the "increasingly concerning" emails coming from the RNC's account.[152] Doe explained that senior individuals at Salesforce effectively ignored their emails about TMAGAC's inflammatory emails[153] and Salesforce ignored the terms of the MSA and permitted the RNC to continue to use its account in this problematic manner.[154] Doe said, "Salesforce very obviously didn't care about anti-abuse."[155]

Ultimately, the Trump Campaign and the RNC let the Big Lie spread because they were making hundreds of millions of dollars from President Trump's supporters who believed that lie. The Big Rip-off needed the Big Lie to motivate unsuspecting individuals to donate their money to a lost cause, and it worked.

## WHERE DID THE MONEY GO?

The Trump Campaign and the RNC had three of their largest fundraising days of the 2020 election cycle immediately after the election.[156] Together, the Trump Campaign and the RNC raised more than one hundred million dollars in three days, telling people they were raising the money for the "Official Election Defense Fund." According to the TMAGAC fundraising pitches, the Trump Campaign and RNC team had created a so-called "Official Election Defense Fund" to help pay for legal challenges to the election results.[157] But there was no "Official Election Defense Fund"—it was simply "a marketing tactic."[158] The TMAGAC fundraisers did not know where the donated money was actually going.[159] The TMAGAC copywriting team simply took the lies that President Trump told them about the need to raise money to overturn the election results and put them into emails to his supporters.

The false claims of election fraud and the "Official Election Defense Fund" were so successful President Trump and his allies raised more than $250 million *after* the election.[160] However, the Trump Campaign was raising too much money to spend solely on their legal efforts to overturn the results of the 2020 election. The Trump Campaign continued to publicly state the election had been stolen by "the Left," while behind closed doors they prepared a new plan to spend their supporters' money.

### A. The Creation of the Save America PAC

On November 9, 2020, President Trump created a separate leadership PAC called Save America that allowed him to keep millions of dollars raised after the election and spend it with very few restrictions in the future. Jared Kushner worked with Alex Cannon, Deputy General Counsel for the Trump Campaign, in creating the entity.[161] Prior to the formation of Save America, any money raised by the Trump Campaign could effectively only be spent on recount and election-contest related expenses, and to pay off campaign debt.[162] But now the money raised into Save America could allow President Trump to pay for his personal expenses, such as travel or hotel stays. After Save America was formed, it was added to the TMAGAC joint fundraising agreement with the RNC, and the percentage of the proceeds allocated to the Trump Campaign began to flow to Save America.[163]

Importantly, Save America, as a leadership PAC, was not even legally permitted to pay for recount and election-contest related expenses in excess of the Federal Election Campaign Act ("FECA") limit of $5,000.[164] Save America never hit that limit in 2020, as it spent no money on recount and election-contest related expenses.[165]

Several reporters noticed the switch and contacted the Campaign asking about the "bait and switch" and the "misleading" nature of the emails. One reporter said directly: "it's misleading to raise money for a committee marked on the website as an 'election defense fund' if it's going to a leadership PAC."[166] Another reporter asked, "Why is the campaign telling its supporters they are contributing toward an 'Election Defense Fund' if only a small percentage of those funds are actually going toward funding legal efforts?" and "How can the campaign justify directing 75% of contributions intended for a 2020 legal fund toward the President's political action committee?"[167]

The Trump Campaign came up with a messaging plan about this tactic, which President Trump personally approved.[168] Tim Murtaugh, the Trump Campaign's communications director, repeatedly asked Justin Clark, the deputy campaign manager, whether they should respond to the reporters.[169] When Murtaugh flagged that the communications team was not responding to the reporters, Justin Clark said, "Good. Don't."[170]

### B. Outlays to Trump-Associated Individuals and Companies

The Trump Campaign spent the money on President Trump, giving donations to his associates, and keeping it for himself in Save America. Hundreds of millions of dollars that were raised to go towards "election defense" and "fighting voter fraud" were not spent that way at all. To the contrary, most of the funds remain unspent, and millions have been paid to companies that are known affiliates of President Trump, or payments to entities associated with former Trump administration officials. Since the election, former Trump officials who are still working for President Trump's PACs, and are publicly receiving salaries as FEC-reported "payroll," are also associated with these companies.

For example, from July 2021 to the present, Save America has been paying approximately $9,700 per month to Dan Scavino,[171] a political adviser who served in the Trump administration as White House Deputy Chief of Staff.[172] Save America was also paying $20,000 per month to an entity called Hudson Digital LLC. Hudson Digital LLC was registered in Delaware twenty days after the attack on the Capitol, on January 26, 2021,[173] and began receiving payments from Save America on the day it was registered.[174] Hudson Digital LLC has received payments totaling over $420,000, all described as "Digital consulting."[175] No website or any other information or mention of Hudson Digital LLC could be found online.[176] Though Hudson Digital LLC is registered as a Delaware company, the FEC Schedule B listing traces back to an address belonging to Dan and Catherine Scavino.[177]

Nick Luna, President Trump's former personal assistant and "body man," was being paid from April 2021 to December 2021 approximately $12,000 per month by Save America for "payroll."[178] The Make America Great Again PAC (MAGA PAC)—formerly the authorized committee of President Trump's reelection campaign, Donald J. Trump for President—paid $20,000 per month to a limited liability corporation called Red State Partners LLC from April 2021 through October 2021, and Save America paid Red State Partners LLC $20,000 in February 2022.[179] The company was registered in Delaware on March 11, 2021[180] and has received a total of $170,000.[181] Though it is registered in Delaware, disclosures filed with the

Federal Election Committee (FEC) list Red State Partners at an address in Miami, Florida, that is an address for Nick Luna and his wife, Cassidy Dumbauld.[182]

Further, Vince Haley, Taylor Swindle, and Ross Worthington are corporate officers of a company known as Pericles LLC.[183] Haley is a former policy advisor to President Trump,[184] Swindle is the Chief Financial Officer for Gingrich 360,[185] and Ross Worthington is the former White House speechwriter[186] who wrote the speech President Trump delivered on the Ellipse on January 6th.[187] Pericles LLC was registered on January 27, 2021,[188] the day after Scavino's Hudson Digital LLC, and, since then, has received payments from Save America totaling at least $352,700.[189]

Another former speechwriter for President Trump, Robert Gabriel, Jr., has also been receiving payments from Save America. Gabriel was involved in writing the speech President Trump delivered on the White House Ellipse on January 6th, and specifically told the speechwriters, including Worthington, to reinsert previously removed incendiary lines about Vice President Pence into the speech.[190] This direction came after Vice President Pence told President Trump that he would not try to change the outcome of the election.[191] In September 2021, Gabriel formed called Gabriel Strategies LLC,[192] which began receiving payments from Save America the following month.[193] Since October 2021, Save America has paid Gabriel Strategies LLC at least $167,674.00.[194] For both Pericles and Gabriel Strategies, the description of the payments is always for "consulting" in political strategy or communications, and some payments are purported to include travel expenses.

Through October 2022, Save America has paid nearly $100,000 in "strategy consulting" payments to Herve Pierre Braillard,[195] a fashion designer who has been dressing Melania Trump for years.[196]

From January 2021 to June 2022, Save America has also reported over $2.1 million in "legal consulting." Many firms perform different kinds of practice, but more than 67% of those funds went to law firms that are representing witnesses involved in the Select Committee's investigation who were subpoenaed or invited to testify.

Additionally, Save America has reported other expenditures, like:

- $1,000,000 donation to America First Policy Institute, home to several former Trump officials and witnesses subpoenaed to testify before the Committee.[197]
- $1,000,000 donation to Conservative Partnership Institute, a conservative nonprofit organization where Mark Meadows is a senior partner.[198]
- More than $10.6 million to Event Strategies, Inc., the preferred staging company for President Trump that staged the January 6th rally.[199]

- More than $327,000 in payments to the Trump Hotel Collection and Mar-A-Lago Club since the 2020 election.[200]
- An "event sponsorship fee" of $165,937.50 to American Conservative Union,[201] the Chairman of which is Matt Schlapp. Schlapp and his wife have offered to pay the legal fees of witnesses called to testify before the January 6th Committee and have extensive ties with former President Trump.
- A little over $140,000 to National Public Affairs, LLC,[202] a consulting company started by former Trump Campaign Manager Bill Stepien and Deputy Campaign Manager Justin Clark.[203] Stepien testified that he knew the claims of voter fraud were false, that he didn't think what was happening was necessarily honest, and that he was stepping away from the Trump Campaign.[204] However, he continues to work and receive hundreds of thousands of dollars consulting for President Trump and several other congressional candidates who continue to spread false voter fraud claims related to the 2020 election.[205]

### C. Payments to 2M Management LLC

As described above, the Trump Campaign, after paying off its general election debt, raised millions of dollars that flowed into a segregated recount account ("Recount Account") by encouraging donors to help pay for legal challenges to the election results. Pursuant to the FECA, the Trump Campaign could only spend these funds on a few limited purposes (e.g., for actual recounts and election-contest expenses or, in the case of surplus funds, donations to charitable organizations or transferring the funds to a national party committee's separate, segregated account for election recounts).[206]

Justin Clark told the Select Committee that he understood that, "[a]fter election day, . . . you can raise money for a recount and to pay off debt,"[207] and that "[t]he money going into the campaign, principal campaign committee, at that point, [after the election] was dead money. It couldn't be spent on things."[208] Alex Cannon agreed.[209] That's why, after the election, the Trump Campaign set up the Recount Account—"a segregated restricted account [held] by the campaign"[210]—and raised money for the Recount Account through TMAGAC.[211]

In February 2021, the Trump Campaign was converted into MAGA PAC.[212] In March 2021, MAGA PAC began disclosing on required FEC forms that it was paying millions of dollars to an eDiscovery vendor called 2M Document Management & Imaging LLC ("2M Management") for what MAGA PAC described as "recount" and "Recount: Research Consulting."[213]

Although the MAGA PAC reported that 2M Management was being paid for recount-related expenses, 2M Management was primarily processing and reviewing documents slated to be produced by the National Archives and Records Administration in response to subpoenas from (1) the House Select Subcommittee on the Coronavirus Crisis ("Covid Subcommittee") and (2) the Select Committee to Investigate the January 6th Attack.[214]

From just March 2021 to May 2021, MAGA PAC paid 2M Management almost $1 million from the Recount Account to review documents related solely to the Covid Subcommittee.[215] Alex Cannon confirmed that he understood these payments to 2M Management came from the Recount Account.[216] Federal campaign finance law requires committees to accurately report information related to expenditures, including the purpose of payments. FEC regulations provide that the "purpose" be described in relevant reports through a brief statement of why the disbursement was made and must be sufficiently specific to make the purpose of the disbursement clear.[217]

## IMPACT OF THE TRUMP CAMPAIGN'S FALSE CLAIMS

Between the election and January 6th, the Trump Campaign sent out hundreds of emails urging President Trump's supporters to "fight the Liberal MOB" and "join the Trump army." Users on the same extreme social media platforms used to plan the attack on the Capitol repeatedly shared the "Official Election Defense Fund" donation links in the week following election day.[218] Links to donate were often accompanied by mentions of voter fraud and calls to save the country, mirroring the language of the fundraising emails and the countless discussions being held by the President's supporters of coming to Washington, DC, on January 6th to "Stop the steal."[219]

On January 6th, while President Trump was speaking at the Ellipse rally and directing his supporters to march to the Capitol, his Campaign was also sending fundraising emails inflaming people to "fight back." One email stated, "100 Members of Congress. . . . Join them in the FIGHT to DEFEND the Election. . . . *This is our last line of defense.*"[220] Another email stated, "TODAY will be a historic day in our Nation's history. Congress will either certify, or object to, the Election results. Every single Patriot from across the Country must step up RIGHT NOW if we're going to successfully DEFEND the integrity of this Election."[221] A third email stated, "TODAY. This is our LAST CHANCE . . . The stakes have NEVER been higher. President Trump needs YOU to make a statement and publicly stand with him and FIGHT BACK."[222]

Thirty minutes after the last fundraising email was sent, the Capitol was breached. It was then and only then that TMAGAC fundraisers decided to stop sending emails containing baseless claims of election fraud.[223] Boedigheimer explained, "And at some point during that time, I don't know if it was right then, if it was a little after, maybe a little before, but either

Gary or Kevin kind of directed us to stop sending fundraising messages out."[224] Cannon stated, "[O]n January 6th, Gary called me and said, ['']are you seeing what's happening? I'm obviously turning everything off.[']"[225]

After raising $250 million dollars on false voter fraud claims, mostly from small-dollar donors, President Trump did not spend it on fighting an election he knew he lost. Instead, a significant portion of the money was deposited into the Save America account and not used for the purposes the Campaign claimed it would be. President Trump got a war chest with millions of dollars, and the American people were left with the U.S. Capitol under attack.

There is evidence suggesting that numerous defendants charged with violations related to the January 6th attack on the U.S. Capitol and others present on the Capitol grounds that day were motivated by false claims about the election.[226]

Further, J. Doe, the Salesforce employee interviewed by the Select Committee, provided insight into the action that Salesforce took after the attack. Doe explained that after they became aware of the ongoing attack, they (Doe) took unilateral action to block the RNC's ability to send emails through Salesforce's platform.[227] Doe noted that the shutdown lasted until January 11, 2021, when senior Salesforce leadership directed Doe to remove the block from RNC's Salesforce account.[228] Doe stated that Salesforce leadership told Doe that Salesforce would now begin reviewing RNC's email campaigns to "make sure this doesn't happen again."[229]

**CONCLUSION**

In the weeks after the 2020 election leading up to January 6, 2021, President Trump's Campaign and his allies sent his supporters a barrage of emails and text messages pushing lies about a stolen election and asking for contributions to challenge the outcome of the election. In reality, the funds raised went primarily towards paying down the Trump Campaign's outstanding 2020 debt, financing President Trump's newly created Save America PAC, and raising money for the RNC.

Overall, only a small amount of the contributions ever went to President Trump's recount account or were otherwise obviously used in connection with post-election recounts or litigation. As President Trump used the Big Lie as a weapon to attack the legitimacy of the 2020 election, his Campaign used that same Big Lie to raise millions of dollars based on false claims and unkept promises.

Not only did President Trump lie to his supporters about the election, but he also ripped them off.

# MALIGN FOREIGN INFLUENCE

## INTRODUCTION

In the wake of the 2020 U.S. Presidential election, President Donald J. Trump and his apologists attempted to blame his loss on foreign interference. They falsely claimed that foreign-manufactured voting machines had been manipulated so that votes cast for Trump were instead recorded as votes for Joseph R. Biden, Jr.[1] No one has ever, either at the time or since, offered any evidence to support Trump's assertion. On the contrary, ample evidence collected by the Intelligence Community (IC) and reviewed by the Select Committee disproves those claims.

That is not to say foreign actors made no attempt to influence the American political climate during and after the 2020 Presidential election. This appendix evaluates the role foreign influence played in the circumstances surrounding the insurrection.[2]

## DISCUSSION

### ELECTION MEDDLING IN 2020:
### FOREIGN INTERFERENCE? NO. FOREIGN INFLUENCE? YES.

In its postmortem assessment of the 2020 U.S. Presidential election, the Intelligence Community comprehensively examined two types of foreign meddling: interference and influence. The distinction between the two is critical in evaluating President Trump's repeated public assertions that there had been massive and widespread "fraud" that had the effect of "stealing" the election for then-candidate Biden.

For its analytic purposes, the Intelligence Community defines election *interference* as "a subset of election influence activities targeted at the technical aspects of the election, including voter registration, casting and counting ballots, or reporting results."[3] That definition notes that election interference is a subset of election *influence*, which the Intelligence Community defines to include "overt and covert efforts by foreign governments or actors acting as agents of, or on behalf of, foreign governments intended to affect directly or indirectly a US election—including candidates, political parties, voters or their preferences, or political processes."[4]

The Intelligence Community's Assessment (ICA) found no factual basis for any allegation of technical interference with the 2020 U.S. election: "We have no indications that any foreign actor attempted to interfere in the 2020 US elections by altering any technical aspect of the voting process, including voter registration, ballot casting, vote tabulation, or reporting results."[5] Put simply, allegations that foreign powers rigged voting machines and swapped ballots were false and unsupported.

Although there is no evidence of foreign technical interference in the 2020 election, there is evidence of foreign influence. Specifically, the Intelligence Community's Assessment concluded that "Russian President Putin authorized, and a range of Russian government organizations conducted, influence operations aimed at denigrating President Biden's candidacy and the Democratic Party, supporting former President Trump, undermining public confidence in the electoral process, and exacerbating sociopolitical divisions in the US."[6] The two Intelligence Community analytic conclusions about the 2020 U.S. Presidential election—that there was evidence of foreign influence, but not foreign interference—are completely consistent.

## MALIGN FOREIGN EFFORTS TO INFLUENCE THE 2020 U.S. ELECTIONS

The 2020 U.S. elections saw an increase in the number of foreign state and non-state entities that attempted to influence the U.S. electorate. The U.S. Intelligence Community suggests, as a possible explanation, that more such foreign entities "may view influence operations as important tools for projecting power abroad."[7] More ascertainably, "[t]he growth of internet and social media use means foreign actors are more able to reach US audiences directly, while the tools for doing so are becoming more accessible."[8]

The United States' principal foreign adversaries—Russia, China, and Iran—all of them autocracies, engage, to varying degrees, in disguised efforts to influence U.S. public opinion.[9] In the context of these overarching efforts,[10] U.S. elections offer special opportunities.

For Russia, "[e]lections…often serve as an opportune target. But attacks on elections are typically just one part of ongoing, multi-pronged operations."[11] The U.S. Intelligence Community's definitive post-election assessment of foreign influence activities during the 2020 Presidential election concluded that Russia was deeply engaged in disinformation activities intended to influence the outcome by supporting President Trump while disparaging then-candidate Biden; Iran also engaged in efforts to influence the election's outcome, but unlike Russia, did not actively promote any candidate; and that China considered opportunities to influence the election's outcome, but ultimately decided that potential costs outweighed any foreseeable benefits.[12] Both Russia and Iran worked to undermine the American public's confidence in U.S. democratic processes and to deepen socio-political divisions in the United States.[13]

## RUSSIA'S MALIGN INFLUENCE EFFORTS TARGETING THE UNITED STATES

Russian malign disinformation efforts are both strategic in scope and opportunistic in nature. They aim to corrode the power and appeal of the U.S. democratic processes, worsen U.S. domestic divisions, and weaken America at home and abroad. The Intelligence Community's February 2022 unclassified "Annual Threat Assessment" puts this sustained Russian threat in a nutshell:

> Russia presents one of the most serious foreign influence threats to the United States, using its intelligence services, proxies, and wide-ranging influence tools to try to divide Western alliances, and increase its sway around the world, while attempting to undermine U.S. global standing, amplify discord inside the United States, and influence U.S. voters and decisionmaking.[14]

### RUSSIAN DISINFORMATION AND THE 2020 PRESIDENTIAL ELECTION

Foreign adversaries' influence campaigns routinely push disinformation to U.S. audiences. Elections offer an important forum for Russia and other U.S. adversaries to seek to deepen divisions within American society through disinformation campaigns.[15] The Intelligence Community projects that both Russia and China will, for the foreseeable future, continue to press their disinformation campaigns attempting to undermine the U.S. population's confidence in their government and society.[16] Russia certainly did so in the period following the election and preceding the January 6th attack.

The disinformation spread by Russia and its messengers during that time was not, however, entirely original. The Intelligence Community Assessment found that Russia's disinformation engine borrowed President Trump's own words to achieve its goals:

> Russian online influence actors generally promoted former President Trump and his commentary, including repeating his political messaging on the election results; the presidential campaign; debates; the impeachment inquiry; and, as the election neared, US domestic crises.[17]

Indeed, President Trump's messaging during and after the 2020 election was reflected in Russian influence efforts at the time. In September of 2020, the Department of Homeland Security's Office of Intelligence and Analysis warned that Russia was engaged in pre-election activity targeting the U.S. democratic process.[18] The bulletin advised that "Russia is likely to continue amplifying criticisms of vote-by-mail and shifting voting processes amidst the COVID-19 pandemic to undermine public trust in the electoral process."[19]

Deliberately spreading disinformation to discredit a U.S. election was not new to Russia's influence arsenal. In the judgment of the U.S. Intelligence Community, it is a tactic Russia was prepared to deploy after the 2016 U.S. Presidential election:

Even after the [2020] election, Russian online influence actors continued to promote narratives questioning the election results and disparaging President Biden and the Democratic Party. These efforts parallel plans Moscow had in place in 2016 to discredit a potential incoming Clinton administration, but which it scrapped after former President Trump's victory.[20]

Russian influence efforts in the 2016 and 2020 elections, while distinct in their particulars, shared some similarities. Historically, Russia has engaged in near-industrial scale online influence efforts.[21] The Intelligence Community Assessment states that in 2020, Russia again relied on internet trolls to amplify divisive content aimed at American audiences:

The Kremlin-linked influence organization Project Lakhta and its Lakhta Internet Research (LIR) troll farm—commonly referred to by its former moniker Internet Research Agency (IRA)—amplified controversial domestic issues. LIR used social media personas, news websites, and US persons to deliver tailored content to subsets of the US population. LIR established short-lived troll farms that used unwitting third-country nationals in Ghana, Mexico, and Nigeria to propagate these US-focused narratives....[22]

The threats posed by Russia's influence efforts are not new, nor are they diminishing. The latest unclassified Intelligence Community Annual Threat Assessment throws this into sharp relief:

Moscow has conducted influence operations against U.S. elections for decades, including as recently as the 2020 presidential election. We assess that it probably will try to strengthen ties to U.S. persons in the media and politics in hopes of developing vectors for future influence operations.[23]

### PROXIES AMONG US: MALIGN FOREIGN INFLUENCE AND U.S. AUDIENCES

Tech-enabled or not, if ever there was a "people business," foreign influence is it. People working on behalf of a foreign government—foreign government officials, their agents, and proxies—work to influence, directly or indirectly, a target audience in another country—its officials and citizens at large. Most who are engaged in those efforts act overtly: ambassadors, consuls general, government delegations and so forth. Their foreign influence efforts are not, however, focused on philanthropy or foreign aid. Moreover, the perspectives they seek to embed in their target audiences may be intentionally and materially inaccurate, propagandistic, or driven by unstated motives. In such instances, foreign influence may amount to injecting foreign disinformation into the U.S. media ecosystem for re-branding and onward transmission to an American audience.[24]

Foreign state adversaries of the United States generally disguise their efforts to influence U.S. audiences, particularly when they seek to influence U.S. voters' views in the run-up to an election. Among the many ways of concealing the foreign-state origin or sponsorship of such a message is to use unattributable proxies—"cut-outs"—or fully independent ideological allies in the United States as messaging organs. A cooperative American messenger—a proxy for the foreign government itself—may be needed to make the foreign-origin message congenial to the target American audience.

Malign foreign influencers, including foreign governments, used an additional such masking tool during the Trump administration: amplifying U.S.-originated messages so that they reached a broader audience. These influencers often took advantage of the algorithms by which social media platforms bring congenial messages and other information to users whose views are likely to be similar or compatible.

Shortly after the January 6th attack, the National Intelligence Council summarized the scope and significance of Russia's use of proxies in the 2020 U.S. Presidential election:

> A key element of Moscow's strategy this election cycle was its use of proxies linked to Russian intelligence to push influence narratives— including misleading or unsubstantiated allegations against President Biden—to US media organizations, US officials, and prominent US individuals, including some close to former President Trump and his administration.[25]

The success of the proxy depends on shielding its foreign sponsorship. For that reason, it can be difficult or impossible to determine conclusively whether someone parroting a foreign government adversary's point of view to a U.S. audience is that government's controlled proxy or a volunteer taking full advantage of U.S. First Amendment freedoms.

### ANTI-U.S. FOREIGN STATE PROPAGANDA AND THE JANUARY 6TH ATTACK

U.S. adversaries use anti-American propaganda and disinformation to advance their strategic foreign policy objectives. They aim to corrode U.S. influence abroad while diluting U.S. citizens' trust in their democratic institutions and processes. They hope to deepen and sharpen the sociopolitical divisions in American society.[26] In doing so, foreign adversaries hope not only to limit U.S. ability to influence the policy choices of other foreign states, but also to help immunize their own populations against the attractions of American-style democracy.

That matters, as Russia and other adversaries of the United States well know. If the United States has long demonstrated such a globally effective cultural power to attract, its corrosion must be a primary strategic objective of Russia or any other of the United States' principal adversaries. Accordingly, over the next 20 years, the Intelligence Community expects that "China and Russia probably will try to continue targeting domestic audiences in the United States and Europe, promoting narratives about Western decline and overreach."[27] The January 6th attack played into their hands.

### PRESIDENT TRUMP AND THE 2020 ELECTION AS AN OPPORTUNITY FOR FOREIGN INFLUENCE

With President Trump in the White House, Russia benefited from a powerful American messenger creating and spreading damaging disinformation it could amplify. The Intelligence Community's comprehensive March 2021 assessment noted that throughout the 2020 Federal election cycle, "Russian online influence actors generally promoted former President Trump and his commentary...."[28]

President Trump's relentless propagation of the Big Lie damaged American democracy from within and made it more vulnerable to attack from abroad. His actions did not go unnoticed by America's adversaries, who seized on the opportunity to damage the United States. According to the Intelligence Community's March 2021 assessment, "[e]ven after the election, Russian online influence actors continued to promote narratives questioning the election results...."[29] What President Trump was saying was, in sum, exactly what the Russian government wanted said—but he was doing it on his own initiative and from the trappings of the Oval Office.

# Acknowledgments

Special thanks to Wilson Andrews, Dean Baquet, Rebecca Blumenstein, Cecilia Bohan, Luke Broadwater, Steve Brown, Mark Bulik, Elisabeth Bumiller, Anika Burgess, Jordan Cohen, Phil Corbett, Julie Hirschfeld Davis, Kelly Doe, Steve Duenes, Sunhee Evans, Alan Feuer, Beth Flynn, Hannah Fowler, Jaclyn Gallucci, Guilbert Gates, Augusta Greenbaum, Danielle Rhoades Ha, Maggie Haberman, Nakyung Han, Joe Kahn, Inyoung Kang, Thomas Kaplan, Aisha Khan, Nancy Lee, Alexis Loinaz, Meaghan Looram, Bill Marsh, Lara McCoy, Greg Miller, Abby Perpich, Caroline Que, Michael S. Schmidt, Erika Sommer, Dick Stevenson, Alice Ting, Archie Tse, Trenitee Wesley, Susan Wessling and many others at The Times. And deep appreciation to our partners at Twelve, including Bob Castillo, Jim Datz, Sean Desmond, Michael Gaudet, Kristen Lemire, Megan Perritt-Jacobson and Albert Tang.